D1611207

360/370 PROGRAMING IN ASSEMBLY LANGUAGE

360/370 PROGRAMING

in Assembly Language

Second Edition

NED CHAPIN, Ph.D.

Consultant

McGRAW-HILL BOOK COMPANY

New York · San Francisco · St. Louis · Düsseldorf · Johannesburg
Kuala Lumpur · London · Mexico · Montreal · New Delhi · Panama
Rio de Janeiro · Singapore · Sydney · Toronto

This book was set in Times Roman by Holmes Typography, Inc. The editors were Richard F. Dojny and Michael A. Ungersma, the designer was James Mennick, and the Production supervisor was Michael A. Ungersma. The drawings were done by Reprographex.

The author is pleased to acknowledge the assistance of the following people and firms in helping to make this a better book: IBM for assistance and for permission to reproduce some of their copyrighted materials, as listed below; Sperry-Rand Univac and RCA for their assistance; Peggy Luce for writing and revising most of the command example programs; Dean Akey for testing many of the programs; Helen McNeill for typing assistance on the various drafts; my students for patience in trying out revisions; my colleagues for reviews of some chapters; the reviewer for many helpful comments and suggestions that have contributed to the book; and my wife and children for their encouragement and consideration.
The following materials are reprinted with permission, and with modifications from publications copyrighted in 1971, 1970, 1969, 1968, 1967, and 1966 by International Business Machines Corporation as IBM form numbers GC24-3354, GC24-3361, GC24-5036, GC24-5037, GC24-5070, GC24-5072, GC28-6514, GC28-6703, GC28-6704, GA22-6821, GA22-7000, and other materials: Frontispiece; Figures 7-14, 7-15, 7-16, 7-17, 11-2, 11-10, 11-11, 11-13, 11-14, 11-15, and 11-25; and Appendixes A, B, C, and D.

360/370 PROGRAMING IN ASSEMBLY LANGUAGE

Copyright © Ned Chapin 1968, 1973. All rights reserved. No part of this publication may be reproduced, stored in a retrieval system, or transmitted, in any form or by any means, electronic, mechanical, photocopying, recording, or otherwise, without the prior written permission of the publisher.

Printed in the United States of America.

Library of Congress Cataloging in Publication Data.

Chapin, Ned.
    360/370 programing in assembly language.

    1968 ed. published under title: 360 programing in assembly language.
    1. Assembler language (Computer program language) 2. IBM 360 (Computer)—Programming. 3. IBM 370 (Computer)—Programming. I. Title.
QA76.73.A8C48 1973   001.6'42   72-3675
ISBN 0-07-010552-9

23456789-MAMM-76543

Preface

The objective of this book is to help the reader learn to program a "byte" computer (such as the IBM System/370, the IBM System/360, the Univac-9000 series, the Univac (formerly RCA Spectra) 70 series, the Interdata, for example) in assembly language. The motive for writing this book has been to provide an easily understood, well-organized, and carefully graded text covering both the syntax and the semantics. A careful eye has been given to the needs of the self-study reader. The reader is assumed to know nothing about "byte" computers, but is assumed to know a minimum about data processing. The only mathematical knowledge assumed is the ability to add, subtract, multiply, and divide. The book has been used succesfully from community college to graduate school.

This second edition provides an updating of all the coverage the prior edition offered—and more. That more is: A—coverage of the IBM System/370, B—coverage of the large Operating System (OS), C—coverage of the user macro language, D—more coverage of input, output, and debugging, E—some coverage of subroutine linkage conventions, and F—coverage of virtual storage, dynamic address translation, OS/VS1, OS/VS2, DOS/VS, and VSAM.

In using or reviewing this text, several points should be kept in mind:
=X'1'   COBOL, RPG, FORTRAN, ALGOL, and PL/1 programers can do a better job if they know how to program in assembly language. The reason for this is that assembly-language programing puts the programer closer to the computer,

giving the programer a better knowledge of how the computer works and what affects the efficiency of the computer's operation. Also, the diagnostic and compilation records produced by the higher-level languages require a knowledge of assembly language for their full interpretation. For example, a procedure map, linkage map, or dump typically is at the assembly-language level.

$=$X$'$2$'$ A workbook accompanies this text, giving additional explanation, examples, and exercises. The workbook thus serves as an aid to the reader, but is not essential. Successful use of the text does not require the workbook, but is helped by it.

$=$X$'$3$'$ It is assumed that the reader will refer to the computer manufacturers' reference manuals for additional detail on points as they are raised. This text thus serves as a cumulative introduction to the manufacturers' manuals, and helps build the reader's skills and understanding to the point at which the reader can, on his own, make sense out of many of the manuals.

$=$X$'$4$'$ Programing involves skills and attitudes as well as understandings. The text attempts to help the reader develop appropriate attitudes by example and by the manner of presentation. It attempts to help the reader gain understanding by what it presents and by the order of presentation. But the reader can acquire skill only if he actually tries seriously to work the exercises. The Do It Now Exercises are an integral part of this book.

$=$X$'$5$'$ The computer manufacturers continually change their software. They provide an endless stream of improvements, alternatives, and additional conveniences. This book will not be rendered obsolete by these changes since it concentrates upon a selection of the most basic, the most general, and the most widely useful aspects of the software. It presents few of the finer frills, extra conveniences, or short cuts that the manufacturers have made available, in order to whet the reader's appetite and motivate him to tackle the manufacturers' most recent manuals.

$=$X$'$6$'$ Illustrations and examples in this book have been chosen for their didactic value. In nearly every case, other ways of doing things are available and possible. The ways presented are not represented as the best or the only ways. The reader is to be commended for finding or developing other ways and then contrasting them with those presented. In this way, the reader will learn more.

$=$X$'$7$'$ An exceptionally extensive index has been provided. However, since the different manufacturers and authorities use different terms for the same thing, the reader should check several possibilities and, if needed, even related terms when he has difficulty finding what he seeks.

$=$X$'$8$'$ The author is pleased to acknowledge his debt to all who have helped in the preparation of this book, as detailed on page iv. Any shortcomings in this book are not the fault of those who have helped or contributed ideas and comments but are the responsibility of the author.

$=$X$'$9$'$ The author welcomes comments and notices of errors or ambiguities. He invites the reader to write to him in care of the publisher.

NED CHAPIN

Contents

CHAPTER 1

The Computer

SYSTEM/370, SYSTEM/360, UNIVAC-9000, AND OTHERS

In April 1964 IBM announced the System/360 as an entry in what has been termed "the third generation" of automatic computers. The new IBM computers were arranged in a series from small to large, and all bore a family resemblance. To computers in the series, IBM gave model numbers such as 20, 25, 30, 40, 50, 65, and so on, using the higher numbers to designate the larger models.

In June 1970 IBM announced the IBM System/370, retaining nearly all of the features of the IBM System/360 but adding new features to provide even better performance. Among the more popular models have been numbers 135, 145, 155, and 165, again using higher numbers to designate the larger models.

In capability, the members of the family spanned a wide range. The smallest was roughly on a par with the smaller members of IBM's former lines of computers, but was priced to offer more data processing power per dollar of cost. The largest member of the new family was more capable per dollar of cost than the largest members of IBM's former lines.

A significant feature of the members of this family is "upward compatibility." Jobs prepared (programed) for execution on any smaller member of the family can also be performed with little or no change on any larger member of the family equipped with at least the same configuration of equipment and features. Thus computer users can change upward in their use of members of the family, without having to extensively reprepare (reprogram) the jobs. However, a computer user can go downward in the family only if the job requires equipment and features possessed by the smaller members of the family. Hence the user often cannot go downward. This situation is diagramed in Fig. 1-1.

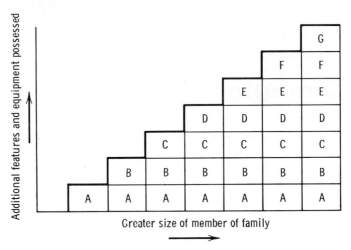

FIG. 1-1. Diagram of feature and equipment relationship among members of computer families.

Within a year following the **IBM** announcement of the System/360, RCA announced the Spectra-70 family of computers. This family covered at first the lower middle part of the same range as the System/360 and had the same type of upward compatibility. And, significantly from a programing point of view, the symbolic languages for programing both the System/360 and the Spectra-70 were identical on many points. The electronic design and construction features of the Spectra-70 family were in many ways very different from those of the System/360, but to a programer the two families of computers appear to be essentially the same on many points. In terms of function, and in terms of the way the programer gives directions to the computer, the members of the two families often appear so much alike as to be almost interchangeable.

A little more than two years after the **IBM** System/360 announcement, the Univac division of Sperry-Rand announced the Univac-9000 family of computers. This family also covered at first the lower and middle parts of the same range as the System/360 and had the same type of upward compatibility. Again, significantly from a programing point of view, the basic symbolic language for programing the Univac-9000 series appeared in many respects identical to those for the System/360 and for the Spectra-70. Even though the design and construction features of the Univac-9000 series are, in many respects, quite different, a programer directs the

Univac-9000 series in much the same way he directs the System/360 or the Spectra-70.

In September 1971 RCA retired from the computer market, and subsequently Univac took over providing support for RCA's Spectra-70 and related computers. In major part, this was possible and acceptable to users because the symbolic language for the Spectra-70 and the Univac-9000 series was so similar. In short, the Univac-9000 series, the Spectra-70, the System/360, and the System/370 families of computers often appear to programers so much alike as to be almost indistinguishable. Programs directing the computer and written in the symbolic language for one member of one of these families can usually be used with only minor modifications on an equivalent member of one of the other computer families.

Since the time of the original System/360 announcement, other computer manufacturers have announced computers having some features in common with the members of the IBM, RCA, and Univac families of computers. The Interdata and the Xerox Data Systems Sigma computers are examples.

Because of the family relationship of features of the IBM System/360, the System/370, the Spectra-70 series, the Univac-9000 series, and the computers of other manufacturers, and because of the deliberate upward compatibility within the members of each family, this book does not concentrate on any one manufacturer's family or on any one specific model of computer. Instead this book concentrates upon the language, the techniques, and the methods of programing applicable to all these families of computers. Since the IBM System/360 and System/370 families are the most widely used, more attention is given to those families than to the others. Since the smaller members of each of the families are the more popular, more attention is given to them than to the larger members. In particular this book stresses the basic symbolic programing language, often called the "assembly language." This language puts the programer closer to the hardware of the computer.

Such languages as COBOL, FORTRAN, RPG, and PL/1 are not covered directly in this book. Such "high-level" languages are implemented on the computer in terms of the assembly language, and to use the troubleshooting output produced by these languages for the assistance of the programer often requires him to have a knowledge of assembly language. Therefore this book can be very helpful to a user of COBOL, FORTRAN, RPG, and PL/1. For example, to interpret the common storage dump produced for a program written in any language for the computer requires a knowledge of assembly language. Or, for example, to interpret a COBOL "Procedure Map," or a "Data Map," requires a knowledge of assembly language. Even the common "linkage editor" listing is more meaningful to a programer with a knowledge of assembly language.

Because of the computer and language stress in this book, it does not seem fair to identify continually the computer being talked about as any one particular manufacturer's computer. The exception is when the book talks about features that are unique to a particular manufacturer's particular model. In that case, it may be important to know what manufacturer's model has those features. In other cases, in which the discussion applies to more than one model and especially to models produced by different manufacturers, this book uses the general term "the computer."

Because these differences among models of the computer do exist, this book has been designed to be read in conjunction with a machine reference or programer manual obtainable from the computer manufacturer for the model of most interest to the reader. Then, as this book presents each feature, with examples, diagrams, and exercises, the reader should check the index in the manufacturer's manual to find the description of the feature as it applies to the specific model of the computer.

In this connection, the term "the programer" may need explanation. As used in this book, a programer is a person who designs, writes, and tests programs in the computer's assembly language. A program is the set of directions the programer prepares for the computer telling or specifying to the computer what the computer is to do, and exactly how it is to do it. The object of this book is to help you become a programer for the computer.

A definition of assembly language, with some explanation, is given in Chapter 2. Subsequent chapters provide the details.

PLAN OF THE BOOK

The first part of this book presents some basic facts about features of the computer. The computer is sufficiently complex that to present all the details at once would result in a snowstorm of information. To avoid such a confusing presentation, this book presents the major facts about the computer and the assembly language in small doses. Chapter 2 contains the most concentrated dose; later chapters are less concentrated. Each, however, builds on some or all of what precedes it.

Chapter 3 presents the ways in which data are represented in the computer. This is not a simple topic, because the computer has the ability to represent data in many ways. This ability is very convenient for the user of the computer, and adds power and efficiency to the computer's handling of data when the programer uses the alternative ways sagaciously.

Data representation links directly to the vital matter of data arrangement in storage. Data can be arranged in storage in ways that are limited mostly by the skill of the programer. The programer can specify exactly how data are to be arranged, and can change the arrangement at any time by data-movement operations. Some of these operations can at the same time change the way data are represented. Since all the operations the computer can do require the data to be correctly arranged in storage, all of Chapter 4 is devoted to data-movement operations.

With this knowledge about data arrangement and data movement, a programer can have the computer do some fundamental arithmetic operations, such as add, subtract, multiply, and divide. Because these operations are easy to understand, they provide a natural way of integrating the material from the earlier chapters into Chapter 5 (Arithmetic Operations).

For a programer to make the computer do what he wants, arithmetic and data-movement operations are not enough. The programer also needs some control operations. The most important of these are the logic operations and the transfer operations. These make repetition of operations possible, as well as providing an ability to take action to fit different alternatives that may be needed to process data correctly. These operations are the topic of Chapter 6.

Chapter 7 presents ways of getting data into the computer to be processed (the input), and ways of getting data that result from its processing (the output) from the computer. The programer can have the computer do input and output operations at various levels. Chapter 7 treats this at a simple level, a more comprehensive treatment being given later.

Chapter 7 also presents "job-control" operations and some conventions for use by the programer in controlling the way the computer translates his assembly language program to machine (object) language and then executes his program. After Chapter 7, the programer can prepare complete programs.

Then in Chapter 8 comes the vital matter known as debugging—finding and correcting the programer's mistakes. A programer who writes a program nearly always overlooks something. That oversight causes the computer to fail to produce a correct output. As a part of learning to program in assembly language, the programer must learn to find and correct his own mistakes.

Chapter 9 presents the very important topic of problem analysis. This presentation is independent of the make or model of the computer, and the four main examples illustrate techniques the programer can use in attacking most programing jobs to which he may be assigned.

Then in Chapters 10 and 11, this book covers more deeply and intensively topics introduced earlier. Chapter 10 presents additional logic operations and more complex forms of data movement. Chapter 11 presents additional input and output operations, and also conventions on the handling of data on magnetic tapes and magnetic disks. Operations for handling input and output operations at the machine level (without macros) are reserved for the workbook.

Chapter 12 covers floating-point operations. These find wide use in research, engineering, statistical, and scientific work. Chapter 13 covers macros and subroutines written in assembly language.

The book gives attention throughout to how the programer does his work, how the computer and programs operate, and (when reasons can be easily given) to why things are done in a particular way. The book gives attention to techniques the programer can use to obtain faster and more efficient computer performance. After all, computer operation depends largely upon how the programer has written the program. If the programer writes it in a way that makes effective use of the capability of the computer, then the computer will probably be able to operate rapidly and efficiently. Since, in computer work, time and money are often synonymous, anything the programer can do to speed the operation of the computer, or speed the programing operation normally results in direct savings for his employer.

PROGRAMING SKILLS

In learning programing, it is important to keep in mind that programing is primarily a skill. To learn any skill requires exercising that skill. Your object or purpose in reading this book is probably to learn how to program. A wide gap separates understanding how to program from being able to do programing. If the reader intends to do programing, he must do more than understand programing. To learn to do programing, he should work out carefully each of the "Do It Now" exercises as he encounters it in the book.

These "Do It Now" exercises have been selected and placed in this book at places where it is important to consolidate the reader's understanding and convert that understanding into an ability to do—to start building a skill, in other words. He will only acquire skill by actually trying to do programing, and these exercises provide the initial opportunity to "try one's wings." The Do It Now exercises often require the reader to refer back to earlier parts of the book to review important points.

These Do It Now exercises are also important preparation for the end-of-chapter exercises in the workbook. These end-of-chapter exercises are highly cumulative in nature and require the reader to use the knowledge and skill gained from previous chapters. In practice, these exercises provide a major part of the chapter-to-chapter tie-in after Chapter 4. Time and effort spent in mastering them will be repaid in more rapid acquisition of skill in programing the computer in assembly language.

EXERCISE

This is the appropriate time for an introduction to the workbook. If you have one, read now the preface and Chapter 1 before continuing to the next chapter in this book. In preparation for later work, please acquire the following items:

5 pads of assembly-language coding forms
1 flowchart template and ruler marked in tenths of an inch and with the ANSI Standard flow diagram symbols
1 reference manual from the computer manufacturer of the model of the computer that is of most interest to you.

CHAPTER 2

Computer and Language Features

PLAN OF THE CHAPTER

The first four sections of this chapter are a brief and simple summary of some computer and programing language features. Some basic technical terms are introduced. If the reader finds all the material familiar, he should skim ahead to the last sections of the chapter, such as Addressing or Coding Form.

If the reader finds the terms and conceptions in the first four sections of this chapter unfamiliar, he should temporarily set this book aside and turn to a general introductory book on computers and data processing.* Then, having strengthened his background, the reader can return to this book with greater comprehension.

If the reader finds the first four sections of this chapter to be familiar in content but not in terminology, he will profit by reading them. In particular, he should note the descriptions of the addressing, and of the internal and peripheral configurations of the computer.

COMPUTER ORGANIZATION

The computer is a machine for processing data at very high speed and very low cost. The computer's great speed, high accuracy, and great economy of perform-

---

* See, for example, Ned Chapin. *Computers*. New York: Van Nostrand Reinhold Company, 1971. 686 pp.

ance result from the features of its design. Many of these directly influence the way the programer programs (directs) the different models of the computer. The general plan of organization in the computer is common to computers generally, and is summarized in Fig. 2-1 in functional terms.

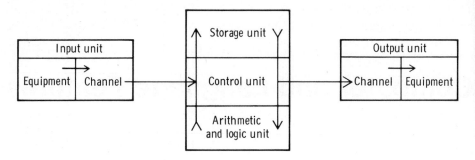

FIG. 2-1. Functional organization of the computer.

In order to be able to use the computer, a programer needs some means of telling the computer what data it is to process. This is basic; the programer must have some way of communicating to the computer the data going into the computer's processing. These data are called the "input data," and the part of the computer that takes in the input data is known as the "input unit." Input is the first function.

Once the computer has received the data to be processed, an important question arises: What does the computer do with the data? It must do two things: (1) process the data, and (2) hold portions of the data until they are needed in the processing. Since it cannot process all the data at once, simultaneously, the computer must hold parts of the data for later use as it needs them. This second function, the ability to hold data for later use, or to remember data, is referred to as the "storage" function. This function is carried out by the "storage unit."

This storage function is extremely important because all of the input data are transmitted to the storage unit and held there until such time as other parts of the computer need them. From a programer's point of view, the storage unit of the computer can be thought of as being like a chalk board on which the input unit of the computer writes the input data, and from which the other parts of the computer read data as needed. The data on the chalk board (in storage) may be copied at any time, or erased at any time and new data brought in (written) to replace the old.

To make the analogy more realistic for the computer, and to introduce the concept of "byte," visualize the chalk board as being ruled into squares, as in Fig. 2-2. This is like breaking a large piece of chalk board into "bite-size" pieces. Each of these "squares" or "cells" or "bites areas" (more correctly spelled "bytes") should be thought of as having identification numbers assigned in sequence. For convenience, a programer can think of the squares (cells or bytes areas) in a row as being numbered from left to right (column numbers) and the rows as being numbered from top to bottom. To substitute for the numbers 10 through 15, let us use the letters A through F, since these use only one position rather than two. Thus any particular square (cell or byte) in the set could be identified (addressed) by giving the row and column identification as if it were all one number. For example, the fourth row down (3) and the tenth column over (9) might be designated (addressed) as "39." This is the square which starts the word "cells" in Fig. 2-2. Note that in the computer, counting starts with 0, not with 1.

	0	1	2	3	4	5	6	7	8	9	A (10)	B (11)	C (12)	D (13)	E (14)	F (15)
0		P	L	E	A	S	E		D	0		N	0	T		
1		S	T	E	P		0	N		T	H	E				
2		L	I	N	E	S	.			J	U	S	T			
3		U	S	E		T	H	E		C	E	L	L	S		
4					C	0	X	P	U	T	E	R				

FIG. 2-2. Ruled chalk-board analogy for internal storage in the computer.

Another modification making the analogy more realistic for the computer calls for the chalk-board user to write only within the boundaries of each cell (byte area or square). Each byte area (cell or square) might, for example, be permitted to hold only one character, such as one letter or one number. Thus to write the word "computer" would require eight byte areas (cells or squares), one for each letter of the word. The user of the chalk board, if he should happen to misspell the word "computer," could erase the erroneous data in the byte area (cell or square) and correct it by writing in the new letter. Thus if the user of the chalk board had spelled "computer" as "coxputer," as in Fig. 2-2, he could change the X to M by erasing the X from the byte area (cell or square) at 46 and then writing there the letter M.

Do It Now Exercise 2-1. *From a study of Fig. 2-2, write down in a column the address identification (row and column number) of the first letter of each word. After each address, write the number of bytes occupied. For the purposes of this exercise, do* not *include the spaces or punctuation between the words as parts of the words.*

Thinking of the storage unit of the computer as if it were a chalk board ruled off into byte-size squares, each capable of holding one letter, number, or other symbol will often help us think more clearly about the way data are represented in the computer. The basic function of the storage unit is to hold data in particular arrangements. The programer can define and prescribe that arrangement by observing some rules and conventions as explained in Chaps. 3 and 4.

The computer takes the data to be processed, as needed, from the storage unit to the unit of the computer that does most of the actual processing, the arithmetic and logic unit, as shown by arrows in Fig. 2-1. Arithmetic and logic manipulations are the third function. Figure 2-1 also indicates that data typically also flow from the arithmetic and logic unit back to the storage unit. These data are the results obtained by the computer from doing arithmetic and logic operations, such as additions, multiplications, subtractions, divisions, and comparisons.

Whenever the processing of the data is complete, the computer can communicate the results of the processing. This is the fourth function, for the computer would be useless indeed if it kept secret the results of processing the data. The programer must have some way for the computer to present the results of the processing. The data presented by the computer are known as the "output data," and the part of the computer that presents the data is known as the "output unit."

The remaining functional unit of the computer is the control unit. Control is the fifth function. The control unit interprets the program which is held in storage just as if it were data. This is a vital feature, for it enables the computer to operate on its own. The control unit, as it takes the program part by part in sequence, calls into action the other parts of the computer, and monitors their performance for accuracy and completeness. A few of the functions performed by the control unit are listed later in this chapter.

FUNCTIONAL UNITS AND EQUIPMENT

The computer can use any of a range of equipment (see Fig. 2-3) for performing the input function. These include punched-card readers, magnetic-tape drives, magnetic-disk drives, keyboards, optical character readers, paper-tape readers, magnetic-ink character readers, communication adapters, data-cell drives, magnetic drums, and data-collection equipment. Let us look briefly at the more important of these at this time and defer the others.*

Card readers translate the data represented as patterns of holes in a punched card into data represented as electrical pulses that can be sent to the storage unit. The punched cards are not altered by the reading process while they pass through the reader mechanism.

Magnetic-tape drives serve as storage devices as well as input equipment. The drive unwinds magnetic tape from one reel past a reading head and then to a take-up reel. During that process, the data recorded on the tape are read, converted to

---

* For a comprehensive discussion of these items of equipment and other features, and how they operate, see, for example, Ned Chapin. *Computers*. New York: Van Nostrand Reinhold Company, 1971. 686 pp.

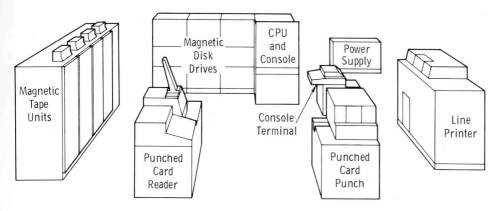

Fɪɢ. 2-3. Key to the items of equipment shown in the frontispiece. (IBM System/370 Model 135.)

electrical pulses, and sent to the storage unit. The tape is similar in form to that used with home tape recorders but is of higher quality, and has a different width, thickness, and recording pattern.

Magnetic-disk drives also serve as storage devices. They serve as input equipment too in that data can be read from the moving disk as the disk surface passes under a reading head attached to an arm that can position the reading head over selected places on the disk surface. Data on magnetic disks are typically recorded and read in nested concentric circles. The reading process is much the same as for magnetic tape, but on magnetic tape the data are typically recorded as a continuous series of characters down the length of the tape, not in concentric circles.

Keyboards are found as part of the control unit of the computer, as well as on inquiry stations such as those used by bank tellers or executives to supply data to the computer. Some of these keyboards look very similar to typewriter keyboards and operate in much the same fashion. Some keyboards have rows of toggle switches, and some have lighted buttons which can be pressed to turn them off or on.

Storage in the computer is accomplished by several devices. Major devices are the magnetic core matrix and the monolithic circuit array for internal storage. The capacity (number of bytes) of the internal storage varies from model to model of the computer, but normally provides for the storage (holding) of from about 4K (4,000) bytes of data to more than three million bytes, each of which can hold a character, such as a letter of the alphabet, a digit, or some special symbol such as a mark of punctuation. The place or location in storage of each byte of data is assigned an identifying number called the "address," so that each place in storage where data can be stored can be identified uniquely and differentiated from any other place in storage. Any one of as many as 256 different characters can be represented by one byte of internal storage, with one character per byte, or sometimes more, as described in Chap. 3.

Supporting the internal storage are four major types of devices for external storage: magnetic-tape drives, magnetic-disk drives, data-cell drives (mass storage), and magnetic drums. The magnetic-tape drives provide rapid reading and writing (copying) of data to and from internal storage. The disks and the mass storage cells provide for random access to large quantities of data, and the magnetic drums provide access to smaller quantities. The magnetic drums provide the most rapid, magnetic disks the next most rapid, and data cells the slowest access to the stored data.

In contrast to the lengthy list of equipment available for doing input and storage operations, the equipment available for doing arithmetic and logic operations is much more limited. Most models of the computer are equipped with from eight to twenty special places where the numbers and other data can be held while they are being operated on arithmetically or logically at high speed. These special places are known as "registers" and often hold data used in performing additions, subtractions, multiplications, divisions, and comparisons. If the data for arithmetic and logic operations are obtained directly from and returned directly to internal storage, the result is a slower speed of operation. Some models of the computer have no actual registers, but can use some parts of storage in a manner very much like using a register.

The equipment used for output parallels that used for input, but with differences. The major items of output equipment are printers, magnetic-tape drives, magnetic-disk drives, data-cell drives, magnetic drums, punched-card punches, paper-tape punches, visual displays, graph plotters, communications adapters, and audio communicators. Let us look briefly at the more common of these.

The printers are very common and provide for writing data on paper or reproduction masters in human-readable characters, as English letters and Arabic numerals. A great variety of data formats are possible, and this is one of the reasons for the popularity of printers. Control over these formats is a major concern of the programer.

Punched-card output is typically less complex because the formats for data are much more restricted, and data usually must be punched more slowly than they can be printed. Since the magnetic-tape drives, magnetic-disk drives, data-cell drives, and magnetic drums are also storage devices, their output operation is normally parallel to, but the reverse of, their input operation. The other output devices are much less commonly encountered.

In considering both output and input equipments, data flows are of great importance to the programer. Input data flow from the input equipment to internal storage. All the data received by and produced (put out) by the output equipment come from internal storage. The connection equipment that ties together the input, storage (both external and internal), and output, is known as "channels." A channel is partly a protected bus for the flow of data and partly the associated controlling equipment for regulating the flow of data.

As used with the computer, a channel can be thought of as a data pathway combined with a buffer (converter and synchronizer), which together provide for the communication and translation of data passing between input and internal storage, internal storage and output, and back and forth between internal and external storage. Because of this channel connection, the input, output, the external storage equipment can together be termed "peripheral equipment." The channels make it possible for several peripheral pieces of equipment to be operating in an essentially simultaneous way (and in an overlapping fashion), providing data to and taking data from internal storage. To make this possible, the channels provide a communication link between the peripheral equipment and the rest of the computer. Thus when the peripheral equipment is ready to provide or receive data, other operations involving internal storage in the computer are briefly stopped until the data movement is complete. This stopped or "lockout" time (from reference to internal storage) is only a small part of the time during which the peripheral equipment operates.

On all but small models of the computer, the channel has two forms, the multiplexor channel and the selector channel. The selector channel is used for high-speed input and output equipment such as magnetic-tape drives and magnetic-disk files. The multiplexor channel is used for slower equipment such as card readers and line printers. The multiplexor channel also provides for time-sharing of the capability of the channel, permitting several input and output equipment units to appear to be using one channel at essentially the same time. To this extent the multiplexor channel can be thought of as being composed of a number of subchannels, one to service each item of equipment, whereas a selector channel can be thought of as having only one subchannel, which operates in the "burst mode"—i.e., fully utilizes the capacity of the channel.

The brief lockouts and extensive overlapping operations resulting from the use of channels add greatly to the power and flexibility of the computer's processing ability. They also complicate the job of the programer, for he must organize and direct these functions in order to obtain efficient operation from the computer. For many simple jobs, however, these lockout and overlap features of the channels can be ignored. It is only when the job requires several types of peripheral equipment that the programer must give careful attention to obtaining effective utilization of the channel capabilities.

The channel capabilities also represent one important aspect of control within the computer. A great variety of control functions is provided in the computer but, except for the channels, are not usually identifiable with any specific equipment. For instance, the control unit meshes, specifies, starts, and stops the operation of the equipment and devices used for input, storage, arithmetic and logic, and output, including the channels. The control unit provides order and direction among these numerous operations, while at the same time the control unit watches for errors. When the control unit detects these, it interrupts automatically the operations being done.

Some of the specific features of the control unit's operation are worthy of mention at this point. These typically influence the way the programer must do his work, because of their pervasive influence upon the way the computer works. The implications of these features will appear frequently in later chapters.

Basic among the control functions of importance to the programer are the channel capabilities cited previously. These affect input and output operations which are presented in Chaps. 7 and 11.

A second control function of importance to the programer is the interrupt upon termination of a peripheral operation. The channel provides these interrupt signals. The result of the interrupt is to cause a change in the program "control sequence." This allows the programer to provide ways of handling peripheral error conditions as well as the completion of the input or output operation. Most programers rely on the "Input-Output Control System" (IOCS) to assist them in handling these peripheral interrupts.

A third control function of importance to the programer is the automatic change in program "control sequence" upon interrupt. Interrupts may arise from invalid addresses, invalid data, and other error conditions. If the control unit interrupts the computer in performing one job, then the computer attempts to go on and perform the next job or, in the small models, the computer may halt or stop operating. This ability, although it facilitates computer operation in the larger models, places a burden of accuracy on the programer. If the programer is to have the computer do his job, he must write the program in such a way that no error condition can arise as the computer executes the job, or so that those conditions which can arise are specifically provided for. This is only good policy anyway, but the computer helps enforce it with the interrupts. In practice, the skillful programer can use this feature to advantage for identifying and handling exception cases and alternative processings of the data.

A fourth control function of importance to the programer is storage protection. Certain areas of storage may be protected from being read from, or being written in (altered), or both. Thus, for the "read only" protection, the computer can read data from an area of storage but cannot write there. Hence it becomes impossible for the programer to have the computer alter, either by accident or by deliberate design, the data held in specified places in storage. If the computer makes an attempt, an interrupt occurs. Not all models of the computer come equipped with this storage protection function. Hence the programer is wise to keep in mind the possibility that he may be writing programs for use on a computer with it.

A fifth control function of great importance to the programer is the ability of the control unit for all but the small models of the computer to treat interchangeably any 4,096 bytes (characters) of storage except part of the first 4,096 bytes or storage subject to storage protection. This allows the programer to have the computer arrange data in storage far more flexibly than in the past. The programer, however, pays a price for this flexibility. The reason is that under common operating procedures, the programer rarely can be certain exactly where in storage any group of

4,096 consecutive bytes of data or program will be found, even though the programer can be assured that within the group the arrangement of data is known. For this reason, it is almost essential that the programer do his work in some symbolic language that makes provision for identifying address (location) relationships among items of data in relative, not absolute, terms.

In discussing the functions of the control unit of the computer, no attempt has been made at this early stage to define these functions in full concrete detail or to indicate the full range of the capabilities or limitations. Some of these will be explored in greater detail in later chapters. At this point some discussion of programing languages is called for.

LEVELS OF LANGUAGE

Three levels of language can be used with the computer. Those at the highest level are known as automatic coding languages. Examples are PL/1, FORTRAN, ALGOL, and COBOL. As noted earlier, these languages are not covered in this book.

At the intermediate level, two forms of language are available for use with the computer. One of these is known as "RPG" or "Report Program Generator." Programers use this convenient language to tell the computer how to prepare reports from organized files of data. This book does not describe RPG. A second form of intermediate-level language is known as "assembly" language. This language is technically a symbolic language, and exists in a variety of forms. This book concentrates upon assembly language.

At the lowest level is machine language. For programing the computer, machine language is very difficult for large- and medium-size jobs. For very small jobs, or for making small corrections ("patches") to large programs originally written in other languages, programers can use machine language easily. In this book, therefore, no explicit attention will be given as such to programing in machine language. How to read language at the machine level and how to form it by translating from assembly language are covered in this book, and the workbook provides practice.

Machine language is the only language used by the computer in actually executing the program. Since the programer writes the program in the assembly language, he must have some means of converting or translating his program from the assembly language to the machine language. The programer can do this himself, or far more conveniently and more commonly, he can have it done by the computer under the control of what is known as an "assembler" or "compiler" program, depending upon the particular variety of the assembly language.

In the small models of the computer, the translating program is a true assembly program because it translates the assembly language line for line, producing not more than one instruction in machine language for each imperative instruction the programer wrote in assembly language. In larger models of the computer a compiler program can be, and usually is, used. It translates from assembly language into machine language, and in the process may translate one line of assembly language into several or many instructions in machine language. Since the compiler version of the translating program is commonly used for all models of the computer for which it is available, and since the features of the assembly language that require the compiler version of the translating program are described in this book, the translating program will be referred to here as a compiler. This should cause no concern because the functions of the assembler translating program can also be performed by the compiler translating program—another example of upward compatibility.

The process of going from assembly language to machine language gives rise to the use of special terms to describe the process. The assembly language is also known as the "source" language, and the machine language as the "object" language. The translation process is one of converting the directions about what the computer is to do, expressed in assembly language, into equivalent directions expressed in machine language.

The programer can control the translation done by the compiler just as he also controls the way the computer processes the data when executing his program. To control the compiler in its translation work, the programer uses what are known as "declarative statements." These tell the compiler where to begin the object program (the program in machine-language form) in storage, where in storage to reserve areas of certain sizes, and so on. Declaratives also identify the beginning and end of the assembly-language program, and may tell the compiler how registers are to be used.

By contrast, the imperative statements the programer writes tell the computer how it is to process the input data to produce the output data. Imperative statements are such things as add, multiply, move data, compare, and the like. The compiler translates these statements and incorporates them in translated form in the object (machine) language program. The declarative statements, in contrast, do not appear in the machine language explicitly, although their influence can be seen in the way in which the compiler translates the imperative statements.

ADDRESSING

The way in which the compiler translates the imperative statements depends in large part upon the manner in which the programer identifies or names ("addresses") items of data and parts of the program he writes. For this, the programer has two main ways of addressing: the machine language and the symbolic. As the names suggest, they are used primarily with the corresponding levels of language. However, as noted earlier since all of the symbolic names (addresses) eventually are translated by the compiler program into machine language, the machine-language addressing serves as the fundamental addressing used in the computer. The others are built upon it.

Two forms of machine-language addressing are important for the programer to understand. One of these, which can be called "absolute addressing," uses as the address the identifying numbers assigned to the individual bytes in storage. Figure 2-2 illustrates absolute addressing in a very simple form. The programer rarely uses absolute addressing because it is difficult to use accurately.

Do It Now Exercise 2-2. *Prepare a table showing the absolute address of the leftmost byte of each mark of punctuation, and of each group of spaces. Also show in your table a count (length) of the number of consecutive bytes having the same value as the byte having the address you note. For example, if the first of three consecutive bytes of spaces is in address 2D, show in the table 2D as the address and 3 as the length. Use the same data and format as in Do It Now Exercise 2-1. Include single spaces as if they were groups.*

The other form of machine-language addressing is base-and-displacement addressing. The programer typically uses this more frequently than absolute addressing. Base-and-displacement addressing takes advantage of the fact that in all but the small models of the computer, any group of 4,096 bytes of internal storage can usually be used interchangeably with any other group of 4,096 bytes. The exception is the first group, which is not interchangeable because part of it is used for special purposes. The following are some other factors that affect use of base-and-displacement addressing. (1) Groups of 2,048 bytes may be subject to storage protection in strict absolute-address sequence position, 2,048 bytes at a time. (2) In contrast, the absolute address of the beginning of each group of 4,096 bytes need not be 4,096, 8,192, or the like, but can be anywhere for base-and-displacement addressing. (3) The 4,096 bytes in a group represent the maximum size of the group (groups may be any smaller size and still be conveniently handled in the base-and-displacement manner).

In base-and-displacement addressing, the programer counts from the first byte of the group to the byte for which he wants an address. This count is known as the displacement. For this purpose, the first or base byte of each group is counted as 0000. In practice, the programer just assigns (gives) a symbolic name to the byte he desires to address. The compiler program counts off the number of bytes to determine the displacement for the programer. The programer then uses a register to designate the address of the first or base byte in the group in which the compiler counts the displacement.

An example may make this clearer. The pages in this book are numbered consecutively throughout. The workbook also has the pages numbered consecutively throughout. For example, a page 14 can be found in the workbook as well as in this book. A reference, therefore, to page 14 may mean either page 14 in this book or page 14 in the workbook. The 14 is the equivalent of the displacement address. It names a location in a group of pages (a book) in terms of how far displaced it is from the start of the book. Then, by analogy, the base is the way of designating which book to look in. The base specifies whether it is in the workbook or in this book that the page number is to be sought.

The computer calculates absolute addresses from the base-and-displacement addresses in machine language in the following manner. The computer takes the number that represents the displacement amount (it is assumed to be a positive binary number) and adds to it the binary number that represents the base. That base number is the absolute address of the beginning of the group of bytes—that is, the leftmost or lowest-numbered absolute address of the group. The base address is always the contents of (held in) a register. Thus, adding together the contents of the register holding the base ("the base-register contents") and the displacement amount yields the equivalent absolute address as a binary number ("the effective address"). Either the base amount or the displacement may be zero. The usual practice in order to designate a deliberate base amount of zero is to use register number 0 as the base register. The computer interprets this as meaning "use zero as the base-register amount" and does not use the actual contents of register 0. Any other general-purpose register may be used as a base register, that is, to hold the base address.

One of the advantages of base-and-displacement addresses in machine language can be appreciated from an example. Suppose that the register to be used as a base is register 9, and that the displacement is 4 bytes into the group. If the (base) register 9 contains the binary equivalent of 8,192, then the computer calculates the effective absolute address as 8196. If now for some reason, a group of 3,008 bytes starting at address 8192 is to be used for some other purpose and hence will be unavailable to the program, the computer operator, by using a relocating loader program and without even bothering the programer, can change the contents of the (base) register 9 to some other absolute address, such as 11200, leaving the displacement unchanged at 4. The new effective address is 11204.

Do It Now Exercise 2-3. *Assume that register number 6 is to serve as a base register. Assume that this register contains the binary equivalent of the decimal number 10,000. Find in decimal the absolute address that is equivalent to the base-and-displacement address for each of the following displacements: 25; 198; 0; 4,095. Assume now that register number 6 contains the equivalent of the decimal number 2,048. Using the same displacements as before, find in decimal the equivalent absolute addresses.*

In practice, the programer writes symbolic addresses in his assembly-language program to identify most of the items of data to be operated on by the computer, as well as most of the references to parts of the program. These symbolic addresses are translated by the compiler usually to base-and-displacement addresses, or more rarely to absolute addresses.

The symbolic addresses used by the programer take four main forms: self-defining values, literals, symbolic names, and relative addresses. Let us look at each of these. The self-defining values are substitutes for absolute addresses. The programer commonly uses these to designate, for example, register numbers, as when the programer wants to refer to register 6. Then he typically writes the self-defining number 6. Self-defining addresses are simple and straightforward in their use.

Literals are similar to self-defining values but may use numbers or letters or other characters. Their value is just what it appears to be. However, the address consequences are very unlike self-defining values. A self-defining value typically represents an address, but a literal does not. Instead, the compiler assigns a base-and-displacement address to the literal, and treats it like a piece of data whose own value serves, in effect, as its symbolic name. The compiler collects most literals and puts them in a group called the "literal pool" in internal storage. Literals are not available on the small models of the computer.

Very common, but not quite so simple, are symbolic names. These the programer assigns as he desires. The compiler usually translates these into base-and-displacement addresses. In the small models of the computer, the programer may not use a name more than four characters long. In other models, the programer may use names up to six or eight characters long. For all models, the name typically must begin with an alphabetic letter and be limited to letters of the alphabet and the digits 0 through 9. For the larger models of the computer and for special purposes, some additional characters are possible, such as $ and &.

For example, if a programer wishes to use a particular area of storage for holding input data, he can, if he desires, assign to that area a symbolic name such as INPUT. If he wishes, for example, to have a particular part of storage hold the numeric value +1, he can assign a symbolic name such as PONE. The choice of names available to the programer in assembly language is limited primarily by the programer's imagination and the maximum length of four, six, or eight characters. Some programers use letters of the alphabet in a fixed rotating pattern, such as AAA, AAB, AAC, and so on. Others use names of their friends, such as FRED, JOE, MARY, and BABS. Some use the names of common household or office items, or of automobiles, or of anything that may strike their fancy. Programers generally prefer to use mnemonic symbolic names, or at least names high in personal association value for the data they identify, such as GRSPAY for a gross pay.

The fourth type of symbolic address is the relative address. This is superficially similar in form to the base-and-displacement type of address. A relative address is composed of two parts: the name that designates the origin point, and a number preceded by a plus or minus sign, which designates a count of the number of bytes of distance from that origin (displacement). For example, suppose the programer has given the symbolic name POINT to some particular place in storage, as shown in Fig. 2-4. If the programer wishes now to designate a place five byte locations higher (that is, conceptually to the right) in storage, the programer can write

POINT+5. If the programer desires to designate a place in storage with three byte positions lower in storage (conceptually to the left) from the place named POINT, the programer can write POINT−3.

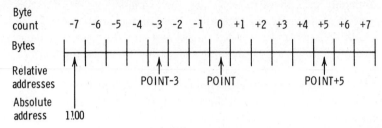

FIG. 2-4. Relative addresses.

In using relative addresses, the programer must keep in mind that the counting of address positions is by byte and that the byte which has the name of the origin is counted as byte number 0. When large byte counts are involved or when tables of data in storage are being used, the programer can also use a multiplication sign after the plus or minus quantity. Then he uses another number to indicate the amount by which he wishes the first number multiplied. For example, if the programer wishes to go 99 bytes to the right of the place named POINT, the programer can write POINT+9∗11.

The programer must make a clear distinction between relative addresses at the symbolic level and base-and-displacement addresses at the machine-language level. In general, symbolic name addresses, literals, and relative addresses are translated by the compiler program to base-and-displacement addresses. Address constants of type A or Y are the major exception. These are always in absolute form, because they may be relocated at the time a program is loaded into internal storage for execution. Furthermore self-defining values are usually translated as absolute addresses. This means that the base-and-displacement address assigned by translation for a relative address will have the name part expressed as a base-and-displacement address and the address count expressed as an additional displacement amount either increasing or decreasing the amount of the original displacement. For example, in Fig. 2-4, assume that register 8 is the base register and contains the absolute address 1100. Then the base-and-displacement equivalent of the symbolic name address POINT is register 8 (containing 1100) and displacement 0007 (here expressed in decimal numbers). For the relative address POINT−3, it is register 8 (containing 1100) and displacement 0004, which is 3 less than the original displacement of 0007.

CODING FORM

With some knowledge of addressing, the programer is now in a position to learn about one of the programer's basic tools, the coding form. The coding form is a means of capturing the input statements for the compiler program. The statements the programer writes on the coding form are typically keypunched into punched cards, which in turn serve as input to the compiler. The output from the compiler run typically is a listing of the programer's program showing the translation from source to object language, and a copy of the machine-language program in the form of data either on magnetic tape, on magnetic disks, or on punched cards. The starting point for this set of steps is, however, the coding form that the programer fills out. A sample of a coding form is shown in Fig. 2-5.

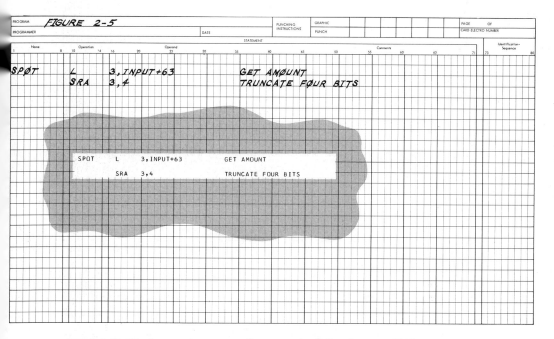

Fig. 2-5. Coding form and corresponding computer listing for assembly language.

The coding form has two major parts, the identification part and the statement part. The identification part across the top of the form provides space for the programer to number the pages, to show the date, to write his name and the name of his program, and to specify some directions to the keypunch operator on how the statement should be punched into cards. None of the identification part has anything to do with the program the computer programer writes. The identification data are for human use only; any or even all of them may be omitted if desired.

The programer uses the statement part of the coding form to list the imperative and declarative statements for the computer and for the compiler program, respectively. This part of the form the programer must fill in with care. It has five parts, called the "name," "operation," "operand," "comment," and "identification-sequence" parts. Normally the programer writes one statement on one line on the coding form, but may under some conditions and for larger models of the computer continue onto other lines.

The first part of a statement is the name assigned to the statement. This the programer writes starting in the first space on the line on the coding form for each statement. Often the programer leaves the name blank. The programer needs to assign a name only to items of data or of the program which are going to be referred to elsewhere in the program. Some of the requirements on names were cited earlier in the chapter. Whenever possible, and except when needed to aid in understanding the program (documentation), the programer should leave the name blank. This is because increasing the number of names increases the length of time required for the computer to translate the program written on the coding form into a program in machine language. Figure 2-5 shows, on the first line of the statement part, an example of a named statement; on the second line, of an unnamed statement.

The operation part of the statement specifies the imperative or declarative operation. This is written in a mnemonic code and must be left-justified in the columns on the coding sheet, with blanks used for fill on the right, as shown in Fig. 2-5.

The operand part of the statement normally specifies by name the data the computer is to operate upon, or provides specifications to the translation program. When more than one operand is permitted in a statement, the operands must be correctly identified and, usually, separated by commas. Blanks (spaces) may not be included in or between operand names. Special characters have some special meanings when used in the operand part of the coding form. At least one blank (one space) must follow the last character of the operand on the coding sheet to separate the operand part of the statement from the comment part.

The programer can use the comment part of the statement to say anything he desires within the space available. The translating program ignores the comments in the process of translating the statements into machine language. Any characters may be used in any quantity. If the programer desires more space for comments, he can place an asterisk (∗) in the first position of the name part, and then use the rest of the statement up through the comment part for more comments.

The identification-sequence part of the coding form may be filled in with any data desired. If the translating program is to check the sequence of the statements while translating them, then the rightmost three digit positions of the identification-sequence part should be numeric (digits 0 through 9). Blanks and special symbols are permitted in the identification-sequence part.

The programer should take note of the small numbers from 1 or 25 through 80 across the top of the statement part of the coding form. These specify the card columns into which the parts of the statements are to be punched, character for character. To separate the name from the operation, a blank is used in card column 9 or 31. To separate the operation from the operand part a blank is used in column 15 or 37. To separate the comment part from the identification-sequence part, a blank is used in column 72, unless the next line is a continuation of the statement on this line. Other formats are possible, but the one illustrated is the standard format. In filling in the coding sheet, a programer should take care to write clearly and put only one character in a box, as illustrated in Figure 2-5. The programer must give special attention to distinguishing zero from the letter O, 1 from I, 2 from Z, 5 from S, and 7 from 1. Neat hand lettering on the coding form helps avoid mistakes.

ANSI STANDARD FLOW DIAGRAM SYMBOLS

To help decide what to write on the coding form, programers generally first make an analysis of a job. For this purpose, programers have found flow diagrams helpful. Such diagrams enable the programer to set down, piece by piece, the essential steps in a job. Since the diagram is graphic in form, revisions are easy, and the entire sequence of steps can be comprehended quickly—sometimes, in simple cases, even at a glance.

Because of the wide acceptance and utility of flow diagraming as an analysis aid, some computer users and manufacturers banded together some years ago and through the American National Standards Institute offered a standard set of flow diagram symbols. These symbols, also known as flowchart symbols, provide separate outlines and conventions to express a variety of data-processing operations as they are commonly implemented on computers. Let us look briefly at the major outlines and their use.

For representing input and output operations, the Standard advances the use of a parallelogram outline, as shown in Fig. 2–6. This outline is independent of the type of equipment used for performing the input-output operations. The diagram, therefore, is presented at a functional level, not at the equipment level, and makes no reference to the particular media used for input or output. Specifications of media and equipment are usually described in system charts prepared by system analysts rather than by programers.

For representing arithmetic and data-movement operations on input, output, or temporary data, the Standard advances the use of a rectangular outline, as shown in Fig. 2–6. If the programer desires to have the computer add, subtract, multiply, divide, or perform any special functions which are arithmetic in nature, this is the outline of choice. The programer does not use different outlines to distinguish among different types of arithmetic operations.

To designate the type of operation, the programer typically writes within the outline some identification, such as the name (address) of the field involved and of the operation. This may be done in words or by the use of symbols, such as + for addition, − for subtraction, * for multiplication, and / for division.

The programer also uses the rectangular outline box for data-movement operation. Again, the box outline makes no distinction between different types or classes of data-movement operation. If he desires, the programer may indicate within the outline of the box, by his choice of words or symbols, the nature of the data-movement operation, and identify the field of data being handled. A right-to-left arrow can be used to specify data movement or name assignment.

For logical processing, arithmetic, and data-movement operations performed on the instructions or constants of a program, the Standard advances the use of a flattened hexagon. By convention, it is not used for decision operations on the instructions or constants of a program.

For comparison operations and other decision operations, the Standard advances the use of the diamond outline, as shown in Fig. 2-6. As shown later, the programer can designate within and beside the outline, by using the appropriate

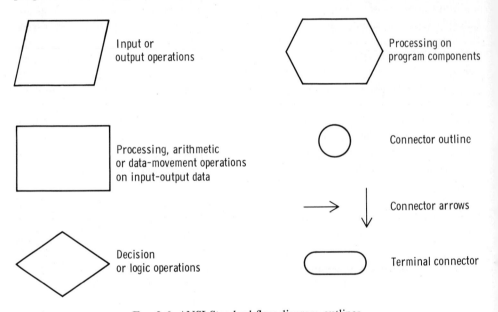

Fig. 2-6. ANSI Standard flow diagram outlines.

symbols, the identification of the fields being tested, and the basis for the resulting action. Within the outline, the programer can use a colon (:) to indicate comparison.

For connection, the Standard advances the use of a small circle, and of arrows. The programer, for example, as he writes diagram outlines down or across the page, soon comes to the bottom or edge of the page. To indicate where on this page or where on some other page the programer has continued the diagram, he uses the circle connector outline as an exit connector, as shown in Fig. 2-6. In this circle the programer places some symbols that identify the corresponding entry point in the program. Elsewhere in the diagram the programer uses the same connector outline and the same symbols as the entry connector. These entry-point symbols may or may not be the same as the symbolic names the programer has used to identify parts of his program. When they are names of parts of his program, the programer can use connector outlines to indicate such program-control operations as unconditional transfers of control. To connect outlines directly, the programer uses the arrows.

One other connector outline is available to the programer. To indicate the termination of a series of steps, such as the beginning or end of a diagram or a major section of one, the programer uses the terminal connector outline. For a beginning terminal, the programer writes within the outline the name of the part of the program which is entered. For the ending termination, the programer writes the type of ending.

DIAGRAM CONVENTIONS

Basic among the conventions for the use of the outlines is that some diagram outlines may have multiple exit arrows. Each such exit must be clearly identified according to the basis on which it is to be used. Other outlines should have only one exit arrow. Arrows may connect to each other but should avoid excessive crossing. All flow diagram outlines may have only one entrance arrow. To avoid unnecessary complexity, the programer should use as few connectors as possible. He can, however, use additional connectors to avoid having crossing arrows in a flow diagram.

By convention, the direction of flow (sequence of control) should be either from top to bottom on the page, or from left to right. The preferred direction is from top to bottom. Thus, by convention, the programer begins to read or prepare diagrams in the upper left-hand corner of the page and proceeds usually downward on the page until he reaches the bottom of the page. At that time, he encounters or writes a connector outline at the bottom with an identifying symbol, and again going to the top of the page, encounters or writes the same connector outline again. He then continues reading or writing diagram outlines down the page.

Where this convention of direction is followed, the arrow lines that connect the boxes need not have arrowheads on them. If for some reason, the programer finds it convenient or necessary to deviate from this conventional flow pattern, the programer should indicate this by means of arrowheads on the arrows, and should use connector outlines more extensively. This the programer can do, for example, if some part of the diagram is to be continued sideways on the page and then downward. To avoid long connecting arrows, or arrows going upward or leftward on a page, the programer should use connector outlines.

By convention, each outline should have only one entry arrow. Although this point is not critical for diagrams drawn at a very detailed level, it becomes important for diagrams drawn at a more general level. When many operations are covered within one outline, and the outline has only one entrance arrow, then there is by definition only one order in which the computer is to perform the operations within the outline. If, on the other hand, there are several entry lines coming into an outline, then it is not clear that there is only one sequence in which the computer is to perform the operations within the outline. To avoid this possible ambiguity, the convention is to use only one entry arrow to an outline. This entry line is typically assumed to come in at the top center of the outline.

The diamond decision outline is one of the two outlines which may have more than one exit arrow. Each exit arrow from the decision outline should be marked immediately above or to the right of its emergence from the outline with an indication of the basis on which this exit line is to be selected from all the others.

To make such a decision selection convenient and possible, the usual convention is to write the testing or compare operation within the decision outline in the form of a standard comparison sequence. In this standard sequence the variable of comparison is on the left of a colon, and the constant of comparison on the right of the colon. An example of this is shown in Fig. 2-7, in which it is assumed that the content of the field called HOUR is to be compared to the literal constant 40. The possible exit lines are less than (i.e., the HOUR amount less than 40); equal to (i.e., the HOUR amount exactly equal to 40); and greater than (i.e., the HOUR amount exceeding 40).

The input-output parallelogram outline may have two exit lines, provided that the operation is an input and that one of those exit lines is clearly labeled as being the "end-of-file" or "end-of-data" condition. An example of this is illustrated in Fig. 2-8. Each of the other outlines may have only one exit line or arrow.

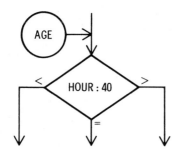

FIG. 2-7. Example of a decision outline.

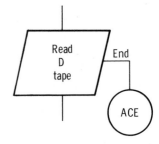

FIG. 2-8. Example of an input-output outline.

The programer should observe the distinction between operations the computer performs on its own program and operations it performs on the input data to produce the output data. For easy debugging, and for logical clarity in the program and diagram, the programer should keep these two sharply separate. By convention, these operations should not be combined within one outline in a flow diagram; distinct outlines are available.

In order to clarify the function of the connector outlines, the usual convention is to write the connector outline above or to the left, if the connector serves as an entry to a sequence of operations. This is illustrated by AGE in Fig. 2-7. The convention also is to write it below or to the right if it serves as an exit from, or as a direction to go to, some other set of operations. This is illustrated by ACE in Fig. 2-8. No arrowheads are needed to indicate the usual direction of "flow," but arrowheads may be included at any time for clarity.

As an example of flow diagram construction and interpretation, consider Fig. 2-9. The routine begins at the point or address SPT. After reading a card of data, the computer is to check the field INB for zero contents. If the field contents are not

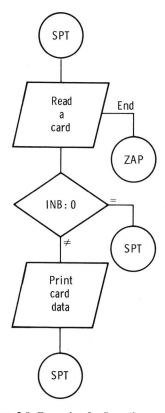

FIG. 2-9. Example of a flow diagram.

zero, the computer is to print the card data. If the field contents are zero, the computer is to go back to read another card. If the computer has read all cards, control is to go to the routine ZAP.

EXERCISES

1. List and identify each part of the coding sheet.
2. Distinguish among the four kinds of symbolic addresses, giving examples of each.

3. Explain how the computer calculates the effective address from a base-and-displacement address.

4. Make a simple diagram in functional terms of how the compiler works. Show in the diagram the input and the output, identifying each carefully.

5. Distinguish between the uses of all the outlines in the ANSI Standard flow diagram symbols.

6. What are the conventions on the use of connecting arrows in flow diagrams?

7. List in the form of a diagram all the items of peripheral equipment the computer can use. Make the diagram an elaboration on, and expansion of, a diagram similar to Fig. 2-1.

CHAPTER 3

Data Representation

DATA HIERARCHY

Programers work with all kinds of data. To carry out their work accurately, programers must make distinctions between the different types and levels of data with which they work. One of the most basic distinctions is the one between data about programs, on the one hand, and data to be processed by the computer under the control of programs, on the other. Data about programs are prepared by programers as they write on coding forms. Data about programs are used by programers as they study the specifications for a job. The data to be processed are the input data for the job. These usually come from an organization's operations: from the sales department, from the accounting department, from the production department, from the research laboratory, or the like.

An analogy may clarify this important distinction. Program data are data the programer uses as tools for directing the computer. For example, the programer writes statements on the coding form to instruct the computer on how it is to process the input data into the output data. Those statements are program data. On the other hand, data to be processed are the raw material the computer accepts for conversion into output data. These data to be processed can be likened to the ingredients of a cake. The flour, sugar, eggs, leavening, spices, and the like are combined into a batter. Then the batter is baked to produce a cake. The raw materials which produce the cake are the ingredients the cook uses to form the batter. These raw ingredients are like the data to be processed. The finished cake is like the output data.

Following this analogy, the program data are like the recipe the cook uses to direct the conversion of the raw ingredients (the input data) into the finished product (the output data). Program data, however, are in practice much more complicated than almost any recipe. Program data have structure, and special terms are used to identify the various components in the structure. Data to be processed also can be thought of as having structure, and different terms are used to describe that structure. A brief review of the major terms may be helpful. Let us look first at the terms for program data structure.

The largest and most inclusive unit in a program data structure is a program library (see Fig. 3-1). A program library is composed of individual programs, just as an ordinary library is composed of individual books. Each program typically has an identifying name just as books have.

A program library may be divided into groups of programs. These groups are called partitions of the program library. Groups of programs can also be known as phases, but a phase typically includes fewer programs than a partition. A phase can even be a group of program sections that are not even a complete program. A program section is typically composed of many routines and subroutines, but a program must be composed of at least one section.

Program sections, in turn, are composed of routines. A programer designs each of the routines in a program—and a program may have from one to many—to handle some particular part of the processing work. Three very common functions for which programers design individual routines are the setup or initialization for doing a job; the actual performance of a job; and the cleanup after, or end of, a job. Long programs may be composed of dozens of routines.

Routines, in turn, are composed of subroutines, but here two usages are common. Sometimes the terms "subroutine" and "routine" are used interchangeably. When a distinction between them is made, then the routine is assumed to be composed of subroutines. Sometimes the term "subroutine" is used to designate a part of the program that is essentially complete in itself and often logically independent from the rest of the program. These are sometimes called closed subroutines. For example, a part of the program that checks the sequence of input data might be thought of as a sequence-checking subroutine.

Routines and subroutines are, in turn, composed of a series of statements. These are of two types, the imperative and the declarative. The declarative statements are the programer's directions to the compiler program that translates the assembly-language program into the object program for the computer to execute. Some declarative statements are described later in this chapter.

The imperative statements are the programer's directions to the computer itself, telling it how to process the input data to produce the output data. The imperative statements are usually called instructions. The imperative statements (instruc-

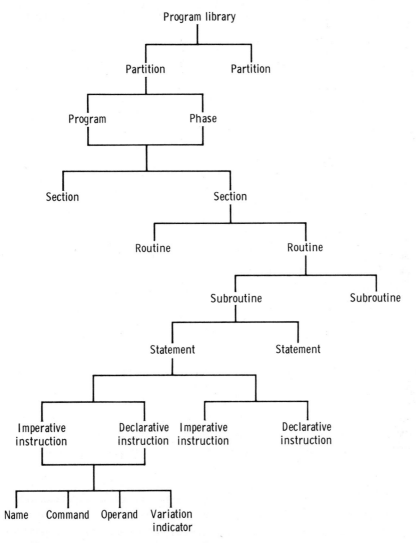

FIG. 3-1. Hierarchy of program data structure. Each level in the hierarchy is composed of a group of items from the next lower level.

tions) tell the computer what it is to do and on which items of data it is to do the work. The individual instructions in a series must be in a specific sequence in order for the computer to take correct action.

Instructions for the computer are composed of names, commands, operands, and variation indicators. The name is the identifying label the programer assigns to an instruction. Often the programer omits the name; this is equivalent to a blank name.

The command is the equivalent of an imperative verb telling the computer what action is to be performed. Here, however, a discrepancy in usage can be noted, especially in dealing with input and output operations. The computer manufacturers use any of several terms for command, including the terms "operation," "instruction," "code," and "order." These terms are used in a manner not fully consistent with traditional usage, or even consistent from one manufacturer to another. Where these discrepancies exist and where the terminology is important, an attempt is made in this book to use traditional terminology.

The operand names the item of data to be acted upon. Usually two or more items of data are involved in an operation, each identified by its address. Thus, for example, an item of data may be in register 2, or in address 2105, or in the address the programer has called (assigned the symbolic name) PLACE. In the assembly language, the programer can sometimes use literals. Here it appears that the programer makes reference to the data in an instruction without giving an address. As noted earlier, however, the computer in practice actually does assign an address—it is just that the programer is not aware of it. Sometimes a one-character literal can be incorporated directly in an imperative instruction.

The variation indicator specifies the length of an operand—that is, how many bytes of data the command is to operate on—and which index register the computer is to use in determining the address of an operand. An instruction may have several variation indicators. These are described in the later chapters of this book.

The terms used to describe operand data structures are considerably different from those used to describe program data structures. In describing the structure of data to be processed, the largest and most inclusive unit of organization typically is the file (see Fig. 3-2). The file is defined as an organized group of related records dealing with a particular subject area. For example, data maintained by a state's motor vehicle department, with a record for each driver who is licensed by the state, can be thought of as a file. Typically, files are identified by header records which appear as the first records in the file. As the last records in the file, one or more trailer records may appear. Files of data typically are organized in the sense that the individual records comprising them come in some particular sequence, referred to as the sort order or sequencing of the file. For example, a file of information on drivers in the state might be sequenced on a "key" of driver name or license number.

For convenience in the physical handling of files, they are typically broken into volumes, each consisting of many records. The volumes are usually the equivalent of the number of records that can be recorded on an individual magnetic tape or a set of magnetic disks. Thus, if the number of records in the file is sufficiently large to require three reels of magnetic tape to carry them, then the file would be considered to consist of three volumes of data. Volumes are sometimes divided into blocks of records. A block may comprise any number of records up to the number in a volume. Most blocks have from two to fifty records.

As noted previously, the fundamental unit of data within the file is the record.

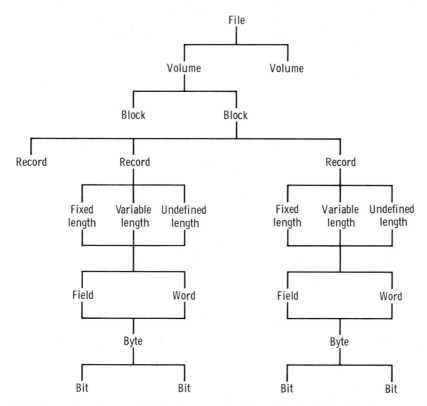

FIG. 3-2. Hierarchy of operand data structure. Each level in the hierarchy is composed of a group of items from the next lower level.

The record is a selection of data items called fields, all pertaining to a single subject, where the data items are organized in a particular format or arrangement. The format or arrangement of the fields in one record in a file is usually the same as for all the other records of the same type in a file. Thus, in the case of a driver's license record, the record might have in sequence fields for the license number, the driver's name, the driver's address, the year the license was first granted, the type of license granted, the expiration data of the license, and a tally of traffic violations.

Three types of records are common: fixed length, variable length, and undefined length. The length of a record is typically measured in terms of the number of bytes of data it comprises. If all of the records in a file are of the same length, the records are called fixed-length records. If the records comprising a file are of varied lengths, some longer and some shorter, the records are called variable-length records. Each such record has a count of its length in bytes as the first field in the record. Undefined records are all records that do not meet the specifications for either fixed or variable length.

Fields are the individual items of data which comprise a record. For example, as we just noted, the license number, the driver's name, the driver's address, and the type-of-license indicator are examples of fields. Fields may be of different lengths in terms of the numbers of characters of data they may contain. Thus a field one character long may be big enough to indicate the type of license issued to the driver, but the driver's address may require a field as long as fifty characters. A field, by definition, has no uniform length. The length of a field is known only when it is specifically stated.

This length factor provides the basic contrast of the term "field" with the term "word." A word is a fixed-length group of characters. In the computer, a word is four characters of data. Therefore a double word is eight characters of data, and a half word is two characters of data. More accurately, a double word is eight bytes of data, a word is four bytes of data, and a half word is two bytes of data. Sometimes the term "quadword" is used to designate the 16 bytes of a pair of double words.

Also in contrast to the definition of field, the definition of word implies alignment of the data by address. That is, a word must have a certain address or it is not properly a word in the computer. By definition a word is four consecutive bytes, so placed in storage that the first byte (that is, the leftmost or lowest-numbered byte of the group) is on a full-word boundary. A full-word boundary is any absolute address divisible by four with a remainder of zero. A double word must be so placed in storage that its leftmost byte is aligned on a double-word boundary which is any absolute address divisible by eight with a remainder of zero. A half word must be aligned on a half-word boundary which is any even absolute address. These length and alignment requirements are summarized in Fig. 3-3. In contrast, a field has no necessary alignment and no prescribed length.

Number of bits	Hexadecimal characters	Number of bytes	Name of the data	Alignment addresses for first byte in hexadecimal
1	1/4	1/8	Bit	Not directly addressed
4	1	1/2	Half byte	Not directly addressed
8	2	1	Byte	Any address
16	4	2	Half word	0, 2, 4, 6, 8, A, C, E
32	8	4	Word	0, 4, 8, C
64	16	8	Double word	0, 8

FIG. 3-3. Data hierarchy and addressing in internal storage in the computer.

A byte, which is the unit of data that comprises words and fields, is the data represented by eight binary bits. Excluded are parity and error checking and correction (ECC) bits which use an additional eight bits for each double word, the equivalent of one per byte. The data represented by an eight-bit byte are typically the equivalent of one character, such as a letter of an alphabet, a digit, or a special symbol like the dollar sign. Sometimes, however, it is convenient to refer to the left or right half of a byte. For convenience, the left half is also known as the zone half, and the right half as the digit half. Since a byte is the data represented by eight bits, and since each group of eight bits that comprise a byte has an absolute address, programers often find it convenient to refer to a byte as if it were an address. This is considered acceptable usage even though it is not precise.

Letters, numbers, and special characters (for example, $) in the computer are represented at the byte level. There are a large number of ways of doing this, but most of these ways suffer from one or more of three very serious defects: they are relatively costly, or they operate slowly, or they do not operate reliably. The computer, to be usable and economical, must be able to represent data inexpensively and reliably, and must be able to operate on the data very quickly.

Bytes are composed of eight bits, the lowest level in the data structure. A bit is the fundamental unit of data and is typically represented in symbol form by a 0 or a 1. These represent the two possible states of a two-state device. Large numbers of such devices are used as the basic electronic components of the computer. Conceptually, these "off-on" circuit elements are very simple. But this very simplicity, in turn, dictates a binary-based way of representing data. This places upon the programer the necessity of learning ways of representing data that are based on the binary system. Fortunately this is not difficult, but the programer does need a good grasp of the binary system. Readers seeking a review of the binary system and of bits will find such a presentation in the workbook.

Numbers in the computer can be represented in the binary system in fields of any length. But if the programer plans to use the same numbers frequently in arithmetic operations, the binary form in full or half words offers the highest computer operating speed. For numbers handled infrequently, for nonnumeric data, and for very large or very small numbers, however, the binary form is inconvenient, for several reasons.

HEXADECIMAL SYSTEM

One reason binary numbers are difficult for human beings to work with is that they appear unconventional and seem awkward in comparison with more compact representations. For example, the binary number 1111111111111111 is equivalent to decimal 65,535. One scheme to circumvent such awkwardness is to code each binary number by breaking it into groups of four bits, and replacing each group with a single symbol. This gives a notation or way of representing data even more compact than the decimal system offers because four bits provide for 16 decimal equivalents. The system and the symbols used are shown in Fig. 3-4 as the hexadecimal system. In that system, the hexadecimal equivalent of binary 1111111111111111 is FFFF.

The four bits of a half byte can be considered as a series of binary numbers with a range of decimal equivalents from numbers 0 through 15. It is inconvenient, however, for human beings to have to use sometimes one and sometimes two decimal digits (two decimal positions) to represent the value of each four-bit group. So that only one character or symbol will be used in one position, the numbers from 10

Binary	Decimal	Hexadecimal
0000	0	0
0001	1	1
0010	2	2
0011	3	3
0100	4	4
0101	5	5
0110	6	6
0111	7	7
1000	8	8
1001	9	9
1010	10	A
1011	11	B
1100	12	C
1101	13	D
1110	14	E
1111	15	F

FIG. 3-4. Table of equivalents for four-bit binary numbers.

through 15 are commonly replaced with the letters A through F as shown in Fig. 3-4 in the hexadecimal system. This system uses all 16 possible combinations of the bits of a half byte. Thus, the hexadecimal system is convenient for representing the data in a half byte by a single symbol, or in a full byte by only two symbols, as shown in Fig. 3-5.

Easy conversion back and forth between binary and hexadecimal is a major advantage of the hexadecimal system, as shown in Fig. 3-5. Figure 3-6 further illustrates these conversions. Note that the first step is to mark off groups for four consecutive bits, starting at the extreme right. Zeros may be used to fill the leftmost

```
                          Full word
          ┌─────────────────────────────────────────┐
                Half word                Half word
          ┌───────────────────┐  ┌───────────────────┐
            Byte       Byte        Byte       Byte
          ┌─────────┐┌─────────┐  ┌─────────┐┌─────────┐
          0010  0100  0101  0111  1001  1010  1011  1111
           2     4     5     7     9     A     B     F
```

FIG. 3-5. Hexadecimal coding and conversions for binary numbers.

00111010	0011	1010	0011 is equivalent to 3 1010 is equivalent to A	00111010
1 byte	1/2 byte	1/2 byte		3 A
				3A
				B2
B2	B	2	B is equivalent to 1011 2 is equivalent to 0010	B 2
1 byte	1/2 byte	1/2 byte		10110010

FIG. 3-6. Binary-hexadecimal conversions for bytes of data.

group. The second step is to find the desired equivalent from the table in Fig. 3-4. The final step is to specify that equivalent in the proper position. Thus, to take the first example, 00111010 can be grouped 0011 and 1010, which by Fig. 3-4 are, respectively, 3 and A. Hence the hexadecimal equivalent of 00111010 is 3A.

Do It Now Exercise 3-1. *What are the hexadecimal equivalents of the following bytes of binary data: 00000000, 00100111, 01000001, 01011010, 01111101, 10011110, 10100011, 10111001, 11001010, 11000111, 11111111, Convert the following hexadecimal numbers to their binary equivalents: 33, B4, 5C, 11, 00, FF, AA, E7, and D6.*

If more than one byte of data is to be worked with, the programer can just continue marking off groups for four bits, starting at the right and converting to the respective hexadecimal equivalent, or converting each hexadecimal character to four binary bits. The only caution, and it is a major one, is to make the groups fit within the bytes, and *not* straddle the boundary between adjoining bytes. Thus, if a byte has the bits 00111100, to pick out the middle four bits and call it equivalent to hexadecimal F would be incorrect. The bits for hexadecimal conversions must have group boundaries that synchronize with byte boundaries.

Do It Now Exercise 3-2. *What are the hexadecimal equivalents of the following binary numbers: 1000000000000001, 1010111010010101010100000, 010011111111101011011011011101110? What are the binary equivalents of 0423, A1B948, 803ADEFC?*

A common problem in working with either binary or hexadecimal numbers is to convert them into their decimal equivalents and to convert decimal numbers into hexadecimal and binary equivalents. Since hexadecimal numbers are more compact, good practice is to convert binary numbers to hexadecimal, and hexadecimal to binary if binary numbers are involved. Those conversions are easy, as has just been shown.

Conversion between decimal and hexadecimal can be done directly, e.g., by the Hartmann method described in Chap. 5. It can also be done conveniently by the use of tables. These tables permit the programer to break a number into parts, convert them, and then combine the conversion parts. For simplicity, let us consider conversion for whole numbers first.

Conversion of numbers from hexadecimal to decimal is most expeditiously handled by doing repeated additions from a conversion table. Suppose, for example, the hexadecimal number to be converted is A3F. Starting with the least significant (farthest to the right) character, which in this case is an F, the programer can search the integer conversion table shown in Appendix A for the decimal equivalent. This proves to be 15 and can be recorded accordingly, as shown in Fig. 3-7.

$$
\begin{array}{rl}
\text{A3F} = & ? \\
\hline
+\text{A00} = & +2560 \\
+\ 30 = & +\ \ 48 \\
+\ \ \text{F} = & +\ \ 15 \\
\hline
+\text{A3F} & +2623
\end{array}
$$

FIG. 3-7. Example of conversion of integer numbers from hexadecimal to decimal.

Since the F character of the number has been taken into account, the remaining next least significant character is 3. But since it is in the second position, it is really 30. According to the table shown in Appendix A, this is equivalent to 48 in decimal, as shown in Fig. 3-6. The remaining portion of the original number A3F in hexadecimal that has not been accounted for yet is the portion A00, since the A is in the third position. A search of the integer table in Appendix A shows this to be the equivalent of 2,560, as shown in Fig. 3-7.

Now comes the step of addition. The numbers F, 30, and A00, can be added as proof to yield the sum A3F. The corresponding decimal equivalents of 15, 48, and 2,560 can be added to obtain the decimal sum of 2,623, which is the decimal equivalent of hexadecimal A3F.

Suppose now the case be reversed. Suppose that the problem is to convert the decimal number 2,623 to its hexadecimal equivalent. The conversion procedure is substantially the same as the one just outlined but consists of subtractions rather than addition. Since subtraction is most conveniently done a step at a time, the process looks longer.

The first step is to search the integer table shown in Appendix A for the largest decimal number equal to or just smaller than the decimal number to be converted. A search of the table shows this decimal number to be 2,560, which is the equivalent of hexadecimal A00. This can be recorded as shown in Fig. 3-7 and the subtraction performed to obtain a difference of 63. This number now serves as the basis for a search of the *next* column of the table to the right of the one in which the first number was found. The largest decimal number equal to or just smaller than the resulting difference can then be recorded.

In the case at hand, a search of the next column to the right yields a decimal equivalent of 48, which is the next smaller number than 63, and is the equivalent of hexadecimal 30, as shown in Fig. 3-8. Subtraction yields a difference between the two decimal numbers of 15.

Again entering the table, the programer can search the next column to the right for the largest decimal number equal to or just smaller than the decimal number remaining. In this case, it is 15, which is the equivalent of hexadecimal F. After subtraction, as shown in Fig. 3-8, the remaining difference is 0. If it were not, it would indicate an error in making the conversion. Since the columns in the integer table shown in Appendix A have been exhausted, and since the difference resulting from

$$
\begin{array}{rl}
2623 & = \ ? \\
+ \quad 2623 & \\
-(+)2560 & = \ +A00 \\
+ \quad \overline{63} & \\
- \quad (+)48 & = \ + \ 30 \\
+ \quad \overline{15} & \\
- \quad (+)15 & = \ + \quad F \\
+ \quad \overline{0} & \quad +A3F
\end{array}
$$

Fig. 3-8. Example of conversion of integer numbers from decimal to hexadecimal.

the subtraction is 0, the conversion is complete. All that remains is to add the column of hexadecimal equivalents. The sum is hexadecimal A3F, which is just the equivalent expected for the decimal number 2,623. Note that integer conversion yields precise equivalents.

Do It Now Exercise 3-3. *Using the integer conversion table in Appendix A, convert the following numbers from hexadecimal to decimal: 9, 22, C6, ED, 4AF, D4B, 6C68E2C, and EA4B35CF. Convert the following numbers to hexadecimal: 11; 14; 17; 176; 245; 1,397; 20,999; 719,634; 5,000,000; 1,000,000; 1,000,000,000; and 4,025,986,437. Show each step in your work.*

Conversion of fractional numbers follows the same general form as the conversion of integer numbers but it requires the use of a different table, and the results usually are not precise. This is probably best illustrated by a sample. Let us consider the case of converting the hexadecimal number 0.A3F to the decimal equivalent. Using the same basic procedure as before, but in the reverse direction, the programer can begin with its first character to the right of the point. A search of the fraction conversion table in Appendix A indicates that the decimal equivalent of hexadecimal 0.A is 0.6250. This can be recorded in an appropriate form such as that shown in Fig. 3-9.

The steps thus far have accounted for the 0.A00 portion of the hexadecimal number, but have left the 0.03F portion unaccounted for. The 0.03 portion, according to a search of the fraction conversion table, has the decimal equivalent 0.0117-1875. The last portion, 0.00F, has the decimal equivalent 0.003662109375. These can be recorded in an appropriate form, as shown in Fig. 3-9. Addition of the

$$
\begin{array}{rcl}
0.A3F &=& ? \\
\hline
+0.A00 &=& +0.6250 \\
+0.\,030 &=& +0.0117\ 1875 \\
+0.\,00F &=& +0.0036\ 6210\ 9375 \\
\hline
+0.A3F &=& +0.6403\ 8085\ 9375
\end{array}
$$

FIG. 3-9. Example of conversion of fractional numbers from hexadecimal to decimal.

equivalents indicates that the decimal number equivalent to hexadecimal 0.A3F is 0.640380859375. If only four fractional places (positions) can be saved, then a round-off to 0.6404 is needed. Thus, as a practical matter, fractional conversions often yield approximate equivalents.

To illustrate more fully this degree of imprecision, let us consider now the case of converting to hexadecimal the decimal number 0.6404 (the rounded-off result of the previous conversion). Essentially the same procedure is followed as that illustrated previously for integer numbers. Starting with the first character to the right of the point (the leftmost position), the programer can search the leftmost column of the table shown in Appendix A. The first step, therefore, is to search the table for the largest decimal number less than or equal to the number to be converted. This can be found in the first column of decimal equivalents as 0.6250, which is the equivalent of hexadecimal 0.A and can be recorded in some suitable form such as that shown in Fig. 3-10.

$$
\begin{array}{rcl}
0.6404 &=& ? \\
\hline
+\quad 0.6404 & & \\
-(+)0.6250 &=& +0.A00 \\
\hline
+\quad 0.0154 & & \\
-(+)0.0117 &=& +0.\,030 \\
\hline
+\quad 0.0037 & & \\
-(+)0.0036 &=& +0.\,00F \\
\hline
+\quad 0.0001 & & +0.A3F
\end{array}
$$

FIG. 3-10. Example of conversion of fractional numbers from decimal to hexadecimal.

As before, the programer now can make a subtraction between the 0.6404 and the 0.6250, yielding a difference of 0.0154. Moving one column to the right in the fraction conversion table, the programer can search again for the decimal equivalent equal to or just smaller than the remaining difference. If this decimal number is all zeros, the conversion is complete. In the case at hand, the programer can find a decimal number, 0.0117 for which the equivalent is hexadecimal 0.03. Note the rounding-off needed to stay within the number of decimal digits available. This the programer can record as shown in Fig. 3-10. The difference of 0.0037 resulting from subtraction serves as the basis for a search of the next column to the right in the table. Here the decimal number of 0.0036 can be found, for which the equivalent is hexadecimal 0.00F. A subtraction yields a difference of 0.0001. The question now arises whether to terminate the conversion operation at this point or to carry it further. Obviously it could be carried further, if additional digits in the number to be converted were available, or if such digits could be properly assumed to be zeros. In this case, however, since the number was obtained by rounding-off a more precise number, there is no point to carrying the conversion any further. The only remaining question, therefore, is how the round-off should be made at this point.

The general rule for determining whether a round-off should be made by truncation (chopping off) or rounding-up (adding 1 to the last place retained) is to compare the difference obtained as the result of the last subtraction with the first two entries in the same column from which the programer obtained the last number subtracted. In this case, a reference to the table shows those decimal numbers to be 0.00000 and 0.00024. Since 0.00010 is less than half of the difference between them, rounding the number up is not appropriate, but truncation is. Hence the hexadecimal equivalents thus far obtained can be added without a round-off factor, to yield a sum of hexadecimal 0.A3F.

Using round-off generally introduces error or imprecision into the affected numbers. Round-off rules commonly give upward (away from zero) bias or error. In extended computation round-off effects can accumulate to the point of making results useless.

To convert mixed integer and fractional numbers, such as 2623.6404, between decimal and hexadecimal, the programer can proceed in the same manner illustrated previously if he treats the integer part (to the left of the point) separately from the fractional part (to the right of the point). Then the programer can combine the parts after conversion to obtain the mixed-number result.

Do It Now Exercise 3-4. *Using the integer and fractional conversion tables in Appendix A, convert the following numbers from hexadecimal to decimal: 5.0, 0.5, A.3, B4.7E, and 92C4.8EA2. Convert the following decimal numbers to hexadecimal: 5.0, 0.5, 3.14159, 2.71828, 62.425, and 0.45359. Carry all fractional work to four places of precision, truncating or rounding-off as required. Show all steps in the work.*

ALPHANUMERIC SYSTEMS

The hexadecimal and binary systems are useful to the programer for describing the data held in the storage unit and operated upon by the arithmetic and logic unit. But they do not by themselves provide an answer to the question of how to represent alphabetic data, special characters of various types, and decimal digits in the computer. The two main ways are referred to as the EBCDIC and the ASCII.

The letters EBCDIC stand for Extended Binary Coded Decimal Interchange Code, a coding system based partly upon the Hollerith punched-card coding system. In Hollerith coding, the alphabetic letters are represented by two punches in a card column, called the "over" or "zone" punch and the "digit" punch. The digit-punch range extends from a 1 punch through a 9 punch. For numeric data it may also be a 0 (zero) punch. A zone punch is a punch in the top two rows of the card, called the Y or X rows, or if it is not the only punch in a column, a punch in the 0 (zero) row.

In EBCDIC coding, the zone punch is represented by the leftmost half of the byte ("zone half") and the digit punch by the rightmost half of the byte ("digit half"). The Y-zone punch is represented by hexadecimal C, the X-zone punch by hexadecimal D, and the 0-zone punch by hexadecimal E. The absence of a zone punch (no zone punch is used for Hollerith coded decimal digits) is represented by hexadecimal F. The digit punches are indicated by hexadecimals 0 through 9, which correspond to the punches 0 through 9. This is summarized in Fig. 3-11, which also shows the special characters used in the EBCDIC code.

To talk of "C," "10," and the like, can cause much confusion unless one specifies the code system. Is "C" in hexadecimal or EBCDIC? Is "10" in binary? To reduce such potential ambiguities in this book, the following aids are used hereafter. A subscript x means that the symbol it follows is shown in hexadecimal code. A subscript b means that the symbol it follows is shown in binary code. The absence of any subscript letter or the presence of c means that the symbol is just what it appears to be and is shown in the EBCDIC code.* Thus, 1010_b is the same as A_x, and 0111_b is the same as 7_x. Where pairs of subscripts follow a symbol, the first letter indicates the code base used, and the second letter indicates how the coded data are intended to be interpreted. Thus 10101000_{bc} is a binary number intended to be interpreted as EBCDIC.

The American National Standards Institute (ANSI) has advanced the ASCII code (American Standard Code for Information Interchange), also called the USASCII code. To avoid ambiguity, ASCII coded data are marked by a subscript k in this book. The ASCII alphabet runs continuously from $A1_x$, for the letter A_k, to BA_x for the letter Z_k, as shown in Fig. 3-12. Thus 10100001_{bk} is a binary number intended as an ASCII character (A_k). The decimal numbers 0 through 9 are represented by 50_x through 59_x. The special characters are also grouped differently. Compare especially the plus-and-minus-sign representation in the ASCII and EBCDIC codes. Note that the representation for a space or blank, i.e., for the deliberate absence of a printable character, is identical in both the EBCDIC and ASCII codes, a 40_x.

---

* The usual practice is to pronounce EBCDIC as *eb*-see-dick, ASCII as *ask*-key, and ANSI as *anne*-see.

Do It Now Exercise 3-5. *Translate the data from Fig. 2-2 to hexadecimal, assuming first that they are in EBCDIC code and then that they are in ASCII. In writing these out, mark the coding off into words and double words by using one blank space before each word and two blank spaces before each double word, with two double words to a line. This causes no confusion in reading the hexadecimal coding, since a blank is* not *a hexadecimal character.*

For representing only numeric data, both the EBCDIC and ASCII codes are redundant and wasteful of storage space in the computer. This is because for numeric data in EBCDIC, the zone half of each byte is an F_x, and in ASCII it is a 5_x. The

Left or zone half of byte in hexadecimal

	0	1	2	3	4	5	6	7	8	9	A	B	C	D	E	F	
0	NULL	DLE	DS		Δ	&	–								0	0	
1	SOH	DC1	SS				/		a	j			A	J		1	1
2	STX	DC2	EFS	SYN					b	k	s		B	K	S	2	2
3	ETX	TM							c	l	t		C	L	T	3	3
4	PF	RES	BYP	PN					d	m	u		D	M	U	4	4
5	HT	NL	LF	RS					e	n	v		E	N	V	5	5
6	LC	BS	ETB	UC					f	o	w		F	O	W	6	6
7	DEL	IL	ESC	EOT					g	p	x		G	P	X	7	7
8		CAN							h	q	y		H	Q	Y	8	8
9		EM							i	r	z		I	R	Z	9	9
A	SMM	CC	SM		¢	!		:									A
B	VT	CU1	CU2	CU3	.	$	,	#									B
C	FF	FS		DC4	<	٭	%	@									C
D	CR	GS	ENQ	NAK	(	)	_	'									D
E	SO	RS	ACK		+	;	>	=									E
F	SI	US	BEL	SUB	|	¬	?	''									F

Right or digit half of byte in hexadecimal

FIG. 3-11. EBCDIC coding chart.

major exception is the plus and minus signs, which traditionally are placed in front of the number, or *over* the last digit. When a Y-zone punch in a card represents a plus, and this plus is over the rightmost digit punch, the card readers interpret the punch combination as a letter and generate for the zone half of the byte not F_x but C_x for EBCDIC, and not 5_x but A_x for ASCII. When an X-zone punch in a card represents a minus, and this minus is over the rightmost digit punch, the card readers interpret the punch combination as a letter, and generate for the left half of the byte not F_x but D_x for EBCDIC, and not 5_x but A_x or B_x for ASCII, depending on the value of the under-punch. This requires translation (a zone conversion) to yield consistently B_x, which is the preferred "minus zone" in ASCII, and to make the digit half

Left half of byte in hexadecimal

	0	1	2	3	4	5	6	7	8	9	A	B	C	D		F	
0	NULL	DLE			Δ	0					@	P			`	p	0
1	SOH	DC1			!	1					A	Q			a	q	1
2	STX	DC2			"	2					B	R			b	r	2
3	ETX	DC3			#	3					C	S			c	s	3
4	EOT	DC4			$	4					D	T			d	t	4
5	ENQ	NAK			%	5					E	U			e	u	5
6	ACK	SYN			&	6					F	V			f	v	6
7	BEL	ETB			'	7					G	W			g	w	7
8	BS	CAN			(	8					H	X			h	x	8
9	HT	EM			)	9					I	Y			i	y	9
A	LF	SUB			*	:					J	Z			j	z	A
B	VT	ESC			+	;					K	[			k	{	B
C	FF	FS			,	<					L	\			l			C
D	CR	GS			-	=					M	]			m	}	D
E	SO	RS			.	>					N	^			n	~	E
F	SI	US			/	?					O	_			o	DEL	F

Right half of byte in hexadecimal

Fig. 3-12. ASCII coding chart.

EXPLANATION OF ASCII AND EBCDIC NON-GRAPHIC SYMBOLS

Δ	Space
SOH	Start of Heading for communication control
STX	Start of Text for communication control
ETX	End of Text for communication control
EOT	End of Transmission for communication control
ENQ	Enquiry for communication control
ACK	Acknowledge for communication control
BEL	Bell or other operator attention signal
BS	Backspace for format control
HT	Horizontal Tabulation or Field Skip for format control
LF	Line Feed for format control
VT	Vertical Tabulation or line skip for format control
FF	Form Feed for format control
CR	Carriage Return for format control
SO	Shift Out
SI	Shift In
DLE	Data Link Escape for communication control
DC1	Device Control 1
DC2	Device Control 2
DC3	Device Control 3
DC4	Device Control 4 or Stop
NAK	Negative Acknowledge for communication control
SYN	Synchronous Idle for communication control
ETB	End of Transmission Block for communication control
CAN	Cancel
EM	End of Medium (as for example, tape or paper)
SUB	Substitute
ESC	Escape
FS	File Separator for information separation
GS	Group Separator for information separation
RS	Record Separator for information separation
US	Unit Separator for information separation
DEL	Delete
PF	Punch off
LC	Lower case shift
SMM	Start manual message
TM	Tape mark
RES	Restore
NL	New line
IL	Idle or wait
CC	Cursor Control
CU1	Customer use code 1
CU2	Customer use code 2
CU3	Customer use code 3
DS	Digit select for Edit

Fig. 3-12 *(continued)*

SS	Significance start for Edit
EFS	Edit field separator
BYP	Bypass
SM	Set mode
PN	Punch on
RS	Reader stop
UC	Upper case shift

Fig. 3-12. (*continued*)

of the byte run from 0 through 9. Thus, for example, 71346 with a plus sign over the 6 would be $F7F1F3F4C6_{xc}$ and $57515354A6_{xk}$ (see Figs. 3-11 and 3-12). For a minus sign over the 6, the representation would be $F7F1F3F4D6_{xc}$ and $57515-354AF_{xk}$ before code correction ("zoned" from conversion).

From these examples, the repeated, redundant F and 5 zones are obvious. To eliminate them, the computer provides the "packed-decimal" or "binary-coded-decimal" representation. In this, only the first 10 hexadecimal characters are used to represent numeric data, with 4 of the other 6 hexadecimal characters being used for plus and minus signs. The data are represented two decimal digits per byte, except that the *rightmost* byte contains only one digit and the sign, with the sign in the right half byte. Thus an odd number of decimal digits is always represented, and the rightmost byte carries the rightmost digit of the number and the sign, as shown in Fig. 3-13. Note that the sign is always the last hexadecimal character, that a zero fill is used to make the number of decimal digits odd, and that the EBCDIC or ASCII zones are eliminated in packed-decimal representation except for the sign.

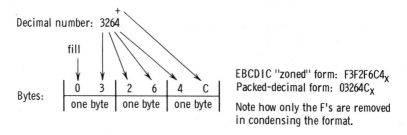

Fig. 3-13. Packed-decimal or BCD data representation.

In practice, packed-decimal numbers in the computer are formed from numbers represented in the EBCDIC or ASCII codes. For an accurate sign character, the zone character in the rightmost byte of the EBCDIC or ASCII number from which the computer forms the packed-decimal number should have the desired sign character in the zone position. To facilitate this in EBCDIC, a "zoned" form is available for numeric data, as described later in this chapter, which has the needed sign character in the zone half of the rightmost byte. For example, if the positive-signed number 346 were in the zoned EBCDIC form of F3F4C6$_{xc}$, the packed-decimal from it would be 346C$_{xp}$, where the subscript p indicates packed-decimal.

Do It Now Exercise 3-6. *Write the phrase BRAZILS—$1.09/LB in hexadecimal, using first the EBCDIC and then the ASCII code. Write the following positive-signed numbers in hexadecimal, using first the zoned EBCDIC code and then packed-decimal from it, and then the ASCII code and the packed-decimal from it: 123; 5; 72; 4; 524; 7398; and 681493. Watch where you put the sign. Using zoned EBCDIC and packed-decimal, try these: 1; 4; 362; 4786; and 62762.*

PLACING DATA IN STORAGE

The programer can get data into internal storage by two means: he can have the computer do an input operation, or he can have the computer place data in storage as part of the program at the time the computer loads (places) the program in storage. The programer uses the first method (which is the topic of later chapters) primarily for data to be processed (the input data); he uses the second for the constant or initial data he wants the computer to use in processing the input data.

To have data in storage available at the time that the computer starts executing a program, and to assign names to fields of data and to places in storage where data may be placed, the programer uses two declarative operations, the "DS" (Define Storage), and the "DC" (Define Constant). Both can link or convert the programer's symbolic names to actual addresses in storage, but the DC also causes values to be loaded in the address when the program is loaded for execution. Let us look first at the DC declarative.

The programer can use the DC declarative to give a symbolic name to an area, location, or place in storage. The areas so named may range from a byte to a record or a block. If the programer assigns a name, he writes it in the name column of the coding sheet, following the usual rules. The programer may assign any one name once and only once; multiple name assignments are an error that will invalidate a compilation. The programer may omit assigning a name by leaving blank the name column for the statement. Multiple blank names are the only repeated names permitted. The name identifies the *leftmost byte of a field or word.*

The programer writes the DC for the declarative in the operation column of the coding form, starting at the left. He writes the operands in the operand column of the coding form, again starting at the left and leaving no blanks.

The programer can use the DC declarative to specify data in a variety of forms and formats. To do this the programer can use, if needed, as many as four operands in each DC statement. The programer writes the operands in a continuous string; he does not write them separated by commas or spaces. The first operand is a duplication factor, which is discussed later and for the moment will be passed over. The second operand is a type indicator for the data to be specified. Considerable variety is possible with binary (B,F,H), hexadecimal (X), EBCDIC (C,Z), packed-decimal (P), and floating-point binary (D,E) formats. The programer can also use address formats (A,Y). The programer may not omit the type operand.

The third operand usually specifies the length of the constant in terms of the number of bytes of storage to be utilized. This operand may often be omitted either because some types of constants can be effectively defined for only certain lengths, or because the fourth operand may provide the length indirectly. When specifying a length, the programer uses the letter L followed by a number in decimal of the count of the bytes of storage he wishes to have the computer use. When a length is specified, it overrides any implied length calculated from the fourth operand. This third operand sometimes does not specify length but for the binary format constants may specify what is known as the "scaling," as noted in Chap. 5.

The fourth operand is the constant value expressed in the form of a literal that is to be placed in storage at the time the program is loaded ready for execution. This fourth operand is written in the form appropriate for the type of constant, and sometimes several may be given. The programer must both precede and follow the fourth operand by a single quote mark (an apostrophe). Where multiple constants are defined, commas must separate them. Examples are given in the next sections of this chapter.

The duplication factor, which is the first operand, specifies how many times the constant that has been defined by the second, third, and fourth operands is to be repeated consecutively in storage. The name, when a name is assigned, applies only to the first constant of the group and, irrespective of the duplication factor, is always the address of the *leftmost byte of storage* used. Where the duplication factor is omitted, it is assumed to be one. When the duplication factor is given as zero, the effect is to convert the DC operation into a DS operation, also with a duplication factor of zero. For this reason, the use of a duplication factor of zero is described in a later section on the DS declaratives.

For convenience and relevance the binary (B), hexadecimal (X), EBCDIC (C), zoned (Z), and packed-decimal (P) types of declaratives are presented first in this book. The more complex DC declaratives of types F and H are presented, then the address constants A and Y are presented. In using DC declaratives of any type, the programer should note that placing the same data in storage can often be done in any of several ways. The choice among the alternatives often hinges on the programer's convenience and the clarity of the documentation. In the small models of the computer the duplication factor must be omitted for the DC declaratives, and only the types C, X, H, and Y are permitted. Type D and type E DC declaratives are covered in Chap. 12. A summary table of DC declaratives is given in Appendix B at the end of the book.

BINARY CONSTANTS, TYPE B

Type B DC declaratives allow the programer to write a constant in binary form. The alignment in storage is by byte. The length in bytes is determined from either the fourth or the third operand and may run from a minimum of one to a maximum of 256 bytes. Any truncation (cutting off) or padding (filling in) occurs on the left side, with 0 bit used for the fill. The fourth operand is written as a string of binary bits. Only one constant can be specified in the fourth operand. Type B DC declaratives are not permitted for the small models of the computer.

Examples of DC declaratives of type B are shown in Fig. 3-14. The first, with the symbolic name BIN1, and the second, named BIN2, are identical in result, yielding eight consecutive 1 bits (a byte of 1 bits) which is also FF_x. When the duplication operand is omitted—the usual case—it is automatically assumed to be one.

OBJECT CODE	NAME	OP	OPERANDS	COMMENT
FF	BIN1	DC	1BL1'11111111'	COMPLETE STATEMENT
FF	BIN2	DC	B'11111111'	DUPLICATION AND LENGTH OF 1 OMITTED
01	BIN3	DC	B'00000001'	LEADING ZEROS SHOWN
01	BIN4	DC	B'1'	LEADING ZEROS FILLED AUTOMATICALLY
000005	BIN5	DC	BL3'101'	FIRST TWO BYTES ARE ZERO FILLED
05	BIN6	DC	B'101'	ONE BYTE OF BINARY FIVE
050505	BIN7	DC	3B'101'	THREE BYTES OF THE SAME VALUE
05	BIN8	DC	BL1'11100000101'	A SPECIFIED LENGTH OVERRIDES

FIG. 3-14. Examples of DC declaratives of type B.

Declaratives BIN3 and BIN4 are also identical in result, yielding a byte of seven 0 bits, with one 1 bit for the rightmost bit. This is because 0-bit fill occurs automatically on the left until the required number of bytes (in this case, one) are filled with bits.

Declaratives BIN5, BIN6, BIN7, and BIN8 illustrate the difference between the length and duplication operands. Either BIN5 or BIN7 generates three bytes of binary data. Both assign the symbolic name to the leftmost byte. But the binary data generated by BIN5 are, in binary, 00000000 00000000 00000101. The data generated by BIN7 with the duplication factor of 3 are these in binary: 00000101 00000101 00000101. This is three repetitions of the constant generated by BIN6. A specified length overrides an implied length, as illustrated in BIN8, which truncates to one byte. When the length operand is omitted, it is assumed to be the minimum of one byte or the implied length, whichever be greater. Note that in all cases the names are assigned to the leftmost byte of the data generated for the constant when more than one byte is built.

Do It Now Exercise 3-7. On a coding form, write DC declaratives of type B to place the first 16 binary numbers in consecutive 3-byte areas of storage. As comments, show in hexadecimal what you expect the contents of storage to be. Give each a name in sequence from the series BEXH0 through BEX15.

HEXADECIMAL CONSTANTS, TYPE X

Type X DC declaratives allow the programer to write a constant in hexadecimal form. The alignment in storage is by byte, not by word. The length in bytes is determined from the fourth operand or the third operand, and may run from a minimum of 1 to a maximum of 256 bytes. Any truncation or padding occurs on the left side, with 0_x used as the fill character. The fourth operand is written as a string of hexadecimal characters. Only one constant can be specified in the fourth operand. Type X DC declaratives are permitted for all models of the computer.

Examples of DC declaratives of type X are shown in Fig. 3-15. Declaratives HEX1 and HEX2 illustrate by example that any EBCDIC or ASCII character can be expressed in hexadecimal form. Because of keypunch difficulties on some older models of keypunches with some special and some ASCII characters, this is

OBJECT CODE	NAME	OP	OPERANDS	COMMENT
F0	HEX1	DC	X'F0'	EBCDIC ZERO
50	HEX2	DC	X'50'	ASCII ZERO
0A	HEX3	DC	X'A'	FILL IS ON THE LEFT
000B	HEX4	DC	XL2'B'	THREE FILLED POSITIONS
40404040	HEX5	DC	4X'40'	FOUR BYTES OF BLANKS

FIG. 3-15. Examples of DC declaratives of type X.

often the most convenient way of expressing them. Declarative HEX3 generates $0A_x$ in storage because one byte is the minimum length, because 0_x is the fill character, and because fill is done on the left. Declarative HEX4 also illustrates the fill action, and results in $000B_x$ in storage because the fill character is 0_x. To generate a string of ASCII or EBCDIC blanks, the programer usually uses the duplication operand, as illustrated by HEX5, which results in 40404040_x in storage.

Do It Now Exercise 3-8. Write 9 four-byte DC declaratives of type X to count by sevens starting at 47_x. Make the length of each field with odd-numbered content five bytes long; each field with even-numbered content three bytes long. Give each three-byte field a name from XVPH2 through XVPH8.

EBCDIC CONSTANTS, TYPE C

Type C DC declaratives allow the programer to write a constant in conventional letters, digits, and special symbols. The translation done by the computer is based upon the EBCDIC coding scheme. The alignment in storage is by byte, not by word. The length in bytes is determined from the fourth operand or the third operand and may run from a minimum of one to a maximum of 256 bytes. Any truncation or padding occurs on the *right* side with blanks used as the fill character (40_x). The fourth operand is written as a string of characters, except for the characters ' and &, which must be written in pairs to generate one character. This is because the single apostrophe and ampersand have special functions in the declaratives. For example, the single apostrophes identify the fourth operand of a DC declarative. Only one constant can be specified in the fourth operand. Type C DC declaratives are permitted for all models of the computer.

Examples of DC declaratives of type C are shown in Fig. 3-16. Declarative EBCH1 generates $4E_x$, which is the EBCDIC plus sign; EBCH2 generates 200 con-

OBJECT CODE	NAME	OP	OPERANDS	COMMENT
4E	EBCH1	DC	C'+'	EBCDIC SPECIAL CHARACTER + SIGN
4040404040404040 (×25 lines)	EBCH2	DC	CL200' '	200 BLANKS
F5F5F5	EBCH3	DC	3C'5'	EBCDIC 5 REPEATED 3 TIMES
C840C840	EBCH4	DC	2CL2'H'	EBCDIC H FOLLOWED BY A BLANK, TWICE
C1F1C1F1	EBCH5	DC	2CL2'A1B2'	THIS TRUNCATES
C1F140C1F140	EBCH6	DC	2CL3'A1'	THIS IS PADDED AND REPEATED
7D7D	EBCH7	DC	C''''''	TWO EBCDIC APOSTROPHES
C150C2	EBCH8	DC	C'A&&B'	A&B TAKES TWO &

FIG. 3-16. Examples of DC declaratives of type C.

secutive bytes of blanks (40_x) in storage; and EBCH3 generates $F5F5F5_x$ in storage because of the duplication operand. Declarative EBCH4, since it has both duplication and length operands, and since padding is on the right, generates H H ‚ ($C840$-$C840_x$). Declarative EBCH5 has a four-character-length fourth operand and a length specification of two bytes. Hence truncation occurs, but on top of that the duplication operand applies. The result generated in storage is C1F1C1F1$_x$. Declarative EBCH6 illustrates padding under similar conditions, with a result of C1F140C1F1-40$_x$. The result of EBCH7 is to place 7D7D$_x$ in storage. Note that the usual apostrophe is still needed on each side of the fourth operand. The result of EBCH8 is to place C150C2$_x$ in storage. Thus EBCH7 and EBCH8 illustrate the two exceptions to the usual string-of-characters rule for the fourth operand.

Do It Now Exercise 3-9. *Write DC declaratives of type C for each of the following names of persons active in the history of the computers: Grace Hopper, Edmund Berkeley, J. Rajchmann, H. H. Goldstine, J. W. Forrester, T. Watson, J. Carr. Put three-byte fillers of blanks between names; leave the name column blank on the coding form. Show in the comments the anticipated contents of storage in hexadecimal, assuming that all names be spelled with all capital letters.*

ZONED CONSTANTS, TYPE Z

Type Z DC declaratives allow the programer to write a numeric constant in conventional decimal digits with an algebraic sign and decimal point if desired. Alignment is by byte, not by word. This zoned format is the usual starting point for a conversion to packed-decimal format and is the result of a conversion from packed-decimal format. Only numbers can be represented with this type, and the number is represented in storage in much the same manner as for type C. One difference is in the handling of the zone half of the rightmost byte of the constant, which with type Z is a sign character like those used in packed-decimal representation, instead of F$_{xc}$ or 5$_{xk}$.

A second difference is that the data are right-justified in the field of storage with any truncation or padding occurring on the left end of the field. Either EBCDIC or ASCII zeros (F0$_x$ or 50$_x$) are the fill, one per byte. A third difference is that the maximum length is 16 bytes for the type Z constant. A fourth difference is that multiple fourth operands may be used if each is given the same length of field. Type Z DC declaratives are not permitted for the small models of the computer.

Examples of DC declaratives of type Z are shown in Fig. 3-17. Declarative

OBJECT CODE	NAME	OP	OPERANDS	COMMENT
F0F1C2	ZON1	DC	ZL3'12'	FILL IS ON THE LEFT
F1F3F9F9C9F1F3F9 F9C9	ZON2	DC	2Z'+13999'	SIGNED AND DUPLICATED
F1F3F9F9D9	ZON3	DC	ZL5'-13999'	NEGATIVES ARE NOT COMPLEMENTS
F9F1F6F0F7D3	ZON4	DC	ZL6'-99.16073'	TRUNCATES, DECIMAL POINTS IGNORED
F1C9F7D8F6C3F0C3	ZON5	DC	ZL2'19,-78,963,+3'	MULTIPLE CONSTANTS,NOTE TRUNCATION

FIG. 3-17. Examples of DC declaratives of type Z.

ZON1 illustrates that fill is with F0$_x$ and occurs on the left. Declarative ZON2 shows that an explicit plus sign is treated just as is the absence of a sign by making the resulting number positive, in contrast to the type C constants. It also illustrates the duplication factor. Declarative ZON3 shows the same number as ZON2, but with a negative sign. Declarative ZON4 shows that any included decimal points are eliminated and ignored, and that any truncation comes on the left, causing a loss of the more significant digits. Declarative ZON5 illustrates the use of a multiple-part fourth operand. Note that all of the four values generated are two bytes long, and hence the 963 truncates on the left to only 63.

Do It Now Exercise 3-10. *Write DC declaratives of type Z for the following numbers, making each as short as possible, and giving each a name in series from ZKH1 through ZKH8: +1, −1, +99, +4093, +743.25, +3.14159. Show as comments the contents of storage in hexadecimal.*

PACKED-DECIMAL OR BCD CONSTANTS, TYPE P

Type P DC declaratives allow the programer to write a numeric constant in decimal form. The data in storage can be interpreted as being in packed-decimal format with a sign following an odd number of digits. The alignment in storage is by byte, not by word. The length in bytes is determined from the fourth operand or the third operand, and may run from a minimum of 1 to a maximum of 16 bytes. Any truncation or padding occurs on the left side, with 0$_x$ used as the fill character. The sign is always the rightmost half of the rightmost byte, and except for that byte, two binary-coded decimal digits of data are placed in each byte. If the sign is omitted, it is assumed to be plus. Multiple constants may be specified in the fourth operand, but each constant must be written as a string of not more than 31 decimal digits because the maximum length is 16 bytes. Multiple constants appear consecutively in storage without separation, but must be separated on the coding sheet by commas, but not blanks. A decimal point may be included in addition to the digits and sign, but is ignored in translating the constant. DC declaratives of type P are not permitted for the small models of the computer.

Examples of DC declaratives of type P are shown in Fig. 3-18. Declaratives

OBJECT CODE	NAME	OP	OPERANDS	COMMENT
229C	PDEC1 *	DC	P'229'	PLUS SIGN IS ASSUMED
229C	PDEC2 *	DC	P'+22.9'	DECIMAL POINTS ARE IGNORED
012D012D	PDEC3 *	DC	2P'−12'	NEGATIVES ARE NOT COMPLEMENTS
234C	PDEC4 *	DC	PL2'1234'	THIS TRUNCATES
5C050C	PDEC5	DC	P'+5,50'	MULTIPLE CONSTANTS

FIG. 3-18. Examples of DC declaratives of type P.

PDEC1 and PDEC2 generate the identical data in storage 229C$_x$, because the absence of a sign is treated as a plus sign. Declarative PDEC3 generates four bytes of data in the form of 012D012D$_x$ because of the duplication operand. Negative numbers differ from positive only in the sign, just as for type Z. Decimal points have no effect. Declarative PDEC4 illustrates the truncation action taken when the specified length is shorter than the length implied from the fourth operand. The result generated is 234C$_x$. Declarative PDEC5 is an example of a multiple constant, with the result generated in storage as 5C050C$_x$. Note that these need not be all the same length, and that the number of digits is always made odd.

Do It Now Exercise 3-11. *Using the data from Do It Now Exercise 3-10, write DC declaratives of type P for each number, assigning the names PKH1 through PKH8. Show as comments the contents of storage in hexadecimal.*

BINARY CONSTANTS, TYPES F AND H

Type F and type H DC declaratives allow the programer to write a constant in decimal form. The constant in storage is in pure binary form. The implied length for a type F is four bytes, which is one full word; for type H it is two bytes, which is one half word. The alignment in storage is by the first available byte (next unassigned byte to the right) that starts a half word for type H ("half word") or a full word for type F ("full word"). A length operand is possible but should be omitted, since alignment becomes the programer's responsibility if he uses a length operand. Instead, scaling factors are possible, as explained in Chap. 5. Any truncation or padding occurs on the left side with the sign bit used as the fill character. This is because negative numbers are shown in two's-complement form, as explained in Chap. 5. The sign bit appears as the leftmost bit of the leftmost byte with the significant data bits right-justified (pushed to the right) in the bytes used. Truncation is on the left and may cut off the sign. Multiple constants may be assigned and appear in successive words or half words in storage, separated on the coding sheet by commas, but not spaces. A decimal point may be included with the decimal digits written on the coding sheet; if so, all digits to the right of the decimal point are ignored, but a binary round-up may occur. Type H DC declaratives are permitted for all models of the computer, but DC declaratives of type F are not permitted for the small models.

Examples of DC declaratives of types F and H are shown in Fig. 3-19. Declarative WD1 generates 00000007$_x$ in storage, and illustrates the automatic alignment on a full word. Declarative WD2 generates FFFFFFF9$_x$, since 0 is the positive sign bit, 1 is the negative sign bit, and the sign bit is the fill bit. The reasons for this are explained in Chap. 5. Declarative WD4 generates 00030003$_x$ because of the decimal point and the duplication factor. Declarative WD5 generates an identical result but illustrates the multiple fourth operand. Declarative WD6 generates 000D$_x$, since the

OBJECT CODE	NAME	OP	OPERANDS	COMMENT
00000007	WD1 *	DC	F'+7'	THE SIGN BIT IS USED AS FILL
FFFFFFF9	WD2 *	DC	F'-7'	NEGATIVES ARE COMPLEMENTS
0000	WD3 *	DC	H'.3'	DECIMAL FRACTIONS ARE IGNORED
00030003	WD4 *	DC	2H'3.'	FILL IS ON THE LEFT
00030003	WD5 *	DC	H'3,3'	MULTIPLE CONSTANTS
0C0D	WD6	DC	H'12.9'	CONVERSION IS TO BINARY, NOT PACKED

FIG. 3-19. Examples of DC declaratives of types F and H.

fourth operand has a decimal point after the 12. Since the digit after the decimal point is a 9, a round-off to 13 takes place, which is D_x.

Do It Now Exercise 3-12. *Using the data from Do It Now Exercise 3-10, write DC declaratives of type F for each number, assigning the names FKH1 through FKH8, and of type H for each number, assigning the names HKH1 through HKH8. Show as comments the anticipated contents of storage in hexadecimal.*

ADDRESS CONSTANTS, TYPES A, V, AND Y

Type A and type Y DC declaratives allow the programer to write a symbolic address and have placed in storage the binary number that is the equivalent absolute address. This ability is very useful for providing constants for control operations, as will be illustrated in Chap. 6 and later chapters.

The type A constant occupies an aligned full word in storage if the programer omits the length operand. The type Y constant occupies an aligned half word under the same conditions. Binary zero fill is used on the left side as needed, and any truncation occurs on the left. Only one operand is permitted. Usually the programer writes it as a symbolic address enclosed in parentheses, with a prefixed A. The operand may include relative address amounts, such as A(SUM-8) for the address eight bytes to the left of the symbolic address (name) called SUM. These are sometimes called "address adjustments." The type A constant should be used in all sizes of the computer that permit its use; the type Y should be restricted to the small models of the computer for which the type A constant is not permitted.

Examples of DC declaratives of type A and Y are shown in Fig. 3-20. Declaratives ADDR1 and ADDR3 both use the same symbolic address and illustrate the difference between the A and Y types of address constant. Declarative ADDR2 illustrates the use of a symbolic relative address (address adjustment). Declarative ADDR4 illustrates the use of what is called a "self-defining" number as an address. Note that such numbers are written as ordinary decimal numbers, but for a type A or Y constant, the computer compiles them to form binary absolute addresses.

Do It Now Exercise 3-13. *(a) Compose a DC statement of type X to represent*

OBJECT CODE	NAME	OP	OPERANDS	COMMENT
00001A02	ADDR1 *	DC	A(ZON1)	ABSOLUTE ADDRESS IN A FULL WORD
00001A48	ADDR2 *	DC	A(WD3+16)	ADDRESS OF WD3+16
1A02	ADDR3 *	DC	Y(ZON1)	ABSOLUTE ADDRESS IN HALF WORD
OFFF	ADDR4	DC	Y(4095)	SELF-DEFINING ABSOLUTE ADDRESS

FIG. 3-20. Examples of DC declaratives of types A and Y, the address constants.

the first three letters of the alphabet in EBCDIC and then in ASCII. Assign them the symbolic addresses (names) CDIC and CII, respectively. (b) Compose DC statements of types C, X, and B to represent the six characters A1$A1$, assigning the names CAT, XBOG, and BUSH, respectively. Note the differences in the statements on the coding sheet needed to achieve the same data in storage. (c) Compose DC statements of types C, P, F, and H to represent the decimal number +9876.42, assigning the names CHAMP, PICKLE, FOXY, and HOPE, respectively. Then restate each as a type X to accomplish the same bit configuration (format) in storage, and with the names preceded by an X (as XCHAMP, and so on). (d) Compose DC statements of types X, C, B, and P to fill 100 consecutive bytes of storage with the one EBCDIC character).

The type V results in no value being assigned by the compiler. Rather, the type V address constant is like a Define Constant for a type F word of zeros. But the operand the programer gives is noted by the compiler and passed on to another program, the link editor, which later will supply a binary absolute address when the program is loaded for execution. In form, the type V address constant is the same as the type A. But the programer only uses the type V address constant for symbolic names of, or in, other programs, not for symbolic names defined in his own program. The programer may specify more than one operand.

DEFINE STORAGE

The format types of the Define Storage (DS) declarative are the same as for the Define Constant (DC) declaratives, with a few exceptions because of the model of the computer. In the small models of the computer, no fourth operand may be included and only types C and H are permitted. In the larger models of the computer, all types are permitted and a fourth operand is permitted to provide only an indication of the desired length. The programer can, however, use the third operand for this. The DS declarative assigns a name (a symbolic address) to the leftmost byte of the area, and reserves the number of bytes of internal storage specified to prevent reassigning the reserved area for other uses.

Define Storage is the preferred declarative to use when the programer will have the computer put data into a field or area before taking data out of the field or area in storage. The fields may range in length from a byte to a record or a block thousands of bytes long. Prime examples are input and output areas, since these receive data before the computer uses them as sources of data. By contrast, for areas of storage the programer wants the computer to take data out of, before (if ever) putting data in, the programer should use Define Constant (DC) declaratives. Using a DC declarative when a DS declarative can serve is wasteful of computer operating time during both compilation and program loading.

The use of the Define Storage declarative is simple and straightforward. It follows closely the pattern of the Define Constant declarative. Thus to define three consecutive areas in storage, one 7 bytes long, one 2 bytes long, and one 4 bytes long, the programer can write three DS declaratives as shown at SVUA1 through SVUA3 in Fig. 3-21, assuming no alignment is needed. To write aligned areas of two, four, or eight bytes in length, the programer can use type H, F, or D, respectively (see SVAL2, for example) in Fig. 3-21. Type D, which has not been previously described, has a usual (implied) length of eight bytes and is aligned as a double word. Using aligned storage areas may leave unutilized areas studded between the reserved fields. These fill areas have no names (symbolic addresses) assigned. An example is at address 002A96 in Fig. 3-23.

LOC	OBJECT CODE	NAME	OP	OPERANDS	COMMENT
001A50		SVUA1	DS	CL7	SEVEN BYTE UNALIGNED AREA
001A57			DS	BL2	TWO BYTE UNALIGNED AREA
001A59		SVUA3	DS	XL4	FOUR BYTE UNALIGNED AREA
001A5D			DS	C	ONE BYTE UNALIGNED AREA
001A5E			DS	H	TWO BYTES ALIGNED ON A HALF WORD
001A60		SVAL2	DS	F	FOUR BYTES ALIGNED ON A FULL WORD
001A68			DS	D	EIGHT BYTES ALIGNED ON A DOUBLE WORD

FIG. 3-21. Examples of DS declaratives.

The programer uses the duplication factor for DS declaratives in the same way as for DC declaratives, and with the same effect. With DS declaratives, however, the zero duplication factor becomes of special importance because it enables the programer to handle easily items of data at different levels. For example, sometimes a programer wishes to assign a name to a field that is a part of another field, which in turn is part of a still larger field. That is, while maintaining the identity of a large field, the programer wants to break the larger field into smaller fields, giving individual names to individual parts.

Such field redefinition requires the use of a duplication factor of zero. In the example shown in Figs. 3-22 and 3-23, the large 10-byte field named HUGHM is broken into two fields, one of 2 bytes and one of 8 bytes, called MEDJ and MEDK, respectively, the latter aligned on a double word. Field MEDK is in turn broken into three fields: one of 1 byte, named QRNV; one of 3 bytes, named QRNW; and one of

4 bytes, named QROL. To attain the proper alignment, an unnamed filler field of 6 bytes is also established.

This illustrates the other major use of the zero duplication factor to force alignment. Thus, if the programer uses a DC or DS declarative of type H, F, or D with a zero duplication factor, and then follows it with any DC or DS declarative, the compiler program will give both declaratives the *same* aligned absolute address. This is because the declarative with the zero duplication factor is assigned the first available aligned address, but is assigned *no* space in storage. Thus that same aligned address is the first available address for the next DC or DS declarative. Each symbolic name, if the programer assigns names, still has, however, an implied or specified length as shown by the DS or DC declarative. All of these points are illustrated in Figs. 3-22 and 3-23.

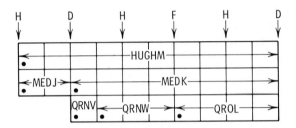

Fig. 3-22. Diagram of levels of field definition.

LOC	OBJECT CODE	NAME	OP	OPERANDS	COMMENT
001A70			DS	0D	FORCES ALIGNMENT TO DOUBLE WORD
001A70		HUGHM	DS	0CL10	NAME OF TEN BYTE MAJOR FIELD
001A70		MEDJ	DS	H	NAME OF TWO BYTE MIDDLE FIELD
001A78		MEDK	DS	0D	NAME OF EIGHT BYTE MIDDLE FIELD
001A78		QRNV	DS	C	NAME OF ONE BYTE MINOR FIELD
001A79		QRNW	DS	CL3	NAME OF THREE BYTE MINOR FIELD
001A7C		QROL	DS	F	NAME OF FOUR BYTE MINOR FIELD
001A80			DS	0F	FORCES ALIGNMENT
001A80		INPUT	DS	80C' '	ALIGNED AREA

Fig. 3-23. Example of use of zero duplication factor to establish levels of field definition.

Do It Now Exercise 3-14. *Write DS declaratives of any appropriate type to define a 16-byte-long area named AQK aligned on a double word, and broken in four subfields of three bytes (AQL3), of five bytes (AQL5), of two bytes (AQL2), and of six bytes (AQL6). Break the five-byte field into two fields, one aligned on a full word and four bytes long named AQM4, and the other named AQMR. Make a diagram like Fig. 3-22 to accompany the declaratives.*

EQUALS-SIGN CONSTANTS AND EQU DECLARATIVES

For medium and large models of the computer, any of the types of constants can be used as part of an imperative instruction without the need for writing a separate DC declarative for the constant. In this way the programer can avoid the need to write separate statements for each constant. Constants written in this manner are termed "literals" and are grouped by the compiler and assigned addresses automatically. To use this literal capability, the programer omits the duplication operand, writes an equals sign (=) in its place, and writes the literal as part of the instruction that uses the literal. For example, to add binary +365 to the contents of a register, the programer could incorporate the =H'365' right in the imperative instruction without writing a separate constant for the number +365. An example of a literal is given in Fig. 3-24.

```
      LOC   OBJECT CODE    ADDR1 ADDR2       NAME    OP   OPERANDS              COMMENT

                           01A34             PLCH    L    3,=H'365'
                                               *
                           01A30                     L    3,=A(F4#1)
      001A30                                          LTORG
      001A30 00001A80                                 =A(F4#1)
      001A34 016D                                     =H'365'
```

FIG. 3-24. Examples of a literal.

For all models of the computer, even those for which no literals are permitted, the programer can use the EQU declarative. For this the programer assigns a symbolic address (name), placing it in the name column. In the operand column he writes either a self-defining value (such as the decimal number that identifies a register, a number, or an absolute address) or another symbolic name, or another symbolic name with address adjustment (relative addressing). Examples of each of these three are given in Fig. 3-25.

```
   LOC   OBJECT CODE              NAME    OP   OPERANDS       COMMENT
   00000F                         EQA3    EQU  15             HEXADECIMAL F
   004388                         EQA4    EQU  INPUT          ANY SYMBOLIC ADDRESS
   00447E                         EQA5    EQU  INPUT+82*3     ADDRESS ADJUSTED BY +246 BYTES
                                    *
```

FIG. 3-25. Examples of EQU declaratives.

Programers find EQU declaratives useful for making substitutions among symbolic names, and to replace numbers with symbolic names. Thus in some installations programers are required to use the letter R in front of any number that identifies a register. To do this, the programer must use EQU declaratives.

Do It Now Exercise 3-15. *(a) Write EQU declaratives to assign the names R8, R9, and R15 to the equivalents of decimal numbers 8, 9, and 15, respectively. (b) Write an EQU declarative to assign the name DIFJ to twice the difference between the absolute-address equivalents of the symbolic addresses HIGHRX and LOWRZ; where LOWRZ is a lower-numbered address. Multiplication is indicated by an *, addition by a +, subtraction by a —, and division by a /.*

Appendix B summarizes the types of DC and DS declaratives. In using the table, the programer should note that different models of the computer may differ in the details of the operands permitted.

EXERCISES

1. Contrast the types of DC and DS declaratives.
2. Attempt to draw from memory the hierarchy of operand data structure. From memory, label each level. Check your own work against Fig. 3-2.
3. Attempt to draw from memory the hierarchy of program data structure. From memory, label each level. Check your own work against Fig. 3-1.
4. Contrast the EBCDIC and ASCII code systems.
5. Using Appendix A, convert the following decimal numbers to hexadecimal: 1, 5, 10, 15, 20, 25, 30, 35, 40, 45, 50, 100, 150, 200, 250. Convert the following hexadecimal numbers to decimal: 1, 8, 10, 18, 20, 28, 30, 38, 40, 48, 50, 58, 60, 68, 70, 78, 80, 90, A0, B0, C0, D0, E0, F0, FF.

CHAPTER 4

Data Movement

OVERVIEW

This chapter introduces imperative statements. It classifies the possible forms and explains the features of the computer that give rise to the different forms. From this general overview, the chapter takes up in detail imperative commands that move data in the computer. To show the effect and significance of these commands, this chapter introduces and explains the interpretation of a storage dump.

CONTENTS OF STORAGE

A programer working with assembly language for the computer usually finds the storage dump one of his most valuable tools for finding and correcting programing mistakes. The storage dump can be likened to a candid photograph which shows the contents of storage as of the exact moment at which the dump was taken. The dump is usually printed by the computer's line printer, and takes a fairly standard format.

To a programer who has never programed with a symbolic language, the usefulness of this "candid camera" dump information may not be obvious. The basis for the value of a storage dump is the role of the data in internal storage at any given time. Before the computer begins the execution of a program, the computer loads the program into internal storage together with such constants as the programer has defined with DC and literal (equals-sign) declaratives. This initial loading gives the starting contents of internal storage. When the program calls for reading in input data, the data read appear at the specified place in internal storage. The operations that the program does to transform or convert the input data into the desired output data appear as a gradual building up of the output data in the output areas and work areas the programer has specified in internal storage. When the output is completely built and ready for sending to the output equipment, the computer copies (as output) the data from internal storage.

In short, data for all of the stages in the transformation of the input data into the output data appear in internal storage at some time or other. This occurs because all output data come from internal storage, and because all input data go to internal storage. Any production of output data from the input data therefore necessarily changes the contents of internal storage. Hence a programer, by inspecting the contents of storage, can determine whether the production of the output data is proceeding correctly and as anticipated, or whether something has gone wrong. By noting the nature of the erroneous (unanticipated) contents of storage, the programer can glean important clues about what in his program or in the input data is causing the unwanted results.

The way a programer typically inspects the contents of internal storage is by obtaining a storage dump. A sample of part of a dump is shown in Fig. 4-1. In its common form the dump for the computer shows the contents of storage in hexadecimal form. Eight or twelve words of storage are shown per line on the dump. For human convenience, each pair of words is separated by some blank space. Since blank is not a hexadecimal character, this causes no confusion. The address of the leftmost byte of storage on each line is shown in the column at the far left of the page. This is shown as an absolute address in hexadecimal form. Each following byte (*two* hexadecimal characters) of internal storage to the right has a sequentially higher address. Since each storage word consists of 4 bytes, each line of 8 words shows 32 bytes of the contents of storage. If the programmer converts to decimal the addresses of the lines in the dump in Fig. 4-1, he finds that $EE0_x$ is 32_c more than $EC0_x$, and $F00_x$ is 32_c more than $EE0_x$. This happens because each row in Fig. 4-1 represents 32 bytes of data. For clarity, the address of each byte in the edge rows is shown. Thus the addresses shown in the leftmost column go up by alternate hexa-

Addresses	00 01 02 03	04 05 06 07	08 09 0A 0B	0C 0D 0E 0F	10 11 12 13	14 15 16 17	18 19 1A 1B	1C 1D 1E 1F
000EA0	40404040	40404040	40404040	40404040	40404046	40404040	40404040	40404040
000EC0	404040F1	F9F7F040	D3C9E2E3	40D6C640	D4C1D5E4	C1D3E240	40404040	F0F5F9F6
000EE0	F740404D	F0404040	40404040	40404040	40404040	40404040	40404040	40404040
000F00	40404040	F0404040	40404040	40404040	40404040	40404040	40404040	40404040
000F20	40404040	F8F1C540	00000000	00008E16	00000001	00008119	40404000	034C0198
000F40	7D404050	55505940	40404040	40404040	40404040	40404040	40404040	40404040
000F60	40404040	40404040	40404040	40404040	40404040	40404040	40404040	40404040
Addresses	00 01 02 03	04 05 06 07	08 09 0A 0B	0C 0D 0E 0F	10 11 12 13	14 15 16 17	18 19 1A 1B	1C 1D 1E 1F

Fig. 4-1. Part of a dump of internal storage.

decimal characters in the second position from the right, as, for example, 60_x, 80_x, $A0_x$, $C0_x$, $E0_x$, 00_x, 20_x, 40_x, 60_x.

A casual inspection of the part of a dump shown as Fig. 4-1 reveals the existence of a substantial number of blanks (represented as 40_x) in storage. EBCDIC alphabetic data are recognizable by the C, D, and E hexadecimal characters in the zone (left) half of some bytes. Binary data are recognizable by the leading 00_x or FF_x in aligned words and half words. EBCDIC numeric data are recognizable by the F_x in the zone (left) half of successive bytes.

As a programing and debugging aid, the programer needs to develop some skill at the interpretation of dumps showing the contents of storage. Under some conditions for the larger models of the computer, it is possible to obtain dumps that also show the contents of storage in ordinary character form, rather than in hexadecimal. Generally, however, the programer will have to inspect dumps in hexadecimal, since the hexadecimal dump is the basic dump for the computer. Thus, for example, the first field has an absolute address of $EC0_x$, is three bytes long, and has the value 404040_x, which is three EBCDIC or ASCII blanks.

Do It Now Exercise 4-1. *Identify in Fig. 4-1 each of the fields. Mark each for its type (blanks, EBCDIC, ASCII, zoned, packed-decimal, or aligned F or H binary), address of the leftmost byte, and field length in bytes. On a coding form, in sequence, and assigning no name, write DC declaratives for each field. If you have no coding forms, use blank paper. If you have no workbook and cannot write in this book, copy Fig. 4-1 carefully and neatly on a sheet of blank or ruled paper. Do not yield to the temptation to skip this Do It Now Exercise. It is very important to do this one now.*

One of the basic techniques the programer has available to alter the contents of storage is moving data around in storage, for example, by copying data from one field in storage to another. Because such data-movement operations for altering the contents of storage are so basic in the transformation of input data into output data, they are covered early in this book. This chapter provides information about the sources and destinations for data movement in the computer, about the nature of the computer's ability to interpret instructions, about the format of the instructions which the computer can execute to move data from one place to another, and about a selection of the more important commands the programer can specify to direct data movement in the computer.

SOURCES AND DESTINATIONS

The destination or receiving area is the place that the data-movement operation alters; the source or sending area supplies a copy of its contents as the data to be moved. The major sources and destinations in the computer for data movement are general-purpose registers, floating-point registers, and addresses in internal storage. Data-movement operations, therefore, may be classified on the basis of whether or not they use a register and whether or not they use a storage address. Thus the data-movement operations available in the computer are from register to register, register to storage, storage to register, and storage to storage.

Most models of the computer are equipped with 16 general-purpose registers, each of which can accommodate four bytes of data. For the small models, only 8 are available, and each can accommodate the equivalent of 2 bytes of data. A few models of the computer have no actual registers but use certain areas of storage as if they were registers. The registers are identified for programing purposes by numbers from 8 through 15 for the small models, and from 0 through 15 for the other models, where it is assumed that the register following register 15 is register 0. That is, when 16 registers are used, register "wrap-around" is possible.

General-purpose registers are used for four major purposes. First, the computer does binary arithmetic operations in the general-purpose registers. For doing this, the leftmost bit of each register is interpreted as an algebraic sign, and the other bits are interpreted as a 15- or 31-bit binary number, depending on the register's length. For all but the small models of the computer, in operations such as multiply or divide, two adjacent registers—an even-numbered one followed by an odd-numbered one— may be used together to form effectively one register having one sign bit at the far left end of the even-numbered register followed by a 63-bit binary number. The usual sign bit in the odd-numbered register then functions as a data bit in this arrangement.

Second, the computer uses the general-purpose registers as index registers to modify instructions at the time they are executed. This is discussed in Chap. 6. Third, the computer uses the general-purpose registers as "base" registers to specify the starting address of areas (locations) in storage where data and instructions may be found. Base-and-displacement addressing was introduced in Chap. 2 and is further discussed later in this chapter.

Fourth, the computer uses some of the registers for particular purposes, and the manufacturer-provided software programs routinely use some registers. For example, the computer hardware uses register 0 and 1 automatically during the execution of some commands, without these registers being cited. The manufacturer's software programs with which all but the small models of the computer are commonly operated may use registers 12, 13, 14, and 15. These uses by the hardware and software of a total of six registers reduce the number of registers usually available without restriction to the programer from 16 to 10—that is, to registers 2 through 11. Unless indicated otherwise, the programer should normally restrict his register usage to these registers.

The general-purpose registers serve both as receivers and as senders of data in data-movement operations. The registers are not cleared to zero or otherwise reset when they are the senders of data. All data movements in the computer are basically copying operations. Thus when the computer moves data from a register to somewhere else in the computer, the data in the register remain unaltered by the move, because the move copies the contents of the register into some place in storage. When the register is a receiver of data, the prior contents of the register are lost. New data replace the prior data in the register that is a receiver of data.

Besides the eight or sixteen general-purpose registers, in some models of the computer there are four double-word registers for floating-point operations, identified as registers 0, 2, 4, and 6. These registers can participate in data-movement operation in much the same manner as the general-purpose registers, but they require separate commands. For arithmetic use, their function is restricted to handling floating-point numbers as described in Chap. 12. The floating-point registers cannot serve as base or index registers.

The internal storage of the computer serves as a sender of data as well as a receiver of data. In order to identify the location or place in storage where the data may be received from or sent to, the leftmost byte of the field is considered the address of the field. In machine language this address is usually in base-and-displacement form; in assembly language, the programer uses a symbolic name. Again, the data movement is essentially a copying operation, as in the case of registers. That is, the sending area remains unchanged, but the prior contents of the receiving area are lost because the copied (incoming) data replace the old contents.

The computer has the ability not only to move data from one place to another in the computer on a copy basis, but also to move data and, while moving it, to translate the code. For example, the computer can copy data from a zoned field, but change the code to packed-decimal for the receiving field. The computer can do other types of translation operations, but for all the general rule is that the area from which the computer gets (copies) the data is unaltered by the data-movement operation. The obvious exception is when the sending field is also the receiving field, as is usually possible but rarely desirable.

COMPUTER FEATURES

Seven features of the computer influence the way data-movement instructions are stated for and executed by the computer. All seven of these are of vital concern to the programer.

First, the computer's instructions vary in length, and are two, four, or six bytes long. Each operation that the computer can do requires an instruction of a particular length. The computer determines the length of each instruction as it prepares to execute it by testing the command (operation code) portion. The computer has *no* delimiters, word marks, flags, or separator symbols to identify the end of one instruction and the start of the next. Since instructions are multiples of one half word in length, instructions must be aligned on half-word boundaries in internal storage in order to avoid error interrupts.

Second, the fields of data the computer is to operate on may be of any length.

The computer has *no* delimiters, word marks, flags, or separator symbols for fields. This means, in practice, that some means must be provided to tell the computer as it executes each instruction how many bytes it is to operate upon at any given time. This is accomplished in two ways. Those commands which use a register normally use all the bytes a register can hold (usually two or four bytes). Those commands which do not use a register normally have as part of the instruction one or more length indicators indicating the number of bytes of data to be handled. As noted earlier, the address of a field in storage is the address of its leftmost byte.

Third, some operands must be aligned. This requirement is imposed by the ways the computer designers have provided for the computer to obtain data from storage rapidly and accurately. The programer can meet this requirement by assigning addresses to fields in storage that begin at the boundaries of half words, words, or double words, as the individual case may demand. Ways of doing this were described in Chap. 3. When operands must be aligned, this book takes note of it.

Fourth, the computer has both general-purpose registers and floating-point registers. Even though these have the same identification numbers, no confusion occurs, since the programer uses entirely different commands for each set of registers.

Fifth, instructions can include indexing. That is, when the computer goes to execute an instruction, it may add automatically a binary-address-adjustment amount to the absolute operand address from which data are to be obtained, or in which data are to be stored. General-purpose registers can hold the index amounts (amounts of automatic address adjustment).

Sixth, the computer uses general-purpose registers as "base" registers to identify the portion of internal storage in which data or instructions are to be found. These registers contain the addresses of the lowest ("base") byte in each portion of internal storage. At the time the computer executes an instruction, it adds together three binary numbers to determine the effective (actual) address in machine language. These three numbers are (1) the contents of the base register; (2) the binary number appearing as the displacement in the instruction; and (3) the contents of the index register. Base-and-displacement addressing has been discussed earlier in this book.

Seventh, the computer is a two-address computer. That is, each instruction normally refers to two operands. This means that normally the programer in writing instructions must specify both of the operands, as explained later in this chapter.

IMPERATIVE FORMAT

The format of the imperative instructions differs from the format of the declarative statements because each serves a different function. As noted earlier, the declaratives serve to tell the compiler program how the translation work (from source to object languages) is to be done. The imperatives, in contrast, tell the computer what to do to transform input data into output data, when it is operating under the control of the object program. Chapter 3 examined two declaratives, the DS and the DC.

To facilitate the computer's execution of the imperative instructions, the command is always in the first byte of each instruction and is represented by two hexadecimal characters (Fig. 4-2). The remaining one through five bytes are then interpreted as operands and variation indicators. If a register holds an operand, then one half byte of the instruction is used to address (name) the register. If the operand is in internal storage, then two bytes of the instruction are used to name each storage address in base-and-displacement form. Hence such operand addresses have two parts: first, the base register, which requires one half byte, and second, the displacement, which uses the three remaining hexadecimal characters of the two bytes.

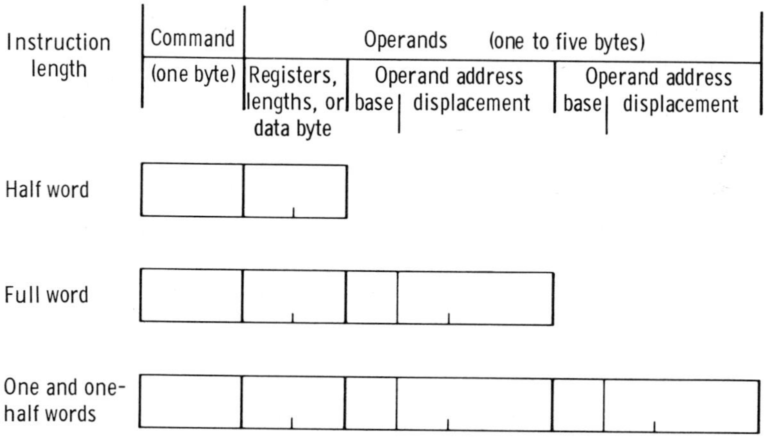

FIG. 4-2. Instructions vary in length, but the command is always first, and the operand addresses last.

Both the displacement and the base register must be specified to cite an address in storage. As noted earlier, the displacement can be thought of as being like a positive relative address which takes the form of a binary number indicating the number of bytes which must be counted off (to the right) in storage to arrive at the address desired. The starting point (origin or base) for the count is the absolute address shown in the base register. Thus the displacement amount plus the contents of the base register is the absolute address of the byte that is the left-hand end of the storage field. An example is shown in Fig. 4-3. Note that this arrangement requires all displacements and base-register components to be positive binary numbers, and the maximum displacement to be FFF_x (4095_c). The absolute address resulting from adding together the base amount, the displacement, and the index amount, if any, is known as the "effective address."

For storage operands (i.e., operands located in internal storage), the computer usually needs a length-of-field indication. When only one storage operand length is

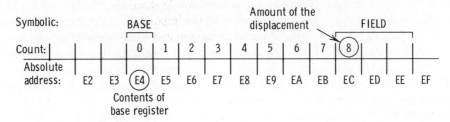

FIG. 4-3. Diagram of relative addressing analogy for base register and displacement addressing. Base address of $E4_x$ plus 08_x displacement yields EC_x absolute address for the field.

used, the length of the storage field is shown as a binary number occupying one byte of the instruction and indicating the number of bytes to be handled. A length of one byte is indicated by 0 in binary; 256 bytes by 255 in binary (FF_x). When two lengths are needed, one for each of two storage operands, each length is represented by one half byte. Such lengths may range from one through sixteen bytes (shown as 0_x through F_x). A length of zero is interpreted as meaning that the computer is to handle only one byte of data, that being the one byte addressed by the base register and displacement, plus any index amount.

When one operand is in a register and another is in storage, no length designation is needed. In such cases, the length of the register automatically determines the length of the storage field, but the field must be aligned. In such cases, one half byte of the instruction is available to designate a general-purpose register to serve as an index register. Any of the general-purpose registers can be used either as index or as base registers except register number 0, since 0 is interpreted to mean "no register" or "zero contents in place of the actual register contents." In order to attain accuracy of addressing, the programer must keep careful track of which registers he desires the computer to use for base registers, which for index registers, and which for arithmetic operations. If the programer confuses these, the result will be chaos.

In writing imperative instructions on the coding sheet, the programer needs to keep in mind the underlying machine-language format of the instructions. The imperative instructions the programer writes in symbolic form on the coding sheet will be translated by the compiler into these machine-language forms. To aid the programer, however, the symbolic format is made simpler than the machine-language format.

IMPERATIVE INSTRUCTION GUIDE

In writing imperative instructions on the coding sheet, the programer will find that observing some guides will help avoid mistakes. Ten of these are listed below, together with a few explanatory remarks on each.

1.   The computer is fundamentally a two-address machine—that is, each im

perative instruction normally names a source operand and a destination operand. Two operands are therefore normally required for the imperative instructions. If the programer specifies less than or more than two, he should check to be sure he is doing so correctly.

2. When an instruction has like source and destination operands, then the programer names the receiver first. For example, when the two operands both name registers, the first register is the address of the receiving operand (the destination), and the second register is the address of the sending operand (the source). That is, the first operand register named will have its contents altered by the operation, whereas the second operand register named will not. The first operand is the leftmost operand cited in the statement as written on the coding form.

When two fields in storage are the two operands named in an instruction, the first operand names the receiving field (the destination) in storage, and the second operand names the sending field in storage (the source). The field in storage named as the first operand will have its contents altered; the field named as the second operand will not have its contents changed by the operation.

3. When an instruction involves both a register and a field in storage, then the programer names the register as the first operand regardless of whether that register be a sender or a receiver. This reflects the underlying machine-language instruction format.

Because of this, the programer cannot, from the listing of the operands on the coding sheet, make any quick-and-easy generalization about the direction of data movement. When he names a register and a field in storage, the programer should look to the nature of the operation being performed and to the nature of the operands involved before attempting to identify the source and the destination—i.e., the direction of data movement.

4. Irrespective of the direction of data movement, the address of a field is always the address of its leftmost byte in storage. The only relation of the length of a field to the address of a field is that the length count starts as one with the byte addressed and goes only to the right toward higher-numbered addresses.

5. Specifying the length of a field in storage must receive the explicit attention of the programer. When a register holds one of the operands, the storage field need have no length specified, because the length of the register determines the number of bytes of storage needed to fill or copy the register. This happens without regard to whether this length fits the intention of the programer or not.

When both operands are in storage, the length of one or both must be specified by the programer in one of two ways: (*a*) The programer can allow the compiler program to determine the length from the declarative defining the field. This is usually the more bug-free and the easier way. To do it, the programer simply omits any reference to the length when writing the imperative instruction. The compiler then supplies it as it translates the instruction. This is why length operands or fourth operands are usually needed in **DC** or **DS** declaratives, even when they have zero duplication factors. The programer must, however, check that the length determined from the declarative is the appropriate length for the operand in the instruction. If it is not, then the programer must use the second method. (*b*) The programer can write the length in parentheses after the symbolic name he writes to identify the operand. This overrides the compiler-provided lengths.

6.   Specifying the registers to serve as the base and the index registers must receive the explicit attention of the programer. When indexing is to be used, the programer can write the index-register identification in parentheses after the operand name. When the programer can use indexing directly, he cannot specify lengths of fields. Hence the material written in parentheses after a symbolic name is never ambiguous. Its use makes it clearly either a length or an index register.

For specifying the base register, the programer has two options. The usual and preferred course of action is to have the compiler supply the base-register designation. To do this, the programer omits all reference to a base register in writing the imperative instruction, but provides a declarative early in his program, naming the base register or registers. Then the compiler automatically uses only these registers as the base registers. To override the compiler assignment, the programer can write the identification of the base register with a comma immediately preceding it, and enclose all within parentheses. Using base registers for indexing—which is possible—is described later in this book.

7.   The sequence of bytes handled in the processing of data within a field or register depends upon the nature of the operation. In practice, it also depends upon the model of the computer, but conceptually it is independent of the model of the computer. Arithmetic operations go from right to left. This is because the computer represents binary and packed-decimal numbers in integer form, justified on the right, and with any fill on the left. Nonarithmetic packed-decimal operations also go from right to left, because the sign is at the right end. All other operations go from left to right—as, for example, movement of data from one place to another in storage. This direction of operation is less expensive in terms of hardware, given the other choices the computer designers have made.

8.   All references to storage fields when a register holds one operand must be aligned, because of design features of the computer that contribute to its fast operating speed. The alignment required depends upon the capacity of the register, and may be on the half, full, or double word. The programer can align data in storage by writing declaratives to define aligned fields in storage, e.g., by using type H, F, or D, with or without zero duplication factors, or by writing imperative move instructions to copy data from nonaligned addresses to aligned addresses.

9.   The programer should be wary of interrupts. In order to facilitate computer operation, the computer manufacturers have provided an automatic interrupt procedure to catch "illegal" situations. These vary with the particular commands the programer specifies and are discussed in Chap. 8.

10.   To simplify the work of the programer, the commands the computer can

Type name	Operand Destination--Source
RR	Register--Register
RS	Registers--Storage Storage--Registers
RX	Register--Storage indexed Storage indexed--Register
SS	Storage--Storage
SI	Storage--Instruction

FIG. 4-4. Summary of command types by source and destination of the data movements.

```
NAME    OP   OPERANDS

 *           R IS REGISTER ADDRESS
 *           S IS STORAGE ADDRESS
 *           B IS BASE REGISTER ADDRESS
 *           D IS DISPLACEMENT AMOUNT
 *           L IS LENGTH AMOUNT
 *           X IS INDEX REGISTER ADDRESS
 *           I IS ONE BYTE OF DATA
 *           1 IS FIRST OPERAND
 *           2 IS SECOND OPERAND
 *           3 IS CONTINUATION OF FIRST OPERAND
 *
 *TYPE   RR   R1,R2              NOTE USE OF COMMAS
 *TYPE   RS   R1,R3,S2           S2 IS D2(B2)
 *TYPE   RX   R1,S2              S2 IS D2(X2,B2)
 *TYPE   SS   S1,S2              S IS D(L,B)
 *TYPE   SI   S1,I2              S1 IS D1(B1)
```

FIG. 4-5. Instruction formats by command type.

execute are normally classified into types, depending upon the pattern of register and storage usage. This is described below and summarized in Fig. 4-4. Figure 4-5 summarizes the general pattern of formats the programer writes on the coding form.

RR. This type of command designates a register-to-register operation. The register identifications can be represented by self-defining decimal numbers on the coding form separated only by a comma.

RS. This designates an operation using one or more registers but with one field in storage—i.e., one operand is in one or more registers, the other in internal storage. The one or more registers are represented as for the RR type. The storage field can be represented on the coding form by a symbolic name for the field in storage, separated only by a comma from the register identifications.

RX. This is like the RS type, but with two differences. One is that one operand is in only one register. The second difference is that only one index register can be designated. All instructions of the RX type can index the storage address, but not the register. That is, the indexing applies only to the operand in storage, not to the one in the register.

SS.   This designates a storage-to-storage operation involving no registers containing operands—i.e., all operand data are in storage. For each field in storage, the displacement-and-base-register assignment is normally written on the coding sheet simply as a symbolic name. One length, the length for the receiving-operand field is needed, except for commands that handle packed-decimal data. For those, each operand needs a length, with the exception of commands for editing data. No index registers are used, but the base register can be used like an index register under some limited conditions, as noted later. In the small models of the computer, this type is also known as the IO type, with input-output equipment and control data replacing two of the register designations.

SI.   This designates an instruction-to-storage operation or control operation that uses a storage address. The storage operand takes the usual base-and-displacement form, with no index-register provision. The other operand is the second byte of the instruction itself, which serves as one byte of data. The byte of data is the equivalent of a literal, and is known as "immediate data," since no address for it is needed. In the small models of the computer, this type (like the SS type) is also known as the IO type, with input-output equipment and control data replacing the byte of immediate data.

DATA-MOVEMENT OPERATIONS

A wide variety of data-movement operations is possible in the computer. Some are relatively simple, others much more complex. Some set indicators in the computer, such as the "condition code" indicator that is also set by comparison operations. For simplicity, all the data-movement operations presented in this chapter have been selected because they do *not* set the "condition code" and because they are unlikely to be subjected to computer interrupts.

The data-movement operations here presented fit into four general groups. The first group moves data from one register to another and thus permits the copying of data from one register to another. The second moves data between registers and storage. This allows new data that is to be operated upon to be moved into the registers and the results of operations from the registers to be copied into internal storage. The third group moves data from one place in storage to another, allowing data in internal storage to be rearranged directly. The fourth group moves data from one place in the computer to another while changing the coding. (Appendix C provides a summary of all commands in the computer.)

REGISTER-TO-REGISTER MOVEMENT

LR—Load Register. This RR command causes all of the data in the register named as the second-operand address to be copied into the register named as the first-operand address, replacing all of the prior contents of the first register. The contents of the second register remain unchanged. Any general-purpose registers may be named as operand addresses; no alignment is needed or possible. No interrupts are permitted, and the condition code remains unchanged. This command is not available in the small models of the computer. An example of Load Register is given in Fig. 4-6, which shows the contents before and after the operation for each of the registers involved.

```
     LOC  OBJECT CODE    ADDR1 ADDR2        NAME    OP    OPERANDS        COMMENT
                                                IMPERATIVES
  00191C 1845                                F4#6    LR    4,5             LOAD A REG. FROM A REG.


                                        REGISTER CONTENTS
                              BEFORE                      AFTER
                                        REGISTER  1
                                        REGISTER  2
                                        REGISTER  3
                              00002748  REGISTER  4   00008F59
                              00008F59  REGISTER  5   00008F59
                                        REGISTER  6
                                        REGISTER  7
                                        REGISTER  8
```

Fig. 4-6. Example of Load Register.

DATA MOVEMENT BETWEEN REGISTERS AND STORAGE

L—Load. This RX command copies the contents of the field in storage into the register named as the first-operand address. The original register contents are replaced by the incoming data; the field in storage is unaffected. The storage address must be aligned on the full word and must be four bytes long. This command is not available on the small models of the computer. The command is subject to interruptions from improper alignment or addresses. An example of Load is given in Fig. 4-7.

Do It Now Exercise 4-2. Write one DC declarative and one Load instruction to provide the binary equivalent of decimal +640 in register 9. Write one DC declarative and one Load instruction to provide the binary equivalent of decimal +28461 in register 9. Show in hexadecimal, in the comments position, the contents of storage for each case.

ST—Store. This RX command copies the data from the register named as the first-operand address into a field in storage named as the second-operand address. The field in storage must be aligned on a full-word boundary. The contents of storage are altered, but the contents of the register are unchanged by the operation. As with Load, any general-purpose register may be designated as the first-operand address. The same interrupts are possible as for Load. The condition code is not altered. This command is not available for the small models of the computer. An example of Store is given in Fig. 4-8. Note that this command is the reverse of Load.

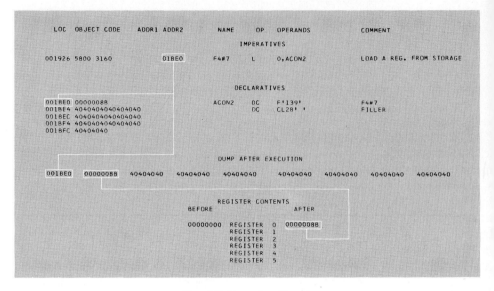

```
    LOC  OBJECT CODE   ADDR1 ADDR2        NAME    OP   OPERANDS            COMMENT
                                         IMPERATIVES

  001926 5800 3160           01BE0       F4#7     L    0,ACON2            LOAD A REG. FROM STORAGE


                                         DECLARATIVES

  001BE0 00000088                        ACON2    DC   F'139'             F4#7
  001BE4 4040404040404040                         DC   CL28' '            FILLER
  001BEC 4040404040404040
  001BF4 4040404040404040
  001BFC 40404040


                                  DUMP AFTER EXECUTION

  001BE0  00000088    40404040   40404040   40404040    40404040   40404040   40404040   40404040


                                    REGISTER CONTENTS
                            BEFORE                  AFTER

                          00000000  REGISTER   0   00000088
                                    REGISTER   1
                                    REGISTER   2
                                    REGISTER   3
                                    REGISTER   4
                                    REGISTER   5
```

FIG. 4-7. Example of Load.

```
    LOC  OBJECT CODE   ADDR1 ADDR2        NAME    OP   OPERANDS            COMMENT
                                         IMPERATIVES

  001938 5060 3200           01C80       F4#8     ST   6,SAVE2            STORE FROM A REG.


                                         DECLARATIVES

  001C80 4040404040404040               SAVE2    DC   CL32' '            USED TO DISPLAY STORAGE
  001C88 4040404040404040
  001C90 4040404040404040
  001C98 4040404040404040


                                  DUMP AFTER EXECUTION

  001C80  000023AC    40404040   40404040   40404040    40404040   40404040   40404040   40404040


                                  DUMP BEFORE EXECUTION

  001C80  40404040    40404040   40404040   40404040    40404040   40404040   40404040   40404040


                                    REGISTER CONTENTS
                            BEFORE                  AFTER

                                    REGISTER   1
                                    REGISTER   2
                                    REGISTER   3
                                    REGISTER   4
                                    REGISTER   5
                          000023AC  REGISTER   6   000023AC
                                    REGISTER   7
                                    REGISTER   8
                                    REGISTER   9
```

FIG. 4-8. Example of Store.

Do It Now Exercise 4-3. Write two DS declaratives and two Store instructions to save in storage the contents of register 9 for the two parts of Do It Now Exercise 4-2. Show the resulting contents of storage in hexadecimal.

LM—Load Multiple. This RS command performs the same function as the Load instruction but can load in sequence more than one register. The first general-purpose register to be loaded is named as the first-operand address; the last register to be loaded is named as the second-operand (R3) address. The computer, in interpreting the operation, assumes that register 0 follows register 15—that is, the registers are assumed to "wrap around." The third-operand address designates the left-most byte of the field which must be aligned on a full word in internal storage from which successive four-byte fields are to be copied. The length of the sending area in bytes is four times the number of registers activated by the other operands. The condition code is not altered, but the same interrupts that occur for Load may occur here. This command is not available in the small models of the computer. An example of Load Multiple is given in Fig. 4-9.

Do It Now Exercise 4-4. Write four DC declaratives and one LM instruction to provide the binary equivalents of decimal +6, +12, +18, and +24 in four consecutive registers, starting with register 7. Show the contents of storage.

STM—Store Multiple. This RS command follows the same pattern and is parallel to the Load Multiple and to the Store described previously. The first-oper-

```
  LOC   OBJECT CODE    ADDR1 ADDR2      NAME    OP   OPERANDS           COMMENT

                                          IMPERATIVES

 001940  9889 3260           01CE0       F4#9    LM   8,9,CON           LOAD MULTIPLE


                                          DECLARATIVES

 001CE0  00004599                         CON     DC   F'17817'         F4#9
 001CE4  000000E1                                 DC   F'225'           USED IN LOAD MULTIPLE
 001CE8  4040404040404040                         DC   CL24' '          FILLER
 001CF0  4040404040404040
 001CF8  4040404040404040


                                     DUMP AFTER EXECUTION

 001CE0   00004599    000000E1    40404040   40404040    40404040   40404040   40404040   40404040


                                     REGISTER CONTENTS
                            BEFORE                        AFTER

                                        REGISTER  1
                                        REGISTER  2
                                        REGISTER  3
                                        REGISTER  4
                                        REGISTER  5
                                        REGISTER  6
                                        REGISTER  7
                          00001DF6       REGISTER  8    00004599
                          00003440       REGISTER  9    000000E1
```

Fig. 4-9. Example of Load Multiple.

and address designates the first register, and the second operand (R3) address designates the last register to be stored from. The leftmost byte of the field in storage into which the data from the registers are to be copied is designated by the third-operand address. The storage field must be aligned, starting on a full-word boundary. The condition code is not altered, but the same interrupts and register wrap-around encountered with Load Multiple may occur here. This command is not available on the small models of the computer. An example of Store Multiple is given in Fig. 4-10.

FIG. 4-10. Example of Store Multiple.

Do It Now Exercise 4-5. *Write one DS declarative and one STM instruction to save in storage the contents of four consecutive registers, starting with register 7. Show the resulting contents of storage in hexadecimal.*

LH—Load Half. This RX command copies one half word of data from storage into the low-order (rightmost) two bytes of the register named as the first-operand address. The field in storage named as the second-operand address is unaltered. The left-hand half of a four-bytes-long register is cleared either to all 0 or to all 1 bits to match the leftmost bit of the data brought into the right-hand half of the register (sign-bit fill from the incoming data). In small models of the computer with registers two bytes long, no such fill is needed or provided. This command does not alter the condition code, but is subject to the same possible interruptions as Load. The storage field must be an aligned half word. An example of Load Half is given in Fig. 4-11.

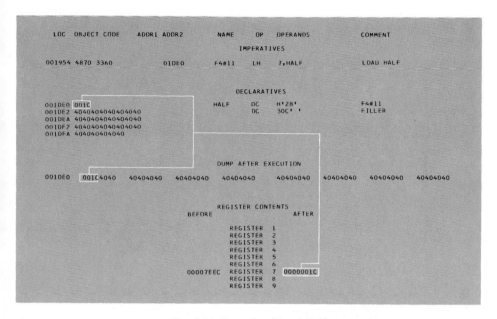

Fig. 4-11. Example of Load Half.

Do It Now Exercise 4-6. *Write two DC declaratives and two LH instructions to provide the binary equivalents of decimal +7643 and +4219 in registers 9 and 11. Show in hexadecimal the contents of storage and of the registers.*

STH—Store Half. This RX instruction is parallel to the other store operations and to the Load Half described previously. The register from which the data are copied is shown as the first-operand address. The field in storage into which the data are to be stored (the field that is to be altered to conform in content) is shown as the second-operand address. Only the right-hand half of a register four bytes long is stored. No verification is made of the contents of the left half of the register. All of the two-bytes-long register is stored in the small models of the computer. The storage address must be an aligned half word. The command does not set the condition code, but is subject to the same possible interruptions as Load. An example of Store Half is given in Fig. 4-12. Note that it is the programer's responsibility to avoid inadvertently changing either the effective sign of a binary number or the apparent number of significant bits, as done in Fig. 4-13.

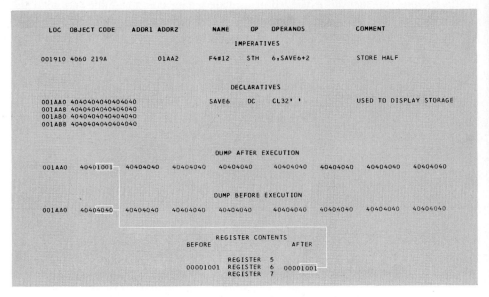

```
  LOC  OBJECT CODE     ADDR1 ADDR2        NAME     OP    OPERANDS              COMMENT
                                                   IMPERATIVES

 001910 4060 219A             01AA2       F4#12    STH   6,SAVE6+2             STORE HALF


                                                   DECLARATIVES

 001AA0 4040404040404040                  SAVE6    DC    CL32' '              USED TO DISPLAY STORAGE
 001AA8 4040404040404040
 001AB0 4040404040404040
 001AB8 4040404040404040


                                               DUMP AFTER EXECUTION

 001AA0    40401001    40404040  40404040   40404040     40404040   40404040   40404040    40404040


                                               DUMP BEFORE EXECUTION

 001AA0    40404040    40404040  40404040   40404040     40404040   40404040   40404040    40404040


                                           REGISTER CONTENTS
                                  BEFORE                      AFTER

                                             REGISTER  5
                                  00001001   REGISTER  6   00001001
                                             REGISTER  7
```

FIG. 4-12. Example of Store Half.

```
  LOC  OBJECT CODE     ADDR1 ADDR2        NAME     OP    OPERANDS              COMMENT
                                                   IMPERATIVES

 001914 4050 21A0             01AA8       F4#13    STH   5,SAVE6+8             STORE HALF. THIS IS STORED AS A NEG.


                                                   DECLARATIVES

 001AA0 4040404040404040                  SAVE6    DC    CL32' '              USED TO DISPLAY STORAGE
 001AA8 4040404040404040
 001AB0 4040404040404040
 001AB8 4040404040404040


                                               DUMP AFTER EXECUTION

 001AA0    40404040    40404040  A53D4040   40404040     40404040   40404040   40404040    40404040


                                               DUMP BEFORE EXECUTION

 001AA0    40404040    40404040  40404040   40404040     40404040   40404040   40404040    40404040


                                           REGISTER CONTENTS
                                  BEFORE                      AFTER

                                             REGISTER  4
                                  032BA53D   REGISTER  5   032BA53D
                                             REGISTER  6
```

FIG. 4-13. Example of errors from using Store Half.

Do It Now Exercise 4-7. *Write one DS declarative and two STH instructions to save in storage the contents of registers 9 and 11 from Do It Now Exercise 4-6. Show the resulting contents of storage in hexadecimal.*

IC—Insert Character. This RX command places in the rightmost byte of the register named as the first-operand address one byte of data obtained from the place in storage named as the second-operand address. No alignment is needed. These data are placed in the register without disturbing the other bytes of data in the register and without altering the area in storage from which the data are copied. This command does not alter the condition code but is subject to the interruption from illegal or improper addressing. This command is not available on the small models of the computer. An example of Insert Character is given in Fig. 4-14.

Do It Now Exercise 4-8. *Write one DC declarative to provide in storage $DAEB_x$. Write two Insert Character instructions to place the DA_x as the rightmost byte in register 9 and the EB_x as the rightmost byte in register 11. Assuming that the registers previously contained all 00_x, show the resulting contents of the registers.*

STC—Store Character. This RX command is the reverse of, and parallel to, the Insert Character. It copies one byte from the rightmost byte of the register named as the first-operand address and places it in storage as a one-byte field at the second-operand address. This command does not alter the condition code, but is subject to the same possible interruptions as Insert Character. This command is not available on the small models of the computer. An example of Store Character is given in Fig. 4-15.

Do It Now Exercise 4-9. *Write one DS declarative and two STC instructions to copy the data from registers 9 and 11 of Do It Now Exercise 4-8 into the storage field reserved by the DS to make its contents $EBDA_x$. Show the resulting contents of storage.*

STORAGE-TO-STORAGE MOVEMENT

The moves in this group begin with two basic operations which move entire bytes of data. The next two move the left-hand halves of bytes and the right-hand halves of bytes separately. The last in the group offsets the data moved by one half byte to the left. No alignment of the operand addresses is needed for the moves in this group.

MVC—Move Characters. This SS command copies data from the second-operand address named to the first-operand address named, both of which must be addresses in internal storage. The copying proceeds from left to right, starting at the named addresses, until each byte of the receiving field has been altered. The one length specified is the length of the receiving field and may range from one through 256 bytes. This command is available on all models of the computer. No code check-

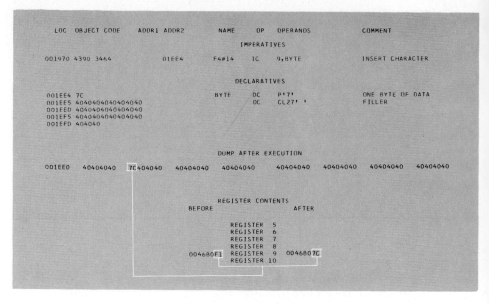

FIG. 4-14. Example of Insert Character.

FIG. 4-15. Example of Store Character.

ing or testing of the data is performed during the move. Improper addresses may cause interrupts, but this command does not alter the condition code. An example of the Move Characters is given in Fig. 4-16. This command is the computer's basic move data command.

```
   LOC  OBJECT CODE    ADDR1 ADDR2        NAME    OP   OPERANDS              COMMENT
                                               IMPERATIVES

   001986 D202 3563 3560 01FE3 01FE0      F4#16   MVC  SEND(3),MOVE          MOVE CHARACTERS


                                               DECLARATIVES

   001FE0 08976C                          MOVE    DC   PL3'8976'             F4#16
   001FE3 E2C5D5C4                         SEND    DC   CL4'SEND'             USED TO MOVE CHARACTERS
   001FE7 4040404040404040                         DC   CL25' '              FILLER
   001FEF 4040404040404040
   001FF7 4040404040404040
   001FFF 40


                                          DUMP AFTER EXECUTION

   001FE0  08976C08   976CC440   40404040   40404040    40404040   40404040   40404040   40404040



                                          DUMP BEFORE EXECUTION

   001FE0  08976CE2   C5D5C440   40404040   40404040    40404040   40404040   40404040   40404040
```

FIG. 4-16. Example of Move Characters.

Move Characters can be used for clearing fields in storage to any given character. If the leftmost byte of the field to be cleared is set to the desired clearing value by some other operation such as Move Immediate, Store Character, or Move Characters, then the entire remainder of the field may be cleared by specifying as the second operand the address of the leftmost byte of the field and as the first operand the address one more than the leftmost byte of the field. This operation therefore typically requires using as the length of the receiving field a count one byte shorter than it actually is. To do this requires overriding the compiler-assigned length by specifying the length in parenthesis for the first operand. An alternative procedure is to set the clearing character in a one-byte field immediately to the left of the field to be cleared. When this is done, no additional length specification is required. These two procedures are illustrated in Figs. 4-17 and 4-18.

Do It Now Exercise 4-10. *Write one DC declarative of type C to place your own name in storage in EBCDIC form. Write one DS of the same length and one MVC to copy your name from the area you defined with the DC into the area you defined with the DS. Show in hexadecimal the resulting contents of storage.*

MVI—Move Immediate. This SI command operates like the Move Characters command, but with two differences. The sending field is only one byte long and is

```
     LOC  OBJECT CODE    ADDR1 ADDR2      NAME   OP  OPERANDS              COMMENT
                                                IMPERATIVES

  001992 D200 35E0 35EA 02060 0206A              MVC  AREA(1),SINGLE       MOVE IN CLEAR CHARACTER
  001998 D204 35E1 35E0 02061 02060     F4#17    MVC  AREA+1(5),AREA       CLEAR 'AREA'



                                               DECLARATIVES

  002060 D6C1D6C1D6C1                    AREA    DC   CL6'OAOAOA'          FIELD TO BE CLEARED
  002066 40404040                                DC   4C' '
  00206A F1                              SINGLE  DC   X'F1'                F4#17
  00206B 404040404040404040                      DC   21C' '
  002073 404040404040404040
  00207B 4040404040


                                          DUMP AFTER EXECUTION

  002060   F1F1F1F1   F1F14040   4040F140   40404040   40404040   40404040   40404040   40404040


                                          DUMP BEFORE EXECUTION

  002060   D6C1D6C1   D6C14040   4040F140   40404040   40404040   40404040   40404040   40404040
```

Fig. 4-17. Example of using two Move Characters instructions to clear a storage area.

```
     LOC  OBJECT CODE    ADDR1 ADDR2      NAME     OP  OPERANDS            COMMENT
                                                  IMPERATIVES

  0019A4 D207 3661 3660 020E1 020E0     F4#18     MVC  WORK,ONE1           CLEAR



                                            DECLARATIVES

  0020E0 AD                              ONE1     DC   X'AD'               CLEARING FIELD
  0020E1 F9F7F6F1C1C6FOD6                WORK     DC   CL8'9761AFOO'       F4#18
  0020E9 404040404040404040                       DC   CL23' '            FILLER
  0020F1 404040404040404040
  0020F9 4040404040404040


                                          DUMP AFTER EXECUTION

  0020E0   ADADADAD   ADADADAD   AD404040   40404040   40404040   40404040   40404040   40404040


                                          DUMP BEFORE EXECUTION

  0020E0   ADF9F7F6   F1C1C6F0   D6404040   40404040   40404040   40404040   40404040   40404040
```

Fig. 4-18. Example of using a leading byte and one Move Characters instruction to clear a storage area.

located in the instruction itself. Hence the second operand for the instruction is not assigned an address in storage nor may it have a symbolic name. The second operand must be written as a one-byte constant on the coding sheet as a part of the instruction, usually as a decimal self-defining value. This command is available on all models of the computer. It does not alter the condition code, but may be subject to interruptions from improper addressing. No alignment of the first-operand address is needed. An example of Move Immediate is given in Fig. 4-19.

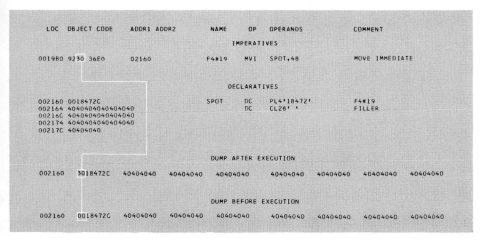

FIG. 4-19. Example of Move Immediate.

MVN—Move Numerics. This SS command copies only the right-hand halves of bytes, starting with the byte named as the second-operand address, into the field named as the first-operand address. The left-hand halves of the bytes in the receiving field and both halves of bytes in the sending field are unaltered. That is, only the right-hand halves of the bytes in the receiving field are changed to be copies of those in the sending field. The length of the receiving field is the only length used. This command is available on all models of the computer. It does not alter the condition code, but may be subject to interruptions from improper addressing. No alignment is needed for either operand address. An example of Move Numerics is given in Fig. 4-20.

```
       LOC   OBJECT CODE    ADDR1 ADDR2       NAME   OP   OPERANDS          COMMENT
                                              IMPERATIVES
     001922  D107 2058 2060  01960 01968      F4#20  MVN  ZERO(8),NUM       MOVE NUMERICS


                                              DECLARATIVES
     001960  0000000000000000                 ZERO   DC   2F'0'             F4#20
     001968  F0F0F1F9F8F5F3C7                 NUM    DC   ZL8'198537'       USED TO MOVE NUMERICS
     001970  4040404040404040                        DC   CL16' '           FILLER
     001978  4040404040404040

                                        DUMP AFTER EXECUTION
     001960  00000109  08050307  F0F0F1F9  F8F5F3C7   40404040  40404040  40404040  40404040

                                        DUMP BEFORE EXECUTION
     001960  00000000  00000000  F0F0F1F9  F8F5F3C7   40404040  40404040  40404040  40404040
```

FIG. 4-20. Example of Move Numerics.

Do It Now Exercise 4-11. *Write one DC to represent in EBCDIC characters the number 67382. Write one DC to represent in ASCII the number 00000. Prepare a flow diagram for the instructions needed to restate the EBCDIC number into the ASCII code, placing it in its own area of storage, while saving the other two areas unaltered. Using one additional DS declarative, write instructions including one MVN. Show the before-and-after contents of storage.*

MVZ—Move Zones. This SS command is the parallel of the Move Numerics, but whereas Move Numerics copies the right-hand half of each byte, Move Zones copies the left-hand half of each byte, leaving untouched the right-hand halves. The length of the receiving field is the only length used. The operation proceeds from left to right in storage from the second operand named to the first operand named. This command is available on all models of the computer. It does not alter the condition code, but may be subject to interruption from improper addressing. No alignment is needed for either operand address. An example of Move Zones is given in Fig. 4-21.

```
    LOC   OBJECT CODE    ADDR1 ADDR2      NAME    OP    OPERANDS           COMMENT

                                                IMPERATIVES

  00192E D307 20F8 2100 01A00 01A08      F4#21   MVZ   REC(8),LAST         MOVE ZONES



                                                DECLARATIVES

  001A00 0000000000000000                REC     DC    2F'0'               USED TO MOVE ZONES
  001A08 F6F1F4F8F8C1C3E9                LAST    DC    CL8'61488ACZ'       F4#21
  001A10 4040404040404040                        DC    CL16' '             FILLER
  001A18 4040404040404040



                                            DUMP AFTER EXECUTION

  001A00   FOFOFOFO   FOCOC0EO   F6F1F4F8   F8C1C3E9    40404040   40404040   40404040   40404040



                                            DUMP BEFORE EXECUTION

  001A00   00000000   00000000   F6F1F4F8   F8C1C3E9    40404040   40404040   40404040   40404040
```

Fig. 4-21. Example of Move Zones.

Do It Now Exercise 4-12. *Write two DS declaratives to match in length the two areas written for Do It Now Exercise 4-11. Prepare a flow diagram for a program of the instructions needed to restate the EBCDIC number as ASCII and the ASCII number as EBCDIC. Use as the starting point the results of Do It Now Exercise 4-11. Write the instructions, and show the resulting contents of storage.*

MVO—Move With Offset. This SS command copies half bytes of data from the second-operand address named to the first-operand address named, shifting the data one half byte to the left (toward lower-numbered addresses). Each operand has its own length, which may be from 1 through 16 bytes. When the length of the receiving field is less than one byte longer than the length of the sending field, truncation occurs on the left, and the truncated half bytes are lost. When the length of the receiving field is more than one byte longer than the length of the sending field, hexadecimal zeros fill out automatically to the left end of the receiving field. This command does not set the condition code but is subject to possible interruption from improper addressing. This command is available on all models of the computer. An example of Move With Offset is given in Fig. 4-22. Remember that the address of a field is the address of its leftmost byte.

```
  LOC  OBJECT CODE     ADDR1 ADDR2       NAME    OP   OPERANDS            COMMENT

                                            IMPERATIVES

 0019D2 F176 3869 3860 022E9 022E0       F4#22   MVO  FIELD,ZCON(7)       MOVE WITH OFFSET



                                            DECLARATIVES

 0022E0 F1F2F3F4F5F6F7F8                 ZCON    DC   CL9'123456789'      F4#22
 0022E8 F9
 0022E9 F0F0F0F0F0F0F0F0                 FIELD   DC   CL8'00000000'       MOVE WITH OFFSET FIELD
 0022F1 4040404040404040                         DC   CL15' '             FILLER
 0022F9 40404040404040


                                       DUMP AFTER EXECUTION

 0022E0   F1F2F3F4    F5F6F7F8    F90F1F2F    3F4F5F6F    70404040    40404040    40404040    40404040


                                       DUMP BEFORE EXECUTION

 0022E0   F1F2F3F4    F5F6F7F8    F9F0F0F0    F0F0F0F0    F0404040    40404040    40404040    40404040
```

FIG. 4-22. Example of Move With Offset.

The Move With Offset command operates as follows: The right-hand half of the rightmost byte of the receiving field (the first operand) is unaffected by the operation, and remains unaltered. The entire sending field (the send operand named) is unaltered. Except for the rightmost half of the right-hand byte, the receiving field is altered to conform in contents to the sending field after being displaced one half byte to the left, with truncation or fill on the left end as necessary.

Since the receiving field's rightmost half byte remains unaltered, the rightmost half byte from the sending field goes into the left-hand half of the rightmost byte of the receiving field. The left-hand half of the rightmost byte of the sending field therefore goes into the rightmost half of the second from the right byte of the receiving field. This pattern continues for the remaining bytes in the sending field.

A primary use for Move With Offset is in modifying packed-decimal fields. For example, Fig. 4-23 illustrates truncating the three lowest-order (least significant) digits from a packed-decimal number, keeping the sign where the sending and receiving fields overlap but are not coextensive. As usual with Move With Offset, this

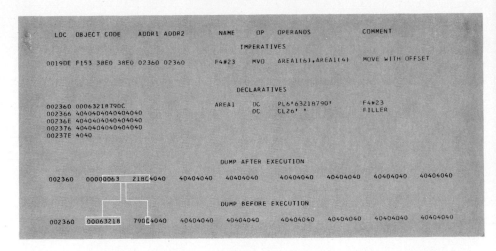

FIG. 4-23. Example of truncating a packed-decimal number by using Move With Offset.

requires specifying explicitly the length of each operand field. Figure 4-24 illustrates annexing two 0s at the right end of a packed-decimal field, an operation that can also be done with Move Zones and Move Numerics.

FIG. 4-24. Example of annexing 0s in packed-decimal by using Move With Offset.

Do It Now Exercise 4-13. *Write two DC declaratives of type P to provide the numbers +731 and +000, and two DS declaratives. Prepare a flow diagram for a routine which will truncate successively the rightmost digits from the +731 field, leaving leading 0s and the sign character. The results should be, successively, +73 and +7. Leave both of the original numbers unaltered in storage. Write instructions to implement the routine as set out in the flow diagram. Show the contents of storage before and after each imperative instruction.*

MOVE AND CHANGE FORMATS

The operations of this group provide for going to and from zoned and packed, and to and from packed and binary data formats. Since all of these operations involve packed-decimal formats, the direction of data handling is from right to left. The two operations that use a register (CVD and CVB) both require alignment. Since the data handled by these operations normally are also thereafter or previously handled by the other two operations, the programer often finds it desirable to align into double words the operands for the Pack and Unpack commands.

PACK—Pack. This SS command converts a field in zoned format and named as the second-operand address into a field in packed-decimal format and named as the first-operand address. Each field must have its own length, which may range from 1 through 16 bytes. Pack goes by the following rule of operation: The two half bytes of the rightmost byte of the sending field are interchanged and copied to the receiving-field rightmost byte. Then the computer copies the rightmost half of each of the remaining bytes in the sending field into the receiving field, with each two bytes of the sending field contributing one byte to the receiving field.

The minimum length needed for the receiving field is the full number of bytes equal to or just greater than one-half of one more than the number of bytes in the sending field. It is obvious from this that an odd number of decimal digits will convert directly into a full number of bytes, but that an even number of decimal digits will convert with the need for a 0-fill hexadecimal character on the left. All truncation and fill occur on the left-hand end of the receiving field. If the receiving field is too short to accommodate all the digits from the sending field, the leftmost (significant) digits of the number being converted will be lost. The computer does not check the data handled for valid codes as it does the conversion work. This command does not alter the condition code, but is subject to interruption from improper addressing. This command is available on all models of the computer. An example of Pack is given in Fig. 4-25.

Do It Now Exercise 4-14. *Write two DS and one DC declarative of type Z for converting the field +8251 into packed-decimal form. Use one of the two DS declaratives to establish the minimum size of the field that the computer can use to hold*

```
   LOC   OBJECT CODE    ADDR1 ADDR2        NAME    OP   OPERANDS              COMMENT
                                                IMPERATIVES
  0019FC F277 39EA 39E0 02468 02460        F4#25   PACK PAC2,ZONED           PACK ZONED FIELD


                                                DECLARATIVES
  002460 F0F1F9F7F6F5F2C8                  ZONED   DC   ZL8'1976528'         F4#25
  002468 004897103018275C                  PAC2    DC   PL8'4897103018275'   PACKED FIELD
  002470 4040404040404040                          DC   CL16' '              FILLER
  002478 4040404040404040


                                           DUMP AFTER EXECUTION

  002460  F0F1F9F7   F6F5F2C8  00000000  1976528C   40404040   40404040   40404040   40404040


                                           DUMP BEFORE EXECUTION

  002460  F0F1F9F7   F6F5F2C8  00489710  3018275C   40404040   40404040   40404040   40404040
  002480 TO THE NEXT LINE ADDRESS CONTAINS 40404040
```

FIG. 4-25. Example of Pack.

the converted number. Use the other to establish an aligned double word. Write two Pack instructions to convert the contents of the DC declarative into packed-decimal form in the two DS fields. For each case, show the contents in storage before and after.

CVB—Convert to Binary. This RX command converts the data in packed-decimal format from an aligned double word in storage named as the second-operand address into the contents of the register named as the first-operand address. Invalid sign or digit codes in the sending operand cause an interrupt. The contents of the register are altered to show the binary equivalent of the packed-decimal number. If the packed-decimal number in the double word is larger than can be converted into a binary number in one register, an interrupt occurs. The packed-decimal number is assumed to be an integer—i.e., the decimal point is assumed to lie between the rightmost digit and the sign character. Where the converted number does not occupy the entire register, the left-hand portion of the register is filled with 0 bits if the sign of the number being converted is plus, and with 1 bits if the sign of the number being converted is minus. The field in storage from which the conversion is done is not affected. The command does not alter the condition code. It is subject to interruption from a number of additional circumstances, including illegal addressing, improper field sizes, invalid sign or digit codes, and improper alignment. This command is not available on the small models of the computer. An example of Convert to Binary is given in Fig. 4-26.

Do It Now Exercise 4-15. *Write a DC declarative of type Z to provide the number +8651. Prepare a flow diagram for a routine to convert the number in the zoned field into a binary number in register 6. Write the necessary Pack and Convert*

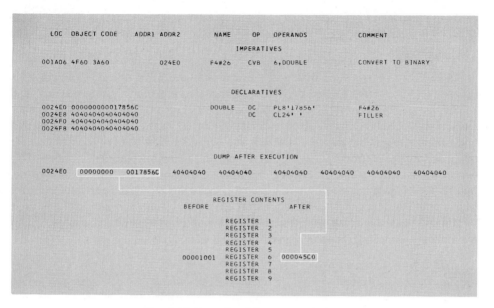

```
LOC   OBJECT CODE    ADDR1 ADDR2        NAME    OP   OPERANDS              COMMENT
                                        IMPERATIVES
001A06 4F60 3A60            024E0       F4#26   CVB  6,DOUBLE              CONVERT TO BINARY


                                        DECLARATIVES
0024E0 000000000017856C               DOUBLE    DC   PL8'17856'            F4#26
0024E8 404040404040404040               DC   CL24' '              FILLER
0024F0 404040404040404040
0024F8 404040404040404040


                                        DUMP AFTER EXECUTION

0024E0  00000000   0017856C  40404040  40404040   40404040  40404040   40404040  40404040


                                        REGISTER CONTENTS
                                BEFORE                      AFTER

                                        REGISTER  1
                                        REGISTER  2
                                        REGISTER  3
                                        REGISTER  4
                                        REGISTER  5
                                00001001 REGISTER  6      000045C0
                                        REGISTER  7
                                        REGISTER  8
                                        REGISTER  9
```

Fig. 4-26. Example of Convert to Binary.

```
LOC   OBJECT CODE    ADDR1 ADDR2        NAME    OP   OPERANDS              COMMENT
                                        IMPERATIVES
001A18 4E70 3B00            02580       F4#27   CVD  7,HOLD5              CONVERT TO DECIMAL


                                        DECLARATIVES
002580 404040404040404040              HOLD5    DC   CL32' '              USED TO DISPLAY STORAGE
002588 404040404040404040
002590 404040404040404040
002598 404040404040404040


                                        DUMP AFTER EXECUTION

002580  00000000   0055744C  40404040  40404040   40404040  40404040   40404040  40404040


                                        DUMP BEFORE EXECUTION

002580 TO THE NEXT LINE ADDRESS CONTAINS 40404040


                                        REGISTER CONTENTS
                                BEFORE                      AFTER

                                        REGISTER  1
                                        REGISTER  2
                                        REGISTER  3
                                        REGISTER  4
                                        REGISTER  5
                                        REGISTER  6
                                0000D9C0 REGISTER  7      0000D9C0
                                        REGISTER  8
                                        REGISTER  9
```

Fig. 4-27. Example of Convert to Decimal.

to Binary instructions, together with any needed DS declaratives. Show the contents of storage and of the register after each operation.

CVD—Convert to Decimal. This RX command is parallel, but opposite in direction, to the Convert to Binary command just described. Overflow, however, is impossible because the packed-decimal field can accommodate a number larger than can be accommodated in the register. The computer converts the binary-format contents of the register named as the first-operand address into a packed-decimal-format field which appears in storage at the second-operand address. Any fill occurs on the left with 0_x. The second-operand address must be for an aligned double word. This command does not include any code checking, and assumes that the position of the binary point is to the right of the rightmost bit in the register ("integer conversion"). This command does not alter the condition code but is subject to interruptions from improper addressing. It is not available on the small models of the computer. An example of Convert to Decimal is given in Fig. 4-27.

Do It Now Exercise 4-16. Write one DC declarative to provide in binary form the equivalent of decimal +2999. Prepare a flow diagram for a routine to convert this number to packed-decimal form. Write any necessary declaratives and imperative instructions. Show the contents of storage and of any registers after each instruction.

UNPK—Unpack. This SS command is parallel to and opposite Pack. The data in the second-operand address are assumed to be in packed-decimal form. The computer converts these into zoned form and places them in storage at the place named as the first-operand address. Each operand has its own length, which may range from 1 through 16 bytes. Any truncation or zero fill occurs as needed on the left end of the receiving field. The length of the receiving field should be at a minimum one byte less than twice the length in bytes of the sending field, to avoid truncation. The data are not checked for valid codes as the conversion work is done.

The operation proceeds in the following manner: The computer interchanges the two parts of the rightmost byte of the sending field and places them in the receiving field's rightmost byte position. The computer then expands the remaining half bytes from right to left in the sending field into full bytes in the receiving field, the data from the sending field being copied into the right-hand half of each of the bytes in the receiving field. The computer fills the left-hand half of each of the bytes in the receiving field, except for the rightmost byte, with the proper zone half byte, which is F_x if the computer is operating in EBCDIC code. The computer provides 0-fill characters as needed to the left in the receiving field. If the receiving field is too short to accommodate the entire field, truncation occurs on the left. This command does not alter the condition code, but is subject to interruption from improper addressing. This command is available on all models of the computer. An example of Unpack is given in Fig. 4-28.

```
  LOC  OBJECT CODE    ADDR1 ADDR2        NAME     OP   OPERANDS              COMMENT
                                                  IMPERATIVES
001A22 F373 3B64 3B60 025E4 025E0        F4#28    UNPK  ZOND(8),PAC          CHANGE A PACKED FIELD INTO ZONED

                                                  DECLARATIVES
0025E0 0194864C                          PAC      DC    PL4'194864'          F4#28
0025E4 0000000000000000                  ZOND     DC    2F'0'
0025EC 4040404040404040                           DC    CL20' '              FILLER
0025F4 4040404040404040
0025FC 40404040

                                           DUMP AFTER EXECUTION
0025E0   0194864C   F0F0F1F9   F4F8F6C4   40404040   40404040   40404040   40404040   40404040

                                           DUMP BEFORE EXECUTION
0025E0   0194864C   00000000   00000000   40404040   40404040   40404040   40404040   40404040
002600 TO THE NEXT LINE ADDRESS CONTAINS 40404040
```

FIG. 4-28. Example of Unpack.

Do It Now Exercise 4-17. *Using the data generated as a result of Do It Now Exercise 4-15, prepare a flow diagram for a routine to convert the binary numbers into character (not zoned) format. Write the declarative and imperative instructions needed to implement the routine. Show the contents of storage after each instruction.*

EXTENDED DATA MOVEMENT

The data-movement commands presented thus far are limited in the amount of data they can move. Thus a Load or Store moves one word, an Insert Character or Store Character moves only one byte, and even a Move Characters can move only 256 bytes at the most. Sometimes the programer wants to have the computer move much more data, such as thousands of characters, and would like to direct it with but a single instruction. A few models of the computer offer a command to do this, the Move Characters Long command, which can move as many as 16,777,216 bytes.

MVCL—Move Characters Long. This RR command copies data from one place in internal storage to another place in internal storage, not to or from the registers. The copying proceeds from left to right, starting at the address as contained in the two specified registers, until the specified number of bytes have been copied. The receiving or destination field may be a different length from the sending or source field, and truncation or fill-padding occurs automatically to handle length differences. No code checking or testing of the data is performed during the move. Improper addresses either of or in the registers may cause interrupts. This command which does set the condition code is available on only a few models of the computer. An example of Move Characters Long is given in Fig. 4-29.

Three aspects of Move Characters Long require the programer's attention: register contents, field overlap and length, and interrupt. The three interact and affect the way the executed command alters the contents of internal storage in the computer.

The programer must use two even-odd pairs of registers for designating the operands. In the instruction, the programer specifies only the even member of each pair; the use of the other member is implied. The three low-order bytes of the even-numbered registers specify the absolute (binary) addresses of the receiving (first operand) and sending (second operand) fields. The three low-order bytes of the associated odd-numbered registers specify the actual lengths of the respective fields. A zero length is permitted for either operand and results in no data movement if it is for the first operand. The leftmost (high-order) byte of three of the registers is unused, but the leftmost bytes of the odd-numbered register of the second-operand pair contains the fill or padding character (in Fig. 4-29 this is the 40_x in register 9). The leftmost bytes in the other registers are ignored. As the computer executes a Move Characters Long, it changes the contents of all four registers by counting up the addresses and counting down the lengths to zero, byte by byte, as it copies each byte from the sending to the receiving field.

Field overlap and length become a problem for Move Characters Long because the command can copy so much data. The programer must specify the length of each field in advance of the computer's executing the command. The computer, as a result of executing the command, sets the condition code to reflect the lengths of the fields: code 0 for equal lengths, code 1 for receiving operand shorter than sending (i.e., truncation occurred), code 2 for receiving operand longer than sending (i.e., padding or fill was used), and code 3 for "destructive overlap." Thus in Fig. 4-29 the condition code would be set to 2.

"Destructive overlap" is said to occur when the receiving field is to the right of but overlaps the sending field. More precisely, it is said to occur when the address in the even-numbered register specifying the receiving operand is equal to or greater than the address in the even-numbered register specifying the sending operand, *and* is less than the sum of the address and the length specified in the register pair used to designate the sending operand. The computer will not execute a Move Characters Long command if the result would be destructive overlap. Destructive overlap should not be confused with storage wrap-around, however. If in executing a Move Characters Long the computer tries to use an address beyond the limits of the internal storage capacity available, an interrupt occurs, and the execution is broken off at that point, just as for an ordinary Move Characters. If, however, the computer happens to have 16,777,216 bytes of internal storage, then the computer treats the next address after address $FFFFFF_x$ as 000000_x and continues the data copying at the low end of internal storage (a "wrap-around"), provided that destructive overlap would not occur.

LOC	OBJECT CODE	ADDR1	ADDR2	NAME	OP	OPERANDS	COMMENT
					IMPERATIVES		
006B0A	91FF 30FB	06900			TM	FLD1,X'FF'	SET CONDITION CODE TO 11
006B0C	0540				BALR	4,0	SAVE CONDITION CODE
006B0E	9869 30BB		06BC0		LM	6,9,CONS	SET UP REGISTERS
006B12	0E68			F4#29	MVCL	6,8	MOVE CHARACTERS LONG
006B14	0550				BALR	5,0	SAVE CONDITION CODE
006B16	9049 30CB		06BD0		STM	4,9,ASAVE	SHOW REGISTER CONTENTS
					DECLARATIVES		
006BC0	00006900			CONS	DC	A(FLD1)	ADDRESS OF RECEIVING FIELD
006BC4	00000020				DC	X'00000020'	LENGTH OF RECEIVING FIELD
006BC8	00006920				DC	A(FLD2)	ADDRESS OF SENDING FIELD
006BCC	4000001B				DC	X'4000001B'	PAD CHAR. AND SENDING LENGTH
006BD0	404040404040404040			ASAVE	DC	CL48' '	USED TO DISPLAY REGISTERS
006BDB	404040404040404040						
006BE0	404040404040404040						
006BEB	404040404040404040						
006BF0	404040404040404040						
006BFB	404040404040404040						
006900	FFFFFFFFFFFFFFFF			FLD1	DC	32X'FF'	RECEIVING FIELD
00690B	FFFFFFFFFFFFFFFF						
006910	FFFFFFFFFFFFFFFF						
006918	FFFFFFFFFFFFFFFF						
006920	E3C8C9E240C6C9C5			FLD2	DC	C'THIS FIELD WILL BE MOVED'	SENDING FIELD
00692B	D3C440E6C9D3D340						
006930	C2C540D4D6E5C5C4						
00693B	7777777777777777				DC	8X'77'	FILLER

DUMP AFTER EXECUTION

006BA0	F0404040	40404040	40404040	40404040	40404040	40404040	40404040	40404040
006BC0	00006900	00000020	00006920	4000001B	70006B0E	60006B16	00006920	00000000
006BE0	0000693B	40000000	40404040	40404040	40404040	40404040	40404040	40404040
006900	E3C8C9E2	40C6C9C5	D3C440E6	C9D3D340	C2C540D4	D6E5C5C4	40404040	40404040
006920	E3C8C9E2	40C6C9C5	D3C440E6	C9D3D340	C2C540D4	D6E5C5C4	77777777	77777777
006940	F0404040	40404040	40404040	40404040	40404040	40404040	40404040	40404040

DUMP BEFORE EXECUTION

006BA0	F0404040	40404040	40404040	40404040	40404040	40404040	40404040	40404040
006BC0	00006900	00000020	00006920	4000001B	40404040	40404040	40404040	40404040
006BE0	40404040	40404040	40404040	40404040	40404040	40404040	40404040	40404040
006900	FFFFFFFF	FFFFFFFF	FFFFFFFF	FFFFFFFF	FFFFFFFF	FFFFFFFF	FFFFFFFF	FFFFFFFF
006920	E3C8C9E2	40C6C9C5	D3C440E6	C9D3D340	C2C540D4	D6E5C5C4	77777777	77777777
006940	F0404040	40404040	40404040	40404040	40404040	40404040	40404040	40404040

FIG. 4-29. Example of Move Characters Long.

The Move Characters Long command is subject to being interrupted. That is, while the computer is in the midst of executing the command, the computer may suddenly cease and instead take care of doing some other operation instead. As explained later in Chap. 8, the computer may later attempt to resume executing the Move Characters Long. This is possible because the register contents change as the operation takes place. But two cautions are in order. First, the programer must be sure that the registers he specifies remain unaltered during any possible interrupts (this is very hard to do even when he uses only registers 4 through 11 inclusive). Second, if another program that can be executed as a result of an interrupt requires that the Move Characters Long be either unexecuted or executed in full, then that other program needs some way of determining whether or not the Move Characters

Long was completed, interrupted, or not yet started. The MVCL command is especially useful for clearing large areas in storage (fill with the padding character) and in doing major rearrangements of storage, as for large input-output buffers or pages in multiprograming.

002660	40404040	40404040	40404040	40404040	40404040	40404040	40404040	40404040
002680	C2C9D5C1	D9E840C3	C1D540D4	C5C1D540	7FD6D560	D6C6C67F	000009E2	00000B68
0026A0	0000011A	00007F34	0000000F	0000DA99	00008AB4	0C6879AA	00000639	0000FABA
0026C0	F2F5F8C4	F7F4C9D3	F1F2F3F4	F5F6F7F8	C9F5D8C7	F8F0F0F0	C0F0F0F0	F0C04040
0026E0	40E3C1D7	E2C2D6E7	E2D1C9C7	E2E2C1E6	E2F2F3C4	F0F0C5F1	F5C6F0F1	C9404040
002700	40404040	40404040	40404040	40404040	40404040	40404040	40404040	40404040

FIG. 4-30. Portion of a dump of internal storage.

Do It Now Exercise 4-18. *Figure 4-30 shows in part a dump of internal storage from the computer. Mark off on this dump the likely boundary between each pair of fields. Then write DC declaratives that would be adequate to establish each field which you have marked off with the contents that you observe in the storage dump. Next, prepare a flow diagram for a routine to convert each binary field you find into a character (not zoned) field, and each zoned or numeric character field into a binary field. Write the instructions needed to implement the routine, but use only the eight-byte field called WOKF, which should be aligned on the double-word boundary. Place the final results of all conversion operations in successive fields in storage, showing in hexadecimal the anticipated contents of storage in each case.*

EXERCISES

1. Why is the computer sometimes called a "two-address" computer?

2. How are four different types of commands fitted into three different lengths of instructions?

3. Why is a storage dump useful to a programer?

4. What are the data sources and destinations in the computer?

5. Propose and defend some rules for determining the direction of data movement for data-movement commands, giving only the name of the command and its type (RR or the like).

6. Which commands presented in this chapter require aligned operands? Why?

CHAPTER 5

Arithmetic Operations

ARITHMETIC IN THE COMPUTER

The computer can perform arithmetic in three major modes: the binary, which is the most rapid; the packed-decimal, which is the most easily understood; and the floating-point, which is the most convenient for extended arithmetic computations. Floating-point operations are taken up in Chap. 12. Before taking up the arithmetic commands presented in this chapter, let us examine some properties of arithmetic operations, as well as five characteristics of the computer.

First, the computer does binary and packed-decimal arithmetic operations in an integer manner. That is, ignoring the algebraic sign, the computer acts as if all numbers (except 0) were 1 or larger, and as if the decimal point always lay to the right of the rightmost digit. To achieve this form, it is assumed that numbers have been multiplied or divided by constants as needed to convert the numbers, as illustrated in Fig. 5-1.

Integer form in turn leads to a right-to-left processing of arithmetic operands. This right-to-left procedure is in line with traditional practice and seems natural to human beings who have been trained in the decimal system. For example, in adding a column of numbers, most of us have been trained to begin with the rightmost column, add that, and make a carry from that column to the next one to the left. After adding that column, we again make a carry into the next column to the left, and so on from right to left, until all of the columns of numbers have been handled.

95

Decimal number	Packed-decimal integer format						Decimal adjustment
1234.	0	1	2	3	4	C	None
1.	0	0	0	0	1	C	None
0.02	0	0	0	0	2	C	100
0.1234	0	1	2	3	4	C	10000

FIG. 5-1. Examples of integer form in packed-decimal format.

In multiplications we are familiar with the same procedure. We begin at the right and gradually work our way to the left until we run out of nonzero digits and carries.

Second, although packed-decimal arithmetic operations do not require it, the binary arithmetic operations all require address alignment of the operands in storage and a proper length. By address alignment is meant that the byte address of the data in storage must be on a half-, full-, or double-word boundary, as the case may require. Thus, for example, if a binary arithmetic operation requires four bytes of data from storage, then the address (leftmost byte) of the storage operand must be on a full-word boundary. Chapter 3 gave examples of how the programer can use the DS declaratives to force alignment, and how the DC and DS declaratives, when used with the F and H types, can automatically result in correct alignment and length.

Third, the arithmetic operations, except for multiply and divide, set the "condition code." The condition code is a control field also used to hold the results of comparison and test operations. This field is not directly addressable in many models of the computer. The condition-code field is two binary bits long, with the following content significance for arithmetic operations: a 0 (00_b) condition code indicates that the prior arithmetic operation had zero (either positive or negative) as a result; a 1 (01_b) that the prior arithmetic operation resulted in a number less than zero (a negative nonzero number); a 2 (10_b) that the prior arithmetic operation resulted in a number greater than zero (a positive nonzero number); and a 3 (11_b) that the prior arithmetic operation resulted in arithmetic overflow.

When it occurs, the overflow condition takes precedence over the other possible condition-code states. The condition of overflow is said to occur when the number generated as a result of an arithmetic operation requires more bit or byte positions than are available in the field. For example, in adding together two positive numbers, a register can hold 31 bits of data. If the sum of an arithmetic operation requires 32 bits to represent it correctly, the result is an arithmetic overflow because the register does not have sufficient capacity to represent correctly the result.

The fact that arithmetic operations set the condition code leads to two consequences of importance to the programer. First, the testable result or record of any prior compare or arithmetic operation is destroyed by the later occurrence of an arithmetic operation. This is because the computer has only one condition-code field. The programer therefore cannot expect to have the computer do a comparison, then do an addition operation, and later use the results of the comparison operation. The condition code from the comparison will have been reset by the arithmetic operation and hence lost.

Second, an arithmetic overflow may cause the computer to interrupt normal program execution, depending upon control settings in the computer. These control settings may be under the programer's control or may be set by the operating environment and procedure (system) under which the program is being run. The occurrence of arithmetic overflow may therefore be, for most practical purposes, fatal to the continuance of the program. Thus the programer needs to avoid directing the computer to do operations that may result in unintentional arithmetic overflow. Some aspects of these matters are discussed in more detail below under the topic of scaling.

An arithmetic overflow can be thought of as the equivalent of moving data to the left beyond the confines of the register or the field boundary. This may be the result of a carry operation being propagated to the left over the end of the field, or of an attempt to move or shift significant characters out of or beyond the left end of the field. The computer detects overflow in a register when an operation attempts to alter a sign bit incorrectly. This occurs when the addition or subtraction results in a carry into the sign-bit position that is different from the carry that would result from adding the sign bits themselves as if they were data bits. In packed-decimal operations in storage, the computer detects an overflow when a carry is generated while handling the leftmost half byte at the left end of the receiving field.

Fourth, binary arithmetic operations are done in the general-purpose registers. The properties of these registers influence the way arithmetic operations are done. As noted previously, in a register the algebraic sign is always assumed to be the bit at the extreme left-hand end, with a 0 bit for plus, a 1 bit for minus. The registers for arithmetic use are 32 bits long. Since the leftmost bit is devoted to the sign, the 31 remaining bits are available for representing data. These 31 bits may represent either a positive or a negative number. The one and only representation of the number binary zero is all 0 bits, and is always positive. The conceptual form of the registers is diagramed in Fig. 5-2.

For some binary arithmetic operations, such as multiply and divide, two registers may be linked together. In such cases, the sign bit of the second (odd-numbered) register ceases to function as a sign bit, but serves instead as a data bit. Thus

S	0000000000000000000000000000000	S	0000000000000000000000000000000
	Register 2		Register 3

FIG. 5-2. Conceptual layout of registers 2 and 3.

arithmetic carry can occur from the high-order (leftmost) bit of the odd-numbered (second) register into the low-order (rightmost) bit in the even-numbered (first) register. When used in this linked manner, the registers effectively contain one sign bit in the far left of the even-numbered register and 63 data bits for representing the results or operands in arithmetic operations.

To function in a linked manner, registers must follow a strict even-odd sequence numbering. The left register of the pair must be an even-numbered register; the right register of the pair must be the next higher odd-numbered register. Thus, for example, registers 8 and 9 can serve as a pair and registers 10 and 11 can serve as a pair, but register 9 cannot be paired with register 10. When pairs of registers are addressed, the *left* (lower and even-numbered) of the two registers is the one named in the instruction.

Fifth, the packed-decimal arithmetic operations require no alignment of either of the operands because the results of the operation are placed immediately in storage and replace one of the two operands. No registers are used for holding the operands or results. Packed-decimal arithmetic operations have a length restriction on the maximum number of decimal digits that may be processed, which is usually 31 digits. And very vitally, each packed-decimal number must have a valid sign character in the right half of the rightmost byte.

ALGEBRAIC SIGN

As described earlier in this chapter and in Chap. 3, the position and form of the sign of a number depend upon the format of the number. Thus, in the binary format, the algebraic sign of a number is represented by the leftmost bit of the number. If this is a 0 bit, the number is considered positive; if it is a 1 bit, it is considered negative. Zero in binary format is considered a positive number.

In the packed-decimal format, the algebraic sign of a number is represented by the rightmost half-byte (hexadecimal) character of the number. If this is a D_{xc} or a B_{xk}, then the number is considered negative (see Fig. 5-3). Any other character is considered a positive-sign, but C_{xc} and A_{xk} are the preferred positive-sign characters. To avoid difficulties in comparison, the programer should consistently use the preferred characters.

0	0	1	2	3	C	is equivalent to decimal +0123
0	0	1	2	3	D	is equivalent to decimal −0123

Fig. 5-3. Packed-decimal format for algebraic signs.

The rules for the manipulation of algebraic signs in the computer follow tradition. Multiplication and division operations with unlike signs for the two operands produce a minus sign in the quotient or product. In division, the sign of the re-

Signs for multiplication "*"

+ 4	- 4	multiplicand	+ 4	- 4
* + 3	* - 3	multiplier	* - 3	* + 3
+12	+12	product	-12	-12

Signs for addition "+"

+ 16	- 16	augend	+ 16	- 16
+ + 08	+ - 08	addend	+ - 08	+ + 08
+ 24	- 24	sum	+ 08	- 08

Signs for subtraction "-"

+ 16	- 16	minuend	+ 16	- 16
- + 08	- - 08	subtrahend	- - 08	- + 08
+ 08	- 08	difference	+ 24	- 24

Signs for division "/"

dividend / divisor = quotient and remainder

```
      + 4
+3 | + 13        + 13  /  + 3  =  + 4          + 1
     + 12
    ─────
     + 1


      + 4
-3 | - 13        - 13  /  - 3  =  + 4          - 1
     - 12
    ─────
     - 1


      - 4
-3 | + 13        + 13  /  - 3  =  - 4          + 1
     + 12
    ─────
     + 1


      - 4
+3 | - 13        - 13  /  + 3  =  - 4          - 1
     - 12
    ─────
     - 1
```

FIG. 5-4. Summary of signs and terminology for arithmetic operations.

mainder is the same as the sign of the dividend. Operations with like signs, be they minus or plus, result in positive signs for quotients and products (see Fig. 5-4).

For addition and subtraction, the sizes of the operands affect the resulting sign of the sum or difference. The sign of the sum or difference is the sign originally associated with the operand that has the largest absolute value, where it is understood that subtraction involves reversing the true sign of the number being subtracted (the subtrahend) prior to beginning the operation (see Fig. 5-4). For binary numbers, changing the sign involves taking the complement of the number, as described later in this chapter.

NEGATIVE NUMBER REPRESENTATIONS

Negative numbers are represented in the computer in three major ways: (1) Floating-point negative numbers are represented in the manner described in Chap. 12. (2) Packed-decimal negative numbers are represented with a negative-sign character at the right half of rightmost byte of the field, with the rest of the field shown in absolute form just as for positive numbers (see Fig. 5-3). No complement notation appears in storage. Negative zero cannot arise as a result of arithmetic operations, but can be created by data-movement operations. (3) Binary negative numbers are represented in a complement form in order to facilitate and speed binary arithmetic operations. The complement is not the one's ("nine's") complement, but is the two's complement of the positive equivalent number. The pencil-and-paper rule for converting a two's complement from a positive binary number is as follows: Change each 0 bit to a 1 bit, each 1 bit to a 0 bit; then add (in binary) a 1 bit in the low-order (i.e., rightmost) place of the resulting binary number. This procedure is illustrated in Fig. 5-5. A brief review of binary addition is given in a later section, and the workbook has a section devoted to the topic.

To convert a negative number in binary to a positive number in binary the procedure is as follows: Subtract a 1 bit from the rightmost (low-order) bit of the negative number; then reverse each 0 bit to a 1 bit and each 1 bit to a 0 bit. This is illustrated in Fig. 5-5.

00000111	Positive number	10000010	Negative number
11111000	Reverse the bits	-00000001	Subtract binary 1
+00000001	Add binary 1	10000001	Difference
11111001	Negative number	01111110	Reverse the bits to get positive number

Fig. 5-5. Binary two's complement notation and conversion.

A study of Fig. 5-4 makes it clear that the high-order or leading bits for binary negative number representations are 1 bits. In hexadecimal, these appear typically as F_x when four consecutive bits occur, since a 1 bit is also the negative sign. This is the reason for using sign bits as the fill bits for binary numbers.

Do It Now Exercise 5-1. *Write DC declaratives of types H, F, Z, P, and X for the decimal numbers −1; −4; −7; −15; −648; −7742; and −0020648. Show in hexadecimal the resulting contents of storage. Using types F, H, and X, write DC declaratives for the largest possible negative and positive binary numbers that can be fitted in full and half words.*

INTEGER AND FRACTIONAL NUMBERS

Basic to a usable understanding of arithmetic operations in the computer is a knowledge of the representation of integer and fractional numbers. An integer number in the decimal system is a number whose digits are all to the left of the decimal point. The first two numbers in the first column of Fig. 5-1 are integers. The second two are fractional. A number obviously may be both integer and fractional; i.e., some of its digits may be to the left of the decimal point and some to the right. Whether it be integer or fractional, the most significant digit of a decimal number is the nonzero digit farthest to the left; the least significant, the digit farthest to the right.

The concepts of integer and fractional numbers and of place significance apply also to the binary and hexadecimal systems. These systems, instead of having a decimal point, have a binary point and a hexadecimal point, respectively, or—in general—a radix point. Thus, in the hexadecimal and binary system, an integer number is one whose characters all lie to the left of the radix point, and a fractional number is one whose characters all lie to the right of the radix point. Again, numbers with both integer and fractional parts are common. The most significant character of a binary or hexadecimal number is the nonzero character farthest to the left; the least significant is the character farthest to the right. An example is given in Fig. 5-6.

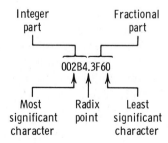

Fig. 5-6. Parts of a mixed number.

The concept of integer and fractional numbers is useful to the programer in doing arithmetic operations, and in converting numbers to and from the binary form by the CVB and CVD commands described in the previous chapter. The arithmetic consequences are described in the section on scaling in this chapter. Let us at this point, therefore, consider the matter of addition of numbers, and of conversion of numbers between decimal and hexadecimal. The conversion from hexadecimal to binary or binary to hexadecimal is a simple recoding and has already been described in introducing the hexadecimal system in Chap. 2.

ADDITION AND SUBTRACTION IN HEXADECIMAL

To check the contents of storage, as shown in a storage dump, the programer must be able to add and subtract hexadecimal numbers. This is necessary because the machine-language addresses—both the absolute addresses and the base-and-displacement addresses—are in hexadecimal form. To a lesser extent, the programer needs to be able to add and subtract binary numbers, since this is convenient for the bits within a byte, and for taking the complement. In each of these cases, however, the programer can convert the binary data to hexadecimal before adding or subtracting. Hence hexadecimal addition and subtraction are the more important to the programer.

For ease in understanding, and to permit addition and subtraction to be presented here by analogy, let us consider first addition and subtraction of decimal numbers. These are the traditional numbers and operations in which the programer has been schooled for many years. Figure 5-7 provides a decimal table. When it is used as an addition table, the augend and the addend are along the left side and the top, with the sum in the center. When it is used as a subtraction table, the subtrahend is along the left side, the minuend is in the center, and the difference is along the top. To add or subtract multiple-digit numbers, the common convention is to begin at the right and handle a position at a time, with a carry or borrow if needed from the next position to the left.

Consider two examples. To find the sum $9 + 14$, the programer reads down the left side to the 9 augend row, and then in to the right to the 4 addend column. The sum is at the intersection and is a 13 (3 with a 1 carry). Then he reads the table again down to the 1 augend row for the prior carry, and across to the 1 addend column (for the 1 from the 14). The sum is a 2 with no carry. To find the difference $8 - 6$, the programer reads down the left side to the 6 (subtrahend) row, and then reads intersections across on the row until he encounters the 08 minuend. Since the 08 is in the column headed 2, the difference is 2.

Do It Now Exercise 5-2. *Using the table in Fig. 5-7, find these sums: $0 + 0$, $2 + 2$, $2 + 6$, $5 + 5$, $7 + 3$, $8 + 7$, $16 + 34$, and $19 + 96$. Again using the table, find these differences: $0 - 0$, $3 - 2$, $9 - 5$, $10 - 4$, $27 - 9$, and $84 - 582$.*

The corresponding table for binary addition and subtraction is shown in Fig. 5-8. This table is used in the same way as the table in Fig. 5-7. Thus the sum $1 + 1$ is 0 with a 1 carry. The sum $01_b + 11_b$ starts as $1 + 1$, which is 0 with a 1 carry for the rightmost position. This gives $1 + 0 + 1$ for the next position because of the

Addend or difference

		0	1	2	3	4	5	6	7	8	9
	0	00	01	02	03	04	05	06	07	08	09
	1	01	02	03	04	05	06	07	08	09	10
	2	02	03	04	05	06	07	08	09	10	11
Augend or subtrahend	3	03	04	05	06	07	08	09	10	11	12
	4	04	05	06	07	08	09	10	11	12	13
	5	05	06	07	08	09	10	11	12	13	14
	6	06	07	08	09	10	11	12	13	14	15
	7	07	08	09	10	11	12	13	14	15	16
	8	08	09	10	11	12	13	14	15	16	17
	9	09	10	11	12	13	14	15	16	17	18

FIG. 5-7. Table for decimal addition and subtraction. Entries in table are sums or minuends.

carry. That sum is also 0 with a 1 carry. Since that is the last position, the full sum is 100_b. To find the difference $10_b - 1_b$, the programer reads down to the 1 subtrahend row and across to the minuend of 10. This is in the column for a difference of 1.

To find sums and differences in hexadecimal, the programer follows the same procedure, but uses a hexadecimal table, as shown in Fig. 5-9. Thus, to find the sum $2B_x + AE_x$, the programer first seeks $B_x + E_x$ in the table. This is 9 with a 1 carry.

Addend or difference

Augend or subtrahend		0	1
	0	00	01
	1	01	10

FIG. 5-8. Table for binary addition and subtraction. Entries in table are sums or minuends.

Then he seeks $1_x + 2_x + A_x$ in the table. Since $1_x + 2_x = 3_x$, and $3_x + A_x = D_x$, the full sum is $D9_x$. To find the difference $32_x - A_x$, the programer first must borrow. To do this, he seeks on the 1_x subtrahend row (since he needs to borrow only a 1_x) the minuend 3_x. This difference $3_x - 1_x$ is 2_x. Hence the programer can then use 12_x as the minuend for the rightmost position and 2_x as the minuend for the next position to the left. Now the programer seeks, on the subtrahend A_x row, the minuend 12_x. Since this is in the 8 column, the difference $12_x - A_x = 8_x$. Since A_x is the same as $0A_x$, the difference for the next position to the left is $2_x - 0_x$, which is 2_x. Hence the full difference is 28_x.

Do It Now Exercise 5-3. *Using the table in Fig. 5-9, find the following sums in hexadecimal: $4 + 5, 7 + 1, 6 + 5, 9 + 9, A + 2, E + 6, F + F, 3B + 94$. Again using the table, find the following differences in hexadecimal: $5 - 4, 8 - 6, 12 - 7, A - 2, E - A, A6 - 2F$.*

Addend or difference

	0	1	2	3	4	5	6	7	8	9	A	B	C	D	E	F
0	00	01	02	03	04	05	06	07	08	09	0A	0B	0C	0D	0E	0F
1	01	02	03	04	05	06	07	08	09	0A	0B	0C	0D	0E	0F	10
2	02	03	04	05	06	07	08	09	0A	0B	0C	0D	0E	0F	10	11
3	03	04	05	06	07	08	09	0A	0B	0C	0D	0E	0F	10	11	12
4	04	05	06	07	08	09	0A	0B	0C	0D	0E	0F	10	11	12	13
5	05	06	07	08	09	0A	0B	0C	0D	0E	0F	10	11	12	13	14
6	06	07	08	09	0A	0B	0C	0D	0E	0F	10	11	12	13	14	15
7	07	08	09	0A	0B	0C	0D	0E	0F	10	11	12	13	14	15	16
8	08	09	0A	0B	0C	0D	0E	0F	10	11	12	13	14	15	16	17
9	09	0A	0B	0C	0D	0E	0F	10	11	12	13	14	15	16	17	18
A	0A	0B	0C	0D	0E	0F	10	11	12	13	14	15	16	17	18	19
B	0B	0C	0D	0E	0F	10	11	12	13	14	15	16	17	18	19	1A
C	0C	0D	0E	0F	10	11	12	13	14	15	16	17	18	19	1A	1B
D	0D	0E	0F	10	11	12	13	14	15	16	17	18	19	1A	1B	1C
E	0E	0F	10	11	12	13	14	15	16	17	18	19	1A	1B	1C	1D
F	0F	10	11	12	13	14	15	16	17	18	19	1A	1B	1C	1D	1E

Augend or subtrahend

FIG. 5-9. Table for hexadecimal addition and subtraction. Entries in table are sums or minuends.

Do It Now Exercise 5-4. *Assume that the programer knows that register 4 should contain the positive difference between $03F6A2B7_x$ and $002ED9A8_x$, and that the field now to be added to the contents of register 4 has an indexed base-and-displacement address as follows: index amount $00000A3C_x$, base amount 00009820_x, displacement amount $F78_x$. What are the correct contents of register 4, and what is the address of the operand now to be added?*

CONVERSION OF INTEGER AND FRACTIONAL NUMBERS

Chapter 2 presented convenient ways for the programer to convert numbers back and forth between decimal and hexadecimal. Such table approaches are not convenient for use in the computer itself. When they are available, the programer can use in the computer the special commands presented in Chap. 4 (Pack, Convert to Binary, Convert to Decimal, and Unpack). Situations can arise, however, in which the programer must use a routine to do conversions. And sometimes the programer needs to do a pencil-and-paper conversion for numbers beyond the range of the tables. To meet these needs, the Hartmann method offers an efficient and easy approach.

The Hartmann method takes a number expressed in one form and then, by a series of additions (or subtractions) and multiplications, converts it to a number in the desired form. To do this, the method uses a "slip number" for the multiplications, and operates on the parts of the number being converted from *left* to *right*. For conversion from decimal to hexadecimal, the slip number is -6_x (that is, $A_x - 10_x$), and all operations are done in hexadecimal. For this purpose, a multiplication table for 6_x is given in Fig. 5-10. For conversion from hexadecimal to decimal, the slip number is $+6_c$ (that is, $16_c - 10_c$), and all operations are done in decimal. To make this possible, a basic step in the Hartmann method is to restate each character in the original number individually into the new form.

The four-step cycle of operations in the Hartmann method is most easily seen from examples. Figure 5-11 summarizes the method for the obvious and trivial case of converting the hexadecimal number 000 to decimal. The first step (A) is to convert the leftmost character to hexadecimal. Since all of the decimal characters have the same values in the hexadecimal system, this is easy: 0_c is equivalent to 0_x.

The second step (B) is to multiply this 0_x by -6_x, the slip number. Figure 5-10 shows the product to be $+0_x$. This product must now be held aside for use in a later step. The third step (C) is to convert the middle character to hexadecimal. This again is 0_x. The fourth step (D) is to shift this converted character one place to the right, and then add it to the number thus far converted. This is an important step, and deserves the programer's careful attention.

The fifth step (E) is to add the product generated three steps earlier to the sum just obtained. The sixth step (F) is to multiply the number thus far converted by -6_x, as shown in Fig. 5-11. The seventh step (G) is to convert the rightmost

Multiplicand or quotient

	0	1	2	3	4	5	6	7	8	9	A	B	C	D	E	F
0	00	00	00	00	00	00	00	00	00	00	00	00	00	00	00	00
1	00	01	02	03	04	05	06	07	08	09	0A	0B	0C	0D	0E	0F
2	00	02	04	06	08	0A	0C	0E	10	12	14	16	18	1A	1C	1E
3	00	03	06	09	0C	0F	12	15	18	1B	1E	21	24	27	2A	2D
4	00	04	08	0C	10	14	18	1C	20	24	28	2C	30	34	38	3C
5	00	05	0A	0F	14	19	1E	23	28	2D	32	37	3C	41	46	4B
6	00	06	0C	12	18	1E	24	2A	30	36	3C	42	48	4E	54	5A
7	00	07	0E	15	1C	23	2A	31	38	3F	46	4D	54	5B	62	69
8	00	08	10	18	20	28	30	38	40	48	50	58	60	68	70	78
9	00	09	12	1B	24	2D	36	3F	48	51	5A	63	6C	75	7E	87
A	00	0A	14	1E	28	32	3C	46	50	5A	64	6E	78	82	8C	96
B	00	0B	16	21	2C	37	42	4D	58	63	6E	79	84	8F	9A	A5
C	00	0C	18	24	30	3C	48	54	60	6C	78	84	90	9C	A8	B4
D	00	0D	1A	27	34	41	4E	5B	68	75	82	8F	9C	A9	B6	C3
E	00	0E	1C	2A	38	46	54	62	70	7E	8C	9A	A8	B6	C4	D2
F	00	0F	1E	2D	3C	4B	5A	69	78	87	96	A5	B4	C3	D2	E1

(left margin label: Multiplier or divisor)

FIG. 5-10. Hexadecimal multiplication table. Entries in table are products or dividends.

character to hexadecimal. The eighth step (H) is to shift this converted character one place to the right, and then add it to the number thus far converted. The ninth step (I) is to add the product generated three steps earlier to the sum just obtained. This completes the procedure, because no more digits of the original number remain to be converted.

Note that the basic four steps are repeated in a cycle—for example, steps C, D, E, and F. The procedure begins by omitting the two middle steps of the cycle, and ends by omitting the final step in the cycle.

To clarify the details of the steps, let us consider a nontrivial case, such as converting the decimal number 527 to hexadecimal. This is shown in Fig. 5-12. The

Decimal number: 000   Slip number: -6_x

Procedure	Result	Step	Comment
$0_c \rightarrow 0_x$	0_x	A	Leftmost character
$0_x * -6_x = -00_x$		B	Multiply by -6_x
$0_c \rightarrow 0_x$		C	Middle character
$+\ \ \dfrac{0_x}{00_x}$		D	Shift and add this character
$+-\ \dfrac{00_x}{00_x}$		E	Add on product from step B
$00_x * -6_x = -000_x$		F	Multiply by -6_x
$0_c \rightarrow 0_x$		G	Rightmost character
$+\ \ \dfrac{0_x}{000_x}$		H	Shift and add this digit
$+-\dfrac{000_x}{000_x}$		I	Add on product from step F

Hence hexadecimal equivalent is 000_x

FIG. 5-11. The Hartmann method.

steps in this conversion are exactly parallel to those in Fig. 5-11. The only difference between the cases is that the numbers being handled are not all zeros in Fig. 5-12. Note again that all arithmetic is done in the number system being converted into.

To clarify still further the Hartmann method, let us consider the example of converting the hexadecimal number $20F_x$ to decimal. This is shown in Fig. 5-13. Here the programer should note that the slip number is a positive decimal 6, and that all the arithmetic operations are done in the decimal system. Since each character in the hexadecimal number is converted individually to decimal before the arithmetic operations are performed, this causes no difficulty, as long as the programer remembers to shift only one place to the right (see step H in Fig. 5-13, for example).

The examples in Figs. 5-12 and 5-13 have dealt with the conversion of integer numbers. The procedure for converting fractional numbers differs in the following ways. The conversion is first made as if the fractional number were expressed in

Decimal number: 527   Slip number: -6_x

Procedure	Result	Step	Comment
$5_c \rightarrow 5_x$	5_x	A	Leftmost character
$5_x * -6_x = -1E$		B	Multiply by -6_x
$2_c \rightarrow 2_x$		C	Middle character
$\begin{array}{r} +\quad 2_x \\ \hline 52_x \end{array} \Big\}$		D	Shift and add this character
$\begin{array}{r} +-1E_x \\ \hline 34_x \end{array} \Big\}$		E	Add on product from step B
$34_x * -6_x = -138_x$		F	Multiply by -6_x
$7_c \rightarrow 7_x$		G	Rightmost character
$\begin{array}{r} +\quad 7_x \\ \hline 347_x \end{array} \Big\}$		H	Shift and add this character
$\begin{array}{r} +-138_x \\ \hline 20F_x \end{array} \Big\}$		I	Add on product from step F

Hence hexadecimal equivalent is $20F_x$

FIG. 5-12. Decimal-to-hexadecimal conversion by the Hartmann method.

two explicit parts, an integer numerator and an integer denominator. The denominator is normally a 1 followed by as many zeros as the number has fractional places. The programer then converts each separately. Then he can change back to the usual notation by dividing the converted denominator into the converted numerator. In converting mixed numbers (having both integer and fractional parts), the programer must convert the parts separately, and then recombine them. This latter procedure applies regardless of the method used to convert the parts.

For example, consider the conversion of 13.5_c to hexadecimal. The 13.5 can be rewritten as 13 and 5/10. Hence conversions are needed for 13_c, 5_c, and 10_c. These are D_x, 5_x, and A_x, respectively. Hence the hexadecimal equivalent is D_x and $5/A_x$ or $D.8_x$, since 0.8_x is the quotient of 5_x divided by A_x. Conversely, to convert $D.8_x$ to decimal, the numbers for which the programer must obtain equivalents are D_x, 8_x, and 10_x. These are 13_c, 8_c, and 16_c, respectively. Hence the decimal equivalent is 13 and 8/16 or 13.5, since 0.5 is the quotient of 8_c divided by 16_c.

Hexadecimal number: 20F   Slip number: $+6_c$

Procedure	Result	Step	Comment
$2_x \rightarrow 2_c$	2_c	A	Leftmost character
$2_c * +6_c = 12_c$		B	Multiply by $+6_c$
$0_x \rightarrow 0_c$		C	Middle character
	$\dfrac{+ \ 0_c}{20_c}$ }	D	Shift and add this character
	$\dfrac{+ \ 12_c}{32_c}$ }	E	Add on product from step B
$32_c * +6_c = 192$		F	Multiply by $+6_c$
$F_x \rightarrow 15_c$		G	Rightmost character
	$\dfrac{+ \ 15_c}{335_c}$ }	H	Shift and add this character
	$\dfrac{+ \ 192_c}{527_c}$ }	I	Add on product from step F

Hence decimal equivalent is 527

FIG. 5-13. Hexadecimal-to-decimal conversion by the Hartmann method.

Do It Now Exercise 5-5. *Convert the following numbers from decimal to hexadecimal, using first the Hartmann method and then, if possible, the table method presented in Chap. 2: 8.5; 17.17; 386.435; 45283.75; 16776959.8745. Convert the following in the same manner to decimal: 9.8, ED.9, 124E3.68A, 1E47ACB25.FFC1.*

FRACTIONAL NUMBERS IN CONSTANTS

The programer can use DC declaratives to set up integer numbers in the manner described in Chap. 3. To use DC declaratives to set up fractional numbers or mixed integer and fractional numbers, the following procedures can be used.

For DC declaratives of types X, B, Z, and P, the programer writes as many integer and fraction digits as desired. These the compiler incorporates directly into the constant, *omitting* the evidence of where the programer wrote or wanted the decimal point. Thus it is the programer's responsibility to remember the implied decimal-point location and the adjustment amount. An example of packed formats was given in Fig. 5-1.

For DC declaratives of type C, special techniques are available and are described in Chap. 10. The reason for this exception is that in type C constants the decimal point appears as a character occupying a full byte. Hence the programer cannot specify arithmetic operations on fields containing numeric data in a type C format.

For DC declaratives of types F and H, and in all but the small models of the computer, the programer has available a special operand to show fractional characters. In place of the length operand L, the programer can substitute the scaling operand S, followed by a decimal number.

The decimal number following the S specifies the number of fractional binary places the programer desires in the data placed in storage. If the programer desires no fractional places, then he should omit the scaling operand entirely. The compiler deducts whatever number of fractional places the programer specifies from the number of integer places available. Thus, with the type H constant, 15 bit positions for data are available. If, in defining a type H constant, the programer specifies S8, then only seven bit positions remain available for holding the integer portion of the number to be converted. Specification by the programer of S15 would provide no integer places at all, only fractional places. The programer must therefore observe caution not to throw away the most significant places in a mixed number when specifying a scaling operand.

For example, suppose the programer desires to have the binary equivalent of the decimal number +12.9 loaded in a full word at the time the program is placed in storage, and to provide for 15 fractional places in the binary number. Then, as illustrated in Fig. 5-14, the resulting contents of storage will be 00067333_x. The reason is that the result of converting decimal +12.9 to hexadecimal is $C.E666_x$. Since that representation provides for 16 fractional binary places, the rightmost binary place which holds a 0 bit must be truncated (or dropped) off. Therefore the data in storage in binary form, reading from left to right, will be 0000000000-000110011100110011001 1. As expected, 67333_x is one-half of $CE666_x$, since dropping one binary place on the right is equivalent to dividing by two. Note also that the binary point need not come between hexadecimal characters.

Do It Now Exercise 5-6. *Write DC declaratives for each of the following decimal numbers, using five different values for S for each number: Omitted S, S4, S5, S8, and S10. The decimal numbers are 2.25; 4.5; 15.8125; 511.073289; 27750.98667984. Can all of these be expressed with a DC declarative of type H, or do any require the use of type F?*

Conversion to hexadecimal by table

+C.	12.90000000
	- 12.
	0.90000000
+ 0.E	- 0.8750
	0.02500000
+ 0.06	- 0.0234375
	0.00156250
+ 0.006	- 0.00146484
	0.00010141
+ 0.0006	- 0.00009155
C.E666	0.00000986

Binary form of hexadecimal number

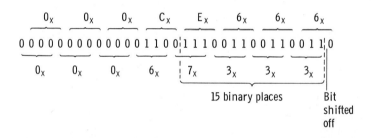

FIG. 5-14. Example of scaling operand in a DC declarative.

SCALING ARITHMETIC OPERATIONS

In programing binary and packed-decimal arithmetic operations for the computer, the programer must continually give attention to two major considerations. One of these is to keep the sizes of the numbers within the confines of the field or register being used—i.e., avoidance of overflow. The other is to align correctly the implied radix points in order to achieve the desired number of significant places in the result. These two considerations are closely related, and in practice the operations the programer does to achieve the one influence what he can do to achieve the other. Handling the two considerations is generally known as scaling.

The scaling for addition and subtraction offers some difficulty. In order to obtain the correct answer by pencil and paper for addition or subtraction, the programer lines up the decimal points in the numbers, each under the other. Thus, to add 6.44 and 3.2 by pencil and paper, the usual procedure would be to write the two numbers one under the other, as shown in Fig. 5-15, with the two decimal points lined up vertically before adding.

$$
\begin{array}{r}
6.44 \\
+\ 3.2 \\
\hline
9.64
\end{array}
$$

FIG. 5-15. Pencil-and-paper addition.

In the computer, in packed-decimal or binary data ready for arithmetic operations, no radix point explicitly appears. Therefore the computer cannot inspect the fields to learn where the radix points are and how to align them. It is up to the *programer* to align them. For example, consider the case of adding two packed-decimal numbers, $+6.44$ and $+3.2$. Their representation in packed-decimal form is shown in Fig. 5-16. Note the absence of decimal points. The programer faces two choices. Either he can have the computer truncate the least significant (rightmost) 4 off the $+6.44$, or he can have the computer annex a 0 to the $+3.2$ to make it $+3.20$.

6	4	4	C
0	3	2	C

} Original numbers

The sum replaces the first operand named in addition.

6	4	4	C
3	2	0	C

} Adjusted operand numbers for addition

9	6	4	C

Sum

FIG. 5-16. Scaling addition for packed-decimal data.

In computer work it is usually desirable to keep as high a degree of precision as a register or field will accommodate, for as long as possible, in order to reduce cumulative round-off and truncation errors. For this reason, the second course of action is preferred. The result of taking this action is shown also in Fig. 5-16, as is the correct resulting sum. Note that the number must be changed in storage prior to the time the computer performs the addition. The process of making such changes, which are called "shifts," is considered part of scaling.

Addition and subtraction present another problem. Suppose, for example, in the preceding case the second number to be added is 9.2. After shifting to annex a

), the computer has the number 9.20. The sum that results from adding is larger han the field can accommodate, since the field is only two bytes long (see Fig. 5-17). In order to avoid a loss of the most significant digit as a result of the addition operation, the programer must provide a field longer than the original operand field o hold the sum. The process of anticipating such overflow problems and providing additional space to accommodate the numbers (or to truncate differently the results or operands) is also part of the scaling process.

Original numbers   Adjusted operands

6 4	4 C	First number

0 9	2 C	Second number

Note: The sum replaces the first operand; the second operand is unchanged; the overflow is lost.

6 4	4 C	First operand

9 2	0 C	Second operand

5 6	4 C	Sum produced

1   Overflow lost

0 1	5 6	4 C	Correct sum

FIG. 5-17. Packed-decimal addition overflow and scaling.

The procedure many programers use to handle overflow is to calculate for each field the largest number possible to be added or subtracted. This typically depends upon the input-data specifications for a job. Where no data to the contrary are available, the usual assumption for packed decimal is to assume that the digits are all 9's. As a general rule, whenever two numbers are added together, the maximum size of the resulting number is at the worst only one significant place longer on the left than the longer of the two operand numbers. This is illustrated in Fig. 5-18. Note that the numbers often have leading 0s because the length of a field must be at least as great as the length of the largest number to be accommodated.

For binary addition and subtraction, the programer can use the same method

Example	Maximum		Equivalent
6.44	9.99	=	10.00−0.01
3.2	9.90	=	10.00−0.10
9.64			

Estimate of maximum field size for addition or subtraction

$$
\begin{array}{l}
+\ 10.00 - 0.01 \\
+\ 10.00 - 0.10 \\
\hline
20.00 - 0.11 = 19.89
\end{array}
\left\{
\begin{array}{l}
\text{2 integer places} \\
\text{2 fractional places}
\end{array}
\right.
$$

FIG. 5-18. Example of finding maximum field sizes for packed-decimal operations.

just illustrated for estimating field sizes. Usually, however, the programer can obtain a closer estimate and more accurate results by working directly in either the binary or the hexadecimal system. Thus, for the same example used previously, $+6.44$ is equivalent to $+6.70A_x$, and 3.2 is equivalent to 3.333_x. If the programer knows the limits on the size of each operand, he should use those in making his estimates of the maximum field size. In the absence of better evidence, the programer usually can use an estimate of 9_x for the leading hexadecimal place, as illustrated in Fig. 5-19.

Example	Maximum		Equivalent
6.70_x	$9.FFF_x$	=	$A.00_x - 0.01_x$
3.33_x	$9.FFF_x$	=	$A.00_x - 0.01_x$

$9.A3_x = 9.63671875$

Estimate of maximum field size for addition or subtraction

$$+ \quad A.00 \; - 0.01$$
$$+ \quad A.00 \; - 0.01$$
$$14.00_x - 0.02_x = 13.FE_x \quad \begin{cases} \text{2 integer places} \\ \text{2 fractional places} \end{cases}$$

Fig. 5-19. Example of finding maximum field sizes for binary operations.

Figure 5-19 illustrates another problem in scaling for binary addition and subtraction. The sum of 6.40_x and 3.33_x is $9.A3_x$. Carried to eight fractional places, this in turn is equivalent to 9.63671875_c. However, as shown in Fig. 5-19, this is not quite equal to the correct answer, 9.64. This illustrates again the approximate precision of fractional conversions, but the degree of precision is under the control of the programer.

To achieve a more precise answer, the programer usually treats mixed integer and fractional numbers as if they were all integer. Since integer conversions are precise, no inaccuracy is introduced by going back and forth between binary and decimal. This is illustrated in Fig. 5-20, where each number is treated as an integer number. This is accomplished by multiplying each decimal number by the necessary power of its base (ten) to make the decimal points for all line up, and then multiplying by another power of the base (ten) to move the decimal point over to the right of the least significant digit. Then, to put the decimal point at the correct place

00000284	hexadecimal equivalent of decimal 644	Addition:
00000020	hexadecimal equivalent of decimal 32	00000284
00000140	hexadecimal equivalent of decimal 320	+00000140
000003C4	hexadecimal equivalent of decimal 964	000003C4

Fig. 5-20. Example of scaling binary addition or subtraction with integer numbers.

in the answer, the programer must divide by the same power of the base (ten) used previously to make all the numbers integral.

The programer can handle such multiplication and division for scaling conveniently in the computer by shifting whenever possible in packed-decimal, and then converting to binary. The commands for doing this are Zero and Add Packed, Move With Offset, Move Zone, Move Numerics, and Shift and Round Packed. After having the computer complete the arithmetic operations, the programer can have the computer convert back to decimal, and again shift if needed to reflect the correct placement of the decimal point. To use this approach, however, the programer needs to consider the effect of carries and leading 0s, especially when applying it to multiplication or division in the computer.

Carries that result in increasing the number of significant characters can occur in binary as well as in decimal when numbers are added, but the carry occurs for powers of 2, not 10, since 2 is the base of the binary system. In the example shown in Fig. 5-20, the binary number resulting as the sum is identical in the number of significant bits to the longer of the two operands, just as in the decimal case. However, if (as shown in Fig. 5-21) the second operand be made the binary equivalent of 9.20, the resulting number of significant bits in the sum is one longer than the longer of the two operands, just as the rule indicates.

00000284   hexadecimal equivalent of 644 $(2_x = 10_b)$ $(3_x = 11_b)$
00000398   hexadecimal equivalent of 920 $(6_x = 110_b)$
_____
0000061C   hexadecimal equivalent of 15.64 and the sum of 6.44 and 9.20

FIG. 5-21. Example of increase in significant bits.

When the computer does binary arithmetic operations in registers, or packed-decimal operations in fields which provide more than sufficient length to accommodate the resulting sum or difference, an appropriate question is "What happens to the leading 0s?" In practice, the answer is that the total number of places in the field or register must remain unchanged. If the number of significant places in the register or field changes as a result of doing a subtraction or addition, then the number of leading 0s must be changed in the opposite direction by the same amount. Thus, if the resulting sum can require one more significant place, the number of leading 0s which can be assured to be always leading 0s will be reduced by one place.

Careful programers find it convenient to keep track of leading 0s and algebraic signs by making a table showing the allocation of the total length of a register or field between sign representation, leading 0s that will always be leading 0s (or the complement), integer-character positions which may be significant, and fractional-character positions. Together these add up to the total number of positions in the field, be it binary or packed decimal.

Figure 5-22 is an illustration of such a table format, showing the number and use of each of the positions for the binary and packed-decimal examples from Figs. 5-17 and 5-20. In the table, "S" stands for sign, "Z" stands for leading 0s (or the complement) which can always be assured to be leading 0s (or the complement), "I" stands for integer (to the left of the implied radix point) positions which may contain significant characters, "F" stands for fractional positions (to the right of the implied radix point) which may contain significant characters, and "T" stands for total number of positions in the field or register.

Packed-decimal addition for Fig. 5-17   Binary addition for Fig. 5-20

$$Z + I + F + S = T \qquad\qquad S + Z + I + F = T$$

Augend 2 + 1 + 2 + 1 = 6   Augend 1 + 21 + 3 + 7 = 32

Addend 0 + 1 + 2 + 1 = 4   Addend 1 + 21 + 3 + 7 = 32

Sum   1 + 2 + 2 + 1 = 6   Sum   1 + 20 + 4 + 7 = 32

FIG. 5-22. Scaling table for examples of addition.

The first line of data in the table shows the place usage for one of the operands, usually the augend or the minuend. The second line for the second operand usually shows the addend or the subtrahend. The third line shows the place usage for the resulting sum or difference. Since in the computer these replace the augend or minuend, the total length for the sum or difference field is normally the same as for the augend or minuend field. Note, therefore, that the numbers in the table are not vertically additive when the table is used for analyzing the scaling of addition or subtraction, and that neither addition nor subtraction changes the number of fractional places in a number. Also, the result needs only one sign.

The scaling of division and multiplication is more complicated. Let us look at the scaling of multiplication first. In the multiplication of decimal numbers, as is illustrated in Fig. 5-23, the programer is accustomed, from pencil-and-paper work, to the fact that the resulting product may occupy more positions than either of the two operands. This situation is also true in computer work, and leads to the rule for the scaling of multiplication:

The total number of places in the product that may hold significant characters (digits and bits) is equal to the number of places in the multiplicand that may hold significant characters, plus the number of places in the multiplier that may hold

$$I + F = T$$

6	Multiplicand	1 + 0 = 1
* 6	Multiplier	1 + 0 = 1
36	Product	2 + 0 = 2

FIG. 5-23. Pencil-and-paper multiplication of integer numbers.

significant characters. Individually the total number of fractional places (to the right of the implied radix point) and the number of integer places (to the left of the implied radix point) that may hold significant characters are subject to the same rule.

Suppose, for example, it is desired to multiply 6 by 6. The resulting product, 36, meets the rule exactly as shown in Fig. 5-23. If the numbers be changed to 60.06 by 60.06, the rule still applies, as can be seen from the example in Fig. 5-24. If these numbers be expressed in packed-decimal or binary form, the rule continues to apply. Here, however, because of the register or field-length limitations, the programer will find it helpful to use the table to summarize the allocation of the field or register. Note that now the table entries are both vertically and horizontally additive.

		I + F = T
60.06	Multiplicand	2 + 2 = 4
⁎ 60.06	Multiplier	2 + 2 = 4
3607.2036	Product	4 + 4 = 8

FIG. 5-24. Pencil-and-paper multiplication of mixed numbers.

If the programer makes the conversion from decimal to binary as if the decimal numbers were integer in form, he then faces the serious problem of locating the radix point correctly in the equivalent binary numbers. Without this knowledge he cannot correctly complete the scaling table. Usually the simplest procedure is to convert separately the original integer parts of each operand number in order to determine the number of significant integer binary places. In the case at hand, from Fig. 5-24, the equivalent of 60 in decimal is $3C_x$, which has six significant integer places, since $3C_x$ is also 00111100_b (see Fig. 5-25). Since 1776_x (000101110-

			S + Z + I + F = T
6006_c =	00001776_x	Multiplicand	1 + 18 + 6 + 7 = 32
6006_c = ⁎	00001776_x	Multiplier	1 + 18 + 6 + 7 = 32
36072036_c =	$0000000002266A64_x$	Product	1 + 37 +12 +14 = 64

FIG. 5-25. Scaling binary multiplication.

1110110_b) has 13 significant binary places, the allocation must be 6 integer places and 7 fractional places. Hence, according to the scaling table, the product has 12 possibly significant integer places and 14 fractional places. How many of these the programer elects to have the computer retain depends on his plans for the subsequent use of the product.

In the face of these difficulties, most programers elect to perform as much as possible of the scaling for multiplication in packed-decimal before converting to binary. When this can be done, the process is simpler, as is illustrated in Fig. 5-26.

Packed decimal

0	0	0	0	0	6	0	0	6	C		
				0	6	0	0	6	C		
0	3	6	0	7	2	0	3	6	C		

	Z + I + F + S = T
Multiplicand	5 + 2 + 2 + 1 = 10
Multiplier	1 + 2 + 2 + 1 = 6
Product	1 + 4 + 4 + 1 = 10

FIG. 5-26. Scaling packed-decimal multiplication.

But the main advantage of the binary operations is their greater speed. When many arithmetic operations are to be done, the programer often has to work primarily with binary data, even though the scaling is more difficult.

In review, for multiplication, the numbers shown in the scaling table are additive vertically to obtain the product length with two exceptions. First, the programer may set the length of the resulting product. Second, only one sign character is needed. The place that would be occupied by the second sign character is allocated to holding a leading 0 unless needed for integer places.

The scaling of division becomes complex if the quotient is to be adjusted to meet any format requirements. The programer is familiar, from working with pencil and paper, with quotients that are endless, like the quotient from dividing 10 by 3 in decimal. In doing long division on paper, he is always able to cut such a quotient off and show the remainder. He knows, from pencil-and-paper work, that the remainder must always be less in absolute value than the divisor, and that the length may not exceed the length of the divisor.

The programer is also familiar, from pencil-and-paper work, with the idea that multiplication and division are essentially the reverse of each other—i.e., if he multiplies together a quotient and the divisor, he obtains the dividend after adding the remainder to the product. Conversely, if he takes the product and divides it by either the multiplicand or the multiplier, he obtains the other operand. For this reason, the scaling rule for division, as would be intuitively expected, follows closely the scaling rule used for multiplication, but with some complications.

When multiplication or division is done in the computer, attention must be given to the length of the fields in which the computer is to do the multiplication or division. In the case of multiplication, the product occupies the field formerly occupied by the multiplicand. In the case of division, the field used to hold the dividend holds, as a result of division, both the quotient and the remainder. The reallocation of dividend places allows the programer to apply the same scaling table used with multiplication, by changing the product to the dividend, the multiplicand to the quotient, and the multiplier to the divisor. For convenience, however, the dividend is usually placed first in the table, and is shown before *and* after any needed adjustment.

The scaling rule for division has two major parts and is as follows: When the computer performs division, the number of possible significant places in the quotient is limited to the number of possible significant places in the dividend minus the number of possible significant places in the divisor. Individually, the number of possible significant integer places and the total number of fractional places follow the same rule. In order to avoid division overflow, a comparison of an equal number counting from the left of the places of the dividend and of the divisor must show those in the divisor to have the larger absolute value (i.e., value ignoring the sign). The length of the remainder is always equal to the length of the divisor, and is always produced, even if it be all zeros.

The application of this rule in practice requires the programer to manipulate the dividend and sometimes also the divisor to obtain a quotient having the desired number of places. To this end, the programer often must have the computer insert additional following 0s after the dividend's least significant original character, and sometimes must prefix leading 0s in front of the dividend before having the computer begin the divide operation.

Assumptions:

At a maximum, the dividend may be 13696 and the divisor 117.
At a minimum, the dividend may be 704 and the divisor 4.
The quotient at a maximum will never exceed 849.99.
Note that 001 of the dividend is less than 117 of the divisor.

Packed decimal

								Label	$Z + I + F + S = T$
		1	3	6	9	6	C	Original dividend	$0 + 5 + 0 + 1 = 6$
0	1	1	3	6	9	6 0	0 C	Adjusted dividend	$1 + 6 + 2 + 1 = 10$
				1	1	7	C	Divisor and remainder	$0 + 3 + 0 + 1 = 4$
1	1	7 0	5 C	1	1	5	C	Quotient	$0 + 3 + 2 + 1 = 6$
Quotient				Remainder					

FIG. 5-27. Example of scaling packed-decimal division.

In determining the adjustment needed, the scaling table is very convenient. This is illustrated in Fig. 5-27 for packed-decimal division. In using the table, it is important to recall that the result of the division operation has one sign allocated to the quotient and one sign allocated to the remainder. Only one sign, however, is found in the dividend, which must be equal in length to the sum of the length of the quotient plus the length of the remainder or divisor. This means that one of the leading 0 places in the dividend is converted into a sign place during division. Examples of using the scaling table for division are given in the workbook and later in this chapter. An example of division overflow is included in Fig. 5-28.

When having the computer do packed-decimal division, the programer must

Assumptions:

Data as for Fig. 5-27, except maximum quotient may be 4999.99, and dividend maximum may be 53696. Then, if divisor is at the minimum of 4, we see that 005 is greater than 004, and the quotient overflows for two reasons: violation of the absolute value rule, and insufficient length to accommodate expected maximum quotient.

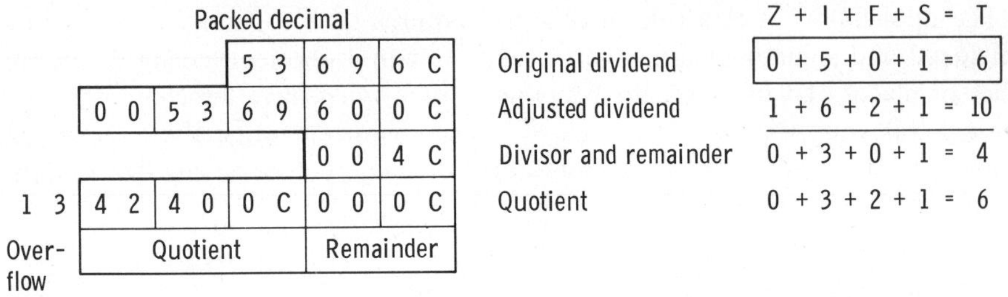

Packed decimal			Z + I + F + S = T
5 3 | 6 9 | 6 C	Original dividend		0 + 5 + 0 + 1 = 6
0 0 | 5 3 | 6 9 | 6 0 | 0 C	Adjusted dividend		1 + 6 + 2 + 1 = 10
0 0 | 4 C	Divisor and remainder		0 + 3 + 0 + 1 = 4
1 3 | 4 2 | 4 0 | 0 C | 0 0 | 0 C	Quotient		0 + 3 + 2 + 1 = 6
Over-flow | Quotient | Remainder			

FIG. 5-28. Example of division overflow.

keep in mind that lengthening a field on the left requires allocation of a full byte of storage. This provides two additional places, not one. If the Move With Offset operation be done in an attempt to provide any following 0s, care must be taken not to leave two signs in the dividend field. The sign of the dividend field in packed-decimal must always be in the right half of the rightmost byte.

BINARY ARITHMETIC OPERATIONS

The commands in this group enable the computer to add, subtract, multiply, and divide numbers in binary form when at least one of them is in a general-purpose register. To enable the programer to scale binary arithmetic operands, the computer has commands for shifting the contents of individual registers and pairs of registers.

AR—Add Register. This RR command adds the contents of the second-register address to the contents of the first-register address, leaving the sum in the first register. The contents of the second-operand register remain unchanged. This command sets the condition code and arithmetic overflow may occur and cause an interruption. In the small models of the computer, this command adds half words, not full words. An example of Add Register is given in Fig. 5-29.

Do It Now Exercise 5-7. Prepare a flow diagram, and then write instructions necessary to do an Add Register operation on the numbers +641 and +728, storing the result as a binary number immediately following the two operand fields in storage. Show the contents of storage for each operand and for the sum.

```
   LOC   OBJECT CODE    ADDR1 ADDR2       NAME    OP   OPERANDS              COMMENT
                                                  IMPERATIVES

 00274C 9867 3000          02940                  LM    6,7,AADD           LOAD TWO REG
 002750 0580                                      BALR  8,0                SAVE CONDITION CODE
 002752 1A67                             F5#29    AR    6,7                ADD TWO REG.
 002754 0590                                      BALR  9,0                SAVE CONDITION CODE
 002756 9069 3020          02960                  STM   6,9,ASAVE          STORE CONTENTS


                                                  DECLARATIVES

 002940 00008000                         AADD     DC    F'32768'           F5#29
 002944 00004000                                  DC    F'16384'
 002948 4040404040404040                          DC    CL24' '            FILLER
 002950 4040404040404040
 002958 4040404040404040
 002960 4040404040404040                 ASAVE    DC    CL32' '            USED TO DISPLAY STORAGE
 002968 4040404040404040
 002970 4040404040404040
 002978 4040404040404040


                                          DUMP AFTER EXECUTION

 002940   00008000   00004000   40404040   40404040   40404040   40404040   40404040   40404040
 002960   0000C000   00004000   40002752   60002756   40404040   40404040   40404040   40404040


                                          DUMP BEFORE EXECUTION

 002940   00008000   00004000   40404040   40404040   40404040   40404040   40404040   40404040
 002960 TO THE NEXT LINE ADDRESS CONTAINS 40404040


                                          REGISTER CONTENTS
                             BEFORE                      AFTER

                             00008000    REGISTER  6    0000C000
                             00004000    REGISTER  7    00004000
                                         REGISTER  8    40002752
                                         REGISTER  9    60002756
```

Fig. 5-29. Example of Add Register. The condition code is the last half of the first hexadecimal character stored by BALR. Thus in register 8 it is a 0, and in register 9 it is a 2.

A—Add. This RX command adds the contents of the second-operand address to the contents of the register named as the first address, leaving the sum as the new contents of the first-operand register. The second operand must be an aligned full word in storage. This command sets the condition code. Arithmetic overflow may occur and result in an interrupt. Interrupts resulting from improper addressing are also possible. This command is not available in the small models of the computer. An example of Add is given in Fig. 5-30.

Do It Now Exercise 5-8. *Using the same data and flow diagram as in Do It Now Exercise 5-7, write the declaratives and imperatives necessary to perform the addition, using an Add instruction. Store the sum as a full word, and show the contents of storage for the sum and for the operands.*

AH—Add Half. This RX command adds the contents of the second-operand address to the contents of the register named as the first-operand address, leaving the sum as the new contents of the first-operand register. Arithmetic overflow can

```
      LOC  OBJECT CODE     ADDR1 ADDR2       NAME    OP   OPERANDS              COMMENT

                                              IMPERATIVES

   00275A 5850 3080              029C0                L    5,AAD1               LOAD A REG.
   00275E 0560                                         BALR 6,0                 SAVE CONDITION CODE
   002760 5A50 3084             029C4         F5#30    A    5,ADD2              ADD A STORAGE WORD TO A REG.
   002764 0570                                         BALR 7,0                 SAVE CONDITION CODE
   002766 9057 30A0             029E0                  STM  5,7,ASAVE2          SAVE REG. CONTENTS


                                              DECLARATIVES

   0029C0 00062FDB                            AAD1    DC   F'405467'           F5#30
   0029C4 FFDF3B65                            ADD2    DC   F'-2147483'
   0029C8 40404040404040404040                        DC   CL24' '             FILLER
   0029D0 40404040404040404040
   0029D8 40404040404040404040
   0029E0 40404040404040404040                ASAVE2  DC   CL32' '             USED TO DISPLAY STORAGE
   0029E8 40404040404040404040
   0029F0 40404040404040404040
   0029F8 40404040404040404040


                                    DUMP AFTER EXECUTION

   0029C0   00062FDB   FFDF3B65   40404040   40404040   40404040   40404040   40404040   40404040
   0029E0   FFE56B40   60002760   50002766   40404040   40404040   40404040   40404040   40404040


                                    DUMP BEFORE EXECUTION

   0029C0   00062FDB   FFDF3B65   40404040   40404040   40404040   40404040   40404040   40404040
   0029E0 TO THE NEXT LINE ADDRESS CONTAINS 40404040


                               REGISTER CONTENTS
                          BEFORE                AFTER

                       00062FDB   REGISTER   5  FFE56B40
                                  REGISTER   6  60002760
                                  REGISTER   7  50002766
```

FIG. 5-30. Example of Add.

occur and cause an interrupt. The second operand must be an aligned half word in storage and is unchanged by the addition operation. Adjoining bytes to the left are also unchanged. The sign of the second operand is assumed to be its leftmost bit, which the computer in all but the small models appears to propagate through the 16-bit position to the left, to extend effective field length to full-word size. This is not done in the small models of the computer, since the registers are only a half word long. This command sets the condition code. Improper addressing may cause interrupts. An example of Add Half is given in Fig. 5-31.

Do It Now Exercise 5-9. *Using the same data and flow diagram as in Do It Now Exercise 5-7, write new declaratives and imperatives to have the computer perform an Add Half operation to achieve the same results. Store the sum as a half word, and show the contents of storage for the sum and the operands.*

SR—Subtract Register. This RR command operates in the same manner as the Add Register command noted previously. The difference is that before beginning

```
     LOC   OBJECT CODE   ADDR1 ADDR2        NAME    OP   OPERANDS          COMMENT

                                            IMPERATIVES

   00276A 5880 3100        02A40                    L    8,FULL            LOAD A REG
   00276E 0560                                      BALR 6,0               SAVE CONDITION CODE
   002770 4A80 3104        02A44           F5#31    AH   8,AHALF           ADD HALFWORD
   002774 0570                                      BALR 7,0               SAVE CONDITION CODE
   002776 9068 3120        02A60                    STM  6,8,AHOLD         SAVE REG. CONTENTS


                                            DECLARATIVES

   002A40 FFFFF530                          FULL    DC   F'-2768'          F5#31
   002A44 0AD0                              AHALF   DC   H'2768'
   002A46 4040404040404040                          DC   CL26' '          FILLER
   002A4E 4040404040404040
   002A56 4040404040404040
   002A5E 4040
   002A60 4040404040404040                 AHOLD   DC   CL32' '           USED TO DISPLAY STORAGE
   002A68 4040404040404040
   002A70 4040404040404040
   002A78 4040404040404040


                                            DUMP AFTER EXECUTION

   002A40  FFFFF530 0AD04040  40404040  40404040    40404040  40404040  40404040  40404040
   002A60  50002770 40002776  00000000  40404040    40404040  40404040  40404040  40404040


                                            DUMP BEFORE EXECUTION

   002A40  FFFFF530 0AD04040  40404040  40404040    40404040  40404040  40404040  40404040
   002A60  TO THE NEXT LINE ADDRESS CONTAINS 40404040


                            REGISTER CONTENTS
                        BEFORE                  AFTER

                                REGISTER  6  50002770
                                REGISTER  7  40002776
                        FFFFF530 REGISTER  8  00000000
```

FIG. 5-31. Example of Add Half.

the operation, the computer forms the two's complement of the second operand. Thereafter, this command proceeds as an Add Register command. An example of Subtract Register is given in Fig. 5-32.

Do It Now Exercise 5-10. *Prepare a flow diagram for a routine to have the computer find the difference between the binary equivalents of decimal +1764 and +843. Assume that the operands are both full words in storage. Store the difference immediately after the two operands in storage. Write the routine, using Subtract Register and any other needed imperatives and declaratives. Show the complement of the second operand as well as the contents of storage for the operands and the difference.*

S—Subtract. This RX command operates in the same manner as the Add command noted previously. The computer, when it begins the operation, takes the two's complement of the second operand. Thereafter the computer proceeds as if under an Add command. An example of Subtract is given in Fig. 5-33.

```
       LOC  OBJECT CODE    ADDR1 ADDR2       NAME    OP    OPERANDS              COMMENT
                                                   IMPERATIVES

     00277A 9889 3180          02AC0                 LM    8,9,SUB              LOAD TWO REG
     00277E 05A0                                     BALR  10,0                 SAVE CONDITION CODE
     002780 1B98                              F5#32   SR    9,8                  SUBTRACT REG.
     002782 05B0                                     BALR  11,0                 SAVE CONDITION CODE
     002784 908B 31A0          02AE0                 STM   8,11,AKEEP           SAVE REG. CONTENTS


                                                   DECLARATIVES

     002AC0 08CA6C00                          SUB     DC    F'147483648'         F5#32
     002AC4 00218425                                  DC    F'2196517'
     002AC8 4040404040404040                          DC    CL24' '              FILLER
     002AD0 4040404040404040
     002AD8 4040404040404040
     002AE0 4040404040404040                 AKEEP   DC    CL32' '              USED TO DISPLAY STORAGE
     002AE8 4040404040404040
     002AF0 4040404040404040
     002AF8 4040404040404040


                                          DUMP AFTER EXECUTION

     002AC0   08CA6C00  00218425  40404040  40404040    40404040   40404040    40404040   40404040
     002AE0   08CA6C00  F7571825  40002780  50002784    40404040   40404040    40404040   40404040


                                         DUMP BEFORE EXECUTION

     002AC0   08CA6C00  00218425  40404040  40404040    40404040   40404040    40404040   40404040
     002AE0 TO THE NEXT LINE ADDRESS CONTAINS 40404040


                                       REGISTER CONTENTS
                                   BEFORE              AFTER

                                   08CA6C00  REGISTER  8   08CA6C00
                                   00218425  REGISTER  9   F7571825
                                             REGISTER 10   40002780
                                             REGISTER 11   50002784
```

FIG. 5-32. Example of Subtract Register.

Do It Now Exercise 5-11. *With the same flow diagram and data as in Do It Now Exercise 5-10, have the computer find the difference, using Subtract. Show the complement and the contents of storage.*

SH—Subtract Half. This RX command operates in the same manner as the Add Half command noted previously. The computer, at the time it begins the subtraction, takes the two's complement of the second operand. Thereafter the computer proceeds as if under an Add Half command. An example of Subtract Half is given in Fig. 5-34.

Do It Now Exercise 5-12. *With the same flow diagram and operands as in Do It Now Exercise 5-9, have the computer find the difference, using Subtract Half. Show the complement and the contents of storage.*

MR—Multiply Register. This RR command does not set the condition code. The register named as the first-operand address must be the even-numbered member of a pair of registers. The contents of this register may be partially replaced by the

```
   LOC   OBJECT CODE    ADDR1 ADDR2      NAME   OP   OPERANDS              COMMENT

                                            IMPERATIVES

 002788 5840 3200         02840                   L    4,SUB2            LOAD A REG.
 00278C 0550                                      BALR 5,0               SAVE CONDITION CODE
 00278E 5840 3204         02844          F5#33    S    4,MIN             SUBTRACT STORAGE WORD FROM A REG.
 002792 0560                                      BALR 6,0               SAVE CONDITION CODE
 002794 9046 3220         02860                   STM  4,6,AKEEP2        STORE RESULTS


                                            DECLARATIVES

 002840 000C2696                         SUB2    DC   F'796310'          F5#33
 002844 000C2696                         MIN     DC   F'796310'
 002848 404040404040404040              DC   CL24' '            FILLER
 002850 4040404040404040
 002858 4040404040404040
 002860 4040404040404040              AKEEP2  DC   CL32' '            USED TO DISPLAY STORAGE
 002868 4040404040404040
 002870 4040404040404040
 002878 4040404040404040


                                       DUMP AFTER EXECUTION

 002840   000C2696   000C2696   40404040    40404040    40404040   40404040   40404040   40404040
 002860   00000000   5000278E   40002794    40404040    40404040   40404040   40404040   40404040


                                       DUMP BEFORE EXECUTION

 002840   000C2696   000C2696   40404040    40404040    40404040   40404040   40404040   40404040
 002860 TO THE NEXT LINE ADDRESS CONTAINS 40404040


                                        REGISTER CONTENTS
                                    BEFORE                    AFTER

                          000C2696    REGISTER  4   00000000
                                      REGISTER  5   5000278E
                                      REGISTER  6   40002794
```

FIG. 5-33. Example of Subtract.

high-order (most significant) part of the product during the operation. For this reason, most programers prefer to clear this register to binary zero with a Load or Subtract Register instruction, before starting the multiplication. The adjacent (next higher) odd-numbered register of the pair must contain the multiplicand, but this register is not named in the instruction. The second-register address contains the multiplier, which may be in any register. The computer destroys the multiplicand during the multiplication. Because the resulting product is right-justified in the pair of registers named as a first operand, the computer has available 63 bits to accommodate a product that at the most will be 62 bits long. Hence overflow is impossible. Interrupt is possible from improper register addressing. This command is not available in the small models of the computer. An example of Multiply Register is given in Fig. 5-35. A further example of multiplication is given later in this chapter.

Do It Now Exercise 5-13. *Prepare a flow diagram, and write the declaratives and imperatives necessary to have the computer find the product in binary of decimal +144 and +55, using the Multiply Register command. Have the resulting product*

```
LOC   OBJECT CODE    ADDR1 ADDR2      NAME    OP   OPERANDS              COMMENT

                                     IMPERATIVES

002798 5880 3280        02BC0                 L    8,SFULL              LOAD A REG.
00279C 0590                                   BALR 9,0                  SAVE CONDITION CODE
00279E 4880 3284        02BC4         F5#34   SH   8,SHALF              SUBTRACT HALF WORD FROM A REG.
0027A2 05A0                                   BALR 10,0                 SAVE CONDITION CODE
0027A4 908A 32A0        02BE0                 STM  8,10,ASAVE3          STORE RESULTS


                                     DECLARATIVES

002BC0 FFFFFFFC                       SFULL   DC   F'-4'                F5#34
002BC4 1963                           SHALF   DC   H'6499'
002BC6 404040404040404040                     DC   CL26' '             FILLER
002BCE 4040404040404040
002BD6 4040404040404040
002BDE 4040
002BE0 4040404040404040         ASAVE3   DC   CL32' '             USED TO DISPLAY STORAGE
002BE8 4040404040404040
002BF0 4040404040404040
002BF8 4040404040404040


                                  DUMP AFTER EXECUTION

002BC0   FFFFFFFC   19634040   40404040   40404040   40404040   40404040   40404040
002BE0   FFFFE699   4000279E   500027A4   40404040   40404040   40404040   40404040


                                  DUMP BEFORE EXECUTION

002BC0   FFFFFFFC   19634040   40404040   40404040   40404040   40404040   40404040
002BE0 TO THE NEXT LINE ADDRESS CONTAINS 40404040
```

FIG. 5-34. Example of Subtract Half.

```
LOC   OBJECT CODE    ADDR1 ADDR2      NAME    OP   OPERANDS              COMMENT

                                     IMPERATIVES

0027A8 9845 3300        02C40                 LM   4,5,MULTC            LOAD TWO REG
0027AC 5880 3308        02C48                 L    11,MULTP             LOAD A REG
0027B0 1C4B                           F5#35   MR   4,11                 MULTIPLY REG.
0027B2 9045 3320        02C60                 STM  4,5,ASAVE4           STORE PRODUCT


                                     DECLARATIVES

002C40 00000000                       MULTC   DC   F'0'                 F5#35
002C44 00326258                               DC   F'3301976'
002C48 000003E9                       MULTP   DC   F'1001'
002C4C 4040404040404040                       DC   CL20' '              FILLER
002C54 4040404040404040
002C5C 40404040
002C60 4040404040404040         ASAVE4   DC   CL32' '              USED TO DISPLAY STORAGE
002C68 4040404040404040
002C70 4040404040404040
002C78 4040404040404040


                                  DUMP AFTER EXECUTION

002C40   00000000   00326258   000003E9   40404040   40404040   40404040   40404040
002C60   00000000   C5028A18   40404040   40404040   40404040   40404040   40404040


                                  DUMP BEFORE EXECUTION

002C40   00000000   00326258   000003E9   40404040   40404040   40404040   40404040
002C60 TO THE NEXT LINE ADDRESS CONTAINS 40404040
```

FIG. 5-35. Example of Multiply Register.

placed in the double word of storage immediately following the two operands. Pre-pare a scaling table. Show the contents of storage for the operands and the product.

M—Multiply. This RX command operates in much the same manner as the Multiply Register command noted previously. The difference is that the computer obtains the second operand (the multiplier) from an aligned full word in storage instead of from a register. Interrupts therefore are also possible from improper addressing. The Multiply command is not available in the small models of the computer. An example of Multiply is given in Fig. 5-36.

```
      LOC   OBJECT CODE      ADDR1 ADDR2        NAME    OP    OPERANDS            COMMENT

                                               IMPERATIVES

      002786  9867 3380           02CC0                 LM    6,7,MULC            LOAD TWO REG
      00278A  5C60 3388           02CC8         F5#36   M     6,MULP              MULTIPLY
      00278E  9067 33A0           02CE0                 STM   6,7,AHOLD2          STORE PRODUCT


                                               DECLARATIVES

      002CC0  00000000                          MULC    DC    F'0'                F5#36
      002CC4  068E37ED                                  DC    F'1099B3725'
      002CC8  00000122                          MULP    DC    F'290'
      002CCC  404040404040404040                        DC    CL20' '             FILLER
      002CD4  404040404040404040
      002CDC  40404040
      002CE0  404040404040404040                AHOLD2  DC    CL32' '             USED TO DISPLAY STORAGE
      002CE8  404040404040404040
      002CF0  404040404040404040
      002CF8  404040404040404040


                                               DUMP AFTER EXECUTION

      002CC0  00000000   068E37ED   00000122    40404040      40404040      40404040      40404040      40404040
      002CE0  00000007   6D1B5A7A   40404040    40404040      40404040      40404040      40404040      40404040


                                               DUMP BEFORE EXECUTION

      002CC0  00000000   068E37ED   00000122    40404040      40404040      40404040      40404040      40404040
      002CE0  TO THE NEXT LINE ADDRESS CONTAINS  40404040
```

Fig. 5-36. Example of Multiply.

Do It Now Exercise 5-14. *Following the same directions as in Do It Now Exercise 5-13, have the computer find the product, using Multiply instead of Multiply Register. Prepare the scaling table and show the contents of storage, assuming that each operand has one fractional place—i.e., that the operands are +14.4 and +5.5.*

MH—Multiply Half. This RX command may name any register as its first-operand address to hold the multiplicand. During multiplication, the computer destroys the multiplicand as it generates the product, since the product replaces the multiplicand in the register (no pair of registers is used). The second-operand address for the multiplier is assumed to be an aligned half word of storage. Here, because the maximum sizes of the operands are 31 bits and 15 bits, arithmetic overflow of the most significant bits can occur. The condition code is *not* set, and no overflow interrupt occurs. Interrupt may occur from improper addressing. This command is not available in the small models of the computer. An example of Multiply Half is given in Fig. 5-37.

```
    LOC   OBJECT CODE    ADDR1 ADDR2      NAME    OP   OPERANDS              COMMENT

                                              IMPERATIVES

    0027C2 5880  3400      02D40                    L    8,MULTHC            LOAD A REG
    0027C6 4C80  3404      02D44          F5#37     MH   8,MULTPH            MULTIPLY HALF
    0027CA 5080  3420      02D60                    ST   8,HOLD3             STORE PRODUCT


                                              DECLARATIVES

    002D40 00000BCB                       MULTHC    DC   F'3019'             F5#37
    002D44 001E                           MULTPH    DC   H'30'
    002D46 4040404040404040                         DC   CL26' '             FILLER
    002D4E 4040404040404040
    002D56 4040404040404040
    002D5E 4040
    002D60 4040404040404040               HOLD3     DC   CL32' '             USED TO DISPLAY STORAGE
    002D68 4040404040404040
    002D70 4040404040404040
    002D78 4040404040404040


                                              DUMP AFTER EXECUTION

    002D40  00000BCB  001E4040  40404040  40404040  40404040  40404040  40404040  40404040
    002D60  000161CA  40404040  40404040  40404040  40404040  40404040  40404040  40404040


                                              DUMP BEFORE EXECUTION

    002D40  00000BCB  001E4040  40404040  40404040  40404040  40404040  40404040  40404040
    002D60  TO THE NEXT LINE ADDRESS CONTAINS 40404040
```

FIG. 5-37. Example of Multiply Half.

Do It Now Exercise 5-15. *With the same data as in Do It Now Exercise 5-13, have the computer find the product, using Multiply Half. Prepare a scaling table. Store the product in a full word immediately after the operands, and show the contents of storage as before.*

DR—Divide Register. In this RR command it is assumed that the dividend to be divided consists of 1 sign bit and 63 data bits, and is located in a double word spread across a pair of adjacent registers. The first-operand address must be the even-numbered (leftmost) register of the pair. The computer obtains the divisor from the second-operand register address. Usually this register is neither of the registers used for the dividend. The computer does not alter the divisor during division.

The resulting quotient replaces the dividend in the odd-numbered register of the pair and is always 31 data bits and 1 sign bit long. The remainder is always equal in length to the divisor, and since the divisor is 1 register long, it also is 31 data bits and 1 sign bit long. The computer generates the remainder in the even-numbered register of the register pair, replacing the dividend. The condition code is not set by the Divide command, but a divide overflow and interrupt can occur if

```
   LOC   OBJECT CODE      ADDR1 ADDR2        NAME    OP    OPERANDS                COMMENT

                                                   IMPERATIVES

  0027CE 9889 3480         02DC0                     LM    8,9,DIVS               LOAD TWO REG
  0027D2 5840 3488         02DC8                     L     4,DIV                  LOAD A REG
  0027D6 1DR4                              F5#38      DR    8,4                    DIVIDE REG.
  0027D8 9089 34A0         02DE0                     STM   8,9,STORE1             STORE REMAINDER AND QUOTIENT
                                                   *
                                                   *            SCALING TABLE FOR F5#38
                                                   *              S +  Z +  I + F =  T
                                                   *DIVD          1 + 51 + 12 + 0 = 64
                                                   *DIVS          1 + 23 +  8 + 0 = 32
                                                   *QUOT          1 + 27 +  4 + 0 = 32
                                                   *REM           1 + 23 +  8 + 0 = 32


                                                   DECLARATIVES

  002DC0 00000000                          DIVS      DC    F'0'                   F5#38
  002DC4 00000E0D                                    DC    F'3597'
  002DC8 000000EF                          DIV       DC    F'239'
  002DCC 4040404040404040                            DC    CL20' '                FILLER
  002DD4 4040404040404040
  002DDC 40404040
  002DE0 4040404040404040                  STORE1    DC    CL32' '                USED TO DISPLAY STORAGE
  002DE8 4040404040404040
  002DF0 4040404040404040
  002DF8 4040404040404040


                                                   DUMP AFTER EXECUTION

  002DC0   00000000   00000E0D   000000EF   40404040   40404040   40404040   40404040   40404040
  002DE0   0000000C   0000000F   40404040   40404040   40404040   40404040   40404040   40404040


                                                   DUMP BEFORE EXECUTION

  002DC0   00000000   00000E0D   000000EF   40404040   40404040   40404040   40404040   40404040
  002DE0   TO THE NEXT LINE ADDRESS CONTAINS 40404040
```

Fig. 5-38. Example of Divide Register.

the absolute-value part of the division scaling rule is not met. The Divide Register command is not available in the small models of the computer.

The programer usually has to adjust the position of the dividend in the registers and occasionally even adjust the divisor in order to have the computer generate the desired number of integer and fractional places in the quotient. The operations needed to do such adjustment are normally the shift operations discussed below.

In utilizing the scaling rule, the programmer must note that the computer provides both the remainder and the quotient with a sign, but the 63 data bits of the dividend have only a single bit for the sign. The effect of this is to use one of the leading 0 bits as a sign position holder in the scaling computation. Figure 5-38 illustrates Divide Register and shows the calculation of the scaling with the aid of a scaling table.

Do It Now Exercise 5-16. *Prepare a flow diagram for a routine to calculate a quotient with two fractional places from dividing decimal 100 by 30. Place the operands in storage and show their contents along with the dividend prior to division. Use a Load to clear to 0s any register that needs clearing. Store the quotient and the remainder in the successive four words of storage immediately following the oper-*

ands. Write the imperatives and declaratives needed to implement this routine. Show the contents of storage and prepare a scaling table.

D—Divide. This RX command operates in much the same manner as the Divide Register command described previously. The major difference is that the second operand, which is the divisor, comes from an aligned full word in storage, not from a register. Improper addressing may cause an interrupt. This command is not available in small models of the computer. An example of Divide is given in Fig. 5-39, along with the scaling table.

```
        LOC   OBJECT CODE    ADDR1 ADDR2        NAME    OP    OPERANDS               COMMENT

                                                IMPERATIVES

      0027DC  9889  3500           02E40               LM    8,9,DIVS1              LOAD A REG
      0027E0  5080  3508           02E48       F5#39   D     8,DIV1                 DIVIDE
      0027E4  9089  3520           02E60               STM   8,9,AHOLD4             SAVE REG. CONTENTS
                                                  *            SCALING TABLE FOR F5#39
                                                  *            S  +   Z  +  I  + F = T
                                                 *DIVD         1  +  43  + 20 + 0 = 64
                                                 *DIVS         1  +  23  +  8 + 0 = 32
                                                 *QUOT         1  +  19  + 12 + 0 = 32
                                                 *REM          1  +  23  +  8 + 0 = 32


                                                DECLARATIVES

      002E40  00000000                          DIVS1   DC    F'0'                   F5#39
      002E44  0006FC88                                  DC    F'457912'
      002E48  00000067                          DIV1    DC    F'103'
      002E4C  404040404040404040                        DC    CL20' '                FILLER
      002E54  404040404040404040
      002E5C  40404040
      002E60  404040404040404040                AHOLD4  DC    32C' '                 USED TO DISPLAY STORAGE
      002E68  404040404040404040
      002E70  404040404040404040
      002E78  404040404040404040


                                                DUMP AFTER EXECUTION

      002E40  00000000  0006FC88  00000067  40404040    40404040   40404040   40404040   40404040
      002E60  0000004D  0001150D  40404040  40404040    40404040   40404040   40404040   40404040

                                                DUMP BEFORE EXECUTION

      002E40  00000000  0006FC88  00000067  40404040    40404040   40404040   40404040   40404040
      002E60  TO THE NEXT LINE ADDRESS CONTAINS 40404040
```

FIG. 5-39. Example of Divide.

Do It Now Exercise 5-17. *Do again Do It Now Exercise 5-16, using Divide rather than Divide Register, but assuming that the divisor is a negative number.*

SLA—Shift Left Algebraic. This RS command operates on the contents of the register named as the first-operand address, moving the bits in that register the number of places to the left specified by the six bits appearing as the rightmost bits of the second-operand address (*not* the contents). This address is calculated in the usual base-and-displacement manner. The second operand is usually expressed as a decimal number on the coding sheet indicating the number of positions to be shifted to the left. The sign bit does not participate in the shift operation; it is left untouched. To fill the vacated places at the right end of the register, the computer uses 0-bit fill. The command sets the condition code, and overflow and interrupt may occur if a bit unlike the sign bit is shifted out of the leftmost data bit position in the register. Shifting to the left in a register is equivalent to multiplying by a power of 2 equal to the number of places shifted. No second-register designation is needed or used, in spite of the RS format of the instruction. This command is not available in the small models of the computer. An example of Shift Left Algebraic is given in Fig. 5-40.

```
LOC   OBJECT CODE    ADDR1 ADDR2     NAME    OP   OPERANDS           COMMENT

                                         IMPERATIVES

0027E8 58A0 3580        02EC0                 L    10,SHIFTL          LOAD A REG
0027EC 0590                                   BALR 9,0                SAVE CONDITION CODE
0027EE 8BA0 0006        00006        F5#40    SLA  10,6               SHIFT REG. CONTENTS LEFT BY 6 BITS
0027F2 0580                                   BALR 8,0                SAVE CONDITION CODE
0027F4 908A 35A0        02EE0                 STM  8,10,ASAVE5        SAVE REG. CONTENTS


                                         DECLARATIVES

002EC0 0000C741                      SHIFTL   DC   F'51009'           F5#40
002EC4 4040404040404040                       DC   CL28' '            FILLER
002ECC 4040404040404040
002ED4 4040404040404040
002EDC 40404040
002EE0 4040404040404040              ASAVE5   DC   CL32' '            USED TO DISPLAY STORAGE
002EE8 4040404040404040
002EF0 4040404040404040
002EF8 4040404040404040


                                     DUMP AFTER EXECUTION

002EC0  0000C741   40404040   40404040   40404040   40404040   40404040   40404040   40404040
002EE0  600027F4   500027EE   00310040   40404040   40404040   40404040   40404040   40404040


                                     DUMP BEFORE EXECUTION

002EC0  0000C741   40404040   40404040   40404040   40404040   40404040   40404040   40404040
002EE0 TO THE NEXT LINE ADDRESS CONTAINS 40404040
```

FIG. 5-40. Example of Shift Left Algebraic.

Do It Now Exercise 5-18. *A binary number that is the equivalent of decimal +2006 occupies an aligned full word of storage. Prepare a flow diagram for a routine to multiply this number by 4, storing the resulting number back in the original field, and showing the contents of storage before and after. Write the declaratives and imperatives necessary to accomplish this.*

SRA—Shift Right Algebraic. This RS command is parallel but opposite in direction to Shift Left Algebraic. This command moves to the right the contents of the register named as the first-operand address by the number of bit positions specified by the rightmost six bits of the second-operand address (*not* contents). No second-register designation is used or needed. On the coding sheet the programer usually writes the second operand as a decimal number. Shifting to the right is equivalent to dividing by a power of 2 equal to the number of places shifted. The places shifted off the right-hand end of the register are lost; the sign bit is used as a fill bit at the left-hand end of the register. This command sets the condition code, but no overflow is possible, and no interrupts may occur. This command is not available in the small models of the computer. An example of Shift Right Algebraic is given in Fig. 5-41.

```
   LOC  OBJECT CODE    ADDR1 ADDR2      NAME   OP   OPERANDS         COMMENT

                                           IMPERATIVES

0027F8 5860 3600       02F40                    L    6,SHIFTR        LOAD A REG
0027FC 0540                                      BALR 4,0            SAVE CONDITION CODE
0027FE 8A60 0008       00008        F5#41        SRA  6,8            SHIFT REG. CONTENTS RIGHT BY 8 BITS
002802 0550                                      BALR 5,0            SAVE CONDITION CODE
002804 9046 3620       02F60                    STM  4,6,ASTORE2    SAVE REG. CONTENTS


                                           DECLARATIVES

002F40 00000060                     SHIFTR DC   F'96'               F5#41
002F44 4040404040404040                     DC   CL28' '            FILLER
002F4C 4040404040404040
002F54 4040404040404040
002F5C 40404040
002F60 4040404040404040             ASTORE2 DC   CL32' '            USED TO DISPLAY STORAGE
002F68 4040404040404040
002F70 4040404040404040
002F78 4040404040404040


                                    DUMP AFTER EXECUTION

002F40  00000060  40404040  40404040  40404040  40404040  40404040  40404040  40404040
002F60  600027FE  40002804  00000000  40404040  40404040  40404040  40404040  40404040


                                    DUMP BEFORE EXECUTION

002F40  00000060  40404040  40404040  40404040  40404040  40404040  40404040  40404040
002F60 TO THE NEXT LINE ADDRESS CONTAINS 40404040
```

FIG. 5-41. Example of Shift Right Algebraic.

Do It Now Exercise 5-19. *The binary equivalent of decimal +47621 is in storage in binary form in an aligned full word. Prepare a flow diagram to truncate seven of the least significant bits off the right-hand end of the number, storing the resulting truncated number back as the contents of the original operand. Then write the declaratives and imperatives necessary to accomplish this. Show the contents of storage after each imperative instruction.*

SLDA—Shift Left Double Algebraic. This RS command operates in the same manner as the Shift Left Algebraic command noted previously. The one difference is that the first-operand address names the even-numbered register of a pair of adjacent registers. In doing the shifting, the computer links these registers. Thus the sign position of the next higher odd-numbered register ceases to function as a sign-bit holder and serves instead as a data-bit position. This command is not available

```
      LOC    OBJECT CODE      ADDR1 ADDR2        NAME     OP    OPERANDS        COMMENT

                                               IMPERATIVES

   002808  9889 3680          02FC0               LM     8,9,SHIFTDL   LOAD TWO REG
   00280C  05A0                                   BALR   10,0          SAVE CONDITION CODE
   00280E  8F80 000C          0000C     F5#42     SLDA   8,12          SHIFT REG. CONTENTS LEFT BY 12 BITS
   002812  05B0                                   BALR   11,0          SAVE CONDITION CODE
   002814  9088 36A0          02FE0               STM    8,11,AKEEP3


                                               DECLARATIVES

   002FC0  00000000                     SHIFTDL   DC     F'0'          F5#42
   002FC4  20C513FB                                DC     F'549786619'
   002FC8  4040404040404040                        DC     CL24' '      FILLER
   002FD0  4040404040404040
   002FD8  4040404040404040
   002FE0  4040404040404040            AKEEP3     DC     CL32' '       USED TO DISPLAY STORAGE
   002FE8  4040404040404040
   002FF0  4040404040404040
   002FF8  4040404040404040


                                            DUMP AFTER EXECUTION

   002FC0   00000000   20C513FB   40404040   40404040   40404040   40404040   40404040   40404040
   002FE0   0000020C   513FB000   4000280E   60002814   40404040   40404040   40404040   40404040


                                           DUMP BEFORE EXECUTION

   002FC0   00000000   20C513FB   40404040   40404040   40404040   40404040   40404040   40404040
   002FE0   TO THE NEXT LINE ADDRESS CONTAINS 40404040
```

Fig. 5-42. Example of Shift Left Double Algebraic.

in the small models of the computer. An example of Shift Left Double Algebraic is given in Fig. 5-42.

Do It Now Exercise 5-20. *The binary equivalent of the decimal number +1089 is to be positioned in the register pair 6 and 7 so that the number has 9 zero bits following it in order to set it up as a dividend for division. Prepare a flow diagram and then write the declaratives and imperatives necessary to accomplish this. Show the contents of storage and of the registers.*

SRDA—Shift Right Double Algebraic. This RS command operates in the same manner as the Shift Right Algebraic command noted earlier. The one difference is that the first-operand address names the even-numbered register of a pair of adjacent registers. In doing the shifting, the computer links these registers. Thus, the sign-bit position of the next higher odd-numbered register serves as a data-bit position. This command is not available in the small models of the computer. An example of Shift Right Double Algebraic is given in Fig. 5-43.

Do It Now Exercise 5-21. *The binary equivalent of +0.65248 is to be multiplied by the binary equivalent of decimal +268435456. The product is to be stored as an aligned double word in storage. Prepare a flow diagram, and then write the declaratives and imperatives necessary to accomplish this, showing the contents of storage for each step.*

```
   LOC   OBJECT CODE    ADDR1 ADDR2        NAME    OP   OPERANDS           COMMENT

                                            IMPERATIVES

002818  9845 3700         03040                   LM   4,5,SHIFTDR       LOAD TWO REG
00281C  0590                                      BALR 9,0               SAVE CONDITION CODE
00281E  8E40 0012         00012      F5#43        SRDA 4,18              SHIFT REG. CONTENTS RIGHT BY 18 BIT
002822  05A0                                      BALR 10,0              SAVE CONDITION CODE
002824  9045 3720         03060                   STM  4,5,AKEEP4        STORE RESULTS
002828  909A 3730         03070                   STM  9,10,AKEEP4+16    STORE CONDITION CODES


                                            DECLARATIVES

003040  00000013                    SHIFTDR  DC   XL4'13'           F5#43
003044  00000000                             DC   F'0'
003048  4040404040404040                     DC   CL24' '           FILLER
003050  4040404040404040
003058  4040404040404040
003060  4040404040404040    AKEEP4  DC   CL32' '           USED TO DISPLAY STORAGE
003068  4040404040404040
003070  4040404040404040
003078  4040404040404040


                                       DUMP AFTER EXECUTION

003040   00000013   00000000   40404040   40404040   40404040   40404040   40404040   40404040
003060   00000000   0004C000   40404040   40404040   6000281E   60002824   40404040   40404040
```

FIG. 5-43. Example of Shift Right Double Algebraic.

Do It Now Exercise 5-22. *Prepare a flow diagram for a routine to find the product in binary of two numbers in packed-decimal format in storage addresses RGR2 and RGR8. Store the integer portion of the binary product in RGR3 and the fractional portion of the product in RGR4, where these are separated by one byte in storage. Use register 6, which contains all F_x. Assume that both numbers are positive and that each has five integer characters and two fractional characters. Prepare a scaling table. Write the imperatives and declaratives needed to implement this routine. Be careful with the algebraic sign. Show the anticipated contents of storage.*

Do It Now Exercise 5-23. *Prepare a flow diagram for a routine to find the quotient and the remainder resulting from dividing the binary equivalents of decimal +7 into +11. The quotient should have the equivalent of five decimal places. Assume that both operands are available in zoned format but that the quotient is desired in binary form as an aligned full word in storage. Write the imperatives and declaratives needed to do the division with the Divide command. Prepare a scaling table, show the contents of storage and the contents of the registers. To clear a register, subtract it from itself.*

PACKED-DECIMAL ARITHMETIC OPERATIONS

The ability to do packed-decimal arithmetic operations is a standard feature on the small models of the computer, an optional feature on the other models. The packed-decimal arithmetic operations include add, subtract, multiply, and divide.

To clear portions of a field to 00_x, a Zero and Add Packed command is available. This command, when used with some of the data-movement commands, such as Move With Offset, Move Numerics, and Move Zones, enables the programer to specify the equivalents of shift operations for doing scaling.

AP—Add Packed. This SS command requires a length for each operand, neither of which may exceed 16 bytes. The contents of the first operand address named are replaced by the sum. The contents of the second operand address named remain unaltered. Neither operand address requires alignment. The command does set the condition code. If the length of the first operand is equal to or less than the length of the second operand, arithmetic overflow may occur, and may cause an interrupt. Interrupt may also arise from improper sign or digit codes, and from improper addressing. Overlapping fields are possible, provided that the rightmost byte of each operand field contains a correctly placed valid sign character. This command is available on all models of the computer. An example of Add Packed is given in Fig. 5-44.

Fig. 5-44. Example of Add Packed.

Do It Now Exercise 5-24. *Prepare a flow diagram for a routine to find the sum in packed-decimal of $+841$ and $+722$ without destroying either operand in storage. Write the routine, using as few imperatives and as little storage as possible. Show the contents of storage for each step.*

SP—Subtract Packed. This SS command operates in the same manner as the Add Packed command noted previously but performs a subtraction instead of addition. No complementing takes place. Subtract Packed can be used to clear to 0 a packed-decimal field by specifying the same operand twice. This command is available in all models of the computer. An example of Subtract Packed is given in Fig. 5-45.

```
    LOC   OBJECT CODE      ADDR1 ADDR2      NAME   OP   OPERANDS        COMMENT

                                         IMPERATIVES

  002840 D208 3820 3800 03160 03140            MVC   ASTORE4(9),SUB1    SHOW CONTENTS OF STORAGE
  002846 0540                                  BALR  4,0                SAVE CONDITION CODE
  002848 FB47 3800 3805 03140 03145   F5#45    SP    SUB1,ASUB2         SUBTRACT PACKED
  00284E 0550                                  BALR  5,0                SAVE CONDITION CODE
  002850 9045 3838             03178           STM   4,5,ASTORE4+24     STORE CONDITION CODES


                                         DECLARATIVES

  003140 015971104C                    SUB1    DC    PL5'15971104'      F5#45
  003145 000765001023440C              ASUB2   DC    PL8'765001023440'
  00314D 404040404040404040                    DC    CL19' '            FILLER
  003155 404040404040404040
  00315D 404040
  003160 404040404040404040            ASTORE4 DC    CL32' '            USED TO DISPLAY STORAGE
  003168 404040404040404040
  003170 404040404040404040
  003178 404040404040404040


                                    DUMP AFTER EXECUTION

  003140  98505233  6D000765  00102344  0C404040   40404040  40404040   40404040  40404040
  003160  01597110  4C000765  00404040  40404040   40404040  40404040   60002848  70002850
  003180  40404040  40404040  40404040  40404040   40404040  40404040   40404040  40404040
```

FIG. 5-45. Example of Subtract Packed.

Do It Now Exercise 5-25. *Prepare a flow diagram for a routine to subtract in packed-decimal −4.61 from +7. Assign each field the minimum length in storage. Retain as much precision as possible in the difference. Leave unaltered both of the two operand fields. Write the imperatives and declaratives needed to implement the routine. Show the contents of storage after each step.*

ZAP—Zero and Add Packed. This SS command clears to packed-decimal 0s the contents of the first operand address specified. It then adds to this cleared field the contents of the second operand address. Each operand has its own length, which may not exceed 16 bytes. Zero and Add Packed can be thought of, therefore, as being either an add following a clearing operation or a movement of data into the field with a fill of packed-decimal 0s on the left, if the receiving field be longer than the sending field. But the movement operation, unlike the usual moves, goes from right to left. This command sets the condition code, and 0s serve as the fill characters. If truncation occurs on the left, overflow is signalled, and an interrupt may occur. Interrupt may also arise from improper sign or digit codes and from improper addressing. This command is available in all models of the computer. Zero and Add Packed is frequently used for clearing the field that is to hold an arithmetic operand in packed-decimal. An example of Zero and Add Packed is given in Fig. 5-46.

```
LOC     OBJECT CODE     ADDR1 ADDR2      NAME    OP   OPERANDS            COMMENT

                                              IMPERATIVES

002854  D20E 38A0 3880 031E0 031C0               MVC  AHOLD5(15),NOZ      SHOW CONTENTS OF STORAGE
00285A  0560                                     BALR 6,0                 SAVE CONDITION CODE
00285C  F8E7 3880 388F 031C0 031CF    F5#46      ZAP  NOZ,APAC            ZERO AND ADD PACKED
002862  0570                                     BALR 7,0                 SAVE CONDITION CODE
002864  9067 3898                 031D8          STM  6,7,AHOLD6+1        STORE CONDITION CODES


                                              DECLARATIVES

0031C0  C4F1F5C5C1F6F9F2                  NOZ    DC   CL15'D15EA692100TJ'  F5#46
0031C8  F1F0F0E3D14040
0031CF  00003144162905C                   APAC   DC   PL8'3144162905'
0031D7  4040404040404040                  AHOLD6 DC   CL9' '               FILLER
0031DF  40
0031E0  4040404040404040                  AHOLD5 DC   CL32' '              USED TO DISPLAY STORAGE
0031E8  4040404040404040
0031F0  4040404040404040
0031F8  4040404040404040


                                              DUMP AFTER EXECUTION

0031A0  F0404040  40404040  40404040  40404040  40404040  40404040  40404040  40404040
0031C0  00000000  00000000  00031441  62905C00  00031441  62905C40  7000285C  60002864
0031E0  C4F1F5C5  C1F6F9F2  F1F0F0E3  D1404040  40404040  40404040  40404040  40404040
003200  F0404040  40404040  40404040  40404040  40404040  40404040  40404040  40404040
```

FIG. 5-46. Example of Zero and Add Packed.

Do It Now Exercise 5-26. *Write a declarative to establish as short a field as possible in packed-decimal format for the decimal number +444. Prepare a flow diagram for a routine to copy this data into a field eight bytes long aligned on a double-word boundary, but have the incoming data right-justified. Write the imperatives and declaratives needed to implement the routine. Show the contents of storage before and after.*

MP—Multiply Packed. This SS command does not set the condition code. The multiplicand, which is the contents of the first operand address, may not have a length exceeding 16 bytes. The multiplier, which is the contents of the second operand, may not have a length exceeding 8 bytes. The contents of the multiplicand field are destroyed during multiplication, since it receives the product. In order to help the programer minimize the likelihood of arithmetic overflow, the length in bytes of the multiplier field must be less than the length in bytes of the multiplicand field. The multiplicand field must have a number of high order (on the left) packed-decimal leading 0s at least equal to the number of significant digits in the multiplier field. Failure to observe these requirements may cause an interrupt. Interrupt may also arise from improper sign or digit codes and from improper addressing. The scaling rule discussed previously holds for Multiply Packed. Overlapping fields are possible, provided that the rightmost byte of each field contains a valid sign code. This command is available in all models of the computer. An example of Multiply Packed is given in Fig. 5-47.

```
        LOC  OBJECT CODE     ADDR1 ADDR2     NAME   OP   OPERANDS              COMMENT

                                                 IMPERATIVES

     002868 D209 3920 3900 03260 03240               MVC  AKEEP5(10),APAC1
     00286E FC93 3900 390A 03240 0324A        F5#47  MP   APAC1,APAC2          MULTIPLY PACKED


                                                 DECLARATIVES

     003240 0000000000329910               APAC1   DC   PL10'329910475'      F5#47
     003248 475C
     00324A 0100111C                       APAC2   DC   PL4'100111'
     00324E 4040404040404040                       DC   CL18' '              FILLER
     003256 4040404040404040
     00325E 4040
     003260 4040404040404040               AKEEP5  DC   CL32' '              USED TO DISPLAY STORAGE
     003268 4040404040404040
     003270 4040404040404040
     003278 4040404040404040


                                            DUMP AFTER EXECUTION

     003220 F0404040  40404040  40404040  40404040  40404040  40404040  40404040  40404040
     003240 00000330  27667562  725C0100  111C4040  40404040  40404040  40404040  40404040
     003260 00000000  00329910  475C4040  40404040  40404040  40404040  40404040  40404040
     003280 F0404040  40404040  40404040  40404040  40404040  40404040  40404040  40404040
```

FIG. 5-47. Example of Multiply Packed.

Do It Now Exercise 5-27. Prepare a flow diagram, and write the declaratives and imperatives necessary to square in packed-decimal the number +169, leaving the original operand in the field untouched. Place the square in a field with not more than one leading 0. Show the contents of storage after each step.

DP—Divide Packed. This SS command does not set the condition code but can result in a divide-overflow interrupt if the scaling is improperly done. Interrupt may also arise from improper sign or digit codes and from improper addressing. Divide Packed is parallel to Multiply Packed because the operations follow a similar pattern. The contents of the dividend field, which is the first operand address, may not exceed 16 bytes in length; the divisor may not exceed 8 bytes in length. The sign of the remainder is the same as that of the dividend. The length of the remainder is the same as the length of the divisor. Both the remainder and the quotient are produced as signed right-justified fields. The quotient field occurs at the left end of the original dividend field; the remainder field occupies the balance of the original dividend field. The division scaling rules noted previously hold for Divide Packed, but the programer must keep in mind that packed-decimal fields can be lengthened or shortened only by full bytes which provide two packed-decimal digits. This command is available in all models of the computer. An example of Divide Packed is given in Fig. 5-48.

Do It Now Exercise 5-28. Prepare a flow diagram for a routine to divide the packed-decimal number +364 by −17 to produce a quotient with two fractional places. Round to one fractional place by the rule of adding 5 to the most significant

LOC	OBJECT CODE	ADDR1	ADDR2	NAME	OP	OPERANDS	COMMENT
				IMPERATIVES			
002874	D21F 39A0 3980	032E0	032C0		MVC	AKEEP6,PAC3	SAVE STORAGE
00287A	FDC5 3980 398D	032C0	032CD	F5#48	DP	PAC3,PAC4	DIVIDE PACKED

				DECLARATIVES			
0032C0	0000000000005049			PAC3	DC	PL13'5049621174635'	F5#48
0032C8	621174635C						
0032CD	00293140135C			PAC4	DC	PL6'293140135'	
0032D3	4040404040404040				DC	CL13' '	FILLER
0032DB	4040404040						
0032E0	4040404040404040			AKEEP6	DC	CL32' '	USED TO DISPLAY STORAGE
0032E8	4040404040404040						
0032F0	4040404040404040						
0032F8	4040404040404040						

			DUMP AFTER EXECUTION					
0032A0	F0404040	40404040	40404040	40404040	40404040	40404040	40404040	40404040
0032C0	00000000	17225C00	28234926	0C002931	40135C40	40404040	40404040	40404040
0032E0	00000000	00005049	62117463	5C002931	40135C40	40404040	40404040	40404040
003300	F0404040	40404040	40404040	40404040	40404040	40404040	40404040	40404040

FIG. 5-48. Example of Divide Packed.

place to be dropped, and then truncate. Write the necessary imperatives and declaratives to do this division and rounding, saving the original operand fields and showing the contents of storage after each operation.

SRP—Shift and Round Packed. This SS command can be used both for left shifting, and for rounding and right shifting packed-decimal numbers. The contents of the first operand named are shifted by the amount and direction specified by the six bits appearing as the rightmost part of the effective second operand address (not the contents). The number of numeric packed-decimal characters to be shifted may range from 0 for no shift, to $+31$ for a maximum left shift, and to -31 for a maximum right shift. The sign character is not affected by the shift, and zeros serve as both left and right fill.

Overflow to the left sets the condition code to 3 and the overflow characters are lost; overflow to the right does not set the condition code and the overflow characters are lost. The command sets the condition code in the usual manner for arithmetic operations. Interrupts may arise from improper sign or digit codes and from improper addressing. This command is available only on some of the newer models of the computer. Two examples of Shift and Round Packed are given in Fig. 5-49.

In writing instructions using this command, the programer has two operands to specify in other than the usual SS form. First is the second operand—the shift direction and amount. One way to do this is to use a zero displacement and an explicit base register. This requires the programer to load the register each time in advance to give the direction and amount of the shift. This is the best alternative when the same instruction must be used many times but each time with a different shift amount. A second way is to use a self-defining number as the operand [the compiler then assigns no (0 as the) base register]. These can only be positive. This is no difficulty for a left shift, since numbers from 0 through 31 can be chosen. But for a right shift, the numbers must be chosen to give a 1 bit as the sixth bit from the right and give the shift amount in 2s complement form. Thus, decimal 63 gives a right shift of 1 place, 62 gives 2, 61 gives 3, 60 gives 4, 56 gives 8, 52 gives 12, 48 gives 16, 44 gives 20, 40 gives 24, 36 gives 28, and 33 gives 31. Both methods are illustrated in Fig. 5-49.

```
   LOC   OBJECT CODE     ADDR1 ADDR2      NAME    OP    OPERANDS            COMMENT

                                    IMPERATIVES

006B1A  1B66                                      SR    6,6                 SET CONDITION CODE TO 00
006B1C  0560                                      BALR  6,0                 SAVE CONDITION CODE
006B1E  5870 3178               06980             L     7,BITS1             LOAD BIT PATTERN
006B22  F055 3180 7000 069B8 00000   F5#49A       SRP   FLD3,0(7),5         SHIFT LEFT THREE POSITIONS
006B28  0580                                      BALR  8,0                 SAVE CONDITION CODE
006B2A  F055 3186 003E 069BE 0003E   F5#49B       SRP   FLD4,62(0),5        SHIFT RIGHT AND ROUND OFF TWO
006B30  0590                                      BALR  9,0                 SAVE CONDITION CODE
006B32  9069 3198               069A0             STM   6,9,AHOLD           SHOW REGISTER CONTENTS


                                    DECLARATIVES

006980  00000003                          BITS1    DC    F'3'               TO SHIFT LEFT THREE POSITIONS
006984  0000003F                          BITS2    DC    XL4'3E'            TO SHIFT RIGHT TWO POSITIONS
006988  0000007B362D                      FLD3     DC    PL6'-78362'        DATA FOR FIG 5-49A
06069BF  00000019587C                     FLD4     DC    PL6'+19587'        DATA FOR FIG 5-49B
006994  0000007B362D                               DC    PL6'-78362'        COPY OF ORIGINAL DATA
06069A  000000019587C                              DC    PL6'+19587'        COPY OF ORIGINAL DATA
0069A0  4040404040404040                  AHOLD    DC    CL32' '            USED TO DISPLAY REGISTERS
0069A4  4040404040404040
0069B0  4040404040404040
0069B8  4040404040404040


                                    DUMP AFTER EXECUTION

006960  F0404040   40404040   40404040   40404040   40404040   40404040   40404040   40404040
006980  00000003   0000003F   0007B362   00000000   0000196C   0000007B   36200000   0019587C
0069A0  4000681E   00000003   50006B2A   60006832   40404040   40404040   40404040   40404040
0069C0  F0404040   40404040   40404040   40404040   40404040   40404040   40404040   40404040
```

Fig. 5-49. Two examples of Shift and Round Packed.

The rounding factor is easily handled. The programer specifies it as the third operand and must do so even for left shifts when no rounding is done. The rounding factor may be any single decimal digit from 0 through 9 inclusive, with 5 being the common choice. In execution, the computer disregards the sign and adds absolutely the rounding factor to the leftmost digit to be truncated off the number to be rounded. The carry, if any, is allowed to propagate to the left before the right shift is completed. This causes no difficulty since a right shift of zero places is not possible.

EXERCISES

1. Demonstrate the use of the addition scaling rule in packed-decimal and in binary formats, where 10 numbers are to be added, the largest of which may not exceed in length 6 decimal digits. Verify by pencil-and-paper computation.

2. Prepare an example in packed-decimal and in binary formats that will illustrate that multiplication and division are opposite processes, provided that the remainder resulting from division is added to the product of the quotient times the divisor. Verify by pencil-and-paper computation. How do fractional characters complicate the relationship?

3. Using zoned numbers and by converting them to binary, prepare a demonstration of multiplication by 8 and division by 8, using Multiply Register and Divide Register instructions. Verify the accuracy by converting the resulting binary numbers back to zoned numbers and comparing with a decimal solution done with pencil and paper. Contrast these operations with shift operations, explaining any differences in the commands used and in the result achieved.

CHAPTER 6

Program Control

PROGRAM CONTROL

Most programs have some parts that the programer wants the computer to execute from a few to many times, as well as parts he wants the computer to skip under some conditions. To be able to write such programs, the programer must know not only what operations are to be skipped or repeated and under what conditions, but also how to cause the computer to skip or repeat selectively those parts of the program as it executes it.

The skipping or repeating of parts of a program applies only to the way in which the computer executes a program, not to the way in which the programer necessarily writes the program originally. These two sequences can be completely independent. The programer can write a program in pieces, skipping around as much as he may desire. Then he can combine the pieces into a coherent program. In his program the programer must provide instructions to enable the computer to skip or repeat parts as needed.

The ability of the computer to execute a program, skipping some parts and repeating other parts, is a fundamental feature of the ability of the computer to adapt a program to the specific input data to be processed. To make this possible, the programer must incorporate in the program ways for the computer to select the parts of the program to be executed and the parts to be skipped. He must also provide in the program ways for the computer to rearrange the sequence of the parts of the program as the computer executes the program. All of these operations are aspects of the general problem of program control.

Selective repetition of parts of a program is introduced later under the title "Iteration." Certain conventional requirements typically must be met for a programer to include iteration in a program. The usual procedure is to consider each repeated part of a program as if it were a loop or cycle of instructions. This loop or cycle of instructions typically has an "entrance," which includes some initialization or setting of control fields at their starting values. It typically also has an "exit" where control leaves the loop to go to some other part of the program. Typically, the loop also contains some tests to determine whether the computer should have control take the exit or should continue executing the instructions in the loop one more time.

Later in this chapter commands will be presented to facilitate the initialization of iterative loops, the test, and the exit. The programer can thus combine these program-control operations with the material from previous chapters to prepare major parts of programs in the exercises.

From a practical point of view, program control has other major aspects. The programer, in writing a program, often finds it convenient to write the program in parts, debugging and finding the mistakes in each part before undertaking the next part. This allows the programer to write each section separately, or a team of programers to write separate sections. But to make such program sectioning possible, the programer must give attention to aspects of program control so that the parts may be put together ("linked") into a meaningful and accurately operating whole.

In writing programs for the computer, the programer also must take into account the possibility of program relocation. Relocatability means that the place in storage where a program section is loaded may differ each time the program is loaded for execution. The instructions in one section that refer to or use data in other sections require the programer to supply specific indications of the way in which this reference is to be done. Thus this too is an aspect of program control.

PROGRAM SECTIONS

Programers who are assigned to work on the same job often divide the work among themselves. The work each programer does must be made to fit with the work done by the others. To avoid overlapping of work, each programer generally works on only a particular part or section of the program, meshing the way he writes his section of the program with the results produced by the other programers. To do this conveniently requires some method of sectioning programs.

Whether a programer works alone or as a member of a team, the programer often must, because of the size of the program he is working on, break the entire job down into parts, programing each part or section separately. The ability to write the program in sections also facilitates debugging work by concentrating the programer's attention on one part of the program at a time. After debugging each section, the programer then combines it with the other debugged sections to form, eventually, an entire program. In doing this, the programer finds it convenient to split the program into parts or sections.

Relocatability of programs also affects program sectioning. In the computer, program parts in sections of up to 4,096 bytes (under some conditions longer) may be relocated to almost any part of internal storage in the computer. The programer, in writing the program, typically has no knowledge of where in storage a particular section of the program will be when it is executed. In other words, when he writes the instructions, he is ignorant of the absolute address to be assigned to any part of the program. Particularly when the computer operates under the control of an operating system, the sections of the program may be placed at different positions in storage each time the operating system loads the program for execution. For example, the first section may be located at one time high in storage, and at another time low in storage. Relocatability of programs is in part achieved by altering the contents of the base registers at the time a program is loaded for execution.

To facilitate program sectioning, the programer can define what are known as "control sections" in a program. A control section is a routine or group of routines loaded physically adjacent in internal storage all at the same time and so organized that address reference is easy to any part, even when the entire section is relocated. The programer provides this organization by the way he directs the compiler and the computer to assign and load base registers, and by his use of program-control declaratives. The latter is also the way the programer controls the method of loading parts of a program in storage.

A short summary will show why base-register usage is vital in a control section. As pointed out in Chap. 2, the programer uses the general-purpose registers for base registers. The computer, when it proceeds to execute an instruction, must calculate each effective storage address. As noted earlier, the computer does this by adding the displacement binary amount shown in the instruction to the contents of the base register. After adding on any index-register contents, the computer uses the resulting sum in binary form as the absolute address (the "effective address").

The situation at compile time is different, however. As diagramed in Fig. 6-1, a compiler program causes the computer to accept as input the source program the programer has written. Under the control of the compiler program, the computer translates the source program the programer has written, and produces the object program. The programer can then take the object program and use it with input data to have the computer produce the desired output data.

At the time of compilation (translation from source to object language) neither the computer nor the programer knows what the contents of a base register will be in absolute terms (as a binary number). The programer can, however, determine— *relative* to landmark points such as the first instruction in the program—how much storage space is needed for parts of the program. Furthermore, the programer can

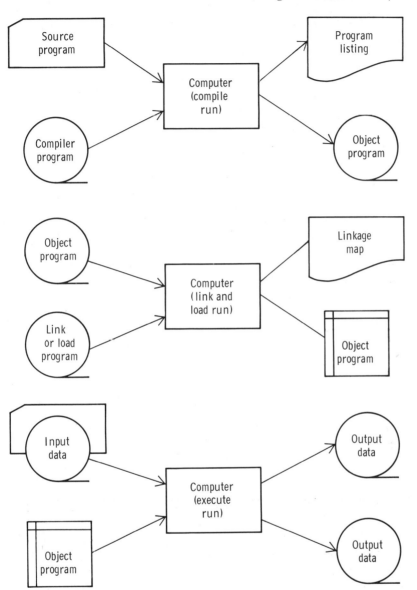

Fig. 6-1. System chart of the compile and execute processes.

specify how the compiler is to use registers at object time (at the time the computer executes the program).

To do this accurately, the programer needs to know how the compiler program determines which registers are available as base registers in compiling a control section, what relative values they will contain, and how much storage space the program uses. To do this, the compiler programer uses a location counter and three general rules.

The location counter is a running tally of the number of bytes of storage needed thus far for the compiled program. Instructions may need two, four, or six bytes, so each compiled instruction adds to the tally of storage space required for the program. DC and DS declaratives take various amounts. Usually at the start of a compilation, the location counter has an initial value of zero. The location counter's current value at any time during a compilation usually is the relative address of the next instruction or constant to be compiled, counting from the start of the program. The programer can himself compose relative addresses using the contents of the location counter by representing its current contents by *. For example, to designate an address one double word less than the address of the current instruction, the programer can write * — 8 and thus avoid giving either storage location a symbolic name.

As it encounters the declarative for each base register, the compiler takes the then-current value of the location counter as the base address unless otherwise specified by the USING declarative. Then the compiler applies the rules. First, all addresses are assumed to be positive binary numbers. No negative numbers for addresses are permitted, and hence no sign is shown. Second, the compiler program uses only those registers that have been identified by the programer as being available for use as base registers. This the programer does by the USING declarative. When the programer desires the compiler program to stop using a register as a base register, the programer signals it by the DROP declarative. This has the effect of making the registers named no longer available to the compiler for use as a base register.

Third, when the compiler has more than one base register available, it determines which base register to use by selecting the base register which yields the *smallest* displacement (see Fig. 6-2). This is an important rule which gives the programer considerable control over which available register will be used. One reason for this rule is that the maximum allowable displacement is only 4,095, since a displacement is represented by three hexadecimal characters in an instruction. This means that a new register must be made available or the contents of an existing register changed whenever the smallest displacement (relative distance) exceeds 4,096 bytes of storage.

Partly for this reason, a programer usually finds it convenient to assign different base registers for use in referring to instructions and to working storage areas such as input-output areas. This is especially true for long programs. In a short program which with all its working storage areas would occupy less than 4,096 bytes, one base register may be enough, but the use of two is a more conservative practice. In larger programs, the use of several base registers may be virtually mandatory.

Assume this assignment of addresses in storage in the computer:

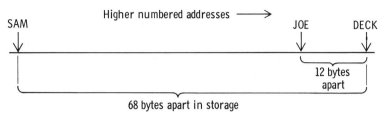

If: USING   SAM,3

Then: a reference to DECK yields a displacement of 68.

If: USING JOE,2

Then: a reference to DECK yields a displacement of 12.

If: USING SAM,3
         USING JOE,2

Then: a reference to DECK uses register 2 as the base register,
         since the displacement is thus made smaller.

If: USING SAM,3

Then: a reference to JOE yields a displacement of 56.

If: USING JOE,3

Then: a reference to JOE yields a displacement of 0.

If: USING JOE,3

Then: a reference to SAM is not possible.

FIG. 6-2. Relationships between base registers and displacements for
         different USING declaratives.

To understand more fully how the compiler program assigns base registers, the programer should note that the compiler program builds during compilation one symbol table for each control section in the program. By the time the compiler program finishes the symbol table, it includes the name of the field, the base register assigned, the length of the field, the displacement amount, and the places where the field is used. In building the symbol table, the compiler program checks that the expected contents of the base register and the displacement together result in a legal effective address.

In order to provide convenient sectioning of a program for the reasons noted earlier, declaratives are available for the programer. One of these, the CSECT declarative, provides for defining and naming a control section in a program. To

START a program and to END a program, two additional declaratives are available. These and other compiler control declaratives are described below, and are illustrated later in this and the next chapter.

SOME PROGRAM-CONTROL DECLARATIVES

USING. This declarative is the programer's means of stating to the compiler program that certain registers are to be made available for use as base registers. The first operand is a symbolic address that specifies in symbolic form the assumed contents of the base register named as the first of the second-operand parts (see Fig. 6-2). The second operand is a list of one or more registers. For small models and some medium models of the computer, the programer may list only one register. Commas separate the two operands and the parts of the second operand. If more than one register is named in the second operand, then the contents of each succeeding register named are 4,096 bytes greater (higher addresses) than the contents of the preceding register named. The symbolic address named as the first operand serves as the origin point the compiler program uses for calculating the displacements (relative address) for symbolic names. The programer can indicate the next available address by using an * as the operand, that is, the current contents of the location counter.

DROP. The one operand lists the registers which are no longer to be used by the compiler program as base registers. Any number of registers, separated by commas, may be specified as being no longer available. For the small models and some medium models of the computer, the programer may list only one register. A DROP statement is not required at the end of a program or of a control section.

CSECT. This declarative identifies the beginning of a control section in the program. For this reason, this declarative always has a name, and blanks are treated by the compiler program as a valid name. Hence it is conservative practice for the programer to assign a specific nonblank name. In programs containing more than one control section, a repeated control-section name is treated as a continuation of the previous control section with the same name. Control sections in a program, assuming adequate base-register use is specified, need not be restricted to less than 4,096 bytes in length. This declarative has no operands and is not required for programs with only one control section if the programer uses the START declarative. A program written for a small model of the computer is assumed to consist of only one control section. Hence, for such programs no CSECT declarative is available, and registers 0, 1, and 2, are permanently assigned in some small models for use as base registers.

START. The START declarative identifies to the compiler program that a compilation is to be begun. It has the effect of initializing the compiler program. For large models of the computer, this declarative has no operand. By giving a self-defining decimal number, divisible by 8 with a 0 remainder as the one operand, the programer can in small and some medium models of the computer specify the left-most (lowest) address in storage in which the compiled program will be placed when loaded for execution. This absolute address is then used by the compiler in preparing the program listing for the programer, and by the program loader. If the translated (compiled) program is then loaded in internal storage for execution, the loader will start it at the address specified. If, however, the program is relocated in storage at the time of program loading, then the programer's attempt to specify a starting address is ignored. Whether or not the programer should use an operand depends on local installation practices and requirements. START serves, in effect, to begin and name the first or only control section in a program. It generally is used without a name but can be used with the name of a control section.

END. This declarative indicates to the compiler program that no further imperative or declarative statements follow—i.e., the END marks the end of a program to be compiled. This declarative has one operand which names the control entry point in the program being compiled. That entry point is normally the name the programer has assigned to the first imperative instruction in the object program to be executed after it has been loaded.

PRINT. This declarative may have from one to three operands to control the data printed at the time the computer compiles assembly language into object language. If the programer omits the PRINT declarative, the usual installation practices will be followed in producing the compilation listings. Standard practice at most installations consists of the equivalents of the operands ON, NOGEN, and NO-DATA, as shown below and illustrated in Fig. 6-3. The programer can override or supplement the installation standard practice by using the PRINT declarative with one or more of the following operands.

```
NAME      OP    OPERANDS           COMMENT
*F6#3     PRINT  ON,NOGEN,NODATA    COMMON INSTALLATION PRACTICE
```

FIG. 6-3. Example of PRINT declarative.

The operand ON causes the computer to print a listing in the usual format. This shows the source language and the object language. OFF causes no listing to be printed. GEN (which stands for generate) causes all of the object language resulting from the use of macrocommands to be printed. NOGEN eliminates the printing of the machine-language expansion of the macro commands and instead prints only the macros in the source-language listing. DATA causes the computer to print in full the hexadecimal equivalents of all literals and DC declaratives in listing. NO-DATA prints only up to the first eight bytes of data in hexadecimal.

ORG. This declarative has one operand, which names the address at which the compiler is to assign the compiled object language. ORG stands for origin. If a program is to be relocatable, only symbolic names may serve as operands, and each name must have been used previously in the program as a name of a DC or DS declarative, or of an imperative instruction. This declarative can be used to reserve areas of storage when the exact length is unknown to the programer, but can be computed for the object language, as shown in Fig. 6-4. The * is the address of the next-higher byte of storage available for assignment. Usually this is the address of the imperative instruction in which the * appears, or of the next DC or DS declarative.

NAME	OP	OPERANDS	COMMENT
F6#4	ORG	*+SPOT2-SPOT1	JUMP AHEAD BY DIFFERENCE SPOT2-SPOT1

Fig. 6-4. Example of ORG declarative.

LTORG. This declarative causes the compiler to use storage space, starting with the first available aligned double word, for all the literals thus far encountered in the program or since the last prior LTORG declarative. This declarative has no operands but can be assigned a name. This declarative is not available for the small models of the computer. For other models, the programer should use it to control the placement of the literals in storage. Normally the programer uses at least one LTORG in each control section of the program. The programer must use one if he also uses IOCS input-output declaratives, as noted in the next chapter.

CNOP—Conditional No Operation. This macrocommand generates from none to three imperative No Operation instructions (each a half word long) in order that the next available address for placing an instruction in storage will be aligned on a half-word, full-word, or double-word boundary. This macrocommand is not available for the small models of the computer; it has two operands, both of which are written as self-defining decimal numbers. For the second operand, the allowable numbers are 4 and 8, representing alignment desired in relation to a full word and a double word, respectively.

When the second operand is a 4, then the first operand may be either 0 or 2. If the first operand is 0, then the next available byte after the No Operation instruction has an address aligned on a full-word boundary. If it is a 2, then the next available byte after the No Operation instruction has an address aligned on the half-word boundary in the middle of an aligned full word.

If the second operand is an 8, then the first operand may be either 0, 2, 4, or 6. If the first operand be a 0, then the next available byte after the No Operation instruction has an address aligned on a double-word boundary. If it be a 2, it will be aligned on the half-word boundary immediately following the double-word boundary.

Alignment	Double word			
	Word		Word	
	Half word	Half word	Half word	Half word
	Byte : Byte	Byte : Byte	Byte : Byte	Byte : Byte
Operand	0,4 0,8	2,4 2,8	0,4 4,8	2,4 6,8

FIG. 6-5. Table of alignments for the CNOP macrocommand.

If it be a 4, it will be on the full-word boundary that is in the middle of a double word. If it be a 6, it will be the last half-word boundary in the double word. These positions are summarized in Fig. 6-5.

The programer often uses a CNOP macrocommand immediately prior to a Branch and Link Register instruction, in order to make the address stored by it be an aligned address, as explained later in this chapter. If the programer desires this alignment to be on a double word—the usual case, in order to reduce the alignment problems in base-and-displacement addressing—he uses the 6,8 operands. This is done because the Branch and Link Register instruction is one half word long. If he desires alignment on a full word, he uses the 2,4 operands.

ENDING OF PROGRAM

The command repertoire of most of the medium and large models of the computer does not include a halt command as such. Instead, when the computer has completed the work of a program, the computer transfers control to the "supervisor program" by means of a supervisor-call instruction. This philosophy and usage reflect the normal operating practice for all but the small models of the computer.

As noted previously, the computer commonly executes a program in conjunction with an additional program called a "supervisor program." Usually the programer does not write his own supervisor program, since each installation generally has adopted some supervisor program for standard use. The supervisor program provides for handling the equivalent of a halt at the end-of-job condition in processing data in a program. To this end, the programer provides a supervisor call. The programer can identify to the supervisor program the reason or basis for interruption by providing one byte of operand data.

EOJ—End of Job. This macrocommand has no operand, and is available only on medium-size models of the computer. The compiler translates this macrocommand into a Supervisor Call. On the computer models for which it is available, it is the preferred ending for a program in terms of its control sequence, not as the programer has written the program on the coding forms. An example of the EOJ macro (macrocommand) is given in Fig. 7-13 in the next chapter.

On small models, the usual ending for a program is Halt and Branch, or Halt and Proceed, as described below. On large models of the computer, a set of conventions for going from one program to another have been established, as described in Chap. 13. For large models of the computer operated under these conventions, the usual practice for ending a program is to make an unconditional transfer of control to the address in register 14, by the means described later in this chapter. To be sure that this is the correct address, cautious programers save this address as they start their program. One form of this practice is given in Chap. 11.

SVC or SRC—Supervisor Call. This RR command causes the computer to change the program status word (see Chap. 8) and hence to alter the control sequence. No registers are used or altered. The one operand specified with this command is normally written as a decimal number in the range 0 through 255 to provide one byte of data indicating the reason for the change of control or the action to be taken. This command is not available on the small models of the computer. An example of Supervisor Call is shown in Fig. 6-6. Note that the byte of data substitutes for the register numbers.

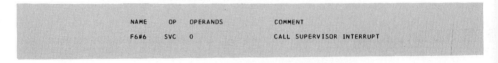

NAME	OP	OPERANDS	COMMENT
F6#6	SVC	0	CALL SUPERVISOR INTERRUPT

FIG. 6-6. Example of Supervisor Call.

HB—Halt and Branch. This SI command halts the computer's operations. The first operand specifies the address at which the computer is to resume program execution if the console operator starts the computer again, and may be any symbolic address. The second operand provides a one-byte identification of the halt. This the programer normally, on the coding form, writes as a decimal number in the range 0 through 255. An example of Halt and Branch is given in Fig. 6-7. This command is available on only a few models of the computer.

NAME	OP	OPERANDS	COMMENT
F6#7	HB	NEXT,13	HALT AND THEN BRANCH

FIG. 6-7. Example of Halt and Branch.

HPR—Halt and Proceed. This SI command is available only on some of the small models of the computer. It causes the computer to halt operations. If the operator presses the start key, the computer resumes operation with the next instruction in sequence. What would normally be the operand address is used as an identification for the halt. The second operand that normally provides a byte of immediate data is ignored. An example of Halt and Proceed is given in Fig. 6-8.

NAME	OP	OPERANDS	COMMENT
F6#8	HPR	RESUME,0	HALT BUT DO NOT BRANCH

FIG. 6-8. Example of Halt and Proceed.

LOGIC OPERATIONS

The programer uses logic operations in the computer primarily to set the condition code. The condition code was explained briefly in Chap. 5. To review, the condition code is a special two-bit binary field. The condition code takes the value of 0 (00_b) if the result of a logic operation indicates equal, 1 (01_b) if the result of a logic operation indicates low, and 2 (10_b) if the result of logic operation indicates high. For logic operations of the type discussed in this chapter, condition code 3 (11_b) is not used.

The logic operations described in this chapter have one characteristic in common and one difference. The characteristic they have in common is that they leave the field or register contents unaltered. For example, a comparison operation, even though it compares the contents of the fields or registers bit by bit, does not result in altering either operand. The only thing a comparison alters is the condition code.

The characteristic the logic operations do not share is the treatment of the sign. For example, the algebraic comparison operations treat separately the sign in the field or register. The logical comparison operations, by contrast, make no distinction between signed and unsigned quantities, since they compare bit by bit without regard to the code format. For that reason, where numeric values which have signs are to be compared, the programer usually chooses an algebraic compare. If the comparison is to be made on data for which the algebraic signs are not a significant factor—for example, on alphabetic fields—a logical compare is the usual choice for comparing fully every bit.

Comparison operations in the computer treat the first operand as the variable of comparison and the second operand as the constant of comparison. This matches the practice recommended by a committee for the American National Standards Institute for representing the variable of comparison on the left-hand side of a colon

COMPARE 9:4 Variable —↑↑— Constant	COMPARE 6:6 Variable —↑↑— Constant
RESULTS	RESULTS
9 > 4 9 is greater than 4	6 ⩾ 6 6 is { greater than or equal to 6 / not less than 6 }
9 ≠ 4 9 is not equal to 4	6 = 6 6 is equal to 6
4 < 9 4 is less than 9	6 ⩽ 6 6 is { not greater than 6 / less than or equal to 6 }

In the computer, the variable of comparison is the first operand. The constant of comparison is the second operand.

Fig. 6-9. Structure of comparison.

and the constant of comparison on the right-hand side. This is illustrated and explained in Fig. 6-9.

The computer performs comparison bit by bit from left to right, except for Compare Packed, which goes from right to left by half bytes. The storage operands for RX commands must be aligned. The condition code is set to reflect whether the first operand be equal to, less than, or greater than the second operand. The respective codes are 0, 1, or 2.

ALGEBRAIC COMPARISON

CR—Compare Register. This RR command provides for comparing the contents of two registers. It treats the leftmost bit of each register as an algebraic sign and the remaining bits of each register as representing a binary number. This command sets the condition code as described previously. No interrupts occur for the command. This command is not available on small models of the computer. An example of Compare Register is given in Fig. 6-10.

Do It Now Exercise 6-1. *Assume that register 7 contains the binary equivalent of +78 and that register 9 contains the binary equivalent of +47. Treating the contents of register 7 as the variable of comparison, write the imperative operations needed to compare the contents, using the CR command. Show the contents of the registers and of the condition code after comparison.*

C—Compare. This RX command compares the contents of the register named as the first-operand address with the contents of the field in storage named as the second-operand address. The leftmost bit of each operand's contents is treated as a sign bit. The storage operand is assumed to be an aligned full word. This command sets the condition code, and improper addressing may cause interrupts. This command is not available on the small models of the computer. An example of Compare is shown in Fig. 6-11.

```
 LOC    OBJECT CODE     ADDR1 ADDR2      NAME    OP    OPERANDS              COMMENT
                                              IMPERATIVES

001A50  9867 3000        01BE0                   LM    6,7,COM1             LOAD TWO REG.
001A54  0580                                     BALR  8,0                  SAVE CONDITION CODE
001A56  1976                            F6#10    CR    7,6                  COMPARE REG.
001A58  0590                                     BALR  9,0                  SAVE CONDITION CODE
001A5A  9069 3020        01C00                   STM   6,9,BHOLD            SAVE REG. CONTENTS


                                              DECLARATIVES

001BE0  05F2FDC9                         COM1    DC    F'99810761'          F6#10
001BE4  05F5A37D                                 DC    F'99984253'
001BE8  4040404040404040                         DC    CL24' '
001BF0  4040404040404040                                                   FILLER
001BF8  4040404040404040
001C00  4040404040404040                BHOLD    DC    CL32' '              USED TO DISPLAY STORAGE
001C08  4040404040404040
001C10  4040404040404040
001C18  4040404040404040


                                    DUMP AFTER EXECUTION

0034C0  F0404040    40404040    40404040    40404040    40404040    40404040    40404040    40404040
0034E0  05F2FDC9    05F5A37D    40404040    40404040    40404040    40404040    40404040    40404040
003500  05F2FDC9    05F5A37D    60003356    6000335A    40404040    40404040    40404040    40404040
003520  F0404040    40404040    40404040    40404040    40404040    40404040    40404040    40404040


                              ADDRESS OF ITEM       001C00
                     PLUS RELOCATION FACTOR         001900
                     YIELDS EFFECTIVE ADDRESS       003500
```

Fig. 6-10. Example of Compare Register.

```
 LOC    OBJECT CODE     ADDR1 ADDR2      NAME    OP    OPERANDS              COMMENT
                                              IMPERATIVES

001A5E  5840 3080        01C60                   L     4,LESS               LOAD A REG
001A62  0550                                     BALR  5,0                  SAVE CONDITION CODE
001A64  5940 3084        01C64        F6#11      C     4,COM2               COMPARE A REG. AND A STORAGE WORD
001A68  0560                                     BALR  6,0                  SAVE CONDITION CODE
001A6A  9046 30A0        01C80                   STM   4,6,BSAVE            SAVE REG. CONTENTS


                                              DECLARATIVES

001C60  00024F69                        LESS     DC    FS8'591.41'          F6#11
001C64  0009FDA5                        COM2     DC    FS16'9.9908'
001C68  4040404040404040                         DC    CL24' '
001C70  4040404040404040                                                   FILLER
001C78  4040404040404040
001C80  4040404040404040                BSAVE    DC    CL32' '              USED TO DISPLAY STORAGE
001C88  4040404040404040
001C90  4040404040404040
001C98  4040404040404040


                                    DUMP AFTER EXECUTION

003540  F0404040    40404040    40404040    40404040    40404040    40404040    40404040    40404040
003560  00024F69    0009FDA5    40404040    40404040    40404040    40404040    40404040    40404040
003580  00024F69    60003364    5000336A    40404040    40404040    40404040    40404040    40404040
0035A0  F0404040    40404040    40404040    40404040    40404040    40404040    40404040    40404040


                              ADDRESS OF ITEM       001C80
                     PLUS RELOCATION FACTOR         001900
                     YIELDS EFFECTIVE ADDRESS       003580
```

Fig. 6-11. Example of Compare.

```
   LOC   OBJECT CODE     ADDR1 ADDR2        NAME    OP   OPERANDS          COMMENT
                                                   IMPERATIVES

001A6E 5060 3120          01D00                    ST   6,BKEEP          STORE REG. CONTENTS
001A72 0570                                        BALR 7,0             SAVE CONDITION CODE
001A74 4960 3104          01CE4        F6#12       CH   6,BHALF          COMPARE A REG. AND A HALF WORD
001A78 0580                                        BALR 8,0             SAVE CONDITION CODE
001A7A 9068 3120          01D00                    STM  6,8,BKEEP        SAVE REG. CONTENTS


                                                   DECLARATIVES

001CE0 0000006F                        BWORD       DC   F'111'           F6#12
001CE4 0501                            BHALF       DC   H'1281'
001CE6 404040404040404040                          DC   CL26' '          FILLER
001CEE 40404040404040404040
001CF6 40404040404040404040
001CFE 4040
001D00 404040404040404040      BKEEP  DC   CL32' '          USED TO DISPLAY STORAGE
001D08 40404040404040404040
001D10 40404040404040404040
001D18 404040404040404040


                                                   DUMP AFTER EXECUTION

0035C0  F0404040  40404040  40404040   40404040    40404040   40404040  40404040  40404040
0035E0  0000006F  05014040  40404040   40404040    40404040   40404040  40404040  40404040
003600  5000336A  50003374  6000337A   40404040    40404040   40404040  40404040  40404040
003620  F0404040  40404040  40404040   40404040    40404040   40404040  40404040  40404040


                              ADDRESS OF ITEM        001D00
                       PLUS RELOCATION FACTOR        001900
                       YIELDS EFFECTIVE ADDRESS      003600
```

FIG. 6-12. Example of Compare Half.

```
   LOC   OBJECT CODE     ADDR1 ADDR2        NAME    OP   OPERANDS          COMMENT
                                                   IMPERATIVES

001A7E 0580                                        BALR 8,0             SAVE CONDITION CODE
001A80 F935 3180 3184 01D60 01D64      F6#13       CP   BAC1,BAC2        COMPARE TWO PACKED FIELDS
001A86 0590                                        BALR 9,0             SAVE CONDITION CODE
001A88 9089 31A0          01D80                    STM  8,9,BSTORE       SAVE REG CONTENTS


                                                   DECLARATIVES

001D60 1936580C                        BAC1        DC   PL4'1936580'     F6#13
001D64 31077152648C                    BAC2        DC   PL6'31077152648'
001D6A 404040404040404040                          DC   CL22' '          FILLER
001D72 40404040404040404040
001D7A 40404040404040
001D80 40404040404040404040      BSTORE DC   CL32' '          USED TO DISPLAY STORAGE
001D88 40404040404040404040
001D90 40404040404040404040
001D98 40404040404040404040


                                                   DUMP AFTER EXECUTION

003640  F0404040  40404040  40404040   40404040    40404040   40404040  40404040  40404040
003660  1936580C  31077152  648C4040   40404040    40404040   40404040  40404040  40404040
003680  60003380  50003388  40404040   40404040    40404040   40404040  40404040  40404040
0036A0  F0404040  40404040  40404040   40404040    40404040   40404040  40404040  40404040


                              ADDRESS OF ITEM        001D80
                       PLUS RELOCATION FACTOR        001900
                       YIELDS EFFECTIVE ADDRESS      003680
```

FIG. 6-13. Example of Compare Packed.

Do It Now Exercise 6-2. *Prepare a flow diagram and write the declaratives and imperatives needed to have the computer compare, using the Compare command, the equivalents of decimal +31.2 and +4.16. Treating the second number as the variable of comparison, show the contents of the operands, and show the condition code after comparison. Hint: Watch those decimal points!*

CH—Compare Half. This RX command compares the contents of the register named as the first-operand address and the contents of an aligned half word as the second-operand address. The leftmost bit of each operand is assumed to be a sign bit. In all but the small models of the computer, the computer performs the operation by extending the two-byte field to a four-byte field internally in the computer by propagating the leftmost bit (the sign bit) of the two-byte field to the left as a sign bit fill. This command sets the condition code. Improper addressing may cause interrupts. This command is available on all models of the computer. An example of Compare Half is shown in Fig. 6-12.

Do It Now Exercise 6-3. *Prepare a flow diagram, and write the imperatives and declaratives necessary to have the computer compare the binary equivalents of decimal +699 and +745. Treat the first number as the variable of comparison, and show the contents of the operands and the condition code after comparison. Use a Compare Half instruction.*

CP—Compare Packed. This SS command names two fields in storage as the operands which are assumed to be in packed-decimal form. Their contents are checked for valid digit and sign codes. The rightmost character of each field must be a sign character. Each operand has a length which may be as long as 16 bytes. The computer lengthens the shorter field internally (not in storage) with leading 0s to equal in length the longer field. No alignment is necessary, and the comparison proceeds from right to left. This command sets the condition code. Invalid digit or sign codes and improper addressing may cause interrupts. The command is available on all models of the computer. An example of Compare Packed is shown in Fig. 6-13.

Do It Now Exercise 6-4. *Write the imperatives and declaratives necessary to have the computer compare, using the Compare Packed command, the numbers −7642 and +1989. Treating the second number as the variable of comparison, show the contents of storage and the condition code after comparison.*

LOGICAL COMPARISON

Logical comparison proceeds from left to right, starting with the leftmost bit of the leftmost byte of each operand. All bits are treated as data bits, and algebraic signs are not recognized as such. In effect, all operands are treated as unsigned binary amounts. EBCDIC data, binary complements, address constants, and the like are not distinguished for their type, and fill bits or characters are treated as part of the unsigned binary amount.

```
LOC   OBJECT CODE    ADDR1 ADDR2        NAME    OP   OPERANDS           COMMENT

                                            IMPERATIVES

001A8C 9878 3200         01DE0                 LM   7,8,COM3          LOAD A REG
001A90 0590                                    BALR 9,0               SAVE CONDITION CODE
001A92 1578                          F6#14     CLR  7,8               LOGICAL COMPARE OF TWO REG.
001A94 05A0                                    BALR 10,0              SAVE CONDITION CODE
001A96 907A 3220         01E00                 STM  7,10,BHOLD2       SAVE REG. CONTENTS



                                            DECLARATIVES

001DE0 FFFFFFFF                      COM3      DC   F'-.909013'       F6#14
001DE4 FFFFFA74                                DC   F'-1420'
001DE8 4040404040404040                        DC   CL24' '           FILLER
001DF0 4040404040404040
001DF8 4040404040404040
001E00 4040404040404040            BHOLD2      DC   CL32' '           USED TO DISPLAY STORAGE
001E08 4040404040404040
001E10 4040404040404040
001E18 4040404040404040



                                       DUMP AFTER EXECUTION

0036C0 F0404040  40404040  40404040  40404040  40404040  40404040  40404040  40404040
C036E0 FFFFFFFF  FFFFFA74  40404040  40404040  40404040  40404040  40404040  40404040
003700 FFFFFFFF  FFFFFA74  50003392  60003396  40404040  40404040  40404040  40404040
003720 F0404040  40404040  40404040  40404040  40404040  40404040  40404040  40404040


                              ADDRESS OF ITEM       001E00
                        PLUS RELOCATION FACTOR      001900
                        YIELDS EFFECTIVE ADDRESS    003700
```

FIG. 6-14. Example of Compare Logical Register.

```
LOC   OBJECT CODE    ADDR1 ADDR2        NAME    OP   OPERANDS           COMMENT

                                            IMPERATIVES

001A9A 5840 3280         01E60                 L    4,BCONZ           LOAD A REG.
001A9E 0550                                    BALR 5,0               SAVE CONDITION CODE
001AA0 5540 3284         01E64       F6#15     CL   4,BCON2           LOGICAL COMPARE - REG. AND STORAGE
001AA4 0560                                    BALR 6,0               SAVE CONDITION CODE
001AA6 9046 32A0         01E80                 STM  4,6,BSAVE2        SAVE REG. CONTENTS



                                            DECLARATIVES

001E60 F9E7C3C1                      BCONZ     DC   CL4'9XCA'         F6#15
001E64 F0F4F0F0                      BCON2     DC   CL4'0400'
001E68 4040404040404040                        DC   CL24' '           FILLER
001E70 4040404040404040
001E78 4040404040404040
001E80 4040404040404040            BSAVE2      DC   CL32' '           USED TO DISPLAY STORAGE
001E88 4040404040404040
001E90 4040404040404040
001E98 4040404040404040



                                       DUMP AFTER EXECUTION

003740 F0404040  40404040  40404040  40404040  40404040  40404040  40404040  40404040
003760 F9E7C3C1  F0F4F0F0  40404040  40404040  40404040  40404040  40404040  40404040
003780 F9E7C3C1  600033A0  600033A6  40404040  40404040  40404040  40404040  40404040
0037A0 F0404040  40404040  40404040  40404040  40404040  40404040  40404040  40404040


                              ADDRESS OF ITEM       001E80
                        PLUS RELOCATION FACTOR      001900
                        YIELDS EFFECTIVE ADDRESS    003780
```

FIG. 6-15. Example of Compare Logical.

CLR—Compare Logical Register. This RR command compares the contents of the register named as the first-operand address with the register named as the second-operand address. No distinction is made between sign and data bits, all bits being treated as data bits. This command sets the condition code as noted earlier. No interruption occurs for the command. This command is not available on the small models of the computer. An example of Compare Logical Register is shown in Fig. 6-14.

Do It Now Exercise 6-5. Prepare a flow diagram, and write the declaratives and imperatives needed to have the computer compare the binary equivalents of decimal −200471 and +300168, where the larger of these two numbers is to be loaded into register 6, the smaller into register 5. Show the register contents and the resulting condition code. Would Compare Register have yielded the same condition-code setting?

CL—Compare Logical. This RX command compares the contents of the register named as the first-operand address with the contents of storage named as the second-operand address. The storage operand must be an aligned full word. No distinction is made between sign and data bits, all bits being treated as data bits. This command sets the condition code. Improper addressing may cause interrupts. An example of Compare Logical is shown in Fig. 6-15.

Do It Now Exercise 6-6. Prepare a flow diagram and write the declaratives and imperatives needed to have the computer compare a field in storage containing the binary equivalent of decimal +600421 with the contents of register 6, from Do It Now Exercise 6-5. Show the contents of storage of the register, and the resulting condition code.

CLC—Compare Logical Characters. This SS command compares two operands in storage. The length of the compare fields is determined by the length of the first operand, which may be as long as 256 bytes. An equal number of bytes from storage is used for the second operand. No alignment is necessary. All combinations of bits are considered legal. No distinction is made between sign and data bits, all bits being treated as data bits. This command sets the condition code. Improper addressing may cause interrupts. This command is the general-purpose compare command for non-numeric data in storage. This command is available on all models of the computer. An example of Compare Logical Characters is shown in Fig. 6-16.

Do It Now Exercise 6-7. Prepare a flow diagram, and write the declaratives and imperatives needed to have the computer compare the EBCDIC field containing the equivalent of decimal +647 with the packed-decimal field containing the equivalent of decimal +648. Show the contents of storage and the resulting condition code. Hint: Watch those codes!

```
LOC   OBJECT CODE      ADDR1 ADDR2       NAME    OP    OPERANDS           COMMENT

                                              IMPERATIVES

001AAA 0570                                     BALR  7,0                SAVE CONDITION
001AAC D507 3305 3300 01EE5 01EE0     F6#16     CLC   BCON3,CON4         LOGICAL COMPARE OF TWO STORAGE FIELDS
001AB2 0580                                     BALR  8,0                SAVE CONDITION CODE
001AB4 9078 3320           01F00                STM   7,8,BKEEP2         SAVE REG. CONTENTS


                                              DECLARATIVES

001EE0 C1F9F0C2F1                       CON4    DC    CL5'A90B1'         F6#16
001EE5 F9C6C6F0C2F1F1F8                  BCON3   DC    CL8'9FF0B118'
001EED 4040404040404040                         DC    19C' '
001EF5 4040404040404040
001EFD 404040
001F00 4040404040404040                  BKEEP2  DC    32C' '            USED TO DISPLAY STORAGE
001F08 4040404040404040
001F10 4040404040404040
001F18 4040404040404040


                                        DUMP AFTER EXECUTION

0037C0  F0404040   40404040   40404040   40404040   40404040   40404040   40404040   40404040
0037E0  C1F9F0C2   F1F9C6C6   F0C2F1F1   F8404040   40404040   40404040   40404040   40404040
003800  600033AC   600033B4   40404040   40404040   40404040   40404040   40404040   40404040
003820  F0404040   40404040   40404040   40404040   40404040   40404040   40404040   40404040


                              ADDRESS OF ITEM        001F00
                       PLUS RELOCATION FACTOR        001900
                   YIELDS EFFECTIVE ADDRESS          003800
```

FIG. 6-16. Example of Compare Logical Characters.

```
 LOC   OBJECT CODE      ADDR1 ADDR2       NAME    OP    OPERANDS           COMMENT

                                              IMPERATIVES

001AB8 0540                                     BALR  4,0                SAVE CONDITION CODE
001ABA 95A1 3380           01F60      F6#17     CLI   BONE,161           COMPARE LOGICAL IMEDIATE
001ABE 0550                                     BALR  5,0                SAVE CONDITION CODE
001AC0 9045 33A0           01F80                STM   4,5,BSTORE2        SAVE REG. CONTENTS


                                              DECLARATIVES

001F60 A1                                BONE    DC    B'10100001'        F6#17
001F61 4040404040404040                          DC    CL31' '           FILLER
001F69 4040404040404040
001F71 4040404040404040
001F79 40404040404040
001F80 4040404040404040                  BSTORE2 DC    CL32' '            USED TO DISPLAY STORAGE
001F88 4040404040404040
001F90 4040404040404040
001F98 4040404040404040


                                        DUMP AFTER EXECUTION

003840  F0404040   40404040   40404040   40404040   40404040   40404040   40404040   40404040
003860  A1404040   40404040   40404040   40404040   40404040   40404040   40404040   40404040
003880  600033BA   400033C0   40404040   40404040   40404040   40404040   40404040   40404040
0038A0  F0404040   40404040   40404040   40404040   40404040   40404040   40404040   40404040


                              ADDRESS OF ITEM        001F80
                       PLUS RELOCATION FACTOR        001900
                   YIELDS EFFECTIVE ADDRESS          003880
```

FIG. 6-17. Example of Compare Logical Immediate.

CLI—Compare Logical Immediate. This SI command compares the one byte in storage named by the first-operand address with the one byte of data that is the second operand. This second operand is in the instruction itself. No alignment of the first operand is needed. This command sets the condition code. Improper addressing may cause interrupts. This command is available on all models of the computer. An example of Compare Logical Immediate is shown in Fig. 6-17.

Do It Now Exercise 6-8. *An input area in storage addressed by the name IN is to be checked for the presence of the letter A in EBCDIC code in the fifth position in the field. Prepare a flow diagram and write the declaratives and imperatives needed to make the comparison. Show the contents of storage and the resulting condition code, on the assumption that the field contains the following 16 characters: HERMXN HOLLERITH.*

CLCL—Compare Logical Characters Long. This RR command compares two operands in storage (not in the registers). Except for the condition code, this command is to Move Characters Long (presented in Chap. 4) as the Compare Logical Characters (CLC) is to the Move Characters (MVC) command. The addresses of the leftmost bytes of the two operands are specified in the named odd-numbered registers. The lengths of the fields compared are specified in the implied even-numbered registers. If the lengths are unequal, the computer extends the right end of the shorter operand by using the specified padding character, but the contents of storage remain unaltered. All combinations of bits are considered legal, and all bytes are treated as data bytes. This command sets the condition code but is available on only a few models of the computer. An example of Compare Logical Characters Long is shown in Fig. 6-18.

The programer must use two even-odd pairs of registers for designating the operands. In the instruction, the programer specifies only the even number of each pair; the use of the odd number is implied. The three low-order bytes of the even-numbered registers specify the absolute (binary) addresses of the variable (first operand) and constant (second operand) of the comparison. The three low-order bytes of the associated odd-numbered registers specify in binary the length in bytes of the respective operands. The leftmost byte of the second operand odd-numbered register (the register that specified its length) contains the padding character, which may be any bit combination. The leftmost bytes in the other registers are ignored.

As the computer executes the Compare Logical Characters Long, it changes the contents of all four registers by counting up the addresses and counting down the lengths toward zero, byte by byte, as it completes the comparison from left to right. But the comparison ceases as soon as the computer finds the operands to be unequal. When both operands have been counted down to (or specified as) zero length with no inequality detected, the computer treats the fields as equal. The contents of the registers indicate the last addresses compared and the lengths still uncompared when the comparison ceases.

```
LOC    OBJECT CODE      ADDR1 ADDR2  ST #  NAME   OP    OPERANDS                COMMENT

                                          IMPERATIVES

000036 91FF 30F8        00100         24          TM    FLD1,X'FF'              SET CONDITION CODE TO 11
00003A 0540                           25          BALR  4,0                     SAVE CONDITION CODE
00003C 9869 31F8        00200         26          LM    6,9,CONC                SET UP REGISTERS
000040 0F68                           27  F6#1R   CLCL  6,8                     COMPARE LOGICAL CHARACTERS LONG
000042 0550                           28          BALR  5,0                     SAVE CONDITION CODE
000044 9049 320R        00210         29          STM   4,9,BSAVE               SHOW REGISTER CONTENTS


                                          DECLARATIVES

000200 00000240                       96  CONC    DC    A(FLD5)                 ADDRESS OF VARIABLE FIELD
000204 00000013                       97          DC    X'00000013'             LENGTH OF VARIABLE FIELD
000208 00000260                       98          DC    A(FLD6)                 ADDRESS OF CONSTANT FIELD
00020C 40000014                       99          DC    X'40000014'             PAD CHAR. AND LENGTH
000210 4040404040404040              100  BSAVE   DC    CL48' '                 USED TO DISPLAY REGISTERS
000218 4040404040404040
000220 4040404040404040
000228 4040404040404040
000230 4040404040404040
000238 4040404040404040
000240 C1D9C540E3C8C5E2              101  FLD5    DC    L'ARE THESE THE SAME?'  VARIABLE OF COMPARISON
000248 C540E3C8C540E2C1
000250 D4C56F
000253 FFFFFFFFFFFFFFFF              102          DC    13X'FF'                 FILLER
00025B FFFFFFFFF
000260 C1D9C540E3C8C5E2              103  FLD6    DC    C'ARE THESE DIFFERENT?' CONSTANT OF COMPARISON
000268 C540C4C9C6C6C5D9
000270 C5D5E36F
000274 FFFFFFFFFFFFFFFF              104          DC    12X'FF'                 FILLER
00027C FFFFFFFF


                                       DUMP AFTER EXECUTION

0069F0 F0404040    40404040    40404040    40404040    40404040    40404040    40404040    40404040
006A00 00006A40    00000013    00006A60    40000014    50006R3C    60006844    0000644A    00000009
006A20 00006A6A    4000000A    40404040    40404040    40404040    40404040    40404040    40404040
006A40 C1D9C540    E3C8C5E2    C540E3C8    C540E2C1    D4C56FFF    FFFFFFFF    FFFFFFFF    FFFFFFFF
006A60 C1D9C540    E3C8C5E2    C540C4C9    C6C6C5D9    C5D5E36F    FFFFFFFF    FFFFFFFF    FFFFFFFF
006A80 F0404040    40404040    40404040    40404040    40404040    40404040    40404040    40404040


                              ADDRESS OF ITEM         000240
                     PLUS RELOCATION FACTOR           006R00
                  YIELDS EFFECTIVE ADDRESS            006A40
```

FIG. 6-18. Example of Compare Logical Characters Long.

Compare Logical Characters Long is subject to being interrupted and later resumed. Upon interrupt, the old PSW stored shows the address of the CLCL as if it had never been executed at all, but the register contents reflect the comparison work still to be done when the PSW is reloaded and execution resumed. For this reason, the programer must take care to protect the contents of the two pairs of registers. If some other program requires knowledge of whether or not a CLCL was completed, the programer may have to set a switch, or a status bit for a Test Under Mask as an indicator, just as with a MVCL.

Compare Logical Characters Long is also subject to specification, addressing, and protection interrupts. For specification errors in the use of the registers, the computer suppresses the operation. For addressing unavailable addresses or protected addresses when both lengths are nonzero, the computer terminates the operation if it encounters those addresses as it counts up the contents of the address registers. An attempt to resume the interrupted operation again results in an interruption.

TRANSFER OF CONTROL

As a result of performing operations that set the condition code, the programer can have the computer take alternative action. This the programer does by having the computer test the state of the condition code and then either continue in sequence to the next instruction or jump to some other place in the program to begin executing a different series of instructions. The process of testing the condition code to ascertain its status does *not* alter the condition code.

The transfer of control takes its name from the way in which the computer determines which instruction to execute next. The computer is designed so that normally the instructions to be executed are taken one after the other sequentially from storage. When this normal operating sequence occurs, the control is said to pass from one instruction to the next in sequence. This is the normal sequence of control. When, however, the computer gets (fetches) the next instruction to be executed from some different address in storage (not the next sequential instruction after the previous one), then a transfer of control is said to take place. This is diagramed in Fig. 6-19.

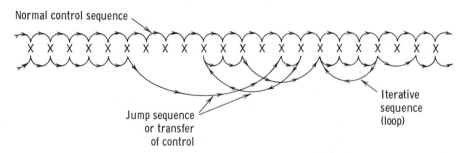

FIG. 6-19. Control-sequence patterns in the computer.

If, while executing instructions in the normal sequence, the computer encounters an instruction that tells it to deviate from this normal sequence, then a transfer of control occurs. The instruction that tells the computer to take its next instruction from some place other than the next sequential instruction address is therefore referred to as a transfer-of-control instruction.

The two types of transfer-of-control instruction are the conditional and the unconditional. For an unconditional transfer of control, the computer ignores conditions and simply executes a transfer of control. For a conditional transfer of control the computer, by contrast, executes the transfer of control only if the particular con-

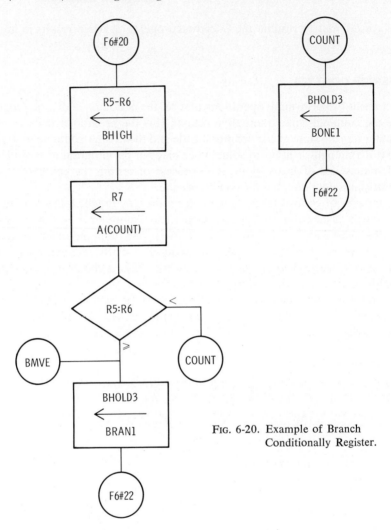

FIG. 6-20. Example of Branch Conditionally Register.

dition described be met. If this condition be met, then the transfer of control occurs. If it be not met, the normal control sequence prevails—i.e., control goes to the next sequential instruction. An unconditional transfer of control—or a conditional transfer that does take place—is sometimes called a "branch" or "jump." A conditional transfer of control that is not executed because the condition specified is not met is sometimes called a "drop through" or a "no operation." Note that a transfer operation is a program-control operation, and not a conventional data-movement or data-rearrangement operation.

```
 LOC  OBJECT CODE      ADDR1 ADDR2      NAME    OP    OPERANDS            COMMENT
                                          IMPERATIVES

001AC4 9856 3400             01FE0              LM    5,6,BHIGH          LOAD REGISTERS
001AC8 0590                                     BALR  9,0                SAVE CONDITION CODE
001ACA 5870 2148             01B94              L     7,=A(COUNT)        LOAD REG. WITH ADDRESS OF  COUNT
001ACE 1556                                     CLR   5,6                COMPARE LOGICAL - REG.
001AD0 05A0                                     BALR  10,0               SAVE CONDITION CODE
001AD2 0747              F6#20                   BCR   4,7                BRANCH TO ADDRESS IN REG. 7 IF
                                *                                        CONDITION 4 IS MET
001AD4 D201 342C 3408 0200C 01FE8  BMVE   MVC   BHOLD3+12(2),BRAN1       BRAN1  WILL EQ= 1 IF COND. 4 WAS
                                *                                        MET. IF IT WAS NOT MET THEN
                                *                                        BRAN1  WILL EQ. 0
001ADA 909A 3420             02000              BMVEZ STM   9,10,BHOLD3   SAVE CONDITION CODE
001ADE 47F0 20A0             01AEC              BC    15,F6#22           BRANCH TO NEXT FIGURE
001AE2 D201 342C 340A 0200C 01FEA  COUNT  MVC   BHOLD3+12(2),BONE1       ADDRESS IN REG. 7
001AE8 47F0 208E             01ADA              BC    15,BMVEZ           BRANCH


                                          DECLARATIVES

001FE0 000C122C                        BHIGH   DC    F'791084'           F6#20
001FE4 FFFE6FDC                                DC    F'-102436'
001FE8 000C                            BRAN1   DC    PL2'0'
001FEA 001C                            BONE1   DC    PL2'1'
001FEC 4040404040404040                        DC    CL20' '             FILLER
001FF4 4040404040404040
001FFC 40404040
002000 4040404040404040      BHOLD3   DC    CL32' '             USED TO DISPLAY STORAGE
002008 4040404040404040
002010 4040404040404040
002018 4040404040404040


                                       DUMP AFTER EXECUTION

0038C0 F0404040    40404040   40404040   40404040    40404040   40404040   40404040   40404040
0038E0 000C122C    FFFE6FDC   000C001C   40404040    40404040   40404040   40404040   40404040
003900 400033CA    500033D2   40404040   000C4040    40404040   40404040   40404040   40404040
003920 F0404040    40404040   40404040   40404040    40404040   40404040   40404040   40404040


                          ADDRESS OF ITEM      002000
                   PLUS RELOCATION FACTOR      001900
               YIELDS EFFECTIVE ADDRESS        003900
```

FIG. 6-20 *(continued)*

Code	Mnemonic	Name of condition
0	NOP	No Operation (No Branch)
1	BO	Branch Ones; Branch Overflow
2	BH	Branch High
2	BP	Branch Plus; Branch Positive
4	BL	Branch Low
4	BM	Branch Minus; Branch Mixed
7	BNE	Branch Not Equal
8	BE	Branch Equal
8	BZ	Branch Zero; Branch Zeros
11	BNL	Branch Not Low
13	BNH	Branch Not High
15	B	Branch Unconditionally; Branch Any Condition

FIG. 6-21. Codes for transfer-of-control conditions.

TRANSFER OPERATIONS

To make programing more convenient, the computer has a number of specialized transfer-of-control operations. Some of these combine a transfer of control with a comparison in one instruction. Others combine a transfer of control with a comparison and arithmetic operation done in a register. Thus one instruction may do two or three operations needed in program-control work. Also, the computer has a provision for storing control-sequence addresses in registers (so they can be used as base registers) at the time a transfer of control takes place.

BCR—Branch Conditionally Register. This RR command specifies as its second-operand address the register which contains the address of the first instruction of a series of instructions to be executed. The first operand is not a register address, but is a number as defined below under Branch Conditionally, which specifies the condition to be met. If the condition be met, a transfer of control takes place; if not, a no operation occurs. The condition code remains unchanged in either case. No interrupts can arise from improper addressing. This command is available for all models of the computer. An example of Branch Conditionally Register is shown in Fig. 6-20. Note that the contents of the branch register must be set in advance of executing the transfer of control.

BC—Branch Conditionally. This RX command causes a transfer of control to be made to the second-operand address if the condition specified as the first operand be met. The condition is specified usually as a decimal number from 0 through 15. The significance of these number combinations is shown in Fig. 6-21. As the table indicates, condition 0 directs the computer to ignore all conditions, and condition 15 directs the computer to accept any and all conditions. Thus condition 0 is a no operation; condition 15 is an unconditional transfer. Conditions 2, 4, and 8, are high, low, and equal, respectively. Conditions 13, 11, and 7, are not high, not low, and not equal, respectively. A branch on arithmetic overflow is specified by condition 1. The condition code remains unchanged. No interrupts can arise from improper addressing. This command is available for all models of the computer. An example of Branch Conditionally is shown in Fig. 6-22.

Do It Now Exercise 6-9. Using the data from Do It Now Exercise 6-8, prepare a flow diagram, and write any needed instructions to replace the character with the letter A if it is not already the letter A. Keep the operation simple.

The choice of numbers to designate the conditions is not without rhyme or reason. The underlying logic is this. The four condition codes can be considered to be enumerated as 0, 1, 2, and 3, as shown in Fig. 6-23. These can be, in turn, matched

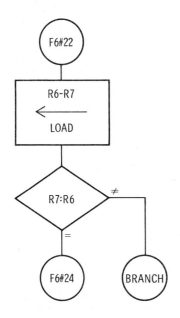

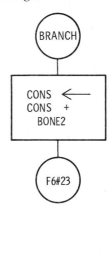

FIG. 6-22. Example of Branch Conditionally.

```
   LOC   OBJECT CODE     ADDR1 ADDR2      NAME    OP    OPERANDS         COMMENT
                                          IMPERATIVES

001AEC  9867 34E0             020C0       F6#22   LM    6,7,LOAD         LOAD REG.
001AF0  0540                                      BALR  4,0              SAVE CONDITION CODE
001AF2  1976                                      CR    7,6              COMPARE REGISTERS
001AF4  0550                                      BALR  5,0              SAVE CONDITION CODE
001AF6  4770 20B6             01B02               BC    7,BRANCH         BRANCH ON COND. 7 TO BRANCH
001AFA  9045 3500             020E0       BMOVE   STM   4,5,BSAVE3       SAVE REG. CONTENTS
001AFE  47F0 20C0             01B0C               BC    15,F6#24         BRANCH TO F6#23
001B02  FA10 34E8 34EA  020C8 020CA       BRANCH  AP    CONS,BONE2       ADD 1 TO 'CONS' IF COND. 7 WAS MET
001B08  47F0 20AE             01AFA               B     BMOVE            BRANCH TO BMOVE



                                          DECLARATIVES

0020C0  0041C7C5                          LOAD    DC    F'4310981'       F6#22
0020C4  04DD8CFA                                  DC    F'81628410'
0020C8  000C                              CONS    DC    PL2'0'           ONE IS ADDED TO 'CONS' IF THE
                                          *                              COMPARE IS NOT EQUAL AND THE PROGRAM
                                          *                              BRANCHES TO BRANCH
0020CA  1C                                BONE2   DC    P'1'
0020CB  4040404040404040                          DC    CL21' '         FILLER
0020D3  4040404040404040
0020DB  4040404040
0020E0  4040404040404040                  BSAVE3  DC    CL32' '         USED TO DISPLAY STORAGE
0020E8  4040404040404040
0020F0  4040404040404040
0020F8  4040404040404040



                                          DUMP AFTER EXECUTION

0039A0  F0404040   40404040   40404040   40404040   40404040   40404040   40404040   40404040
0039C0  0041C7C5   04DD8CFA   001C1C40   40404040   40404040   40404040   40404040   40404040
0039E0  500033F2   600033F6   40404040   40404040   40404040   40404040   40404040   40404040
003A00  F0404040   40404040   40404040   40404040   40404040   40404040   40404040   40404040



                   ADDRESS OF ITEM           0020E0
            PLUS RELOCATION FACTOR           001900
            YIELDS EFFECTIVE ADDRESS         0039E0
```

Equal or zero	Low or minus or mixed	High or plus	Overflow or ones	Result of comparison, test, or arithmetic operations
0	1	2	3	Condition code in decimal
8	4	2	1	BCD place values for hexadecimal

FIG. 6-23. Basis of the transfer-of-control codes.

against a hexadecimal character whose value would be 8, 4, 2, or 1, respectively, according to the decimal values of the four bit positions. Thus a 1 bit in the 8 position would indicate that condition 0 be satisfied ("equal").

For the small models of the computer, the programer is required to use numbers to indicate the condition to be met. Among the other models of the computer, however, and as a convenience for the programer writing in assembly language, the condition indications can usually be combined with the command into what is referred to as an "extended mnemonic," actually a macrocommand. When the macro or extended mnemonic is used, the first operand disappears; the programer uses only the second operand in the instruction. That operand specifies the address to which a transfer of control is to be made if the condition specified is met.

Figure 6-21 summarizes the permissible mnemonics. Note especially the following meanings of the letters and combinations: NOP—No Operation, for condition 0; B—Branch, for condition 15 (the unconditional transfer of control); H—High; L—Low; E—Equal; and N—Not.

As an additional convenience for the programer, the extended mnemonics have been augmented to cover the case of transfer after arithmetic operations, as shown also in Fig. 6-21: O—Overflow; P—Plus; M—Minus, and Z—Zero. An example of two extended mnemonics is given in Fig. 6-24.

Do It Now Exercise 6-10. *Using the data from Do It Now Exercise 6-8, prepare a flow diagram for a routine to have the computer determine and replace the letter in the fifth position if it is from A through I with the letter A, from J through R with the letter J, and from S through Z with the letter S. If any other character be encountered, then the digit 9 is to be inserted. Assume that the input field is in EBCDIC. Using the extended mnemonics, write the imperatives and declaratives needed to implement the routine.*

ITERATION CONTROL

BCTR—Branch on Count Register. This RR command operates in the same ways as the BCT command noted below, except that the second-operand address names a register which contains the absolute address to which the transfer of control is to be made.

BCT—Branch on Count. This RX command combines an arithmetic operation, a comparison operation, and a conditional transfer of control. It does not alter or test the condition code. The contents of the register named as the first-operand address are decremented by 1 and then tested. If the contents are nonzero, control transfers to the second-operand address. No interrupts can occur from improper addressing or from arithmetic errors. This command is not available on small models of the computer. An example of Branch on Count is shown in Fig. 6-25.

The first-operand register is assumed to contain a binary number. The second operand names a transfer-of-control address. Each time the computer executes the command, it subtracts binary 1 from the contents of the register named as the first operand. Afterward the computer tests the contents of that register. If that register then contains binary 0, control drops through to the next instruction in sequence. If the register contains any other contents, be they positive or negative, then control goes to the transfer-of-control address named as the second operand.

A major use of Branch on Count is to control the number of times the computer is to execute a loop of instructions. The initialization for the loop includes loading a binary number into a register to represent the number of times the computer is to execute the loop. Control then enters the loop at the entry point, which is a place such that the computer executes all the operations in the loop once, ending with the exit test. The exit test can be the BCT instruction. The second operand in that instruction is the address of the return or re-entry point. The first operand is the register that was loaded during the initialization.

Consider the example flow-diagramed in Fig. 6-26 and coded in Fig. 6-27. If a number ("LACE") is to be added to itself 6 times, then the initialization of the loop consists of loading a register (in this case, register 4) with the binary number 6, and another register with the contents of LACE. An unconditional transfer of control can then be made, if necessary, as a loop entry. At the entry point in the loop, as shown in Fig. 6-26, the computer adds the number to itself. Then the Branch on Count instruction serves as the loop exit test. If the contents of the count register 4 are not yet equal to zero, then the computer transfers control back to the entry point of the loop. Each time the computer executes the Branch on Count instruction, the computer reduces by 1 the contents of register 4. Hence, after executing the loop of instructions 6 times, the computer will make the contents of the register equal to 0. Hence, on that sixth time, control drops through to the next instruction and hence results in an exit from the loop.

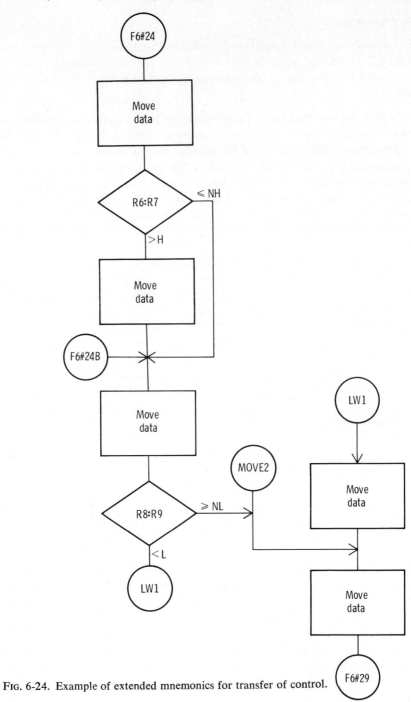

FIG. 6-24. Example of extended mnemonics for transfer of control.

A "leading-decisions" approach offers an interesting alternative. To use it, the programer must make two changes. First, the register named as the first operand must be loaded with a number one greater than the number of times the computer is to execute the loop. Second, the original entry point to the loop is the exit test, and the re-entry or return point is different (see Fig. 6-28). Typically, the leading-decisions approach requires the computer to execute more instructions and the programer to do more writing than is necessary for the ordinary approach, and this is a disadvantage. For example, compare Figs. 6-27 and 6-29.

The major advantage of the leading-decisions approach is its conservatism— the computer does not execute instructions without first verifying that they should be executed. That is, the computer tests whether or not an operation should be done before attempting it. Especially in long programs, this approach simplifies debugging by reducing the numbers of iteration errors likely to be made.

```
  LOC   OBJECT CODE     ADDR1 ADDR2      NAME    OP    OPERANDS              COMMENT

                                             IMPERATIVES

000006  9867 303F              000A0     F6#24   LM    6,7,BCOMP             LOAD REGISTERS
00000A  0540                                     BALR  4,0                   SAVE CONDITION CODE
00000C  1967                                     CR    6,7                   COMPARE REG.
00000E  0550                                     BALR  5,0                   SAVE CONDITION CODE
000010  47D0 2018              0001A             BNH   FIG23B
000014  D200 3063 3047   000C4 000A8             MVC   BKEEP4+4(1),ONE2
00001A  9889 3048              000AC     FIG24B  LM    8,9,BCOMP1
00001E  0560                                     BALR  6,0                   SAVE CONDITION CODE
000020  1989                            COMPAR   CR    8,9                   COMPARE REG
000022  0570                                     BALR  7,0                   SAVE CONDITION CODE
000024  4740 202E              00030             BL    LW1                   IF LOW BRANCH TO LW1
000028  9047 3067              000C8     MOVE2   STM   4,7,BKEEP4+8          SAVE CONDITION CODES
00002C  47F0 2038              0003A             B     F6#29                 BRANCH TO F6#28
000030  D200 305F 3047   000C0 000A8     LW1     MVC   BKEEP4(1),ONE2        MOVE 'ONE2' TO BKEEP4 IF THE COND.
                                           *                                 WAS HIGH
000036  47F0 2026              00028             B     MOVE2                 BRANCH TO MOVE2


                                             DECLARATIVES

0000A0  000F20B0                         BCOMP   DC    F'991408'             F6#24A
0000A4  0001AD2B                                 DC    F'109867'             FILLER
0000A8  1C                               ONE2    DC    P'1'                  FILLER
0000A9  404040                                   DC    3C' '                 FILLER
0000AC  0025958A                         BCOMP1  DC    F'2463114'            F6#24B
0000B0  00256A8E                                 DC    F'2452110'            FILLER
0000B4  4040404040404040                         DC    12C' '                FILLER
0000BC  40404040
0000C0  4040404040404040                 BKEEP4  DC    32C' '                USED TO DISPLAY STORAGE
0000C8  4040404040404040
0000D0  4040404040404040
0000D8  4040404040404040


                                             DUMP AFTER EXECUTION

001980  F0404040   40404040   40404040   40404040   40404040   40404040   40404040   40404040
0019A0  000F20B0   0001AD2B   1C404040   0025958A   00256A8E   40404040   40404040   40404040
0019C0  40404040   1C404040   4000190C   60001910   60001920   60001924   40404040   40404040
0019E0  F0404040   40404040   40404040   40404040   40404040   40404040   40404040   40404040


                            ADDRESS OF ITEM          0000C0
                     PLUS RELOCATION FACTOR          001900
                    YIELDS EFFECTIVE ADDRESS         0019C0
```

FIG. 6-24. *(continued)*

```
      LOC   OBJECT CODE    ADDR1 ADDR2      NAME    OP    OPERANDS              COMMENT

                                              IMPERATIVES

    001B32  5860 3660       02240                    L     6,CNTZ               LOAD 5 INTO REG.
    001B36  4660 20EA       01B36            F6#25   BCT   6,F6#25              EXECUTE 5 TIMES
    001B3A  5060 3668       02248                    ST    6,CNTZ+8             SAVE DECREMENTED COUNT


                                              DECLARATIVES

    002240  00000005                         CNTZ    DC    F'5'                 F6#25 COUNT
    002244  4040404040404040                         DC    CL28' '              SAVE AREA
    00224C  4040404040404040
    002254  4040404040404040
    00225C  40404040


                                          DUMP AFTER EXECUTION

    003B20  F0404040   40404040   40404040   40404040   40404040   40404040   40404040   40404040
    003B40  00000005   40404040   00000000   40404040   40404040   40404040   40404040   40404040
    003B60  F0404040   40404040   40404040   40404040   40404040   40404040   40404040   40404040


                             ADDRESS OF ITEM        002240
                     PLUS RELOCATION FACTOR         001900
                     YIELDS EFFECTIVE ADDRESS       003840
```

FIG. 6-25. Example of Branch on Count.

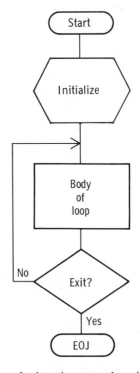

FIG. 6-26. Flow diagram for iteration example, using traditional approach.

```
    LOC   OBJECT CODE      ADDR1 ADDR2       NAME    OP    OPERANDS              COMMENT

                                                   IMPERATIVES

  001B4C  4840 36C0           022A0          F6#27   LH    4,STR                LOAD REG. WITH COUNT
  001B50  1B55                                       SR    5,5                  CLEAR REG. 5 TO ZEROS
  001B52  4A50 36C2           022A2          ENTER   AH    5,LACE               ADD 'LACE' TO REG. 5
  001B56  4640 2106           01852                  BCT   4,ENTER              BRANCH ON COUNT
  001B5A  9045 36E0           022C0                  STM   4,5,BSTORE3          SAVE REG. CONTENTS


                                                   DECLARATIVES

  0022A0  0006                               STR     DC    H'6'                 F6#27
  0022A2  0014                               LACE    DC    H'20'
  0022A4  404040404040404040                         DC    CL28' '              FILLER
  0022AC  404040404040404040
  0022B4  404040404040404040
  0022BC  40404040
  0022C0  404040404040404040             978 BSTORE3 DC    CL32' '              USED TO DISPLAY STORAGE
  0022C8  404040404040404040
  0022D0  404040404040404040
  0022D8  404040404040404040


                                             DUMP AFTER EXECUTION

  003B80  F0404040  40404040  40404040  40404040  40404040  40404040  40404040  40404040
  003BA0  00060014  40404040  40404040  40404040  40404040  40404040  40404040  40404040
  003BC0  00000000  00000078  40404040  40404040  40404040  40404040  40404040  40404040
  003BE0  F0404040  40404040  40404040  40404040  40404040  40404040  40404040  40404040


                                    ADDRESS OF ITEM         0022C0
                            PLUS RELOCATION FACTOR          001900
                           YIELDS EFFECTIVE ADDRESS         003BC0
```

FIG. 6-27. Coding for iteration example, using traditional approach.

Do It Now Exercise 6-11. Prepare a flow diagram for a routine to have the computer subtract in packed-decimal the equivalent of $+2.78$ four times from the equivalent of $+66.37$, using the traditional approach. Write the declaratives and imperatives needed to implement the routine, using the Branch on Count command. Show the starting and resulting contents of storage. Then re-do the diagram and coding, using the leading-decisions approach.

BALR—Branch and Lir◊ Register. This RR command has two operands. The first-operand address names the register that is to be loaded with the address of the next instruction in sequence. The second-operand address names the register that holds the absolute address to which a transfer of control is to be made unconditionally. The computer copies the condition code into the third and fourth bits of the leftmost byte of the first-operand register. If the second operand be shown as 0, then a no operation follows the register loading instead of an unconditional transfer of control—i.e., control drops through. With a nonzero second operand, this command is used for linkage to subroutines, at the same time saving in a register the address of the next instruction in sequence (the return address). With a zero second operand, it is used to set the contents of a base register. As such, it serves as the imperative companion to the USING declarative, especially at the start of a program or control section. This command is not subject to interruption; it is not available on

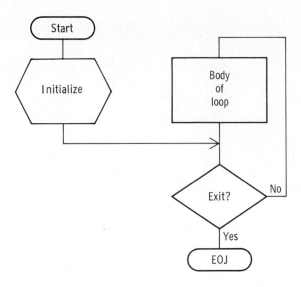

FIG. 6-28. Flow diagram for iteration example, using leading-decisions approach.

```
   LOC   OBJECT CODE    ADDR1 ADDR2      NAME    OP   OPERANDS        COMMENT

                                            IMPERATIVES

 00003A 5860 30BF          00120        F6#29    L    6,STR1          LOAD REG. WITH COUNT
 00003E 1B77                                     SR   7,7             CLEAR REG. 7 TO ZEROS
 000040 47F0 2046          00048                 B    PIG             BRANCH TO PIG
 000044 4A70 30C1          00122        ENTER1   AH   7,LACE1         ADD 'LACE1' TO REG. 7
 000048 4660 2042          00044        PIG      BCT  6,ENTER1        BRANCH ON COUNT
 00004C 9067 30DF          00140                 STM  6,7,BHOLD4      SAVE REG. CONTENTS


                                            DECLARATIVES

 000120 0007                            STR1     DC   H'7'            F6#29
 000122 0014                            LACE1    DC   H'20'           FILLER
 000124 4040404040404040                         DC   CL28' '         FILLER
 00012C 4040404040404040
 000134 4040404040404040
 00013C 40404040
 000140 4040404040404040   BHOLD4    DC    CL32' '            USED TO DISPLAY STORAGE
 000148 4040404040404040
 000150 4040404040404040
 000158 4040404040404040


                                        DUMP AFTER EXECUTION

 001A00 F0404040  40404040   40404040   40404040    40404040  40404040    40404040   40404040
 001A20 00070014  40404040   40404040   40404040    40404040  40404040    40404040   40404040
 001A40 00000000  008C017C   40404040   40404040    40404040  40404040    40404040   40404040
 001A60 F0404040  40404040   40404040   40404040    40404040  40404040    40404040   40404040


                           ADDRESS OF ITEM     000140
               PLUS RELOCATION FACTOR     001900
            YIELDS EFFECTIVE ADDRESS      001A40
```

FIG. 6-29. Coding for iteration example, using leading-decisions approach.

LOC	OBJECT CODE	ADDR1 ADDR2	NAME	OP	OPERANDS	COMMENT
				IMPERATIVES		
000FD4	0700			CNOP	6,8	CONDITIONAL NO OPERATION
000FD6	0530		F6#30	BALR	3,0	SET BASE REGISTER
000FD8				USING	*,3	NOTIFY COMPILER OF BASE REGISTER

FIG. 6-30. Example of Branch and Link Register.

the small models of the computer, and operates differently on some large models. An example with a CNOP and a USING is shown in Fig. 6-30.

Do It Now Exercise 6-12. Write the declaratives and imperatives necessary to start a program with a named control section that is to use register 7 as a base register. Be sure to provide the correct contents of the base register (a double-word boundary address).

BAL—Branch and Link. This RX command is parallel to Branch and Link Register. The first-operand address names the register which will be loaded with the address of the next instruction in sequence. The second-operand address names an address in storage to which a transfer of control is to be made unconditionally. A major use of this command is for saving the address to which a return is to be made when transferring (branching) to execute a subroutine. It also saves the condition code in the third and fourth bits in the leftmost byte of the register. This command is not subject to interruption and is not available on the small models of the computer. Note that the data loaded into the register are a copy of the right half of the program status word (PSW) as described in Chap. 8.

Do It Now Exercise 6-13. Prepare a flow diagram for a routine to save a copy of the condition code as the rightmost bits of one byte of 0 bits (00_x) in storage. Write the declaratives and imperatives needed to implement the routine.

BASR—Branch and Store in Register. This RR command causes the address of the next sequential instruction (part of the program status word) to be stored in the register named as the first-operand address. At the same time, the contents of the second-operand address are copied to become the new address of the new next sequential instruction. If this second-operand register contain all binary zero bits, the address of the next sequential instruction remains unchanged. This command does not alter the condition code and is not subject to interruption. It is available only on the small models of the computer, and for them replaces the BALR command. An example of BASR is given in Fig. 6-31.

BAS—Branch and Store. This RX command operates in the same way as the BASR command previously described, except that the second-operand address names a place in storage which must be aligned on the half word. No indexing is permitted, even though the command is of the RX format.

NAME	OP	OPERANDS	COMMENT
F6#31	BASR	8,9	BRANCH TO CONTENTS OF REG. 9

FIG. 6-31. Example of Branch and Store Register.

INDEXING

The computer provides two ways for handling what are known as index operations. One of these is by means of the RX group of commands which incorporate a specific provision for indexing. The other is by means of altering the contents of base registers in a systematic fashion. Both of these methods are worthy of some attention at this point.

The major limitation on using the RX commands for indexing is that they apply primarily to load register, store register, and binary arithmetic operations. When one is working with data in binary formats, the RX commands provide a convenient way of having the computer perform indexing operations. However, when the programer is working with data in character and packed-decimal formats, the programer finds the indexing capability of the RX commands virtually useless, since all of the character and packed-decimal operations use SS or SI commands. In such cases, if the programer desires to have indexing performed, he must do it by means of altering the contents of base registers. In practice, this is the major method available in the small models of the computer, since the packed-decimal operations are the major arithmetic capability provided.

The situations in which programers find indexing convenient to use are those which involve data arranged in storage in a systematic and symmetric pattern. Consider, for example, having a large number of prices stored in the computer in the form of a table of prices and associated product numbers. If the product number occupies one full word of storage, if the price occupies the adjoining full word in storage, and if each pair occupies an aligned double word in storage, then indexing provides a convenient way of locating and utilizing prices from the table.

The way the programer uses RX commands depends upon the computer's use of base-and-displacement addressing. As noted earlier, the computer calculates the effective absolute address for an operand by adding the displacement amount to the contents specified for the base register. For RX commands, however, one additional factor is added: the contents of the index register. In order to be able to specify the absence of indexing, general register 0 may not be used as an index register, because 0 is the indication to the computer that no indexing is to be performed. Therefore any register except register zero can be used as an index register. Index amounts must be in the binary format, as positive numbers with no explicit sign.

Consider first a simpler form of this price-table situation. Assume that five prices only are in storage in consecutive full words, with no product numbers. Assume that the programer desires to copy out the third and fourth prices. Since the count of the number of items starts with 0, the items desired are numbers 2 and 3. Hence, the programer can load a register with a 2 to access the first price. Then since each price in the table occupies 4 bytes, the programer can have the computer multiply (as by a shift) the position desired (2) by the length of an item (4) to get the index amount (8 bytes). Then he can have the computer load the desired prices, as shown in Fig. 6-32.

Consider now the double-word table originally described of the product numbers and prices. Thus, for example, if the programer in this price-table example wished to obtain the fifteenth price from the table, where the displacement and base register together give the address of the first byte of the table, then he could specify in a register a quantity that was 8 times 14. The first double word in storage for purposes of the table counts as double word 0. Hence, the fifteenth double word in the table counts as double word 14. Since each double word is composed of eight bytes, the double-word count must be multiplied by the number of bytes in a double word to obtain the number of bytes from the beginning of the table to the start of the double word of table data sought. Hence, if the programer loads the product of 8 times 14 into a register (this is easily done by load and shift operations), the programer can then utilize this product as an index amount by specifying that register as the index register.

If, in the situation at hand, the base and displacement together are known by the symbolic name TABLE, the programer can cause the computer to load any available register—for example, register 9—with a full word or half word of data representing in binary the quantity 14, shift this left by 3 bit positions, and then have the computer perform 2 loads into a pair of registers, such as 10 and 11, from the address table indexed by the contents of register 9. Thus, as has been illustrated, indexing in effect adds another level of displacment addressing to the displacement addressing already available.

Do It Now Exercise 6-14. *Starting with the flow diagram in Fig. 6-32, prepare a new flow diagram for getting data from the double-word price table described in the text, assuming the table has 20 entries in it. From your diagram and Fig. 6-32, write a routine to load into registers 10 and 11, respectively, the fifteenth product number and price. Hint: For easy checking, assign each price a number 256 more than the product number, and make the product numbers run consecutively in sequence from 1 through 20.*

The significance of this is perhaps most conveniently illustrated by an example. Consider the case in which 13 binary numbers in storage occupy 13 successive half words, beginning at the symbolic address STZ. The programer wants to write one brief routine to have the computer find the sum in binary of these 13 numbers, plac- in the sum in storage as SUM. One approach to this task is diagramed in Fig. 6-33.

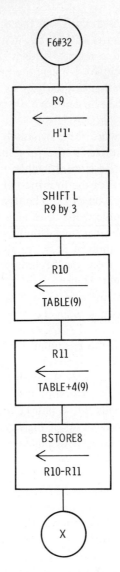

FIG. 6-32. Example of indexed operation. The number enclosed in parentheses is the index register designation.

The initialization consists of clearing the register in which the summing is to be done, loading the value in the count register, and setting the index register to zero as its starting value. The loop itself consists of the addition and the index increment. The exit test is a Branch on Count operation. The cleanup consists of storing the sum. The entire program is shown in complete form in Fig. 6-34.

LOC	OBJECT CODE	ADDR1	ADDR2	NAME	OP	OPERANDS	COMMENT
				IMPERATIVES			
001B74	4890 2150	01B9C		F6#32	LH	9,=H'2'	
001B78	8B90 0002	00002			SLA	9,2	SHIFT REG. TO OBTAIN CORRECT INDEX
001B7C	58A9 37A0	02380			L	10,TABLE(9)	LOAD REG. USING INDEXING.
001B80	58B9 37A4	02384			L	11,TABLE+4(9)	LOAD A REG. USING INDEXING
001B84	909B 3820	02400			STM	9,11,BSTORE8	SAVE REG. CONTENTS

LOC	OBJECT CODE	ADDR1	ADDR2	NAME	OP	OPERANDS	COMMENT
				DECLARATIVES			
002380	001F5E76			TABLE	DC	F'2055798'	F6#32
002384	00016377				DC	F'90999'	
002388	0B0BEA09				DC	F'185330185'	
00238C	0065A23A				DC	F'6660666'	
002390	00003046				DC	F'12358'	
002394	4040404040404040				DC	12C' '	
00239C	40404040						
002400	4040404040404040			BSTORE8	DC	CL32' '	
002408	4040404040404040						
002410	4040404040404040						
002418	4040404040404040						

DUMP AFTER EXECUTION

003C60	F0404040	40404040	40404040	40404040	40404040	40404040	40404040	40404040
003C80	001F5E76	00016377	0B0BEA09	0065A23A	00003046	40404040	40404040	40404040
003CA0	00000000	008C017C	40404040	40404040	40404040	40404040	40404040	40404040
003CC0	F0404040	40404040	40404040	40404040	40404040	40404040	40404040	40404040
003CE0	F0404040	40404040	40404040	40404040	40404040	40404040	40404040	40404040
003D00	00000008	0B0BEA09	0065A23A	40404040	40404040	40404040	40404040	40404040
003D20	F0404040	40404040	40404040	40404040	40404040	40404040	40404040	40404040

ADDRESS OF ITEM	002380	002400
PLUS RELOCATION FACTOR	001900	001900
YIELDS EFFECTIVE ADDRESS	003C80	003D00

FIG. 6-32 *(continued)*

A program begins with a START declarative to identify to the compiler program that an assembly is being begun. The CSECT declarative identifies and names the first and, in this case, only control section in the program. The BALR imperative loads register 2 for use as a base register. A name must be given to the BALR because it is the first imperative operation in the program to be executed, and serves therefore as the control entry point for the program. The USING declarative informs the compiler program of the intended use of register 2 as a base register and specifies the contents as being the address of the next imperative instruction in sequence. This agrees with the data to be loaded into the register by the preceding BALR imperative.

The initialization for the loop consists of several parts. Loading hexadecimal 0s into the registers clears them. Loading the register for the Branch on Count operation comes next, with the number 14 being loaded (since the leading-decisions approach is followed in this example). Control then transfers unconditionally to the exit test in the loop. If the initialization be correct, the count will be nonzero and control will transfer to the re-entry point in the loop. Since the index register is 0 for the first iteration, the computer will add the first number. Then the computer increments the index register by adding 2 (since the data are in half words). Then the exit test is repeated. In this manner the computer will execute one addition instruction 13 times, each time using a different operand. This is summarized in Fig. 6-35.

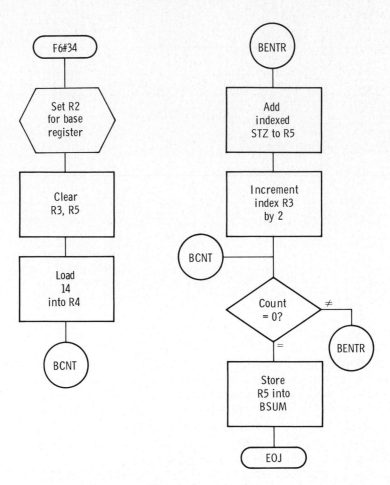

FIG. 6-33. Flow diagram for indexing, using index registers.

***Do It Now* Exercise 6-15.** *Prepare a flow diagram for a complete program to have the computer place in successive full words of storage the binary numbers 1 through 31. Use the Branch on Count command, and use indexing. Prepare a table showing the anticipated contents of storage ("storage map") on the assumption that the contents of storage before execution in the area defined by the DS to receive the 31 words will contain blanks. Write the imperatives and declaratives for ("code") the program.*

```
  LOC   OBJECT CODE        ADDR1 ADDR2   ST #   NAME    OP      OPERANDS                              COMMENT

002AE8                                   1261   F6#34   CSECT
002AE8  070007000700                     1262           CNOP    6,8
002AEE  0520                             1263   BFRST   BALR    2,0
002AF0                                   1264           USING   *,2
002AF0  5830 2030          02820         1265           L       3,=F'0'                               CLEAR A REGISTER BY
002AF4  5850 2030          02820         1266           L       5,=F'0'                               A LITERAL
002AF8  4840 2038          02828         1267           LH      4,=H'14'                              LOAD A REG. USING A LITERAL
002AFC  47F0 2018          02808         1268           BC      15,BCNT
002B00  4A53 2050          02840         1269   BNTER   AH      5,STZ(3)                              USE REG. 3 TO INDEX 'STZ'. USING A
                                         1270   *                                                     REG. TO INDEX A SERIES IS POSSIBLE
                                         1271   *                                                     ONLY ON RX OPERATIONS.
002B04  4A30 203A          02B2A         1272           AH      3,=H'2'                               INCREMENT THE INDEX REG.
002B08  4640 2010          02B00         1273   BCNT    BCT     4,BNTER                               BRANCH ON COUNT
002B0C  5050 206C          02B5C         1274           ST      5,BSUM                                STORE TOTAL SUM
002B10  9035 2074          02B64         1275           STM     3,5,BSUM+8
002B14  5860 2034          02B24         1276           L       6,=A(F6#37)
002B18  07F6                             1277           BR      6
002B20                                   1278           LTORG
002B20  00000000                         1279                   =F'0'
002B24  00002B80                         1280                   =A(F6#37)
002B28  000E                             1281                   =H'14'
002B2A  0002                             1282                   =H'2'
                                         1283   *
                                         1284   *                               CONSTANT SECTION
                                         1285   *
002B30                                   1286           DS      2D
002B40  000F00E100010034                 1287   STZ     DC      H'15,225,1,52,10,48,76,42,88,26,14,4,32'           F6#34
002B48  000A0030004C002A
002B50  0058001A000E0004
002B58  0020
002B5A  0000
002B5C  00000000                         1288   BSUM    DC      F'0'


                                             DUMP AFTER EXECUTION

004180  40404040   40404040   40404040   40404040   40404040   40404040   F0404040   40404040
0041A0  40404040   40404040   40404040   40404040   40404040   40404040   07000700   07000520
0041C0  58302030   58502030   48402038   47F02018   4A532050   4A30203A   46402010   5050206C
0041E0  99352074   58602034   07F61017   41E00010   00000000   00004250   000E0002   F0280A32
004200  43DEF0EB   43C01016   19C04770   F05E9180   000F00E1   00010034   000A0030   004C002A
004220  0058001A   000E0004   00200000   00000279   40404040   0000001A   00000000   00000279


                              RELOCATION FACTOR   0016D0
```

Fig. 6-34. Coding for indexing, using index registers.

When the programer cannot make use of RX commands for indexing, indexing is still possible but more difficult. In such cases, the programer must alter the contents of the base registers or must alter the displacement amounts in the instructions themselves. Either approach can be used; the choice between them usually becomes one of convenience in individual cases. Let us look briefly at the methods used for each.

If the programer elects to index by altering the displacement amount in an instruction, then he must first assign a name to the instruction and determine whether it is the first operand that is to be indexed or the second, or both. If it is the second operand, the correct address is the address of the instruction plus four bytes. If it is the first operand, it is the address of the instruction plus two bytes (see Fig. 6-36).

The major complication of this approach arises from the placement of the base-register identification number, which is in the leftmost half byte of the half word the programer must address for access to the right displacement (see Fig. 6-36). Hence if the programer wishes to index by altering the displacement, he must usually have the computer perform a half-word load, double- and single-register shifts, then addition or subtraction on the three half bytes isolated in one register. After that he must have the computer re-form the base-and-displacement half word and store it back.

Summary of iteration variables

Iteration number	Contents of register 4		Contents of register 3		Effective address	Operand contents	Value of sum
	Before	After	Before	After			
0	14	13	0	0	STZ+0	15	0
1	13	12	0	2	STZ+0	15	15
2	12	11	2	4	STZ+2	225	240
3	11	10	4	6	STZ+4	1	241
4	10	9	6	8	STZ+6	52	293
5	9	8	8	10	STZ+8	10	303
6	8	7	10	12	STZ+10	48	351
7	7	6	12	14	STZ+12	76	427
8	6	5	14	16	STZ+14	42	469
9	5	4	16	18	STZ+16	88	557
10	4	3	18	20	STZ+18	26	583
11	3	2	20	22	STZ+20	14	597
12	2	1	22	24	STZ+22	4	601
13	1	0	24	26	STZ+24	32	633

FIG. 6-35. Analysis of iteration from Figs. 6-33 and 6-34.

Nor is that the only complication. If the programer has difficulty with the control sequence, then to do the debugging work, he must inspect each instruction that has been or could be altered by the program. This means that the programer must give his attention to a larger area of and to more places in the dump, which slows debugging work. Also, if he should make an error in calculating the addresses or should revise the program addresses, he may find that his program is altering displacement amounts in, or even other parts of, instructions other than the ones he

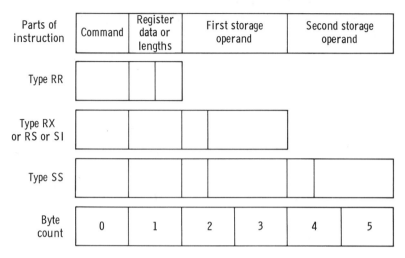

Fig. 6-36. Addressing parts of an instruction.

wishes to have altered. Lastly, if the routine can be executed more than once, the programer may have to provide some way of resetting each altered displacement back to its original starting value ("re-initializing").

In terms of difficulty in debugging, the other approach offers generally more attractive possibilities, and hence should probably be the method of choice for a beginning programer. If the programer attempts to alter the contents of a base register, then the base register used for this purpose must be explicitly assigned, and must be loaded and reloaded at the correct points in the program. For example, suppose the programer has assigned one base register for instructions and another base register for data. Then if he alters the contents of the base register assigned for data, *all* references to data fields will be altered, not just those in the area in which he desires indexing.

Several ways are open to the programer for getting around this difficulty. One way is to assign a separate base register explicitly for the area of storage desired. This can be done, for example, by defining a base register with a USING declarative at the time of introducing the area of storage to be indexed through, and then either assigning a new base register or dropping the use of that register immediately after the declarative defining that area in storage. Even so, it is still the programer's responsibility to load the register with the correct contents. In spite of these difficulties, this approach is probably the preferred approach for a beginner to use, assuming that programer can allocate a separate register specifically for use in this manner.

If a register is not available, then the programer must take action to make a register available by storing and loading its contents repeatedly in a shuttle or a musical-chairs process. This the programer can do with the load and store register instructions, but he must be careful to keep straight in his mind what contents the register has at each point in the program. To help in this, the programer usually finds it convenient to override the compiler's automatic assignment of base registers in an instruction to be indexed with a base register. In order to force the compiler program to use a specific register, the programer can specify the base register after the operand address. This is probably best illustrated in an example.

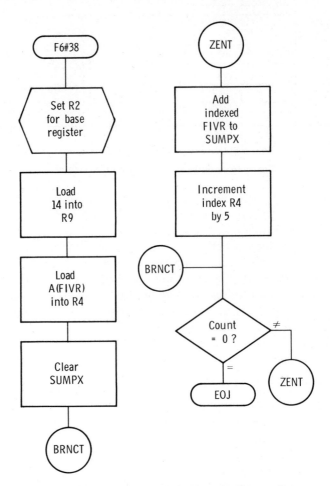

FIG. 6-37. Flow diagram for indexing, using base registers.

Let us consider again the example described previously. However, let us modify it by assuming that the 13 numbers in storage are packed-decimal numbers and occupy successive five-byte fields beginning at the symbolic address FIVR. Let us assume that the programer wants to write one brief routine to have the computer find the sum in packed-decimal of these 13 numbers, placing the sum in storage as a

```
  LOC   OBJECT CODE      ADDR1 ADDR2   ST #  NAME    OP    OPERANDS                  COMMENT

002B80                                 1290  F6#38   CSECT
002B80  070007000700                   1291          CNOP  6,8
002B86  0520                           1292          BALR  2,0
002B88                                 1293          USING *,2
002B88  4890 202C              02BB4   1294          LH    9,=H'14'
002B8C  5840 2028              02BB0   1295          L     4,=A(FIVR)
002B90  FB44 2048 2048 02BD0   02BD0   1296          SP    SUMPX,SUMPX
002B96  47F0 201C              02BA4   1297          B     BRNCT
002B9A  FA44 2048 4000 02BD0   00000   1298  ZENT    AP    SUMPX,0(5,4)
002BA0  4A40 202E              02BB6   1299          AH    4,=H'5'
002BA4  4690 2012              02B9A   1300  BRNCT   BCT   9,ZENT
002BA8  47F0 20EE              02C76   1301          B     END
002BB0                                 1302          LTORG
002BB0  00002BD5                       1303                =A(FIVR)
002BB4  000E                           1304                =H'14'
002BB6  0005                           1305                =H'5'
                                       1306  *             CONSTANT SECTION
                                       1307  *
002BB8                                 1308          DS    3D
002BD0  000000000C                     1309  SUMPX   DC    PL5'0'
002BD5  000000015C000000               1310  FIVR    DC    PL5'15,225,1,52,10,48,76,42,88,26,14,4,32'    F6#38
002BDD  225C000000001C00
002BE5  0000052C00000001
002BED  0C00000048C0000
002BF5  00076C000000042C
002BFD  000000088C000000
002C05  026C000000014C00
002C0D  0000004C00000003
002C15  2C
002C16  0000


                                   DUMP AFTER EXECUTION

004240  40404040  40404040  40404040  10024710  07000700  07000520  4890202C  58402028
004260  F8442048  204847F0  201CFA44  20484000  4A40202E  46902012  47F020D6  12004780
004280  000042A5  000E0005  10280A00  91801002  4710F0CE  0A0707FE  00000000  00000000
0042A0  00000063  3C000000  015C0000  00225C00  0000001C  00000005  2C000000  010C0000
0042C0  00048C00  0000076C  00000004  2C000000  088C0000  00026C00  0000014C  00000000
0042E0  4C000000  032C0000  99999C00  0088888C  00007777  7C000055  555C0000  55555C00


                           RELOCATION FACTOR  0016D0
```

Fig. 6-38. Coding for indexing, using base registers.

five-byte field known as SUMPX. The fundamental nature of the problem has not
changed, but a new diagram is needed (see Fig. 6-37).

The initialization of the program consists of the same operation as before. The
essential structure of the loop is identical. The loop still consists of the addition and
indexing increment. The exit test is still a Branch on Count operation. The cleanup
still consists of storing the sum. The entire program is shown in complete form in
Fig. 6-38. The only major difference between this example and the one in Fig. 6-34,
described previously, is the use of a base register for indexing purposes. Instead of
adding the increment amount onto the index register, the programer has the computer add the increment amount to the base register, since no index registers can be
used. In order to avoid confusing this base register with other possible assignments,
the programer has specifically identified the base register in the instruction to be
indexed.

Do It Now Exercise 6-16. *Prepare flow diagrams for two complete programs
to have the computer place in successive 3-byte fields in storage the packed-decimal
numbers 161 through 201, counting by 4s. Use the Branch on Count command, and*

index by the use of base registers. Have one program assign the base register by a USING declarative. Have the other one assign it by overriding the automatic assignment. Code the programs, and prepare a storage map showing the contents of storage before and after execution.

EXERCISES

1. List and explain three major parts of an iterative loop.
2. What is the difference in function between the BALR and the USING?
3. What is the leading-decisions approach? What are its features and advantages?
4. What are the advantages of sectioning a program? How can it be done conveniently?
5. Explain indexing, illustrating your explanation with an example. Prepare a flow diagram and do the coding for your example.

CHAPTER 7

Input, Output, and Job Control

IO CAPABILITY

The computer is very flexible in its input and output (IO) capabilities because a wide range of input and output equipments can be attached to operate on-line (i.e., under the computer's control). Included among these equipments are disk files, magnetic-tape drives, and random-access devices for storage and retrieval of data, as well as card readers, line printers, and communication equipment. This flexibility means that the computer can be used to meet a great variety of input and output demands. Input and output may be in any code form, but EBCDIC and ASCII are the most common.

This input and output flexibility is enhanced considerably by the channels which provide a high degree of buffering. The buffering makes it possible for a large amount of input and output equipment to operate in what appears to be a simultaneous fashion. Each piece of equipment supplies data to or obtains data from internal storage as needed, and each may operate at full rated speed. The operation of each may overlap some or all of the operation of the central processing unit, as well as that of the other peripheral units.

As part of their buffering capability, the channels accept instructions from the control unit of the computer, execute series of instructions specifically presented to them ("channel program"), arrange the needed connections to supply data to or to obtain data from storage, activate the named input and output equipment units, and monitor the IO operation. The channels provide for the necessary code translation of the information, check the information partially for code validity, and supply information to the computer about the status of the IO operation.

In most medium and large models, the computer has five main input and output commands: Start input-output operation, test channel, test input output, halt device, and halt input output. These operations call into use special data fields such as a channel address word, a channel status word, and one or more channel command words as needed to direct the channel's operation. The data from these fields of storage act as a channel program to supply the direct control over the channel in executing input and output operations. In the small models of the computer from two to seven IO commands are provided, but no channel program is used. The designations of the operations and the items of equipment are incorporated directly into the instructions as operands and variation indicators.

To simplify the programing of input and output operations, input-output control-system (IOCS) software "packages" have been developed for all models of the computer. The major cost of using IOCS is the cost of the additional storage space used by the routines that comprise the package. An additional but usually minor cost is a restriction in the full range of input and output operations. The programer gains, however, in convenience of programing and in ease of debugging, since IOCS provides pretested software for handling input and output operations in a quasi-standardized manner. Especially for beginning programers on the computer, this is certainly a gain in almost every case, even just from the debugging standpoint.

INPUT-OUTPUT CONTROL SYSTEM FOR DOS, BOS, BPS

Because of the availability and convenience of the input-output control-system (IOCS) software package, the input and output stressed in this chapter are in terms of IOCS. But IOCS exists in two major forms, "logical" and "physical." Although either can be used by the programer for input and output, logical IOCS is stressed in this book.

Physical IOCS makes more demands upon the programer than logical IOCS because it handles fewer situations automatically. Physical IOCS is closer to the computer, and hence gives the programer greater and closer control over the way the input and output operations are done. However, physical IOCS places more of a burden upon the programer to prepare routines for handling by programing the various conditions that can arise in input and output operations. Logical IOCS often handles these situations automatically, with the result that the programer is not even aware of their existence.

In its bare form, physical IOCS provides for initiating the input and output operations, handling of interrupts, scheduling of the channel, and detecting of error conditions when they arise. Matters of timing, however, are not covered, nor is the handling of end-of-data conditions and of many detected-error conditions. These are the responsibility of the programer, along with the handling of the data. In short, physical IOCS is limited to the actual physical input and output of data.

Logical IOCS uses physical IOCS to handle the physical input and output of data. Many of the capabilities of physical IOCS can be called into play by logical IOCS. But logical IOCS goes further. It handles the reading and the writing of labels on input and output files, and it handles the end-of-file and end-of-volume conditions. It handles some error conditions. It provides automatically, if necessary, for switching (alternating) of multiple input and output areas, and provides automatically for blocking and unblocking of records, where records are combined to form a physical block of data.

One of the conveniences of logical IOCS is its provision for handling the major types of file organization—that is, the sequence of records within a file and the manner of their processing. The most common of these types is usually known as the serial, sequential, or consecutive method. In this method, the records within a file are usually in a sorted sequence and are to be processed one after the other, one at a time. A disposition must be made of each record in the file before the next record can be processed. Files of this nature are very commonly found in punched-card work and in printing listings or reports. For example, the cards in a deck must be read and processed in sequence from first to last. It is not physically possible to jump around, processing cards at random from a deck of cards. This serial method is stressed in this chapter. Chapter 11 introduces other methods, including input and output under the large operating system OS.

IOCS IMPERATIVES AND DECLARATIVES

The programer uses file definition declaratives to describe the data organization, the IO equipment to be used, and the programer's choice of options. These file definition declaratives are listed in Fig. 7-1 and follow a general format. The pro-

DECLARATIVE	SUBTYPES	USE
DTFBG	FOR DTFSR ONLY	BOS ONLY
DTFBS	COMMUNICATIONS	LOGICAL IOCS
DTFDA	RANDOM	LOGICAL IOCS
DTFIS	INDEXED SEQUENTIAL	LOGICAL IOCS
DTFPH	NO SUBTYPES	PHYSICAL IOCS
DTFRF	COMMUNICATIONS	LOGICAL IOCS
DTFSN	COMMUNICATIONS	LOGICAL IOCS
DTFSR	SUBTYPES BELOW	LOGICAL IOCS
	DTFCD	PUNCHED CARD
	DTFCN	CONSOLE
	DTFDI	DEVICE INDEPENDENT
	DTFMR	MICR MAGNETIC INK
	DTFMT	MAGNETIC TAPE
	DTFOR	OCR—OPTICAL READER
	DTFPR	LINE PRINTER
	DTFPT	PAPER TAPE
	DTFSD	DISK SEQUENTIAL
DTFEN	FOR DTFSR ONLY	FOR DISK OR TAPE

Fig. 7-1. Summary of IOCS declaratives.

gramer gives a name, if required, in the name column on the coding form. This name serves as the name of the file of data. Such names may be chosen by the programer to fit his own convenience and are often chosen for their mnemonic value. The programer writes the file definition declarative in the operation column on the coding sheet. He writes the operands, of which he may use many, to fit the character of the data, the situation, and the input or output equipment. The keyword format is used for these operands to provide flexibility to the programer in omitting or including operands needed to cover particular situations.

The keyword format (see Fig. 7-2) utilizes operands composed of two parts. The first part is a prescribed set of letters called the keyword, followed by an equals sign with no intervening space. These prescribed series of letters are searched for by the compiler program, and recognized upon encounter as being parts of the operands of the file definition declarative. The second part immediately follows the equals sign without any intervening space and is the part supplied by the programer to identify the way in which that operand is to be handled or interpreted. In some cases this consists of selecting the correct alternative from among a group of available alternatives. In others, it consists of supplying the address of the data, or the address of a routine to handle certain operations. In still other cases, it consists of supplying a count of the number of bytes of data to be handled. The options available with the various keywords, and the keywords available, are discussed in some detail in a later section of this chapter.

```
         TYPEFLE=INPUT,
         BLKSIZE=80                                          X
```

FIG. 7-2. Example of keyword operand format.

The imperatives in logical IOCS are termed "macros." The macros cause the computer to perform input and output operations during the course of program execution. They call upon and cause the computer to execute some of the routines that comprise logical IOCS. In turn, these routines use the data provided by the file-description declaratives to control the character and extent of the actual input and output operations.

The term "macro" is short for "macrocommand" or "macroinstruction." Macros get their name from the way the compiler translates them. During compilation, these imperatives are typically translated from one line of source language coding (one statement) into many lines of coding—that is, into many imperative instructions in machine language. The compiler substitutes a routine or a call for a routine in place of a macro. This "one-to-many" relationship is what gives rise to the term macro.

To review, logical IOCS consists of two major parts, the IO macros, which call for the execution of input and output operations, and the file definition declaratives, which prescribe the conditions and circumstances surrounding and controlling the execution of the macros. Logical IOCS, in turn, is built upon and utilizes many features of physical IOCS but extends beyond them in providing automatically for a number of operations which would have to be provided by the programer explicitly if he used only physical IOCS. The following sections in this chapter describe some features of the macros and of the file-definition declaratives for logical IOCS for the serial method.

For convenience of presentation, and because input and output operations in the computer are not always simple, attention is given first to the handling of the simpler input and output operations. Among the simplest that can be done are punched-card input and ouput operations, and printer output operations. For convenience in this presentation, the possibility of combining reading from, and punching data into, the same cards is omitted.

Attention is given in a later chapter to magnetic-tape, magnetic-disk, and mass storage operations. Since the disk and mass storage operations are more complex than the magnetic-tape operations, they are presented last. This allows the presentation to go in a cumulative manner, for some of the operations with disks are closely parallel to operations with magnetic tape, and some tape operations are parallel to those with punched cards.

MACROS FOR CARD AND PRINTER OPERATIONS

When doing input and output operations on a card reader, card punch, or printer, the programer faces five major situations.

The first of these is the need to ready the input or output equipment for use. This initialization prepares the equipment to handle data. It establishes that the equipment is on and ready to operate, and is performed by the macro OPEN.

The second situation arises when the programer determines, usually toward the end of a program, that certain input or output equipment is no longer needed. The programer, in other words, desires to close down or terminate the use of the input or output equipment for the file of data. This is done by the macro CLOSE.

The third situation, and the most common with input equipment, is the need to have that equipment supply data for processing. The input macro GET directs this function. It supplies in internal storage one record from the file of data being read by the input equipment. The GET macro is usually not applicable to card punches and card printer, since they are output equipment.

The fourth situation, and the most common with output equipment, arises when the programer desires to have data copied from storage and included as one record in the output file of data, such as one line of data to be printed. For this, the programer uses the output macro **PUT**. This macro is usually not applicable to input equipment.

These four macros—OPEN, CLOSE, GET, and PUT—cover the basic operations (see Fig. 7-3) and are available in most versions of the operating system, including OS, DOS, BOS, and BPS, as explained later in this chapter. Two additional macros are available, however, to handle equipment control situations. One of these is applicable to all three kinds of equipment and is the CNTRL macro. This the programer can use to cause card readers and card punches to select other than normal stackers. For printers, the programer can use the CNTRL macro to control vertical movement of the paper being printed. Two varieties of such control are possible: space vertically and skip vertically. Space vertically is done independently of the punching of the printer's carriage-control tape, but depends upon the number of lines specified to be spaced vertically. Skip vertically, on the other hand, depends for its operation upon the punches that are in the carriage-control tape on the printer at the time the printer is operating. Both space vertically and skip vertically apply only to vertical movement of the paper, and do not apply to the horizontal placement or format of data along the line of printing.

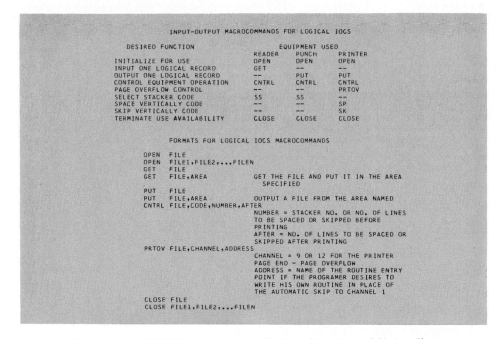

```
                    INPUT-OUTPUT MACROCOMMANDS FOR LOGICAL IOCS

        DESIRED FUNCTION                    EQUIPMENT USED
                                      READER     PUNCH      PRINTER
   INITIALIZE FOR USE                 OPEN       OPEN       OPEN
   INPUT ONE LOGICAL RECORD           GET        --         --
   OUTPUT ONE LOGICAL RECORD          --         PUT        PUT
   CONTROL EQUIPMENT OPERATION        CNTRL      CNTRL      CNTRL
   PAGE OVERFLOW CONTROL              --         --         PRTOV
   SELECT STACKER CODE                SS         SS         --
   SPACE VERTICALLY CODE              --         --         SP
   SKIP VERTICALLY CODE               --         --         SK
   TERMINATE USE AVAILABILITY         CLOSE      CLOSE      CLOSE


              FORMATS FOR LOGICAL IOCS MACROCOMMANDS

        OPEN    FILE
        OPEN    FILE1,FILE2,...FILEN
        GET     FILE
        GET     FILE,AREA                GET THE FILE AND PUT IT IN THE AREA
                                            SPECIFIED
        PUT     FILE
        PUT     FILE,AREA                OUTPUT A FILE FROM THE AREA NAMED
        CNTRL   FILE,CODE,NUMBER,AFTER
                                         NUMBER = STACKER NO. OR NO. OF LINES
                                            TO BE SPACED OR SKIPPED BEFORE
                                            PRINTING
                                         AFTER = NO. OF LINES TO BE SPACED OR
                                            SKIPPED AFTER PRINTING
        PRTOV FILE,CHANNEL,ADDRESS
                                         CHANNEL = 9 OR 12 FOR THE PRINTER
                                         PAGE END - PAGE OVERFLOW
                                         ADDRESS = NAME OF THE ROUTINE ENTRY
                                         POINT IF THE PROGRAMER DESIRES TO
                                         WRITE HIS OWN ROUTINE IN PLACE OF
                                         THE AUTOMATIC SKIP TO CHANNEL 1
        CLOSE FILE
        CLOSE FILE1,FILE2,...FILEN
```

FIG. 7-3. Logical IOCS macros for use with the serial method of file handling.

An additional macro, **PRTOV** ("printer page overflow"), is used only with the printer. The programer uses this macro to override the automatic skipping from one page to the next incorporated in logical IOCS. It allows the programer to substitute a routine which he himself has written. Whether or not the programer specifies PRTOV, the printer must have a carriage tape to skip to the top of a page unless the programer specifies only space operations and keeps a correct count of the lines printed and spaced.

In writing the macros, the programer must meet some format requirements, as summarized in the second part of Fig. 7-3. Each of the macros may have a name assigned in the name column. The operation is the macro itself. The operands go in the operand part of the coding sheet. For OPEN and CLOSE, only the file name is specified. For all but the small models of the computer, the programer may specify multiple files, provided that the file names are separated by commas. That is, one OPEN and one CLOSE may be used to open and close more than one file (see Fig. 7-4 for examples).

```
OPEN   AONE
OPEN   BTWO,CINPUT
CLOSE  BTWO
CLOSE  AONE,CINPUT
```

FIG. 7-4. Examples of OPEN and CLOSE macros.

The operands for the GET and PUT macros are used to specify the file from which or onto which data are to be copied. Multiple operands are not allowed. When the programer has specified a work area as being available in storage, however, he can give the name of the desired work area immediately following the file name, as explained later. The programer should note that both the GET and PUT use the name of the file (as given by the DTF declarative), not the name of the record as the operand.

The CNTRL macro has three or four operands, depending upon the circumstances. For card readers and punches, the programer uses three operands. The first two are the file name and the select stacker code SS, as shown in Fig. 7-3. Note the use of the comma. The third operand, also separated by a comma, is the number of the stacker pocket to be selected. For printer operations (since printers have no stackers to control), the second operand is SP for space and SK for skip.

```
CNTRL AFILE,SK,2      SKIP TO CHANNEL 2 BEFORE PRINTING
CNTRL BOUT,SK,,1      SKIP TO CHANNEL 1 AFTER PRINTING
CNTRL CINPUT, SP,2    SPACE TWO LINES BEFORE PRINTING
CNTRL DFILE,SP,,4     SPACE 4 LINES AFTER PRINTING
CNTRL EFILE,SP,1,3    SPACE 1 LINE BEFORE AND 3 LINES
                      AFTER PRINTING
```

FIG. 7-5. Example of printer skip and space operations.

The remaining two operands indicate whether the spacing or skipping is to be done *before* the next print operation, or after it. (The printer normally spaces one line after print anyway.) An entry in the third operand indicates an operation to be done before printing; one in the fourth operand, an entry to be done after. The "before" operations are done at once, but the "afters" are held in abeyance for execution after the next PUT. If the programer issues two or more consecutive "afters," the computer executes only the last one. The third and fourth operands are usually written as digits, as shown in Fig. 7-5, to specify the number of lines to be spaced or the carriage tape channel to which the carriage is to skip. When the third operand is omitted, the comma separating it from the second operand must still be included to mark its omission. This is not true for an omitted fourth operand.

The PRTOV macro requires three operands. The first is the name of the file and the second is the number of the carriage tape channel which is to be sensed. In practice, the most common channels set up for sensing on most printers are numbers 9 and 12. The third operand is the address of the programer's routine for taking the action desired upon detection of a channel punch—that is, the routine which specifies what the computer is to do when the channel indication has been sensed (see Fig. 7-6).

```
WRITE   PUT    BFILE              PUT BFILE IN THE OUTPUT AREA
        PRTOV  BFILE,12,NEWPAGE   IF PAGE-OVERFLOW GO TO NEWPAGE
        ....   ......
NEWPAGE CNTRL  BFILE,SK,3         SKIP TO CHANNEL 3
        B      JUMP
```

FIG. 7-6. Example of use of PRTOV macro.

Do It Now Exercise 7-1. *Write macros to accomplish the following functions: (a) Open three files, naming them FISH, CHIPS, and PIZZA. (b) Read a record from the file named PIZZA. (c) Write a record as output in the file named FISH. (d) Read a record from the file named CHIPS, having the data placed in a working area in storage called BAG. (e) Close the three files which were opened.*

FILE DEFINITION FOR CARD AND PRINTER OPERATIONS (DOS, BOS, BPS)

Since card readers, card punches, and printers all operate in a sequential or serial manner, the basic file definition declarative applicable is the DTFSR and its subtypes (see Fig. 7-1). DTF and SR are mnemonics for "Define the File" and "Serial," respectively. With some models of the computer, the DTFSR file definition declarative can be replaced with a series of DTF declaratives that identify specifically the type of input or output equipment to be used. For example, the DTFCD indicates punched-card equipment, and the DTFPR identifies line-printer equipment. (A note summarizing the varieties is given in Fig. 7-1.) Where available, the use of these

DTF declaratives is optional as a substitution for the DTFSR and results in a faster assembly. Since the DTFSR is the basic variety of the declarative in question, it is the declarative that receives the major emphasis in this chapter. The name specified with the DTFSR declarative is the name assigned to the file. This is the name which is used as the file operand in the macros. The operands used with the DTFSR declarative for card readers, card punches, and printers are summarized in Fig. 7-7. Operands applicable only to combined card read and punch operations have been omitted, as have a few specialized operands.

FUNCTION DESIRED	INPUT-OUTPUT EQUIPMENT USED		
	CARD READER	CARD PUNCH	PRINTER
REQUIRED OPERANDS			
SPECIFY LENGTH OF BLOCK	BLKSIZE=N	BLKSIZE=N	BLKSIZE=N
SPECIFY THE EQUIPMENT BY THE SYS IDENTIFICATION	DEVADDR= SYSNNN	DEVADDR= SYSNNN	DEVADDR= SYSNNN
SPECIFY THE EQUIPMENT TYPE XX IF NOT IN THE DTF	DEVICE= READXX	DEVICE= READXX	DEVICE= PRINTER
SPECIFY THE IO AREA RESERVED IN STORAGE	IOAREA1= ADDRESS	IOAREA1= ADDRESS	IOAREA1= ADDRESS
SPECIFY THE RECORD BLOCKING FIXUNB IS ASSUMED IF THIS OPERAND BE OMITTED	RECFORM= FIXUNB --- ---	RECFORM= FIXUNB VARUNB UNDEF	RECFORM= FIXUNB VARUNB UNDEF
SPECIFY INPUT OR OUTPUT STATUS OF THE FILE	TYPEFLE= INPUT	TYPEFLE= OUTPUT	TYPEFLE= OUTPUT
OPTIONAL OPERANDS			
SPECIFY USE OF CNTRL MACRO (THEN MAY NOT USE CTLCHR)	CONTROL= YES	CONTROL= YES	CONTROL= YES
SPECIFY USE OF CONTROL CHARACTERS (THEN MAY NOT USE THE CNTRL MACRO)	---	CTLCHR= ASA	CTLCHR= ASA
SPECIFY ADDRESS OF THE END OF FILE ROUTINE ON INPUT	EOFADDR= ADDRESS	---	---
SPECIFY ALTERNATIVE IO AREA AVAILABILITY	IOAREA2= ADDRESS	IOAREA2= ADDRESS	IOAREA2= ADDRESS
SPECIFY REGISTER NUMBER FOR BLOCKED RECORDS OR ALTERNATE AREAS IN STORAGE	IOREG=(R)	IOREG=(R)	IOREG=(R)
SPECIFY USE OF PRTOV MACRO	---	---	PRINTOV=YES
SPECIFY RECORD LENGTH FOR FIXED LENGTH BLOCKED RECORDS, OR A REGISTER FOR LENGTH OF UNDEFINED RECORDS	---	RECSIZE=N OR =(R)	RECSIZE=N OR =(R)
SPECIFY SEPARATE COMPILE OF DTF	SEPASMB= YES	SEPASMB= YES	SEPASMB= YES
SPECIFY A WORK AREA FOR USE WITH GET AND PUT MACROS	WORKA=YES	WORKA=YES	WORKA=YES

FIG. 7-7. DTFSR operands for use with card and printer equipment.

All of the operands shown in Fig. 7-7 are of the keyword type. They are divided into two groups, required and optional. The required operands (the first group) always must be included in full—i.e., the programer must use them with the DTFSR declarative. One partial exception is RECFORM=, which if it is omitted, is assumed by default to be FIXUNB, as noted in Fig. 7-7. A second partial exception is the DEVICE= operand, which can be omitted if the programer uses the subtypes of DTFSR, such as DTFCD and DTFPR. When the programer uses more than one line on the coding form for operands, he must place a nonblank character in column 72 of the coding form on each line to be continued, and resume on the next line of the coding form at the first-operand position. A review of the data summarized in Fig. 7-7 is helpful to indicate the way in which each of these operands defines the environment in which the logical IOCS macros are to operate.

In writing the DTFSR declaratives, the programer must use a comma after each operand. The programer may write as many operands per line on the coding form as he can fit on, or write only one per line. The latter is the preferred practice, since the programer can then make changes more easily.

The BLKSIZE operand must be specified as the number of characters (bytes of data) to be taken as input or output. For most card readers and punches this is normally 80, and for printers this is normally a full line, generally 120 or 132. The default options are 80 and 121, respectively, if the programer omits the BLKSIZE operand. Data are normally read, punched, or printed in EBCDIC form, and hence one byte is normally required for each character to be handled.

The IOAREA1 operand specifies the name (address) given by the programer to the area in storage which is to serve as the general input or output area. Thus if the programer, in order to receive data from a card reader, has specified some particular area in storage, that is the area to be named in this operand. The programer must define the address elsewhere in the program by use of a DS or DC declarative of the length specified for the BLKSIZE operand.

The RECFORM operand for all card readers, card punches, and printers is assumed to be some variety of unblocked record, and FIXUNB is the default option. Blocked records are not handled by logical IOCS for card readers, card punches, and printers. (If the programer actually has blocked records, then the blocking and unblocking must be handled by the programer himself in the routines that he writes.) In particular, card readers are assumed to operate always with the fixed-length variety of unblocked records. Printers and card punches may operate with records that are of the variable-length, the fixed-length, or the undefined-length varieties of unblocked record. This reflects the fact that some card punches may be used to punch less than a full card of data, and printers less than a full line of data. Where variable or undefined lengths are specified, then other action must be taken to define more fully for logical IOCS the amount of data to be handled. The standard practice is to use only fixed-length card records and printer records.

The TYPEFLE operand specifies whether the data are to be handled as input or output. Card readers are assumed to have only input data files, printers and card punches only output data files. These are respectively the default options. The combination case for punched cards, as noted previously, is not discussed here.

The DEVADDR operand specifies what is known as the "SYS" identification of the input or output equipment. What these are can vary from one installation to another, depending upon the configuration and upon local practice. In general, the non-numeric identifications are as follows: SYSRDR for the card reader for reading job control cards; SYSLST for printer; SYSIPT for the usual input equipment (such as magnetic-tape or punched-card); SYSOPT for the usual output equipment (such as magnetic-tape or printer); and SYSLOG for the control-card-logging typewriter or printer. Most other units of equipment are assigned numerals in the range from SYS000 through SYS254. These are described further in the section on job control.

The DEVICE operand may be omitted entirely if the programer can use the variation of the DTF declaratives that identify the equipment directly, such as DTFPR for printer. Otherwise, the DEVICE operand specifies the type of equipment to be used for input or output. The number and letters used to identify the equipment vary from configuration to configuration, and from model to model of the computer. For the didactic purposes of this chapter, the following will be used: READ20 for card reader or card punch, and PRINTER for printer.

Among the optional file definition operands available are some that in practice must be used by the programer to meet conditions very commonly encountered. Among these, a prime example is sensing the end-of-file condition on the input equipment. Some other operands are relatively little used.

The CONTROL operand specifies that the programer desires to override the logical IOCS automatic control functions and to provide his own by use of the CNTRL macro noted previously. If the programer uses the CONTROL operand for a file, he may not also use the CTLCHR operand.

The CTLCHR operand specifies that the programer does not desire to use the CNTRL macro, but does desire to override the automatic control features of logical IOCS for a printer or card machine by including a control character as a prefix character for each record. The choice of the control character must reflect the particular item of equipment as well as the function desired. A list of the functions performed by such control characters is shown in Fig. 7-8. Where the control character alternative is used, the BLKSIZE must be specified as one byte longer per record

Δ	Single space before print	1	Skip to channel 1 before print
0	Double space before print	2	Skip to channel 2 before print
-	Triple space before print		.
+	No space before printing (suppress usual single space after)		.
		9	Skip to channel 9 before print
V	Select stacker 1	A	Skip to channel 10 before print
W	Select stacker 2	B	Skip to channel 11 before print
		C	Skip to channel 12 before print

FIG. 7-8. List of ASA control characters for use with CTLCHR operand.

than would normally be the case, and the **DS** or **DC** declaratives must reserve the first byte position for holding the control character.

The **EOFADDR** operand specifies the address of the programer's input end-of-file routine. This operand makes **IOCS** sensitive to the end-of-file condition on an input file being read in a serial manner. The end-of-file condition is not applicable to card-punch or printer equipment.

The **IOAREA2** operand specifies the address (name) of the alternate storage area which the programer may provide by means of the **DS** or **DC** declaratives. The programer should, as a general rule, specify either an **IOAREA2** or a **WORKA** operand in order to avoid increasing input and output delays. The use of an alternative (swap) input or output area (sometimes called "programed buffer area") is particularly advantageous when the average time required to process a record is shorter than the average time required to read or write a record if the processing of the records individually will vary in time, some taking longer than read or write time. In order to keep the input or output equipment operating at full speed, it is desirable to insulate the timing of the input or output operations from the timing of the processing operation. This can be done by setting up an alternative (swap) input or output area which can be used by logical **IOCS**. Thus logical **IOCS** can be filling or emptying one area while the programer uses data in the other area. When the **IOAREA2** operand is specified, **IOREG** operand must also be used, but **WORKA** may not be used.

The **IOREG** operand specifies in parentheses the number of the general-purpose register which is to be made available to logical **IOCS** for keeping track of the alternate areas in storage. Since only unblocked records are permitted for the printers and the card equipment, the use of **IOREG** is limited to this function. The register number must be chosen from the group 2 through 11.

The **PRINTOV** operand specifies that the programer desires to use the **PRTOV** macro to override the automatic logical **IOCS** provision for between-page skips on the printer. If the automatic provision is used, the programer must have available a carriage-control tape. If the programer overrides the automatic provision by the **PRTOV** macro, he may still have to provide a carriage tape for use in the printer.

The **RECSIZE** operand specifies, in parentheses for card and printer files, the register that contains the length in bytes of the current record if the **RECFORM** operand specifies variable or undefined length. It is then the responsibility of the programer to provide the correct contents of the register. The register may be any general-purpose register from 2 through 11.

The **SEPASMB** operand permits the programer to compile **DTFSR** declaratives separately from the rest of his program. This affords substantial savings in compilation time, because the programer typically makes few mistakes on the **DTFSR** declaratives and because the declaratives may take several minutes to compile. The procedures for making separate assemblies differs in detail from installation to installation, because full efficiency is obtained only if portions of the **IOCS** routines exist as already-compiled "logic modules." This can be done by a MOD declarative, but it is beyond the scope of this book. MOD declaratives or logic modules are required when using the specialized DTF varieties shown in Fig. 7-1. An illustration of using a SEPASMB operand is given in Fig. 7-9.

The WORKA operand specifies that the programer desires to have made available to IOCS one or more work areas in storage to receive input data or supply output data. Such areas are in addition to the main input and output area, but for practical purposes the records in the main areas are effectively unavailable to the programer if he uses work areas. Any area in storage may be used as a work area, but the programer may not then use the IOREG operand.

The file-definition declaratives are normally placed in the program immediately after the START or CSECT declarative. They must be the first thing in a control section if they are present at all. They must begin with a DTFBG declarative if the programer has used DTFSR, with an operand of DISK if the computer has magnetic-disk files. They must end with the DTFEN declarative, which may have an operand of OVLAY that under BOS can save storage space. Both are shown with no name. This placement assures correct handling by the compiler program of the IOCS material if the programer also uses a LTORG declarative later in the control section. Examples of a logical IOCS file definition for a card punch and of one for a printer are shown in Fig. 7-9. The DTFBG and DTFEN declaratives may be omitted when the programer uses the specialized DTF varieties. Summaries of the operands for the DTFSR declarative that may be used for card-reader, card-punch, and printer files, are shown in Figs. 7-10 to 7-12.

***Do It Now* Exercise 7-2.** *Prepare a flow diagram for a complete program to have the computer perform an "80-80" card-to-printer operation. Assume that the printer requires a print line 132 characters long, that only card images (data from one card with no format changes) are to be printed one per line, and that lines are to be triple-spaced (two blank lines between one line of print and the next). Number the pages as they are printed, in the upper right-hand corner. Code the program. Hint: Prepare the complete program first without the triple-space feature and without the page-number feature. Then add the triple-spacing, and lastly add the page-numbering. Hint: What about those 52 characters?*

OPERATING SYSTEM CONTROL

In order for the programer to have the computer compile and execute his program, he must give attention to the "operating system program" or "supervisor program." Several different types of operating systems are used with the different models of the computer, and each type performs differently.

For the larger models of the computer the two major varieties of operating systems are OS and VM, standing for (Full) Operating System and Virtual Machine (Operating System), respectively. These provide a wide range of convenient func-

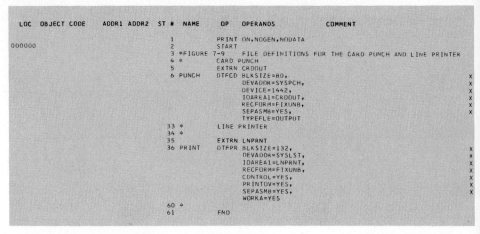

```
  LOC  OBJECT CODE   ADDR1 ADDR2  ST #  NAME    OP    OPERANDS                    COMMENT
                                    1            PRINT ON,NOGEN,NODATA
000000                              2            START
                                    3  *FIGURE 7-9      FILE DEFINITIONS FOR THE CARD PUNCH AND LINE PRINTER
                                    4  *         CARD PUNCH
                                    5            EXTRN CRDOUT
                                    6  PUNCH     DTFCD BLKSIZE=80,                                              X
                                                       DEVADDR=SYSPCH,                                         X
                                                       DEVICE=1442,                                            X
                                                       IOAREA1=CRDOUT,                                         X
                                                       RECFORM=FIXUNB,                                         X
                                                       SEPASMB=YES,                                            X
                                                       TYPEFLE=OUTPUT
                                   33  *         LINE PRINTER
                                   34  *
                                   35            EXTRN LNPRNT
                                   36  PRINT     DTFPR BLKSIZE=132,                                             X
                                                       DEVADDR=SYSLST,                                         X
                                                       IOAREA1=LNPRNT,                                         X
                                                       RECFORM=FIXUNB,                                         X
                                                       CONTROL=YES,                                            X
                                                       PRINTOV=YES,                                            X
                                                       SEPASMB=YES,                                            X
                                                       WORKA=YES
                                   60  *
                                   61            END
```

FIG. 7-9. Example of DTFCD and DTFPR declaratives for a card punch and a line printer.

```
BLKSIZE=N
CONTROL=YES
DEVADDR=SYSNNN
DEVICE=READXX
EOFADDR=ADDRESS
IOAREA1=ADDRESS
IOAREA2=ADDRESS
IOREG=(N)
RECFORM=FIXUNB
TYPEFLE=INPUT
WORKA=YES
```

FIG. 7-10. Checklist of DTFSR operands for a card reader, excluding the combination read-punch capability.

```
BLKSIZE=N
CONTROL=YES
CTLCNR=YES
DEVADDR=SYSNNN
DEVICE=READXX
IOAREA1=ADDRESS
IOAREA2=ADDRESS
IOREG=(N)
RECFORM=RECORD TYPE
RECSIZE=N
TYPEFLE=OUTPUT
WORDA=YES
```

FIG. 7-11. Checklist of DTFSR operands for a card punch, excluding the combination read-punch capability.

```
BLKSIZE=N
CONTROL=YES
CTLCHR=YES
DEVADDR=SYSNNN
DEVICE=PRINTER
IOAREA1=ADDRESS
IOAREA2=ADDRESS
IOREG=(N)
PRINTOV=YES
RECFORM=RECORD TYPE
RECSIZE=N
TYPEFLE=OUTPUT
WORKA=YES
```

FIG. 7-12. Checklist of DTFSR operands for line printers.

tions for the programer, including handling of most possible interrupt conditions. These also provide an extensive variety of messages to the operator about conditions, errors, and the status of a program the computer may be executing. To direct and control OS or VM, the programer prepares in a specific format "job control" cards or messages. The OS and VM systems are used mostly with the large models of the computer, which are in much less common use than the medium and small models.

More commonly encountered are the TOS, DOS, BOS, TDOS, and BPS, which are, respectively, the Tape, Disk, Basic, and Tape-Disk Operating Systems, and the Basic Programing Support Systems. When an installation of the computer is equipped with disk drives, DOS is the most commonly used. When disks are not available but magnetic tapes are, TOS is usually used. In small configurations of the medium-size models of the computer, BOS and BPS are common. These do not provide the extensive and comprehensive interrupt handling and operator messages provided by TOS or DOS, but they accomplish many of the same basic functions. With BPS, for example, a program must be specifically assembled with a supervisor routine in order to provide for a normal handling of the interrupts. Because of their common use, the BPS, BOS, TDOS, TOS, and DOS job control cards are described later in this chapter and their use briefly explained. Summary coverage for large models of the computer operated under OS (full Operating System) is also given.

For small models and the smaller medium models of the computer, common practice is to operate the computer with only a supervisor program, or in some cases with only IOCS routines. The regular supervisor program provides for a basic handling of interrupts, and on some models of the computer provides for some functions included in DOS or TOS. Examples are locating and loading a program stored on magnetic tape, and keeping track of internal storage available for executing other programs.

In considering the functional capability of an operating system, the programer must distinguish clearly between job control cards for making a program compilation, and job control cards for executing a compiled program. The choice of the second depends in part upon the first. The cards for making a program compilation also involve the interaction of the compiler program with the declaratives the programer has written, and with the operating system. For control of this interaction, the programer can use OPTION or AOPTN cards with the compiler.

JOB CONTROL WITH BPS

Using the example program discussed earlier, in Do It Now Exercise 7-2, the programer can contrast the job control cards for BPS (Basic Programing Support), and those for other levels of the operating system. For compilation under BPS, the programer needs the cards shown in Fig. 7-13. Program execution is described later, as are the TOS or DOS job control cards.

On the front of the deck and in the first position is the LOG job control card.

This card is not required, but if it is present, it causes the console typewriter or on-line printer to list the job control cards (see Fig. 7-14 for the format of the job control cards). Then comes the JOB card. This card is required because it directs the computer to perform an assembly (ASSEMB) language compilation. The remainder of the card, up through column 71, may be used for comments or identifying information.

The next card which may be omitted, if previously supplied to the supervisor program, is a date card. The first two digits following the space after DATE represent the year; the next three represent the day of the year.

The ASSGN cards come next. These cards may be omitted if the installation's standard practice is acceptable to the programer. For safety and clarity, however, the programer should normally include them, and should always do so if he wishes to give the console operator flexibility in running the computer. The function of the ASSGN cards is to identify items of input and output equipment in terms of their use in a program. An example of ASSGN cards for a magnetic-tape-equipped model of the computer is shown in Fig. 7-13.

For making a compilation using the assembly language and a magnetic-tape-equipped model of the computer, two tape units beyond the systems residence tape unit are required to hold the intermediate steps in the compilation. If the programer has used literals, then a third tape unit beyond the systems residence unit is required for them; i.e., a total of four magnetic tape units are required.

The operands for the ASSGN cards are worth close inspection because they reveal how the identification is made. The first operand specifies the item of input or output equipment in terms of the arbitrary SYS code mentioned earlier in this chapter. The key part of this operand is the group of letters SYS. The following letters or numerals in the operand designate the use or conceptual (logical) position of the item of input or output equipment. Thus RES (for "resident") designates the input or output equipment which has recorded on it the operating system. The

```
// LOG
// JOB ASSEMB
// DATE 78002
// ASSGN SYSRES,X'121',T2,X'00'
// ASSGN SYSRDR,X'00C',R3
// ASSGN SYSLST,X'00E',L1
// ASSGN SYSOPT,X'00C',R3
// ASSGN SYSLOG,X'00A',C1
// ASSGN SYS000,X'122',T2,X'00'
// ASSGN SYS001,X'123',T2,X'00'
// ASSGN SYS002,X'124',T2,X'00'
// EXEC
       ALOG
       AOPTN LITERAL
       AOPTN IPL
       SUPVR CONFG=00000010
       SYMUN 0
       IOCFG MPX=YES,R3=YES
       SEND
```

FIG. 7-13. Example of BPS job control cards for compiling an assembly-language program.

```
LOC     OBJECT CODE     ADDR1 ADDR2  ST #   NAME      OP     OPERANDS              COMMENT

                                             IMPERATIVES

                                      1             PRINT  ON,NOGEN,NODATA
000000                                2             START
                                      3   #FIGURE 7-13  DTF SECTION
                                      4  *
                                      5  *                INPUT FILE  -  CARD READER
                                      6  *
                                      7  INPUT    DTFCD  BLKSIZE=80,                           X
                                                         DEVADDR=SYSRDR,                       X
                                                         DEVICE=1442,                          X
                                                         IOAREA1=CARDIN,                       X
                                                         RECFORM=FIXUNB,                       X
                                                         TYPEFLE=INPUT,                        X
                                                         EOFADDR=LAST
                                     28  *                OUTPUT FILE  -  PRINTER
                                     29  *
                                     30  PRINTOT  DTFPR  BLKSIZE=132,                          X
                                                         DEVADDR=SYSLST,                       X
                                                         DEVICE=1443,                          X
                                                         IOAREA1=PRINT,                        X
                                                         RECFORM=FIXUNB,                       X
                                                         CONTROL=YES,                          X
                                                         PRINTOV=YES,                          X
                                                         WORKA=YES
                                     51  *
                                     52  #FIGURE7-13   CARD TO PRINTER LISTING
                                     53  *
000068                               54  FIG7#13  CSECT
000068  070007000700                 55             CNOP   6,8
00006E  0520                          56             BALR   2,0
000070                                57             USING  *,2
000070  5830 20F0          00160      58             L      3,=A(CARDIN)
000180                                59             USING  CARDIN,3
                                      60             OPEN   INPUT,PRINTOT
                                      69  FIRST    CNTRL  PRINTOT,SK,2
                                      75             PUT    PRINTOT,PAGE
0000A4  FA10 315C 2108 002DC 00178    81             AP     PAGENO,=P'1'
0000AA  F331 314C 315C 002CC 002DC    82             UNPK   NUMBER,PAGENO
                                      83  READ2    GET    INPUT
0000BC  9240 3050         001D0       88             MVI    PRINT,64            CLEAR PRINT AREA
0000C0  D282 3051 3050 001D1 001D0    89             MVC    PRINT+1(131),PRINT
0000C6  D24F 3050 3000 001D0 00180    90  MOVEI    MVC    PRINT(80),CARDIN
                                      91             CNTRL  PRINTOT,SP,3
                                      97             PRTOV  PRINTOT,12,OVRFLW
                                     103             PUT    PRINTOT,PRINT
                                     109             PRTOV  PRINTOT,12,OVRFLW
00010A  47F0 2040          00080     115             B      READ2
                                     116  OVRFLW   CNTRL  PRINTOT,SK,2
                                     122             PUT    PRINTOT,PAGE
00012C  FA10 315C 2108 002DC 00178   128             AP     PAGENO,=P'1'
000132  F331 314C 315C 002CC 002DC   129             UNPK   NUMBER,PAGENO
000138  47F0 2056          000C6     130             B      MOVEI
                                     131  LAST     CLOSE  INPUT,PRINTOT
                                     140             EOJ
000150                               143             LTORG
000150  5B5B8C2D6D7C5D540            144             =C'$$BOPEN '
000158  5B5B8C2C3D3D6E2C5            145             =C'$$BCLOSE'
000160  00000180                     146             =A(CARDIN)
000164  00000038                     147             =A(PRINTOT)
000168  00000258                     148             =A(PAGE)
00016C  00000000                     149             =A(INPUT)
000170  0000010E                     150             =A(OVRFLW)
000174  000001D0                     151             =A(PRINT)
00017B  1C                           152             =P'1'
                                             DECLARATIVES
000180                               153             DS     0D             ALIGN INPUT AREA
000180  4040404040404040             154  CARDIN   DC     CL80' '        CARD INPUT
0001D0                               155             DS     0D             ALIGN PRINT AREA
0001D0  4040404040404040             156  PRINT    DC     CL132' '       PRINT LINE OUTPUT
000258                               157             DS     0D             ALIGN HEADING LINE
000258                               158  PAGE     DS     0CL132         HEADING LINE OUTPUT
000258  4040404040404040             159             DC     38C' '
00027E  C6C9C7E4D9C5F760             160             DC     CL26'FIGURE7-13, 80-80 LISTING'
000298  404040404040404040           161             DC     47C' '
0002C7  D7C1C7C540                   162             DC     CL5'PAGE '
0002CC  404040F1                     163  NUMBER   DC     CL4'   1'
0002D0  404040404040404040           164             DC     12C' '
0002DC  001C                         165  PAGENO   DC     PL2'1'
000068                               166             END    FIG7#13
```

```
/*
/&
```

FIG. 7-13   *(continued)*

letters RDR designate the equipment from which job control cards are to be read. The letters IPT designate the equipment from which the source deck and any data decks are to be read. The letters LST designate the item of output equipment upon which the programer desires to have the computer list the source program in printed form, or in a form ready for printing. The letters OPT designate the output equipment which will punch or record the object program. The letters LOG designate the equipment used by the computer to provide error messages to the console operator. The number designations (such as 041) depend for their significance on the programer's DTFSR assignments and upon local practice at any particular installation.

The second operand on the ASSGN cards designates, in the form of a hexadecimal constant, the channel and device number of an item of input or output equipment. This is in terms of the hardware available at the particular installation, and depends upon how the particular computer is equipped and how the input and output equipment is connected physically. The channel designator is the first hexadecimal character. The next two hexadecimal characters designate the position of the device or equipment on the channel. Slow-speed equipment such as card readers, line printers, card punches, console typewriters, and the like are normally placed on channel 0, the multiplexor channel. High-speed devices such as magnetic tapes or magnetic disks are normally assigned to channel 1 or channel 2, which are usually selector channels.

Thus, since the first operand specifies the use the programer is to make of the equipment and the second operand designates the item of hardware, the ASSGN card links use to equipment. It permits the programer to assign or allocate an item of equipment to a particular use.

The third operand for the ASSGN cards designates the particular type of equipment utilized. A table of such equipment is incorporated in Fig. 7-14. The fourth operand takes the form of a hexadecimal constant and designates, for magnetic tapes only, the type of magnetic tape utilized. The interpretation table for this is also shown in Fig. 7-14.

After the ASSGN cards, which are optional for the programer, comes the EXEC job control card, which is required. This card directs the computer to begin execution of the job named by the job card.

At this point, the programer can begin to introduce more explicitly the way in which he wishes the operating system to interact with the compiler program. To this end, it is helpful for the programer to keep in mind that the usual practice is to produce the following items as a part of a compilation: (1) a listing of the source program also showing the object language translation; (2) a symbol table showing the names (symbolic addresses) the programer has used to designate instructions or items of data; (3) a listing of errors or diagnostics, informing the programer where he has violated some of the rules in utilizing the assembly language; (4) an object program in machine-language form; (5) an external symbol dictionary, which identifies those names the programer has used which are not fully

Identifier (cols. 1-2)	One or more blanks	Operation	One or more blanks	Operand (or parameters) (may not exceed col. 71)		
//		JOB		Progname (only six characters are processed)		
//		ASSGN		SYSxxx,X'cuu',dd,X'ss'	or	SYSxxx,UA
						col. 72
//		ASSGN		SYSxxx,		c
Continuation card				c = Continuation punch (any nonblank character)		
			col. 16			
(Columns 1 to 15 are blank)				X'cuu',dd,X'ss'	or	col. 16-17 UA

UA = Unassign (to unassign an I/O device from a symbolic unit)

xxx = RDR for a card reader
     LST for a printer
     IPT for an input unit
     OPT for an output unit
     LOG for a control-card logging device
     000 to 254 for any unit

X'cuu' = Channel and unit number (in hexadecimal)
     c = 0 for a multiplexor channel
          1 for selector channel 1
          2 for selector channel 2
     uu = 00 to FF (0 to 255)

dd = Device type
     BS - 2701 with SDA II (BSC)
     C1 - 1052 printer-keyboard
     L1 - 1403 or 1404 printer
     L2 - 1443 or 1445 printer
     P1 - 2540 card read-punch (punching only)
     P2 - 1442 card read-punch (punching only)
     P3 - 2520 card read-punch (punching only)
     R0 - 2671 paper tape reader
     R1 - 2540 card read-punch (reading only)
     R2 - 2540 using punch-feed-read feature
     R3 - 1442 card read-punch (reading, or reading and punching
          for combined files)
     R4 - 2501 card reader
     R5 - 2520 card read-punch (reading, or reading and punching
          for combined files)
     RR - 1285 optical reader or 1287 optical reader (in journal tape
          mode)
     RD - 1287 optical reader (in document mode)
     ST - 2701 with SDA I (STR)
     T1 - 2400 seven-track Tape
     T2 - 2400 nine-track Tape

X'ss' = Device specifications (in hexadecimal)
     ss = 00 unless 7-track tape, 9-track tape or a 1403 printer with the
          UCS (Universal Character Set) special feature is specified.

FIG. 7-14. Job control card formats for BPS and AOPTN operands.

Identifier (cols. 1-2)	One or more blanks	Operation	One or more blanks	Operand (or parameters) (may not exceed col. 71)			

		ASSGN (continued)		Seven-track Tape Specifications				
//				Density (bytes per inch)	Parity	Convert feature	Translate	ss
				200	odd	on	off	10
				200	odd	off	off	30
				200	odd	off	on	38
				200	even	off	off	20
				200	even	off	on	28
				556	odd	on	off	50
				556	odd	off	off	70
				556	odd	off	on	78
				556	even	off	off	60
				556	even	off	on	68
				800	odd	on	off	90
				800	odd	off	off	B0
				800	odd	off	on	B8
				800	even	off	off	A0
				800	even	off	on	A8

Nine-track Tape Specifications		
Density (bytes per inch)		ss
800		C8
1600		C0

If this operand is omitted, a density of 800 bytes per inch will be assumed.

For a 1403 printer with the UCS feature:

Printer Specifications	
ss	Meaning
73	Ignore data check
7B	Accept data check

//		DATE		yyddd

yy = Year (two digits)

ddd = Day of the year (three digits)

//		CONFG		nnnnnnnn

n = 0 or 1
If a 1 is not specified, a zero is assumed.
Positions 0-3: machine size
0000 = 8 K bytes
0010 = 16 K bytes
0011 = 24 K bytes
0100 = 32 K bytes
0110 = 64 K bytes
1000 = 128 K bytes
1010 = 256 K bytes

FIG. 7-14 *(continued)*

Identifier (cols. 1-2)	One or more blanks	Operation	One or more blanks	Operand (or parameters) (may not exceed col. 71)
				Position 4: Model (for diagnostic scan-out area) 0 = Model 30 1 = Other models
				Position 5: floating point feature 0 = Feature not present 1 = Feature present
				Position 6: decimal feature 0 = Feature not present 1 = Feature present
				Position 7: 1052 printer-keyboard 0 = Device not present 1 = Device present
//		PAUSE		(Any operand is treated as a comment)
//		LOG		(Any operand is treated as a comment)
//		NOLOG		(Any operand is treated as a comment)
//		EXEC		(Any operand is treated as a comment)

One or more blanks	Operation	One or more blanks	Operand	Meaning
	AOPTN		NODECK	The object deck will not be produced, in cards, or on tape or disk. This will not affect the appearance of the program listing. Also, no cards will be reproduced as a result of REPRO or PUNCH instructions.
	AOPTN		NOESD	No External Symbol Dictionary data will appear in the object deck or the program listing. (Program will not be acceptable to a basic operating system or an operating system.)
	AOPTN		NORLD	No Relocation Dictionary data will appear in the object deck or the program listing. (Program may not be relocatable.)
	AOPTN		NOLIST	The program listing will not appear.
	AOPTN		NOERR	The error listing will not appear in the program listing.
	AOPTN		NOSYM	The symbol table will not appear in the program listing.
	AOPTN		IPL	An IPL routine (for loading as independent supervisor from a card reader) will precede the object program.
	AOPTN		PCHSYM	The symbol table is put out on the device specified for text output. This table is required by the Auto-test program, if its symbolic testing capabilities are to be used.
	AOPTN		CROSSREF	A cross-reference listing will appear instead of the symbol table listing. The cross-reference listing contains all the symbols used in the program and the statement numbers of statements in which they were used.
	AOPTN		ENTRY	An ENTRY card will be produced at the end of the output text. Otherwise it must be placed there manually, before link-editing.

FIG. 7-14   *(continued)*

defined in the portion of the program being compiled, and which therefore require linkage edit or other resolution; and (6) a relocation dictionary, which lists the major points that serve as benchmarks for the relocation in internal storage of the program at the time it is loaded.

In addition to these items which are normally provided, there are some items normally not provided. Thus an initial program loading or bootstrap routine is normally not provided with the object program. Provision for handling literals—i.e., constants incorporated as part of an instruction—is normally not provided. A cross-reference list showing where each symbolic name is used in the program is normally not provided. And a supervisor program is normally not provided as part of the object program.

The programer has the ability, by the use of various control statements, to alter or reverse any of these items. To provide for literals and for most of the other options, except for a supervisor, the programer can use AOPTN cards (see Fig. 7-15). To suppress those items normally provided, the programer can cite, usually with one operand per AOPTN card, the following operands: NOLIST, NOSYM, NOERR, NODECK, NOESD, and NORLD. If the programer wishes to provide for literals, he can do it by specifying an AOPTN card with an operand of LIT-ERAL. If he wishes to obtain a cross-reference list, he can cite the operand CROSSREF. This replaces the symbol table. If he wishes an initial program loading or bootstrap routine to be included in the deck, he can cite the operand IPL. This is normally utilized only when a supervisor is also to be incorporated in the deck.

A supervisor and an initial program loader or bootstrap are normally not required when the object program is to be stored on a program tape (library tape). The reason is that because the first program on the program tape normally provides for an initial program loader and a supervisor program. Then, when a call is made to execute a program from the program tape, the initial program loader and the supervisor program are automatically provided.

Since the purpose of making a compilation is usually to translate a program from source language into object language, an object deck is normally provided. Whether the object program appears as a deck of cards or as the equivalent on magnetic tape depends upon whether the programer has specified a card-punch or a magnetic-tape unit on the ASSGN card for SYSOPT. Since the program listing showing the translation from source to object language is useful for correcting errors, most programers desire the program listing. They also desire the error list and either a cross-reference table or a symbol table to help them trace errors in their use of symbolic names. If a linkage edit such as that described later is to be performed, the external symbol dictionary is helpful for checking symbol usage to avoid linkage errors.

To have a supervisor routine included in the object program, the programer must supply four macrocommands and their associated operands. These are shown in Fig. 7-15 and commented on below. In practice, in any given installation these cards will normally be punched and used in standard form for the installation. Therefore a programer should obtain these cards from his immediate supervisor or from another programer before attempting to make them up himself. In this way the programer can easily observe the installation's standard practice.

The four operands for the SUPVR macro provide information about the computer configuration, and about whether or not checkpoint records are to be utilized. The operands may be included in any order, but must be separated by commas without intervening spaces. The CONFG= operand, which is required, must be completed by eight numeric characters which must be 0s or 1s. The first three designate the amount of storage capacity available. The range of these is from 000 for 8K of storage through 101 for 256K of storage (like a binary number). Position 4 should always be a zero. Position 5 should be a zero for the smaller of the medium-size models of the computer and a 1 for all larger models. Positions 6, 7, and 8 designate, respectively, whether or not the computer is equipped with floating-point commands, decimal commands, or a console typewriter. If these features are present, the programer uses a 1; if they are absent, a 0.

The programer completes the TR= operand with the words YES to indicate that an interval-timer routine must be included in the supervisor. This operand is required only when the problem (programer's) program utilizes the interval timer provided in the hardware.

The operand CR=YES is needed whenever the program requires communication between the console operator and the programer by means of the console typewriter. For example, if the computer under the control of the program requests that the console operator supply the input card count (as a checking operation), then this operand must be included.

The CHKPT=YES operand is needed for any program that is to utilize the checkpoint macro or to attempt to utilize checkpoint data for restarting the program.

The SYMUN macro provides the support for the ASSGN job control cards. The first operand is always a decimal number designating the number of items of peripheral equipment which may be referenced by the program beyond (i.e., over and above) the five basic items of equipment normally supplied. The basic five are SYSRDR, SYSLST, SYSIPT, SYSOPT, and SYSLOG. For each of the other SYS identifications which the programer wishes to utilize in his program, the programer must supply for the SYMUN macro a pair of hexadecimal constants. The first one uses two hexadecimal characters to designate the channel number and two hexadecimal characters to designate the unit or item of equipment number—i.e., the unit address. The second constant uses two hexadecimal characters to designate the type of input-output equipment, and for computer magnetic tapes, the second two characters, which are otherwise 0, are used in the same fashion as for the ASSGN cards. The programer should note, in utilizing the SYMUN macro, that the designations are effective only for the execution of the program and do not effect the manner of the compilation of the program. As such, the use of the SYMUN macro makes it possible to eliminate, if desired, the use of ASSGN job control cards when executing the object program.

Any operands not utilized, as in the case of the SUPVR macro, may be omitted, since they are keyword operands. If operands be present, then they must be separated by commas with no intervening space. The first operand of the SYMUN macro must always be present. An example is shown in Fig. 7-13.

The IOCFG macro uses keyword operands to specify in more detail the input-output equipment configuration available with the computer. An operand of MPX=n designates the number of multiplexor queues desired. The operand SEL=, with a number, indicates the number of selector channels available, usually 1 or 2. If the operand TAU=YES is included, it indicates that a tape control unit is available which has the ability to read while writing. If a magnetic tape is available, it is designated by T=YES. If the tape has nine tracks, the additional operand TKR9= YES is used. For seven-track tape, it is TRK7=YES. A full listing of these is given in Fig. 7-15.

The final macrocommand of the group of four needed to yield a supervisor program with the object program is the SEND macro. The function of the SEND macro is to call the program loader routine in order to load the following object program. The first operand of the SEND macro is optional and specifies the number of bytes of internal storage to be left at the end of the supervisor program as a separation of it from the beginning object program. Two hundred bytes is an amount of space commonly used to permit possible later changes in the supervisor program without thus forcing a recompilation of the source program.

The second operand, REP, of the SEND macro is also optional. It causes the program loader routine to include a "replacement" capability. This permits the programer to make "patches" (corrections) to his program which are incorporated at program load time by replacing part of the program previously compiled and loaded. If used with discretion, this is a convenience to the programer in saving compilation time, but it should not be used for production operations or on a routine basis by programers. The format for the patch cards is shown later in this chapter.

The next card normally incorporated in the compilation may be the card TITLE. The first four characters of the first operand of this card are used to identify the program listing and the cards, if any, which are punched by the compiler program as a result of compilation. As such, it offers the programer a convenient way to identify both his deck and the listing.

The next card is typically the first card of the programer's source program, the START card. With the BPS job control, the programer can avoid the necessity of executing the link-edit by designating an appropriate starting address as the

SUPVR Macro

CONFG=nnnnnnnn,TR=YES,CR=YES,CHKPT=YES

CONFG=nnnnnnnn: This operand is the same as the configuration byte (byte 9) of the communication region. It must consist of eight "0" or "1" digits. The eight digits indicate the machine configuration for which the supervisor is being assembled, as follows (numbering from the left):

Digit positions	Configuration			
1-4	Number of bytes of main storage:	5	Model * 30=0 other=1	
	8K-0000			
	16K-0010	6	Floating-point option	} Present=1
	24K-0011	7	Decimal feature	
	32K-0100	8	Printer-keyboard	} Not present=0
	48K-0101			
	64K-0110			
	128K-1000			
	256K-1010			

TR=YES: This operand (timer routine) must be included if the supervisor being assembled is to be used for any problem program that contains routine(s) for the interval timer. If this operand is omitted, the interval timer (INT TMR) switch must be set OFF for any program(s) that uses this supervisor.

CR=YES: This operand (communication routine) must be included if the supervisor being assembled is to be used for any problem program that contains routine(s) for operator-initiated communication from the 1052.

CHKPT=YES: This operand (checkpoint) must be included if the supervisor being assembled is to be used for any problem program that included the checkpoint macro or that requires restarting from checkpointed records.

SYMUN Macro

n,X'ccuu',X'ddss',X'ccuu',X'ddss',.....

When devices are assigned by the SYMUN macro, a separate <u>pair</u> of parameters (x'ccuu',x'ddss') is entered for each device in this exact order:

SYSRDR—card reader for control statements
SYSLST—printer
SYSIPT—main data input device
SYSOPT—main data output device
SYSLOG—printer for control statements
SYS000
  thru } other peripherals if and as available
SYS254

The operand n is five less than the total number of parameter pairs cited. The programer should keep the number of parameter pairs used as few as possible, and avoid using high numbers and skipping numbers in the series SYS000-SYS254.

The parameters (x'ccuu',x'ddss') for each assigned device are two four-position hexadecimal numbers indicating the channel (cc) and unit (uu) address, the device type (dd), and specifications (ss), as follows:

cc—Channel number
    00—multiplexor channel
    01—1st selector channel
    02—2nd selector channel

uu—00-FF—unit address (0-255)

FIG. 7-15. Operands for supervisor macros.

dd—Device type

00—2401, 2402, 2403, 2404 magnetic tape unit	14—2501 card reader
02—1052 printer-keyboard	16—2520 read-punch
04—1442 card read-punch	18—1285 optical reader
06—1403, 1404 printer	1A—2520 card punch
08—2540 card read-punch (read)	1C—2701 communication unit with
0A—2540 card punch or punch feed read	Synchronous Data Adapter I
0E—1015 inquiry display terminal	1E—1287 OCR in document mode
10—2671 paper tape reader	20—2701 communication unit with
12—1443, 1445 printer	Synchronous Data Adapter II

ss—Specifications

These two hexadecimal characters are 00 unless seven-track tape is specified. In this case they provide four different options: Density, Parity, Translate, and Convert. A code is specified to represent a valid combination of options, as shown in the table below.

Options for Seven-track Tape				
Density (bytes per in.)	Parity	Convert feature	Translate	ss
200	odd	on	off	10
200	odd	off	off	30
200	odd	off	on	38
200	even	off	off	20
200	even	off	on	28
556	odd	on	off	50
556	odd	off	off	70
556	odd	off	on	78
556	even	off	off	60
556	even	off	on	68
800	odd	on	off	90
800	odd	off	off	B0
800	odd	off	on	B8
800	even	off	off	A0
800	even	off	on	A8

IOCFG Macro

keyword=YES,keyword=YES, ...

Operand	Object program(s) requires
MPX=n	Multiplexor channel queues desired (if omitted, 1 is assumed)
SEL=n	One selector channel (n is "1") or both selector channels (n is "2")
TAU=YES	Two-channel read-while-write tape control unit
DVE=n	Test for carriage channel 9 or 12 overflow, or for a 2540 punch error (n=maximum number of printers and 2540 punches to be tested for these conditions by any problem program using the supervisor).

FIG. 7-15 *(continued)*

operand for the START declarative. What this is can vary from installation to installation. If this operand be zero or be omitted, then the programer must use the link-edit program in order to supply a usable starting address, as noted later in this chapter.

After the last card of the source deck, which is the END card, the programer needs two job control cards. The first is a /∗ card, which indicates the end of the

A carriage channel 9 punch should not be used for overflow under two conditions:

1. The supervisor used for the problem program does not include the DVE specification.
2. The supervisor does include the DVE specification, but the PRTOV or CCB macro instruction in the problem program does not request posting of device end in the command control block (CCB).

If a 9 punch is used under either condition, a physical IOCS error message results.

T=YES	2401, 2402, 2403, or 2404 magnetic tape unit
R1=YES	2540 reader
R2=YES	2540 punch feed read
R3=YES	1442 read, or read and punch
R4=YES	2501 reader
R5=YES	2520 reader or read and punch for combined files
P1=YES	2540 punch only
P2=YES	1442 punch only
P3=YES	2520 punch only
L1=YES	1403 or 1404 printer
L2=YES	1443 or 1445 printer
C1=YES	1052 printer-keyboard
S1=YES	1015 inquiry display terminal
R0=YES	2671 paper tape reader
RR=YES	1285 or 1287 OCR in any mode
BACKWRD=YES	Backward reading of magnetic tape
TRK7=YES	7-track magnetic tape
TRK9=YES	9-track magnetic tape (if omitted and T=YES is specified, TRK9=YES is assumed)
ST=YES	2701 communication unit with Synchronous Data Adapter I
ANSWR=n	n is number of lines to be monitored
BSC=YES	2701 communication unit with Synchronous Data Adapter II
BTAB=n	n is number of BSC CCBs permitted, up to 12

Fig. 7-15 *(continued)*

group (in this case, the source deck), and the second is the /& card which indicates the end of the entire job. These are shown in Fig. 7-13.

As a result of compilation, the computer produces as output an object program together with some other information. Usually the computer punches the object program into cards, but it may, depending upon the ASSGN cards, place the object program instead on tape or disk, or it may only print it. If cards are produced (or card images recorded on tape or disk), the first cards are for the IPL—that is, the initial program loader or bootstrap routine, if it was requested. These are followed by the external symbol dictionary (ESD) cards, which are the first cards if no IPL cards were specified and if ESD cards were not suppressed. The format for these cards is shown in Fig. 7-16. The information in the listing shows the name of the symbol (the name given by the programer), and the type. The ESID (external symbol identifications) letters are used as follows: SD indicates a named control section, PC indicates an unnamed control section, LD indicates a symbolic name that may be an entry point, and ER indicates an external reference (symbolic name) not defined in this program. Then comes the address of the symbol without any consideration of relocation. This is followed by the length in bytes of the area

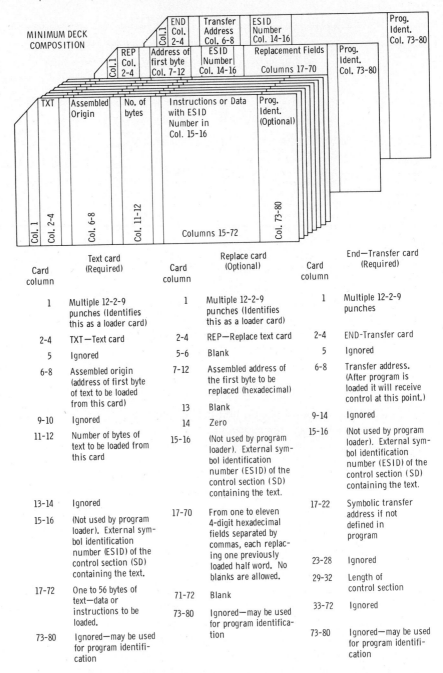

FIG. 7-16. Formats for assembly output cards and link-edit input cards.

COMPLETE DECK COMPOSITION

Columns	Contents
ACTION card (punched by the user; only one used)	
	One or more blanks
	ACTION Selects options.
	One or more blanks
	MAP, NOMAP, CLEAR, or NOAUTO
	Blanks
73-80	Ignored—may be used for program identification
PHASE card (punched by user; one for each phase)	
	One or more blanks
	PHASE Assigns a phase name.
	One or more blanks
	name,* [,NOAUTO] name is the identifying name desired for the phase when it is catalogued into the program library. * specifies loading of the program in internal storage at the next available double word (other options are available). NOAUTO indicates that the AUTOLINK function is to be suppressed. The [ ] indicate to the programer that this operand is optional; the programer omits the [ ] in writing the operand.
	Blanks
73-80	Ignored—may be used for program identification
INCLUDE card (punched by user; one or more for each phase if needed)	
	One or more blanks
	INCLUDE Includes modules in a phase
	One or more blanks
	[module] [,(list-of-names)] module is the name of a module or phase available in the program library, to be incorporated into the phase. list-of-names is a list of one to five CSECT names separated by commas, from which a phase is to be constructed. Note: One or both of the two operands must be present The programer omits the [] in writing the operands, but does show the ( ) and the commas.
	Blanks
73-80	Ignored—may be used for program identification

FIG. 7-16 *(continued)*

Columns	Contents
ESD card (assembly output for the phase)	
1	Multiple punch (12-2-9)
2-4	ESD External Symbol Dictionary
11-12	Number of bytes of information contained in this card
15-16	External symbol identification number (ESID) of the first SD, PC, or ER on this card.
17-72	Variable information:

8 positions	Name		
1 position	Type code in hex as follows:		

Code	ID	Description
00	SD	Section Definition, from named START or CSECT
01	LD	Label Definition, from ENTRY
01	LR	Label Definition, from matched ENTRY and EXTRN
02	ER	External Reference, from EXTRN
04	PC	Private Code, from blank START or CSECT
05	CM	Common storage to more than one module
0A	WX	Weak External Reference (DOS only)

Columns	Contents
73-80	Ignored—may be used for program identification
TXT card (assembly output for the phase)	
1	Multiple punch (12-2-9)
2-4	TXT Text to be loaded.
6-8	Assembled origin (address of first byte to be loaded from this card)
11-12	Number of bytes of text to be loaded
15-16	External symbol identification number (ESID) of the control section (SD) containing the text
17-72	Up to 56 bytes of text (data or instructions to be loaded)
73-80	Ignored—may be used for program identification
REP card (punched by user; one or more for each phase if needed)	
1	Multiple punch (12-2-9)
2-4	REP Replace or Program Patch
5-6	Blank
7-12	Assembled address of the first byte to be replaced (hexadecimal)
13	Blank
14-16	External symbol identification number (ESID) of the control section (SD) containing the text with leading zero.
17-72	From one to eleven 4-digit hexadecimal fields separated by commas, each replacing one previously loaded halfword. A blank indicates the end of information in this card.
73-80	Ignored—may be used for program identification

FIG. 7-16 *(continued)*

Columns	Contents
XFR card (assembly output; may be none or more than one for a phase)	
1	Multiple punch (12-2-9)
2-4	XFR Transfer
6-8	Assembled origin of entry point (after the program is loaded, it receives control at this point)
15-16	ESID number of the control section to which this XFR card refers
17-22	Symbolic label supplied to the assembler if this label was not defined within the assembly
73-80	Ignored—may be used for program identification
RLD card (assembly output; one or more for each phase)	
1	Multiple punch (12-2-9)
2-4	RLD Relocation list dictionary
11-12	Number of bytes of information contained in the card
17-72	Variable information (multiple items)
	2 positions Pointer to the ESID number for the relocation factor of the address constant.
	2 positions Pointer to the ESID number for the position of the address constant.
	1 position Flag indicating type of constant and action needed
	3 positions Assembled address of load constant
73-80	Ignored—may be used for program identification
END card (assembly output; one per phase)	
1	Multiple punch (12-2-9)
2-4	END End of text to be loaded
6-8	Assembled origin of the label supplied to the assembler in the END card (optional)
15-16	ESID number of the control section to which this END card refers
17-22	Symbolic label supplied to the assembler if this label was not defined within the assembly.
23-72	Ignored
73-80	Ignored—may be used for program identification
ENTRY card (punched by the user; only one used, and must be last)	
	One or more blanks
	ENTRY Starting control entry point
	One or more blanks
	Entry point—symbolic name of an entry point. This parameter is optional. If used, it must be a symbol defined in the program with the assembler ENTRY statement, or it must be the name of a START or CSECT statement. It must be followed by at least one blank.
73-80	Ignored—may be used for program identification

FIG. 7-16   *(continued)*

Columns	Contents
SYM card (assembly output; punched only if AOPTN PCHSYM is specified)	
1	Multiple punch (12-2-9)
2-4	SYM Symbol table
11-12	Number of bytes of information contained in this card
14-16	ESID number of the control section to which this SYM card refers.
17-72	Variable information

<table>
<tr><td></td><td colspan="2">ID is EQU, DC, or DS:</td></tr>
<tr><td></td><td>1 position</td><td>type ID</td></tr>
<tr><td></td><td>3 positions</td><td>value attribute (displacement within CSECT)</td></tr>
<tr><td></td><td>8 positions</td><td>symbol name</td></tr>
<tr><td></td><td>1 position</td><td>constant type</td></tr>
<tr><td></td><td>1 position</td><td>length (one less than constant)</td></tr>
<tr><td></td><td>3 positions</td><td>multiplicity</td></tr>
<tr><td></td><td colspan="2">ID is machine or assembler instruction other than EQU, DC, or DS:</td></tr>
<tr><td></td><td>1 position</td><td>type ID</td></tr>
<tr><td></td><td>3 positions</td><td>value attribute (displacement within CSECT)</td></tr>
<tr><td></td><td>8 positions</td><td>symbol name</td></tr>
</table>

73-76	Program identification taken from the name field of the first TITLE statement before the START card.
77-80	Sequence number starting with 0001

FIG. 7-16   *(continued)*

identified by the symbol, and the number of the control section in which the name of the symbol appears.

The next cards produced, if they were specified, are for the supervisor and the program loader. If the programer did not request these by a macro, then these cards, like the IPL cards, are absent from the deck. If a supervisor is present, then the IPL cards should also be present. If neither are present, then the ESD (external symbol dictionary) cards are the first cards in the deck, unless the programer has specified an AOPTN of NOESD.

The next group of cards consist of the object program itself. This is comprised mostly of TXT cards, whose format is shown in Fig. 7-16. The TXT cards carry the actual translated program in machine language. They identify the control section and up to 56 bytes of instructions or data to be loaded. They also include the basic origin address prior to relocation.

In the case of the small and medium models of the computer, the next card usually is an XFR (transfer of control) card. The XFR card, in contrast to the TXT cards, provides information about the place in the program where control should enter in order for the computer to begin execution correctly. This information is calculated from the operand of the END card in the source program.

The next group of cards in the object deck is the relocation dictionary. These cards are omitted if they are suppressed by the AOPTN card with an operand of NORLD. The relocation dictionary (RLD) cards provide information for the linkage editor program on the relocation of constants which serve as operands for instructions. The function of the RLD cards is to make it possible for the programer to use a constant in one control section which may be subject to relocation when the constant itself is defined in another control section, which may also be subject to relocation. The listing of the RLD cards shows which control section contains the constant, which control section contains the address of the constant, and what is the address of the constant prior to relocation.

The last card of the deck is an END card, which may repeat the information available in the last XFR card if any was present.

During the course of assembly, unless they are suppressed by an AOPTN card, the computer will print diagnostic statements. A directory of the meaning of the more common of these statements is shown in Fig. 7-17. In interpreting diagnostics from a compilation, the programer should recognize that an error in one point in the program will normally generate not one but several diagnostic statements at later points in the program. Thus, for example, if the programer makes an error in defining a constant, any reference to that constant will also generate error diagnostics at those points where the other references are made. Therefore the programer, when he peruses for the first time a compilation listing containing diagnostics, should search first for those which are most basic. To this end he usually should give his first attention to the diagnostics on the declaratives, especially the DC and DS declaratives. Only afterward should he turn his attention to diagnostics pertaining to the imperative instructions. In this manner he will save time in making corrections to his program.

Once the programer has achieved a compilation that yields no diagnostic messages, he is ready to test the program. For this, he needs test data (see Chap. 8) and different job control cards. The choice of the latter depends on the type of deck the programer has. If it is a complete deck (IPL, supervisor, and object program) that was compiled with a START card that had a suitable operand, then the programer can use the job control cards shown in Fig. 7-18. It is there assumed that no DATE or ASSGN cards are needed.

If the deck is incomplete, the programer must make it a complete deck by placing the IPL and supervisor decks (obtained from his immediate supervisor) on the front of the object deck. This is the common practice at some installations and is workable if the programer has specified input and output operations in a manner conforming to the standard practice at his installation.

If the object deck does not have a suitable origin point (because the START card lacked a suitable operand), then the programer must pass his program through the linker or link-edit program. This relocates the program in storage and either

Flag	Cause
* A	Expression not simply relocatable
* B	START, EXTRN, ENTRY or ICTL out of order
* C	Location counter overflow
* E	More than 14 EXTRNs
* F	Operand field format error or self-defining value in operand field too large
* G	DC, D, or E range error
I	Expression can not be mapped into base and displacement
* J	Symbol table full
K	Relocation list dictionary buffer table full
* L	Name field error
* M	Multiple-defined symbol
* N	Statement not used. This flag is normally accompanied by other flags which define the reason the statement was not used. If it appears alone, it indicates that the statement was completely extraneous. If the flag (N) appears by itself when a 1442 card option system is being used, it indicates that the source statement has been modified since a previous assembly but the intermediate text field (columns 1-24) has not been left blank.
* O	Invalid OP code
R	Expression not absolute
* S	Specification error
* T	Value too large
U	Undefined symbol
* V	ORG or EQU symbol not previously defined
W	Unused mask bits (37-39) in CCW not zero
X	Duplicate entry statement
* Y	Negative expression
* Z	Column 72 not blank

Note: The * indicates those flags which may be punched in the intermediate text cards produced by phase 1 in card-option systems. For systems without the ability to produce program listings, these flags provide a limited form of error notification. It should be noted that the intermediate text cards produced by phase 1 contain an A, B, or C in column 1 if they are error free. Cards in error have a J, K, L, or M in column 1. Error flags are located in columns 23-24 on cards with a J or K in column 1. The error flags appear in columns 21-24 on cards beginning with L or M.

FIG. 7-17. List of common diagnostics for BPS assemblies on card-oriented models of the computer

loads it for execution or produces a deck ready for loading. This operation is also needed if the program is to be combined with other programs, such as separately assembled DTF declarations. The use of the link edit program is described later in this chapter.

```
// LOG
// JOB
// EXEC
   OBJECT DECK GOES HERE
   DATA DECK GOES HERE
/*
/&
```

FIG. 7-18. BPS job control cards to execute a compiled program.

JOB CONTROL WITH A CARD-ORIENTED SYSTEM

For compilation of an assembly-language program on a no-magnetic-tapes and no-magnetic-disks system, the programer can dispense with many of the job control cards. Often the only remaining job control cards are the /* and the /& cards. Also, for small models of the computer, the programer can often dispense with the macros for the supervisor program.

To make a compilation on a model of the computer equipped with no tapes and no disks, the programer must use a card version of the compiler program. This card version permits fewer option and control cards than would be typical for the BPS version. It comes in two parts, referred to as phase 1 and phase 2. In brief form, phase 1 builds a symbol table, and phase 2 uses it to translate operand addresses. For phase 1, the programer supplies the source deck as input to the computer. The computer produces intermediate information and a symbol table. The input for phase 2 is the intermediate information produced by phase 1 and the symbol table generated by phase 1. The output produced by phase 2 is the object program.

The actual operating practice for making the compilation depends heavily upon the particular configuration of input-output equipment available. For this reason, the programer should rely upon local practice and the programing or operation manager of his installation for assistance on this point. Some general description is possible, however, depending upon the size of the computer to be used.

If the card-only computer is equipped with an interrupt system, which is such that it requires a supervisor program to be present in storage when an object program is executed, no job control cards are needed for the compilation beyond /* or /&, but the programer must provide the ALOG, AOPTN, and supervisor macro cards. If, in contrast, the computer is not equipped with an interrupt system, the programer need supply only the source deck itself, since usually no options are permitted. The /* or /& cards may still be needed.

The compilation procedure for the small models of the computer relies on punching information into the source deck itself. For this reason, with small models of the computer which are card-oriented, a "short" version of the coding form is used, part of the original form being omitted. One popular style leaves the first 24 columns of the card blank and available for receiving the information to be punched during compilation. For larger models of the computer, the computer produces new decks of intermediate information which serve as input for the second phase. In some models of the computer, however, because of their input-output configurations, the programer must insert a blank card following each source card in the source deck to receive the output information.

In general terms, the operating procedure for compilation on a small model of the computer is as follows: The programer supplies the phase 1 compilation deck, which includes its own IPL or bootstrap routine. Immediately following this, the programer provides the source deck, beginning with the START card.

Usually no job control cards are required. Part of the output from the phase 1 operation is data punched into the source deck cards themselves, or into the blank cards fed with the source deck.

For phase 2, the programer supplies the phase 2 compilation deck, which includes its own IPL routine. Immediately following that, the programer again provides the source deck with its partially punched information produced during the first phase. The output data from the second phase consists of the object deck and the program listing. Included in the object deck, usually, is a clear storage routine and an IPL or bootstrap loader routine. The object program may be produced by punching in the original source deck, or may be produced in the blank cards that were fed with the source deck in the first phase.

For larger models of the computer without tapes or disks, the procedure differs slightly. The programer supplies the phase 1 compilation deck, which includes its own IPL or bootstrap routine. Immediately following this, he supplies the source deck, together with any ALOG, AOPTN, and supervisor cards that he may desire. As a result of processing the source deck, the computer produces, as output from phase 1, an intermediate text deck, which serves as input for the phase 2, and if the programer requested it with an AOPTN of PCHSYM, a symbol table deck.

For phase 2, the programer supplies the phase 2 compilation deck, which includes its own IPL routine, and the intermediate text deck produced as the output of the phase 1. As a result of the processing action, the computer produces an object deck punched into a separate set of cards, independent of those read by the computer as input for either of the phases.

The symbol table information in both cases remains in internal storage in the form of a table for reference by the phase 2 compilation deck. As such, phase 1 communicates symbol definition information to phase 2 by means of the contents of storage. For this reason, it is important that the programer make the phase 2 part of his compilation immediately following the phase 1. If he does not, then he must have the compiler punch out the symbol table in order to be able to perform phase 2 later. The usual procedure, in this case, is to supply the symbol table in front of the partially punched source deck or in front of the intermediate text deck in phase 2. Practice is not uniform, however, and some versions of the compiler program do not permit interrupted compilations.

On some of the small models of the computer, the programer has an additional complication: the assembly program for the IOCS is separate from the main assembly program. This means that the programer must make two additional passes of his source deck in order to produce a complete object deck when using those models of the computer. First he compiles the IOCS routines in a two-pass operation similar to that just sketched. Then, incorporating that object deck data into his source deck, he compiles his program again, but this time he uses the main assembly deck.

JOB CONTROL WITH TAPE OR DISK OPERATING SYSTEM (TOS OR DOS)

For compilations on models of the computer equipped with magnetic disks or tapes and 32K (32,000) bytes or more of internal storage capacity, different job control cards are used. The job control cards for the DOS or Disk Operating System are shown in Fig. 7-19. The task is the one shown previously in Fig. 7-13.

Taking the job control cards in groups clarifies the functions they perform in directing the operating system. From JOB through the first /*, the cards provide directions for doing the compilation. From TITLE to END are the cards of the source program to be compiled. The TITLE card is optional but, if used, results in printing the program name (the operand for TITLE) on the output. But that title is only for use on the printed pages; if the computer is to refer to the program by name, it must be assigned by means of a PHASE card. A "phase" is one or more control sections compiled together all at one time. The ENTRY card specifies the control entry point and also must be specified in the program itself by an ENTRY declarative (see later in this chapter) or by a named CSECT or START declarative. The ENTRY card when present overrides the entry point specified as the operand for the END declarative.

The group of control cards beginning with ACTION and ending two cards later with EXEC LNKEDT provides directions for doing the link-edit. Specifying an ACTION of MAP results in a printed summary of the placement of programs in storage. The INCLUDE is needed if the link-edit step in the run is to link together the program just compiled with other programs. If these other programs exist as decks in object language, the INCLUDE needs no operand, but the decks must immediately follow the INCLUDE card. If these other programs are to come from the operating system maintained library, then they must be named as the operands of the INCLUDE cards, one per card.

The group of control cards beginning with EXEC and ending with /& pro-

```
// LOG
// JOB
* ANY COMMENTS
// OPTION LIST,ERRS,DECK,LINK
   ENTRY ENTR
   PHASE POGO
// EXEC ASSEMBLY
          TITLE POGO
          START
   SOURCE DECK GOES HERE
          END    ENTR
/*
 ACTION MAP
 INCLUDE
// EXEC LNKEDT
// EXEC
   TEST DATA GOES HERE IF ON CARDS
/*
/&
```

FIG. 7-19. Job control cards to compile and execute under DOS.

vides directions for running the compiled and edited programs against the test data. The EXEC needs no operand when it is the just-compiled program with a specified control entry point, as by an operand for an END or ENTRY. The /* marks the end of a job step; the /& marks the end of the job initiated by the JOB card.

A comparison of the job control cards for TOS or DOS with those of BPS, as shown in Fig. 7-13, reveals several noteworthy differences (see also Figs. 7-20 and 7-15). In the first place, the JOB card need not identify the program to be executed; this is now handled by the execute card. Comments can be made by the use of an asterisk card. In order to specify some of the options for controlling the interaction between the compiler and the operating system, the programer has available under TOS or DOS the OPTION card. The OPTION card, shown in Fig. 7-19, asks for a listing of the source deck, a listing of the errors and diagnostics, an output deck, and a list on tape or disk of the input needed for the linkage editor program. The programer could add other options to the list—for example, XREF—to obtain the cross-reference list in place of a symbol table.

In the case of TOS or DOS the object deck is normally provided directly on tape or disk, where it can later be called for execution. Before it can be called for execution, however, it must pass through a linkage-edit operation in order to make the correct storage relocation. Loading (placing) the program, ready for execution, in internal storage is done automatically under DOS, complete with a supervisor. For this reason, a deck should be asked for only if manual patches are to be performed, or if it is desired to keep the tape or disk clear of a permanent record of the program.

```
IN APPENDIX D, NOTE
        JOB
        EXEC
        ASSGN
        DATE
        OPTION
```

FIG. 7-20. Job control card formats for DOS or TOS.

If the programer desires to make the program a permanent part of the program library tape or disk, he can do this by including as an option the CATAL operand. Then he must supply on the immediately following card, after the word PHASE, the name that he wishes to have assigned to the program so it can be called later for execution from the library tape or disk.

The particular choice of options open to the programer varies from installation to installation. Some installations, for example, wish to maintain close control over those programs which are cataloged into the program library. In such cases, the programer is normally not permitted free use of the CATAL option. In order to utilize his own installation's standard operating procedure, the programer can omit the OPTION card entirely. In such cases, the standard option set is automatically utilized. Only if the programer finds that the standard option set provided by the installation does not meet his needs, should he supply an OPTION card to request a change in the standard pattern. If he does supply one, the operands that he lists are the only operands affected. The other portions of the standard set of options remain unchanged. The programer also need not worry about confusing or disturbing other programers' operations, since whenever the computer encounters another JOB card or a /& card, the original listing of options is automatically restored.

The programer should note that under TOS or DOS the function of the EXEC card is changed. Instead of being placed on the EXEC card, comments are now placed on the * card. It is now on the EXEC card that the programer identifies the program he wishes to have executed. If he wishes to make a compilation, the operand he specifies is ASSEMBLY.

For program execution under TOS or DOS, a supervisor program is provided automatically without a request by the programer. Hence the compiler provides none, and the programer need not provide supervisor macros. Nor are AOPTN cards needed. Literals are part of the normal repertoire at most installations at the TOS or DOS level, and to use them no special action is required. If the programer finds that literals have not been correctly compiled, the most likely trouble is the placement of the LTORG card. The remaining cards in the deck are the normal source cards, as shown previously.

The programer may also have to provide ASSGN cards immediately prior to the EXEC card, with a blank operand in order to correctly identify the way in which the operating system is to use the input and output equipment. No ASSGN cards are required for making the compilation, because normally this uses either the standard areas on disk or "scratch" tapes which have been mounted for the compilation.

For execution of the object program, the console operator may at any time interrupt the operation and type in from the control console new ASSGN statements to modify the equipment the program is to use. To facilitate the console operator's reassignment, as in the case of equipment malfunction, it is helpful if the programer supplies ASSGN cards for the program he wishes to have the computer execute. This gives a basis for more intelligent assignment by the console operator of the equipment than would be possible if the console operator were left uninformed about the significant items of equipment to be used. Comment (*) cards telling the console operator how to set up the computer are, for the same reason, recommended at some installations, for these print out on the console for the console operator's information.

JOB CONTROL WITH OPERATING SYSTEM (OS)

For compilations on models of the computer equipped with magnetic disks (or magnetic tapes or both) and at least 64 K bytes of internal storage, still different

job control cards may be required. A larger, more comprehensive, and more powerful operating system may be used, called OS (Operating System), that offers more
conveniences to the programer but requires a more extensive job control language
(JCL) to call them into play.

A comparison of the job control cards needed for OS, as shown in Fig. 7-21,
with those for DOS reveals a difference in philosophy and practice as well as differences in card formats (compare with Fig. 7-19). To lay a groundwork, a brief review of the philosophy and practice is in order.

OS offers the programer many options on a variety of operational matters. Yet
most programers most of the time select the same options, run after run, with only
minor variations. To save the programer the effort of repeating himself endlessly in
writing JCL, OS makes frequent use of default options. These are set by the installation management and hence may vary from one installation to another and from one
time to another. Users' choices even on the default options do not show enough uniformity to permit summarizing them briefly. Hence the options available are not described in an appendix to this book. To do so would give a falsely simplistic impres-
sion of the JCL for OS and fail to reveal the wide extent of the choices open to the
programer. At least initially, the programer should seek and follow the advice of his
supervisor on JCL for OS, for OS JCL is a very common source of bugs.

OS offers the programer more assistance than do the other operating systems
described earlier. It provides a greater variety of diagnostic messages to help in debugging. It provides more options for the programer in using assembly language, as
summarized in this book's Assembly Language Comparison in Appendix B. It uses
itself as a supervisor. It gives the programer a larger and more capable library of
routines to draw upon in link-edit. It permits a more flexible use of input and output equipment. And in some versions, it allows the programer to take advantage of
multiprograming.

In practice, at most computer installations using OS, the programer finds that
the JCL cards he usually needs are available as a "cataloged procedure." These pre-
prepared sequences of JCL cards, maintained in callable form in a library ready for
use, strongly reflect individual installation practices and computer configurations.
What goes well at one installation may be unacceptable or unworkable at another.
The presentation given in Fig. 7-21 and the comments below are but a few of the
many alternatives that may be acceptable.

The three main JCL cards in OS are the JOB, EXEC, and DD. These must be
used in that sequence, but the JOB card is needed only once as the first JCL card for
a job. The other cards may be repeated in groups consisting of one EXEC card followed by one to many DD cards for each job step. A job step in OS is the execution
of one program, such as a linkage editor. A job typically requires the execution of
several programs, such as the assembly language compiler, the linkage editor, and
then the compiled program.

```
//FIG#7 JOB (V46-39),'A. USER'.MSGLEVEL=1
//FSTPR EXEC ASMGCLG
//ASM.SYSIN DD *
              * SOURCE DECK GOES HERE
/*
//GO.D7K DD DSNAME=&TTOD,DISP=(NEW,PASS),UNIT=2314,             X
//            SPACE=(CYL,(9)),DCB=(BLKSIZE=200,RECFM=FB)
//GO.T7W DD DSNAME=TDFL,DISP=(OLD,PASS),UNIT=2400,              X
//            DCB=(BLKSIZE=200,RECFM=FB,DEN=3)
//GO.SYSUDUMP DD SYSOUT=A
/*
```

FIG. 7-21. JCL example to compile, link, and go (execute) under OS, with a dump requested if the execution fails.

The JOB card identifies the job and the user. The JOB card must begin with // in the first two positions—a general requirement for most OS JCL cards that is the same as that for DOS and TOS. The programer must assign a name to the job, placing it immediately after the //. The length may not exceed eight characters. Then after one or more spaces, the programer must put JOB (see Fig. 7-21). Nearly all installations require after one or more spaces that the programer provide as operands at least an account or charge number in parentheses, a comma, and in single quotes, his name. Optionally but often required are one or more operands in keyword format. These separated by commas and no intervening spaces must, if present, immediately follow the user's name after a comma. A common operand is MSGLEVEL=1, which directs the operating system to print a copy in the output of all the JCL cards when the computer executes a job.

The EXEC card calls for the execution of a program. On the EXEC card immediately after the usual //, the programer may specify a name for the job step or may leave the name blank. After at least one space, the programer must place EXEC. After at least one space, the programer must begin the operands by placing either the name of a cataloged procedure or one or more keyword operands. One common mnemonic used in specifying cataloged-procedure names in OS is to let ASM stand for assembly language, C for compile, L for load or link-edit, and G for go to execution of the compiled and linked program. Thus, for a compiler identified as the "F" version of the compiler, a cataloged procedure named as the first operand on the EXEC card might be ASMFCLG. Sometimes the keyword PROC= is catenated to the procedure name to make a keyword parameter, as PROC= ASMFCLG.

Thus the first operand on the EXEC card identifies the program to be executed. To identify the program, the programer may catenate PGM= to the program name. For example, to call for the execution of a program named LOADER, the programer may write PGM=LOADER. Sometimes the programer wants to give special directions or to select nondefault options for a program's execution. To do this, the programer can follow the program or cataloged name by a comma and then write the keyword PARM.name= followed by the value or name desired. The "name" must be for a step in a job, usually as a practical matter, a step in a cataloged procedure. Thus, in an ASMFCLG, the job step for the link-editor might be called LKED. Then to obtain a link-edit map (see Fig. 7-22), the programer might specify ASMFCLG,PARM.LKED=MAP, if the usual practice at his installation was not to print the map. Since many operands can be specified, the programer may have to continue citing them on a following card. The format is // followed by from 2 to 14 spaces, followed by the operands. The last or rightmost operand character on the continued card should be the comma that separates successive keyword operands.

The DD cards needed with each EXEC card are more complex in format and usually numerous. The DD (data definition) card specifies the peripheral equipment for each "data set" and how the data are to be handled. Jobs with little or simple input and output usually require few DD cards; jobs with many inputs and out-puts, or with many steps where an output of one may serve as an input for another, usually require many DD cards. A "data set" is a file or collection of data assigned a name and treated by OS as a coherent whole but accessed a part at a time. Cataloged procedure and installation conventions for handling input and output ease part of the burden on the programer preparing DD cards, but usually they cause pro-gramers the most trouble.

After the usual //, the programer writes a name for the DD card, not more than eight characters long. If the programer has written a DCB (data control block, see Chap. 11), this name may be the same as the name used in the program for the DCB. After at least one space, the programer places the DD and at least one following space. Then the programer writes from one to many operands. If the operand DATA or * be the programer's choice, then it must be the first oper-and. Both indicate that the following cards are not JCL cards but are data cards for the program to be executed. But DATA also indicates that the data cards may have // in the first two columns—not generally a good practice. After a comma, the programer can cite other operands as needed. Continuation cards may be used in the format described previously.

The common operands for the DD card are DCB=, DSN= or DSNAME=, UNIT=, DISP=, and VOL=. A brief look at each can help show their functions. The DCB= is followed by keyword operands describing the data. These must be consistent with the description given in the program. In practice, the programer needs to provide on the DD card only those items of description not included in the data control block (DCB) and not available in the label recorded in computer-readable form with the data. For example, data in an indexed-sequential organiza-tion with fixed-length records 120 bytes long in blocks of five records could be shown as DCB=(DSORG=IS,RECFM=FB,BLKSIZE=600,LRECL=120).

The DSN= or DSNAME= is the data set name. If the programer uses two &'s before the name, it marks the data as temporary "scratch storage" to be re-tained only for the duration of the job. An example is DSNAME=&&SCRCH3.

The DISP= operand (disposition) specifies the initial and final status of the data, both for a normal and an aborted job termination, in that order. The initial status commonly is NEW for an output and OLD for an input. The disposition at normal termination is PASS if the data are to be used in a later job step, KEEP if the data are to be retained for other jobs and no longer needed for this job, and DELETE if the data are to be discarded. For aborted termination, PASS is 1.ᵗ allowed, but KEEP and DELETE are. If OLD data are to be retained and NEW eliminated, then the termination operands may be omitted. Thus DISP=(OLD, KEEP,KEEP) is usually equivalent to DISP=OLD. Temporary data (&& in the name) may only have PASS or DELETE as terminal dispositions.

The UNIT= and VOL= operands refer, respectively, to the item of peripheral equipment and the identification given to the storage medium holding the data. These operands depend heavily upon installation practices and the computer configuration. The UNIT= operand permits the computer operator to reassign peripheral equipment to fit operational needs. The VOL= operand permits the computer to check on the identification recorded on the data medium for the data prior to reading or writing data on it.

In addition to the differences in the JOB and EXEC cards between DOS and OS job control language, the programer should note the DD card which has no direct equivalent in DOS. OS has also still other JCL cards not touched on here and other differences from DOS, TOS, BOS, and BPS. One of them, for instance, is the non-use in OS of /& cards to mark the end of a job or data.

PROGRAM LINKAGE

Mention has been made at several points in the preceding sections of the common need to link-edit the compiled program. This need arises when parts of a program are to be combined before execution or when it is necessary to establish the location of the program in storage. The link-edit program adjusts the addresses in a program to locate the program in a particular area of storage and to permit one control section to reference data or instruction in another control section.

The input to the link-editor program is the object program, complete with the relocation dictionary and the external symbol dictionary (see Fig. 7-16). The output from the link-editor program is the object program ready for execution and under DOS loaded in internal storage. To record the way in which the program has been made ready for execution, the link-editor program provides as output a printed summary called a "map" of the action it has taken. A sample is shown in Fig. 7-22.

The input for the link-edit program is, in the sequence shown, the following cards: ACTION, PHASE, INCLUDE, ESD, TXT, REP, RLD, END or XFR, and ENTRY. The formats of these cards have been shown in Fig. 7-16. The IN-

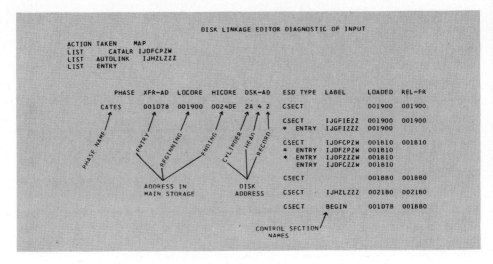

Fig. 7-22. Link-edit map.

CLUDE card is needed only if this program is to be combined with other programs. The output is a punched deck or is listed on tape or disk ready for loading and execution.

The printed output from the link-editor program shows the name of each phase (program), the beginning and ending locations in internal storage, and the control entry (transfer) address in absolute form. The disk storage addresses, if any, of the program are shown next. Then follow typically several columns of information showing the entry points noted in the external symbol dictionary with the symbolic name (label) used in the program for the entry point. Then, under the column "loaded," is the absolute address to which the link-editor has assigned the entry point. The relocation factor immediately follows that and shows the amount by which the symbolic address was relocated in storage. When only one program has been loaded, and it has been loaded in a continuous area of storage, the loaded address and the relocation factor will be identical.

If the programer wishes to have cross referencing between separately compiled control sections, or wishes to compile a program in portions and later link them together for execution, he must give specific attention to ways of providing information to the link-editor enabling it to identify the symbolic names (the entry points) in the sections that are used by other sections. To do this, the programer has available two declaratives, ENTRY and EXTRN, for use in his program. These are for the purpose of identifying, respectively, the entry points and the external symbols. An external symbol is a name not defined in the control sections being compiled at any one time. Some external symbols may be defined in programs stored in

NAME	OP	OPERANDS	COMMENT
	EXTRN	IJDFCZZZ	
	ENTRY	INPUTB	

FIG. 7-23. Example of ENTRY and EXTRN declaratives.

the operating system maintained library. These can be called upon by an EXTRN declarative but not by a WXTRN which is otherwise identical in function. EXTRN and ENTRY are not needed for type V constants. The use of the EXTRN and ENTRY declaratives is not difficult but does require the attention of the programer.

By convention, the name of an item of data or an instruction in programing is referred to as an entry point in the control section in which it is defined. Thus, for example, if the name APPLE identifies a particular field in control section TWO, then for that control section it is an entry point.

If in some other control section, such as section THREE, the programer wishes to use the contents of the field APPLE, he must identify this data name by an EXTRN declarative as being an external symbol—i.e., its definition is external to the control section in which it is being used. Then in control section TWO he must identify APPLE as an entry point with an ENTRY declarative. The use of ENTRY and EXTRN declaratives is shown in Fig. 7-23. The programer must be careful to place ENTRY and EXTRN declaratives in the program immediately after the start of the control section. Figure 7-9 provides an example of EXTRN usage.

When the relative positions among items of data in storage are important, and these items are in a different control section that is to be or has been compiled at a different time, the programer can avoid some of the limitations of the ENTRY and EXTRN declaratives by the use of a DSECT (dummy control section). The compiler uses a DSECT to obtain the relative addresses, but does not compile it in the usual manner for ordinary control sections. The dummy section serves as a stand-in for an ordinary control section, and the compiler produces no TXT or other object language output for it.

The programer writes a dummy section as he would write an ordinary control section, but he replaces the CSECT declarative with a DSECT declarative. Since the dummy section serves only as a replacement for a separately compiled control section, the programer usually includes only DS or DC declaratives. If the programer provides in the control section he is writing a way of setting the contents of a base register to provide coverage of the dummy section, e.g., by loading an address constant for the name of the dummy section and giving a USING declarative, he can reference in his program any symbolic name in the dummy section without an EXTRN or ENTRY declarative. Other arrangements are possible. An example of the use of a dummy section is given in a later chapter.

Do It Now Exercise 7-3. *Check with the Standard Operating Practice manual or the supervisor at your installation on the job control cards needed to compile and execute the program you wrote for Do It Now Exercise 7-2. Prepare the cards, and then compile and execute the program using at least 70 data cards listing the names of your favorite baseball players, your local civic leaders, your favorite recording artists, and your supervisor or instructor. How do the control cards you use differ from those shown in this text?*

Do It Now Exercise 7-4. *Revise the program for Do It Now Exercise 7-2 to place the DTF declaratives in a separate control section. Then incorporate EXTRN and ENTRY declaratives for each data name. Compile the control sections separately, obtaining separate program decks. Then link-edit these together and execute them.*

EXERCISES

1. List the advantages of utilizing IOCS macros for performing input and output operations.

2. What are the functions handled or specified by the required operands for the DTFSR declarative for a printer? For a card reader? How do these contrast with the functions handled or specified by the optional operands?

3. Why do the small models of the computer have a halt command, whereas the larger models do not?

4. What is job control and how is it accomplished?

5. What is the use of each type of job control card?

6. How do the job control cards for TOS or DOS differ from those for BPS?

CHAPTER 8

Debugging

FINDING MISTAKES IN PROGRAMS

In the normal course of events the programer rarely writes a perfect program. Except on the most small and trivial applications, the programer usually finds he has written a program that directs the computer inaccurately. It is then the responsibility of the programer to correct his mistakes and make the program direct the computer correctly.

Evidence of mistakes comes in two main ways: First and the easiest to correct, the output data produced by the computer do not agree with what was expected. If this difference is small, a small correction in the program will normally fix it. If the difference is large, such as the nearly entire absence of correct output data, then major remedies may be necessary. In either case, however, since the output data show the fault, the programer has something he can see and relate back to the program. Since the programer knows which parts of the program produce each part of the output data, he can find the place in the program where correction is needed.

The second type of evidence of mistakes is more subtle—the absence of output data, or output data that indicate errors that consist of skipping or repeating parts of the program. The computer may be unable to execute the instructions in the desired sequence in the program for any of a wide variety of reasons. The evidence indicating what the reasons were and where in the program the computer was trying to execute the instructions is often difficult to obtain, and the causes are sometimes difficult to correct. This situation is influenced by the interrupt system provided in the computer and by the execution of the programer's program ("the problem program") in conjunction with the supervisor program or operating system.

The supervisor program or operating system takes over control of the computer when the computer is unable to execute the instructions in a program the programer has written. When this happens, what the computer does depends upon several things: the standard operating procedure at the installation; the action taken by the console operator; and the nature of the difficulty the computer encountered. From the point of view of the programer, however, these boil down essentially to a situation which can be pictured briefly in the following terms.

When the computer is unable to execute a program ("dies," "blows up," or "goes into an endless loop") the programer normally finds handed to him a dump of internal storage from the computer in a format similar to that described in Chaps. 3 and 4 (a "post mortem" dump); and a few or no comments from the console operator about the symptoms the computer exhibited at the time (of "death"). The interpretation the programer makes of these materials depends upon his knowledge of the data (usually the "test data") that served as input, and of the way in which the computer operates. Much of this knowledge pertains to how the computer operates in general, and how it executes each command in particular, as described elsewhere in this book. But the programer, for an adequate interpretation, also needs an understanding of the interrupt system in the computer, and how it can affect the data provided in the dump.

To that end, the following sections in this chapter deal with the choice of test data, the way the computer maintains control, the nature of the operating states in the computer, the way the interrupt system operates, and the interpretation of the dumps from the point of view of debugging.

TEST DATA

The ease or difficulty the programer experiences in doing debugging work depends in part upon his choice of test data. To save himself work, the programer must be very careful in his selection of test data. The first input data with which he attempts to test his program should be data for which the output data, if the program processes these input data at all, will be obviously accurate or obviously inaccurate. Fields whose contents are especially critical should be the ones emphasized by the test data. All data combinations should be easy, and all exceptions should be avoided. The workbook gives several examples of how to select initial test data.

Once the program processes correctly the initial test data, the programer can try more elaborate test data to evaluate the program's ability to handle a greater variety of conditions. Even here, however, the programer must be careful which conditions he selects for the program to try to process. The programer should know what the correct results are for each test case he has supplied. If he does not, he may fail to recognize erroneous processing action by the computer.

Of particular concern is the correct processing of the first of anything, such as the first record of a group or the first line of output data. Also of particular concern is the correct processing of the last of anything, such as the last record of a file of input data or the final line on a report. Also of particular concern are the iterative loops in a program. The test data should check their ability to be executed zero, one, two, and three times.

After the computer processes all the intermediate test data correctly, the programer is ready for extensive live data tests. These the programer rarely attempts to evaluate directly himself; instead he gives the output to the data user, who makes the evaluation for him. The data user may say, "This does not look reasonable to me, what should it be?" Then he and the programer can attempt to reach a conclusion about what the correct output should have been. If this agrees with what the computer produced, most data users are willing to assume that the program is operating correctly. If it differs, the error may lie in the manual estimate of what the correct output should be, or it may lie in the computer program.

The extensiveness and nature of the bugs the programer detects depend partly upon the program and partly upon the programer's selection of test data. In order to avoid being overwhelmed by bugs that are difficult to catch at first, the programer is wise to select easy test data for his initial attempt. When the program operates successfully on these, then is the time to introduce more elaborate test data. If the programer attempts to use elaborate test data from the beginning, the result may be to slow seriously the debugging.

In practice, the control-sequence arrangement and the interrupt systems of the computer help preserve evidence of mistakes. This helps the programer detect the mistakes and devise corrective action. For an appreciation of the help this can be, some background on the program status word is basic.

PROGRAM STATUS WORD OPERATIONS

Not all models of the computer use a program status word (PSW). All models of the computer do, however, have portions of their storage and control units devoted to performing the control functions that are accomplished by the presence of and changes in the program status word (PSW) of those models that have them. Prime attention in this chapter is therefore devoted to the PSW and its significance to the programer.

The functions of the PSW in the small models of the computer are similar to those in medium and larger models. These functions include maintaining the sequence of control and regulating the interrupts. The PSW maintains the sequence of control by incorporating in it the address of the next instruction the computer is to execute.

The PSW regulates interrupts by incorporating in itself the channel mask bits. To identify specifically the functions of the PSW, it is convenient to examine the fields in the PSW.

In the small models of the computer, the PSW is one full word (four bytes) long, and is divided into seven fields, as shown in Fig. 8-1. The numbers in the diagram denote bit positions in the word. The function of each of these is explained in more detail later in this section. Starting at the extreme left, the first field is unused. The next to the leftmost field, two bits long, serves as the condition code. The next field is unused. The following field, also two bits long, serves as the ASCII mode bit and as the channel mask bit. The next field is one half byte long and serves as the device address for an input or output operation, thus identifying the active item of input or output equipment. The following half-byte field is the function specification for an input or output operation, thus identifying the operation being performed by the I-O equipment. The rightmost two bytes of the PSW consist of the address of the next instruction to be executed.

```
0 1 2 3 4 5 6 7 8   11 12  15 16                    31
```

J   Not used (should be 0 bits)
F   Condition code
J   Not used (should be 0 bits)
M   Channel mask bits
K   Device or equipment address
L   Function specification
H   Instruction address (address of next instruction)

FIG. 8-1. Fields in the program status word for the small models of the computer.

The primary command for changing the PSW in the small model of the computer is the Set PSW command. In using it to replace an existing PSW with data to serve as a new PSW, the programer must recognize a few restrictions. First, the instruction address must be greater than 144. The reason is that the first 144 bytes of internal storage are considered to be protected and may not contain instructions for execution. Second, the instruction address in the new PSW being loaded must be within the limits of available internal storage within the computer. In practice, this means that there must be at least one leading 0 at the left end of the instruction address field, depending on the size of internal storage available in the small model of the computer at the installation. Third, the address of the word to be loaded as a PSW should be aligned on the full-word boundary, but this is not required. Alignment on the half-word boundary is satisfactory. Fourth, even though the Set PSW command is of the SI type, no immediate data need be supplied, and none are utilized. Hence only one operand need be written.

SPSW—Set Program Status Word. This SI command causes one full word of data from the operand address to replace and become the current program status word (PSW). No part of the old PSW is retained. This command may result in altering the condition code, because the new PSW loaded contains its own condition code. This command is available only on the small models of the computer and serves as a substitute for the Load PSW command available on the medium and large models.

In the medium and large models of the computer, the operations on, and the functions performed by, the PSW differ from those in the small models of the computer. With two exceptions, and except for the commands that set the condition code, the commands the programer can use to alter the PSW are normally not available to the programer because they are "privileged" in some models of the computer. Nevertheless, it is helpful to know what are the components of the PSW, and what is the role of the PSW, in order to be able to interpret and understand better the other operations which can be performed by the computer. This is more easily understood if we examine how the PSW controls the computer's operation.

The program status word (PSW) in the medium and large models of the computer is a double word composed of eight fields. Each of these eight fields has its own role in controlling the way in which the computer executes instructions. A diagram of the PSW in the common basic control (BC) mode is shown in Fig. 8-2. The numbers in that diagram denote the bit positions in the double word.

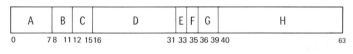

A	B	C	D	E	F	G	H
0	7 8	11 12	15 16	31 33	35 36	39 40	63

A System mask bits
B Key for storage protection
C XMWP control bits
D Interruption code
E Instruction length code
F Condition code
G Program mask bits
H Instruction address (address of next instruction)

FIG. 8-2. Fields in the PSW for the BC mode (see also Appendix E).

Let us examine the PSW in terms of the function of each field. The rightmost field of the PSW is the instruction address. This is the address of the next instruction to be executed after the computer completes the execution of the current instruction. If the computer executes a transfer of control instruction, then the normal content of this field is replaced by the new address from which the next instruction to be executed is to be obtained. The computer actually uses this field of the PSW to obtain the next instruction. Ignoring the unintentional interrupts, the programer has three ways of altering the sequence of control: change this field in the existing PSW by executing a transfer of control; replace the entire PSW; or permit an interrupt operation to replace the entire PSW.

The next field to the left in the PSW is the program mask. This is a four-bit field (one hexadecimal character). Each bit has a particular significance and function. A 1 bit permits an interrupt; a 0 bit suppresses an interrupt. For convenience of identification, the bits are normally numbered from 36 through 39 in this field. Bit 36 indicates by a 0 or 1 status whether an interruption is to be taken in the event of arithmetic overflow in a binary arithmetic operation. Bit number 37 performs the same function, but for packed-decimal arithmetic operations. Bits 38 and 39 are used in floating-point operation and are discussed in Chap. 12. The programer can alter the program mask field by specifying a Set Program Mask instruction.

The next field to the left in the PSW is the condition code field. This two-bit field has been described earlier in this book. The programer can set it directly by means of the Set Program Mask command.

The next field to the left is the instruction-length code field. This length code is expressed in terms of half words with the following significance: (01_b) The current instruction is one half word long and is in the RR format. (10_b) The current instruction is one full word long and is in the RX format, or the current instruction is one full word long and is in the RS or SI format. (11_b) The current instruction is three half words long and is in the SS format. A code of 00_b indicates the absence of any specific length. The RX is distinguished from the RS or SI formats by the first bit in the command code, which is 0_b for the RX format. The programer should note that the instruction length is not for the next instruction but for the length of the *current* instruction being executed. This determines the amount by which to increase the instruction address portion of the PSW to adjust it to contain the address of the next sequential instruction for a normal sequence of control.

The four fields just reviewed (instruction address, program mask, condition code, and instruction length) comprise the second (right) full word of the double-word PSW in the medium and large models of the computer. The left word of the double-word PSW also consists of four fields, but their use and significance are different.

The rightmost field of the first half of the PSW is the interruption code. The interpretation and significance of this code are commented upon later in this chapter.

The XMWP field is, for convenience, identified by bit positions 12 through 15. In some of the older models of the computer, bit 12 indicates the use of an ASCII (a 1 bit) or EBCDIC (a 0 bit) input-output code. This was never fully implemented, and for the newer models has been dropped entirely and a 0 bit must be used here in the PSW to indicate the BC mode.

Bit 13 is the Machine-check mask bit. If the bit is 1, an interrupt occurs on the detection of a machine failure. If the bit is 0, no interrupt occurs. Bit 14 indicates whether or not the computer is in the Wait state. A 1 bit indicates the wait state; a 0 bit indicates the absence of the wait state. Bit 15 indicates whether or not the computer is in the Problem state. If the bit is a 1, the computer can execute no "privileged" commands—i.e., the computer is in the problem program state. A 0 bit indicates the absence of the problem program state, i.e., the presence of the supervisor state. The MWP states are described later in this chapter.

The next field to the left in the PSW is the protection key. This field is used in conjunction with the storage protection capability, which is an optional feature with various models of the computer. Privileged operations are available for altering the protection key. These and the nature of the storage protection feature are beyond the scope of this chapter but are briefly covered in Appendix E.

The leftmost field in the PSW is the system mask. Each bit in this field is associated with a particular channel or external interrupt source. Bit numbers 0 through 6 are associated with channels 0 through 6. Bit number 7 is a multiple-use bit referring to the external interrupt key and to any other external signals. Privileged commands are available for altering the PSW, such as Load PSW.

LPSW—Load PSW. This SI command has one operand, the address of the aligned double word in storage which contains the data to be used as the new PSW. This command copies the contents of that field, making those contents the new PSW. The former PSW is not stored or saved. The condition code is set because a new condition code is part of the new PSW. This command is a privileged operation, and no example of its use is included here. In the small models of the computer, the command Set PSW is available instead.

SPM—Set Program Mask. This RR command uses only one operand, which is named as the address of a register. Bits 2 and 3 of that register are copied into and become the condition code in the current PSW. Bits 4 through 7 are copied into and become the program-mask field in the PSW. In the BC mode, these same bits are copied from the PSW by the Branch and Link commands. An example of Set Program Mask is given in Fig. 8-3. No equivalent command is available for the small models of the computer.

TS—Test and Set. This SI command sets entirely to 1 bits the one byte of storage which is named as the only operand. This address cannot be directly indexed. Before the one byte of storage is altered, the leftmost bit of the byte is copied into the PSW in bit position 35, and bit 34 is set to 0. This command is useful for setting program switches, since the effect is to set the condition code to match the leftmost bit of the byte in storage before changing that byte to contain FF_x. An example of Test and Set is given in Fig. 8-4. No equivalent command is available for the small models of the computer since they are not used for time sharing.

```
    LOC    OBJECT CODE      ADDR1 ADDR2  ST #   NAME    OP    OPERANDS              COMMENT

                                               IMPERATIVES

  000008  5840 3058        00060           8            L     4,QOLD               LOAD MASK
  00000C  0550                             9            BALR  5,0
  00000E  0440                            10  F8#3      SPM   4                     SET THE PROGRAM MASK
  000010  0560                            11            BALR  6,0
  000012  9046 3078        00080          12            STM   4,6,QSAVE


                                               DECLARATIVES

  000060  3F000000                        29  QOLD      DC    X'3F000000'          F8#3 CC AND MASK
  000064  404040404040404040              30            DC    28C' '               FILLER
  00006C  4040404040404040
  000074  4040404040404040
  00007C  40404040
  000080  4040404040404040                31  QSAVE     DC    CL32' '              DISPLAY STORAGE
  000088  4040404040404040
  000090  4040404040404040
  000098  4040404040404040


                                          DUMP AFTER EXECUTION

  001940  F0404040    40404040   40404040   40404040   40404040   40404040   40404040   40404040
  001960  3F000000    40404040   40404040   40404040   40404040   40404040   40404040   40404040
  001980  3F000000    4000190E   7F001912   40404040   40404040   40404040   40404040   40404040
  0019A0  F0404040    40404040   40404040   40404040   40404040   40404040   40404040   40404040


                                       RELOCATION FACTOR    001900
```

FIG. 8-3. Example of Set Program Mask.

```
    LOC    OBJECT CODE      ADDR1 ADDR2  ST #   NAME    OP    OPERANDS              COMMENT

                                               IMPERATIVES

  000016  0550                            14            BALR  5,0
  00001B  D200 30F8 30D8  00100 000E0     15            MVC   QSTORE(1),QYTE
  00001E  9300 30D8        000E0          16  F8#4      TS    QYTE                 TEST AND SET
  000022  0560                            17            BALR  6,0
  000024  9056 30FC        00104          18            STM   5,6,QSTORE+4


                                               DECLARATIVES

  0000E0  02                              37  QYTE      DC    B'00000010'          F8#4
  0000E1  404040404040404040              38            DC    CL31' '
  0000E9  4040404040404040
  0000F1  4040404040404040
  0000F9  4040404040404040
  000100  4040404040404040                39  QSTORE    DC    CL32' '              DISPLAY STORAGE
  000108  4040404040404040
  000110  4040404040404040
  000118  4040404040404040


                                          DUMP AFTER EXECUTION

  0019C0  F0404040    40404040   40404040   40404040   40404040   40404040   40404040   40404040
  0019E0  FF404040    40404040   40404040   40404040   40404040   40404040   40404040   40404040
  001A00  02404040    7F001918   4F001924   40404040   40404040   40404040   40404040   40404040
  001A20  F0404040    40404040   40404040   40404040   40404040   40404040   40404040   40404040


                                       RELOCATION FACTOR    001900
```

FIG. 8-4. Example of Test and Set.

COMPUTER STATES

In the small model of the computer, only two operating states are available; the stopped and the operating. The stopped is indicated by the presence of a light at the stop key indicator. The computer enters the stop state when it senses an error condition, or when the operator presses the stop key.

These states and operations are in contrast with those of larger models of the computer. A programed halt in operations as such is not possible, because most models of the computer lack a halt command. Also, many states are available in the large and medium models of the computer—such as wait, run, supervisor, and problem—which are not available in the small model of the computer. These larger models respond to a wide range of interrupts.

The only interrupt provided in the small model of the computer is one to signal the completion of an input-output operation. When this condition arises in the small model of the computer, an automatic interrupt takes place. The current PSW is stored as the old PSW at address 144, and a new PSW is obtained from address 148. A diagram of this is shown in Fig. 8-5.

This simplicity of operating states in the small model of the computer forces more operating responsibility upon the console operator of the computer, while at the same time relieving the programer of none of the difficulty of handling different conditions that may arise. In contrast, in the medium and large models of the computer, the supervisor program or operating system (with which most users operate

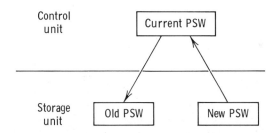

FIG. 8-5. When an interrupt occurs, a copy of the current PSW replaces the former old PSW, and a copy of the new PSW then replaces the former current PSW.

the computer) provides automatic action under many conditions that are likely to arise. This aids both the programer and the console operator. Since these actions are not possible with the small model of the computer because of the limited number of states it can recognize, the programer of the small models of the computer must make provision in his own program, and in his directions to the console operator, for the adequate disposition of these various conditions.

What some of these conditions are can perhaps best be seen by examining in broad outline the states and interrupts in the medium and large models of the computer.

The computer has three pairs of states (see Fig. 8-6). One member of each pair exists simultaneously with one member of each other pair, but each member of each pair is mutually exclusive with the other member. That is, the computer at all times exists in one state or the other of each of the three pairs of states available. These are the three pairs of states: stopped vs. operating; supervisor vs. problem; and wait vs. run. For example, at any given moment in time, the computer may be in the operating state, the problem state, and the run state. Or it may be in the operating state, the supervisor state, and the wait state. The computer cannot, however,

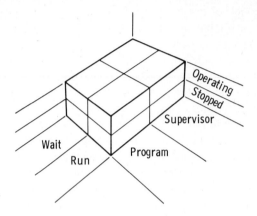

FIG. 8-6. Summary of computer states.

be at the same moment in both the wait state and the run state, or in both the stopped state and the operating state, or in both the supervisor state and the problem state. At any given point of time, only one member of each pair can exist but one member from each of the three pairs must exist.

For the interpretation of dumps and for the general assistance it provides in program debugging, it is important for the programer to know the states of the computer and how they affect the way the computer executes a program. To that end, a brief review of each of the states is provided below.

STOPPED VERSUS OPERATING STATES

In the stopped state, the computer does not execute any instructions and is not subject to being interrupted. Input and output operations may be going on, but are stopped as soon as the current equipment cycle has been completed. The stopped state is indicated on the control console by the manual light, which is on.

The operating state is the alternative to the stopped state. In the operating state the computer can execute instructions one after the other, can be interrupted, and can continue input or output operations beyond one equipment cycle, if so directed. In the operating state, the manual light on the control console is off.

To change the computer from the operating to the stopped state or vice versa requires manual intervention or a console setting by the console operator. In other words, the choice between the stopped or the operating state is fundamentally a choice of the console operator. Only in the small models of the computer can the programer stop the computer by his choice of instructions.

From the point of view of program debugging, only the operating state is significant. In the stopped state the computer does not execute instructions, and hence it cannot initiate the production of output, nor can it accept input data into internal storage. It cannot alter the contents of the internal storage because no instructions can be executed. Thus, as long as the computer is in the stopped state, nothing in the programmer's program can cause any difficulty. It is only in the operating state that the computer can work through (or attempt to work through) the program that the programer has prepared. For this reason, if the programer receives information that his program did not run correctly, he can safely assume that the computer was in the operating state up to the instant of failure. A partial exception to this can arise if the programer is preparing real-time applications. In such programs, timing matters are vital.

SUPERVISOR VERSUS PROBLEM STATE

The supervisor and problem states are distinguished by the setting of bit 15 in the current program status word (PSW). If this bit is set to 0, then the computer is said to be in the supervisor state. If this bit is set to 1, then the computer is said to be in the problem state. Neither the supervisor nor the problem state is indicated by a console light. In the supervisor state, all the commands are valid and may be executed, whereas in the problem state "privileged" commands cannot be executed, and an attempt to execute them results in an interrupt. Among the privileged commands are all the input and output operations, operations changing storage protection, operations involving direct control (as one computer by another computer), and most operations that deal directly with the PSW. This means that a programer will normally be preparing programs to operate in the problem state. If the programer were preparing input and output routines in place of the IOCS routines, or preparing routines to handle interrupts, he would have to use the supervisor state. Normally such routines are written by experienced programers, and often the same routines are used throughout the installation by all programers as common routines fixed by installation standard. For this reason, the beginning programer normally writes programs for execution only in the problem state.

The change to and from the supervisor and problem states can only be made by changing the active PSW. This cannot usually be done unless the supervisor state already exists, or unless the computer is interrupted, since an interrupt automatically changes the PSW. In practice, the transition from supervisor to problem state is made by a deliberate alteration of the PSW as directed by the program, whereas the change from problem to supervisor state is made by the supervisor call command (SVC) or by the occurrence of an interrupt. Unwanted interrupts are a prime indicator of mistakes ("bugs") in the program.

The choice of the supervisor vs. the problem state is of prime significance to the programer in debugging. The programer, especially the beginning programer, will nearly always be writing his program for execution in the problem state. That program will, however, be executed in conjunction with a supervisor program or operating system which operates in the supervisor state. All input and output operations require the presence of the supervisor state for their execution.

Since the programer normally uses IOCS routines for input and output operations, he will indirectly also use the supervisor state. The change from problem to supervisor state to handle input and output is taken care of automatically by the IOCS routines. Hence, if in studying a dump the programer learns that the computer was operating in the supervisor state at the time the difficulty arose, he can assume that the problem lies in input or output operations, or in the relationship of the supervisor program to the program he has prepared. If on the other hand, the evidence indicates that the computer was operating in the problem state, then in the absence of evidence of input or output interrupt the programer can safely rule out input and output operations as the cause of difficulty. He can also safely assume that the supervisor program's relationship to his program was not the cause of the difficulty. The difficulty in such cases must lie within the program that the programer himself has prepared.

A word of caution is in order, however. The taking of a dump on the computer typically requires that the computer be in the supervisor state. This means that any dump the programer receives normally has been prepared for him by a program which operates in the supervisor state. When interpreting the information presented to him in the dump, the programer must keep in mind the fact that some of the information presented in the dump reflects the dump program itself, not the program that the programer has written. Distinguishing between these two depends upon the particular choice of dump program used at the installation, and upon the skill and operating practices followed by the console operator. That is, the quality of the information in the dump may depend upon the factors beyond the control of the programer.

WAIT VERSUS RUN STATE

The distinction between the wait state and the running state is partly a programing matter and partly an operating matter. These states are also mutually exclusive; one or the other but not both must be present. The wait state may occur while input and output operations are taking place, and indicates that the computer is temporarily idle until the occurrence of some event such as the termination of an input or output operation. The running state indicates that the computer is executing instructions one after the other. For this reason, the programer is normally concerned with the presence or absence of the wait or running state only when he be writing input and output routines. A change to or from the wait state may only be made by changing the active PSW either deliberately or by interrupt.

In either of these states the computer may be subject to interrupt. When the computer is in the wait state, it does not execute instructions but is for all practical purposes temporarily idle. During the running state the computer executes instructions one after the other without a pause or idle period between them. The choice between the wait and the run state is determined by bit 14 in the PSW. When this bit is 0, the computer is in the run state. When this bit is 1, the computer is in the wait state. In normal practice, the wait state is used when the computer must idle pending the completion of an input or output operation. The wait state is indicated by the wait light on the console. The run state is used for normal processing work.

Since the choice between the wait state and the run state depends upon a bit in the PSW, to change to and from the wait and run states requires altering the PSW. This can be done by loading a new PSW deliberately or by means of interrupt. In practice, because the wait state is used primarily to fill idle time arising from input and output operations, the change between the wait and run states is in practice nearly always handled by the interrupt system. When, however, the computer is operating in the supervisor state, the change between wait and run states can be made deliberately by the programer's choice of instructions.

States	Operating		Stopped	
	Run	Wait	Run	Wait
Supervisor	S	S	Q	Q
Problem	M	M	Q	Q

Notes: M   This situation is of major concern to the programer.
        S   This situation usually is of some concern to the programer.
        Q   This situation is of concern to the operator.

Fig. 8-7. Programer significance of computer operating states.

A summary of the six states of the computer is presented in Fig. 8-7. The number of possible combinations is large, but only half of these combinations are of relevance to the programer. Any that involve the stopped state are normally of concern to the console operator but not to the programer. The major exceptions to this are programs designed to operate in real time. In these cases, the existence of the stopped state can seriously impair correct program execution. Such cases, however, are not among the usual job assignments of the beginning programer.

OVERVIEW OF THE INTERRUPT SYSTEM

While the computer is executing the instructions of a program, the computer can be made to stop executing those instructions and begin executing a different series of instructions. This can be in response to some conditions in the program or data, or outside of and having no relation necessarily to the program or the data being processed at the time. This ability of the computer to stop executing the series of instructions associated with one program and change to execute a series of instructions associated with a different program is referred to as an interrupt. That is, the computer's execution of the instructions of one program can be interrupted, thus causing the computer to begin executing the instructions of a different program. The interrupt can be for a variety of external causes such as, for example, action taken by the console operator, or by an item of input or output equipment signalling that it is ready to receive or transmit data. It can also have any one of a variety of internal causes, such as machine failures, or illegal situations—e.g., trying to divide by zero.

Computers of older design usually just halted when such situations arose. Manual intervention by the operator then was required to get the computer back into operation. Or, as in the case of input and output operations, the computer was required to be waiting and ready at whatever time the input and output equipment was ready to send or receive data. In short, to whatever extent the central processing unit's operation was interruptable, the result of the interrupt was to cause a halt or stop in the operations. This older arrangement did not make it possible for the computer to attempt automatically to continue operations in the face of adversities. Console operator intervention was required to handle them.

In order to decrease the need for operator intervention, the computer has been provided with an interrupt system. The effect of this interrupt system is to enable the computer to take action itself to meet some conditions, and to accept a wider range of timing situations in input and output equipment operations. But the effect of this interrupt system is also to provide more complex operations in the computer. This presents an additional challenge to the programer, and it both facilitates and complicates the finding of mistakes ("bugs") in a program.

The responsiveness of the computer to being interrupted is controlled in many cases by what are known as "masks." The two major masks used in the computer are the program mask and the system mask. In both cases, these masks are fields of bits in the PSW. If these fields have a 1 bit present in specified positions, then an interrupt is permitted to occur if the need for it should arise. If the bit in the specified position is 0, then the interrupt is not permitted and the computer ignores the interrupt request. This means that the programer can control to some extent the degree to which the computer is subject to interrupt from a variety of causes. He can do this by the way he specifies the program and system masks in the new PSW's. In some installations, however, these masks are specified for the programer by installation policy and by "store protection." In such cases, the programer may have no effective control over them.

The program mask controls the responsiveness of the computer to arithmetic overflow situations. The program mask is a four-bit field in the PSW running from bits 36 through 39 (see Fig. 8-2). Bit 36 controls the responsiveness of the computer to binary arithmetic overflows, and bit 37 controls its responsiveness to packed-decimal arithmetic overflows. Bits 38 and 39 control the responsiveness to underflow and significance in floating-point operations, respectively (see Chap. 12).

Arithmetic overflow is a relatively serious situation involving the loss of significant data. The programer, at least while his program is being debugged, should normally permit interruption for overflow. That is, program mask bits 36 and 37 should normally be set to 1. This will help the programer find and correct errors in arithmetic scaling that he might have inadvertently permitted.

The system mask is an eight-bit field in the PSW running from bits 0 through 7 (see Fig. 8-2). The system mask controls the responsiveness of the computer to interrupt from input and output operations and from external causes. Bits 0 through 6 refer to the corresponding input-output channels with which the particular model and configuration of computer may be equipped. The assignment of particular items of input and output equipment to the respective channels may differ from installation to installation, and no general guidance can be offered other than that bit position 0 normally refers to the multiplexor channel which normally is used for the lower-speed input and output equipment, such as card readers, printers, and card punches. Bit number 7 is referred to as the external interrupt bit in the mask. The three external causes of interrupt are summarized later in this chapter.

The timing of interrupt action is of considerable significance to the programer and can greatly alter the symptoms of program difficulty that the programer may find in the dump. In practice, three different timing arrangements are likely to occur. These are the normal completion, the aborted termination, and the suppressed operation. Let us look briefly at each in turn.

In the normal completion, interrupts occur only when the computer has completed executing one instruction and before it begins executing the next instruction. It is at this point that the control unit normally checks to determine whether or not interrupt action has been requested. External interrupts, supervisor call interrupts, and input and output interrupts occur at this point and this point only. In other words, the computer has completed one instruction normally ("normal termination"), and before beginning to execute the next instruction it takes any requested interrupt action.

In the case of machine-check and program interrupts, two additional timing situations may arise. One of these is the premature or aborted termination. In this situation, the computer detects during the course of executing an instruction that a condition has arisen which requires it to stop the execution of the instruction. It cuts off the execution before the execution is complete. The result is that the contents of the receiving operand may only be partially altered. The extent to which they may have been altered varies from command to command and with the particular data being handled and the timing of the interrupt. The resulting contents of the receiving operand are unpredictable, therefore. An instruction that suffers this aborted or premature termination is often referred to simply as "terminated."

In some cases, the computer detects the need to abort execution before any of the contents of the receiving operand have been altered. For example, if the computer is asked to execute a command that is not available in the computer, it is able, before it alters storage, to determine that an illegal situation has arisen. In such cases the computer is able to abort the execution before any of the contents of storage have been altered. The operation is "suppressed," and no result is produced. In effect, the computer executes the instruction as if it were a "no operation" instruction. The contents of the registers and of storage are as they were before the computer began attempting to execute the instruction.

When an interrupt request is made, a very definite pattern of action takes place in the central processing unit of the computer. In the first place, the appropriate PSW mask bit is tested. If that permits interrupt or if no mask bit applies, and if the execution of the current instruction has been completed, terminated, or suppressed as appropriate, then the computer stores a copy of the current PSW. If these conditions are not met, normal operation continues. When the computer stores a copy of the current PSW, it stores it in internal storage to make it a matter of record so that the programer can have the computer program test it. The place where the PSW is stored is determined by the classification of the cause of the interrupt. For this purpose, five major classes of program interruption are recognized, and the PSW is

PRIORITY	CLASS OF INTERRUPT	OLD PSW ADDRESS	NEW PSW ADDRESS
1	MACHINE CHECK	30_x	70_x
2	SUPERVISOR CALL	20_x	60_x
2	PROGRAM	28_x	68_x
3	EXTERNAL	18_x	58_x
4	INPUT-OUTPUT	38_x	78_x

OTHER FIXED STORAGE LOCATIONS	ADDRESS
CHANNEL STATUS WORD	40_x
CHANNEL ADDRESS WORD	48_x
TIMER	50_x
DIAGNOSTIC SCAN AREA	80_x

NOTE   ALL ADDRESSES ARE SHOWN IN ABSOLUTE FORM.

Fig. 8-8. Internal-storage fixed-address assignments (see also Appendix E).

stored accordingly in one of five different double-word locations in storage, as summarized in Fig. 8-8.

When the computer stores an old PSW, the computer stores seven of the eight fields exactly as they are in the current PSW. But the computer alters the interruption code field to reflect the nature and circumstances of the interruption. This field provides valuable data to the programer in determining why the interruption occurred. The interpretation of these codes and the relationship of the codes to various conditions in the program are described in more detail later in this chapter.

Storing the old PSW, however, is not enough, nor is it the only operation that takes place. The computer also replaces the former PSW by copying into the current PSW position a double word from internal storage. This provides a new current PSW. The specific location in storage from which the computer copies (loads, fetches, or obtains) this new PSW reflects the class of the interruption. For this purpose, the same five classes noted before are again recognized. The locations in storage which supply the new PSW's are shown in summary form in Fig. 8-8.

When it loads a new PSW, the computer sets the interruption code and the instruction length codes to zero. The remaining fields of the new PSW are accepted exactly as they are shown in the new PSW location in storage. This means that the programer can store in these locations, in advance of their use, whatever data he might desire. Hence the programer can control the action the computer takes when an interrupt occurs. For example, the programer can set the instruction address, the condition code, the program mask, and the systems mask. However, he should be wary. In some models of the computer and in some installations because of the operating system used, the new PSW locations are not accessible to the programer. In some installations he may not have the computer put the data into them. In others he may move data neither into nor out of them. This is part of the store-protect feature with which some models of the computer are equipped.

INTERRUPT PRIORITY AND CLASS

More than one request for an interrupt may occur at any given point in time in the computer. When a request has been made, but no interrupt action has been permitted, the interrupt is said to be "pending." Since the computer is designed to be able to receive an interrupt request from a number of sources, the result is that a number of interrupt requests may be pending at any given time. The question then arises: Which request will be honored first? This depends in part on the interrupt requests themselves and in part upon an established system of priorities among the classes of interrupts.

The highest-priority interrupt (level 1) is the machine-check interrupt. If masked off, the interrupt remains pending only during the execution of the current instruction, after which it is canceled (nullified or dropped). When this interrupt request is made and not masked off, any pending program and supervisor-call interrupts are canceled. The machine-check interrupt is then taken. Immediately afterward, and depending upon the new PSW system mask, the computer may be subject to external or input-output interrupts.

The result can be a limited chain or cascade of interrupts. Assuming that a program interrupt, an external interrupt, and an input-output interrupt are all pending, the occurrence of the machine-check interrupt causes the PSW to be stored in the old machine-check PSW area and a new PSW to be loaded from the new machine-check PSW area. If that PSW does not mask off the external interrupt, then the computer becomes at once interruptable from the pending external interrupt, since the program interrupt was canceled. This causes the PSW to be stored in the old external-interrupt PSW area and a new PSW to be loaded from the new external-interrupt PSW area. Again assuming that this PSW does not mask off input-output interrupt, the pending input-output interrupt will be taken. This will cause the just-loaded PSW to be stored the old input-output PSW area and a new PSW to be loaded from the input-output new PSW area.

During this chain of three successive interrupts, no imperative instructions have been executed by the computer. It is only after the last interrupt of the chain has occurred that the computer finally attempts to execute an instruction. The instruction to be executed is the one specified by the PSW loaded as the result of the most recent interrupt (in this case, the input-output interrupt). That this state of affairs has occurred is evident to the programer only by comparing the old and new PSW areas in the dump. The content of the new machine-check PSW is the same except for the interrupt code as the content of the old external PSW. The content of the new external PSW is the same except for the interrupt code as the content of the old input-output PSW.

Such chains or cascades of interrupts are not helpful at all to the programer, but he can limit them by the masks. At the minimum, the programer usually specifies masks to prevent further interrupts of the same class. In practice, this depends upon the use of privileged commands, or upon access to an area of storage that may be unavailable to a programer in some installations. This may leave the programer at the mercy of the supervisor program or the operating system. The possibility of a chain of interrupts therefore should be watched for the programer.

At the second level of priority among interrupts (level 2) are the supervisor-call and program interrupts. Both of these are at the same level. Since a supervisor-call interrupt arises from the execution of a supervisor-call command and cannot be masked off, no conflict arises from assigning these two interrupts the same priority level.

The supervisor-call and program interrupts remain pending only during the execution of one instruction, and both can be canceled by the occurrence of a machine-check interrupt. This means that each time the computer starts executing an instruction, both the program interrupts and the supervisor-call interrupts outstanding are canceled. Each instruction starts afresh with regard to these interrupts.

The only major complication of interrupts at this second level is again the occurrence of a chain of interrupts. Since the machine-check interrupt occurs at a higher level of priority, it is remotely possible that a machine-check interrupt may take precedence, cancel the program interrupt, and give rise to the same kind of a situation described previously. It is more likely, however, that the condition that gives rise to a program interrupt will, in turn, give rise to another program interrupt, and another, and still another to form an endless chain.

For example, suppose the cause of the program interrupt be a non-valid instruction address in a PSW that was loaded from the program new PSW area. This situation, in turn, gives rise to a program interrupt, which results in storing that PSW into the program interrupt old PSW area and loading the same new PSW again from the program new PSW area. Since this PSW is identical to the one that was just loaded and which gave rise to an interrupt, this one gives rise to the same interrupt. It will therefore be stored again and reloaded again. This chain is endless and can be broken only by operator intervention. It can be recognized on the dump by the fact that nearly all of the program-old PSW area and the program-new PSW area are identical in content, that the interrupt code identifies an illegal addressing situation, and that the instruction address is not legal.

At the third level of interrupt (level 3) are the external interrupts. External interrupts remain pending until the computer accepts them or the console operator cancels them. The external interrupts can be masked off (held pending) and are a primary means of communication for the console operator and other computers.

At the fourth level of priority (level 4) are the input and output interrupts. These interrupts remain pending until accepted and may be masked by the system mask. Since a large number of input and output items of equipment can be attached, some means is needed to provide detailed information about the cause of the interrupt. This is provided by the channel status word (CSW), which the computer stores at hexadecimal address 40_x at the time of interrupt. The interpretation of the CSW is briefly discussed later in this chapter.

INSTRUCTION ADDRESS AND LENGTH

In studying the old and new PSW areas in the dump, the programer can glean useful information from the instruction addresses and the instruction length codes. To be able to interpret these, the programer needs to know at what addresses in storage his program was loaded. He needs to find out the absolute machine-language addresses, since these determine the part of the dump that shows the program, and since these addresses may appear in the instruction-address portion of a PSW in the old and new PSW areas in storage as shown on the dump.

This information is available from the lists provided by the computer at the time of program compilation and link-edit. Since the lists produced at compilation time show the relative addresses of points in the program (relative to the beginning of the program), the programer can find any absolute machine-language address by adding together two numbers, the relative address as shown on the compilation listings, and the base address at which the section of the program was loaded as shown by the link-edit listing. The base address serves in effect as a relocation factor.

The programer should then check the dump at that absolute address to establish that the contents of storage match what he expected. For example, if the address is an instruction address, the content of storage at that address is normally shown in the machine-language column of the compilation lists to the left of the source language.

Since the instruction address shown in a PSW is the address of the next instruction to be executed—not the one that was executed—the programer can learn from this where in the program execution would be started. In the case of an old PSW, this is the instruction that would have been executed next if the interrupt had not occurred. In the case of a new PSW, this is the instruction that would be executed if this and only this interrupt occurred. If this next instruction is also an entry point for one or more transfers of control, the programer may have to use other clues to determine the last instruction executed.

In interpreting instruction addresses, the programer needs to make a distinction between those which fall within the imperative coding he himself wrote and those which fall outside of it. Those which fall outside of it most likely fall in the supervisor-program or operating-system area, or in the IOCS routines area. Thus, looking at the PSW areas, the programer normally expects to find an IOCS or supervisor address in the input-output new PSW, a supervisor address in the machine-check new PSW, a supervisor address in the program new PSW, a supervisor address in the supervisor-call new PSW, and a supervisor address in the external new PSW. The programer normally expects to find an address from his own program or from the supervisor in the input-output old PSW, an address from any place in internal storage in the machine-check old PSW, an address from his own program in the program old PSW, and an address from any place in internal storage in the supervisor-call old PSW and in the external old PSW.

In order to find the last instruction executed before an interrupt, the programer can make use of the instruction length code. If the instruction length code is 0, it supplies no useful information on this point to the programer. Length codes of 1, 2, or 3 are associated with specific lengths of instructions, as described previously. By subtracting from the instruction address in the old PSW the length in bytes associated with the corresponding instruction length code, the programer can often, but not always, find the address of the last instruction executed by the computer before the interrupt.

To test the information for validity, the programer should verify that the type of instruction (RR, RX, RS, SS, or SI) found at that location in storage does agree with the instruction length code and that the address is for the left byte of an instruction. If not, the information should be questioned. If the address be acceptable, then the programer should verify that the instruction address in the old PSW is an address which can be reached only by a normal control sequence. It should be remembered that the instruction address in the PSW is altered by a transfer of control. Hence, if the last instruction executed was a transfer control, the instruction address and the instruction length code may be useless in obtaining information about where the computer was in the program before it executed the transfer of control. Lastly, the programer should attempt to establish whether the apparent last instruction was executed completely. If it was not, as is possible for machine-check and program interrupts, then the instruction length code may be misleading.

INTERRUPT CODES BY CLASS

The interrupt codes found in any new PSW are normally insignificant. This is because when a new PSW is loaded that field in the PSW is cleared to 0 bits, replacing whatever bits were there before. In the case of an old PSW, however, the interrupt codes are significant. The presentation that follows, therefore, pertains only to the interpretation of interrupt codes in the old PSW areas.

Since the interrupt code in an old PSW depends upon the class of interrupt, the presentation is broken down into the five classes noted previously. Information is given in each case about the situation giving rise to the interrupt identified by each particular interrupt code.

The machine-check interrupt code is 0000_x. The instruction length code is unpredictable, and the command being executed has usually been terminated prematurely. This interrupt may cause the computer, in addition to storing the old PSW and loading the new PSW, to execute a diagnostic procedure. This copies into the diagnostic area of storage (see Fig. 8-8) selected information from elsewhere in storage and from the registers of the computer. What this information and its format are depends upon the particular model of the computer, the particular configuration of input and output equipment, and the nature of the machine failure. The diagnostic area therefore can provide additional information to the programer about the nature of the machine failure.

In interpreting machine-check interrupt information, the programer should be aware that the console operator's use of the system reset button may give rise to a machine failure if the programer has not been careful. When the console operator presses the system reset button, the contents of the registers and sometimes of storage may be affected. The result may be to produce some non-valid parity bits. In practice, this is of most concern with registers. If the programer in his program has specified using data from a register, as in an addition operation or in storing data from a register, and the register contains non-valid parity, a machine-check interrupt may occur. To avoid this situation, the programer can follow the practice of clearing the registers before their use by loading them with a constant from storage of 00000000_x. To clear a register by subtracting it from itself may give rise to the machine check if bad parity exists. As a matter of conservative practice, therefore, the programer should put something into a register before attempting to use that information or to copy it out. The same rule applies to areas of storage defined with a DS declarative, but not with a DC declarative.

The supervisor-call interrupt arises from the execution of a supervisor-call instruction. Hence it is normally completed without being subject to interrupts from other sources. The interruption code in the old PSW is normally $00HH_x$, where HH represents the one byte of data provided as the operand of the supervisor-call command by the programer. The instruction length code is normally 1, and the operation is almost always completed.

Twenty-one different sets of situations can give rise to a program interrupt, and each is identified by its own interrupt code in the old PSW. These interruption codes take the general form of $000H_x$, where H is one half byte identifying the interruption. Each of these is described below, or in Appendix E.

Code 1 identifies the operation interrupt. No mask is available. This occurs when the programer has specified a command which is not available on the particular model and configuration of the computer. The operation normally is suppressed; the instruction length code may be 1, 2, or 3.

Code 2 identifies the privileged operation interrupt. Privileged commands may only be executed in the supervisor state. If an attempt is made to execute them in the problem state, an interrupt occurs. No mask is available. The operation is normally suppressed; the instruction length code is 1 or 2. The privileged commands are listed in Fig. 8-9 for those models that have them.

CODE	NAME	MNEMONIC	FORMAT
0A	SET STORAGE KEY	SSK	RR
09	INSERT STORAGE KEY	ISK	RR
80	SET SYSTEM MASK	SSM	SI
82	LOAD PSW	LPSW	SI
83	DIAGNOSE	---	SI
84	WRITE DIRECT	WRD	SI
85	READ DIRECT	RDD	SI
9C	START I/O	SIO	SI
9C	START I/O FAST REL	SIOF	SI
9D	TEST I/O	TIO	SI
9E	HALT I/O	HIO	SI
9E	HALT DEVICE	HDV	SI
9F	TEST CHANNEL	TCH	SI
B2	STORE CPU ID	STIDP	SI
B2	STORE CHANNEL ID	STIDC	SI
B2	SET CLOCK	SCK	SI
B6	STORE CONTROL REG	STCTL	RS
B7	LOAD CONTROL REG	LCTL	RS

FIG. 8-9. List of privileged commands.

Code 3 identifies the execute interrupt. The operation is suppressed with an instruction length code of 2. This interruption occurs when the instruction referenced by an Execute instruction is another Execute instruction. No mask is available (see Chap. 10).

Code 4 identifies the storage-protection interrupt. Three varieties of this exist. Some models of the computer are equipped with storage "write" protection against copying data into an area of storage—i.e., altering the contents of storage. Some are provided with "fetch" protection against reading data from storage—i.e., copying or loading data from storage. Some are equipped with both. The commands which can attempt to violate storage protection in the computer are summarized in Figs. 8-10 to 8-12. The instruction length code may be either 0, 2, or 3. Storage protection is determined by the storage key mask in the PSW. The commands subject to protec-

CODE	NAME	MNEMONIC	FORMAT	ACTION
0E	MOVE CHARACTERS LONG	MVCL	RR	TERMINATED
40	STORE HALFWORD	STH	RX	SUPPRESSED
42	STORE CHARACTER	STC	RX	SUPPRESSED
4E	CONVERT TO DECIMAL	CVD	RX	SUPPRESSED
50	STORE	ST	RX	SUPPRESSED
60	STORE (LONG)	STD	RX	SUPPRESSED
70	STORE (SHORT)	STE	RX	SUPPRESSED
83	DIAGNOSE	---	SI	UNPREDICTABLE
85	READ DIRECT	RDD	SI	TERMINATED
90	STORE MULTIPLE	STM	RS	TERMINATED
92	MOVE IMMEDIATE	MVI	SI	SUPPRESSED
93	TEST AND SET	TS	SI	TERMINATED
94	AND IMMEDIATE	NI	SI	SUPPRESSED
96	OR IMMEDIATE	OI	SI	SUPPRESSED
97	EXCLUSIVE OR IMMEDIATE	XI	SI	SUPPRESSED
B2	STORE CPU ID	STIDP	SI	TERMINATED
B2	STORE CLOCK	STCK	SI	TERMINATED
B6	STORE CONTROL REGISTERS	STCTL	RS	TERMINATED
BE	STORE CHARACTERS MASKED	STCM	RS	TERMINATED
D1	MOVE NUMERICS	MVN	SS	TERMINATED
D2	MOVE CHARACTERS	MVC	SS	TERMINATED
D3	MOVE ZONES	MVZ	SS	TERMINATED
D4	AND CHARACTERS	NC	SS	TERMINATED
D6	OR CHARACTERS	OC	SS	TERMINATED
D7	EXCLUSIVE OR CHARACTERS	XC	SS	TERMINATED
DC	TRANSLATE	TR	SS	TERMINATED
DE	EDIT	ED	SS	TERMINATED
DF	EDIT AND MARK	EDMK	SS	TERMINATED
F1	MOVE AND OFFSET	MVO	SS	TERMINATED
F2	PACK	PACK	SS	TERMINATED
F3	UNPACK	UNPK	SS	TERMINATED
F8	ZERO AND ADD PACKED	ZAP	SS	TERMINATED
F0	SHIFT AND ROUND PACKED	SRP	SS	TERMINATED
FA	ADD PACKED	AP	SS	TERMINATED
FC	MULTIPLY PACKED	MP	SS	TERMINATED
FD	DIVIDE PACKED	DP	SS	TERMINATED

FIG. 8-10. Commands subject to storage protection.

tion interruptions are detected by the computer control unit based upon the bit pattern in the command byte, not upon the logic of the operation directly.

Code 5 identifies the addressing interrupt. This interrupt arises when the control unit attempts to reference an address that lies beyond the limits of the available storage in the particular computer. No mask is available. For example, if the computer has only 32K bytes of storage, an attempt to obtain or place data or instructions at address $E9B6_x$ will result in an address interruption. The instruction length code may be 0, 1, 2, or 3, and in most cases the operation is terminated prematurely. A list of the commands subject to address interrupt is shown in Fig. 8-13.

Code 6 identifies the specification interrupt. For the beginning programer, this is one of the most frequent types of interrupt. The instruction code is 1, 2, or 3, and the operation is suppressed. No mask is available. A list of the commands subject to the specification interrupt is shown in Fig. 8-14.

The situations giving rise to the specification interrupt are fairly numerous and vary with the command and operands presented for execution. They may be summarized as follows: For a command that requires data to be aligned, the data are aligned incorrectly (a common beginner's fault). Where an even-odd pair of registers is used, the operand fails to specify the even-numbered register. In packed-decimal division or multiplication, the multiplier or divisor is longer than eight bytes, or the multiplicand or dividend fields are too short. A storage-protection key has been used that does not correspond to the storage-protection key in the PSW, or a nonexistent floating-point register has been named.

CODE	NAME	MNEMONIC	FORMAT	ACTION
0E	MOVE CHARACTERS LONG	MVCL	RR	TERMINATED
0F	COMPARE LOGICAL CHAR. LONG	CLCL	RR	TERMINATED
43	INSERT CHARACTER	IC	RX	TERMINATED
44	EXECUTE	EX	RX	SUPPRESSED
49	COMPARE HALFWORD	CH	RX	TERMINATED
4A	ADD HALFWORD	AH	RX	TERMINATED
4B	SUBTRACT HALFWORD	SH	RX	TERMINATED
4C	MULTIPLY HALFWORD	MH	RX	TERMINATED
4F	CONVERT TO BINARY	CVB	RX	TERMINATED
54	AND	N	RX	TERMINATED
55	COMPARE LOGICAL	CL	RX	TERMINATED
56	OR	O	RX	TERMINATED
57	EXCLUSIVE OR	X	RX	TERMINATED
58	LOAD	L	RX	TERMINATED
59	COMPARE	C	RX	TERMINATED
5A	ADD	A	RX	TERMINATED
5B	SUBTRACT	S	RX	TERMINATED
5C	MULTIPLY	M	RX	TERMINATED
5D	DIVIDE	D	RX	TERMINATED
5E	ADD LOGICAL	AL	RX	TERMINATED
5F	SUBTRACT LOGICAL	SL	RX	TERMINATED
68	LOAD (LONG)	LD	RX	TERMINATED
69	COMPARE (LONG)	CD	RX	TERMINATED
6A	ADD NORMALIZED (LONG)	AD	RX	TERMINATED
6B	SUBTRACT NORMALIZED (LONG)	SD	RX	TERMINATED
6C	MULTIPLY (LONG)	MD	RX	TERMINATED
6D	DIVIDE (LONG)	DD	RX	TERMINATED
6E	ADD UNNORMALIZED (LONG)	AW	RX	TERMINATED
6F	SUBTRACT UNNORMALIZED (LONG)	SW	RS	TERMINATED
78	LOAD (SHORT)	LE	RX	TERMINATED
79	COMPARE (SHORT)	CE	RX	TERMINATED
7A	ADD NORMALIZED (SHORT)	AE	RX	TERMINATED
7B	SUBTRACT NORMALIZED (SHORT)	SE	RX	TERMINATED
7C	MULTIPLY (SHORT)	ME	RX	TERMINATED
7D	DIVIDE (SHORT)	DE	RX	TERMINATED
7E	ADD UNNORMALIZED (SHORT)	AU	RX	TERMINATED
7F	SUBTRACT UNNORMALIZED (SHORT)	SU	RX	TERMINATED
80	SET SYSTEM MASK	SSM	SI	TERMINATED
82	LOAD PSW	LPSW	SI	TERMINATED
84	WRITE DIRECT	WRD	SI	TERMINATED
91	TEST UNDER MASK	TM	SI	TERMINATED
95	COMPARE LOGICAL IMMEDIATE	CLI	SI	TERMINATED
98	LOAD MULTIPLE	LM	RS	TERMINATED
B2	SET CLOCK	SCK	SI	TERMINATED
B7	LOAD CONTROL REGISTERS	LCTL	RS	TERMINATED
BD	COMPARE LOGICAL MASKED	CLM	RS	TERMINATED
BF	INSERT CHARACTERS MASKED	ICM	RS	TERMINATED
D5	COMPARE LOGICAL CHARACTERS	CLC	SS	TERMINATED
DD	TRANSLATE AND TEST	TRT	SS	TERMINATED
F8	ZERO AND ADD PACKED	ZAP	SS	TERMINATED
F9	COMPARE PACKED	CP	SS	TERMINATED

FIG. 8-11. Commands subject to fetch protection.

CODE	NAME	MNEMONIC	FORMAT	ACTION
0E	MOVE CHAR. LONG	MVCL	RR	TERMINATED
83	DIAGNOSE	---	SI	UNPREDICTABLE
93	TEST AND SET	TS	SI	TERMINATED
D1	MOVE NUMERICS	MVN	SS	TERMINATED
D2	MOVE CHARACTERS	MVC	SS	TERMINATED
D3	MOVE ZONES	MVZ	SS	TERMINATED
D4	AND CHARACTERS	NC	SS	TERMINATED
D6	OR CHARACTERS	OC	SS	TERMINATED
D7	EXCLUSIVE OR CHAR.	XC	SS	TERMINATED
DC	TRANSLATE	TR	SI	TERMINATED
DE	EDIT	ED	SS	TERMINATED
DF	EDIT AND MARK	EDMK	SS	TERMINATED
F1	MOVE WITH OFFSET	MVO	SS	TERMINATED
F2	PACK	PACK	SS	TERMINATED
F3	UNPACK	UNPK	SS	TERMINATED
F8	ZERO AND ADD PACKED	ZAP	SS	TERMINATED
FA	ADD PACKED	AP	SS	TERMINATED
FB	SUBTRACT PACKED	SP	SS	TERMINATED
FC	MULTIPLY PACKED	MP	SS	TERMINATED
FD	DIVIDE PACKED	DP	SS	TERMINATED

FIG. 8-12. Additional commands subject to both store and fetch protection.

CODE	NAME	MNEMONIC	FORMAT	ACTION
08	SET STORAGE KEY	SSK	RR	SUPPRESSED
09	INSERT STORAGE KEY	ISK	RR	TERMINATED
0E	MOVE CHARACTERS LONG	MVCL	RR	TERMINATED
0F	COMPARE LOGICAL CHAR.LONG	CLCL	RR	TERMINATED
40	STORE HALFWORD	STH	RX	SUPPRESSED
42	STORE CHARACTER	STC	RX	SUPPRESSED
43	INSERT CHARACTER	IC	RX	TERMINATED
44	EXECUTE	EX	RX	SUPPRESSED
48	LOAD HALFWORD	LH	RX	TERMINATED
49	COMPARE HALFWORD	CH	RX	TERMINATED
4A	ADD HALFWORD	AH	RX	TERMINATED
4B	SUBTRACT HALFWORD	SH	RX	TERMINATED
4C	MULTIPLY HALFWORD	MH	RX	TERMINATED
4E	CONVERT TO DECIMAL	CVD	RX	SUPPRESSED
4F	CONVERT TO BINARY	CVB	RX	TERMINATED
50	STORE	ST	RX	SUPPRESSED
54	AND	N	RX	TERMINATED
55	COMPARE LOGICAL	CL	RX	TERMINATED
56	OR	O	RX	TERMINATED
57	EXCLUSIVE OR	X	RX	TERMINATED
58	LOAD	L	RX	TERMINATED
59	COMPARE	C	RX	TERMINATED
5A	ADD	A	RX	TERMINATED
5B	SUBTRACT	S	RX	TERMINATED
5C	MULTIPLY	M	RX	TERMINATED
5D	DIVIDE	D	RX	TERMINATED
5E	ADD LOGICAL	AL	RX	TERMINATED
5F	SUBTRACT LOGICAL	SL	RX	TERMINATED
60	STORE (LONG)	STD	RX	SUPPRESSED
68	LOAD (LONG)	LD	RX	TERMINATED
69	COMPARE (LONG)	CD	RX	TERMINATED
6A	ADD NORMALIZED (LONG)	AD	RX	TERMINATED
6B	SUBTRACT NORMALIZED (LONG)	SD	RX	TERMINATED
6C	MULTIPLY (LONG)	MD	RX	TERMINATED
6D	DIVIDE (LONG)	DD	RX	TERMINATED
6E	ADD UNNORMALIZED (SHORT)	AW	RX	TERMINATED
6F	SUBTRACT UNNORMALIZED (LONG)	SW	RX	TERMINATED
70	STORE (SHORT)	STE	TX	SUPPRESSED
78	LOAD (SHORT)	LE	RX	TERMINATED
79	COMPARE (SHORT)	CE	RX	TERMINATED
7A	ADD NORMALIZED (SHORT)	AE	RX	TERMINATED
7B	SUBTRACT NORMALIZED (SHORT)	SE	RX	TERMINATED
7C	MULTIPLY (SHORT)	ME	RX	TERMINATED
7D	DIVIDE (SHORT)	DE	RX	TERMINATED
7E	ADD UNNORMALIZED (SHORT)	AU	RX	TERMINATED
7F	SUBTRACT UNNORMALIZED (SHORT)	SU	RX	TERMINATED
80	SET SYSTEM MASK	SSM	SI	TERMINATED
82	LOAD PSW	LPSW	SI	TERMINATED
83	DIAGNOSE	---	SI	SUPPRESSED
84	WRITE DIRECT	WRD	SI	TERMINATED
85	READ DIRECT	RDD	SI	TERMINATED
90	STORE MULTIPLE	STM	RS	TERMINATED
91	TEST UNDER MASK	TM	SI	TERMINATED
92	MOVE IMMEDIATE	MVI	SI	TERMINATED
93	TEST AND SET	TS	SI	TERMINATED
94	AND IMMEDIATE	NI	SI	SUPPRESSED
95	COMPARE LOGICAL IMMEDIATE	CLI	SI	TERMINATED
96	OR IMMEDIATE	OI	SI	SUPPRESSED
97	EXCLUSIVE OR IMMEDIATE	XI	SI	SUPPRESSED
98	LOAD MULTIPLE	LM	SI	SUPPRESSED
B2	STORE CPU ID	STIDP	SI	TERMINATED
B2	SET CLOCK	SCK	SI	TERMINATED
B2	STORE CLOCK	STCK	SI	TERMINATED
B6	STORE CONTROL REGISTERS	STCTL	RS	TERMINATED
B7	LOAD CONTROL REGISTERS	LCTL	RS	TERMINATED
BD	COMPARE LOGICAL MASKED	CLM	RS	TERMINATED
BE	STORE CHARACTERS MASKED	STCM	RS	TERMINATED
BF	INSERT CHARACTERS MASKED	ICM	RS	TERMINATED
D1	MOVE NUMERICS	MVN	SS	TERMINATED
D2	MOVE CHARACTERS	MVC	SS	TERMINATED
D3	MOVE ZONES	MVZ	SS	TERMINATED
D4	AND CHARACTERS	NC	SS	TERMINATED
D5	COMPARE LOGICAL CHARACTERS	CLC	SS	TERMINATED
D6	OR CHARACTERS	OC	SS	TERMINATED
D7	EXCLUSIVE OR CHARACTERS	XC	SS	TERMINATED
DC	TRANSLATE	TR	SS	TERMINATED
DD	TRANSLATE AND TEST	TRT	SS	TERMINATED
DE	EDIT	ED	SS	TERMINATED
DF	EDIT AND MARK	EDMK	SS	TERMINATED
F0	SHIFT AND ROUND PACKED	SRP	SS	TERMINATED
F1	MOVE WITH OFFSET	MVO	SS	TERMINATED
F2	PACK	PACK	SS	TERMINATED
F3	UNPACK	UNPK	SS	TERMINATED
F8	ZERO AND ADD PACKED	ZAP	SS	TERMINATED
F9	COMPARE PACKED	CP	SS	TERMINATED
FA	ADD PACKED	AP	SS	TERMINATED
FB	SUBTRACT PACKED	SP	SS	TERMINATED
FC	MULTIPLY PACKED	MP	SS	TERMINATED
FD	DIVIDE PACKED	DP	SS	TERMINATED

FIG. 8-13. Commands subject to addressing interrupt.

LIST OF CAUSES OF INTERRUPT

1	EVEN VS. ODD REGISTER SPECIFICATION
2	TWO-BYTE UNIT OF INFORMATION SPECIFICATION (ALIGNMENT)
3	FLOATING-POINT REGISTER SPECIFICATION
4	FOUR-BYTE UNIT OF INFORMATION SPECIFICATIONS (ALIGNMENT)
5	DECIMAL MULTIPLIER OR DIVISOR SIZE SPECIFICATIONS
6	ZERO PROTECTION KEY SPECIFICATION
7	BLOCK ADDRESS SPECIFICATION
8	EIGHT-BYTE UNIT OF INFORMATION SPECIFICATION (ALIGNMENT)

CODE	NAME	MNEMONIC	FORMAT	CAUSE
08	SET STORAGE KEY	SSK	RR	7
09	INSERT STORAGE KEY	ISK	RR	7
0E	MOVE CHARACTERS LONG	MVCL	RR	1
0F	COMPARE LOGICAL CHAR. LONG	CLCL	RR	1
1C	MULTIPLY REGISTER	MR	RR	1
1D	DIVIDE REGISTER	DR	RR	1
20	LOAD POSITIVE (LONG)	LPDR	RR	3
21	LOAD NEGATIVE (LONG)	LNDR	RR	3
22	LOAD AND TEST (LONG)	LTDR	RR	3
23	LOAD COMPLEMENT (LONG)	LCDR	RR	3
24	HALVE (LONG)	HDR	RR	3
28	LOAD (LONG)	LDR	RR	3
29	COMPARE (LONG)	CDR	RR	3
2A	ADD NORMALIZED (LONG)	ADR	RR	3
2B	SUBTRACT NORMALIZED (LONG)	SDR	RR	3
2C	MULTIPLY NORMALIZED (LONG)	MDR	RR	3
2D	DIVIDE (LONG)	DDR	RR	3
2E	ADD UNNORMALIZED (LONG)	AWR	RR	3
2F	SUBTRACT UNNORMALIZED (LONG)	SWR	RR	3
30	LOAD POSITIVE (SHORT)	LPER	RR	3
31	LOAD NEGATIVE (SHORT)	LNER	RR	3
32	LOAD AND TEST (SHORT)	LTER	RR	3
33	LOAD COMPLEMENT (SHORT)	LCER	RR	3
34	HALVE (SHORT)	HER	RR	3
38	LOAD (SHORT)	LER	RR	3
39	COMPARE (SHORT)	CER	RR	3
3A	ADD NORMALIZED (SHORT)	AER	RR	3
3B	SUBTRACT NORMALIZED (SHORT)	SER	RR	3
3C	MULTIPLY NORMALIZED (SHORT)	MER	RR	3
3D	DIVIDE (SHORT)	DER	RR	3
3E	ADD UNNORMALIZED (SHORT)	AUR	RR	3
3F	SUBTRACT UNNORMALIZED (SHORT)	SUR	RR	3
40	STORE HALFWORD	STH	RX	2
44	EXECUTE	EX	RX	2
48	LOAD HALFWORD	LH	RX	2
49	COMPARE HALFWORD	CH	RX	2
4A	ADD HALFWORD	AH	RX	2
4B	SUBTRACT HALFWORD	SH	RX	2
4C	MULTIPLY HALFWORD	MH	RX	2
4E	CONVERT TO DECIMAL	CVD	RX	8
4F	CONVERT TO BINARY	CVB	RX	8
50	STORE	ST	RX	4
54	AND	N	RX	4
55	COMPARE LOGICAL	CL	RX	4
56	OR	O	RX	4
57	EXCLUSIVE OR	X	RX	4
58	LOAD	L	RX	4
59	COMPARE	C	RX	4
5A	ADD	A	RX	4
5B	SUBTRACT	S	RX	4
5C	MULTIPLY	M	RX	1,4
5D	DIVIDE	D	RX	1,4
5E	ADD LOGICAL	AL	RX	4
5F	SUBTRACT LOGICAL	SL	RX	4
60	STORE (LONG)	STD	RX	3,8
68	LOAD (LONG)	LD	RX	3,8
69	COMPARE (LONG)	CD	RX	3,8
6A	ADD NORMALIZED (LONG)	AD	RX	3,8
6B	SUBTRACT NORMALIZED (LONG)	SD	RX	3,8
6C	MULTIPLY (LONG)	MD	RX	3,8
6D	DIVIDE (LONG)	DD	RX	3,8
6E	ADD UNNORMALIZED (LONG)	AW	RX	3,8
6F	SUBTRACT UNNORMALIZED (LONG)	SW	RX	3,8
70	STORE (SHORT)	STE	RX	3,4
78	LOAD (SHORT)	LE	RX	3,4
79	COMPARE (SHORT)	CE	RX	3,4
7A	ADD NORMALIZED (SHORT)	AE	RX	3,4
7B	SUBTRACT NORMALIZED (SHORT)	SE	RX	3,4
7C	MULTIPLY (SHORT)	ME	RX	3,4
7D	DIVIDE (SHORT)	DE	RX	3,4
7E	ADD UNNORMALIZED (SHORT)	AU	RX	3,4
7F	SUBTRACT UNNORMALIZED (SHORT)	SU	RX	3,4
82	LOAD PSW	LPSW	SI	8
83	DIAGNOSE	----	SI	
8C	SHIFT RIGHT DOUBLE LOGICAL	SRDL	RS	1
8D	SHIFT LEFT DOUBLE LOGICAL	SLDL	RS	1
8E	SHIFT RIGHT DOUBLE	SRDA	RS	1
8F	SHIFT LEFT DOUBLE	SLDA	RS	1
90	STORE MULTIPLE	STM	RS	4
98	LOAD MULTIPLE	LM	RS	4
B2	STORE CPU ID	STIDP	SI	8
B2	SET CLOCK	SCK	SI	8
B6	STORE CONTROL REGISTERS	STCTL	RS	4
B7	LOAD CONTROL REGISTERS	LCTL	RS	4
FC	MULTIPLY PACKED	MP	SS	5
FD	DIVIDE PACKED	DP	SS	5

FIG. 8-14. Commands subject to specification interrupt.

LIST OF CAUSES

1	IN OLDER MODELS, INVALID SIGN OR DIGIT CODES CAUSE TERMINATION. IN NEWER MODELS, INVALID SIGNS CAUSE SUPPRESSION, AND IF SIGNS ARE VALID, INVALID DIGIT CODES CAUSE TERMINATION.
2	OVERLAPPING FIELDS
3	MULTIPLICAND LENGTH

CODE	NAME	MNEMONIC	FORMAT	CAUSE
4F	CONVERT TO BINARY	CVB	RX	1
DE	EDIT	ED	SS	1
DF	EDIT AND MARK	EDMK	SS	1
FO	SHIFT AND ROUND PACKED	SRP	SS	1
FA	ADD PACKED	AP	SS	1,2
FB	SUBTRACT PACKED	SP	SS	1,2
FC	MULTIPLY PACKED	MP	SS	1,2,3
FD	DIVIDE PACKED	DP	SS	1,2
F8	ZERO AND ADD PACKED	ZAP	SS	1,2
F9	COMPARE PACKED	CP	SS	1,2

FIG. 8-15. Commands subject to packed-decimal data interrupt.

CODE	NAME	MNEMONIC	FORMAT
10	LOAD POSITIVE REGISTER	SPR	RR
13	LOAD COMPLEMENT REGISTER	LCR	RR
1A	ADD REGISTER	AR	RR
1B	SUBTRACT REGISTER	SR	RR
4A	ADD HALFWORD	AH	RX
4B	SUBTRACT HALFWORD	SH	RX
5A	ADD	A	RX
5B	SUBTRACT	S	RX
8B	SHIFT LEFT SINGLE	SLA	RS
8F	SHIFT LEFT DOUBLE	SLDA	RX

FIG. 8-16. Commands subject to binary overflow interrupt.

Code 7 identifies the packed-decimal data interrupt. No mask is available. The instruction length code is 2 or 3. The operations are terminated prematurely if the sign code is valid but any digit code is invalid. The operations are suppressed if a sign code is invalid or not in the last half byte of both operand fields. The commands subject to this interrupt are listed in Fig. 8-15. The causes of this interrupt are sign codes where digit codes should be or vice versa, improper field overlap (the signs must be at the right-hand ends of the fields for correct overlap), or too long a multiplicand in packed-decimal multiplication.

Code 8 identifies the binary arithmetic-overflow interrupt. When this interrupt occurs, a high-order 1 bit has been lost. This interrupt can be masked by the PSW bit 36. The instruction length code is 1 or 2, and the operations are carried to completion but with a loss of the overflow data. The commands subject to this interruption are listed in Fig. 8-16.

Code 9 identifies the binary divide interrupt. The instruction length code is 1 or 2. No mask is available. This interrupt situation arises when an attempt is made to divide by zero, or to divide when the dividend and divisor have not been correctly scaled to fit the register capacity available. In these cases the Divide or Divide Register operation is suppressed. In the case of Convert to Binary, the interruption occurs when the result exceeds 31 bits in length. In such cases the operation is carried to completion, but the additional most significant (overflow) bits are discarded. The commands subject to this interruption are listed in Fig. 8-17.

CODE	NAME	MNEMONIC	FORMAT	ACTION
1D	DIVIDE REGISTER	DR	RR	SUPPRESSED
4F	CONVERT TO BINARY	CVB	RX	COMPLETED
5D	DIVIDE	D	RX	SUPPRESSED

FIG. 8-17. Commands subject to binary divide interrupt.

Code A identifies the packed-decimal arithmetic-overflow interrupt. Operations are carried to completion, and the overflow characters are discarded. The interruption may be masked off by PSW bit 37. The instruction length code is always 3, since the SS commands that can give rise to this interrupt are Add Packed, Subtract Packed, Zero and Add Packed, and Shift and Round Packed.

Code B identifies the packed-decimal divide interrupt. This interrupt arises when the quotient exceeds the field size available or an attempt is made to divide by zero. The operation is suppressed; the length code is 3. The only command subject to this interruption is Divide Packed. No mask is available.

Codes C, D, E, and F identify conditions that can arise only in floating-point operations. The interpretation of these is described in Chap. 12.

The programer will find that in debugging a program the program interrupts are common and nearly always identify conditions in need of the programer's corrective action. They are for the same reason rare in programs which have been adequately debugged. These interrupts are a blessing in disguise to the programer and provide invaluable assistance in identifying failures to observe the rules associated with the accurate use of the commands.

The external interrupts may come from three main sources and may be masked by bit 7 in the PSW system mask. The most common source of an external interrupt is a console operator pressing the interrupt key on the control console. A second major source of external interrupt is the timer changing from positive to negative (the timer reads in terms of "time yet to run"). The timer is an optional feature on some models of the computer and standard on others. Even on those models on which it is standard, its form and manner of operation may differ from one model to another. The exact manner in which the timer operates is beyond the scope of this book. In general, it may be said that the timer permits the programer to have available the equivalent of a clock which can yield the value of the time in the form of a binary number. This clock can then be used by the programer for measuring intervals of time or for use as a continuously running clock. The third source of external interrupt is the connection to another computer. The beginning programer will rarely be called upon to deal with this source of external interrupts.

In the case of an external interrupt, the nature of the source is indicated by the second byte of the interrupt code. The interrupt code takes the general form of

00HH$_x$, where HH stands for a hexadecimal pair in which the position of a 1 bit identifies the source. The timer is indicated by the presence of a 1 bit as the leftmost bit of the byte, and the interrupt key by a 1 bit as the second bit from the left. Other external signals in sequence from 2 through 7 are indicated by 1 bits in successive positions from 2 through 7 in the byte.

KEY	0000	COMMAND ADDRESS	STATUS BITS	RESIDUAL BYTE COUNT
0	3 4	7 8 31	32 47	48 63

FIG. 8-18. Fields in the channel status word (CSW).

BIT	SIGNIFICANCE
32	ATTENTION BIT
33	STATUS MODIFIER BIT
34	CONTROL UNIT END BIT
35	BUSY BIT
36	CHANNEL END BIT
37	DEVICE END BIT
38	UNIT CHECK BIT
39	UNIT EXCEPTION BIT
40	PROGRAM-CONTROLLED INTERRUPTION BIT
41	INCORRECT LENGTH BIT
42	PROGRAM CHECK BIT
43	PROTECTION CHECK BIT
44	CHANNEL DATA CHECK BIT
45	CHANNEL CONTROL CHECK BIT
46	INTERFACE CONTROL CHECK BIT
47	CHAINING CHECK BIT

FIG. 8-19. Significance of some status bit settings in the CSW.

Input-output interrupts may be masked by bits 0 through 6 in the PSW system mask. At the time when the computer accepts an input-output interrupt, the channel status word (CSW) associated with the interruption is stored in the standard address 40$_x$ before the old PSW is stored and the new PSW loaded. The interruption code in the old PSW identifies the channel and the input or output equipment that gave rise to the interruption. Its format is 0HJJ$_x$, where H stands for the number of the channel and JJ stands for the identification number of the equipment at the installation. An input-output interrupt never cuts off the execution of an instruction. But since the input and output action is controlled by a subprogram in a different (channel) programing language, the interrupt code alone is of only moderate help.

The interpretation of the channel status word (CSW) is only infrequently a matter of much concern to the programer who uses logical IOCS for input and output operations. The CSW is used only on the medium and large models of the computer. A diagram of the fields in the channel status word or CSW is shown in Fig. 8-18. These fields are briefly summarized below.

The first byte consists of a storage-protection key and a half byte of 0 bits. The next three bytes are an address eight bytes higher than the address of the last "channel command word" (CCW) used in the input or output operation. A CCW is an instruction in the channel subprogram. The next two bytes are of status bits, which are of value to the programer as evidence on the cause of interrupt. A table briefly summarizing the meaning of the status bits is given in Fig. 8-19. The last two bytes are a count of the remaining bytes of data to be handled by the input or output operation.

The bits in the status field of the CSW are normally read from left to right and numbered accordingly from 32 through 47. Bit 32 is the attention bit. This is set to 1 to indicate that a timing difficulty exists with the equipment or channel which may prevent satisfactory operation. Bit 33 is a status-modifier bit. This is set to 1 when the channel or equipment cannot respond correctly to a request for status information. Bit 34 is the control-unit end bit. This is set to 1 to indicate that an input-output control unit (such as a magnetic-tape control) has completed its operation.

Bit 35 of the CSW is the busy bit. This bit is set to 1 when the equipment or its associated control unit is already executing an instruction and has not yet completed it. Bit 36 is the channel end bit. This bit is set to 1 when the channel is free for other work because it has completed the work it was doing. Bit 37 is the device end bit. This bit is set to 1 when the input or output equipment has completed the work it was performing. Bit 38 is the unit-check bit. This bit is set to 1 when an error condition of some type has been detected in the equipment or control unit. Bit 39 is the unit-exception bit. This bit is set to 1 when the input or output equipment detects a condition that is not common but is not an error—for example, the sensing of a tape mark in the case of magnetic tape.

Bit 40 is the program-controlled interruption bit. This bit is set to 1 when the channel subprogram controlling the input or output operations has a program-control interruption flag on. Bit 41 is the incorrect-length bit. This bit is set to 1 when the number of bytes being handled does not agree with that anticipated (residual count not 0 at the end of the operation). Bit 42 is the program check bit. This bit is set to 1 when an error has been detected in the channel subprogram controling the input or output operations. Bit 43 is a protection check bit. This bit is set to 1 when an attempt is made to violate the storage protection provided in the computer.

Bit 44 is the channel-data check bit. This bit is set to 1 when a parity error is detected by the channel in the data being handled. Bit 45 is the channel-control check bit. This bit is set to 1 when an error other than parity is detected in the channel operation. Bit 46 is the interface-control check bit. This bit is set to 1 when the channel detects some difficulty in handling the data from or to the input or output equipment. Bit 47 is the chaining check bit. This bit is set to 1 when an error is detected in the relationship between the parts of the channel subprogram controlling the input or output operation.

The programer should note that the presence of a nonzero CSW does not mean that an input or output situation is the cause of an interrupt. The CSW is stored automatically on the occurrence of any of a variety of conditions which are handled normally by the logical IOCS routines. These require no specific attention from the programer, since they are handled automatically by the IOCS routines. For this reason, it is normal to find a nonzero CSW in a dump of internal storage. A programer should inspect and study the CSW for indications of error only if he can determine from other sources that an input-output interrupt has occurred that is significant for him.

INTERPRETATION OF DUMPS

For assistance in debugging, the programer needs a correctly taken dump of internal storage, a listing of the program compilation, a listing of the output produced by the program (this may require "dumping" a tape to get the data it carries, for example), a listing of the input read by the program, a link-edit listing ("map") if a link-edit was performed on the object program, and a statement from the console operator listing the contents of the current PSW and the symptoms of program failure. Console operators, when they terminate the computer's operation on a job, often neglect to note the contents of the current PSW. If the supervisor program or the operating system terminates the computer's operation on a job, the contents of current PSW may not be relevant, since the data usually have been saved in an old PSW area anyway.

Programers also need translations of the test data into hexadecimal form. For ease of comparison with the storage dump, these listings are most convenient if they show both the EBCDIC code and the hexadecimal code. For ease in recalling the logic of the program, the programer needs a flow diagram, as described elsewhere in this book.

With these materials at hand, the programer can begin debugging. Additional examples and additional comments on the examples given in this chapter will be found in the workbook. Let us take as a first example a program from a previous chapter, Fig. 6-33, but modified to introduce a few programing errors.

First, the programer must calculate the address of the program. This he can do from the link-edit map, as shown. The console operator reports he has terminated the job, since it appeared to be in an endless loop and was producing no output. The contents of the current PSW, a compilation list, and the dump are shown in Fig. 8-20.

Since the console operator provided a current PSW, the programer can check it. Where is the instruction address? A check of this establishes that the computer was executing the program, since it falls among the instruction addresses shown on the compilation list. The length code agrees with the length of the instruction last executed, the Add Half at address 001918. Since the console operator terminated the program's execution for lack of output, the programer can try to "play computer" by following the control sequence to establish why the computer may have been in a loop and why it was producing no output—since these are both usually control-sequence bugs.

```
// JOB
// OPTION DECK,ERRS
// EXEC ASSEMBLY


                              EXTERNAL SYMBOL DICTIONARY

SYMBOL  TYPE ID  ADDR  LENGTH LD ID


         PC   01 000000 000000
F8#20    SD   02 000000 0000A8


    LOC  OBJECT CODE    ADDR1 ADDR2  ST #  NAME   OP    OPERANDS              COMMENT
                                            IMPERATIVES

                                      1            PRINT ON,GEN,DATA
000000                                2            START
000000                                3 F8#20      CSECT
000000  070007000700                  4            CNOP  6,8
000006  0520                          5 BFRST      BALR  2,0
000008                                6            USING *,2
000008  5830 2030          00038      7 BSCND      L     3,=F'4'              CLEAR A REGISTER BY
00000C  5850 2034          0003C      8            L     5,=F'0'              A LITERAL
000010  4840 2038          00040      9            LH    4,=H'14'             LOAD A REG. USING A LITERAL
000014  47F0 201A          00020      10           B     BCNT                ENTER LOOP
000018  4A53 2040          00048      11 BNTER     AH    5,STZ(3)            USE REG. 3 TO INDEX 'STZ', USING A
                                      12 *                                   REG. TO INDEX A SERIES IS POSSIBLE
                                      13 *                                   ONLY ON RX OPERATIONS.
00001C  4A30 203A          00042      14           AH    3,=H'2'             INCREMENT THE INDEX REG.
000020  4640 2010          0001B      15 BCNT      BCT   4,BNTER             BRANCH ON COUNT
000024  47E0 2000          00008      16           BC    14,BSCND            ITERATE 13 TIMES USING
                                      17 *                                   LEADING DECISIONS
000028  5050 2060          00068      18           ST    5,BSUM              STORE TOTAL SUM
00002C  9035 2068          00070      19           STM   3,5,BSUM+8
                                      20           EOJ
                                      21** 360N-CL-453  EOJ    CHANGE LEVEL  2-0
000030  0A0E                          22+          SVC   14
00003B                                23           LTORG
000038  00000004                      24                 =F'4'
00003C  00000000                      25                 =F'0'
000040  000E                          26                 =H'14'
000042  0002                          27                 =H'2'
                                      28 *
                                      29 *   DECLARATIVES
                                      30 *
000048                                31           DS    0D
000048  000F00E100010034              32 STZ       DC    H'15,225,1,52,10,48,76,42,88,26,14,4,32'
000050  000A0030004C002A
000058  0058001A000E0004
000060  0020
000062  0013002F                      33           DC    H'19,47'
000066  0000
000068  00000000                      34 BSUM      DC    F'0'
00006C  404040404040404040            35           DC    28C' '                         FILLER
000074  404040404040404040
00007C  404040404040404040
000084  40404040
000000                                36           END   F8#20



                              CROSS-REFERENCE

SYMBOL   LEN  VALUE  DEFN

BCNT     00004 000020 0015   0010
BFRST    00002 000006 0005
BNTER    00004 00001B 0011   0015
BSCND    00004 000008 0007   0016
BSUM     00004 00006B 0034   001B 0019
F8#20    00001 000000 0003   0036
STZ      00002 000048 0032   0011


NO STATEMENTS FLAGGED IN THIS ASSEMBLY


// PAUSE
// OPTION LINK,DUMP
    INCLUDE
// EXEC LNKEDT
```

FIG. 8-20. First debugging example.

```
                        DISK LINKAGE EDITOR DIAGNOSTIC OF INPUT

        ACTION TAKEN    MAP
        LIST    ENTRY



              PHASE  XFR-AD  LOCORE  HICORE  DSK-AD  ESD TYPE  LABEL     LOADED  REL-FR
          PHASE***  001900  001900  001987  2A 4 2  CSECT               001900  001900
                                                    CSECT    F8#20      001900  001900

    CONTROL SECTIONS OF ZERO LENGTH IN INPUT



    // EXEC


REG0   00000000  00001900  40001908  00000004  0000000D  00000001  00000000  00001888
REG8   80003410  0A0107F1  00002000  00002000  00002C18  00003C18  0000017B  0000008B

40-CSW  KEY-00  ADDR-000088  STATUS-0000110000000000  COUNT-000000    48-CAW  KEY-00  ADDR-00009B

PSW CONTENTS              EXTERNAL INTERRUPT    SUPERVISOR CALL      PROGRAM CHECK        MACHINE CHECK        INPUT/OUTPUT
FIELD          FORMAT-OLD 18    -NEW 58    -OLD 20    -NEW 60    -OLD 28    -NEW 68    -OLD 30    -NEW 70    -OLD 38    -NEW 78
SYSTEM MASK    BIT-11111111  -00000000  -11111110  -00000000  -11111111  -00000000  -01011011  -00000000  -11111110  -00000000
PROTECTION KEY HEX-0         -0         -0         -0         -0         -0         -5         -0         -0         -0
AMWP           BIT-0110      -0100      -0100      -0100      -0101      -0100      -1011      -0000      -0100      -0100
INTERRUPT CODE HEX-0040      -0000      -0000      -0000      -0006      -0000      -C2C5      -0000      -0090      -0000
INSTR LENGTH   DEC-2         -0         -1         -0         -2         -0         -3         -0         -2         -0
CONDITION CODE DEC-0         -0         -1         -0         -2         -0         -1         -0         -0         -0
PROGRAM MASK   BIT-0000      -1111      -0000      -0000      -0000      -0000      -0110      -0000      -0000      -0000
INSTR ADDRESS  HEX-000000    -000ADE    -000BCC    -000924    -001910    -000A86    -D1F340    -000726    -0008D0    -0001FC

4C-UNUSED-00000000    50-TIMER-FFFFFFFF    54-UNUSED-00FFFFFF

000300  91003006  07194820  30009120  30064710  008C0202  00491009  9C002000  47700334
000320  90230F60  96803006  91023006  07899602  030107F9  47300362  91060045  4770071A
000340  913F0045  4770034E  91AF0044  07894020  003A5860  0048A4A0  0DAC5060  004047F0
 ?360   03A64710  052A07F9  4190014C  91060045  4770071E  94F00039  D501003A  0F624780
        050A4570  05124820  003A4220  03A14570  03A04133  0008D500  3000003A  47200460
        ?083001   07774570  04849102  00444710  05429139  00454770  05369180  00444780
001460       ?4   0044910A  01B14770  030E9500  30044770  030E9603  0F484190  01069110
001480  41...     03F69500  00440789  06020041  00414770  049C9104  00444770  040C9550
0014A0  1002417.. ?477      300607F9  94773006  91043006  4780044A  D6011004  00449473
0014C0  09000076  ...       042E9200  30039680  100292FF  500C4370  30020200  30024000
0014E0  080002DB  0000U..   ?95FF     30024780  045A9198  30064780  04809102  30060789
001500  1E0002F8  30000081  .         D5003000  003A0729  95FB3002  07879198  30060777
001520  C74B40E3  D9C1D5E2  48+..     ?5481A44  1A444144  0F785810  400007F7  02011000
001540  5858C2D7  C3C8D240  5B5BC2C1  ?01       50004720  04E25870  00404870  00AC5877
001560  C9E2F0C1  D6E2C4C3  F1D604E2  C,.       0F5A4770  04E29620  30069640  10029601
001580  40C9D1E2  E8E2F0F1  40E2E8E2  E3C5D4+   ?444770   041E9680  30069104  10024780
0015A0  40404040  40404040  40404040  ??        4320003A  48300186  43223000
0015C0  00420100  0000E2C4  D6E24040  40404040  40U.      0DA99204  05A19109  00454780
0015E0  00BD0003  01010000  C901E2E8  E2F0F140  0000800.. ?006      4780057C  94F005A1
001600  00000000  00C70000  0B00C700  000B2C00  60000000  U.        94FD0301  48600DF6
001620  TO THE NEXT LINE ADDRESS CONTAINS 00000000
                                                    ?000040   40306008
001660  00000000  00000000  00000000  00000000  00000000  00000000  ?F        40800D62
001680  00BD0003  00000000  00000000  00000000  00000000  00000000  00U..     ?004780
0016A0  00680000  03001888  00F50000  43012100  00001580  80002E50  D7C8C1E+  ?F0
0016C0  D7C8C1E2  C55C5C5C  00190001  0019002A  04020088  40404040  40404040  4U.
0016E0  TO THE NEXT LINE ADDRESS CONTAINS 40404040
001820  40404040  40404040  C2C740F0  D7F0F8C1  40404040  40C9D5E3  C5D9E540  D9C5D840
001840  E2E8E2D9  C4D97EF0  F0C14040  40404040  404040C3  C3E2E67E  F0F2F0F0  F0F0F2F2
001860  F4F0F0C2  F0F0F0F0  F0F040E2  D5E27EF4  F0F0F0F0  F0F0F0F0  C3C3C27E  C3C3C27E
001880  F0F0F2F2  F2F040E2  D27EC2C2  C2C2C3C3  C3C3C8C8  C8C84000  00002220  C14040C9
0018A0  D5E3C5D9  E5400DC5  D810C2C7  00000000  FF050001  00001900  0A0107F1  00007FFF
0018C0  00002000  00002C18  00003C18  0000017B  00000088  80003410  00001900  00002238
0018E0  00001900  00007F74  FFFFFF8C  00000000  00001888  80003410  00001900  00002238
001900  07000700  07000520  58302030  58502034  48402038  47F02018  4A532040  4A30203A
001920  46402010  47E02000  50502060  9035206A  0A0E205C  0A0E1017  00000004  00000000
001940  000E0002  00010034  000F00E1  00010034  000A0030  004C002A  0058001A  000E0004
001960  00200013  002F0000  00000000  40404040  40404040  40404040  40404040  40404040
001980  40404040  40404040  00000000  00000000  00000000  00000000  00000000  00000000
0019A0  TO THE NEXT LINE ADDRESS CONTAINS 00000000
007FE0  00000000  00000000  00000000  00000000  00000000  00000000  00000000  00000000
```

PSW- FF050000A00019IC

FIG. 8-20 *(continued)*

```
// JOB
// OPTION LISTX,ERRS,DECK
// EXEC ASSEMBLY


                              EXTERNAL SYMBOL DICTIONARY

SYMBOL  TYPE ID  ADDR  LENGTH LD ID


           PC  01 000000 000000
F8#21      SD  02 000000 000080


  LOC  OBJECT CODE    ADDR1 ADDR2  ST #  NAME    OP    OPERANDS            COMMENT

                                    IMPERATIVES

                                    1              PRINT  ON,GEN,DATA
000000                              2              START
000000                              3  F8#21       CSECT
000000 070007000700                 4              CNOP   6,8
000006 0520                         5  BFRST       BALR   2,0
000008                              6              USING  *,2
000008 5A20 205A      00060         7              A      2,INCR           SET INCREMENT AMOUNT
00000C 5830 2030      00038         8              L      3,=F'0'          CLEAR A REGISTER BY
000010 5450 2030      00038         9              L      5,=F'0'          A LITERAL
000014 4840 2034      0003C        10              LH     4,=H'14'         LOAD A REG. USING A LITERAL
000018 47F0 201C      00024        11              B      BCNT             ENTER LOOP
00001C 4A53 2038      00040        12  BNTER       AH     5,STZ(3)         USE REG. 3 TO INDEX 'STZ', USING A
                                   13  *                                  REG. TO INDEX A SERIES IS POSSIBLE
                                   14  *                                  ONLY ON RX OPERATIONS.
000020 4A30 2036      0003E        15              AH     3,=H'2'          INCREMENT THE INDEX REG.
000024 4640 2014      0001C        16  BCNT        BCT    4,BNTER          BRANCH ON COUNT
000028 5050 2054      0005C        17              ST     5,BSUM           STORE TOTAL SUM
00002C 9035 205C      00064        18              STM    3,5,BSUM+8
                                   19              EOJ
                                   20+* 360N-CL-453           EOJ          CHANGE LEVEL  2-0
000030 0A0E                        21+             SVC    14
000038                             22              LTORG
000038 00000000                    23                     =F'0'
00003C 000E                        24                     =H'14'
00003E 0002                        25                     =H'2'
                                   26  *
                                   27  *  DECLARATIVES
                                   28  *
000040                             29              DS     0D
000040 000F00E100010034            30  STZ         DC     H'15,225,1,52,10,48,76,42,88,26,14,4,32'
000048 000A0030004C002A
000050 0058001A000E0004
000058 0020
00005A 0000
00005C 00000000                    31  BSUM        DC     F'0'
000060 00000001                    32  INCR        DC     F'1'             TAKE NUMBERS ONE AT A TIME
000064 404040404040404040          33              DC     28C' '           FILLER
00006C 404040404040404040
000074 404040404040404040
00007C 40404040
000000                             34              END    F8#21


                              CROSS-REFERENCE

SYMBOL    LEN  VALUE   DEFN

BCNT    00004 000024 0016    0011
BFRST   00002 000006 0005
BNTER   00004 00001C 0012    0016
BSUM    00004 00005C 0031    0017 0018
F8#21   00001 000000 0003    0034
INCR    00004 000060 0032    0007
STZ     00002 000040 0030    0012


NO STATEMENTS FLAGGED IN THIS ASSEMBLY


// OPTION LINK,DUMP
// PAUSE
   INCLUDE
// EXEC LNKEDT
```

FIG. 8-21. Second debugging example.

```
                              DISK LINKAGE EDITOR DIAGNOSTIC OF INPUT

         ACTION TAKEN    MAP
         LIST   ENTRY


              PHASE  XFR-AD  LOCORE  HICORE  DSK-AD  ESD TYPE  LABEL     LOADED  REL-FR

            PHASE***  001900  001900  00197F  2A 4 2  CSECT              001900  001900

                                                      CSECT     F8#21    001900  001900

      CONTROL SECTIONS OF ZERO LENGTH IN INPUT


      // EXEC



      0S031 PROGRAM CHECK INTERRUPTION - HEX LOCATION 00190C - CONDITION CODE 2 - SPECIFICATION EXCEPTION
      0S00I JOB          CANCELLED


REG0   00000000   00001900   40001909   00001900   00007F74  FFFFFFBC   00000000   000018BB
REG8   80003410   0A0107F1   00002000   00002000   00002C18  00003C18   00000178   0000008B

40-CSW KEY-00 ADDR-000000  STATUS-0000001000000000 COUNT-000000   48-CAW KEY-00 ADDR-000090

PSW CONTENTS         EXTERNAL  INTERRUPT SUPERVISOR CALL   PROGRAM CHECK      MACHINE CHECK       INPUT/OUTPUT
FIELD       FORMAT-OLD 18   -NEW 58  -OLD 20   -NEW 60  -OLD 28   -NEW 68  -OLD 30   -NEW 70  -OLD 38   -NEW 78
SYSTEM MASK    BIT-11111111  -00000000 -11111111 -00000000 -11111111 -00000000 -01011011 -00000000 -11111110 -00000000
PROTECTION KEY HEX-0         -0        -0        -0        -0        -0        -5        -0        -0        -0
AMWP           BIT-0110      -0100     -0111     -0100     -0101     -0100     -1011     -0000     -0100     -0100
INTERRUPT CODE HEX-0040      -0000     -0007     -0000     -0006     -0000     -C2C5     -0000     -0090     -0000
INSTR LENGTH   DEC-2         -0        -1        -0        -2        -0        -3        -0        -2        -0
CONDITION CODE DEC-0         -0        -0        -0        -2        -0        -1        -0        -0        -0
PROGRAM MASK   BIT-0000      -1111     -0000     -0000     -0000     -0000     -0110     -0000     -0000     -0000
INSTR ADDRESS  HEX-00000     -000ADE   -001526   -001910   -000AB6   -D1F340   -000726   -0008CC   -0001FC

4C-UNUSED-00000000     50-TIMER-FFFFFFFF    54-UNUSED-00FFFFFF

000300  91003006  07194820  30009120  30064710  00ACD202  00491009  9C002000  47700334
000320  90230F60  96803006  91023006  07899602  030107F9  47300362  91060045  4770071A
000340  913F0045  4770034E  91AF0044  07894020  003A5860  00484A60  0DAC5060  004047F0
00?360  03A64710  052A07F9  4190014C  91060045  4770071E  94F00039  0501003A  0F624780
001?    050A4570  05124820  003A4220  03A14570  03A04133  0008D500  3000003A  47200460
0015A0  ?0?3001   07774570  04849102  00444710  05429139  00454770  05369180  004447A0
0015C0  60??  ?4  0044910A  01B14770  03DE9500  30044770  03DE9603  0F484190  01069110
0015E0  D706C9D?  ?3F69500  00440789  06020041  00414770  049C9104  004447F0  040C9550
001600  C4C5C3C9  ?  ?477  300607F9  94773006  91043006  4780044A  06011004  00449473
001620  070AD5C5  D5E34?   042E9200  30039680  100292FF  500C4370  30020200  30024000
001640  E6E2C9C7  D5C9C6C9  ?095FF    30024780  0454919B  30064780  04809102  30060789
001660  C4C50000  00000000  00?  ?    D5003000  003A0729  95FF3002  07879198  30060777
001680  008D0003  00000000  0000000?  ?5A81A44  1A444144  0F785810  400007F7  D2011000
0016A0  00680000  03001888  00F50000  4?  ?01    50004720  04E25870  00404870  0DAC5877
0016C0  5858C2C5  D9D9E3D5  00000001  00000?  ?   0F5A4770  04E29620  30069640  10029601
0016E0  00000004  0A0102A6  5858C2D9  E2E3D9E3  ?444770  041E9680  30069104  10024780
001700  C5E3C6C6  00000001  00000004  09010442  5b?  ??   4320003A  48300186  43223000
001720  09020480  5858C2E2  C5E3D340  00000001  000000u?  ?0A99204  05A19109  00454780
001740  00000001  00000005  010202CC  5858C105  C5D9D906  ?  ?006   4780057C  94F005A1
001760  5858C105  C5D909E5  00000001  00000005  030101EB  585b??  94F00301  48600DF6
001780  00000005  030203CE  5858C2C4  E4D407C6  00000001  00000005  ?00040   40306008
0017A0  E2E3C9D6  00000001  00000005  04020398  5858C2C4  09E2E3D9  0?? ?    40800062
0017C0  05010480  5858C2D1  C3D607E3  00000001  00000005  05020300  5858C2C?  ?00447A0
0017E0  00000001  00000005  960103D1  5858C2C1  E3E3D5C2  00000001  00000005  ?  7F0
001800  5858C2C1  E3E3D5C3  00000001  00000005  07010104  5858C2C1  E3E3D5C4  0000u?
001820  00000005  07020147  C2C740F0  D7F0F8C1  40404040  40C9D5E3  C5D9E540  D9C50840
001840  E2E8E2C9  07E37EF0  F0C14040  40404040  404040C3  C3E2E67E  F0F2F0F0  F0F0F2C1
001860  F2F8F0C5  FDF0F0F0  F5F040E2  05E27EF4  F0F0F0F0  F0F0F040  F0F0F040  C3C3C27E
001880  F0F0F2F9  C2F040E2  D27EC2C2  C2C2C3C3  C3C3CACR  C8C84000  000029B0  C14040C9
0018A0  D5E3C5D9  E540D9C5  0810C2C7  00000000  FF050006  A0001910  0A0107F1  00020000
0018C0  00002000  00002C18  00003C18  0000017B  0000008B  00000000  00001900  40001909
0018E0  00001900  00007F74  FFFFFF8C  00000000  000018BB  80003410  00001900  00001909
001900  07000700  07000520  5A202058  58302030  5F502030  48402034  47F02020  47F02020
001920  4A53203B  4A302036  46402018  50502054  9035205C  0A0E1017  00000000  000E0002
001940  000F00E1  00010034  000A0030  004C002A  0058001A  000E0004  00200000  00000000
001960  00000001  40404040  40404040  40404040  40404040  40404040  40404040  40404040
001980 TO THE NEXT LINE ADDRESS CONTAINS 00000000
007FE0  00000000  00000000  00000000  00000000  00000000  00000000  00000000  00000000
```

FIG. 8-21 *(continued)*

Since no interrupts were reported, the programer can trace the control sequence directly by starting at the PSW shown address and going down the program compilation list to the next transfer of control, the BCT instruction. The programer can check the register contents for the registers cited. Since the contents of the count register (number 4) are not yet 1, the programer can assume that a transfer of control would take place to execute the loop again. Assuming that this has indeed happened the required D_x (thirteen) more times, the programer can ask what would happen when the contents of the count register went to 0. Control falls through to the next instruction in sequence. This is a transfer of control back to the very start of the program. But should not this transfer have gone to the end of the program? Here then is the cause of the endless loop.

While a programer has a dump, he should always search for evidence of other bugs, even after finding the bug that may appear to be the cause of the immediate difficulty. To that end he should, in general, check the output area in storage, the sequence control fields, if any, any intermediate work areas, and the input areas. To find the addresses, the programer can refer to the compilation listing and the link-edit, if any. Here the sum register contains some data. But is it correct? To check it, the programer can add the input values. This total is not the same as the contents of the sum register. What has caused this bug?

This type of bug is usually not a control-sequence difficulty, but arises usually from logic error or clerical error by the programer. To find this bug, the programer can again play computer. This time, he must check each operand address and contents, not just the control sequence. Turning to the point shown in the dump, he can check the operand addresses and contents in the instruction that is the heart of the program, the indexed Add Half. To do this, the programer must add together the contents as shown in the dump of the base and index register and then add on the displacement. Since these values are for the first of 13 iterations, do they agree with what the programer would expect?

No, they do not, since the field being added is not the very first field in the input. Then either the displacement amount, the index amount, the base amount, or all of them, must be wrong. In this case the base and the displacement were determined by the compiler and hence are more likely to be correct than the index amount. A check of the index register makes it appear to be correct, but a check of the initial loading of the index register reveals a clerical error.

A second example is shown in Fig. 8-21. This is another modification of the program shown in Fig. 6-33, and was link-edited. In this instance, the console operator has provided the materials shown with no comments and no current PSW contents. The programer approaches this problem much as he did the former example. The first step is to calculate the base address of the program from the program list and from the linkage map, as shown in Fig. 8-21. The computer-produced error message indicates that a program check interruption has occurred.

A comparison of the old and new PSW areas shows that an interrupt did occur, since one of the old PSW areas contains an instruction address from the program. The interrupt code in the program old PSW is 6_x. Since the command is a Load, the probable bug is an incorrect alignment. Since a check of the declaration indicates that the programer used a type H or F and the compilation list verifies the address, that is not the bug. Perhaps, then, it is the contents of the index register. The dump and the listing show the index amount to be 0. A check of the base-register contents, however, reveals the difficulty. The register should cite an address on a full- or, even better, double-word boundary, but does not. The bug comes, therefore, from the loading of the register, or from modifying its contents. Since it was loaded by a BALR with a double-word boundary address, that is not the bug, but why is there a later instruction in the initialization adding $+1$ to the base-register contents?

Additional explanation of the interpretation of dumps will be found in the workbook. More extensive comments on debugging procedures will also be found there.

EFFECTS OF THE OPERATING SYSTEM

Debugging problems, aids, and techniques change with different supervisors or operating systems used. Thus, under BPS, the supervisor provides very little assistance in debugging, only infrequently causes bugs in the programer's programs, and can be largely ignored in doing debugging.

At the other extreme is OS. It can provide three varieties of dumps, in addition to the stand-alone dump. It can provide hundreds of diagnostic messages and completion codes. It has available debugging routines that the programer can call. And the dump itself may contain special data to help in debugging, such as a "trace table."

An extensive operating system such as OS is also a source of bugs. The programer has more conventions to observe, and failure to observe them correctly and in full can give bugs. The programer has available more than 100 system macros that call into play the capabilities of the operating system. Failure to use them in accord with their proscription results in bugs. And changes in the operating system itself can give bugs, even in such simple things as the operands for SVC commands, for instance.

The effects on debugging of an extensive operating system such as OS cannot be ignored. The programer has additional areas in storage to check. For example, in OS he has the Task Control Block (TCB), the Request Blocks (RB, which come in seven varieties), the Task Input-Output Tables (TIOT), the Data Control Blocks (DCB), the Unit Control Blocks (UCB), the Event Control Blocks (ECB), the Input-Output Control Blocks (IOB), the Data Extent Blocks (DEB), and the Communications Vector Table (CVT). Not all are relevant each time, but the programer often must check them anyway. He has the problem of locating them on the dump, finding what he needs to know out of each (and each has a different format), and interpreting the codes they contain. And he may have to examine a series of saved register contents. And the whole picture is complicated by the fact that the operating system may be multiprograming the programer's program with other programs.

In debugging programs that have died under an extensive operating system such as OS, the programer first must determine what program the computer was executing at the time—it may be a part of the operating system, a library program or routine, or the programer's program. If it is any but the last, the programer needs to find out what it was and what relation its execution has to his program. It was called by some kind of interrupt, perhaps even an SVC. The TCB and RB are usually helpful in the identification. So are the diagnostic messages and completion codes.

The programs may be executed in a series, with the operating system calling one after another. For example, on input and output operations, over a half dozen routines may be called before an IO operation is complete, and interrupts for other causes, even other IO operations, may have occurred. To find the correction needed, the programer must trace the series back to his own program. To find out what caused the trouble, he may have to check the TIOT, the CSW, and the control blocks affected by the operation such as the DCB, UCB, ECB, IOB, and DEB (the DCB is described briefly in Chap. 11). A look at the coding and byte count of the data themselves is usually worthwhile—it may not be what the programer wrote the program to handle.

EXERCISES

1. What is the priority system established among interrupts?
2. What happens when an interrupt is honored?
3. What is meant by calling an interrupt "pending"?
4. What is a PSW? How does the computer use it?
5. What is the significance of each type of program interrupt?
6. How do dumps help in debugging?

CHAPTER 9

Problem Analysis

NEED FOR ANALYSIS AID

The exercises given thus far in this book and in the workbook are sufficiently simple that some programers will be able to keep track mentally of all the parts of the problem statement. Other programers have probably had to refer back occasionally to the problem statement, reviewing details as they worked.

On the job, some of the problems a programer will work on are as simple as the exercises given thus far in this book. However, most programers spend the majority of their time working on more complex problems. On these problems, it becomes difficult for the programer to retain in his head at all times all the aspects of the problem that are important for doing the programing. The job gets too big, and the programer cannot do the entire job in five or ten minutes, or even in half an hour. He may require instead, for example, a year and a half of concentrated work. In such a time period, he will have to give attention to many things, not all at one time, but in relation to one another.

With increasing problem complexity, therefore, the programer finds a growing need for analysis aids. Ideally these analysis aids should bring to the programer's mind, easily and quickly, the essential aspects of the task to be performed and the way in which the programer has elected to do them. In particular, they must ease the appearance of complexity for the programer, and make it possible for him to concentrate his attention on particular parts of the program and job specifications in a way that is consistent with the guidance of his superior and the job specification of other parts of the job.

The programer also needs the help of analysis aids when he revises or modifies a program that he or some other programer has written previously. This requires that the analysis aids have the quality of documenting the programer's work. The use of analysis aids should yield good written records suitable for use by other programers. These records should describe the way in which the computer processes the input data to produce the output data.

Good program documentation helps the programer in three main ways: If the programer prepares it as he does the programing, it reminds the programer himself about the way he has done his work thus far. It improves the ability of the programer to remember his work, and to determine what he has done and how he has done it.

Second, good program documentation helps the programer who is revising a program by bringing to light easily and quickly the essential facts he needs to make the revision correctly. By putting everything in its place and providing a place for everything, adequate documentation helps the programer avoid overlooking important aspects of making the revision.

Third, good documentation helps the programer learn from his own mistakes by reviewing programs that he and other programers have written. In the light of the experience obtained in using the program, the programer can determine which things he did that should be done differently and which things he did that proved successful. Used in this way, documentation provides a valuable training aid for the programer.

Analysis aids, therefore, should not only ease the programer's path through the complexities of large problems, but should also yield good documentation. Among the aids commonly recommended as meeting these requirements are the use of mathematical formulas and numerical analysis techniques which may be particularly appropriate to some engineering and scientific applications, decision tables which may be appropriate for logically complex situations such as handling real-time data streams, and flow diagrams or flow charts which may be widely applicable.

FLOW DIAGRAM CONVENTIONS

The programer should know the ANSI flow diagram symbols and understand how to use them, thus making his flow diagrams conform more closely to the Standard and hence improving the communication value of the diagrams he prepares. Some of these conventions and the symbols were presented in Chap. 2. Now let us look briefly at some additional conventions. Figure 9-1 reviews the outline and notation symbols.

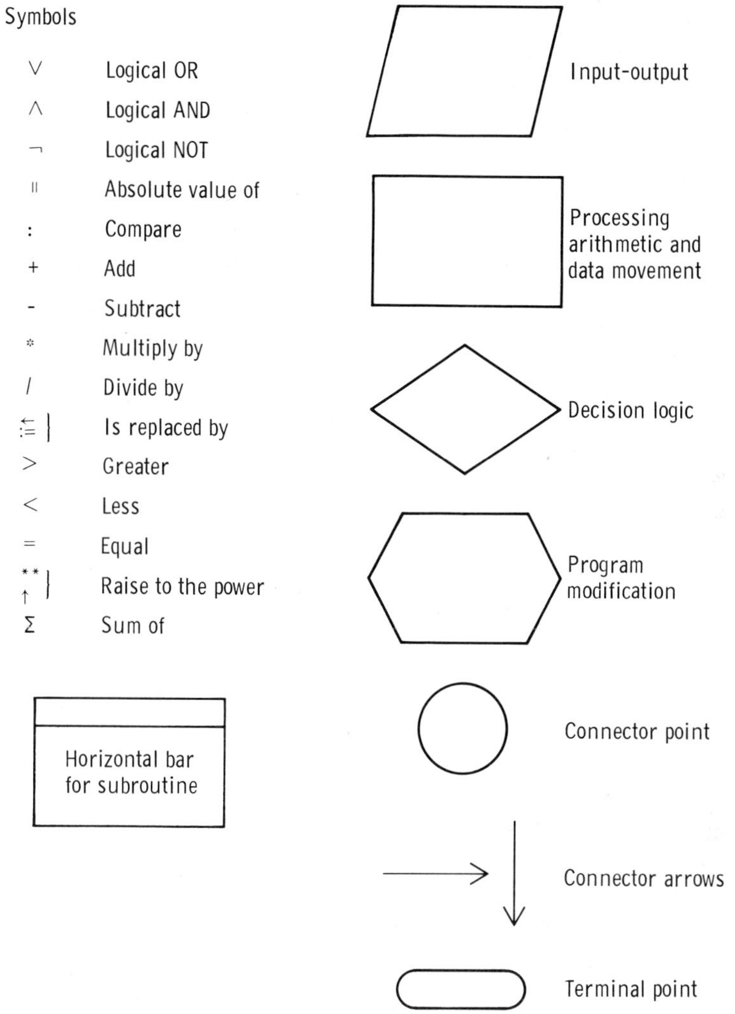
Symbols
∨ Logical OR
∧ Logical AND
¬ Logical NOT
| | Absolute value of
: Compare
+ Add
- Subtract
* Multiply by
/ Divide by
← := Is replaced by
> Greater
< Less
= Equal
** ↑ Raise to the power
Σ Sum of
Horizontal bar for subroutine
Input-output
Processing arithmetic and data movement
Decision logic
Program modification
Connector point
Connector arrows
Terminal point

FIG. 9-1. ANSI Standard flow diagram outlines and some notation for use within the outlines.

As long as the number of steps in a program remains small, the programer may be able to fit the entire diagram for the program on one or two sheets of paper. With large programs, however, this is not possible. Serious questions can then arise about the "whereabouts" of particular connectors among the many pages. Wherever such questions are likely to arise, the programer should annotate above and immediately to the right of each exit connector the page and column or row reference of the place where that same connector symbol will be found as an entry point. This is illustrated by 9B and 13C in Fig. 9-2.

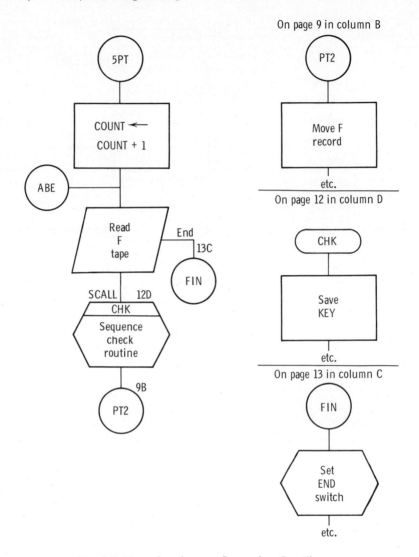

Fig. 9-2. Examples of cross reference in a flow diagram.

For clarification, the programer can use the same convention of writing the page designation above and immediately to the right of the subroutine outline to designate where in the diagram the subroutine name will be found. This becomes particularly useful when the programer has used many routines in his program. This is illustrated by 12D in Fig. 9-2 for the subroutine CHK. Subroutines cross referenced in this manner must begin and end in the flow diagram with terminal outlines.

Although it is of little help to the programer in using the flow diagram as an analysis aid, many programers find that cross referencing between the flow diagram and the coding clearly improves the diagram as program documentation. To do this cross referencing, the programer can write a connector outline at the appropriate places in the diagram for every name given to an instruction in the coding, whether or not each be an entry point. Thus, for example, if the programer has assigned the name ABE to some instruction in the program, he can show in his flow diagram an entry connector with the name ABE, as shown in Fig. 9-2. As an alternative, and one that is particularly useful in diagrams at the summary level, the programer can indicate, above and to the left of an outline, the name he assigns to the instruction or an instruction in a group at that point in the program. This is illustrated by SCALL in Fig. 9-2.

In preparing flow diagrams, programers usually find it convenient to refer to items of data by the names which they have assigned ("first-level" addressing). For literals ("zero-level" addressing), the programer may use apostrophes around the literal to call attention to its literal status, but need not do so if the context makes it clear, as is usually the case for a numeric literal. Neither of these two notations has the status of an ANSI Standard but is, like the following one, convenient for programers who work with assembly language.

Where the programer needs to designate a field whose address is the contents of another ("pointer") field, the programer can place the address (name) of the

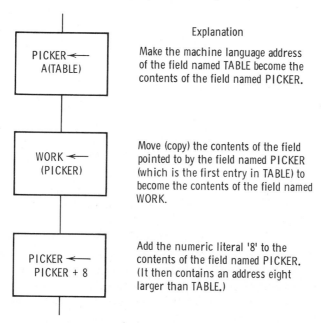

FIG. 9-3. Address conventions for flow diagrams.

pointer field in parentheses. This is then read as the contents of the field pointed to by the first address ("second-level" addressing). To refer to the address itself of a field, the programer can place an A in front of the parentheses just as in the case of an address constant. All of these conventions are illustrated in Fig. 9-3.

Persons with mathematical backgrounds sometimes find no sense at all in some of the statements programers commonly use in flow diagrams. For example, to a person with mathematical training, PICKER = PICKER + 8 looks like sheer nonsense; how can something be set equal to itself plus or minus something? This convention is a notation for expressing an operation the programer wants the computer to do on an item of data, returning that item of data to its original address in storage. Thus, in the example at hand, the programer wishes the value of PICKER to be increased by eight, with this new increased amount replacing the old amount at the address called PICKER. Some programers prefer an arrow with the arrowhead pointing to the left for use in place of the equal sign for this purpose, as shown in Fig. 9-3. Others use a := combination of symbols in place of the leftward pointing arrow, in preference to an equal sign.

An arrow pointing to the left in a rectangular outline is sometimes used to indicate a data-movement operation, as illustrated in Figure 9-3. In such cases the receiving field is named first in the outline, and the sending field is named second in the outline. Some programers prefer to reverse the direction of the arrow and the sequence of the operands.

With this basic information about the use of the ANSI flow diagram outlines, the programer is now in position to attempt using them. First, however, a few words are probably in order about the usual way in which programers approach or analyze the problem, as well as some guidelines to doing programing in general.

PROGRAMING GUIDELINES

The experience of programers has given rise to a wide diversity of opinion about the best ways of doing programing work. Some argue that no guidelines are necessary, and that each job's characteristics are sufficiently different that no useful guidelines can be formulated. Others argue for the use of standardized approaches as guidelines and claim that strict adherence to these approaches is helpful. The practice at the particular installation where a programer works must guide the programer. The comments on programing guidelines offered here must, of necessity, be very general and may in particular instances be countermanded by local practices.

A major guideline for programing is to concentrate the essential logic of the program in a particular part of the program. All the basic comparisons used to select the specific work the computer is to do from among the alternatives the programer provides should be concentrated in a relatively brief section of coding in the program. If the programer scatters this logic throughout his program, the difficulties of debugging and of later modification of the program are greatly increased.

A second guideline is to use a subroutine approach as much as possible in writing the program. The programer should write individual subroutines for handling particular functions, and then have the computer exit to the subroutines and return to the program after the subroutine execution is complete. This makes program modification relatively easy, because the individual subroutines can be removed, repaired, and then re-inserted without damage to the operational efficiency of the rest of the program.

A third guideline, related to the second, is to utilize only one routine for reading input data from any given piece of input equipment. Thus, if records are to be read from a magnetic-tape file, the programer should write a subroutine to handle this reading operation. Whenever the programer wants the computer to read data from the magnetic tape, he should program an exit to the subroutine and then a return after the data reading has been accomplished.

A fourth guideline, applicable whenever the programer works with organized files of data, is to sequence-check the data as it is read, whether or not the problem statement asks for it. Many a programer has found that his program died a premature death because of out-of-sequence data. Sequence checking is the process of verifying the sort order of an organized file. It is illustrated later in this chapter.

A fifth guideline, applicable whenever the programer works with multiple files of data, is to read and sequence-check before deciding whether or not a logical break in the data occurs. If it occurs, then the programer should provide for completing the processing of the sequence break prior to beginning the processing of the record just read. This is in contrast to the so-called "look-ahead" read and hold for processing, where the program reads one record ahead of the record it is processing. "Look-ahead" uses more storage space and increases logical complexity, but may yield faster execution.

A sixth guideline is to concentrate in one place in storage all of the DS declaratives for work areas, including any input and output areas. This saves the programer time in reading a dump and makes register usage easier.

A seventh guideline is to construct all program switches as fields to be tested in working storage. This saves the programer much time in studying a dump. It reduces the number of program bugs because the programer has not asked the computer to alter the instructions themselves in a piecemeal fashion.

An eighth guideline is to initialize a subroutine immediately before its use, not afterward. This assures that the initialization is correct each time the computer goes to execute the subroutine, and leaves a record in storage of the action a subroutine took.

A ninth guideline is to incorporate in the program specific provisions for a restart in event some difficulty or operator option results in aborting the run before it has gone to a natural conclusion. In long programs this is essential; in short programs it is a convenience. In programs that do cumulative processing, it is difficult because the restart must be such that no input data are processed more than once, and that all input data are processed without gaps or skipped data.

A tenth guideline is to make specific provision in the program for the end-of-file or end-of-data condition, and for the start-of-file or start-of-data condition. The end-of-data or end-of-file is traditionally considered "tricky" and worthy of the programer's best efforts. It is a common source of bugs.

An eleventh guideline is to check each iterative loop for correct performance when the computer should not execute it at all (entrance followed by immediate exit), or should execute it once, twice, or three times. The value of this has been pointed out elsewhere.

A twelfth guideline is to incorporate record counters for both input and output files to count the number of records read and written. These are valuable in debugging, because they enable the programer to check more easily for redundant and missing input handling and for skipped or multiple output.

A thirteenth guideline is to find out about—and observe—the standard operating practices at the installation where the programer works. Some of these contribute to the smooth working of programers in groups by reducing confusion, inconsistency, and duplication. Others contribute to the efficiency of the individual programer.

ANALYSIS APPROACHES

Over the course of more than a decade, programers have developed scores of analysis approaches to programing problems. Entire books can be written on the subject. The presentation here is limited to four analysis approaches which are among the most commonly used by programers at the present time. These can be briefly typified as "highlight and detail fill," "simplify and augment," "fragment and combine," and "fit into a canned algorithm." The choice among these analysis approaches is a subjective one on the part of the programer. What is comfortable, convenient, and helpful to one programer may not be to another working on the same problem.

The "highlight-and-detail-fill" approach gets its name and its general styling from journalism. A newspaper writer, in writing a news story, typically attempts to give in the first paragraph a highlight of the news, and in his second and following paragraphs he restates this same information in more detail. In the next group of paragraphs, the writer again fills in more detail, covering the same ground all over again. The newspaper writer continues this process until he feels he has exhausted his subject or his editor cuts him off.

In the "highlight-and-detail-fill" approach, therefore, the programer first attempts to search for the things about the task at hand that strike his attention as being the most significant, the things he should be most aware of. These he notes in a simple, brief flow diagram. This diagram he then uses as the organizing or focal point around which he will base his work. For each of these highlights that he has selected, he then proceeds to look for details which support or fill out, or which provide a context of relationship between one highlight and the next. For example, if the programer has selected as a highlight reading a record from magnetic tape, then some of the details might be the identification of the record, the kind of data it can provide, the conditions under which it can provide these data, the conditions under which it should be read, and what to do when end-of-file occurs.

In the "fragment-and-combine" approach, the programer examines the entire job as originally defined, searching for natural division points. If the job is large, he searches for many such points. If the job is small, a few such points will do. Ideally he searches for a large enough number of division points to permit breaking the job into a series of small jobs (fragments), each small enough that he can keep most of its own details in mind all the time as he works on the individual parts separately.

After having considered the way in which the parts can later be combined, the programer then approaches each part individually. In the "fragment-and-combine" approach, the programer typically makes no or little attempt to simplify and then augment the original definitions of the work to be done in each fragment. Rather, he takes the original specifications, working with them in full detail right from the start. The programer, in the fragment and combine approach, does not look for the particular highlights of the job, but looks only for places where the job can be broken into parts which are workably small. These parts may be, and usually are, the mundane day-to-day elements of getting the total job done—rarely are they the most important things. The programer, in fragmenting the job, typically makes no attempt to recognize or to reflect the relative importance of the different parts of the total work to be done.

The work the programer wants the computer to do in one fragment must relate to, and provide the necessary data for, the work the computer is to do in some subsequent parts. To make this possible, the programer must give thought in each part, as he breaks or fragments the job into pieces, to what data will be needed for the later parts. The programer then uses these data for tying the fragments of the total job together into a coherent whole. That is, he then combines the parts in a sequence which enables him to use the data that each part builds or provides as data necessary for the operation of later parts. The programer thus usually, but not always, works on the parts in the order in which they provide data to each other.

In combining the fragments, the programer must give careful thought to the way in which he proposes to test the program. A program written in fragments and then combined cannot be tested in full until the entire program has been written. Until the program is complete, the programer must test it in parts. In contrast, a program written by the "simplify-and-augment" approach may be able to produce output data very early in the programing process, but these output data will be only partial. The "highlight-and-detail-fill" approach, in contrast, typically permits the production of output data only after the program is nearly complete.

In the "simplify-and-augment" approach, the programer attempts to reduce the problem by condensing it and making out of it a smaller series of less complicated operations. In doing the condensing, the programer does not strive to hit the highlights. Instead he takes the things that represent the most essential operations from a pragmatic point of view, while taking into account the fact that one set of operations must of necessity follow another.

Thus, for example, if the programer is handed a five-page written specification on a job to program, the programer may search through it to determine what he feels to be the mundane essentials of the job. These might be, for example, read data from three input files, accumulate data in tables, print reports when matching records are found, note sequence errors, write an error analysis of all records of a particular type, and update and produce as output the data from one of the input tapes.

Then in the augment phase, the programer attempts to look at each of the simplified points he has enumerated, and ask about each what needs to be added to make the program less "simplified" and more realistic. The programer finds that adding realism to each point typically suggests ways of making the other points more realistic. The programer carries this augment phase out in waves, until he finds that further analysis yields no significant additional realism. The augmenting phase, therefore, consists of applying less and less of the simplifying procedure to each part of the job again and again. In the simplify-and-augment approach, therefore, the programer is in effect using a form of iteration in his own analysis work.

In the "canned-algorithm" approach, the programer relies upon and adapts the analysis work done by other programers or by others working in the field. For example, if the installation in which the programer works has previously prepared a program for handling inventory-control operations in a certain warehouse, the programer may find it useful to study this program carefully, in order to utilize major parts of it when he is assigned to write a program for handling inventory control in another warehouse. The work that was done for one program may be in a large part applicable to the new program.

The canned-algorithm approach gets its name from the fact that other programers or analysts have developed procedures for the computer to use on given jobs. Such procedures are known as algorithms. The programer, when he wishes to use an algorithm developed by someone else, must interpret it and restate it to fit the requirements of the particular computer he is working with, and of the particular job at hand. In this fourth analysis approach, unlike the other three, it is assumed that the programer will adapt an existing algorithm. In the other three analysis approaches it is assumed that the programer will create his own algorithm. The use of algorithms developed by someone else means that they are available "off the shelf," ready to be adapted.

One branch of mathematics known as "numerical analysis" is in part concerned with the development of algorithms to yield results of satisfactory accuracy in mathematical operations. Numerical analysts have studied extensively such areas as differential equations, matrix algebra, series, and the like, and have, over the years, discovered many useful algorithms. When a programer is assigned a job in the area of mathematics, he often will find it helpful to review the available information from numerical analysis before attempting to begin his programing.

The four examples that follow illustrate these four analysis approaches. The first example, dealing with a file problem, illustrates the use of the highlight-and-detail-fill approach. The second example, dealing with table search, illustrates the fragment-and-combine approach. The third example, dealing with the preparation of a summary report, illustrates the simplify-and-augment approach. The fourth example, dealing with the computation of a square root, illustrates the canned-algorithm approach.

Each of these examples has been structured and set up to be generally within the limits of the command repertoire and the programer's assumed knowledge of the computer at this point in this book. Each example is a problem which could be approached differently if the programer had a full knowledge of the computer's commands. The analysis and the programs presented in the following sections have been done to strengthen the didactic value of the examples. They are *not* represented as being the most efficient or the best way of doing the programing in each of the individual cases. They are given here as examples, and as ways of stimulating the programer to think for himself. The discussion of them intentionally raises more questions than it answers.

FILE EXAMPLE

The problem is this: Two files of shipping data exist in the form of large decks of punched cards. The data format for both files is the same and is shown in Fig. 9-4. Both files have been sorted into an ascending sequence by product number. Both files have header records but no trailer records. A header record identifies the file; a trailer record indicates that the previous card was the last data card in the file. The problem facing the programer is to merge the two files to produce one file in the same ascending sort sequence as the two original files. He is to have the computer create the new, merged file as a separate deck of cards without altering or disturbing the physical integrity of the two original card decks. A system chart is given in Fig. 9-6. For the purposes of this example, the computer can be assumed to be equipped with two card readers and one card punch.

The general form for a systems chart is shown in Fig. 9-5. The chart lists the input data by their identifying names, and shows them as entering the computer.

Card columns	Field name
Data cards	
1-5	Product number
6-80	Other data
Header cards	
1-4	HDR1
5-21	SHIPPING FILE 010
Trailer cards	
1-2	/*
3-80	Blank

FIG. 9-4. Data formats for merge-highlight example.

The chart enters, in the processing outline, the name of the program to be executed. The chart lists the output data by their identifying names, and shows them emerging from (or produced by) the computer. To specify the type of medium used, the programer typically uses the outlines shown in Fig. 9-5, which have been designed for this purpose by the ANS Institute.

The highlight of this file problem is the merge operation, as diagramed in Fig. 9-7. Merging typically requires making comparisons between the keys of records from the two files and selecting the next item to be placed in correct sequence as the result of the comparison. The highlight of this job, therefore, is the process of making the comparison. Note that the product number serves as the key field.

The second highlight of the job is the need to read data from two files and to write (punch) data into one file. This second highlight, therefore, means that the programer will have to provide two separate and distinct read operations and one write operation. But the write operation and the read operation both depend for their control upon the merge logic, which is the primary highlight. This can be summarized in the form of a flow diagram, as shown in Fig. 9-8. This figure bears some resemblance, even though it is at the program level, to the system charts shown in Fig. 9-6.

With the two highlights clearly in mind, the programer is now ready to begin filling in the details. Turning attention to the second highlight, the programer can give some thought to how the computer could do the read. It is usually desirable to sequence-check any sorted file. It is essential to do so when the processing to be performed later depends upon the sequence of items in the file, as in this example. This means that the programer will have to make the computer save from each record read the previous product-number key. Then as each new record is read,

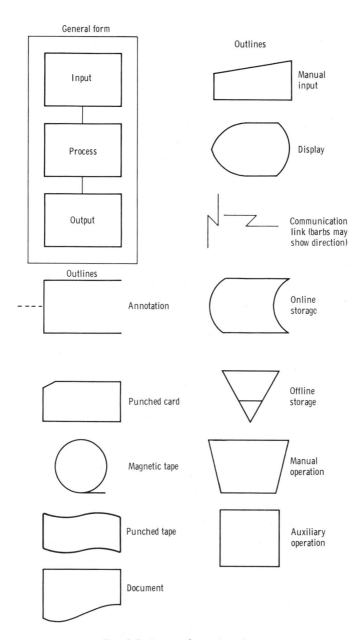

FIG. 9-5. Format for system charts.

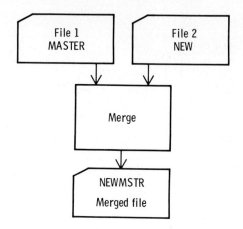

FIG. 9-6. System chart for merge-highlight example.

he can have the computer compare the previous key (old key) with the present key (new key). If the file is in correct sorted sequence, the new key should be the same as, or greater than, the prior key. If it is less, a sort-sequence failure has been detected. The outline of a procedure for doing this is shown in Fig. 9-9, under the assumption that sequence errors are to be punched separately and a count maintained.

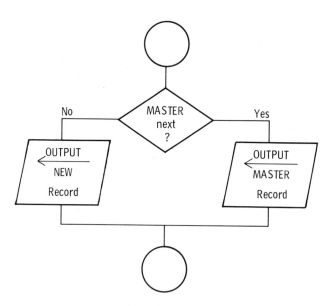

FIG. 9-7. First highlight for merge-highlight example.

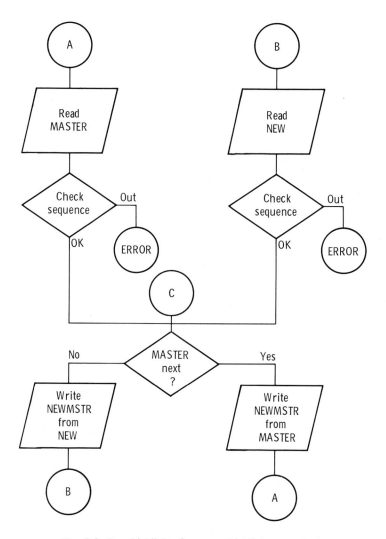

FIG. 9-8. Two highlights for merge-highlight example.

The programer can turn his attention to the major highlight of the program, the merge operation itself. Since this output file is to be written in ascending sequence, the next record to be placed in the output file should always be the one of the two input records that has the lower key. This means that the programer must have the computer compare the keys in the two input areas, and then either move the record with the lower key to the output area or have the computer write from the input area having the lower key. This is shown in Fig. 9-10.

As an aid in debugging, the programer can have the computer check for sort reversals in the output file by use of a sequence check on the output file. One procedure is much the same as that used on the input read. The key from each record, as it is written, must be saved to be compared to the key of the next record to be written. If the next record to be written has a lower key than the record last written, a sequence error has been detected. The major value of this is not in pre-

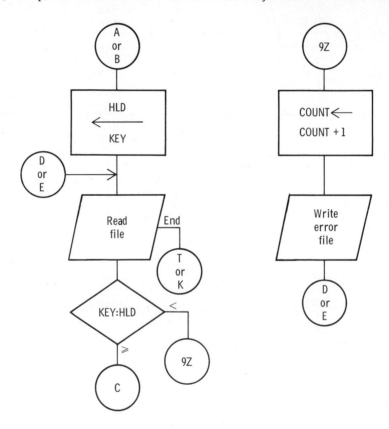

FIG. 9-9. Sequence check fill for merge-highlight example.

venting sequence errors in the output file, but in pointing up programing bugs and errors in the programer's logic. If the input files are correctly sequenced and the programer's selection logic is correct, the output file will also be correct in sequence. From that point of view, the output sequence checking is unnecessary and is not incorporated in the example.

In summary, then, the algorithm thus far is to compare the keys from the two records, one from each file. The record with the lower key is then to be copied onto the output file and a new record read from the input file, from which the last

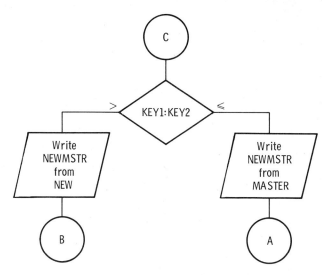

FIG. 9-10. Selection comparison fill for merge-highlight example.

record was obtained in order to replenish that record area in storage. The process then repeats.

In order to make the program complete, however, some initialization setup and some cleanup must be done. This initialization routine must load each of the two input areas correctly, set up the necessary work controls, and load the necessary registers, besides preparing the output files to receive records. Clearing the control fields by a move instruction (rather than by a DC declarative) makes it possible for the operator to run the program repeatedly without reloading it. In the initialization, each file must be opened, a record read from each of the two input files, and provision made to set up the sequence checking on the input. This is shown in Fig. 9-11.

The programer also must give attention to how to finish (clean up) the job. What happens, for example, when one of the input files becomes exhausted? Of necessity, one of them will always become exhausted before the other. What does the programer want the computer to do when an end-of-file condition has been sensed on an input file? On the one hand, no more records can be read from that file; on the other, all the records remaining in the other file must be copied without change into the output file but need to be sequence-checked. Handling this alteration of usual procedure can conveniently be done by what is known as a program switch. Commands specifically for handling these have not been covered in the previous chapters, but are covered in subsequent chapters. A less refined method, consisting of comparison, can be used here as a substitute.

Incorrect switch placement and setting are common bugs in programs. In the case at hand, the switch must be set in three places. It is set, first, in each end-of-

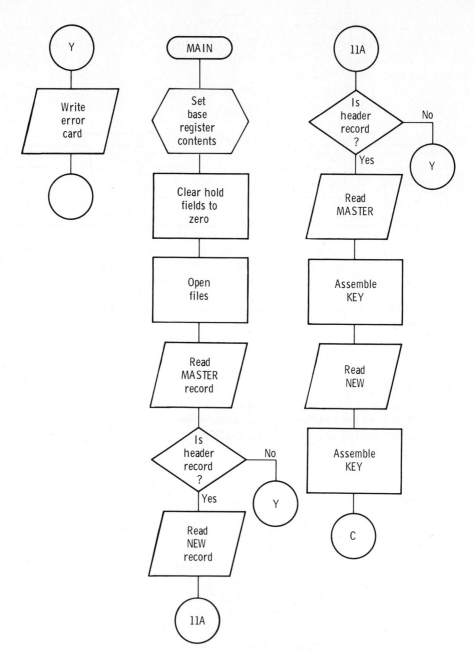

Fig. 9-11. Setup fill for merge-highlight example.

file routine for the opposite file, in order to cause an end-of-job operation when the reading operation on a file is complete. The third place is in the selection operation. This has the effect of making program control go through the selection operation on the same route. These can be combined by setting one of the selection-test-key fields to all FF$_x$. This is shown in Fig. 9-12. The end-of-job operation itself consists of punching an error-count card, closing the files, and calling the supervisor with an EOJ macro.

With the analysis now apparently complete, the programer is in a position to begin the coding. Up to this time the programer should not have begun coding at all, even though he has kept in mind how he is going to implement by coding the operation that he has been diagraming. The process of actually performing the coding requires the programer to take each outline in the flow diagram and restate it in terms of instructions to the computer. In the course of doing this, the programer typically encounters some areas which need elaboration, and he may uncover oversights in program logic. Very frequently, he may discover the need for additional initialization. As he encounters each of these situations, he should incorporate it as needed in the diagram and in the coding. An example of the coding prepared for the diagram in question is shown in Fig. 9-13. Note that the two read operations after the header reads are written as subroutines, with the BAL call for the subroutine and a BR for the return. The Load Address command provides the address for the transfer of control (see Chap. 10). Note also that the compile was done in this instance in two parts to save recompilation time.

Do It Now Exercise 9-1. Prepare a program to match two files of data from cards, printing all records that are unmatched. A match exists wherever the two files each have a record with the same key. Identify the records printed according to which file it is that is missing the key. Assume that the key is four EBCDIC characters long. Prepare a detailed flow diagram before starting the coding.

TABLE-SEARCH EXAMPLE

The problem is this. A deck of cards has been prepared showing stock numbers of items to be priced. Each number is eight digits long, starting in column 1 on the cards. The cards, however, do not contain the prices. The task is to locate the price for each item in a price table, listing the stock number and the associated price on the printer. The input deck is in a random sequence—it is not in sorted order by stock number. The input deck, however, does have an identifying header card and an end-of-file trailer card. A system chart for this example is given in Fig. 9-14.

In using the fragment-and-combine approach, the first operation is to break the total job into fragments. A quick review of the job indicates that it can be

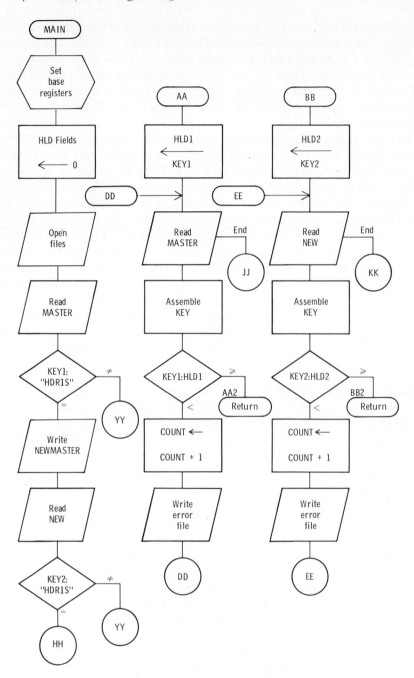

FIG. 9-12. Flow diagram for merge-highlight example.

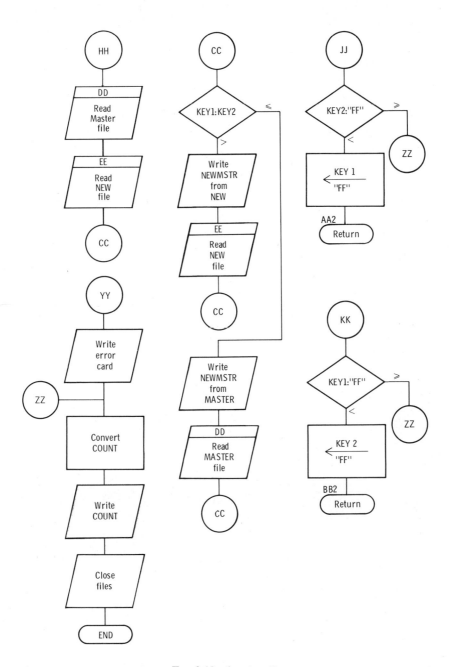

Fɪɢ. 9-12 *(continued)*

```
// JOB
// OPTION NODECK,LISTX,ERRS,SYM
// EXEC ASSEMBLY


                            EXTERNAL SYMBOL DICTIONARY

   SYMBOL  TYPE ID  ADDR   LENGTH LD ID


           PC   01 000000 000000
   MERGE    ER   02
   KK       ER   03
   OUTPT    ER   04
   NEWC     SD   05 000000 000032
   NEW      LD      000000        05
   IJCFZIZO ER   06
   NEWMSTRC SD   07 000038 000088         .
   NEWMSTR  LD      000038        07
   IJCFCOW4 ER   08
                    .

   LOC  OBJECT CODE   ADDR1 ADDR2  STMT   SOURCE STATEMENT

                                    1          PRINT ON,NOGEN,NODATA
   000000                           2          START
                                    3          EXTRN MERGE
                                    4          EXTRN KK
                                    5          EXTRN OUTPT
                                    6 NEW      DTFCD BLKSIZE=80,              X
                                                     DEVADDR=SYSRDR,         X
                                                     DEVICE=2540,            X
                                                     EOFADDR=KK,             X
                                                     IOAREA1=MERGE,          X
                                                     RECFORM=FIXUNB,         X
                                                     TYPEFLE=INPUT,          X
                                                     SEPASMB=YES
                                   30 *
                                   31 NEWMSTR  DTFCD BLKSIZE=80,             X
                                                     CRDERR=RETRY,           X
                                                     CONTROL=YES,            X
                                                     DEVADDR=SYSPCH,         X
                                                     DEVICE=2540,            X
                                                     IOAREA1=OUTPT,          X
                                                     RECFORM=FIXUNB,         X
                                                     TYPEFLE=OUTPUT,         X
                                                     WORKA=YES,              X
                                                     SEPASMB=YES
                                   58          END


                             CROSS-REFERENCE

   SYMBOL    LEN   VALUE  DEFN

   IJCX0001 00008 000020 0025    0015
   IJCX0002 00008 000060 0054    0040
   IJJZ0001 00001 000032 0029
   IJJZ0002 00001 0000C0 0057
   KK    •  00001 000000 0004    0024
   MERGE    00001 000000 0003    0023 0025
   NEW      00006 000000 0012    0010
   NEWC     00001 000000 0009
   NEWMSTR  00006 000038 0037    0035
   NEWMSTRC 00001 000038 0034
   OUTPT    00001 000000 0005    0048 0054


   NO STATEMENTS FLAGGED IN THIS ASSEMBLY
```

FIG. 9-13. Coding for merge-highlight example. Note the separate compile of part of the IOCS declarative.

RELOCATION DICTIONARY

POS.ID	REL.ID	FLAGS	ADDRESS
05	05	0C	000008
05	06	18	000011
05	02	0C	000018
05	03	0C	00001C
05	02	08	000021
07	07	0C	000040
07	08	18	000049
07	04	0C	000050
07	04	08	000061
07	07	08	000069

EOJ

```
// JOB
// OPTION LISTX,ERRS,DECK
// EXEC ASSEMBLY
```

EXTERNAL SYMBOL DICTIONARY

SYMBOL	TYPE	ID	ADDR	LENGTH	LD ID
	PC	01	000000	000000	
MERGE	LD		000274		04
KK	LD		000142		04
OUTPT	LD		0002C4		04
NEW	ER	02			
NEWMSTR	ER	03			
MAIN	SD	04	000000	0003F3	

```
LOC      OBJECT CODE        ADDR1 ADDR2 ST #  NAME    OP     OPERANDS              COMMENT

                                IMPERATIVES

                                   1           PRINT  ON,NOGEN,NODATA
                                   2  *
                                   3  *FIGURE 9-13     MERGE THE FILES
                                   4  *
000000                             5           START
                                   6           ENTRY  MERGE
                                   7           ENTRY  KK
                                   8           ENTRY  OUTPT
                                   9           EXTRN  NEW
                                  10           EXTRN  NEWMSTR
                                  11  *
                                  12           DTFBG  DISK
                                  13 MASTER    DTFSR  BLKSIZE=80,                         X
                                                      DEVADDR=SYS010,                     X
                                                      DEVICE=READ01,                      X
                                                      EOFADDR=JJ,                         X
                                                      IOAREA1=INPUTB,                     X
                                                      RECFORM=FIXUNB,                     X
                                                      TYPEFLE=INPUT
                                  14           DTFEN
                                  15  *
                                  16  *
000000                            17 MAIN      CSECT
                                  18  *                PROCEDURE SECTION
000000 070007000700              19           CNOP   6,8
000006 0530                      20           BALR   3,0
000008                           21           USING  *,3
000008 5820 31F8         00200   22           L      2,=A(INPUTB)
000224                           23           USING  INPUTB,2
00000C D202 214C 214F 00370 00373 24          MVC    COUNT,ZERO       INITIALIZE WORK FIELDS
000012 D202 2146 214F 0036A 00373 25          MVC    HLD1,ZERO
000018 D202 2149 214F 0036D 00373 26          MVC    HLD2,ZERO
                                  27           OPEN   MASTER           PREPARE FILES
                                  35           OPEN   NEW
                                  43           OPEN   NEWMSTR
00004E 4140 31FC         00204   51           LA     4,=A(YY)         PROTECT AGAINST UNWANTED EOF
                                  52           GET    MASTER
00005E D514 2152 2000 00376 00224 57          CLC    HDM(21),INPUTB
000064 4770 3186         0018E   58           BNE    YY               NO HEADER
                                  59           PUT    NEWMSTR,INPUTB
```

FIG. 9-13 *(continued)*

```
000084 D514 2167 2050 0038B 00274   65        GET   NEW
                                    70        CLC   ADM(21),MERGE
00008A 4770 3186             0018E  71        BNE   YY                    NO HEADER
00008E 4540 309A             000A2  72        BAL   4,DD                  READ FIRST MASTER RECORD
000092 4540 30F6             000FE  73        BAL   4,EE                  READ FIRST NEW RECORD
000096 4140 314C             00154  74        LA    4,CC                  SET SWITCH
00009A 07F4                         75        BR    4                     GO TO CC
00009C D202 2146 2140 0036A 00364  76 AA      MVC   HLD1,KEY1             SAVE OLD MASTER KEY
                                    77 DD      GET   MASTER
0000AE F224 2140 2000 00364 00224  82        PACK  KEY1,PRODNO
0000B4 D502 2140 2146 00364 0036A  83        CLC   KEY1,HLD1             CHECK SEQUENCE
0000BA 47B0 30EE             000F6  84        BNL   AA2                   OK
0000BE FA22 214C 3218 00370 00220  85        AP    COUNT,=PL3'+1'
                                    86        CNTRL NEWMSTR,SS,2          SELECT STACKER 2
                                    92        PUT   NEWMSTR,INPUTB        PUNCH OUT OF SEQ. CARD
0000E2 47F0 309A             000A2  98        B     DD
0000E6 D502 2143 21CC 00367 003F0  99 JJ      CLC   KEY2,HIGH            END SWITCH
0000EC 47B0 31A4             001AC 100        BNL   ZZ                    EOJ
0000F0 D202 2140 21CC 00364 003F0 101        MVC   KEY1,HIGH            SET SWITCH
0000F6 07F4                        102 AA2     BR    4                     RETURN TO CC
0000F8 D202 2149 2143 0036D 00367 103 BB      MVC   HLD2,KEY2           SAVE OLD NEW KEY
                                   104 EE      GET   NEW
00010A F224 2143 2050 00367 00274 109        PACK  KEY2,IDENT
000110 D502 2143 2149 00367 0036D 110        CLC   KEY2,HLD2            CHECK SEQUENCE
000116 47B0 314A             00152 111        BNL   BB2                   OK
00011A FA22 214C 3218 00370 00220 112        AP    COUNT,=PL3'+1'
                                   113        CNTRL NEWMSTR,SS,2          SELECT STACKER 2
                                   119        PUT   NEWMSTR,MERGE        PUNCH OUT OF SEQ CARD
00013E 47F0 30F6             000FE 125        B     EE
000142 D502 2140 21CC 00364 003F0 126 KK      CLC   KEY1,HIGH            END SWITCH
000148 47B0 31A4             001AC 127        BNL   ZZ                    EOJ
00014C D202 2143 21CC 00367 003F0 128        MVC   KEY2,HIGH            SET SWITCH
000152 07F4                        129 BB2     BR    4                     RETURN TO CC
000154 D502 2140 2143 00364 00367 130 CC      CLC   KEY1,KEY2           SELECT ROUTINE
00015A 4720 316E             00176 131        BH    CC1
                                   132        PUT   NEWMSTR,INPUTB
00016E 4540 3094             0009C 138        BAL   4,AA                  READ ANOTHER MASTER
000172 47F0 314C             00154 139        B     CC
00018A 47F0 314C             00154 140 CC1     PUT   NEWMSTR,MERGE
000186 4540 30F0             000F8 146        BAL   4,BB                  READ ANOTHER NEW
00018A 47F0 314C             00154 147        B     CC
                                   148 YY      CNTRL NEWMSTR,SS,2          SELECT STACKER 2
                                   154        PUT   NEWMSTR,HDMSG
0001AC F342 20F0 214C 00314 00370 160 ZZ      UNPK  TOT,COUNT
0001B2 D300 20F4 321B 00318 00223 161        MVZ   TOT+4(1),=X'FF'
                                   162        CNTRL NEWMSTR,SS,2
                                   168        PUT   NEWMSTR,WORK         WRITE OUT ERROR COUNT
                                   174        CLOSE MASTER,NEW,NEWMSTR
                                   184 *
                                   185        EOJ
                                   188        LTORG
0001F0                             189            =C'$$BOPEN '
0001F0 5858C2D6D7C5D540            190            =C'$$BCLOSE'
0001F8 5858C2C3D3D6E2C5            191            =A(INPUTB)
000200 00000224                    192            =A(YY)
000204 0000018E                    193            =A(MASTER)
000208 00000000                    194            =A(NEWMSTR)
00020C 00000000                    195            =A(NEW)
000210 00000000                    196            =A(MERGE)
000214 00000274                    197            =A(HDMSG)
000218 000003A0                    198            =A(WORK)
00021C 00000314                    199            =PL3'+1'
000220 00001C                      200            =X'FF'
000223 FF                          201 *
                                   202 *     DECLARATIVES
                                   203 *
000224                             204 INPUTB  DS   0CL80
000224                             205 PRODNO  DS   CL5
000229                             206        DS   CL75
                                   207 *
000274                             208 MERGE   DS   0CL80
000274                             209 IDENT   DS   CL5
000279                             210        DS   CL75
0002C4                             211 OUTPT   DS   CL80
000314                             212 WORK    DS   0CL80
000314 4040404040                  213 TOT     DC   CL5' '
000319 40D9C5C3D6D9C4E2            214        DC   C' RECORDS WERE OUT OF SEQUENCE'
000336 4040404040404040            215        DC   46C' '
                                   216 *
```

FIG. 9-13 *(continued)*

```
000364 00000C                    217 *
000367 00000C                    218 KEY1     DC    PL3'0'
00036A 00000C                    219 KEY2     DC    PL3'0'
00036D 00000C                    220 HLD1     DC    PL3'0'
000370                           221 HLD2     DC    PL3'0'
000373 00000C                    222 COUNT    DS    PL3
000376 C8C4D9F1E2C8C9D7          223 ZERO     DC    PL3'0'
00038B C8C4D9F1E2C8C9D7          224 HDM      DC    CL21'HDR1SHIPPING FILE 010'
0003A0 40E6D9D6D5C740C6          225 ADM      DC    C'HDR1SHIPPING FILE 020'
0003F0 FFFFFF                    226 HDMSG    DC    CL80' WRONG FILE OR HEADER RECORD MISSING '
000000                           227 HIGH     DC    X'FFFFFF'
                                 228          END MAIN
```

RELOCATION DICTIONARY

POS.ID	REL.ID	FLAGS	ADDRESS
04	02	0C	000038
04	03	0C	000048
04	02	0C	0001E4
04	03	0C	0001E8
04	04	0C	000200
04	04	0C	000204
04	03	0C	00020C
04	02	0C	000210
04	04	0C	000214
04	04	0C	000218
04	04	0C	00021C

CROSS-REFERENCE

```
SYMBOL     LEN    VALUE  DEFN

AA         00006  00009C 0076   0138
AA2        00002  0000F6 0102   0084
ADM        00021  00038B 0225   0070
BB         00006  0000F8 0103   0146
BB2        00002  000152 0129   0111
CC         00006  000154 0130   0074  0139  0147
CC1        00004  000176 0142   0131
COUNT      00003  000370 0222   0024  0085  0112  0160
DD         00004  0000A2 0079   0072  0098
EE         00004  0000FE 0106   0073  0125
HDM        00021  000376 0224   0057
HDMSG      00080  0003A0 0226   0157  0197
HIGH       00003  0003F0 0227   0099  0101  0126  0128
HLD1       00003  00036A 0220   0025  0076  0083
HLD2       00003  00036D 0221   0026  0103  0110
IDENT      00005  000274 0209   0109
IJJC0019   00004  0001DC 0179
IJJ00001   00004  000024 0032
IJJ00002   00004  000034 0040
IJJ00003   00004  000044 0048
INPUTB     00080  000224 0204   0022  0023  0057  0062  0095  0135  0191
JJ         00006  0000E6 0099
KEY1       00003  000364 0218   0076  0082  0083  0101  0126  0130
KEY2       00003  000367 0219   0099  0103  0109  0110  0128  0130
KK         00006  000142 0126   0007
MAIN       00001  000000 0017   0228
MASTER                          0033  0054  0079  0180  0193
MERGE      00080  000274 0208   0006  0070  0122  0143  0196
NEW        00001  000000 0009   0041  0067  0106  0181  0195
NEWMSTR    00001  000000 0010   0049  0061  0088  0094  0115  0121  0134  0142  0150  0156  0164  0170  0182  0194
OUTPT      00080  0002C4 0211   0008
PRODNO     00005  000224 0205   0082
TOT        00005  000314 0213   0160  0161
WORK       00080  000314 0212   0171  0198
YY         00004  00018E 0150   0051  0058  0071  0192
ZERO       00003  000373 0223   0024  0025  0026
ZZ         00006  0001AC 0160   0100  0127
```

NO STATEMENTS FLAGGED IN THIS ASSEMBLY

EOJ

FIG. 9-13   *(continued)*

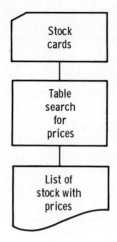

FIG. 9-14. System chart for search-fragment example.

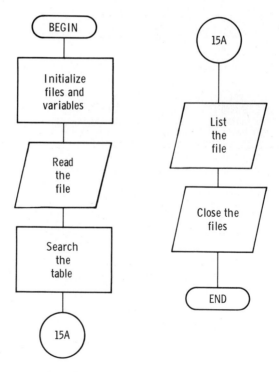

FIG. 9-15. Fragments for search-fragment example.

broken into the following fragments: initialize, read, search the table, list, and clean up, as summarized in Fig. 9-15. Other fragments could be made by breaking up the job differently.

Each of these fragments can be approached independently. The order in which the programer takes the individual fragments for detailed consideration is arbitrary, and is primarily a matter of convenience. Experience, however, has indicated that it is usually wise to take the initialization and the cleanup section last and to concentrate attention initially on those fragments which compose the main body of the program. Let us then consider those in the order read, search, and list.

The read operation does not need to incorporate any sequence checking because the file is in a random sequence. The read operation need only make available the next stock number and provide the data for the listing. A simple read should provide this adequately, as shown in Fig. 9-16.

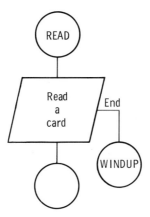

Fig. 9-16. Read fragment for search-fragment example.

The search operation is more difficult. Classically, a table search can be performed on one of four bases: a sequential search, an interval search, a calculated search, or a binary search. The sequential search will be used here since the data are randomly ordered. The selection among alternative search methods is beyond the scope of this book, being more appropriate to a book on systems analysis or design.

In the sequential-search approach, a table is assumed to exist in storage. This table may be organized in any of several ways; one of the more common ways is to have the search argument and the table function in alternate fields. The argument is the basis by which the computer identifies the appropriate table entry. The function is the data desired from the table. Thus, in the case at hand, the stock numbers are the arguments, and the associated prices are the function values. A series of pairs of stock number and price fields comprise the table.

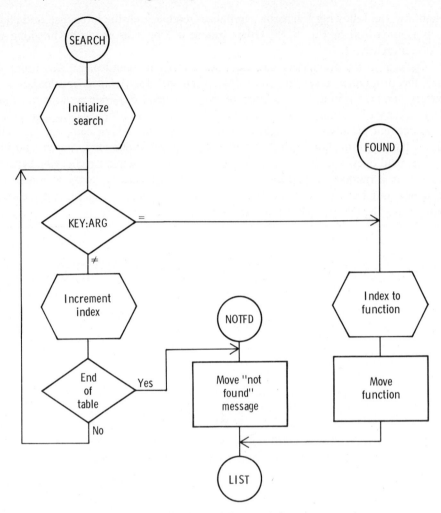

FIG. 9-17. Search fragment for search-fragment example.

For the table format in this example, a convenient arrangement is one double word for the stock number in EBCDIC, and one full word in a packed-decimal format for the price. For table search, the computer must have the address of the start of the table and some way of identifying the end of the table, such as the number of entries in the table, or an indicator in the last table position or the last address used for the table.

The sequence of arguments in the table can have considerable effect upon the time the computer requires to search the table. Thus, if the computer is to search the table randomly (as in the case at hand), arranging the items in the table in order of frequency (most popular first) gives the most efficient sequential search. If the items of the table are in a sorted order on the basis of the argument, the result for unsorted input data is a longer search time.

To handle a table search, the programer typically relies upon iteration techniques. The program is to compare the field from the input area (the "key") with successive argument fields in the table. Thus, if a key and an argument are unequal, and if the table is being searched for an equality condition, the programer directs the computer to index to the next position in the table and repeat the comparison. If the comparison is equal, the programer has the computer index to the associated price function and copy that item of data into the output. As each argument index operation occurs, the programer must have the computer check that it has not exceeded the boundaries of the table. If it has exceeded the boundaries of the table, it must produce as output an indication that the item could not be found in the table. This is summarized in Fig. 9-17.

The key to the search operation is the indexing. The programer must provide for indexing from one argument-function pair to the next in the table. As he does this, the programer must also provide for a way of keeping the comparison within the table. The Branch on Count command could be used for this, but the programer may be able to save operations by the use of a Branch on Index High or a Branch on Index Low or Equal. When the comparison of the argument and the key indicates an equality condition, the programer will wish to have the computer index by only two words in order to be able to copy the price function from the table. Since the operations here are to be done in packed-decimal and in EBCDIC, the programer knows the indexing will have to be accomplished through the base register.

The next fragment is the list operation. The input data provide the stock number, and the table search yields the price or an indication that the price could not be found. If a price can be found, it must be printed with the stock number. If the price cannot be found, the programer can mark this price field, e.g., by having the computer put in asterisks in place of a price. Then a write-out on the printer finishes the list operation. To avoid running off the end of the page, the programer should provide a count of the number of lines printed. For this example, the programer can assume 54 lines per page. He can use this to determine the choice of carriage-control character. At this point, a return of control back to the read operation is required to read the item of input data. This is shown in Fig. 9-18.

The next fragment of the program is the cleanup at the end of file. Since no totaling is needed, and no summary is to be prepared, a simple close of the files and an end-of-job operation will do. This is shown in Fig. 9-19.

The last fragment of the program is the initialization. Ignoring, for the time being, the problem of loading the table into storage, we find that the major operations are to set the contents of the base and control registers and open the files. But the programer should also have the computer check the identification of the input file and skip to a new page for the printing after setting the line-count field to 0s. These operations are shown in Fig. 9-20.

It should be noted in passing, however, that the programer could make the computer operator's job easier. The programer could, for example, at the end of the job have the computer skip the paper in the printer by about five pages in order to give blank sheets for tearing off the job that has just been completed. The programer could also notify the console operator with messages about errors such as "wrong input file" and with control counts accumulated during the run, such as a count of the number of records processed or a count of the number of prices not found. These frills smooth the operation of the job, even though they do not fundamentally change the nature of the job being performed. They are not included in the example.

A more fundamental consideration is the provision for a restart. If a machine failure or other operating difficulty should arise that causes the program to halt while the computer is executing a job, the operator must have some way of resuming the job. The worst way, in terms of operating time and expense, is to restart the job

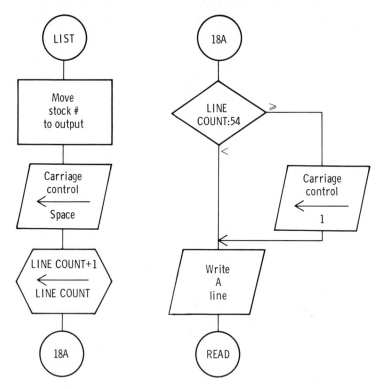

Fig. 9-18. List fragment for search-fragment example.

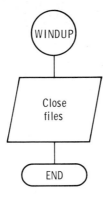

FIG. 9-19. Cleanup fragment for search-fragment example.

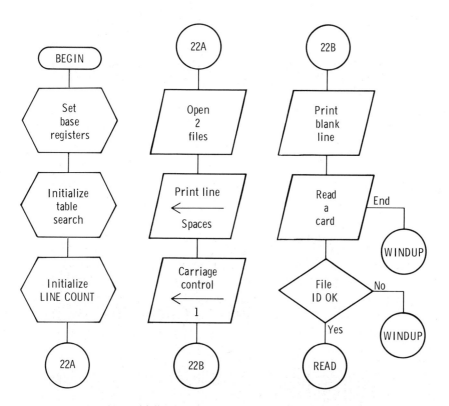

FIG. 9-20. Initialization fragment for search-fragment example.

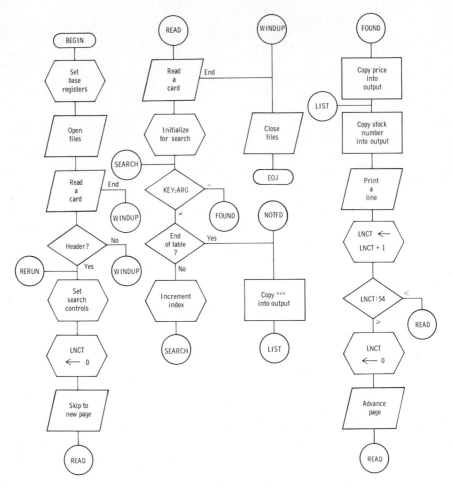

FIG. 9-21. Flow diagram for search-fragment example.

from the beginning and repeat the entire job from the processing of the first input record. It is cheaper in terms of operating time and expense, but more expensive in terms of programing time, to provide a way of resuming a job in the middle. This can become very complex when cumulative processing is being done. In this example, no cumulative processing is being done. Hence a restart can be made by reorganizing the original initialization routine and providing an entry point, as at RERUN in Fig. 9-21.

With the analysis of the job complete and put together in the form of a flow diagram, as shown in Fig. 9-21, the programer can begin the coding. This is not difficult, but the programer must watch his use of registers. The search is an iterative loop and must therefore be initialized before it is entered. Since the loop must always

```
// JOB
// OPTION LISTX,DECK,SYM
// EXEC ASSEMBLY


                        EXTERNAL SYMBOL DICTIONARY

   SYMBOL  TYPE  ID  ADDR  LENGTH  LD  ID


           PC   01  000000  000068
   IJCFZIZ1 ER  02
   IJDFCZZZ ER  03
   FIG9#22  SD  04  000068  000246


   LOC  OBJECT CODE       ADDR1 ADDR2  ST #  NAME    OP    OPERANDS              COMMENT

                                       IMPERATIVES

                                         1            PRINT  ON,NOGEN,NODATA
   000000                                2            START
                                         3  *FIGURE 9-22   SEARCH EXAMPLE
                                         4  *FILE-DEFINITIONS
                                         5  INPUT    DTFCD  BLKSIZE=80,                        X
                                                            DEVADDR=SYSRDR,                    X
                                                            DEVICE=1442,                       X
                                                            EOFADDR=WINDUP,                    X
                                                            IOAREA1=CARD,                      X
                                                            RECFORM=FIXUNB,                    X
                                                            TYPEFLE=INPUT
                                        26  *
                                        27  PRINT    DTFPR  BLKSIZE=132,                       X
                                                            CONTROL=YES,                       X
                                                            DEVADDR=SYSLST,                    X
                                                            DEVICE=1443,                       X
                                                            IOAREA1=OUTPUT
                                        48  *
                                        49  *FIGURE 9-22   SEARCH THE TABLE
   000068                               50  FIG9#22  CSECT
   00006B 0530                          51           BALR  3,0
   00006A                               52           USING *,3
   00006A 5820 3226             00290   53           L     2,=A(CARD)
   000146                               54           USING CARD,2
                                        55           OPEN  INPUT,PRINT
                                        64           GET   INPUT
   00008E D514 2000 2116 00146 0025C    69           CLC   CARD(21),ID          CHECK HEADER
   000094 4770 30C6             00130   70           BNE   WINDUP
   000098 5850 2152             00298   71  RERUN    L     5,=A(TABLE)          INITIALIZE TABLE SEARCH
   00009C 5880 2156             0029C   72           L     8,=F'1'
   0000A0 5890 215A             002A0   73           L     9,=F'3'
   0000A4 D203 210E 210A 00254 00250    74           MVC   LNCT,ZERO
                                        75           CNTRL PRINT,SK,1
                                        81  READ     GET   INPUT
   0000C4 1845                          86           LR    4,5
   0000C6 5870 2112             00258   87           L     7,ZEROS
   0000CA D507 2000 4000 00146 0025C    88  SEARCH   CLC   KEY,0(4)             COMPARE KEY AND ARGUMENT
   0000D0 4780 3076             000E0   89           BE    FOUND
   0000D4 8678 3086             000F0   90           BXH   7,8,NOTFD            END OF TABLE
   0000D8 4A40 2162             002A8   91           AH    4,=H'12'
   0000DC 47F0 3060             000CA   92           B     SEARCH
   0000E0 F373 2060 4008 001A6 00008    93  FOUND    UNPK  PRICE(8),8(4,4)      MOVE PRICE TO OUTPUT RECORD
   0000E6 D300 2067 2166 001AD 002AC    94           MVZ   PRICE+7(1),=X'FF'
   0000EC 47F0 308C             000F6   95           B     LIST
   0000F0 D207 2060 212B 001A6 00271    96  NOTFD    MVC   PRICE,MESS
   0000F6 D207 2050 2000 00196 00146    97  LIST     MVC   STKNO,KEY
                                        98           PUT   PRINT
   000108 FA30 210E 2167 00254 002AD    103          AP    LNCT,=P'1'
   00010E F931 210E 2164 00254 002AA    104          CP    LNCT,=P'54'
   000114 4740 304E             000B8   105          BL    READ
   000118 D203 210E 210A 00254 00250    106          MVC   LNCT,ZERO
                                        107          CNTRL PRINT,SK,1
   00012C 47F0 304E             000B8   113          B     READ
                                        114 *
```

FIG. 9-22. Coding for search-fragment example.

```
000142                              115 WINDUP   CLOSE INPUT,PRINT
                                    124         EOJ
                                    125 *
                                    126 *     DECLARATIVES
                                    127 *
000146                              128 CARD     DS    OCL80
000146                              129 KEY      DS    CL8
00014E                              130          DS    CL72
                                    131 *
000196                              132 OUTPUT   DS    OCL132
000196                              133 STKNO    DS    CL8
00019E 404040404040404040          134          DC    CL8' '
0001A6                              135 PRICE    DS    CL8' '
0001AE 404040404040404040          136          DC    CL108' '
                                    137 *
                                    138 *PRICE TABLE
000220                              139          DS    OD              FORCE ALIGNMENT
000220 F0F1F8F7F1F3F3F4             140 TABLE    DC    CL8'01871334'   ITEM
000228 0000726C                     141          DC    PL4'726'        PRICE
00022C F0F2F6F4F3F8F7F1             142          DC    CL8'02643871'   ITEM
000234 0014621C                     143          DC    PL4'14621'      PRICE
000238 F0F3F4F7F6F1F2F6             144          DC    CL8'03476126'   ITEM
000240 0000037C                     145          DC    PL4'37'         PRICE
000244 F0F9F7F4F3F8F6F2             146          DC    CL8'09743862'   ITEM
00024C 0038643C                     147          DC    PL4'38643'      PRICE
                                    148 *
                                    149 *
000250 0000000C                     150 ZERO     DC    PL4'0'
000254                              151 LNCT     DS    PL4
000258 00000000                     152 ZEROS    DC    F'0'
00025C C8C4D9F1E2C5C1D9             153 ID       DC    CL21'HDR1SEARCH F9#22'
000271 5C5C5C5C5C5C5C5C             154 MESS     DC    CL8'********'
                                    155 *
000280                              156          LTORG
000280 5B5BC2D6D7C5D540             157          =C'$$BOPEN '
000288 5B5BC2C3D3D6E2C5             158          =C'$$BCLOSE'
000290 00000146                     159          =A(CARD)
000294 00000000                     160          =A(INPUT)
000298 00000220                     161          =A(TABLE)
00029C 00000001                     162          =F'1'
0002A0 00000003                     163          =F'3'
0002A4 0000003B                     164          =A(PRINT)
0002A8 000C                         165          =H'12'
0002AA 054C                         166          =P'54'
0002AC FF                           167          =X'FF'
0002AD 1C                           168          =P'1'
                                    169 *
000068                              170          END   FIG9#22
```

RELOCATION DICTIONARY

POS.ID	REL.ID	FLAGS	ADDRESS
01	01	0C	000008
01	02	18	000011
01	04	0C	000018
01	04	0C	00001C
01	04	08	000021
01	01	0C	000040
01	03	18	000049
01	04	0C	000050
01	04	08	000061
04	01	0C	000078
04	01	0C	00007C
04	01	0C	000138
04	01	0C	00013C
04	04	0C	000290
04	01	0C	000294
04	04	0C	000298
04	01	0C	0002A4

FIG. 9-22   *(continued)*

```
                                         CROSS-REFERENCE
SYMBOL    LEN   VALUE  DEFN

CARD      00080 000146 0128    0019  0021  0053  0054  0069  0159
FIG9#22   00001 000068 0050    0170
FOUND     00006 0000E0 0093    0089
ID        00021 00025C 0153    0069
IJCX0001  00008 000020 0021    0011
IJJC0009  00004 000134 0120
IJJO0003  00004 000074 0060
IJJZ0001  00001 000032 0025
IJJZ0002  00001 000068 0047
INPUT     00006 000000 0008    0061  0066  0083  0121  0160
KEY       00008 000146 0129    0088  0097
LIST      00006 0000F6 0097    0095
LNCT      00004 000254 0151    0074  0103  0104  0106
MESS      00008 000271 0154    0096
NOTFD     00006 0000F0 0096    0090
OUTPUT    00132 000196 0132    0041  0046
PRICE     00008 0001A6 0135    0093  0094  0096
PRINT     00006 000038 0030    0062  0077  0100  0109  0122  0164
READ      00004 0000B8 0083    0105  0113
RERUN     00004 000098 0071
SEARCH    00006 0000CA 0088    0092
STKNO     00008 000196 0133    0097
STOP      00004 000142 0124    0124
TABLE     00008 000220 0140    0071  0161
WINDUP    00004 000130 0118    0020  0070
ZERO      00004 000250 0150    0074  0106
ZEROS     00004 000258 0152    0087



NO STATEMENTS FLAGGED IN THIS ASSEMBLY



// OPTION LINK,DUMP
// PAUSE
   INCLUDE
// EXEC LNKEDT



                    DISK LINKAGE EDITOR DIAGNOSTIC OF INPUT

ACTION TAKEN    MAP
LIST       CATALR IJDFCPZZ
LIST       AUTOLINK  IJCFZIZ1
LIST       ENTRY


          PHASE  XFR-AD LOCORE  HICORE  DSK-AD   ESD TYPE  LABEL      LOADED  REL-FR

       PHASE*** 0019E8 001900  001C7F  2A 4 2   CSECT                001900  001900

                                                CSECT    IJDFCPZZ    001900  001900
                                                *  ENTRY IJDFZPZZ    001900
                                                *  ENTRY IJDFZZZZ    001900
                                                   ENTRY IJDFCZZZ    001900

                                                CSECT                001980  001980

                                                CSECT    IJCFZIZ1    001C30  001C30

                                                CSECT    FIG9#22     0019E8  001980

CONTROL SECTIONS OF ZERO LENGTH IN INPUT



// EXEC



02643871        00014621
09743862        00038643
01871334        00000726
05384215        ********
03476126        00000037
```

FIG. 9-22   *(continued)*

be executed at least once, a leading-decisions approach has not been used. The logical IOCS macros and declaratives differ from those of the previous example in that a printer operation is called for, with the use of a CNTRL macro for the carriage control, as shown in Fig. 9-22.

Do It Now Exercise 9-2. *Add to the program just presented a routine to load the price table into storage. Prepare a detailed flow diagram before starting the coding. Hint: What would be a good format for the input on cards? Watch the start-of-table and end-of-table file carefully!*

Do It Now Exercise 9-3. *Add to the program presented in Figs. 9-21 and 9-22 all of the "frills" discussed earlier for this example but not included in the program. Prepare a detailed flow diagram before starting the coding. Can you add some other "extras" or "frills" to the program that are not discussed here? Why would each be a useful addition to the program?*

REPORT EXAMPLE

The task is as follows: A deck of cards exists, sorted in an ascending sequence by salesman within territory. Each card shows an individual sale made by a salesman during the month (see Fig. 9-23). These sales are to be listed and summed to a grand total, with a total printed for each salesman and for each territory. Data for each territory and each salesman are to start on a separate page. The grand total is to be on a page by itself. Pages should be headed as "Sales Reports" and numbered sequentially.

Card column	Field name
Data cards	
1-4	Territory
5-8	Salesman
9-16	Sales
17-80	Other data
Header cards	
1-4	HDR1
5-21	Sales detail pack
Trailer cards	
1-2	/*
3-80	Blank

FIG. 9-23. Input format for report-simplify example.

FIG. 9-24. System chart for report-simplify example.

For this task, the computer can be assumed to be equipped with a card reader and a line printer (printing 6 lines, 10 characters to the inch), but the carriage-control tape in the line printer is marked only for top-of-form. The paper to be used in the printer is 11 in. wide and 8½ in. deep, in terms of printable surface. A 1-in. margin is to be allowed at the top, a ½-in. margin (minimum) at the bottom, with side margins of at least 1 in. Page numbers are to be at the upper right-hand corner of the printed area. The title is to be printed at the upper left-hand corner. The programer is to do no financial format editing on the sales data, which can be assumed to be reported to the nearest whole dollar.

For this task, the simplify-and-augment approach is illustrated. Simplified down to its barest essentials, with the frills and auxiliary details ignored for the moment, the task can be assumed to be reading and listing data from cards, as is shown in system-chart form in Fig. 9-24.

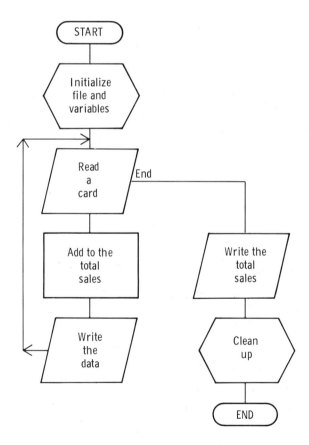

FIG. 9-25. First augmentation for report-simplify example.

This is a start, but too simple to be useful. The programer can therefore augment this very simple conception by including some additional feature—for example, the totaling operation. In this view, the job would consist of reading data from cards, building the total, listing the individual sales cards, and, at the end of the job, printing the grand total. This is shown in Fig. 9-25. However, this is still too simple to be adequate. The programer, therefore, can elaborate it again.

In attempting to elaborate the analysis again, the programer is immediately faced with a major difficulty. The time at which he needs to know whether or not total data are to be printed for a salesman or for a territory is after he has already finished processing the last item of data for the salesman or the territory. Information, therefore, about the need to print totals is not available at the time the totals are to be printed, but becomes available after they are to be printed. The programer, therefore, must provide some different sequence of doing the work in this program in order to have the needed data available at the time desired.

One approach is to use the sorted sequence of the input data. Since the input data are to be in sorted order, the programer should provide a sequence-check operation anyway. This sequence check can also incorporate a provision for testing whether or not the salesman is the same for the new record as for the last record read, and whether the territory is the same for this new record as for the last record read. If either the salesman or the territory changes, the programer can have the computer print totals for the prior salesman or the prior territory *and* salesman, as the case may be, before attempting to begin processing the data for the new salesman.

An additional complication arises at once, however: how are the separate levels of totals to be retained? The programer could have the computer, each time it reads the data from a card, add to each of the levels of totals for salesman, territory, and grand total. This has disadvantages, such as the longer operating time.

What alternatives does the programer have to keep the various levels of totals separate? And what are the more efficient ways of building such totals. Experience has indicated that for most situations a good procedure is to set up a separate area for each level of total. In this case, an area for salesman, an area for territories, and an area for grand totals will do. For efficiency and in order to save computer time, the usual practice is to build totals directly only in the lowest level—in this case, the salesman level—until such time as that level should be printed. Then the lower level totals are "rolled out"—that is, added onto the totals for the next higher level, thus increasing those. This procedure then continues, after resetting the lower levels totals to 0, until the next break in the low-level sequence occurs—that is, data for another salesman appears. At that time, the process repeats again.

When the territory level changes, the territory totals are in turn rolled into the grand total, after which the territory totals are printed and cleared. Then the process of building new territory totals repeats all over again.

The algorithm can be summarized in simplified form, as shown in Fig. 9-26.

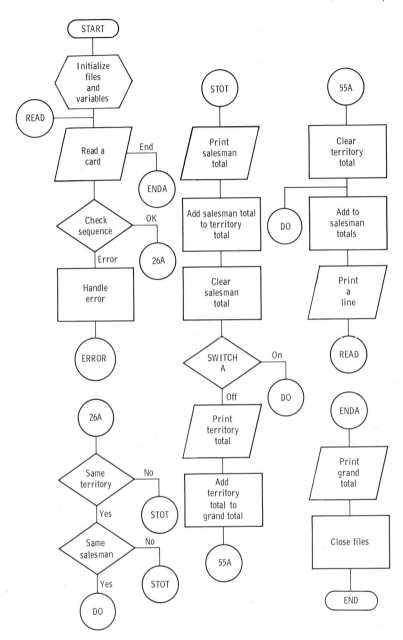

FIG. 9-26. Second augmentation for report-simplify example.

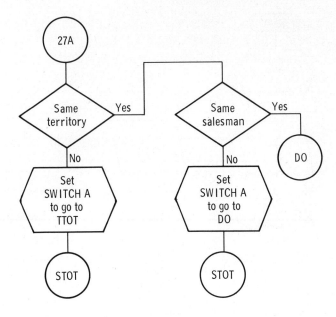

FIG. 9-27. Form for switches in report-simplify example.

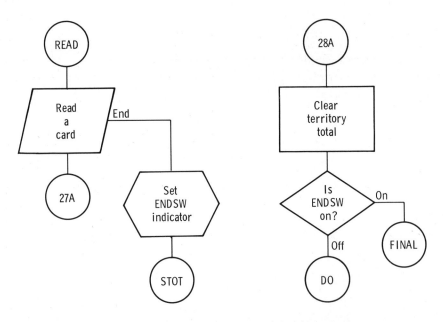

FIG. 9-28. Switch placement in report-simplify example.

There data on the individual sales are added to the salesman total. If the salesman has changed, then the salesman total data are rolled into the territory total, and the salesman total set to zero after being printed. If the territory has changed, the territory total is printed and rolled into the grand total before the territory total is cleared to zero. The printing of the grand total occurs, it should be noted, only at the end of the job (end of file on input).

The approach shown in Fig. 9-26 requires a careful use of program switches. At the point at which the program tests to determine whether or not the salesman has changed, the programer can place a switch-setting operation. One form for such a switch is to load a register with a transfer of control and then later transfer control (branch) to that address. With this in mind, the programer can attempt a recasting of the switch logic shown previously. He can establish, as shown in Fig. 9-27, a way of setting the correct exit address.

The algorithm needs to be augmented still further to handle the end-of-file condition. When the computer detects an end-of-file condition on the input data, the record that was just read (which had salesman data in it, and which contributed data to the salesman total), will have to be printed. Then the salesman total will have to be printed, then the territory total, and finally the grand total. In order to avoid repeating the same instructions on the coding form, the programer can again use a program switch, as shown in Fig. 9-28.

The algorithm thus far, while it may adequately take care of the data to be handled, does not meet the requirements of the print format outlined in the problem statement, as shown in Fig. 9-29. It is time, therefore, to augment the algorithm again to produce the print format.

Basic to a control of the print format is the problem of keeping track of where on the page the computer will put the next line of printing. This must reflect some arbitrary decisions about data format on the page. For example, if it is necessary to move the salesman's total to another page, then at least one additional line of sales data should also be printed on that page for good appearance. A territory total may, however, be alone on a page. Printing should not occur too close to the bottom of the page, and a heading must be put on the page as well as the page number.

To keep track of the vertical position on the page, the programer can establish a line counter. Since most computers print 6 lines to the inch, since approximately 7 in. of the page are to be printed vertically, and since approximately ½ in. can be devoted to heading (one line followed by two blank lines), 6½ in. of printable distance will remain. To allow distance for one blank line and a salesman total at the bottom would take an additional third of an inch, leaving one line more than 6 in. of printable area on the page, which means that a total of 37 lines of printing can be accommodated. Thus each time the computer begins printing on a new page after the heading is complete, the line counter must be set to count once for each line printed. Any time the line count exceeds 37, a new page must be headed as before and the data continued, unless the line to be printed is a salesman total. Since there

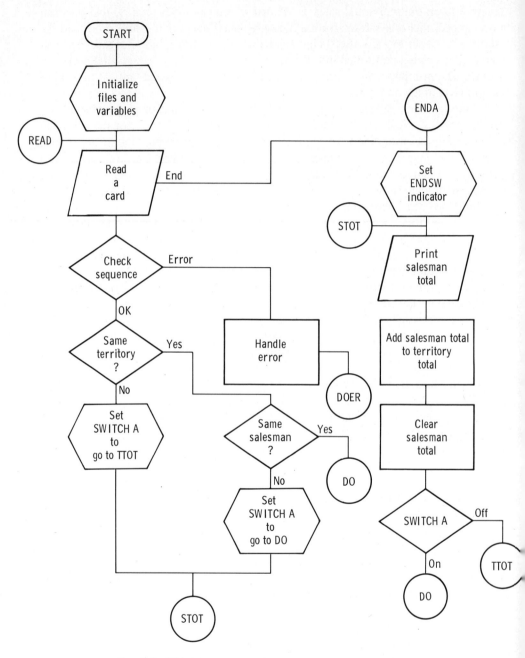

FIG. 9-29. Third augmentation for report-simplify example before including print format provisions.

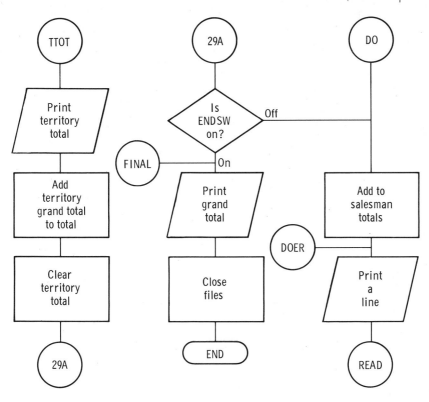

Fig. 9-29 *(continued)*

is always space at the bottom of the page to accommodate that total, there is no problem in bringing the total over to the top of the following page. This is true only if the programer does not have the computer advance the page until such time as the program has established that there is no need to print the salesman total on a page. This calls, therefore, for careful placement of the test to determine whether or not to jump to a new page.

This need to augment the algorithm suggests two things: One is a routine to head pages. It can be written as a subroutine to be called by a branch-and-link operation and hence provide for a return address. This is shown in Fig. 9-30 as a closed subroutine.

This operation of testing and adding to the line counter must take place when each line is printed. Since the grand total is to be printed on a page by itself, that printing always follows execution of the head-page routine. For the salesman and territory totals, however, the picture is different. Here the programer must test the line counter to determine whether or not the line should be printed in the next available position on the page, or whether the page must be skipped (advanced) to a new

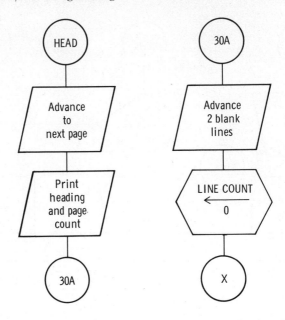

FIG. 9-30. Page head subroutine for report-simplify example.

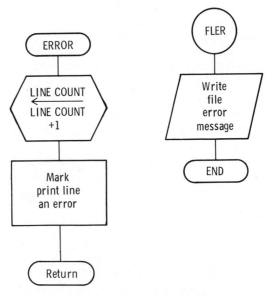

FIG. 9-31. Error routines for report-simplify example.

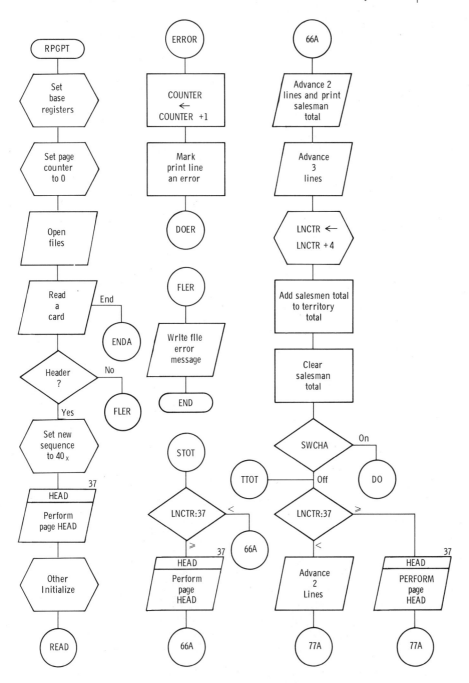

FIG. 9-32. Flow diagram for report-simplify example.

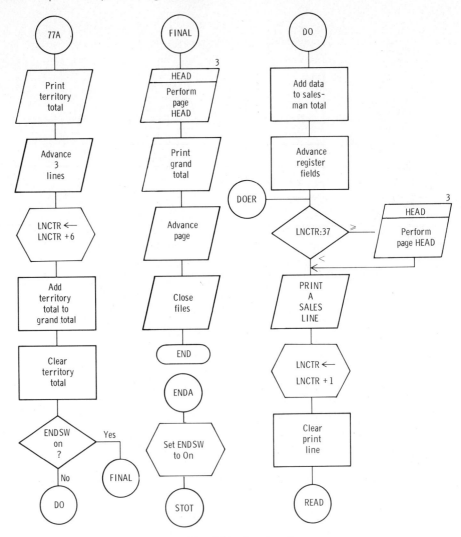

FIG. 9-32 *(continued)*

page, reheaded, and then printed. When it is time to print the territory total, the same procedure can be followed, but the territory total may be alone on a page.

Second, the programer must provide for handling error conditions. One simple way to do this is to count the errors and to mark the print lines that include errors, as shown in Fig. 9-31. The most likely errors are from input sequence, or from an improper header or data deck.

All of these operations can be incorporated in the detailed flow diagram, as shown in Fig. 9-32. This information is sufficiently detailed to permit the coding to be done. As before, the process of doing the coding uncovers the need for some ad-

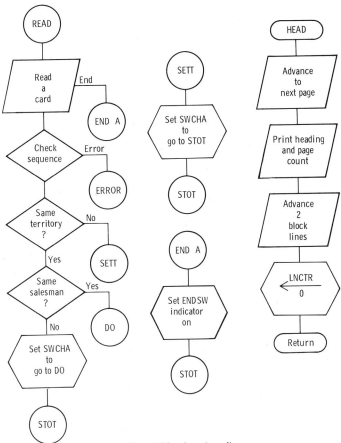

FIG. 9-32 *(continued)*

ditional initialization and cleanup, as shown in Fig. 9-33 on the following pages.

A study of the final flow diagram and the coding emphasizes one very basic point. In this example, two cycles of action are present. One is the cycle accumulating sales data in a pattern determined by the data itself. The other is the cycle of placing lines of print on the page. These two cycles are fundamentally independent. Hence the programer must select one of them as the dominant cycle—in this case, the accumulation cycle. Also, the programer must check for any links between the two cycles—in this case, the placement of totals and the starting of new pages for new territories. Programers have found such situations to be common.

Do It Now Exercise 9-4. *Modify the example just presented by making the input number a quantity rather than a value of sales. Then establish a price table and a table search to obtain a price for each product. Multiply this by the quantity to obtain an extension. Put the quantity, price, and extension under suitable column headings. Prepare a detailed flow diagram before starting the coding.*

```
// JOB
// OPTION DECK,ERRS
// EXEC ASSEMBLY


                          EXTERNAL SYMBOL DICTIONARY

    SYMBOL  TYPE ID  ADDR  LENGTH LD ID


            PC  01 000000 000068
IJCFZ1Z1    ER  02
IJDFCZZW    ER  03
BEGIN       SD  04 000068 000696



  LOC   OBJECT CODE    ADDR1 ADDR2  ST #  NAME    OP    OPERANDS                COMMENT

                                          IMPERATIVES

                                     1           PRINT  ON,NOGEN,NODATA
000000                               2           START
                                     3  *
                                     4  *FIGURE 9-33   REPORT EXAMPLE
                                     5  *
                                     6  REPORT  DTFCD  BLKSIZE=80,                      X
                                                       DEVADDR=SYSRDR,                  X
                                                       DEVICE=1442,                     X
                                                       EOFADDR=ENDA,                     X
                                                       IOAREA1=INPUTA,                  X
                                                       RECFORM=FIXUNB,                  X
                                                       TYPEFLE=INPUT
                                    27  PRINTR  DTFPR  BLKSIZE=132,                     X
                                                       DEVADDR=SYSLST,                  X
                                                       DEVICE=1443,                     X
                                                       IOAREA1=OUTA,                    X
                                                       WORKA=YES,                        X
                                                       CONTROL=YES
                                    48  *
000068                              49  BEGIN   CSECT
000068 0530                         50           BALR   3,0
00006A                              51           USING  *,3
00006A 5820 32C6          00330     52           L      2,=A(TITLE)
00003DE                             53           USING  TITLE,2
00006F 58A0 32CA          00334     54           L      10,=A(SALE1)
0005DC                              55           USING  SALE1,10
000072 D201 A094 A081 00670 0065D   56           MVC    PGNO,ZERO+2             START PAGE COUNT
                                    57           OPEN   REPORT                  OPEN FILES
                                    65           OPEN   PRINTR
000096 9240 21E6          005C4     73  .        MVI    FILE,64                 CLEAR PRINT LINE
00009A D282 21E7 21E6 005C5 005C4   74           MVC    FILE+1(131),FILE
                                    75           GET    REPORT
0000AC 0514 2196 A0F6 00574 006D2   80           CLC    INPUTA(21),HDRID        TEST FOR CORRECT FILE
0000B2 4770 3082          000EC     81           BNE    FLER
0000B6 D201 A08D 32EA 00669 00354   82           MVC    LNCTR,=P'40'            SET LINE COUNTER
0000BC 4540 31DC          00246     83           BAL    4,HEAD                  HEAD FIRST PAGE
0000C0 D203 A099 A07A 00675 00656   84           MVC    PTERR,SPACE             SET FILE SEQUENCE
0000C6 D203 A09D A07A 00679 00656   85           MVC    PSLSMN,SPACE            SET FILE SEQUENCE
0000CC D202 A096 A080 00672 0065C   86           MVC    IRR,ZERO+1              SET ERROR COUNT TO ZERO
0000D2 927A A093          0066F     87           MVI    ENDSW,122               SET END OF FILE SWITCH
0000D6 D203 A08F A07F 0066B 0065B   88           MVC    TOTS,ZERO               ZERO THE TOTAL FIELD
0000DC D204 2191 A083 0056F 0065F   89           MVC    TOTT,ZERO5              ZERO THE TOTAL FIELD
0000E2 D204 A08B A083 00664 0065F   90           MVC    TOTG,ZERO5              ZERO THE TOTAL FIELD
0000E8 47F0 30A4          0010E     91           B      READ
0000EC D216 2084 A10B 0D462 006E7   92  FLER    MVC    IDENT,EMESS             WRONG FILE ROUTINE
                                    93           PUT    PRINTR,TOTAL
000102 47F0 3290          002FA     99           B      FINER
000106 9200 3081          0011B    100  FIRST   MVI    FRSTSW+1,0
00010A 47F0 318A          001F4    101           B      DO
                                   102  READ    GET    REPORT
00011A 47F0 309C          00106    107  FRSTSW  B      FIRST                   FIRST CARD SWITCH
00011E D507 2196 A099 00574 00675  108           CLC    INPUTA(8),PTERR         CHECK SEQUENCE
000124 4740 3226          00290    109           BL     ERROR
000128 D503 A099 2196 00675 00574  110           CLC    PTERR,TERR
00012E 4770 30DA          00144    111           BNE    SETT                    TERRITORY CHANGED
000132 D503 A09D 219A 00679 0057B  112           CLC    PSLSMN,SLSMN            HAS SALESMAN CHANGED
000138 4780 318A          001F4    113           BE     DO
00013C 5850 32DA          00344    114           L      5,=A(DO)                NEED A SALESMAN TOTAL
000140 47F0 30DE          00148    115           B      STOT
000144 5850 32DE          00348    116  SETT    L      5,=A(TTOT)              NEED BOTH TOTALS
000148 4540 31DC          00246    117  STOT    BAL    4,HEAD                  HEAD NEW PAGE
                                   118           CNTRL  PRINTR,SP,1,3
00015E F383 20A5 A08F 00483 0066B  125           UNPK   TOT1,TOTS
000164 D300 20AD 32EC 0048B 00356  126           MVZ    TOT1+8(1),=X'FF'
00016A D216 2084 A0AC 00462 00688  127           MVC    IDENT,SMESS
                                   128           PUT    PRINTR,TOTAL           PRINT SALESMAN TOTAL
```

FIG. 9-33. Coding for report-simplify example.

```
000180 FA10 A08D 32ED 00669 00357    134           AP    LNCTR,=P'4'
000186 FA43 2191 A08F 0056F 0066B     135           AP    TOTT,TUTS        ROLL SALES TO TERRITORY
00018C FB33 A08F A08F 0066B 0066B     136           SP    TOTS,TOTS        CLEAR SALES TOTAL
000192 07F5                           137  SWCHA     BR    5                GOES TO TTOT OR DO
000194 4540 310C              00246    138  TTOT     BAL   4,HEAD           HEAD NEW PAGE IF NEEDED
                                       139           CNTRL PRINTR,SP,1,3
0001AA F384 20A5 2191 00483 0056F     146           UNPK  TOT1,TOTT
0001B0 D300 20AD 32EC 00488 00356     147           MVZ   TOT1+8(1),=X'FF'
0001B6 D216 2084 A0C3 00462 0069F     148           MVC   IDENT,TMESS
                                       149           PUT   PRINTR,TOTAL     PRINT TERRITORY TOTAL
                                       155           CNTRL PRINTR,SP,2
0001DA FA10 A08D 32EE 00669 00358     161           AP    LNCTR,=P'6'
0001E0 FA44 A088 2191 00664 0056F     162           AP    TOTG,TOTT        ROLL TERRITORY TO GRAND
0001E6 FB44 2191 2191 0056F 0056F     163           SP    TOTT,TOTT
0001EC 957A A093         0066F         164           CLI   ENDSW,122        END SWITCH GOES TO DO OR FINAL
0001F0 4770 323E              002A8    165           BNE   FINAL
0001F4 F247 A0A1 219E 0067D 0057C     166  DO       PACK  ASALES,SALES
0001FA FA34 A08F A0A1 0066B 0067D     167           AP    TOTS,ASALES      ACCUMULATE SALES DATA
000200 D203 A099 2196 00675 00574     168           MVC   PTERR,TERR       SAVE OLD KEYS
000206 D203 A090 219A 00679 00578     169           MVC   PSLSMN,SLSMN
00020C D203 21F0 2196 005CE 00574     170  DOER     MVC   TERR1,TERR       BUILD PRINT LINE
000212 D203 21F5 219A 005D3 00578     171           MVC   SLSMN1,SLSMN
000218 D207 A000 219E 005DC 0057C     172           MVC   SALE1,SALES
00021E 4540 310C              00246    173           BAL   4,HEAD           HEAD NEW PAGE IF NEEDED
                                       174           PUT   PRINTR,FILE
000232 FA10 A08D 32EF 00669 00359     180           AP    LNCTR,=P'1'      ADD 1 TO LINE COUNTER
000238 9240 21E6         005C4         181           MVI   FILE,64          CLEAR PRINT LINE
00023C D282 21E7 21E6 005C5 005C4     182           MVC   FILE+1(131),FILE
000242 47F0 30A4              0010E    183           B     READ
000246 F911 A08D A0A6 00669 00682     184  HEAD     CP    LNCTR,BOTTOM     PAGE HEAD ROUTINE
00024C 4740 3224              0028E    185           BL    OUT
                                       186           CNTRL PRINTR,SK,1     SKIP TO NEXT PAGE
00025E FA10 A094 32EF 00670 00359     192           AP    PGNO,=P'1'
000264 F321 2074 A094 00452 00670     193           UNPK  PAGE,PGNO
00026A D300 2076 32EC 00454 00356     194           MVZ   PAGE+2(1),=X'FF'
                                       195           CNTRL PRINTR,SP,,3    DOUBLE SPACE AFTER PRINT
                                       199           PUT   PRINTR,TITLE
000288 D201 A08D A081 00669 0065D     205           MVC   LNCTR,ZERO+2     RESET LINE COUNT
00028E 07F4                           206  OUT      BR    4                RETURN TO MAIN PROGRAM
000290 FA20 A096 32EF 00672 00359     207  ERROR    AP    IRR,=P'1'        COUNT ERRORS
000296 D203 A06C A0A8 00648 00684     208           MVC   ERR,AST          MARK PRINT LINE
00029C 47F0 31A2              0020C    209           B     DOER             HOLD OLD KEYS, TRY A READ
0002A0 92E7 A093         0066F         210  ENDA     MVI   ENDSW,231
0002A4 47F0 30DE              00148    211           B     STOT
0002A8 FA11 A08D 32EA 00669 00354     212  FINAL    AP    LNCTR,=P'40'     EOJ ROUTINE
0002AE 4540 310C              00246    213           BAL   4,HEAD
0002B2 F384 20A5 A088 00483 00356     214           UNPK  TOT1,TOTG
0002B8 D300 20AD 32EC 00488 00356     215           MVZ   TOT1+8(1),=X'FF'
0002BE D216 2084 A00A 00462 00686     216           MVC   IDENT,GMESS
                                       217           PUT   PRINTR,TOTAL     PRINT GRAND TOTAL
0002D4 FA11 A08D 32EA 00669 00354     223           AP    LNCTR,=P'40'
0002DA 4540 310C              00246    224           BAL   4,HEAD
0002DE F342 2137 A096 00515 00672     225           UNPK  IRR1,IRR         COPY ERROR COUNT
0002E4 D300 213B 32EC 00519 00356     226           MVZ   IRR1+4(1),=X'FF'
                                       227           PUT   PRINTR,ERRM
                                       233  FINER    CNTRL PRINTR,SK,1
                                       239           CLOSE REPORT,PRINTR
                                       248           EOJ
                                       251  *
000320                                 252           LTORG
000320 5858C2D6D7C5D540                253                =C'$$BOPEN '
000328 5858C2C3D3D6E2C5                254                =C'$$BCLOSE'
000330 000003DE                        255                =A(TITLE)
000334 000005DC                        256                =A(SALE1)
000338 00000000                        257                =A(REPORT)
00033C 0000003B                        258                =A(PRINTR)
000340 00000462                        259                =A(TOTAL)
000344 000001F4                        260                =A(DO)
000348 00000194                        261                =A(TTOT)
00034C 000005C4                        262                =A(FILE)
000350 000004E6                        263                =A(ERRM)
000354 040C                            264                =P'40'
000356 FF                              265                =X'FF'
000357 4C                              266                =P'4'
000358 6C                              267                =P'6'
000359 1C                              268                =P'1'
                                       269  *
                                       270  *
                                       271  *     DECLARATIVES
                                       272  *
00035A                                 273  OUTA     DS    CL132
                                       274  *
0003DE                                 275  TITLE    DS    OCL132
0003DE D9C5D7D6D9E340C6                276           DC    CL12'REPORT FILE '
0003EA 404040404040404040              277           DC    99C' '
00044D D7C1C7C540                       278           DC    CL5'PAGE '
000452                                 279  PAGE     DS    CL3
000455 404040404040404040             280           DC    13C' '
                                       281  *
```

FIG. 9-33 *(continued)*

```
000462                     282 TOTAL   DS    0CL132
000462                     283 IDENT   DS    CL23
000479 4040404040404040    284         DC    10C' '
000483                     285 TOT1    DS    CL9
00048C 4040404040404040    286         DC    90C' '
                           287 *
0004E6                     288 ERRM    DS    0CL132
0004E6 4040404040404040    289         DC    9C' '
0004EF E3C8C540E3D6E3C1    290         DC    CL38'THE TOTAL NUMBER OF SEQUENCE ERRORS - '
000515                     291 IRR1    DS    CL5
00051A 4040404040404040    292         DC    80C' '
                           293 *
00056A 000000000C          294 TOT5    DC    PL5'0'
00056F 000000000C          295 TOTT    DC    PL5'0'
                           296 *
                           297 *                 CONSTANT SECTION
                           298 *
000574                     299 INPUTA  DS    0CL80
000574                     300 TERR    DS    CL4
000578                     301 SLSMN   DS    CL4
00057C                     302 SALES   DS    CL8
000584                     303         DS    CL64
                           304 *
0005C4                     305 FILE    DS    0CL132
0005C4 4040404040404040    306         DC    10C' '
0005CE                     307 TERR1   DS    CL4
0005D2 40                  308         DC    1C' '
0005D3                     309 SLSMN1  DS    CL4
0005D7 4040404040          310         DC    5C' '
0005DC                     311 SALE1   DS    CL8
0005E4 4040404040404040    312         DC    100C' '
000648                     313 ERR     DS    CL4
00064C 4040404040404040    314         DC    10C' '
000656 4040404040          315 SPACE   DC    CL5' '
00065B 0000000C            316 ZERO    DC    PL4'0'
00065F 000000000C          317 ZERO5   DC    PL5'0'
000664 000000000C          318 TOTG    DC    PL5'0'
000669 000C                319 LNCTR   DC    PL2'0'
00066B 0000000C            320 TOTS    DC    PL4'0'
00066F 40                  321 ENDSW   DC    C' '
000670 000C                322 PGNO    DC    PL2'0'
000672 00000C              323 IRR     DC    PL3'0'
000675                     324 PTERR   DS    CL4
000679                     325 PSLSMN  DS    CL4
00067D                     326 ASALES  DS    PL5
000682 037C                327 BOTTOM  DC    PL2'37'
000684 5C5C5C5C            328 AST     DC    CL4'****'
000688 E3D6E3C1D340C6D6    329 SMESS   DC    CL23'TOTAL FOR THE SALESMAN '
00069F E3D6E3C1D340C6D6    330 TMESS   DC    CL23'TOTAL FOR THE TERRITORY'
0006B6 4040404040404040    331 GMESS   DC    12C' '
0006C2 C6C9D5C1D340E3D6    332         DC    CL11'FINAL TOTAL'
0006CD 4040404040          333         DC    5C' '
0006D2 C8C4D9F1E2C1D3C5    334 HDRID   DC    CL21'HDR1SALES DETAIL PACK'
0006E7 4040E6D9D6D5C740    335 EMESS   DC    CL23'  WRONG INPUT FILE     '
00006B                     336         END   BEGIN
```

```
                    RELOCATION DICTIONARY

POS.ID   REL.ID   FLAGS   ADDRESS

  01       01      0C     000008
  01       02      18     000011
  01       04      0C     00001B
  01       04      0C     00001C
  01       04      08     000021
  01       01      0C     000040
  01       03      18     000049
  01       04      0C     000050
  01       04      08     000061
  04       01      0C     000080
  04       01      0C     000090
  04       01      0C     000310
  04       01      0C     000314
  04       04      0C     000330
  04       04      0C     000334
  04       01      0C     000338
  04       01      0C     00033C
  04       04      0C     000340
  04       04      0C     000344
  04       04      0C     000348
  04       04      0C     00034C
  04       04      0C     000350
```

FIG. 9-33   *(continued)*

```
                                    CROSS-REFERENCE

SYMBOL    LEN   VALUE  DEFN

ASALES    00005 00067D 0326   0166  0167
AST       00004 000684 0328   0208
BEGIN     00001 000068 0049   0336
BOTTOM    00002 000682 0327   0184
DO        00006 0001F4 0166   0101  0113  0114  0260
DOER      00006 00020C 0170   0209
EMESS     00023 0006E7 0335   0092
ENDA      00004 0002A0 0210   0021
ENDSW     00001 00066F 0321   0087  0164  0210
ERR       00004 000648 0313   0208
ERRM      00132 0004E6 0288   0230  0263
ERROR     00006 000290 0207   0109
FILE      00132 0005C4 0305   0073  0074  0074  0177  0181  0182  0182  0262
FINAL     00006 0002A8 0212   0165
FINER     00004 0002FA 0235   0099
FIRST     00004 000106 0100   0107
FLER      00006 0000EC 0092   0081
FRSTSW    00004 00011A 0107   0100
GMESS     00001 0006B6 0331   0216
HDRID     00021 0006D2 0334   0080
HEAD      00006 000246 0184   0083  0117  0138  0173  0213  0224
IDENT     00023 000462 0283   0092  0127  0148  0216
IJCX0001  00008 000020 0022   0012
IJJC0020  00004 00030C 0244
IJJ00003  00004 00007C 0062
IJJ00004  00004 0000AC 0070
IJJZ0001  00001 000032 0026
IJJZ0002  00001 000068 0047
INPUTA    00080 000574 0299   0020  0022  0080  0108
IRR       00003 000672 0323   0086  0207  0225
IRR1      00005 000515 0291   0225  0226
LNCTR     00002 000669 0319   0082  0134  0161  0180  0184  0205  0212  0223
OUT       00002 00028E 0206   0185
OUTA      00132 00035A 0273   0041  0046
PAGE      00003 000452 0279   0193  0194
PGNO      00002 000670 0322   0056  0192  0193
PRINTR    00006 000038 0030   0071  0095  0120  0130  0141  0151  0157  0176  0188  0197  0201  0219  0229
                              0235  0246  0258
PSLSMN    00004 000679 0325   0085  0112  0169
PTERR     00004 000675 0324   0084  0108  0110  0168
READ      00004 00010E 0104   0091  0183
REPORT    00006 000000 0009   0063  0077  0104  0245  0257
SALES     00008 00057C 0302   0166  0172
SALE1     00008 0005DC 0311   0054  0055  0172  0256
SETT      00004 000144 0116   0111
SLSMN     00004 000578 0301   0112  0169  0171
SLSMN1    00004 0005D3 0309   0171
SMESS     00023 000688 0329   0127
SPACE     00005 000656 0315   0084  0085
STOT      00004 000148 0117   0115  0211
SWCHA     00002 000192 0137
TERR      00004 000574 0300   0110  0168  0170
TERR1     00004 0005CE 0307   0170
TITLE     00132 0003DE 0275   0052  0053  0202  0255
TMESS     00023 00069F 0330   0148
TOTAL     00132 000462 0282   0096  0131  0152  0220  0259
TOTG      00005 000664 0318   0090  0162  0214
TOTS      00004 00066B 0320   0088  0125  0135  0136  0136  0167
TOTT      00005 00056F 0295   0089  0135  0146  0162  0163  0163
TOT1      00009 000483 0285   0125  0126  0146  0147  0214  0215
TOT5      00005 00056A 0294
TTOT      00004 000194 0138   0116  0261
ZERO      00004 00065B 0316   0056  0086  0088  0205
ZERO5     00005 00065F 0317   0089  0090


NO STATEMENTS FLAGGED IN THIS ASSEMBLY


// OPTION LINK,DUMP
// PAUSE
   INCLUDE
// EXEC LNKEDT


                        DISK LINKAGE EDITOR DIAGNOSTIC OF INPUT

ACTION TAKEN    MAP
LIST       CATALR IJDFCPZW
LIST   AUTOLINK   IJCFZIZ1
LIST   ENTRY
```

FIG. 9-33   *(continued)*

```
    PHASE  XFR-AD  LOCORE  HICORE  DSK-AD   ESD TYPE  LABEL    LOADED  REL-FR

  PHASE***  001A08  001900  0020EF  2A 4 2   CSECT    IJDFCPZW  001900  001900
                                             *  ENTRY  IJDFZPZW  001900
                                             *  ENTRY  IJDFZZZW  001900
                                                ENTRY  IJDFCZZW  001900

                                             CSECT             0019A0  0019A0

                                             CSECT    IJCFZIZ1  0020A0  0020A0

                                             CSECT    BEGIN     001A08  0019A0
```

// EXEC

REPORT FILE   PAGE 001

        0020 0120   00003841
        0020 0120   00012002
TOTAL FOR THE SALESMAN   000015843

        0020 0150   00038713
TOTAL FOR THE SALESMAN   000038713

        0020 0380   00022384
        0020 0380   00056735
        0020 0380   00013456

TOTAL FOR THE SALESMAN   000092575

TOTAL FOR THE TERRITORY   000147131

        0042 0140   00050007
TOTAL FOR THE SALESMAN   000050007

TOTAL FOR THE TERRITORY   000050007

        0068 0170   00003908
        0068 0170   00083009

REPORT FILE   PAGE 002

TOTAL FOR THE SALESMAN   000086917

TOTAL FOR THE TERRITORY   000086917

REPORT FILE   PAGE 003

        FINAL TOTAL   000284055

REPORT FILE   PAGE 004

        THE TOTAL NUMBER OF SEQUENCE ERRORS - 00000

FIG. 9-33   *(continued)*

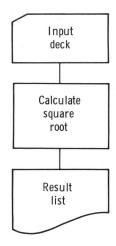

Fig. 9-34. System chart for square-canned example.

SQUARE-ROOT EXAMPLE

The task is as follows: Each card of a deck of cards has from one through four numbers for which square roots are needed. Each number is right-justified, with leading 0s in a field 10 characters long, with no blank space on a card between the fields. The square roots are desired to an accuracy of no decimal places, and no rounding off is requested. The numbers of which the square roots are desired are all integers with no fractional digits. The output is to be listed on a printer with one line for each input card. A system chart is shown in Fig. 9-34.

The approach illustrated here is the canned-algorithm approach. Since the operation being performed is a mathematical operation of finding the square root, the first action is to turn to some reference work on numerical analysis. These have discussions of appropriate techniques for the determination of a square root to varying degrees of accuracy.

The method selected here is one derived from Newton's method, or the Newton-Raphson method as it is sometimes called, and represents essentially a special case of that method.* It is one of the most rapidly converging methods for calculating the square root and entails only a small amount of uncorrectable error. The algorithm is simple and straightforward, as shown in Fig. 9-35.

$$X_{n+1} = \frac{X_n + (L/X_n)}{2}$$

Fig. 9-35. Formula for square-canned example.

*See, for example, Daniel D. McCracken and William S. Dorn, *Numerical Methods and FORTRAN Programming*. New York: John Wiley & Sons, Inc. 1964, pp. 133-139.

The value of the number for which the square root is desired is represented by L. The value of X can be chosen *initially* as any number whatever. As a convenient starting point, experience has shown that about one-fourth of the input number is an expeditious first approximation for integers. This can then be substituted into the formula to attain a new approximation, X_{n+1}. This new approximation can then be used as the X_n element, in the right-hand half of the formula again, to attain still

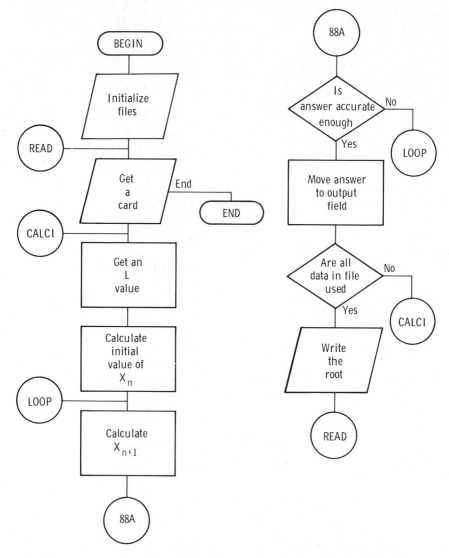

FIG. 9-36. Summary flow diagram for square-canned example.

another new approximation. This procedure can be continued until successive values of X_{n+1} are identical, to whatever degree of precision is desired.

The programer can prepare a summary diagram following the general pattern of setup, do, and cleanup, as shown in Fig. 9-36. The initialization consists of calculating the initial approximation. This requires selecting the first L number from the input. Since as many as four L numbers may occur per input card, the program must test for the presence of a valid number before accepting the contents of an input field. Also—though this relates to a later matter—the programer must provide for a way of indexing from one field to the next.

After selecting the L number, the initialization part of the program for the actual computation must calculate an initial value of X_n. For this, the programer can use one-fourth of the value of L, provided that this value is equal to not less than $+1$. In almost all computer work it is more rapid and more efficient to have the computer multiply by a reciprocal than it is to have it divide. Since in the computer binary operations are the most rapid, and since successive computation is required here, the appropriate choice of number representation is binary. Dividing by four in binary is easily done by use of a shift, as shown in Fig. 9-37.

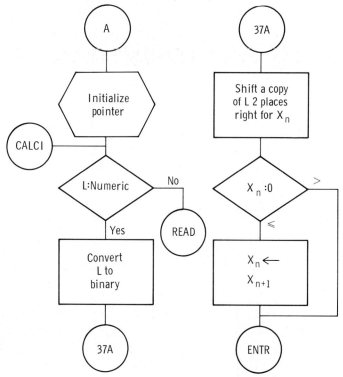

Fig. 9-37. Initial approximation for square-canned example.

The basic computation-loop operation, as shown in Fig. 9-38, is to add the approximation of the value of X_n to the quotient of X_n divided into L. This yields the numerator to be divided by 2. Since division by two in binary can be handled by a shift, the result yields the next approximation, X_{n+1}. Then the operation can be repeated, using X_{n+1} as the old X_n. Calculating the first approximation can be done either outside of the main loop or incorporated in the main loop, as at ENTR.

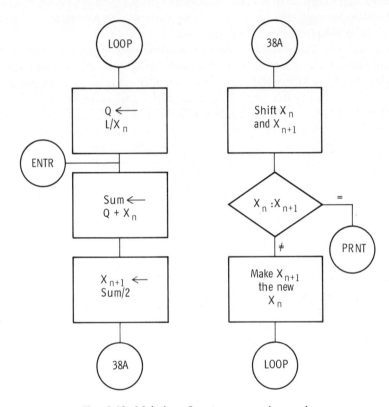

FIG. 9-38. Main loop for square-canned example.

The exit test for the main loop can be a comparison of one approximation of the series with the next, to determine whether or not another iteration should be performed. Note that the exit from the loop is not fixed at any particular number of iterations, but is determined by the accuracy desired and the closeness of the successive approximations. In binary operations it cannot be reasonably expected that the operation will agree more closely than one place (the last bit position on the right). The comparison, therefore, should ignore at least this bit position. This can be conveniently handled by a shift.

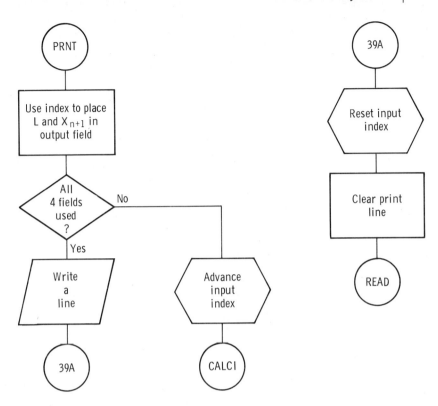

F<small>IG</small>. 9-39. Output routine for square-canned example.

As shown in Fig. 9-36, the remaining operations are to test whether all possible L values from an input card have been processed, and to do the output. A companion problem arises, in that indexing will be needed to determine the position on the print line in which to print these square roots (see Fig. 9-39). The position on the page in which it should be printed depends in turn upon the position on the card on which the number was originally obtained. Therefore the same indexing factor used to obtain the number from the card can be used as the indexing factor for placing the resulting root on the output form. This provides a tie into the CALCI routine noted earlier in Fig. 9-37. For easy-to-read output, some extra space between the roots is helpful.

The setup and cleanup operations here are quite simple. End-of-file consists only of closing the files and calling the supervisor after advancing the paper. Setup consists of loading the initial register contents and opening the files.

From the diagrams already presented, a detailed flow diagram can be prepared, as shown in Fig. 9-40. With this, the programer is ready to do the coding. This he

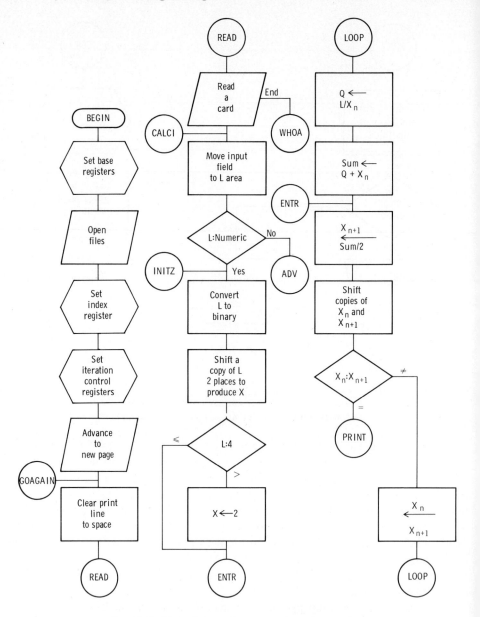

FIG. 9-40. Flow diagram for square-canned example.

can do in a straightforward manner directly from the diagram, as shown in Fig. 9-41. The major difficulties lie in the heavy demands upon the registers—a common

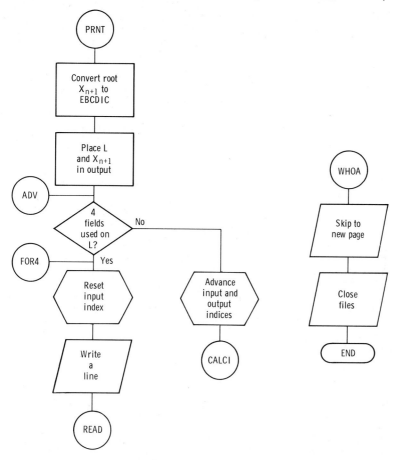

Fɪɢ. 9-40 *(continued)*

situation when the registers are used for arithmetic computation and for iteration control, as well as for addressing.

Do It Now Exercise 9-5. *Figure 9-41 indicates that the program has a bug. Identify the bug. Prepare a revised flow diagram to correct it. Code and test your revision.*

Do It Now Exercise 9-6. *Write a program to find the natural logarithm to 10 fractional places of any positive number greater than +1.0, which may have up to 12 integer and fractional places. Be sure to prepare a detailed flow diagram before starting the coding. Hint: Seek out several references on numerical analysis and numerical (digital) approximations, and compare the algorithms they suggest before selecting one.*

```
// JOB
// OPTION DECK,ERRS
// EXEC ASSEMBLY


                        EXTERNAL SYMBOL DICTIONARY

    SYMBOL  TYPE ID  ADDR  LENGTH LD ID


             PC  01 000000 000068
    IJCFZIZI ER  02
    IJDFCZZZ ER  03
    F9#41    SD  04 000068 000254


    LOC   OBJECT CODE   ADDR1 ADDR2 ST #  NAME    OP   OPERANDS                COMMENT

                                          IMPERATIVES

                                      1           PRINT ON,NOGEN,NODATA
    000000                            2           START
                                      3  *FIGURE 9-41   SQUARE ROOT EXAMPLE
                                      4  *
                                      5  INPUT    DTFCD BLKSIZE=80,                      C
                                                        DEVADDR=SYSRDR,                  C
                                                        DEVICE=1442,                     C
                                                        EOFADDR=WHOA,                    C
                                                        IOAREA1=XVALUE,                  C
                                                        RECFORM=FIXUNB,                  C
                                                        TYPEFLE=INPUT
                                     26  OUTPUT   DTFPR BLKSIZE=132,                      C
                                                        DEVADDR=SYSLST,                  C
                                                        DEVICE=1443,                     C
                                                        IOAREA1=LISTX,                   C
                                                        RECFORM=FIXUNB,                  C
                                                        CONTROL=YES
    000068                           47  F9#41    CSECT
    000068 0520                      48           BALR  2,0
    00006A                           49           USING *,2
    00006A 4130 217E           001E8 50           LA    3,XVALUE          BASE FOR INPUT
    0001E8                           51           USING XVALUE,3
    00006E 4140 3050           00238 52           LA    4,LISTX           BASE FOR OUTPUT
    000238                           53           USING LISTX,4
    000072 4150 2156           001C0 54           LA    5,HOLD            BASE FOR CONSTANTS
    0001C0                           55           USING HOLD,5
                                     56  *
                                     57  *        REG   7                 X QUOTIENT
                                     58  *        REG   6                 X REMAINDER
                                     59  *        REG   8                 NEW X
                                     60  *        REG   9                 OLD X SHIFTED  ITERATION CONTROL
                                     61  *        REG   10                NEW X SHIFTED  ITERATION CONTROL
                                     62  *
                                     63           OPEN  INPUT,OUTPUT
                                     72           CNTRL OUTPUT,SK,1        EJECT TO NEW PAGE
    000098 9240 4000        00238    78  GOAGAIN  MVI   LISTX,64          CLEAR PRINT LINE
    00009C D282 4001 4000 00239 00238 79          MVC   LISTX+1(131),LISTX
                                     80  READI    GET   INPUT
    0000AE D209 5008 3000 001C8 001E8 85  CALC1   MVC   L,VAL
    0000B4 D509 5008 213E 001C8 001A8 86          CLC   L,=C'0000000000'   ZERO OR NON-NUMERIC
    0000BA 4740 20CA           00134 87           BL    ADV
    0000BE F279 5000 5008 001C0 001C8 88  INITZ   PACK  HOLD,L
    0000C4 4F80 5000           001C0 89           CVB   8,HOLD            L IN BINARY
    0000C8 1888                      90           LR    11,8              L IN BINARY
    0000CA 1878                      91           LR    7,8
    0000CC 5890 5014           001D4 92           L     9,BZERO
    0000D0 5970 2136           001A0 93           C     7,=F'0'
    0000D4 4740 20CA           00134 94           BL    ADV               AVOID NEGATIVE NUMBERS
    0000D8 4770 207A           000E4 95           BNE   *+12              AVOID DIVISION BY ZERO
    0000DC 4870 214B           001B2 96           LH    7,=H'4'
    0000E0 47F0 207C           000E6 97           B     *+6
    0000E4 1878                      98           LR    7,8
    0000E6 8A70 0001           00001 99           SRA   7,1
    0000EA 47F0 2096           00100 100          B     ENTR
    0000EE 187B                     101  LOOP     LR    7,11             PICK UP L IN BINARY
    0000F0 1866                     102           SR    6,6
    0000F2 8F60 0001           00001 103          SLDA  6,1
    0000F6 1D68                     104           DR    6,8              DIVIDE L BY OLD X
    0000F8 1866                     105           SR    6,6              DISCARD REMAINDER
    0000FA 8E60 0001           00001 106          SRDA  6,1
    0000FE 1A78                     107          AR    7,8               ADD ON OLD X
    000100 8A70 0001           00001 108  ENTR    SRA   7,1              DIVIDE BY TWO
    000104 1887                     109          LR    8,7               NEW X
    000106 18A7                     110          LR    10,7
    000108 8AA0 0001           00001 111          SRA   10,1             NEW X SHIFTED
    00010C 199A                     112          CR    9,10              EXIT TEST
    00010E 4780 20AE           00118 113          BE    PRNT
```

FIG. 9-41. Coding for square-canned example.

```
000112 189A                        114        LR    9,10            OLD X SHIFTED
000114 47F0 2084           000EE   115        B     LOOP
000118 D209 4005 5008 0023D 001C8  116 PRNT   MVC   VALL,L          MOVE L TO OUTPUT
00011E 4E80 5000           001C0   117        CVD   8,HOLD          CONVERT ROOT TO EBCDIC
000122 F397 5008 5000 001C8 001C0  118        UNPK  L,HOLD
000128 D300 5011 214E 001D1 00188  119        MVZ   L+9(1),=X'FF'   CORRECT ZONE
00012E D205 4011 500C 00249 001CC  120        MVC   VALX,L+4        MOVE ROOT TO OUTPUT
000134 5930 213A           001A4   121 ADV    C     3,=A(XVALUE+25) EXIT TEST
000138 4720 20DE           00148   122        BH    FOR4
00013C 4A30 214A           00184   123        AH    3,=H'10'        INDEX INPUT
000140 4A40 214C           001B6   124        AH    4,=H'25'        INDEX OUTPUT
000144 47F0 2044           000AE   125        B     CALC1
000148 5830 5020           001E0   126 FOR4   L     3,ADXVAL        RESET INDEX
00014C 5840 5024           001E4   127        L     4,ADLISTX
                                   128        PUT   OUTPUT          WRITE OUTPUT
00015C 47F0 202E           00098   133        B     GOAGAIN         RECYCLE
                                   134 WHOA   CNTRL OUTPUT,SK,1     END OF INPUT
                                   140        CLOSE INPUT,OUTPUT
                                   149        EOJ
                                   152 *
000188                             153        LTORG
000188 5858C2D6D7C5D540            154              =C'$$BOPEN '
000190 5B5BC2C3D3D6E2C5            155              =C'$$BCLOSE'
000198 0000003B                    156              =A(OUTPUT)
00019C 00000000                    157              =A(INPUT)
0001A0 00000000                    158              =F'0'
0001A4 00000201                    159              =A(XVALUE+25)
0001A8 F0F0F0F0F0F0F0F0F0          160              =C'0000000000'
0001B2 0004                        161              =H'4'
0001B4 000A                        162              =H'10'
0001B6 0019                        163              =H'25'
0001B8 FF                          164              =X'FF'
                                   165 *
                                   166 *   DECLARATIVES
                                   167 *
0001C0                             168        DS    0D
0001C0                             169 HOLD   DS    PL8
0001C8                             170 L      DS    CL10
0001D2 0000                        171 BZERO  DC    F'0'
0001D4 00000000                    172        DC    8C' '
0001D8 404040404040404040          173 *
0001E0 000001E8                    178 ADXVAL DC    A(XVALUE)
0001E4 00000238                    179 ADLISTX DC   A(LISTX)
0001E8                             180 XVALUE DS    0CL80
0001E8                             181 VAL    DS    4CL10
000210                             182        DS    CL40
                                   183 *
000238                             184 LISTX  DS    0CL132
000238 4040404040                  185        DC    5C' '
00023D                             186 VALL   DS    CL10
000247                             187        DS    2C' '
000249                             188 VALX   DS    CL6
00024F                             189        DS    7C' '
000256                             190        DS    CL102
                                   191 *
000068                             192        END   F9#41
```

RELOCATION DICTIONARY

POS.ID	REL.ID	FLAGS	ADDRESS
01	01	0C	000008
01	02	18	000011
01	04	0C	000018
01	04	0C	00001C
01	04	08	000021
01	01	0C	000040
01	03	18	000049
01	04	0C	000050
01	04	08	000061
04	01	0C	000080
04	01	0C	000084
04	01	0C	000178
04	01	0C	00017C
04	01	0C	000198
04	01	0C	00019C
04	04	0C	0001A4
04	04	0C	0001E0
04	04	0C	0001E4

FIG. 9-41 *(continued)*

```
                                    CROSS-REFERENCE

     SYMBOL    LEN   VALUE  DEFN

     ADLISTX   00004 0001E4 0179    0127
     ADV       00004 000134 0121    0087  0094
     ADXVAL    00004 0001E0 0178    0126
     BZERO     00004 0001D4 0171    0092
     CALC1     00006 0000AE 0085    0125
     ENTR      00004 000100 0108    0100
     FOR4      00004 000148 0126    0122
     F9#41     00001 000068 0047    0192
     GOAGAIN   00004 000098 0078    0133
     HOLD      00008 0001C0 0169    0054  0055  0088  0089  0117  0118
     IJCX0001  00008 000020 0021    0011
     IJJC0008  00004 000174 0145
     IJJO0003  00004 00007C 0068
     IJJZ0001  00001 000032 0025
     IJJZ0002  00001 000068 0046
     INITZ     00006 0000BE 0088
     INPUT     00006 000000 000A    0069  0082  0146  0157
     L         00010 0001C8 0170    0085  0086  0088  0116  0118  0119  0120
     LISTX     00132 000238 0184    0040  0045  0052  0053  0078  0079  0079  0179
     LOOP      00002 0000EE 0101    0115
     OUTPUT    00006 000038 0029    0070  0074  0130  0136  0147  0156
     PRNT      00006 000118 0116    0113
     READI     00004 0000A2 0082
     VAL       00010 0001E8 0181    0085
     VALL      00010 00023D 0186    0116
     VALX      00006 000249 0188    0120
     WHOA      00004 000160 0136    0020
     XVALUE    00080 0001E8 0180    0019  0021  0050  0051  0121  0159  0178


     NO STATEMENTS FLAGGED IN THIS ASSEMBLY


     // OPTION LINK,DUMP
     // PAUSE
        INCLUDE
     // EXEC LNKEDT


                        DISK LINKAGE EDITOR DIAGNOSTIC OF INPUT

     ACTION TAKEN    MAP
     LIST   AUTOLINK  IJCFZIZ1
     LIST   ENTRY


              PHASE  XFR-AD  LOCORE  HICORE  DSK-AD  ESD TYPE  LABEL     LOADED  REL-FR

              PHASE***  001980  001900  001C57  2A 4 2  CSECT             001900  000000

                                                        CSECT   IJDFCZZZ  001900  000000

                                                        CSECT             001948  001948

                                                        CSECT   IJCFZIZ1  001C08  001C08

                                                        CSECT   F9#41     001980  001948

     CONTROL SECTIONS OF ZERO LENGTH IN INPUT


     // EXEC


     0000000016  000004       0000000049  000007     0000000009  000003      0000000025  000005
     0000000036  000006
     0000000004  000001       0000000144  000012     0000000421  000020
     0000000081  000009
     0000007396  000086       0000986049  000993     0000376996  000614      0000037249  000193
```

Fig. 9-41 *(continued)*

EXERCISES

1. Draw each outline in the ANSI Standard flow diagram group.
2. Explain the use of each.
3. List and contrast four main approaches to problem analysis.
4. Explain what is meant by "initialization."
5. Explain the use of program switches. Illustrate your explanation with an example of your own creation.

CHAPTER 10

Data Manipulation

NONARITHMETIC FUNCTIONS

The basic arithmetic operations were presented in Chap. 5. Those operations enable the computer to shift, add, subtract, multiply, and divide data. The basic data-movement operations were presented in Chap. 4. Those operations enable the computer to rearrange data in storage and to move data from place to place. Such data-movement and arithmetic operations are vital and important in data-processing work.

Even in combination, however, they fall short of the demands of the more complex data-processing jobs. To meet the needs of such jobs without using extensive subroutines, the computer must be able to rearrange the bits within a byte and to treat data in nonarithmetic ways, such as changing a number from negative to positive, doing a financial edit, or performing logic operations. Data manipulation and logic operations of these types are the topic of this chapter.

Before launching into a discussion of these operations, it is worth while to review and sharpen the distinctions among logical, data-movement, and arithmetic operations. An arithmetic operation performs data changing according to one or more of the rules of arithmetic (addition, subtraction, multiplication, or division) on data assumed to be represented in a numeric format with an algebraic sign. In contrast, logical operations do not perform data changing according to any of the four rules of arithmetic and do not necessarily assume the data to be represented in a numeric format. Data for logic operations are assumed to be a string of bits or characters.

Logic operations typically involve altering or modifying data by more than just copying data from one place to another in the computer. Data-movement operations typically involve altering or modifying data by means of copying data from one place to another. Arithmetic operations typically involve altering or modifying data according to the rules of arithmetic.

The operations described in this chapter fall into seven major groups. The first group is concerned with the loading of registers in special ways. The second group has two parts, one concerned with logical shifts and the other with logical add and subtract. The third group is concerned with operations on the bits in a byte. The fourth group is concerned with financial editing and code translation. The fifth group is concerned with data-replacement operations. The sixth group is concerned with operations that alter the control sequence in the program, either by providing iteration exits or by the indirect execution of instructions. The seventh group provides ways of specifying noncontiguous bytes to be moved or compared.

In reading the presentation of each of these groups of operations, the programer should note the role of the condition code, and the locations of the data. Some operations set the condition code, some do not. Some operate on data in registers, some on data in storage.

REGISTER LOADS

The commands in this group in effect combine a load and a compare, or a load, a code conversion, and a compare. This enables the programer to write a program using fewer instructions than would otherwise be possible. All of these commands, in part because of register sizes, are unavailable on the small models of the computer.

LTR—Load and Test Register. This RR command loads one register from another or a register from itself. The first-operand address names the receiving register; the second, the sending register. The command, in its operation, differs from the ordinary Load Register only in that the condition code is set. If, after the operation, the receiving register contains only 0 bits, the condition code is set to 0. If the register contains a negative number, the condition code is set to 1. If the register contains a positive number greater than 0, the condition code is set to 2. No overflow is possible, and hence condition code 3 is not used. This command is not subject to interruption, and is not available on small models of the computer. An example of Load and Test Register is shown in Fig. 10-1.

Do It Now Exercise 10-1. *Write one imperative instruction that will set the condition code to reflect the sign of the contents of register 7 without altering the content of any register or any place in storage.*

LPR—Load Positive. This RR command names the receiving register as the first-operand address and the sending register as the second-operand address. After

```
     LOC   OBJECT CODE    ADDR1 ADDR2   ST #   NAME    OP    OPERANDS         COMMENT

                                               IMPERATIVES

   00000E  9867 F000            00200    11             LM    6,7,TEST1       LOAD REG.
   000012  0580                          12             BALR  8,0             SAVE CONDITION CODE
   000014  1276                          13  F10#1      LTR   7,6             LOAD AND TEST REG.
   000016  0590                          14             BALR  9,0             SAVE CONDITION CODE
   000018  9069 F020            00220    15             STM   6,9,CHOLD       SHOW REG. CONTENTS



                                               DECLARATIVES

   000200  FFFE8123                     178  TEST1      DC    F'-98013'       F10#1
   000204  00019339                     179             DC    F'103225'       FILLER
   000208  4040404040404040             180             DC    CL24' '         FILLER
   000210  4040404040404040
   000218  4040404040404040
   000220  4040404040404040             181  CHOLD      DC    CL32' '         USED TO DISPLAY  STORAGE
   000228  4040404040404040
   000230  4040404040404040
   000238  4040404040404040


                                     DUMP AFTER EXECUTION

   001AE0  TO THE NEXT LINE ADDRESS CONTAINS 40404040
   001B00    FFFE8123  00019339  40404040  40404040    40404040  40404040  40404040  40404040
   001B20    FFFE8123  FFFE8123  40001914  5000191B    40404040  40404040  40404040  40404040
   001B40    F0404040  40404040  40404040  40404040    40404040  40404040  40404040  40404040


                                   RELOCATION FACTOR   001900
```

FIG. 10-1. Example of Load and Test Register.

```
     LOC   OBJECT CODE    ADDR1 ADDR2   ST #   NAME    OP    OPERANDS         COMMENT

                                               IMPERATIVES

   00001C  9845 F080            00280    17             LM    4,5,POS         LOAD REG.
   000020  0560                          18             BALR  6,0             SAVE CONDITION CODE
   000022  1054                          19  F10#2      LPR   5,4             LOAD POSITIVE
   000024  0570                          20             BALR  7,0             SAVE CONDITION CODE
   000026  9047 F0A0            002A0    21             STM   4,7,CKEEP       SHOW REG. CONTENTS



                                               DECLARATIVES

   000280  FFFFFBB1                     187  POS        DC    F'-1103'        F10#2
   000284  0000210C                     188             DC    F'8460'         FILLER
   000288  4040404040404040             189             DC    CL24' '         FILLER
   000290  4040404040404040
   000298  4040404040404040
   0002A0  4040404040404040             190  CKEEP      DC    CL32' '         USED TO DISPLAY STORAGE
   0002A8  4040404040404040
   0002B0  4040404040404040
   0002B8  4040404040404040


                                     DUMP AFTER EXECUTION

   001B60    F0404040  40404040  40404040  40404040    40404040  40404040  40404040  40404040
   001B80    FFFFFBB1  0000210C  40404040  40404040    40404040  40404040  40404040  40404040
   001BA0    FFFFFBB1  0000044F  50001922  60001926    40404040  40404040  40404040  40404040
   001BC0    F0404040  40404040  40404040  40404040    40404040  40404040  40404040  40404040


                                   RELOCATION FACTOR   001900
```

FIG. 10-2. Example of Load Positive.

the operation, the contents of the receiving register are usually a positive number. If the sending register contains a negative number (the leftmost bit is a 1 bit), that number will be complemented to obtain the positive equivalent in the receiving register, and the condition code set to 2. If the sending register contains a positive number (the leftmost bit is a 0 bit), the operation proceeds as an ordinary Load Register, but the condition code is set to 2. In either case, however, if the receiving register, after the operation is done, contains 0, the condition code is set to 0, not 2. Overflow condition code 3 may occur if the sending register contains the maximum negative number. In that case an interrupt occurs, and the receiving register contents remain unchanged. This command is subject to interrupt because of overflow and is not available on small models of the computer. An example of Load Positive is shown in Fig. 10-2.

Do It Now Exercise 10-2. *Assume that register 4 contains in binary form the negative number −643. Write one imperative operation which will replace the register contents with the positive equivalent. Show the before-and-after contents of the register and the new status of the condition code.*

LNR—Load Negative. This RR command names the receiving register as the first-operand address, and the sending register as the second-operand address. The resulting contents of the receiving register are always a negative number. If the leftmost bit in the sending register is a 0, the contents are complemented to yield the binary negative equivalent for entry into the receiving register. If the leftmost bit is a 1, the operation proceeds as an ordinary Load Register, but the condition code is set. If the receiving register, after the operation, contains only 0 bits, the condition code is set to 0. If the contents of the receiving register are a negative number, the condition code is set to 1. Condition codes 2 and 3 are not used. No overflow is possible, because the maximum negative number that can be represented in a register is larger than the maximum positive number that can be represented in a register. This command is not subject to interruption and is not available on small models of the computer. An example of Load Negative is shown in Fig. 10-3.

Do It Now Exercise 10-3. *Prepare a flow diagram for a routine to place in register 3 the positive equivalent of the number in register 6, and in register 5 the negative equivalent of the number in register 6. Code the routine, and show the contents of the registers in each case if the quantity in register 6 is the binary equivalent of either plus or minus 9998. Make the routine as short as possible.*

LCR—Load Complement. This RR command names the receiving register as the first-operand address and the sending register as the second-operand address. The resulting contents of the receiving register are the complement of the contents of the sending register, be they positive or negative. The command works like a combination of Load Positive and Load Negative in that whatever the sending register

```
    LOC  OBJECT CODE   ADDR1 ADDR2  ST #  NAME   OP   OPERANDS          COMMENT
                                           IMPERATIVES

  00002A 9889 F100           00300   23           LM   8,9,NEG          LOAD REG.
  00002E 0560                        24           BALR 6,0              SAVE CONDITION CODE
  000030 1198                        25 F10#3     LNR  9,8              LOAD NEGATIVE
  000032 0570                        26           BALR 7,0              SAVE CONDITION CODE
  000034 9069 F120           00320   27           STM  6,9,CSAVE        SHOW REG. CONTENTS


                                           DECLARATIVES

  000300 00000001                    196 NEG      DC   F'1'             F10#3
  000304 000022EF                    197          DC   F'8943'          FILLER
  000308 4040404040404040            198          DC   CL24' '          FILLER
  000310 4040404040404040
  000318 4040404040404040
  000320 4040404040404040            199 CSAVE    DC   CL32' '          USED TO DISPLAY STORAGE
  000328 4040404040404040
  000330 4040404040404040
  000338 4040404040404040


                                           DUMP AFTER EXECUTION

  001BE0  F0404040  40404040  40404040  40404040  40404040  40404040  40404040  40404040
  001C00  00000001  000022EF  40404040  40404040  40404040  40404040  40404040  40404040
  001C20  60001930  50001934  00000001  FFFFFFFF  40404040  40404040  40404040  40404040
  001C40  F0404040  40404040  40404040  40404040  40404040  40404040  40404040  40404040


                                   RELOCATION FACTOR   001900
```

Fig. 10-3. Example of Load Negative.

```
    LOC  OBJECT CODE   ADDR1 ADDR2  ST #  NAME   OP   OPERANDS          COMMENT
                                           IMPERATIVES

  000038 9845 F180           00380   29           LM   4,5,COM          LOAD REG.
  00003C 0560                        30           BALR 6,0              SAVE CONDITION CODE
  00003E 1354                        31 F10#4     LCR  5,4              LOAD COMPLEMENT, REGISTER
  000040 0570                        32           BALR 7,0              SAVE CONDITION CODE
  000042 9047 F1A0           003A0   33           STM  4,7,CSTORE       SHOW REG. CONTENTS


                                           DECLARATIVES

  000380 0000A80D                    205 COM      DC   F'43021'         F10#4
  000384 00000000                    206          DC   F'0'             FILLER
  000388 4040404040404040            207          DC   CL24' '          FILLER
  000390 4040404040404040
  000398 4040404040404040
  0003A0 4040404040404040            208 CSTORE   DC   CL32' '          USED TO DISPLAY STORAGE
  0003A8 4040404040404040
  0003B0 4040404040404040
  0003B8 4040404040404040


                                           DUMP AFTER EXECUTION

  001C60  F0404040  40404040  40404040  40404040  40404040  40404040  40404040  40404040
  001C80  0000A80D  00000000  40404040  40404040  40404040  40404040  40404040  40404040
  001CA0  0000A80D  FFFF57F3  5000193E  50001942  40404040  40404040  40404040  40404040
  001CC0  F0404040  40404040  40404040  40404040  40404040  40404040  40404040  40404040


                                   RELOCATION FACTOR   001900
```

Fig. 10-4. Example of Load Complement.

contains is changed as it is copied into the receiving register, and the condition code is set. All 0-bit contents are simply copied unchanged from one register to the other. If the receiving register, after the operation, contains only 0 bits, the condition code is set to 0. If the receiving register contains a negative number, the condition code is set to 1. If it contains a positive number, the condition code is set to 2. Overflow is possible if the sending register contains the maximum negative number. In that case, an interrupt occurs, the receiving register contents are unaltered, and the condition code is set to 3. This command is subject to interrupt because of overflow, and is not available on small models of the computer. An example of Load Complement is shown in Fig. 10-4.

Do It Now Exercise 10-4. *Using the data and situation for Do It Now Exercise 10-3, prepare a flow diagram and the coding, using Load Complement to accomplish the operation. Show the resulting contents of the registers, and compare the number of imperative instructions needed to accomplish the job with those needed in Do It Now Exercise 10-3.*

LA—Load Address. This RX command differs considerably from the other load operations. The receiving-operand address is a register, but the sending-operand address does not name a field in storage in the usual way. A usual load register would copy the contents of the address named in storage into the register. In contrast, Load Address loads the absolute address itself as a positive binary number, and no data are copied from storage by the load-address operation. The contents of the register after a load-address operation are the address in the three low-order bytes. The leftmost byte of the register contents is eight 0 bits. The condition code is not set.

As the absolute address to be stored, the computer takes the effective address it calculates as the sending operand address. Hence, the address loaded by Load Address depends upon the contents of the base and index registers specified. And hence, in practice, the results of a Load Address change when the program containing the command is relocated in storage.

The major use for the Load Address command is to obtain in the form of a single binary number the absolute machine-language address of some field of data. This is convenient in loading base registers and in performing arithmetic and logic operations on an absolute address, since usually addresses are in a base-and-displacement form unusable as arithmetic or logic operands. Arithmetic and logic operations on addresses are sometimes essential for control purposes in programs. This command is not subject to interruption, and is not available on small models of the computer. An example of Load Address is shown in Fig. 10-5.

Do It Now Exercise 10-5. *Write one imperative operation needed to obtain in register 9 the absolute address of the instruction called GOTO.*

```
    LOC   OBJECT CODE    ADDR1 ADDR2  ST #   NAME    OP    OPERANDS              COMMENT
                                             IMPERATIVES

000046  5880 F200             00400   35             L     8,CCNT               LOAD A REG. WITH THE CONT. OF COUNT
00004A  4190 F200             00400   36 F10#5       LA    9,CCNT               LOAD REG. WITH ADDRESS OF 'COUNT'
00004E  9089 F220             00420   37             STM   8,9,CHOLD2           SHOW REG. CONTENTS


                                             DECLARATIVES

000400  000E5922                      214 CCNT       DC    F'940322'            F10#5
000404  404040404040404040            215            DC    CL28' '              FILLER
00040C  404040404040404040
000414  404040404040404040
00041C  40404040
000420  404040404040404040            216 CHOLD2     DC    CL32' '              USED TO DISPLAY STORAGE
000428  404040404040404040
000430  404040404040404040
000438  404040404040404040


                                             DUMP AFTER EXECUTION

001CE0  F0404040   40404040   40404040   40404040   40404040   40404040   40404040   40404040
001D00  000E5922   40404040   40404040   40404040   40404040   40404040   40404040   40404040
001D20  000E5922   00001D00   40404040   40404040   40404040   40404040   40404040   40404040
001D40  F0404040   40404040   40404040   40404040   40404040   40404040   40404040   40404040


                              RELOCATION FACTOR    001900
```

FIG. 10-5. Example of Load Address.

```
    LOC   OBJECT CODE    ADDR1 ADDR2  ST #   NAME    OP    OPERANDS              COMMENT
                                             IMPERATIVES

000052  5870 F280             00480   39             L     7,SHIFTLL            LOAD A REG
000056  8970 0008             00008   40 F10#6       SLL   7,8                  SHIFT LEFT LOGICAL
00005A  5070 F2A0             004A0   41             ST    7,CKEEP2             SHOW REG. CONTENTS


                                             DECLARATIVES

000480  05582F82                      222 SHIFTLL    DC    F'89665410'          F10#6
000484  404040404040404040            223            DC    CL28' '              FILLER
00048C  404040404040404040
000494  404040404040404040
00049C  40404040
0004A0  404040404040404040            224 CKEEP2     DC    CL32' '              USED TO DISPLAY STORAGE
0004A8  404040404040404040
0004B0  404040404040404040
0004B8  404040404040404040


                                             DUMP AFTER EXECUTION

001D60  F0404040   40404040   40404040   40404040   40404040   40404040   40404040   40404040
001D80  05582F82   40404040   40404040   40404040   40404040   40404040   40404040   40404040
001DA0  582F8200   40404040   40404040   40404040   40404040   40404040   40404040   40404040
001DC0  F0404040   40404040   40404040   40404040   40404040   40404040   40404040   40404040


                              RELOCATION FACTOR    001900
```

FIG. 10-6. Example of Shift Left Logical.

LOGICAL SHIFT

The logical-shift commands enable the programer to position bits in a register prior to or following other operations, using 0 bits for fill. For example, if the programer desires to move a condition-code setting, he can have the condition code copied into a register by a Branch and Link instruction. But to store it by itself in one byte of storage, the programer must shift left or right until the condition-code bits are isolated in a register in a byte with 0 bits. Then he can store the condition code by a Store Character or other instructions. Or he can use it without isolating it by means of a Test Under Mask as discussed later.

SLL—Shift Left Logical. This RS command functions in a manner very similar to the Shift Left Algebraic command described previously in Chap. 5. The major difference is that the sign bit in the register is treated not as a sign bit but as a data bit, and hence is shifted along with the other bits. Zero bits serve as fill on the right. The condition code is not set. The base-and-displacement portions of the instruction are not used as an address but are used as an indicator of the amount of the shift. This command is not subject to interruption, and is not available on small models of the computer. An example of Shift Left Logical is shown in Fig. 10-6.

SRL—Shift Right Logical. This RS operation is parallel in function to Shift Left Logical and to Shift Left Algebraic, as noted earlier. The content of the register is not assumed to be an algebraic magnitude, for the normal sign bit is treated as a data bit. Zero bits serve as fill on the left. The condition code is not set. This command is not subject to interruption, and is not available on small models of the computer. An example of Shift Right Logical is shown in Fig. 10-7.

Do It Now Exercise 10-6. *Prepare a flow diagram for a routine to take a full word of 1 bits and produce from it, through the use of shift logical operations, a word consisting of one byte of 0 bits, two bytes of 1 bits, and one byte of 0 bits, with the two bytes of 1 bits in the center of the word. Code the routine, and show the contents of the registers after each step in the process.*

SLDL—Shift Left Double Logical. This RS command operates in a manner parallel to Shift Left Logical and Shift Left Double Algebraic. The two registers are linked, and the register named as the operand address must be an even-numbered register. The odd-numbered register participating is the next-higher-numbered register. All bits are treated as data bits, and 0 bits are used as fill bits on the right. The condition code is not set. This command is subject to interruption from incorrect register specification, and is not available on small models of the computer. An example of Shift Left Double Logical is shown in Fig. 10-8.

SRDL—Shift Right Double Logical. This RS command operates in a manner parallel to Shift Right Logical and to Shift Right Double Algebraic, as described

```
      LOC   OBJECT CODE      ADDR1 ADDR2  ST #  NAME   OP   OPERANDS            COMMENT
                                                        IMPERATIVES

   00005E 5860 F300            00500    43            L     6,SHIFTRL          LOAD A REG.
   000062 8860 0002            00002    44  F10#7     SRL   6,2                SHIFT RIGHT LOGICAL
   000066 5060 F320            00520    45            ST    6,CSAVE2           SHOW REG. CONTENTS



                                                       DECLARATIVES

   000500 00008785                      230  SHIFTRL  DC    F'46981'           F10#7
   000504 4040404040404040              231           DC    CL28' '            FILLER
   00050C 4040404040404040
   000514 4040404040404040
   00051C 40404040
   000520 4040404040404040              232  CSAVE2   DC    CL32' '            USED TO DISPLAY STORAGE
   000528 4040404040404040
   000530 4040404040404040
   000538 4040404040404040



                                       DUMP AFTER EXECUTION

   001DE0   F0404040   40404040   40404040   40404040   40404040   40404040   40404040   40404040
   001E00   00008785   40404040   40404040   40404040   40404040   40404040   40404040   40404040
   001E20   00002DE1   40404040   40404040   40404040   40404040   40404040   40404040   40404040
   001E40   F0404040   40404040   40404040   40404040   40404040   40404040   40404040   40404040



                                 RELOCATION FACTOR    001900
```

FIG. 10-7. Example of Shift Right Logical.

previously. Two registers are linked, and the register named as the first operand must be an even-numbered register. The following odd-numbered register is the other register of the pair. All bits are treated as data bits, and 0 bits serve as fill on the left. The condition code is not set. This command is subject to interruption from incorrect register specification, and is not available on small models of the computer. An example of Shift Right Double Logical is shown in Fig. 10-9.

Do It Now Exercise 10-7. Prepare a flow diagram for a routine to have the computer convert a double word of alternating 0 and 1 bits (a 0 bit is the leftmost bit) into a half word of 0 bits, followed by four bytes of alternating 1 and 0 bits (a 1 bit is the leftmost bit), followed by one half word of 0 bits. Code the routine, using shift-double commands. Show the contents of the registers after each step in the operation.

LOGICAL ADD AND SUBTRACT

Binary arithmetic operations can be performed on the contents of registers or on data obtained from storage. Such arithmetic operations have been described previously in this book. However, in addition to doing those operations, the computer can also add and subtract data in a binary manner without regard to the actual code (EBCDIC, packed, or whatever) or to the presence of a bit serving as the algebraic sign. These add and subtract operations, referred to as logical add and logical sub-

```
  LOC   OBJECT CODE   ADDR1 ADDR2  ST #  NAME    OP   OPERANDS          COMMENT

                                          IMPERATIVES

00006A 9867 F380            00580   47            LM   6,7,DOUBLEL      LOAD REG.
00006E 8D60 000E            0000E   48  F10#8     SLDL 6,14             SHIFT LEFT DOUBLE LOGICAL
000072 9067 F3A0            005A0   49            STM  6,7,CSTORE2      SHOW REG. CONTENTS


                                          DECLARATIVES

000580 00DFFFDF                     238  DOUBLEL  DC   F'14680031'      F10#8
000584 FFFFFFFF                     239           DC   F'-1'            FILLER
000588 4040404040404040            240           DC   CL24' '          FILLER
000590 4040404040404040
000598 4040404040404040
0005A0 4040404040404040            241  CSTORE2  DC   CL32' '          USED TO DISPLAY STORAGE
0005A8 4040404040404040
0005B0 4040404040404040
0005B8 4040404040404040


                                      DUMP AFTER EXECUTION

001E60  F0404040   40404040   40404040   40404040   40404040   40404040   40404040   40404040
001E80  00DFFFDF   FFFFFFFF   40404040   40404040   40404040   40404040   40404040   40404040
001EA0  FFF7FFFF   FFFFC000   40404040   40404040   40404040   40404040   40404040   40404040
001EC0  F0404040   40404040   40404040   40404040   40404040   40404040   40404040   40404040


                                      RELOCATION FACTOR   001900
```

FIG. 10-8. Example of Shift Left Double Logical.

```
  LOC   OBJECT CODE   ADDR1 ADDR2  ST #  NAME    OP   OPERANDS          COMMENT

                                          IMPERATIVES

000076 9845 F400            00600   51            LM   4,5,DOUBLER      LOAD A REG.
00007A 8C40 0009            00009   52  F10#9     SRDL 4,9              SHIFT RIGHT DOUBLE LOGICAL
00007E 9045 F420            00620   53            STM  4,5,CHOLD3       SHOW REG. CONTENTS


                                          DECLARATIVES

000600 FFFFFFFF                     247  DOUBLER  DC   F'-1'            F10#9
000604 00000000                     248           DC   F'0'             FILLER
000608 4040404040404040            249           DC   CL24' '          FILLER
000610 4040404040404040
000618 4040404040404040
000620 4040404040404040            250  CHOLD3   DC   CL32' '          USED TO DISPLAY STORAGE
000628 4040404040404040
000630 4040404040404040
000638 4040404040404040


                                      DUMP AFTER EXECUTION

001EE0  F0404040   40404040   40404040   40404040   40404040   40404040   40404040   40404040
001F00  FFFFFFFF   00000000   40404040   40404040   40404040   40404040   40404040   40404040
001F20  007FFFFF   FF800000   40404040   40404040   40404040   40404040   40404040   40404040
001F40  F0404040   40404040   40404040   40404040   40404040   40404040   40404040   40404040


                                      RELOCATION FACTOR   001900
```

FIG. 10-9. Example of Shift Right Double Logical.

tract, recognize no algebraic sign. The computer treats all bits as data bits and handles the contents of the field or register without regard to algebraic signs.

Under these circumstances, the computer also sets the condition code differently. If the addition or subtraction produces a 1-bit carryout of the leftmost bit position (which would be partly the equivalent of arithmetic overflow), then the condition code is set to 2 or 3. If 0-bit carryout occurs, the condition code is set to 0 or 1. The choice between the numbers of these pairs depends on the resulting sum or difference. If the receiving register, after the operation, contains only 0 bits, the condition code is set to 0 or 2. If it contains any 1 bits the condition code is set to 1 or 3.

Among other uses, logical add and subtract commands make it possible for the programer to write routines for doing binary arithmetic operations on strings of bits of any length. For example, using logical add and subtract, the programer can write routines to add, subtract, multiply, and divide binary numbers 75 bits long.

ALR—Add Logical Register. This RR command performs a binary add operation on the contents of the register named as the first-operand address with the contents of the register named as the second-operand address. The sign bits are treated as data bits, not as sign bits. The contents of the second-operand register remain unchanged. The carry and the resulting zero or nonzero status of the first-operand register determine the setting of the condition code in the manner noted previously. This command is not subject to interrupt, and is not available on small models of the computer. An example of Add Logical Register is shown in Fig. 10-10.

AL—Add Logical. This RX command performs a binary add operation on the contents of the register named as the first-operand address. The second-operand address names an aligned full word in storage, which is unaltered by the operation. Sign bits are treated as if they were data bits. The condition code is set as a result of the carry and the zero or nonzero contents of the first-operand register, as noted above. This command is subject to interrupt from improper addressing, and is not available on small models of the computer. An example of Add Logical is shown in Fig. 10-11.

Do It Now Exercise 10-8. *Write the imperatives and declaratives needed to have the computer perform a logical add with the binary equivalents of the following numbers: -7, $+8$. Use the positive number as the contents of the first operand. Show the before-and-after contents of both operands. What is the decimal equivalent of the resulting logical sum?*

SLR—Subtract Logical Register. This RR command operates in the same manner as the Add Logical command, except that a subtraction is done instead of an addition. Condition code 0 is not used, however, since that combination of circumstances cannot arise in subtraction. Condition codes 1, 2, and 3 are set in the manner described previously. This command is not subject to interruption, and is

```
   LOC   OBJECT CODE    ADDR1 ADDR2  ST #  NAME    OP   OPERANDS         COMMENT
                                         IMPERATIVES

 000082  9845 F480         00680     55          LM   4,5,DADD         LOAD REG.
 000086  0530                        56          BALR 3,0              SAVE CONDITION CODE
 000088  1E54                        57  F10#10  ALR  5,4              ADD LOGICAL
 00008A  0560                        58          BALR 6,0              SAVE CONDITION CODE
 00008C  9036 F4A0         006A0     59          STM  3,6,DSAVE2       SHOW REG. CONTENTS


                                         DECLARATIVES

 000680  03D37D9F                    256 DADD    DC   F'64191903'      F10#10
 000684  48F0C1F6                    257         DC   CL4'.0A6'        FILLER
 000688  4040404040404040            258         DC   CL24' '          FILLER
 000690  4040404040404040
 000698  4040404040404040
 0006A0  4040404040404040            259 DSAVE2  DC   CL32' '          USED TO DISPLAY STORAGE
 0006A8  4040404040404040
 0006B0  4040404040404040
 0006B8  4040404040404040


                                     DUMP AFTER EXECUTION

 001F60  F0404040  40404040  40404040  40404040  40404040  40404040  40404040  40404040
 001F80  03D37D9F  48F0C1F6  40404040  40404040  40404040  40404040  40404040  40404040
 001FA0  50001988  03D37D9F  4FC43F95  5000198C  40404040  40404040  40404040  40404040
 001FC0  F0404040  40404040  40404040  40404040  40404040  40404040  40404040  40404040


                          RELOCATION FACTOR   001900
```

FIG. 10-10. Example of Add Logical Register.

```
   LOC   OBJECT CODE    ADDR1 ADDR2  ST #  NAME    OP   OPERANDS         COMMENT
                                         IMPERATIVES

 000090  5870 F500         00700     61          L    7,DADD1          LOAD REG.
 000094  0560                        62          BALR 6,0              SAVE CONDITION CODE
 000096  5E70 F504         00704     63  F10#11  AL   7,DADD2          ADD LOGICAL
 00009A  0580                        64          BALR 8,0              SAVE CONDITION CODE
 00009C  9068 F520         00720     65          STM  6,8,DSTORE2      SHOW REG. CONTENTS


                                         DECLARATIVES

 000700  00FF00FF                    265 DADD1   DC   X'00FF00FF'      F10#11
 000704  FF761D72                    266 DADD2   DC   F'-9036430'
 000708  4040404040404040            267         DC   CL24' '          FILLER
 000710  4040404040404040
 000718  4040404040404040
 000720  4040404040404040            268 DSTORE2 DC   CL32' '          USED TO DISPLAY STORAGE
 000728  4040404040404040
 000730  4040404040404040
 000738  4040404040404040


                                     DUMP AFTER EXECUTION

 001FE0  F0404040  40404040  40404040  40404040  40404040  40404040  40404040  40404040
 002000  00FF00FF  FF761D72  40404040  40404040  40404040  40404040  40404040  40404040
 002020  50001996  00751E71  7000199C  40404040  40404040  40404040  40404040  40404040
 002040  F0404040  40404040  40404040  40404040  40404040  40404040  40404040  40404040


                          RELOCATION FACTOR   001900
```

FIG. 10-11. Example of Add Logical.

```
        LOC  OBJECT CODE    ADDR1 ADDR2  ST #  NAME    OP    OPERANDS              COMMENT

                                                IMPERATIVES

      0000A0  9878 F580           00780   67            LM    7,8,DSUB             LOAD REG.
      0000A4  0560                        68            BALR  6,0                  SAVE CONDITION CODE
      0000A6  1F78                        69  F10#12    SLR   7,8                  SUBTRACT LOGICAL REG.
      0000A8  0590                        70            BALR  9,0                  SAVE CONDITION CODE
      0000AA  9069 F5A0           007A0   71            STM   6,9,DKEEP3           SHOW REG. CONTENTS


                                                DECLARATIVES

      000780  FFFFF43D                   274  DSUB      DC    F'-3011'             F10#12
      000784  FFFFF43D                   275            DC    F'-3011'             FILLER
      000788  4040404040404040           276            DC    CL24' '              FILLER
      000790  4040404040404040
      000798  4040404040404040
      0007A0  4040404040404040           277  DKEEP3    DC    CL32' '              USED TO DISPLAY STORAGE
      0007A8  4040404040404040
      0007B0  4040404040404040
      0007B8  4040404040404040


                                             DUMP AFTER EXECUTION

      002060  F0404040   40404040   40404040   40404040   40404040   40404040   40404040   40404040
      002080  FFFFF43D   FFFFF43D   40404040   40404040   40404040   40404040   40404040   40404040
      0020A0  700019A6   00000000   FFFFF43D   600019AA   40404040   40404040   40404040   40404040
      0020C0  F0404040   40404040   40404040   40404040   40404040   40404040   40404040   40404040


                                       RELOCATION FACTOR    001900
```

FIG. 10-12. Example of Subtract Logical Register.

```
        LOC  OBJECT CODE    ADDR1 ADDR2  ST #  NAME    OP    OPERANDS              COMMENT

                                                IMPERATIVES

      0000AE  5890 F600           00800   73            L     9,DSUB1              LOAD REG.
      0000B2  0580                        74            BALR  8,0                  SAVE CONDITION CODE
      0000B4  5F90 F604           00804   75  F10#13    SL    9,DSUB2              SUBTRACT LOGICAL
      0000B8  05A0                        76            BALR  10,0                 SAVE CONDITION CODE
      0000BA  908A F620           00820   77            STM   8,10,DHOLD3          SHOW REG. CONTENTS


                                                DECLARATIVES

      000800  FFFFFFFC                   283  DSUB1     DC    F'-4'                F10#13
      000804  000F6736                   284  DSUB2     DC    F'1009462'
      000808  4040404040404040           285            DC    CL24' '              FILLER
      000810  4040404040404040
      000818  4040404040404040
      000820  4040404040404040           286  DHOLD3    DC    CL32' '              USED TO DISPLAY STORAGE
      000828  4040404040404040
      000830  4040404040404040
      000838  4040404040404040


                                             DUMP AFTER EXECUTION

      0020E0  F0404040   40404040   40404040   40404040   40404040   40404040   40404040   40404040
      002100  FFFFFFFC   000F6736   40404040   40404040   40404040   40404040   40404040   40404040
      002120  600019B4   FFF098C6   700019BA   40404040   40404040   40404040   40404040   40404040
      002140  F0404040   40404040   40404040   40404040   40404040   40404040   40404040   40404040


                                       RELOCATION FACTOR    001900
```

FIG. 10-13. Example of Subtract Logical.

not available on small models of the computer. An example of Subtract Logical Register is shown in Fig. 10-12.

SL—Subtract Logical. This RX command is parallel in its operation to Subtract Logical Register, described previously. The first-operand address named is a register, and the second-operand address, which is not altered by the operation, is an aligned full word in storage. The setting of the condition code follows the same pattern as for Subtract Logical Register. This command is subject to interrupt from improper addressing, and is not available on small models of the computer. An example of Subtract Logical is shown in Fig. 10-13.

Do It Now Exercise 10-9. *Using the same data and situation as in Do It Now Exercise 10-8, have the computer perform a Subtract Logical operation. Show the operand contents before and after. What is the decimal equivalent of the logical difference?*

BIT MANIPULATION

TM—Test Under Mask. This SI command uses a literal called a mask (the second operand) in the instruction itself to test the 0 or 1 status of the bits in one byte of storage (the first operand). The condition code is set. If the bits selected by the mask are all 0 bits, the condition code is set to 0. If no bits are selected, the condition code is also set to 0. If the bits selected are some 0 and some 1 bits, the condition code is set to 1. If all of the bits selected are 1 bits, the condition code is set to 3. Condition code 2 is not used. This command is subject to interrupt from improper addressing, and is available on all models of the computer.

The operation of Test Under Mask merits some discussion. The mask itself consists of one byte incorporated in the instruction itself as the second operand. Typically this operand is written as a decimal number in the range of 0 through 255 to correspond with the bit positions of the binary number needed to represent the decimal number. Thus, if the decimal number written as the second operand be zero, then the mask consists only of 0 bits (00_x). If the decimal number, for example, be written as 15, the mask will consist of four 0 bits followed by four 1 bits ($0F_x$). If, for example, the mask be specified as 255, then the resulting bit pattern will consist of eight 1 bits (FF_x).

In function, the 0 bits in the mask are interpreted as meaning that the corresponding bit positions in the byte in storage are not to be tested. A 1 bit in the mask is interpreted as meaning that the bit in the corresponding position in the storage byte is to be tested. A programer can think of the 0 bits in the mask as being like doors hinged on their centers. If he can see the face of the door (a 0), he cannot see past it to the corresponding bit position in storage—the door is closed. If the door is in the open position, so that he see the edge (a 1), not the face, then he can see through beyond the door to the corresponding bit position in storage. The bits he can

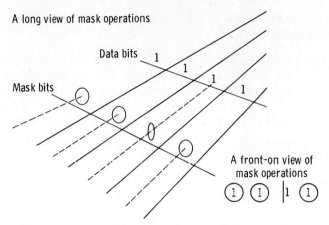

A long view of mask operations

Data bits

Mask bits

A front-on view of
mask operations

Note: Zero (0) bits in the mask are like closed doors; one (1) bits in
the mask are like open doors permitting a view of the corresponding
data bit.

FIG. 10-14. Relation of mask bits and data bits.

```
        LOC   OBJECT CODE      ADDR1 ADDR2  ST #  NAME    OP    OPERANDS              COMMENT

                                                        IMPERATIVES

        0000BE 0560                           79          BALR  6,0                  SAVE CONDITION CODE
        0000C0 9123 F680        00880          80  F10#15  TM    TEST2,35             TEST UNDER MASK
        0000C4 0570                            81          BALR  7,0                  SAVE CONDITION CODE
        0000C6 9067 F6A0              008A0    82          STM   6,7,CKEEP3           SHOW REG. CONTENTS
        0000CA D200 F6B4 20BF  00884 000C1    83          MVC   CKEEP3+20(1),F10#15+1  SHOW THE MASK USED


                                                        DECLARATIVES

        000880 BC                             292  TEST2   DC    X'BC'                F10#15
        000881 000000                         293          DC    X'000000'            FILLER
        000884 4040404040404040              294          DC    CL28' '              FILLER
        00088C 4040404040404040
        000894 4040404040404040
        00089C 40404040
        0008A0 4040404040404040              295  CKEEP3  DC    CL32' '              USED TO DISPLAY STORAGE
        0008A8 4040404040404040
        0008B0 4040404040404040
        0008B8 4040404040404040


                                                     DUMP AFTER EXECUTION

        002160  F0404040     40404040    40404040    40404040     40404040    40404040    40404040    40404040
        002180  BC000000     40404040    40404040    40404040     40404040    40404040    40404040    40404040
        0021A0  700019C0     500019C6    40404040    40404040     40404040    23404040    40404040    40404040
        0021C0  F0404040     40404040    40404040    40404040     40404040    40404040    40404040    40404040


                                              RELOCATION FACTOR    001900
```

FIG. 10-15. Example of Test Under Mask.

see are said to be the "selected bits" in storage. For a bit to be selected, therefore, the mask bit in the corresponding position of the mask must be a 1 bit. This is illustrated in Fig. 10-14. Thus, for example, the condition code in a word produced by a Branch and Link can be determined using two Test Under Mask instructions. An example of Test Under Mask is shown in Fig. 10-15.

For use with the Test Under Mask command, three mnemonic conditional transfer of control commands are available for medium or large models of the computer. All of these are actually Branch Conditionally instructions with the first operand omitted. BO (Branch on Ones) tests whether the condition code is set to 3, BM (Branch on Mixed) tests whether the condition code is set to 1, and BZ (Branch on Zeros) tests whether the condition code is set to 0. It should be noted that these are identical to BO (Branch on Overflow), BM (Branch on Minus), and BZ (Branch on Zero), used for arithmetic operations as shown in Fig. 6-20. The availability of these extended mnemonics is only a convenience to the programer and does not in any way alter the way in which the computer tests or alters the condition code.

The programer typically uses the Test Under Mask in conjunction with the logical operation of AND, OR, and Exclusive OR. These logical operations are available in the medium and large models of the computer in the form of four commands for each operation, one of each of the types RR, RX, SS, and SI. In small models of the computer only the SI type is available and that only for AND and OR. These logical operations enable the programer to have the computer alter or set the value of any bit in storage or in a register. In each of the sections that follow, a presentation is first made of the bit changes done by the logical operation involved. Then the four commands capable of doing this bit manipulation are presented. Each has two operands and the receiving operand is altered.

Each sets the condition code as follows: 0 if all of the resulting bits are 0 bits and 1 if any of the resulting bits is a 1 bit. Condition codes 2 and 3 are not used for logical AND, OR, Exclusive OR.

A logical AND operation can be described as follows: If a 1 bit is combined with a 1 bit, the result is a 1 bit. All other combinations of bits result in 0 bits. This is summarized in Fig. 10-16. A major value of logical AND is that it can be used to set a bit to 0 by combining whatever it is now with a 0 bit in a logical AND operation.

Bits In		Result
1st	2d	
0	0	0
0	1	0
1	0	0
1	1	1

Fɪɢ. 10-16. Logical AND.

```
   LOC  OBJECT CODE      ADDR1 ADDR2  ST #  NAME    OP   OPERANDS        COMMENT

                                            IMPERATIVES

 0000D0 9867 F700          00900     85            LM   6,7,ANDRR       LOAD REG.
 0000D4 0580                         86            BALR 8,0             SAVE CONDITION CODE
 0000D6 1476                         87  F10#17    NR   7,6             AND REG.
 0000D8 0590                         88            BALR 9,0             SAVE CONDITION CODE
 0000DA 9069 F720          00920     89            STM  6,9,CSAVE3      SHOW REG. CONTENTS


                                            DECLARATIVES

 000900 00000400                     301 ANDRR     DC   F'1024'         F10#17
 000904 000004F9                     302           DC   F'1273'         FILLER
 000908 4040404040404040             303           DC   CL24' '         FILLER
 000910 4040404040404040
 000918 4040404040404040
 000920 4040404040404040             304 CSAVE3    DC   CL32' '         USED TO DISPLAY STORAGE
 000928 4040404040404040
 000930 4040404040404040
 000938 4040404040404040


                                       DUMP AFTER EXECUTION

 0021E0 F0404040  40404040  40404040  40404040  40404040  40404040  40404040  40404040
 002200 00000400  000004F9  40404040  40404040  40404040  40404040  40404040  40404040
 002220 00000400  00000400  500019D6  500019DA  40404040  40404040  40404040  40404040
 002240 F0404040  40404040  40404040  40404040  40404040  40404040  40404040  40404040


                                   RELOCATION FACTOR   001900
```

Fig. 10-17. Example of AND Registers.

NR—AND Registers. This RR command performs the logical AND operation on the contents of the registers named as the two operand addresses. The contents of the first-operand address are altered. The contents of the second-operand address are unaffected by the operation. The condition code is set as described previously. This command is not subject to interrupt, and is not available on small models of the computer. An example of AND Registers is shown in Fig. 10-17.

Do It Now Exercise 10-10. *Prepare a flow diagram for a routine to make every other bit in register 6 a 0 bit, starting with the bit at the leftmost position. Leave the other bits unchanged. Code the routine and show the contents of the registers before and after the operation for whatever data you assume them to contain.*

N—AND. This RX command performs the logical AND operation on the contents of the register named as the first-operand address. The word of data named as the second-operand address is unaffected by the operation. The condition code is set as described previously. This command is subject to interrupt from improper addressing, and is not available on small models of the computer. An example of AND is shown in Fig. 10-18.

Do It Now Exercise 10-11. *Prepare a flow diagram for a routine to set the leftmost bit of each byte in a word to 0. Store this word back, replacing its original form in storage. Code the routine, and show the contents of storage before and after.*

```
   LOC   OBJECT CODE     ADDR1 ADDR2   ST #   NAME      OP    OPERANDS           COMMENT

                                              IMPERATIVES

  0000DE 5850 F780              00980   91              L     5,ANDRS            LOAD A REG.
  0000E2 0560                           92              BALR  6,0                SAVE CONDITION CODE
  0000E4 5450 F784              00984   93 F10#18       N     5,ANDRS2           AND REG. AND STORAGE
  0000E8 0570                           94              BALR  7,0                SAVE CONDITION CODE
  0000EA 9057 F7A0              009A0   95              STM   5,7,CSTORE3        SHOW REG. CONTENTS



                                              DECLARATIVES

  000980 00000101                      310 ANDRS        DC    F'257'            F10#18
  000984 00000208                      311 ANDRS2       DC    F'520'
  000988 4040404040404040              312             DC    CL24' '            FILLER
  000990 4040404040404040
  000998 4040404040404040
  0009A0 4040404040404040              313 CSTORE3      DC    CL32' '            USED TO DISPLAY STORAGE
  0009A8 4040404040404040
  0009B0 4040404040404040
  0009B8 4040404040404040



                                        DUMP AFTER EXECUTION

  002260  F0404040    40404040    40404040    40404040    40404040    40404040    40404040    40404040
  002280  00000101    00000208    40404040    40404040    40404040    40404040    40404040    40404040
  0022A0  00000000    500019E4    400019EA    40404040    40404040    40404040    40404040    40404040
  0022C0  F0404040    40404040    40404040    40404040    40404040    40404040    40404040    40404040


                                   RELOCATION FACTOR   001900
```

FIG. 10-18. Example of AND.

```
   LOC   OBJECT CODE        ADDR1 ADDR2    ST #   NAME     OP    OPERANDS            COMMENT

                                                  IMPERATIVES

  0000EE D204 F820 F802 00A20 00A02       97              MVC   CHOLD4(5),ANC1-1   SHOW CONTENTS OF STORAGE
  0000F4 0580                             98              BALR  8,0                SAVE CONDITION CODE
  0000F6 D402 F803 F800 00A03 00A00       99 F10#19       NC    ANC1(3),ANDC       AND CHARACTERS
  0000FC 0590                            100              BALR  9,0                SAVE CONDITION CODE
  0000FE 9089 F830             00A30     101              STM   8,9,CHOLD4+16      SHOW REG. CONTENTS



                                                  DECLARATIVES

  000A00 00F611                          319 ANDC        DC    XL3'F611'          F10#19
  000A03 034A0C                          320 ANC1        DC    XL3'34A0C'
  000A06 4040404040404040                321             DC    CL26' '            FILLER
  000A0E 4040404040404040
  000A16 4040404040404040
  000A1E 4040
  000A20 4040404040404040                322 CHOLD4      DC    CL32' '            USED TO DISPLAY STORAGE
  000A28 4040404040404040
  000A30 4040404040404040
  000A38 4040404040404040



                                          DUMP AFTER EXECUTION

  0022E0  F0404040    40404040    40404040    40404040    40404040    40404040    40404040    40404040
  002300  00F61100    42004040    40404040    40404040    40404040    40404040    40404040    40404040
  002320  11034A0C    40404040    40404040    40404040    400019F6    500019FE    40404040    40404040
  002340  F0404040    40404040    40404040    40404040    40404040    40404040    40404040    40404040


                                     RELOCATION FACTOR   001900
```

FIG. 10-19. Example of AND Characters.

NC—AND Characters. This SS command performs the logical AND operation on bytes of data in storage. The contents of the first-operand address are altered; the contents of the second-operand address named are unaltered by the operation. The length of the receiving first operand determines the number of bytes used by both operands. The condition code is set as by the And Register command. This command is subject to interrupt from improper addressing, and is not available on small models of the computer. An example of AND Characters is shown in Fig. 10-19.

Do It Now Exercise 10-12. *Taking the data and situation of Do It Now Exercise 10-11, code the routines, using And Characters to perform the same operation. Show the contents of storage. Compare the count of the number of declaratives and imperatives needed in both exercises to accomplish the job.*

NI—AND Immediate. This SI command performs the logical AND operation on the one byte of storage data named by the first-operand address. The second operand is a literal which is normally written as a decimal number in the range of 0 through 255 and is unaffected by the operation. The condition code is set as by the AND Register command. This command is subject to interruption from improper addressing, and is available on all models of the computer. An example of AND Immediate is shown in Fig. 10-20.

```
     LOC   OBJECT CODE      ADDR1 ADDR2   ST #   NAME     OP    OPERANDS              COMMENT
                                                IMPERATIVES
    000102 D200 F8A0 F880 00AA0 00A80    103             MVC   CKEEP4(1),CBYTE       SHOW CONTENTS OF STORAGE
    000108 0540                          104             BALR  4,0                   SAVE CONDITION CODE
    00010A 9418 F880        00A80        105   F10#20    NI    CBYTE,24              AND IMMEDIATE
    00010E 0550                          106             BALR  5,0                   SAVE CONDITION CODE
    000110 9045 F8A4              00AA4  107             STM   4,5,CKEEP4+4          SHOW REG. CONTENTS
    000114 D200 F8B0 2109 00AB0 0010B    108             MVC   CKEEP4+16(1),F10#20+1 SHOW IMMEDIATE BYTE


                                                DECLARATIVES

    000A80 1B                            328   CBYTE     DC    X'1B'                 F10#20
    000A81 4040404040404040              329             DC    CL31' '               FILLER
    000A89 4040404040404040
    000A91 4040404040404040
    000A99 40404040404040
    000AA0 4040404040404040              330   CKEEP4    DC    CL32' '               USED TO DISPLAY STORAGE
    000AA8 4040404040404040
    000AB0 4040404040404040
    000AB8 4040404040404040


                                                DUMP AFTER EXECUTION

    002360  F0404040    40404040    40404040    40404040    40404040    40404040    40404040    40404040
    002380  1B404040    40404040    40404040    40404040    40404040    40404040    40404040    40404040
    0023A0  1B404040    50001A0A    50001A10    40404040    1B404040    40404040    40404040    40404040
    0023C0  F0404040    40404040    40404040    40404040    40404040    40404040    40404040    40404040


                               RELOCATION FACTOR    001900
```

FIG. 10-20. Example of AND Immediate.

Do It Now Exercise 10-13. *Write the imperatives and declaratives needed to alter the two middlemost bits of the second to the rightmost byte in a word to consist of 0 bits. For whatever data you assume, show the before-and-after contents of storage.*

The logical OR operation can be described as follows: If a 1 bit is combined with a 0 bit or a 1 bit, the result is a 1 bit. Only if a 0 bit is combined with a 0 bit is the result a 0 bit. This is summarized in Fig. 10-21. From that table it is apparent that the logical OR operation can be used to set any bit to a 1 bit, because a 1 bit plus either a 0 or a 1 bit becomes a 1 bit. Thus the OR operations can be used as a substitute for Move Zones when the zones are F_x.

Bits		Result
1st	2d	
0	0	0
0	1	1
1	0	1
1	1	1

Fig. 10-21. Logical OR.

OR—OR Registers. This RR command performs the logical OR operation on the contents of the registers named as the two operands. The contents of the first-operand address are altered. The contents of the second-operand address are un-affected by the operation. The condition code is set as described previously. This command is not subject to interrupt, and is not available on small models of the computer. An example of OR Registers is shown in Fig. 10-22.

Do It Now Exercise 10-14. *Using the data from Do It Now Exercise 10-10, write the imperatives and declaratives needed to cause the bits that were to be 0 bits to become 1 bits. Show the content of the registers for each step.*

O—OR. This RX command performs the logical OR operation on the contents of the register named by the first-operand address. The word of data named by the second-operand address is unaffected by the operation. The condition code is set as described previously. This command is subject to interrupt from improper address-ing, and is not available on small models of the computer. An example of OR is shown in Fig. 10-23.

Do It Now Exercise 10-15. *Code again the operations in Do It Now Exercise 10-11, substituting 1 bits for 0 bits. Show the content of storage and of the registers for each step.*

OC—OR Characters. This SS command performs the logical OR operations on bytes of data in storage. The contents of the first-operand address are altered

```
     LOC   OBJECT CODE    ADDR1 ADDR2  ST #  NAME    OP    OPERANDS           COMMENT
                                          IMPERATIVES

   00011A 9856 F900             00B00   110          LM    5,6,ORR1          LOAD REG.
   00011E 0570                          111          BALR  7,0               SAVE CONDITION CODE
   000120 1665                          112 F10#22   OR    6,5               OR REG.
   000122 0580                          113          BALR  8,0               SAVE CONDITION CODE
   000124 9058 F920             00B20   114          STM   5,8,CSAVE4        SHOW REG. CONTENTS


                                          DECLARATIVES

   000B00 00313184                       336 ORR1    DC    F'3223940'        F10#22
   000B04 00313184                       337         DC    F'3223940'        FILLER
   000B08 4040404040404040               338         DC    CL24' '           FILLER
   000B10 4040404040404040
   000B18 4040404040404040
   000B20 4040404040404040               339 CSAVE4  DC    CL32' '           USED TO DISPLAY STORAGE
   000B28 4040404040404040
   000B30 4040404040404040
   000B38 4040404040404040


                                      DUMP AFTER EXECUTION

   0023E0  F0404040   40404040   40404040   40404040   40404040   40404040   40404040   40404040
   002400  00313184   00313184   40404040   40404040   40404040   40404040   40404040   40404040
   002420  00313184   00313184   50001A20   50001A24   40404040   40404040   40404040   40404040
   002440  F0404040   40404040   40404040   40404040   40404040   40404040   40404040   40404040


                                  RELOCATION FACTOR   001900
```

FIG. 10-22. Example of OR Registers.

```
     LOC   OBJECT CODE    ADDR1 ADDR2  ST #  NAME    OP    OPERANDS           COMMENT
                                          IMPERATIVES

   000128 5890 F980             00B80   116          L     9,ORS1            LOAD A REG.
   00012C 0570                          117          BALR  7,0               SAVE CONDITION CODE
   00012E 5690 F984             00B84   118 F10#23   O     9,ORS2            OR A REG. AND STORAGE
   000132 0580                          119          BALR  8,0               SAVE CONDITION CODE
   000134 9079 F9A0             00BA0   120          STM   7,9,CSTORE4       SHOW REG. CONTENTS


                                          DECLARATIVES

   000B80 00000000                       345 ORS1    DC    F'0'              F10#23
   000B84 00000000                       346 ORS2    DC    F'0'
   000B88 4040404040404040               347         DC    CL24' '           FILLER
   000B90 4040404040404040
   000B98 4040404040404040
   000BA0 4040404040404040               348 CSTORE4 DC    CL32' '           USED TO DISPLAY STORAGE
   000BA8 4040404040404040
   000BB0 4040404040404040
   000BB8 4040404040404040


                                      DUMP AFTER EXECUTION

   002460  F0404040   40404040   40404040   40404040   40404040   40404040   40404040   40404040
   002480  00000000   00000000   40404040   40404040   40404040   40404040   40404040   40404040
   0024A0  50001A2E   40001A34   00000000   40404040   40404040   40404040   40404040   40404040
   0024C0  F0404040   40404040   40404040   40404040   40404040   40404040   40404040   40404040


                                  RELOCATION FACTOR   001900
```

FIG. 10-23. Example of OR.

by the operation; the contents of the second-operand address are unaltered. The length of the first operand controls the number of bytes utilized in both operands. The condition code is set as described previously. This command is subject to interrupt from improper addressing, and is not available on small models of the computer. An example of OR Characters is shown in Fig. 10-24.

```
  LOC  OBJECT CODE      ADDR1 ADDR2  ST #  NAME   OP   OPERANDS              COMMENT

                                           IMPERATIVES

000138 D202 FA20 FA04 00C20 00C04   122           MVC  CHOLD5(3),ORC2       SHOW CONTENTS OF STORAGE
00013E 0560                         123           BALR 6,0                  SAVE CONDITION CODE
000140 D602 FA04 FA00 00C04 00C00   124  F10#24   OC   ORC2(3),ORC1         OR CHARACTERS
000146 0570                         125           BALR 7,0                  SAVE CONDITION CODE
000148 9067 FA30            00C30   126           STM  6,7,CHOLD5+16        SHOW REG. CONTENTS


                                           DECLARATIVES

000C00 0009C10F                     354  ORC1     DC   XL4'9C10F'           F10#24
000C04 A11B09                       355  ORC2     DC   XL3'A11B09'
000C07 404040404040404040           356          DC   CL25' '              FILLER
000C0F 404040404040404040
000C17 404040404040404040
000C1F 40
000C20 404040404040404040           357  CHOLD5   DC   CL32' '              USED TO DISPLAY STORAGE
000C28 404040404040404040
000C30 404040404040404040
000C38 404040404040404040


                                           DUMP AFTER EXECUTION

0024E0 F0404040    40404040    40404040   40404040   40404040   40404040   40404040   40404040
002500 0009C10F    A11BC940    40404040   40404040   40404040   40404040   40404040   40404040
002520 A11B0940    40404040    40404040   40404040   40001A40   50001A48   40404040   40404040
002540 F0404040    40404040    40404040   40404040   40404040   40404040   40404040   40404040


                          RELOCATION FACTOR   001900
```

FIG. 10-24. Example of OR Characters.

Do It Now Exercise 10-16. *Perform again the operation in Do It Now Exercise 10-12, placing 1 bits where the 0 bits were called for. Show the contents of storage.*

OI—OR Immediate. This SI command performs the logical OR operation on the one byte of storage data named by the first-operand address. The second operand is a literal, which is normally written as a decimal number within the range 0 through 255, and is unaffected by the operation. The condition code is set as described previously. This command is subject to interruption from improper addressing, and is available on all models of the computer. An example of OR Immediate is shown in Fig. 10-25.

Do It Now Exercise 10-17. *Code again the operation specified in Do It Now Exercise 10-13, placing 1 bits wherever 0 bits were specified. Show the contents of storage.*

The Exclusive OR operation can be described as follows: If a 0 bit is combined with a 1 bit, the result is a 1 bit. If two 1 bits or two 0 bits are combined, the

```
     LOC   OBJECT CODE      ADDR1 ADDR2  ST #  NAME   OP   OPERANDS                COMMENT

                                         IMPERATIVES

   00014C D200 E020 E000 00CA0 00C80    128          MVC  CKEEP5(1),CONE          SHOW CONTENTS OF STORAGE
   000152 0580                          129          BALR 8,0                     SAVE CONDITION CODE
   000154 96FF E000          00C80      130  F10#25  OI   CONE,255                OR IMMEDIATE
   000158 0590                          131          BALR 9,0                     SAVE CONDITION CODE
   00015A 9089 E024          00CA4      132          STM  8,9,CKEEP5+4            SHOW REG. CONTENTS
   00015E D200 E030 2153 00C80 00155    133          MVC  CKEEP5+16(1),F10#25+1   SHOW IMMEDIATE BYTE


                                        DECLARATIVES

   000C80 00                            363  CONE    DC   X'00'                   F10#25
   000C81 4040404040404040              364          DC   CL31' '                 FILLER
   000C89 4040404040404040
   000C91 4040404040404040
   000C99 4040404040404040
   000CA0 4040404040404040              365  CKEEP5  DC   CL32' '                 USED TO DISPLAY STORAGE
   000CA8 4040404040404040
   000CB0 4040404040404040
   000CB8 4040404040404040


                                     DUMP AFTER EXECUTION

   002560 F0404040  40404040   40404040   40404040    40404040  40404040   40404040   40404040
   002580 FF404040  40404040   40404040   40404040    40404040  40404040   40404040   40404040
   0025A0 00404040  50001A54   50001A5A   40404040    FF404040  40404040   40404040   40404040
   0025C0 F0404040  40404040   40404040   40404040    40404040  40404040   40404040   40404040


                             RELOCATION FACTOR    001900
```

FIG. 10-25. Example of OR Immediate.

Bits	In	Result
Ist	2d	
0	0	0
0	1	1
1	0	1
1	1	0

FIG. 10-26. Exclusive OR.

result is a 0 bit. This is summarized in Fig. 10-26. As can be seen from the table, a 1 bit, when combined with either a 0 or a 1 bit, will yield the opposite of what the 1 bit was combined with. Thus Exclusive OR can be used to invert bits.

XR—Exclusive OR Registers. This RR command performs the Exclusive OR operation on the contents of the registers named as the two operands. The contents of the first-operand address are altered. The contents of the second-operand address are unaffected. The condition code is set as described previously. This command is not subject to interrupt, and is not available on small models of the computer. An example of Exclusive OR Register is shown in Fig. 10-27.

Do It Now Exercise 10-18. *Prepare the flow diagram for a routine for the taking of a two's complement of the binary equivalent of +10006 in register 7, placing the two's complement in register 8. Code the routine, using the Exclusive OR*

```
    LOC   OBJECT CODE     ADDR1 ADDR2  ST #   NAME     OP   OPERANDS              COMMENT
                                                IMPERATIVES

  000164  9845 E080             00D00  135             LM   4,5,EXOR             LOAD REG.
  000168  0560                          136            BALR 6,0                  SAVE CONDITION CODE
  00016A  1754                          137  F10#27    XR   5,4                  EXCLUSIVE OR REG.
  00016C  0570                          138            BALR 7,0                  SAVE CONDITION CODE
  00016E  9047 E0A0             00D20   139            STM  4,7,CSAVE5           SHOW REG. CONTENTS


                                                DECLARATIVES

  000D00  000001F3                      371  EXOR      DC   F'499'               F10#27
  000D04  00000808                      372            DC   F'2056'              FILLER
  000D08  404040404040404040            373            DC   CL24' '              FILLER
  000D10  404040404040404040
  000D18  404040404040404040
  000D20  404040404040404040            374  CSAVE5    DC   CL32' '              USED TO DISPLAY STORAGE
  000D28  404040404040404040
  000D30  404040404040404040
  000D38  404040404040404040


                                             DUMP AFTER EXECUTION

  0025E0  F0404040   40404040   40404040   40404040   40404040   40404040   40404040   40404040
  002600  000001F3   00000808   40404040   40404040   40404040   40404040   40404040   40404040
  002620  000001F3   000009FB   50001A6A   50001A6E   40404040   40404040   40404040   40404040
  002640  F0404040   40404040   40404040   40404040   40404040   40404040   40404040   40404040


                                     RELOCATION FACTOR   001900
```

FIG. 10-27. Example of Exclusive OR Registers.

Registers command and such other imperatives and declaratives as are needed to do this by instructions (not including Load Complement).

X—Exclusive OR. This RX command performs the logical Exclusive OR operation on the contents of the register named as the first-operand address. The contents of the word of data in storage named as the second-operand address are unaffected by the operation. The condition code is set as described previously. This command is subject to interrupt from improper addressing, and is not available on small models of the computer. An example of the Exclusive OR is shown in Fig. 10-28.

Do It Now Exercise 10-19. *Taking the data and situations from Do It Now Exercise 10-18, code again the operation, using RX rather than RR commands. Show the contents of storage.*

XC—Exclusive OR Characters. This SS command performs the logical Exclusive OR operation on bytes of data in storage. The contents of the first-operand address named are altered by the operation; the contents of the second-operand address are unaltered. The length of the first operand determines the number of bytes used by both operands. The condition code is set as described previously. This command is subject to interrupt from improper addressing, and is not available on small models of the computer. An example of Exclusive OR Characters is shown in Fig. 10-29. Exclusive ORing an operand with itself clears it to 0 bits.

```
LOC   OBJECT CODE   ADDR1 ADDR2  ST #  NAME     OP    OPERANDS          COMMENT
                                     IMPERATIVES

000172 5860 E100          00D80  141           L     6,EXOS1           LOAD A REG.
000176 0570                      142           BALR  7,0               SAVE CONDITION CODE
000178 5760 E104          00D84  143  F10#28   X     6,EXOS2           EXCLUSIVE OR REG. AND STORAGE
00017C 0580                      144           BALR  8,0               SAVE CONDITION CODE
00017E 9068 E120          00DA0  145           STM   6,8,CSTORE5       SHOW REG. CONTENTS


                                     DECLARATIVES

000D80 00000080                  380  EXOS1    DC    F'176'            F10#28
000D84 00000080                  381  EXOS2    DC    F'176'
000D88 40404040404040            382           DC    CL24' '           FILLER
000D90 4040404040404040
000D98 4040404040404040
000DA0 4040404040404040          383  CSTORE5  DC    CL32' '           USED TO DISPLAY STORAGE
000DA8 4040404040404040
000DB0 4040404040404040
000DB8 4040404040404040


                                 DUMP AFTER EXECUTION

002660  F0404040  40404040  40404040  40404040     40404040  40404040  40404040  40404040
002680  00000080  00000080  40404040  40404040     40404040  40404040  40404040  40404040
0026A0  00000000  50001A78  40001A7E  40404040     40404040  40404040  40404040  40404040
0026C0  F0404040  40404040  40404040  40404040     40404040  40404040  40404040  40404040


                          RELOCATION FACTOR  001900
```

FIG. 10-28. Example of Exclusive OR.

```
LOC   OBJECT CODE        ADDR1 ADDR2  ST #  NAME    OP    OPERANDS         COMMENT
                                       IMPERATIVES

000182 0203 E1A0 E184  00E20 00E04  147          MVC   CHOLD6(4),EXOC2  SHOW CONTENTS OF STORAGE
000188 0540                         148          BALR  4,0              SAVE CONDITION CODE
00018A D703 E184 E180  00E04 00E00  149  F10#29  XC    EXOC2(4),EXOC1   EXCLUSIVE OR CHARACTERS
000190 0550                         150          BALR  5,0              SAVE CONDITION CODE
000192 9045 E1A8             00E28  151          STM   4,5,CHOLD6+8     SHOW REG. CONTENTS


                                    DECLARATIVES

000E00 00099D62                     389  EXOC1   DC    F'630114'        F10#29
000E04 A911CD8B                     390  EXOC2   DC    XL4'A911CD8B'
000E08 40404040404040               391          DC    CL24' '          FILLER
000E10 4040404040404040
000E18 4040404040404040
000E20 4040404040404040             392  CHOLD6  DC    CL32' '          USED TO DISPLAY STORAGE
000E28 4040404040404040
000E30 4040404040404040
000E38 4040404040404040


                                DUMP AFTER EXECUTION

0026E0  F0404040  40404040  40404040  40404040     40404040  40404040  40404040  40404040
002700  00099D62  A91850E9  40404040  40404040     40404040  40404040  40404040  40404040
002720  A911CD8B  40404040  40001A8A  50001A92     40404040  40404040  40404040  40404040
002740  F0404040  40404040  40404040  40404040     40404040  40404040  40404040  40404040


                          RELOCATION FACTOR  001900
```

FIG. 10-29. Example of Exclusive OR Characters.

Do It Now Exercise 10-20. *Prepare a flow diagram for a routine to invert the bits in a 16-bit mask field aligned on the half word. Code the routine to save the contents of both the inverted and the uninverted fields so that either can be used for a later operation. Show the contents of storage.*

XI—Exclusive OR Immediate. This SI command performs the logical Exclusive OR operation on a single byte of storage data named by the first-operand address. The second operand is a literal which is normally written as a decimal number in the range 0 through 255 and is unaffected by the operation. The condition code is set as described previously. This command is subject to interrupt from improper addressing, and is not available on small models of the computer. An example of Exclusive OR Immediate is shown in Fig. 10-30.

```
LOC    OBJECT CODE      ADDR1 ADDR2  ST #   NAME    OP    OPERANDS             COMMENT

                                            IMPERATIVES

000196 D200 E220 E200 00EA0 00E80   153            MVC   CKEEP6(1),CONE1      SHOW CONTENTS OF STORAGE
00019C 0570                         154            BALR  7,0                  SAVE CONDITION CODE
00019E 979E E200       00E80        155  F10#30    XI    CONE1,158            EXCLUSIVE OR IMMEDIATE
0001A2 0580                         156            BALR  8,0                  SAVE CONDITION CODE
0001A4 9078 E224             00EA4  157            STM   7,8,CKEEP6+4         SHOW REG. CONTENTS
0001A8 D200 E230 219D 00EB0 0019F   158            MVC   CKEEP6+16(1),F10#30+1  SHOW IMMEDIATE BYTE


                                            DECLARATIVES

000E80 9E                           398  CONE1     DC    X'9E'                F10#30
000E81 4040404040404040             399            DC    CL31' '              FILLER
000E89 4040404040404040
000E91 4040404040404040
000E99 4040404040404040
000EA0 4040404040404040             400  CKEEP6    DC    CL32' '              USED TO DISPLAY STORAGE
000EA8 4040404040404040
000EB0 4040404040404040
000EB8 4040404040404040


                                      DUMP AFTER EXECUTION

002760 F0404040   40404040   40404040   40404040   40404040   40404040   40404040   40404040
002780 00404040   40404040   40404040   40404040   40404040   40404040   40404040   40404040
0027A0 9E404040   50001A9E   40001AA4   40404040   9E404040   40404040   40404040   40404040
0027C0 F0404040   40404040   40404040   40404040   40404040   40404040   40404040   40404040


                                      RELOCATION FACTOR    001900
```

Fig. 10-30. Example of Exclusive OR Immediate.

Do It Now Exercise 10-21. *Assume that a Test Under Mask instruction has been assigned the name TEST in a program. Write the imperatives and declaratives necessary to invert the bits in the mask.*

FINANCIAL EDIT OPERATIONS

In working with data representing amounts of money, the programer will often be asked to prepare reports in formats that call for printing the numbers with periods, commas, dollar signs, minus signs, credit symbols, asterisks, and the like.

The use of such symbols dresses up an otherwise plain-looking list of numbers and improves readability, but to the programer it can be a headache.

In the absence of financial edit capability, the programer can write his own routines to do the work. From experience it can be said that these routines typically are not short, and because of the arbitrary character of some financial edit work, the logic of the routines is not clean. Fortunately, the computer is equipped, as a part of the decimal or commercial instruction set, with two commands which greatly facilitate financial edit work. One of these, Edit, can be used for all major financial edit operations except the insertion of a floating dollar sign. The other, Edit and Mark, allows an address to be saved which can be used to indicate the appropriate position for a floating dollar sign.

To develop an understanding of the way in which these commands work, let us examine briefly the situation in which the programer usually tries to use them. The programer desires to have a number in storage printed on a line printer in financial format. If the number was produced as output directly in EBCDIC form after conversion from packed-decimal, it would look as shown in the top part of Fig. 10-31. In edited form ("check protect"), the number should be as shown in the bottom part of Fig. 10-31, with an asterisk first, then a dollar sign, a comma after the first digit, a period to separate the dollars and cents, and an asterisk at the end.

EBCDIC format	000428174
Packed-decimal format	000428174+
Pencil-and-paper format	4‸281‸74
Check protect edited format	****$4,281.74*
General edit format	*$9,999,999.99*

FIG. 10-31. An illustration of financial editing operations.

Let us review step by step the operation necessary for this editing operation. First, the programer can visually scan the number from *left to right*, looking for the change from leading 0s to significant digits. In this case, he can note that there are three leading 0s. These three leading 0s, therefore, can be replaced with asterisks or blanks, as shown in the pencil-and-paper format in Fig. 10-31. The programer can also take note of (mark) the place where the last leading 0 was encountered. The remaining digits to the right in the number are therefore significant, but now the programer must determine where to insert the commas and the decimal point.

For this purpose he can scan the number from *right to left*, counting off and marking the places for the decimal point and the commas. The traditional rule, as shown by the pencil-and-paper format in Fig. 10-31, is to mark off two places for pennies and tens of pennies, and then insert a decimal point to set those off separately from the dollars. Then he can count three more places to the left and mark again the insert position for the comma, to separate hundreds of dollars from thousands of dollars. This will complete the operation, since further counting goes beyond the first significant digit. Now he can place a blank or an asterisk after the number to replace the plus sign. If the sign is a minus, he can put on a minus sign or the DR or CR symbols for debit or credit as needed. Turning now to the dollar sign, he can insert this at the place he marked previously just to the left of the most significant digit. Such a dollar sign is referred to as a floating dollar sign because it is positioned immediately before the number with which it is to be associated.

It is obvious from this that in order to do the work of the financial edit by manual means, a human being typically scans the number to be edited in both directions—from left to right and from right to left—doing different things during each scan. Once he has scanned the number and marked positions, he must rewrite (copy) the number, physically inserting additional characters, and altering others—replacing them with blanks, asterisks, or other fill characters.

The computer and the programer share the work of the financial edit. The computer performs the left-to-right scan on a specific instance-by-instance basis, and does the copying operation, while translating a packed-decimal number to EBCDIC when the computer executes the program ("at run time"). The programer performs the right-to-left scan on a general basis when writing the instructions, and specifies the choice of characters to precede and to follow the number. The programer must also determine the maximum length of numbers to be handled and whether or not the computer is to suppress all leading 0s.

The programer tells the computer the results of his scan by preparing a control field when he writes the program. It is most convenient to prepare this control field in hexadecimal form with one byte position for each character of edited output data to be produced. Let us examine how the programer determines the contents of this control field as he scans in general form the number to be edited from right to left.

Since the field to be scanned from right to left is a packed-decimal field, the first thing the programer encounters is the sign. In practice, this is also disposed of first by the programer for that reason, but here for ease of explanation let us skip it and return to it later. Reading on to the left, the programer next encounters the two numeric characters that represent the cents. To stand for these as place holders, the programer writes in the control field two hexadecimal character pairs of 20. Each hexadecimal pair is referred to as the "digit select" indicator. It notifies the compiler that it is to insert in this position the corresponding digit, as noted at point "P" in Fig. 10-32.

0000000S	Packed decimal format to be edited
⌒"P"	
206B2020206B2020204B2020	Partial control field in hexadecimal
40206B2020206B2020214B202040C3D9	Complete edit control field

Fig. 10-32. Construction of an edit control field.

For the dot to serve as a decimal point, the programer can write the normal EBCDIC equivalent of a period, which is $4B_x$. Then, since the programer typically wants three digits to the left of the decimal point, he can use as place holders three bytes of 20_x. This is shown, approximately, in Fig. 10-32.

If at this point the programer desires to have the computer insert a comma, he can place a byte of $6B_x$, which is the usual EBCDIC coding for a comma. The digits next to the left should be digits from the field to be edited, so again the programer can insert the place-holder pairs 20_x. Since the maximum size of the number in this case is nine significant digits (five bytes in packed format), the programer can provide a pair of place holders flanking a comma to provide for the handling of all the characters of the numeric field except the sign.

Let us review now the content of the resulting (partial) control field, reading from left to right, as shown in Fig. 10-32. The control field begins with groups of hexadecimal 20_x to indicate that digits are to be taken from the field to be edited and expanded to EBCDIC and placed here, one for each byte in the control field marked by the 20_x. The number of 20_x pairs must equal the number of packed-decimal digits in the field to be edited (in this case seven). Wherever a $6B_x$ is shown, a comma is to be inserted. Wherever a $4B_x$ is shown, a decimal point is to be inserted.

The programer has not yet specified what character the computer is to use for replacing the leading 0s. This the programer writes as the leftmost byte of the control field. Usually a blank, 40_x, is used as this substitution character, but any printable character can be used. Asterisks and dashes are also fairly common, but blank is illustrated in Fig. 10-32.

The programer can also indicate whether he desires that some or all leading 0s be retained. To do this he can "force the start of significance" by substituting the hexadecimal pair 21_x for a 20_x in the numeric position where significance is to be forced to start. Often this is the dollars position just to the left of the decimal point. It then prints as 0 dollars when the dollar amount is 0, as illustrated in Fig. 10-32.

The data in Fig. 10-32 do not yet include handling of the algebraic sign which follows to the right of the last digit copied over from the field to be edited. The usual practice is to blot out any plus sign by using the same character used to substitute for the leading 0s. If the sign is a minus, then practice is diverse. Sometimes a minus sign is desired (60_x). Sometimes a CR ($C3D9_x$), a DR ($C4D9_x$), or an asterisk ($5C_x$) is desired. Sometimes these are printed immediately adjoining the rightmost digit, but sometimes a space separates them.

The usual practice, therefore, is to specify in the control field the data to be provided if the sign is minus, with the understanding that if the sign is plus, the 0-suppress character will replace those data. Thus, in the case at hand, let us assume that a blank, a C, and an R are to be shown if the field to be edited has a minus sign. In that case, the programer adds three bytes to the right end of the control field, $40C3D9_x$.

In brief summary and by analogy, the programer has the responsibility for providing the computer with the information obtained from a right-to-left scan of the data to be edited. To do this, the programer prepares a control field in which he indicates how each byte of data is to appear after editing. The hexadecimal characters which have special significance in the control field are the leftmost byte of the control field, which serves as the 0-suppression character; the hexadecimal pair 20_x, which serves on an indicator for use of one numeric character from the field to be edited (digit select); and the hexadecimal pair 21_x, which serves as a significance start indicator, as well as serving like a 20_x.

Let us look now at the way in which the computer performs the scan from left to right, using the packed-decimal field to be edited and the data provided by the programer in the form of the control field. The computer, as it performs the scan, needs to have a significance status indicator of whether or not a significant digit has been encountered. That determines whether or not 0 suppression is to be done, for example. For that purpose, the computer has a built in 1-bit indicator known as the "significance trigger." The significance trigger is initialized to the value of 0 each time the computer starts an edit operation and each time the computer encounters the hexadecimal pair 22_x (a "field separator"). The significance trigger is then either altered or left unchanged as the computer reads from left to right in the field to be edited and in the control field. In general, the significance trigger has the value of 0 when insignificant data are being handled, and the value of 1 when significant data are being handled.

At the start of the scan from left to right, the significance trigger has the value of 0. The computer brings one character of data over from the field to be edited for each 20_x in the control field. As the computer brings it over, it tests the character for a 0 value. If it encounters a nonzero character from the field to be edited, the significance trigger is set to 1, and the character of data is accepted, translated to EBCDIC and placed in the control field. Thus the computer destroys the control field as it performs the edit operation. If the status of the significance trigger is 0 and the character brought over has a value of 0, then the computer does not translate the character and does not enter it into the control field, but instead copies the 0-suppress character into that position in the control field, blotting out whatever was there.

Let us examine the process in more detail. In beginning the scan from left to right, the computer accepts the first byte of the control field without alteration and without taking action upon it. It sets the significance trigger to 0, and then proceeds to the second byte in the control field. If that character is a hexadecimal pair 20_x, then the first digit half byte from the field to be edited is obtained and compared for 0. If the digit is 0 and the significance trigger is also 0, then the digit is rejected. The computer then copies the 0-suppress character into the control field position, replacing the 20_x. If the digit is not 0, then the computer accepts the digit from the field to be edited, translates it, and places it in the control field, replacing the 20_x, and sets the significance trigger to 1.

If the computer encounters in the control field the hexadecimal pair 20_x while the significance trigger is 1, then the computer accepts the digit from the field to be edited, translates it, places it in the control field without testing it for a 0 value, and sets (reaffirms) the significance trigger to 1. This same action is taken if the computer encounters the hexadecimal pair 21_x. That is, the digit from the field to be edited is accepted and incorporated into the control field without testing.

If, in performing the scan from left to right of the control field, the computer encounters a hexadecimal pair other than 20_x, 21_x, or 22_x, and has not yet encountered a sign character in the field to be edited, it treats the bytes in the control field in one of two ways, depending upon the state of the significance trigger. If the significance trigger is 0, then the computer replaces the data in the control field byte by copying the 0-suppress character in the control field. If the significance trigger is 1, then the computer accepts the byte in the control field and leaves it unchanged. It does not replace the byte with the 0-suppress character.

FIG. 10-33. Edit of a positive number.

FIG. 10-34. Edit of a negative number.

When the byte containing the sign character is encountered in the field to be edited, the computer sets the significance trigger to 0 as soon as the digit part of the byte has been brought over and handled. Then the computer tests the sign character from the field to be edited. If the sign is positive, the significance trigger remains set to 0. If the sign is negative, the signficance trigger is set to 1. Then the same rule used before is applied to the remaining bytes in the control field. That is, if the significance trigger is 1, the computer accepts the remaining bytes in the control field. If the significance trigger is 0, the computer replaces the remaining bytes in the control field with the 0-suppress character. Two examples of this financial edit operation are shown in Figs. 10-33 and 10-34, one with a positive number and one with a negative number.

ED—Edit. This SS command uses as its first operand a control field in storage and as its second operand a packed-decimal field in storage. Under the control of the data in the control field named by the first-operand address, the computer brings the data from the packed-decimal field named in the second-operand address, one half byte at a time, and matches them against the control field contents to determine the action. The first-operand (control) field is altered by the edit operation; the second-operand field remains unchanged—i.e., the control field becomes the edited result field. Processing proceeds from left to right. The length associated with the command is the length in bytes of the control field. This length must conform to the contents of the second operand, but not in terms of a byte count. The condition code is set to reflect the sign of the field to be edited. It is 0 if the field is all 0s, 1 if the sign is negative, and 2 if the field is nonzero positive. This command is subject to interruption from improper length and addressing, and is available on all models of the computer. An example of Edit is shown in Fig. 10-35.

```
LOC   OBJECT CODE       ADDR1 ADDR2  ST #  NAME   OP    OPERANDS            COMMENT

                                           IMPERATIVES

000006 D20C 811E 80FE  00120 00100   11           MVC   CHOLD7(13),CCON2    SHOW CONTENTS OF STORAGE
00000C 0530                          12           BALR  3,0                 SAVE CONDITION CODE
00000E DEOC 80FE 810B  00100 0010D   13  F10#35   ED    CCON2,NUMB3         EDIT 'NUMB3' INTO 'CCON2'
000014 0540                          14           BALR  4,0                 SAVE CONDITION CODE
000016 9034 8132             00134   15           STM   3,4,CHOLD7+20       SHOW REG. CONTENTS


                                           DECLARATIVES

000100 40202168202020 4B              77  CCON2   DC    XL13'4020216B2020204B202040C3D9'  CONTROL FIELD
000108 202040C3D9
00010D 0000191C                       78  NUMB3   DC    PL4'191'            F10#35
000111 4040404040404040                79          DC    CL15' '             FILLER
000119 4040404040404040
000120 4040404040404040                80  CHOLD7  DC    CL32' '             USED TO DISPLAY STORAGE
000128 4040404040404040
000130 4040404040404040
000138 4040404040404040


                                      DUMP AFTER EXECUTION

0019E0  F0404040   40404040   40404040   40404040   40404040   40404040   40404040   40404040
001A00  4040406B   FOFOF14B   F9F14040   40000019   1C404040   40404040   40404040   40404040
001A20  4020216B   20202048   202040C3   D9404040   40404040   4000190E   60001916   40404040
001A40  F0404040   40404040   40404040   40404040   40404040   40404040   40404040   40404040


                   RELOCATION FACTOR    001900
```

FIG. 10-35. Example of Edit.

Do It Now Exercise 10-22. *Write the imperatives and declaratives needed to have the computer perform a financial edit without a floating dollar sign on the following packed-decimal fields:* +000768432 *and* −798932468. *Use the same control field for both with a double asterisk as a negative indication, and use blank* *as the 0-suppression character. Show the contents of storage before and after for each field. Be sure to leave the control field undestroyed in storage for later use.*

More than one field of data may be edited at a time, provided that the fields to be edited are arranged in storage in the same sequence as the control fields in storage, and that the lengths correctly correspond. In such a case, the hexadecimal pair 22_x serves as a field separator. This serves to set the significance start trigger back to 0, and thereafter is treated as if it were identical to a hexadecimal pair 20_x. For this reason, when multiple fields are being handled, the leading 0-suppress character need not be repeated, but need only be shown once as the leftmost byte of the multiple-part control field.

EDMK—Edit and Mark. This SS command operates in the same manner as the Edit command described previously, but with one additional feature. The point at which the significance starts—i.e., at which the significance trigger first changes from 0 to 1—is recorded as an absolute machine-language address in binary form and is stored in register 1. This address can be used, by subtracting 1_b from it, to indicate the address at which a floating dollar sign should be inserted. The condition code is set as in Edit. This command is subject to interruptions from improper

```
   LOC   OBJECT CODE    ADDR1 ADDR2  ST #  NAME   OP    OPERANDS          COMMENT

                                            IMPERATIVES

00001A  D209 819E 817E 001A0 00180  17          MVC   CKEEP7(10),CCON3  SHOW CONTENTS OF STORAGE
000020  4110 8182        00184     18          LA    1,CCON3+4         LOAD $ ADDRESS FOR 1 CASE
000024  5010 81B2        001B4     19          ST    1,CKEEP7+20       SAVE $ ADDRESS
                                   20  *                                 OF FORCED (21) SIGNIFICANCE
000028  05A0                       21          BALR  10,0              SAVE CONDITION CODE
00002A  DF09 817E 8188 00180 0018A 22  F10#36  EDMK  CCON3,NUMB4       EDIT AND MARK 'NUMB4'
000030  05B0                       23          BALR  11,0              SAVE CONDITION CODE
000032  90AB 81AA        001AC     24          STM   10,11,CKEEP7+12   SHOW REGISTER CONTENTS
000036  0610                       25          BCTR  1,0               SUB. 1 FROM REG. 1
000038  5010 81B6        001B8     26          ST    1,CKEEP7+24       SHOW $ ADDRESS
00003C  9258 1000        00000     27          MVI   0(1),91           MOVE A DOLLAR SIGN TO ADDR.
                                                                         IN REG. 1


                                            DECLARATIVES

000180  402020214B202040           86  CCON3   DC    XL10'402020214B202040C3D9'    CONTROL FIELD
00018A  07361C                     87  NUMB4   DC    PL3'7361'         F10#36
00018D  4040404040404040           88          DC    CL19' '          FILLER
000195  4040404040404040
00019D  404040
0001A0  4040404040404040           89  CKEEP7  DC    CL32' '          USED TO DISPLAY STORAGE
0001A8  4040404040404040
0001B0  4040404040404040
0001B8  4040404040404040


                                     DUMP AFTER EXECUTION

001A60  F0404040  40404040  40404040  40404040  40404040  40404040  40404040  40404040
001A80  405BF7F3  4BF6F140  40400736  1C404040  40404040  40404040  40404040  40404040
001AA0  40202021  4B202040  C3D94040  6000192A  60001932  00001A84  00001A81  40404040
001AC0  F0404040  40404040  40404040  40404040  40404040  40404040  40404040  40404040


                              RELOCATION FACTOR    001900
                                           *
```

FIG. 10-36. Example of Edit and Mark.

lengths and addressing, and is not available on small models of the computer. An example of Edit and Mark is shown in Fig. 10-36.

Do It Now Exercise 10-23. *Have the computer perform a financial edit, including a floating dollar sign, on the following data: +73642897 and −99. Use an asterisk as the 0-suppress character and DR as a minus indicator. For fields of less than one dollar, show a 0 in the dollar position. Use one control field for editing both fields. Show the contents of storage, assuming the data are in packed-decimal form.*

CODE TRANSLATION

The computer has two commands of considerable assistance in handling the translating of one type of code to another. The computer does this translation by searching a table in storage. Then, as a result of this search, the original data are replaced or the contents of some registers altered to reflect the data found in the table.

In order to understand the translation operation, the programer needs to understand first the way the computer does the search. To do the table search, the computer takes the starting address of the table in storage and arithmetically *adds* to it one byte of data (the byte of data to be translated). Since one byte of data is in binary the equivalent of the decimal number from 0 through 255, the resulting sum may be an address between the start of the table in storage and as many as 255 bytes later. At this address in the table, the computer finds one byte of data which the computer uses as specified by the command.

To be able to use the translate commands, the programer normally sets up in storage a table up to 256 bytes long. This table normally contains only the data the computer should find as a result of its search. Consider the following simple example, shown in Fig. 10-37. The data to be translated consist of a series of bytes which may be between 00_x and FF_x. The algorithm is that if the byte in the data to be translated has a 1 bit in the rightmost position, the result data should have two 1 bits in the center portion of the right half byte, that is, 6_x. If not, the result should be 0_x. If the data to be translated have a 1 bit in the leftmost bit position, then F_x should be used as the left half of the result byte. Otherwise, A_x should be used. Thus all possible bytes are to be assigned to one of four categories: $A0_x$, $A6_x$, $F0_x$, and $F6_x$. Since the table is so simple, it is also very repetitious.

TR—Translate. This SS command substitutes, byte by byte, for the bytes in the field named by the first-operand address, the bytes selected from the table named by the second-operand address. The computer takes the bytes from the first-operand field in a left-to-right sequence. The first operand is altered by the translate command; the second operand is unaltered. The length applies to the first operand only and determines the number of bytes to be altered. The condition code is not set. The table searched normally is 256 bytes long, but may be less if some first-operand bit combinations are known never to occur. Improper addressing may cause an interruption. This command is available on all models of the computer. An example of Translate is given in Fig. 10-38.

Do It Now Exercise 10-24. *Prepare the flow diagram for a program to read data from cards, then translate the data, one card at a time, from EBCDIC to*

Logic table

Output / Input		Left half byte	Right half byte
Odd-numbered input	Y	••	6
	N	••	0
Last half of 256	Y	F	••
	N	A	••

Notes for conceptual table

K — Position in table shown as a hexadecimal form (argument)

M — Byte of data in the table in hexadecimal form (function)

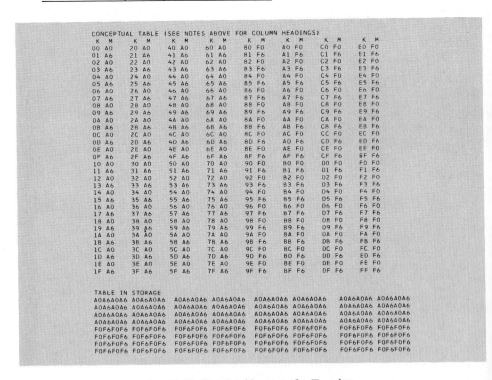

FIG. 10-37. Search table set up for Translate.

ASCII, and punch the translated data (assuming the punch can handle ASCII). Be sure to prepare a table layout before starting the coding.

TRT—Translate and Test. This SS command uses successive bytes from the field named by the first-operand address to search a table designated by the second-operand address. If the byte located in the second-operand table consists only of 0 bits, the operation continues to the next byte in the first operand. The operation proceeds from left to right until a byte with nonzero bits is detected in the second oper-

```
  LOC  OBJECT CODE      ADDR1 ADDR2  ST # NAME    OP   OPERANDS          COMMENT

                                        IMPERATIVES

000040 D206 821E 81FE  00220 00200   29          MVC  DKEEP1(7),TRANS   SHOW CONTENTS OF STORAGE
000046 DC06 81FE 823E  00200 00240   30 F10#38   TR   TRANS,TABLE       TRANSLATE


                                        DECLARATIVES

000200 7903A6F0760081                95 TRANS    DC   XL7'7903A6F0760081'  F10#38
000207 4040404040404040              96          DC   CL25' '              FILLER
00020F 4040404040404040
000217 4040404040404040
00021F 40
000220 4040404040404040              97 DKEEP1   DC   CL32' '           USED TO DISPLAY STORAGE
000228 4040404040404040
000230 4040404040404040
000238 4040404040404040
000240 A0A6A0A6A0A6A0A6              98 TABLE    DC   64XL2'A0A6'       F10#38, TRANSLATING TABLE
000248 A0A6A0A6A0A6A0A6
000250 A0A6A0A6A0A6A0A6
000258 A0A6A0A6A0A6A0A6
000260 A0A6A0A6A0A6A0A6
000268 A0A6A0A6A0A6A0A6
000270 A0A6A0A6A0A6A0A6
000278 A0A6A0A6A0A6A0A6
000280 A0A6A0A6A0A6A0A6
000288 A0A6A0A6A0A6A0A6
000290 A0A6A0A6A0A6A0A6
000298 A0A6A0A6A0A6A0A6
0002A0 A0A6A0A6A0A6A0A6
0002A8 A0A6A0A6A0A6A0A6
0002B0 A0A6A0A6A0A6A0A6
0002B8 A0A6A0A6A0A6A0A6
0002C0 F0F6F0F6F0F6F0F6              99          DC   64XL2'F0F6'       TRANSLATING TABLE
0002C8 F0F6F0F6F0F6F0F6
0002D0 F0F6F0F6F0F6F0F6
0002D8 F0F6F0F6F0F6F0F6
0002E0 F0F6F0F6F0F6F0F6
0002E8 F0F6F0F6F0F6F0F6
0002F0 F0F6F0F6F0F6F0F6
0002F8 F0F6F0F6F0F6F0F6
000300 F0F6F0F6F0F6F0F6
000308 F0F6F0F6F0F6F0F6
000310 F0F6F0F6F0F6F0F6
000318 F0F6F0F6F0F6F0F6
000320 F0F6F0F6F0F6F0F6
000328 F0F6F0F6F0F6F0F6
000330 F0F6F0F6F0F6F0F6
000338 F0F6F0F6F0F6F0F6


                                    DUMP AFTER EXECUTION

001AE0  F0404040   40404040   40404040   40404040   40404040   40404040   40404040   40404040
001B00  A6A6F0F0   A0A0F640   40404040   40404040   40404040   40404040   40404040   40404040
001B20  7903A6F0   76008140   40404040   40404040   40404040   40404040   40404040   40404040
001B40 TO THE NEXT LINE ADDRESS CONTAINS A0A6A0A6
001BC0 TO THE NEXT LINE ADDRESS CONTAINS F0F6F0F6
001C40  F0404040   40404040   40404040   40404040   40404040   40404040   40404040   40404040


                        RELOCATION FACTOR   001900
```

FIG. 10-38. Example of Translate (see also Fig. 10-37).

and, or until the first-operand field is exhausted. If the byte located in the table does not contain only 0 bits, the computer inserts, right-justified into three bytes of register 1, the absolute binary address of the byte just inspected in the first operand. The computer also inserts into the right end of register 2 the corresponding byte found from the table. Other bytes in registers 1 and 2 remain unaltered by the insert operations.

The condition code is set to 0 only if bytes containing only 0 bits were encountered in the table, and if all bytes in the first operand were inspected. The condition code is set to 1 if the computer finds a nonzero entry in the table before inspecting the last byte in the first operand. The condition code is set to 2 if the computer finds a nonzero byte which is also the last byte in the first operand. The length for the instruction is the length of the first operand, and may be as much as 256 bytes. In contrast to Translate, neither the first nor the second operand is altered by Translate and Test. Improper addressing may cause an interruption. This command is not available on small models of the computer. An example of Translate and Test is shown in Fig. 10-39.

The major use of Translate and Test is to locate bytes containing particular bit combinations. This is useful in breaking messages into parts, such as into words, and in scanning for the presence of certain characters, such as commas, blanks, and the like. The repeated successive use of Translate and Test is usually done with the Execute command, which is described later.

Do It Now Exercise 10-25. *Prepare the flow diagram for a program to have the computer read data from a deck of cards and list the data, using one line for each card read, but with all the numeric information and all periods deleted and replaced by blanks. The numeric information and periods may occur anywhere on the card and may be in fields of any length. Be sure to prepare a table layout before starting the coding. What address does the computer need to resume a Test and Translate? How is the condition-code setting helpful?*

ITERATION EXITS

The computer provides two commands which are very convenient for controlling the exits from iteration. These two commands are in addition to the Branch on Count operation introduced earlier. That operation, it will be recalled, allowed the programer to set up a count in a register. The computer then decreased this count by one each time it executed the Branch on Count operation. As long as the count was not 0, control went to a transfer address.

The limitations of the Branch on Count operation are that the count may only be decreased, not increased; that the amount of decrement is always 1; and that the test condition is zero vs. nonzero only. In the two additional operations provided by the computer, all three of these limitations are removed.

In order to remove these three limitations, the computer uses three registers. One register, which is named as the first-operand address, serves as a counter. This register may be either an even- or an odd-numbered register, and it is treated in the usual arithmetic (binary) manner. The second register (named as the second-oper-

```
  LOC  OBJECT CODE    ADDR1 ADDR2  ST #  NAME    OP   OPERANDS          COMMENT

                                          IMPERATIVES

00004C D207 839E 837E 003A0 00380   32            MVC  DHOLD(8),TRANS1   SHOW CONTENTS OF STORAGE
000052 1B22                         33            SR   2,2               CLEAR REG. 2
000054 4110 837E            00380   34            LA   1,TRANS1          LOAD STARING ADDRESS
000058 9207 805D       0005F        35            MVI  F10#39+1,7        INSERT LENGTH BYTE
00005C 0530                         36            BALR 3,0               SAVE CONDITION CODE
00005E DD00 1000 83BE 00000 003C0   37  F10#39    TRT  0(0,1),TABLE1     TRANSLATE AND TEST
000064 0540                         38            BALR 4,0               SAVE CONDITION CODE
000066 9200 805D       0005F        39            MVI  F10#39+1,0        CLEAR LENGTH BYTE
00006A 9014 83A6            003A8   40            STM  1,4,DHOLD+8       SHOW REG. CONTENTS
00006E D207 83B6 837E 003B8 00380   41            MVC  DHOLD+24(8),TRANS1  SHOW CONTENTS OF STORAGE


                                          DECLARATIVES

000380 178313BF1C746410           105 TRANS1   DC   XL8'178313BF1C746410'  F10#39
000388 404040404040404040        106          DC   CL24' '                FILLER
000390 404040404040404040
000398 404040404040404040
0003A0 404040404040404040        107 DHOLD    DC   CL32' '                USED TO DISPLAY STORAGE
0003A8 404040404040404040
0003B0 404040404040404040
0003B8 404040404040404040
0003C0 A000A000A000A000          108 TABLE1   DC   64XL2'A000'            F10#39, TRANSLATING TABLE
0003C8 A000A000A000A000
0003D0 A000A000A000A000
0003D8 A000A000A000A000
0003E0 A000A000A000A000
0003E8 A000A000A000A000
0003F0 A000A000A000A000
0003F8 A000A000A000A000
000400 A000A000A000A000
000408 A000A000A000A000
000410 A000A000A000A000
000418 A000A000A000A000
000420 A000A000A000A000
000428 A000A000A000A000
000430 A000A000A000A000
000438 A000A000A000A000
000440 F0F6F0F6F0F6F0F6          109          DC   64XL2'F0F6'            TRANSLATING TABLE
000448 F0F6F0F6F0F6F0F6
000450 F0F6F0F6F0F6F0F6
000458 F0F6F0F6F0F6F0F6
000460 F0F6F0F6F0F6F0F6
000468 F0F6F0F6F0F6F0F6
000470 F0F6F0F6F0F6F0F6
000478 F0F6F0F6F0F6F0F6
000480 F0F6F0F6F0F6F0F6
000488 F0F6F0F6F0F6F0F6
000490 F0F6F0F6F0F6F0F6
000498 F0F6F0F6F0F6F0F6
0004A0 F0F6F0F6F0F6F0F6
0004A8 F0F6F0F6F0F6F0F6
0004B0 F0F6F0F6F0F6F0F6
0004B8 F0F6F0F6F0F6F0F6


                                      DUMP AFTER EXECUTION

001C60  F0404040   40404040   40404040   40404040   40404040   40404040   40404040   40404040
001C80  178313BF   1C746410   40404040   40404040   40404040   40404040   40404040   40404040
001CA0  178313BF   1C746410   00001C81   000000F6   4000195E   50001966   178313BF   1C746410
001CC0  TO THE NEXT LINE ADDRESS CONTAINS A000A000
001D40  TO THE NEXT LINE ADDRESS CONTAINS F0F6F0F6
001DC0  F0404040   40404040   40404040   40404040   40404040   40404040   40404040   40404040


                   RELOCATION FACTOR   001900
```

FIG. 10-39. Example of Translate and Test.

and address) is normally an even-numbered register which holds the amount by which the count is to be increased or decreased. If this register holds a positive number, then that amount is added to the first-operand register, thus increasing the contents. If this second register holds a negative number, then since adding a negative number is the same as subtracting a positive one, the contents of the first-operand register are decreased. By specifying the sign and magnitude of the contents of the second register, the programer can cause the change in the count register to go either upward or downward by whatever amount the programer chooses.

The third register is not explicitly named as an operand. This register is the odd-numbered register one more than the second-operand register. (If the second-operand register was odd-numbered, then the second- and third-operand registers are identical.) That is, usually the second and third register are an adjoining pair of registers, such as 8 and 9. This third odd-numbered register holds the contents to which the contents of the first register are to be compared. It holds, in other words, the constant of comparison. The programer may set this to 0 or any other value that may suit his convenience to meet the needs of the program at hand.

The transfer-of-control condition for these two operations follows the same pattern as that for Branch on Count. It will be recalled that the Branch on Count operation properly could be termed "Branch on Count Not Equal to Zero." That is, the condition to be satisfied in order for the transfer of control to occur is that the count be nonzero. For the two operations at hand, the same philosophy is followed. When the condition specified in the title of the commands be met, a transfer of control takes place.

An additional feature of these two operations is that the condition code is not altered. Overflow and other conditions that may arise are all ignored both in the changing of the count and in the making of the comparison. This means that these two branch operations can be performed without disturbing the condition code and with good assurance that interruptions will not occur.

BXLE—Branch on Index Low or Equal. This RS command utilizes three registers and one transfer-of-control address. The transfer-of-control address is named as the third-operand address. The first-operand address is a register used to maintain a count. The second-operand address is a register which contains the amount by which the count is to be increased or decreased—i.e., the increment or decrement. This second-operand register normally is specified as an even-numbered register. The third register used is normally the odd-numbered register immediately following the second-operand register. If the third register is odd-numbered, then that one register serves as both the second and third registers. This third register, however, is not cited in the instruction; its use is implied in the instruction itself. This third register holds the limit or address value that serves as the constant of comparison.

```
    LOC   OBJECT CODE      ADDR1 ADDR2   ST #   NAME     OP    OPERANDS              COMMENT

                                                IMPERATIVES

  000074 989B 84FE              00500     43            LM    9,11,DCNT            LOAD REG.
  000078 D203 8522 850A 00524 0050C       44            MVC   DSAVE+4(4),DSUM      SHOW CONTENTS OF STORAGE
  00007E 47F0 8086              00088     45            B     *+10                 BRANCH TO F10#40
  000082 FA31 850A 80D6 0050C 000D8       46  DENTER    AP    DSUM,=P'14'          ADD 14 TO SUM
  000088 879A 8080              00082     47  F10#40    BXLE  9,10,DENTER          BRANCH ON INDEX LOW OR EQUAL
  00008C 909B 852E              00530     48            STM   9,11,DSAVE+16        SHOW REG. CONTENTS


                                                DECLARATIVES

  000500 FFFFFFFF                        115  DCNT      DC    F'-1'                F10#40 - INDEX COUNTER
  000504 00000006                        116            DC    F'6'                 DECREMENT
  000508 00000020                        117            DC    F'32'                LOWER LIMIT
  00050C 0000000C                        118  DSUM      DC    PL4'0'               SUM HOLDER
  000510 4040404040404040                119            DC    CL16' '              FILLER
  000518 4040404040404040
  000520 4040404040404040                120  DSAVE     DC    CL32' '              USED TO DISPLAY STORAGE
  000528 4040404040404040
  000530 4040404040404040
  000538 4040404040404040


                                             DUMP AFTER EXECUTION

  001DE0  F0404040   40404040   40404040   40404040   40404040   40404040   40404040   40404040
  001E00  FFFFFFFF   00000006   00000020   0000070C   40404040   40404040   40404040   40404040
  001E20  40404040   0000000C   40404040   40404040   00000023   00000006   00000020   40404040
  001E40  F0404040   40404040   40404040   40404040   40404040   40404040   40404040   40404040


                              RELOCATION FACTOR    001900
```

FIG. 10-40. Example of Branch on Index Low or Equal.

```
    LOC   OBJECT CODE      ADDR1 ADDR2   ST #   NAME     OP    OPERANDS              COMMENT

                                                IMPERATIVES

  000090 9857 857E              00580     50            LM    5,7,COUNT2           LOAD REG.
  000094 D203 85A2 858A 005A4 0058C       51            MVC   DSTORE+4(4),TOTAL    SHOW CONTENTS OF STORAGE
  00009A 47F0 80A2              000A4     52            B     *+10                 BRANCH TO F10#41
  00009E FB30 858A 80DA 0058C 000DC       53  ZBRAN     SP    TOTAL,=P'5'          SUBTRACT PACKED
  0000A4 8656 809C              0009E     54  F10#41    BXH   5,6,ZBRAN            BRANCH ON INDEX HIGH
  0000A8 9057 85AE              005B0     55            STM   5,7,DSTORE+16        SHOW REG. CONTENTS


                                                DECLARATIVES

  000580 0000001D                        126  COUNT2    DC    F'29'                F10#41 - INDEX COUNTER
  000584 FFFFFFFD                        127            DC    F'-3'                INCREMENT
  000588 0000000F                        128            DC    F'15'                UPPER LIMIT
  00058C 0000037C                        129  TOTAL     DC    PL4'37'              DIFFERENCE HOLDER
  000590 4040404040404040                130            DC    CL16' '              FILLER
  000598 4040404040404040
  0005A0 4040404040404040                131  DSTORE    DC    CL32' '              USED TO DISPLAY STORAGE
  0005A8 4040404040404040
  0005B0 4040404040404040
  0005B8 4040404040404040


                                             DUMP AFTER EXECUTION

  001E60  F0404040   40404040   40404040   40404040   40404040   40404040   40404040   40404040
  001E80  0000001D   FFFFFFFD   0000000F   0000017C   40404040   40404040   40404040   40404040
  001EA0  40404040   0000037C   40404040   40404040   0000000E   FFFFFFFD   0000000F   40404040
  001EC0  F0404040   40404040   40404040   40404040   40404040   40404040   40404040   40404040


                              RELOCATION FACTOR    001900
```

FIG. 10-41. Example of Branch on Index High.

In operation, the command adds the contents of the second-operand address (a register) to the contents of the first-operand address (a register) and stores the new sum back in the first-operand address. Before storing the new sum, the computer compares the new sum and the contents of the unnamed operand register. If the new sum is less than or equal to the contents of the unnamed operand register, a transfer of control takes place to the address named as the third operand. If the new sum is greater than the contents of the unnamed operand register, then the next instruction in sequence is taken, and no transfer of control takes place. This command is not subject to interrupt, and is not available on small models of the computer. An example of Branch on Index Low or Equal is shown in Fig. 10-40.

BXH—Branch on Index High. This RS command operates in the same manner as Branch on Index Low or Equal, except that the condition of transfer of control is high instead of not high. An example of Branch on Index High is shown in Fig. 10-41.

Do It Now Exercise 10-26. *Using a leading-decisions approach, assume that storage contains 100 bytes of data organized into 5-byte groups. The last two bytes, which are in binary format, of each group are to be added to form a sum, which is to be stored at the address SUM. Prepare a flow diagram for a routine to accomplish this, and then code it. Be sure to prepare a storage map or layout.*

INDIRECT EXECUTION OF INSTRUCTIONS

In more complicated programs, the programer occasionally finds it convenient to have the computer execute an instruction which is not the next instruction in sequence. A Translate and Test instruction is a common example. For instance, consider the following situation. The programer may cause the computer to build an instruction in storage as if it were an ordinary piece of data. Then the programer would like to have the computer execute that instruction. One way this can be done is to reserve an area in the sequence of instructions but leave it blank, and then have the computer build in that space the instruction to be executed. The computer would then execute it in the normal sequence. This requires no special commands.

Another situation is that in which the programer has provided, in another routine or at some other place in the program, an instruction which is appropriate for execution a number of times, but with slightly differing values for the operands in each case. In order to save the trouble of defining fields within imperative instructions and then modifying their contents many times, the programer can set up the definitions once, and then cause the instruction to be modified and executed directly from its position in storage without executing the neighboring instructions. This requires no special instructions, but can be done more conveniently with a special command.

Other instructions
in normal sequence

Instructions in sequence
of execution

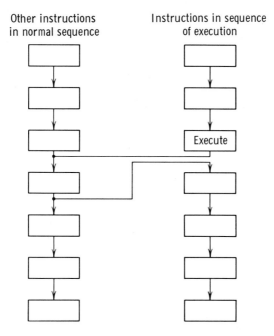

FIG. 10-42. Diagram of control sequence for Execute.

Still another situation is that in which the programer has caused the computer to build, in working storage outside of the normal instruction stream, an instruction. Rather than have the computer transfer control to it, execute the instruction, and then transfer control unconditionally back again, the programer would like to have some more convenient way of getting the computer to execute the instruction. To obtain this convenience requires the use of a special command.

Such a special command exists. It is the Execute command. With it, the computer can execute instructions outside of the normal sequence of instructions. This Execute command can be used quite complexly, because included with it is a Logical OR operation which allows part of the instruction to be executed to be modified by the logical OR operation immediately before execution without altering the actual contents of storage (i.e., the instruction).

EX—Execute. This RX command transfers control for the execution of one instruction only to the second-operand address. This address may include indexing. The first-operand address designates a register from which the low-order byte is used in a logical OR operation with the second byte of the instruction to be executed. When this first-operand register is specified as register 0, no logical OR operation takes place. Once the instruction named by the second operand has been executed, control returns to execute the next instruction in the normal sequence. A diagram of this situation is shown in 10-42. The condition code may be set, and any interrupt is possible, depending upon the instruction executed by the Execute. This command is not available on the small models of the computer. An example of Execute is shown in Fig. 10-43.

```
      LOC   OBJECT CODE        ADDR1 ADDR2   ST #   NAME    OP    OPERANDS                COMMENT

                                                           IMPERATIVES

    0000AC  4A10 80D8              000DA      57             AH    1,=H'1'                 MOVE POINTER OVER 1 BYTE
    000080  4160 8385              00387      58             LA    6,TRANS1+7              GET END ADDRESS
    000084  1B61                              59             SR    6,1                     COMPUTE REMAINING LENGTH
    0000B6  5060 8616              00618      60             ST    6,DKEEP2+24             SAVE LENGTH INDICATOR
    0000BA  4740 80C6              000C8      61             BM    *+14                    JUMP OUT IF DONE
    0000BE  1822                              62             SR    2,2                     CLEAR REGISTER 2
    0000C0  4460 805C              0005E      63   F10#43    EX    6,F10#39                EXECUTE TRANSLATE INSTRUCTION
    0000C4  9014 85FE              00600      64             STM   1,4,DKEEP2              SHOW REG. CONTENTS
    0000C8  D207 860E 837E  00610 00380       65             MVC   DKEEP2+16(8),TRANS1     SHOW CONTENTS OF STORAGE


                                                           DECLARATIVES

    000600  4040404040404040                 137  DKEEP2    DC    CL32' '                 STORAGE
    000608  4040404040404040
    000610  4040404040404040
    000618  4040404040404040


                                             DUMP AFTER EXECUTION

    001EE0  F0404040   40404040   40404040   40404040     40404040   40404040   40404040   40404040
    001F00  00001C83   000000F6   4000195E   50001966     178313BF   1C74641D   00000005   40404040
    001F20  F0404040   40404040   40404040   40404040     40404040   40404040   40404040   40404040


                                    RELOCATION FACTOR   001900
```

FIG. 10-43. Example of Execute.

The instruction which is performed by means of the Execute must be an ordinary assembly-language instruction. It may not be a macro instruction. It is also generally unwise to make the instruction executed by the Execute instruction a conditional or unconditional transfer of control without also having some clear way of establishing and recording the conditions under which the Execute takes place. This is a problem not of machine organization but of program logic. In general, the Execute command makes it possible to complicate the program logic considerably. This makes debugging more difficult, and the programer should beware.

Do It Now Exercise 10-27. *Prepare a flow diagram for a subroutine to Store Multiple the contents of all the registers in 16 consecutive full words of storage after adding 17 to the contents of registers 1, 4, 7, 12, and 16. Code the routines to use the address in register 13 as the address at which to store the data, and then adjust the contents of register 13 without using a DC constant or a literal.*

BYTE MANIPULATION

Masked operations together with logical AND, OR, and Exclusive OR give the programer ways to have the computer manipulate the bits within fields, words, and single bytes. But they do not provide the programer ways to have the computer manipulate entire bytes as units under a mask, or to treat together nonconsecutive bytes. To do these operations, the programer can write subroutines using the bit-manipulating commands. But some of the more recent models of the computer provide commands for doing such operations directly on up to four bytes if one of the operands is in a general purpose register.

For these commands, the computer uses as a mask the four bits of one hexadecimal character from the instruction. The four bits of this mask correspond from left to right with four consecutive bytes in a register. The bytes in the register that correspond to the 1 bits in the mask serve as the first operand; the other bytes do not participate in the operation and are ignored.

The operand is a field of contiguous bytes in storage. The length of this field is equal to the number of selected bytes in the register, which is equal to the number of 1 bits in the mask. This may make the operands be from zero through four bytes long, and both the storage and register operands are always the same length.

Whether or not the computer alters the contents of storage or the register depends upon the operation. The operation also determines whether or not the computer sets the condition code. The three commands provided are Insert Characters Under Mask, Store Characters Under Mask, and Compare Logical Characters Under Mask.

ICM—Insert Characters Under Mask. This RS command places in the register at the byte positions indicated by 1 bits in the mask from none to four bytes copied

```
   LOC   OBJECT CODE     ADDR1 ADDR2   ST #  NAME   OP   OPERANDS             COMMENT

                                            IMPERATIVES

 000048  91FF 32BC       002C4          31          TM   CMA,X'FF'           SET CONDITION CODE TO 11
 00004C  0540                           32          BALR 4,0                 SAVE CONDITION CODE
 00004E  5850 32BC             002C4    33          L    5,CMA               LOAD DATA FIELD
 000052  BF56 32BB             002C0    34  F10*44  ICM  5,6,CMB             INSERT CHARACTERS MASKED
 000056  0560                           35          BALR 6,0                 SAVE CONDITION CODE
 00005B  9046 32C8             002D0    36          STM  4,6,CHOLD           SHOW REGISTER CONTENTS


                                            DECLARATIVES

 0002C0  08803333                      113  CMB    DC   X'08803333'         BYTES FOR INSERTION
 0002C4  FFFFFFFF                      114  CMA    DC   X'FFFFFFFF'          BYTES FOR REGISTER CONTENTS
 0002C8  4040404040404040              115         DC   CL8' '              FILLER
 0002D0  4040404040404040              116  CHOLD  DC   CL16' '             USED TO DISPLAY REGISTERS
 0002D8  4040404040404040


                                         DUMP AFTER EXECUTION

 006AA0  F0404040   40404040   40404040   40404040    40404040   40404040   40404040   40404040
 006AC0  08803333   FFFFFFFF   40404040   40404040    7000684E   FF0880FF   6000685B   40404040
 006AE0  F0404040   40404040   40404040   40404040    40404040   40404040   40404040   40404040


                               RELOCATION FACTOR    006800
```

FIG. 10-44. Example of Insert Characters Under Mask.

from consecutive bytes of the operand in storage. The byte positions in the register corresponding to 0 bits in the mask are not altered. The first operand specifies the register. The second operand is the mask. The programer usually writes this as a decimal number from 0 through 15, depending upon the pattern of mask bits desired. The third operand specifies the address in storage of the leftmost byte to be copied. This command is available on some of the newer models of the computer. An example of Insert Characters Under Mask is given in Fig. 10-44.

The computer sets the condition code when performing an Insert Characters Under Mask to reflect the bit pattern in the bytes handled. The condition code is 0 if the mask has no (zero) 1 bits or if all the bits inserted into the register are 0 bits. When the bytes inserted include at least one 1 bit, then the code is 1 if the leftmost bit inserted is a 1 bit and is a 2 if the leftmost bit inserted is a 0 bit. Condition code 3 is not used. At first sight, this pattern of condition code settings makes little sense, but reasons exist for the pattern. First, if the leftmost byte of a register be replaced by an Insert Characters Under Mask, then the condition code indicates the algebraic sign of the resulting binary number. Second, if the mask is 0_x, then the command becomes a No Operation, but the 0 condition code indicates it. Third, if the mask is F_x, then the command sets the condition code and behaves like a Load and Test command, except for alignment. The Insert Characters Under Mask command is subject to interruption for storage protection and for addressing beyond the limits of available storage, even when the mask is 0_x.

STCM—Store Characters Under Mask. This RS command copies selected bytes from the register to form a field of contiguous bytes in storage. The condition code

```
      LOC   OBJECT CODE      ADDR1 ADDR2  ST #  NAME    OP   OPERANDS        COMMENT

                                           IMPERATIVES

    00005C 91FF 331C         00324         38            TM   CMD,X'FF'       SET CONDITION CODE TO 11
    000060 0540                             39            BALR 4,0             SAVE CONDITION CODE
    000062 5850 331B         00320         40            L    5,CMC           LOAD INSERT FIELD
    000066 BE5A 331C         00324         41 F10#45      STCM 5,10,CMD        STORE CHARACTERS MASKED
    00006A 0560                             42            BALR 6,0             SAVE CONDITION CODE
    00006C 9046 332B         00330         43            STM  4,6,CSAVE       SHOW REGISTER CONTENTS


                                           DECLARATIVES

    000320 204B216B                        125 CMC       DC   X'204B216B'     BYTES FOR INSERTION
    000324 FFFFFFFF                        126 CMD       DC   X'FFFFFFFF'     BYTES FOR STORAGE FIELD
    000328 404040404040404040              127           DC   CL8' '          FILLER
    000330 404040404040404040              128 CSAVE     DC   CL16' '         USED TO DISPLAY REGISTERS
    000338 404040404040404040


                                        DUMP AFTER EXECUTION

    006B00 F0404040  40404040  40404040  40404040   40404040  40404040  40404040  40404040
    006B20 204B216B  2021FFFF  40404040  40404040   70006B62  204B216B  70006B6C  40404040
    006B40 F0404040  40404040  40404040  40404040   40404040  40404040  40404040  40404040


                              RELOCATION FACTOR      006B00
```

FIG. 10-45. Example of Store Characters Under Mask.

is not set. Otherwise, the command operates substantially as the reverse of the Insert Characters Under Mask, and the programer specifies the operands in the same manner. This command is available on some of the newer models of the computer. This command is subject to interruption for storage protection and for addressing beyond the limits of available storage, but not when the mask is 0_x. An example of Store Characters Under Mask is shown in Fig. 10-45.

CLM—Compare Logical Characters Under Mask. This RS command compares selected bytes from the register named as the first operand address with a field of bytes in storage named as the third operand address. The second operand is the mask, which the programer usually specifies as a decimal number from 0 through 15, depending upon the pattern of mask bits desired. Byte positions in the register corresponding to the 0 bits in the mask are not included in the comparison. The register named as the first operand address serves as the source of the bytes for the variable of the comparison. The third operand address specifies the leftmost byte of the constant of the comparison. The length of the third operand is always the same as the length of the first operand and is equal to the number of 1 bits in the mask. Since the comparison is logical, not algebraic, the computer accepts all bit combinations and makes no distinction between sign and data bits or characters. This command is available on some of the newer models of the computer. An example of Compare Logical Characters Under Mask is given in Fig. 10-46.

This command sets the condition code. The setting is to zero if the mask is 0_x, or if the comparison indicates equal. The other settings are the usual for a logical

```
   LOC   OBJECT CODE    ADDR1 ADDR2  ST #   NAME   OP    OPERANDS              COMMENT

                                         IMPERATIVES

  000070 91FF 331C      00324          45          TM    CMD,X'FF'             SET CONDITION CODE TO 11
  000074 0540                          46          BALR  4,0                   SAVE CONDITION CODE
  000076 5850 337B      00380          47          L     5,CME                 LOAD VARIABLE OF COMPARISON
  00007A BD54 337C      00384          48  F10#46  CLM   5,4,CMG               COMPARE LOGICIAL CHAR. MASKED
  00007E 0560                          49          BALR  6,0                   SAVE CONDITION CODE
  000080 9046 338B      00390          50          STM   4,6,DSAVE             SHOW REGISTER CONTENTS


                                         DECLARATIVES

  000380 D4C1E2D2                     137  CME      DC    C'MASK'               VARIABLE OF COMPARISON
  000384 C1C2C3C4                     138  CMG      DC    C'ABCD'               CONSTANT OF COMPARISON
  000388 4040404040404040             139          DC    CL8' '                FILLER
  000390 4040404040404040            140  DSAVE    DC    CL16' '               USED TO DISPLAY REGISTERS
  000398 4040404040404040


                                    DUMP AFTER EXECUTION

  006B60  F0404040   40404040   40404040   40404040   40404040   40404040   40404040   40404040
  006B80  D4C1E2D2   C1C2C3C4   40404040   40404040   50006876   D4C1E2D2   40006B80   40404040
  006BA0  F0404040   40404040   40404040   40404040   40404040   40404040   40404040   40404040


                              RELOCATION FACTOR    006800
```

Fig. 10-46. Example of Compare Logical Characters Under Mask.

comparison (1 is for low, 2 is for high, and 3 is unused). The command is subject to interruption for storage protection and for addressing beyond the limits of storage, even when the mask is 0_x.

EXERCISES

1. How does add logical differ from a normal algebraic add?
2. Under what conditions could a table of less than 256 bytes be safely used in Translate or Translate and Test?
3. What is meant by a mask?
4. Distinguish between logical OR and Exclusive OR.
5. Distinguish between logical OR and logical AND.
6. Describe a financial edit.
7. Define a floating dollar sign.
8. What is meant by check-protect format?
9. Make a list of all the operations that have been described thus far in this book that have the effect of altering the condition code. Show the basis for the setting in each instance.

CHAPTER 11

Tape and Disk Operations

DATA ORGANIZATION

Chapter 7 presented input and output operations as done under the simpler versions of the operating systems available, such as BPS, BOS, TOS, and DOS. In those, the IOCS routines are such a significant portion of the operating system as to make their presence obvious to the programer. In the larger versions of the operating systems, such as OS, the IOCS routines fade in importance to the level of another important portion of the operating system. Programers working under OS usually do not even refer to "IOCS" as such. For generality in this book, however, the term IOCS is used to designate the input-output control routines available in the operating system, irrespective of the choice of operating system (OS, DOS, TOS, etc.). In particular, this chapter stresses input and output under both DOS and OS for magnetic tape and magnetic disk.

Chapter 7 also presented the serial (or consecutive or sequential) form of input-output, since the most widely used types of input and output equipment, e.g., card readers and printers, require the use of the serial organization. Other types of input and output equipment, such as magnetic disks, can use other forms of IOCS.

The data organizations and the supporting IOCS routines available to the programer depend in part upon the size and model of computer and upon its complement of input and output equipment. If the programer has access only to a relatively small computer, then serial may be the only form of data organization and IOCS

381

available. If a programer is working with a large model of the computer equipped with a large operating system and with a wide variety of input and output equipment, including communications equipment, he may have a choice of more than 10 data organizations and supporting IOCS routines.

Physical IOCS, which is independent of the data organization, underlies all of the varieties of logical IOCS. The programer can use physical IOCS with any data organization and to support and implement his own unique data organizations.

When the programer selects physical IOCS, he assumes much of the control over the input and output equipment. Physical IOCS is closer to the machine operations in content and approach than logical IOCS. In physical IOCS, the programer is responsible for handling directly and deliberately many of the conditions and timing situations that can arise in input and output operations. The programer must provide for each step and must do so in terms that are closer to machine language than the IOCS terms described previously. By way of contrast, in logical IOCS the programer can concentrate his attention upon the logical aspects of the structure of the data to be processed and can rely on logical IOCS to handle many or all of the details of timing, error conditions, use of storage space, buffer queues, and the like.

Within logical IOCS two major varieties exist, the queued and the basic. The queued is the most distant from the machine language of the computer; the basic is closer. Basic places upon the programer the responsibility for some timing considerations and for some error handling. Basic goes beyond physical IOCS in that the programer need not concern himself with the preparation of subroutines for the control of the input and output operations. As such, it does not permit the programer as much detailed control over the input and output operations as physical IOCS does, but it provides more than queued logical IOCS does.

In queued logical IOCS, which is the most distant from machine language, the timing of data movements and manipulation of data in storage are handled automatically, as are most error conditions. The result is that whenever the programer wishes another logical record of data to be read or written, that logical record and its buffer queue are handled without further attention from the programer.

Within both basic and queued logical IOCS, five main types exist, depending upon the data organization assumed. These five types of data organization are the serial (sequential or consecutive), the direct access, the indexed sequential, the partitioned, and the communications. Some of these are dependent upon the choice of input and output equipment to be used, others relatively independent. The distinctions between these five types are presented briefly below.

The serial (also called consecutive or sequential) data organization has been described in Chap. 7. In this organization, each record in a file is assumed to be placed in a series based upon an ascending sequence of some key field. One record follows the next in the input-output medium in strict order. To insert or to delete a record from the file requires rewriting the entire set of records in the file, copying them with the insertion added or the deletion accomplished. The normal processing sequence utilized by the serial IOCS routines is to take each record in strict sequence. Records may not be skipped, and it is impossible to go back to a record with a lower key.

The serial data organization is required with some types of input and output equipment. Thus, for example, card readers, card punches, and line printers all require it. Magnetic tape, in practice, is usually used with it, and magnetic disks may also be used with it, but to do so usually sacrifices some of the major advantages of magnetic disks.

The direct-access IOCS routines assume an essentially random data organization. In practice this data organization requires that the programer have some way of determining where in the file the particular record to be processed can be found. This is often done by a locator or randomizing routine which can calculate the location (address) of the record from the key of the record. Making insertions, therefore, may require the use of "overflow" areas if the insertions are numerous and have bunched keys.

The direct-access data organization requires the use of magnetic-disk, magnetic-drum, or mass-storage devices. With this data organization, the programer can insert and delete records without copying the entire file of records. Because of the need to search for each record before it can be processed, the processing time with the direct-access IOCS may be longer than with the serial IOCS. Where the records to be processed are in a random order, however, a direct-access data organization and IOCS make possible a far more rapid handling than can be obtained by the use of the serial organization and IOCS.

The indexed-sequential IOCS routines are based upon an essentially serial organization of the records in the file data. To supplement this basically serial organization of the records, a hierarchy of indexes is established. These indexes usually are in terms of the same key used to sequence the records in the file. By searching the indexes, the computer can find the addresses of a record in any sequence.

Insertions of a few records to the file can be made through the use of overflow areas without rewriting the entire file. Deletions are commonly done by rewriting the entire file. Since the records are organized essentially in serial form, serial processing can be done efficiently. When a random access to the records is desired, it can be accomplished quickly by the use of the index. The cost of this indexed organization is a greater use of storage space for the serial organization. This organization requires magnetic-disk, magnetic-drum, or mass-storage devices.

The partitioned IOCS routines rest upon a partitioned data organization. In that organization, groups of records are arranged in a serial organization in the file. Within each group, the order of the records may be essentially random and is supported by an index or directory covering only that particular group. No master index exists. Individual records may be inserted or deleted in any one partition, but the insertion or deletion of a partition requires rewriting the entire file. The partitioned organization is sometimes used for storing subroutines and programs, where it is known that the need for one program is often associated with the need for another program. In such cases, the programs that are likely to be used together are put in the same partition.

Where communication equipment is used with the computer, a separate set of IOCS routines and supporting data organizations are available. Communication equipment often involves coding and format restrictions and commonly operates in a serial manner. This data organization finds increasing use as communication equipment becomes more widely tied to computers for input and output.

Because magnetic tape is used usually with the serial IOCS, the following sections on serial IOCS stress the use of magnetic tape. Since the indexed-sequential IOCS can be used with magnetic disks and mass storage, the later sections of this chapter stress disks. The random- or direct-access IOCS is not further discussed in this book because many users apparently find the indexed-sequential about as convenient for most applications, or more so. Parts of this chapter are applicable only to models of the computer produced by particular manufacturers, and may not reflect improvements recently introduced.

INPUT AND OUTPUT UNDER OS

If the programer has access to a medium or large model of the computer, he may find it used with OS. OS (Operating System) is a computer operating system that offers the programer more assistance and flexibility (see Chaps. 7 and 8). But to accomplish this, it imposes upon the programer a different way of specifying input and output declaratives.

In OS, the programer may place input-output declarative operands partly in his program and partly in the DD job control cards. The preferred practice is to specify in the program the declarative operands that reflect the nature of the data, and to specify in the DD cards the declarative operands that reflect the input-output equipment. The reason for this is to give the computer operator flexibility in reassigning equipment as demands upon the computer change, and as equipment may be available. For example, if a printer is being repaired, the operator can divert temporarily the to-be-printed output data to magnetic disk, and then have the computer do the actual printing later when the printer is back in service.

To replace the DTF declarative, OS offers a DCB macro which generates a series of Define Constant declaratives, depending upon the operands the programer specifies. The constants are arranged in a specific tablelike pattern in storage, called a Data Control Block (DCB). The programer must specify a DCB for each input or output file (often called "data set" in OS). The programer uses the same DCB macro in his program as in the DD job control cards, but the operands may be different. When the operands specified in the DD card conflict with or are inconsistent with those specified in the program, those in the DD card usually take precedence, overriding those the programer specified in his program. The macros to direct input and output operations, however, are similar under both DOS and OS.

MACROS FOR QUEUED SERIAL INPUT AND OUTPUT

The macros for the queued serial IOCS for both magnetic tape and magnetic disks are often the same as those used with printers, card punches, and card readers, as described in Chap. 7. The functions performed by the various macros differ a little because of the nature of the input and output equipment involved. A brief review of each of these macros is appropriate; a summary of them is given in Fig. 11-1.

The OPEN macro initializes the input and output equipment for use. In addition to the functions described in Chap. 7, one major additional function is performed for magnetic tape and magnetic disk: the checking of labels against the data provided by the DTF declarative or DD. The format of the standard labels is described in Fig. 11-2. When the OPEN macro is given for a magnetic-tape input file, the IOCS routine checks the status of the magnetic-tape drive; if it is operational, the routine attempts to read the first record from the file. This first record is typically the volume label identifying the reel of tape. The IOCS routine, after checking that this label (record) meets the IOCS specifications, reads the next record from the file, the file header label.

The purpose of this header label (record) is to identify the information contained in the file. Normally only one file header label (record) will be processed by the IOCS routines. If additional header labels (records) are encountered, the IOCS routines do not process them but skip over them, searching for the first nonlabel record. The first nonlabel record in the file is then entered into the buffer to prepare for the first GET operation. This first record may actually be an additional tape label created by the user ("user label"), but this fact is not checked for by the IOCS routines, since the IOCS routines recognize a label word by the identifications shown in Fig. 11-2.

In the case of magnetic disks and mass storage devices, a similar pattern of labeling is followed. The volume label, which is encountered first, identifies the storage or disk unit. On magnetic disks, however, this is usually the third record on the first track of the first cylinder—i.e., record two in track zero in cylinder zero—since the other two are needed for other purposes, such as IPL routines. If additional volume labels follow, and they may, the IOCS routines do not process them but search instead for the first file header label.

The first file header label on disk and mass-storage follows the same general format used for magnetic-tape labels. The programer rarely uses one magnetic tape to hold more than one file, but commonly does so for other storage devices. When multiple logical files occur in one storage device, the checking of the file header label becomes particularly important. Each file header label for disk or mass storage con-

386 | *360/370 Programing*

INPUT-OUTPUT MACROCOMMANDS

DESIRED FUNCTION TO BE PERFORMED	SEQUENTIAL DOS	OS	INDEXED-SEQUENTIAL DOS	OS
INITIALIZE FILES FOR USE	OPEN	OPEN	OPEN	OPEN
INITIALIZE FOR SEQUENTIAL PROCESS	---	---	SETL	SETL
INPUT ONE LOGICAL RECORD	GET	GET	GET	GET
OUTPUT ONE LOGICAL RECORD	PUT	PUT	PUT	PUT
TERMINATE SEQUENTIAL PROCESSING	---	---	ESETL	ESETL
OUTPUT ONE MODIFIED RECORD	---	PUTX	---	PUTX
INSERT-OUTPUT RECORDS RANDOMLY	---	---	WRITE	WRITE
	---	---	WAITF	CHECK
ACCESS-INPUT RECORDS RANDOMLY	---	---	READ	READ
	---	---	WAITF	CHECK
CREATE-LOAD AN IS FILE	---	---	SETFL	---
TERMINATE CREATE-LOAD OF IS FILE	---	---	ENDFL	---
RELEASE INPUT BLOCK	RELSE	RELSE	---	RELSE
TRUNCATE OUTPUT BLOCK	TRUNC	TRUNC	---	---
FORCE END OF VOLUME	FEOV	FEOV	---	---
CONTROL EQUIPMENT OPERATION	CNTRL	CNTRL	---	---
WRITE CHECKPOINT RECORDS	CHKPT	CHKPT	CHKPT	CHKPT
TERMINATE USE OF FILES	CLOSE	CLOSE	CLOSE	CLOSE

```
SYNTAX UNDER OS
OPEN   (DCBN,(INPUT))
OPEN   (DCBN,(OUTPUT))
OPEN   (DCB1,(OUTPUT),DCB2,...)
SETL   DCBN,B
GET    DCBN
GET    DCBN,WAREA
PUT    DCBN,WAREA
PUT    DCBN
PUTX   DCBN
PUTX   DCB2,DCB1
ESETL  DCBN
READ   NDECB,KU,MF=E
READ   NDECB,KU,DCBN,'S','S',KEYAD,MF=L
WRITE  NDECB,K,MF=E
WRITE  NDECB,KN,MF=E
CHECK  NDECB,DSORG=IS
---    ---
---    ---
RELSE  DCBN
TRUNC  DCBN
CNTRL  DCBN,SX,N
---    ---
CHKPT  DCBN
FEOV   DCBN
CLOSE  DCBN
CLOSE  (DCB1,DCB2,...)
---    ---
```

```
SYNTAX UNDER DOS
OPEN   FILE
OPEN   FILE1,FILE2,...
---    ---
SETL   FILE,BOF
GET    FILE
GET    FILE,WAREA
PUT    FILE
PUT    FILE,WAREA
---    ---
---    ---
ESETL  FILE
READ   FILE,KEY
READ   (1),KEY
WRITE  FILE,KEY
WRITE  FILE,NEWKEY
WAITF  FILE
SETFL  FILE
ENDFL  FILE
RELSE  FILE
TRUNC  FILE
CNTRL  FILE,AAA
CNTRL  FILE,SX,N,M
CHKPT  SYSNNN,RSTRT,HIGH
FEOV   FILE
CLOSE  (DCBN)
CLOSE  FILE
CLOSE  FILE1,FILE2,...
```

FIG. 11-1. Macros for serial file organization.

tains the file limits within which the records comprising the file will be found. More than one standard file header label per file may be used and checked by the IOCS routines, depending upon the manner in which the file is recorded. Other records are bypassed until the first nonlabel record to be processed is encountered. This is then prepared for the first GET operation.

In the case of tape output files, the OPEN macro writes the standard volume label and the standard header label appropriate to identify accurately the file to be written. Since these labels are the labels checked as volume and header labels when the file is later read as an input file, it is important that these be written accurately by the OPEN routine. The information written by the OPEN macro is obtained from the DTF or DD card data, as described later, and from the labels already on the tape or disk. In the case of mass-storage or disk files, the OPEN macro updates— that is, corrects to reflect the new use—the existing labels, and creates new ones only if the needed labels do not exist.

In summary, therefore, the major additional functions performed by the OPEN macro in the case of magnetic tape, mass storage, and disk files, are to check and create volume and header labels. This operation has no equivalent for line printers, card readers, or card punches.

OPEN—Open the File. This macrocommand under OS normally has three operands. The first is the name of the DCB. The second may be (INPUT) or (OUTPUT) or (UPDAT) and is assumed to be input if this operand is omitted with the omission marked by a comma. The third is normally omitted without marking commas to indicate that the DISP option cited in the DD card is to determine the position of the access mechanism of the equipment after the use of the data is complete. All operands must be enclosed as a group within parentheses. The programer may assign a name if he wants to and may OPEN more than one file if desired with one macrocommand.

This macrocommand under DOS has one operand, the name of the file. The programer may OPEN more than one file if desired with one macrocommand. If the program is to be easily relocated in storage, the programer should put an R on the end of the macro, as OPENR. No parentheses are used.

To terminate the availability of a file of data ("data set"), the programer uses the CLOSE macro. Its functions with magnetic tape, mass storage, and magnetic disk, are very similar to those for line printers, card readers, and card punches, as described in Chap. 7. The major additional functions performed by CLOSE for magnetic tape and disk are the handling of labels.

In the case of an input file, the CLOSE macro checks the trailer label at the end of the input file and compares it with information (typically a count of the records read) which has been accumulated during the course of reading the input file. If no error has occurred in processing or in input operations, the data will agree. If an error has occurred, a disagreement may be detected and an error signaled. In the case of magnetic-tape files, the tape is also rewound.

As in the case of card punches, card readers, and printers, the programer must give an OPEN macro prior to any other macro specifying action on a given logical file of data. Before the end of the program, the programer should give a CLOSE macro for the files in order to have the trailer records written or checked correctly. After the programer has had the computer execute the CLOSE macro, he cannot again use that file for input or output operations in the program without first again giving an OPEN macro.

CLOSE—Close the File. This macrocommand under OS normally has two operands. The first is the name of the DCB. The second is normally omitted to indicate that the DISP option cited in the DD card is to determine the position of the access mechanism of the equipment after the use of the data is complete. All operands must be enclosed as a group within parentheses. The programer may assign a name to the CLOSE if he wants to and may CLOSE more than one file if desired with one macrocommand. For basic (not queued) access, other operands may be needed.

This macrocommand under DOS has one operand, the name of the file. The programer may CLOSE more than one file if desired with one macrocommand. If the program is to be easily relocated in storage, the programer should put an R on the end of the macro, as CLOSER. All files given an OPEN must be given a CLOSE before terminating the program, regardless of the choice of operating system.

To do input or output operations, the two macros used for magnetic tape and magnetic disk are the same as those described earlier. GET enables the IOCS routines to make available in storage the next logical record of input data for processing. PUT enables the IOCS routines to copy one logical record of data as output from internal storage. Buffering and any blocking or unblocking needed are performed automatically by the queued IOCS routines for the programer.

GET—Get a Record. This macrocommand under OS may have one or two operands. The first operand is the name of the DCB. When this is the only operand used, then the operating system assumes that data will be used from its position in the buffer and sets the contents of register 1 to serve as a pointer to the left end of the record. This is known as the "locate" mode for a GET. A second mode is the "move" mode. For this, the programer specifies as a second operand the address of a work area in storage. The operating system copies the record from the buffer into the work area. Under OS, the programer indicates his intention of using work areas when he writes the MACRF operands for the DCB, and having once made a choice, he must adhere to it for that DCB. If the GET fails because the end of data file has been reached, control goes to the address specified as the operand for the EODAD in the DCB. If the GET fails for any other reason, control goes to the address specified as the operand for the SYNAD in the DCB. The programer may assign a name to a GET.

This macrocommand under DOS may have one or two operands. If processing is to be done directly in the assigned input area of storage, only one operand, the name of the file, is needed. If the programer wants to have the processing done in a work area instead, then the address of the work area is the second operand. If the programer elects to use work areas, he must have specified WORKA= in the DTF, and use them consistently. If the GET fails because the EOF (end-of-data file) has been reached, control goes to the address the programer specifies as the completion for the EOFADDR in the DTF. If the GET fails for any other reason, control goes

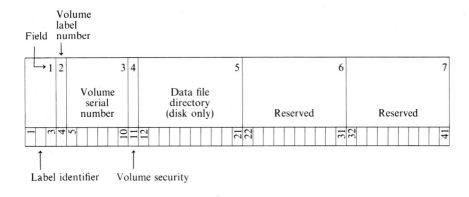

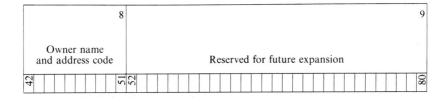

Volume Label Format for Tape or Disk

Field	Name and length	Description
1.	Label identifier 3 bytes	Must contain VOL to indicate that this is a volume label.
2.	Volume label number 1 byte	Indicates the relative position (1–8) of a volume label within a group of volume labels.
3.	Volume serial number 6 bytes	A unique identification code which is assigned to a volume when it enters an installation. This code may also appear on the external surface of the volume for visual identification. It is normally a numeric field 000001 to 999999; however, any or all of the 6 bytes may be alphameric.
4.	Volume security 1 byte	Indicates security status of the volume: 0 = no further identification for each file of the volume is required. Non-0 = further identification for each file of the volume is required before processing.

FIG. 11-2. Tape and disk file label formats.

Volume Label Format for Tape or Disk (Continued)

Field	Name and length	Description
5.	VTOC pointer 10 bytes	For DASD only. The first 5 bytes contain the starting address (CCHHR) of the VTOC. The last 5 bytes are blank. For tape files, this field is not used and should be recorded as blanks.
6.	Reserved: 10 bytes	Reserved; at present, show blanks.
7.	Reserved: 10 bytes	Reserved; at present, show blanks.
8.	Owner name and address code: 10 bytes	Indicates a specific customer, installation and/or system to which the volume belongs. This field may be a standardized code, name, address, etc.
9.	Reserved: 29 bytes	Reserved; at present, show blanks.

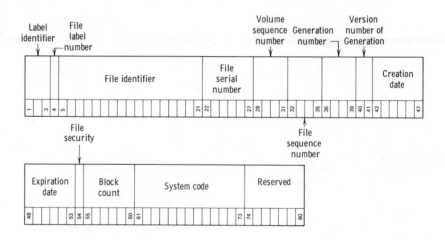

Magnetic tape labels

Field	Name and length	Description
1.	Label identifier 3 bytes	Identifies the type of label: HDR = Header – beginning of a data file EOF = End of file – end of a set of data EOV = End of volume – end of the physical reel
2.	File label number 1 byte	Always a 1 for the first label.
3.	File identifier 17 bytes	Uniquely identifies the entire file, may contain only printable characters except apostrophe.

FIG. 11-2. (*continued*)

Field	Name and length	Description
4.	File serial number or set identifier 6 bytes	Uniquely identifies a file/volume relationship. This field is identical to the volume serial number in the volume label of the first or only volume of a multi-volume file or a multi-file set. This field will normally be numeric (000001 to 999999) but may contain any six alphameric characters.
5.	Volume sequence number or file section number 4 bytes	Indicates the order of a volume in a given file or multi-file set. The first must be numbered 0001 and subsequent numbers must be in proper numeric sequence.
6.	File sequence number 4 bytes	Assigns numeric sequence to a file within a multi-file set. The first must be numbered 0001.
7.	Generation number 4 bytes	Uniquely identifies the various editions of the file. May be from 0001 to 9999 in proper numeric sequence, or blank.
8.	Version number of generation 2 bytes	Indicates the version of a generation of a file.
9.	Creation date 6 bytes	Indicates the year and the day of the year when the file was created:

Position	Code	Meaning
1	blank	none
2-3	00-99	year
4-6	001-366	day of year

(For example, January 31, 1978 would be entered as 78031.)

Field	Name and length	Description
10.	Expiration date 6 bytes	Indicates the year and the day of the year when the file may be erased. The format of this field is identical to field 9. On a multi-file reel, processed sequentially, all files are considered to expire on the same day.
11.	Accessibility or file security 1 byte	Indicates security status of the file. 0 = No security protection Non-0 = Security protection. Additional identification of the file or user is required before the file can be processed.
12.	Block count 6 bytes	Indicates the number of data blocks written on the file from the last header label to the first trailer label exclusive of tape marks. Count does not include checkpoint records. This field is used in trailer labels.
13.	System code 13 bytes	Identifies the operating system or programing language.
14.	Reserved 7 bytes	Reserved; at present, show as blanks.

Fɪɢ. 11-2. (*continued*)

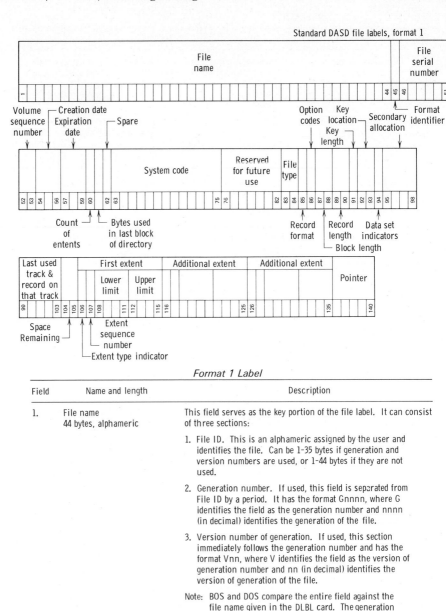

Standard DASD file labels, format 1

Format 1 Label

Field	Name and length	Description
1.	File name 44 bytes, alphameric	This field serves as the key portion of the file label. It can consist of three sections:

1. File ID. This is an alphameric assigned by the user and identifies the file. Can be 1-35 bytes if generation and version numbers are used, or 1-44 bytes if they are not used.

2. Generation number. If used, this field is separated from File ID by a period. It has the format Gnnnn, where G identifies the field as the generation number and nnnn (in decimal) identifies the generation of the file.

3. Version number of generation. If used, this section immediately follows the generation number and has the format Vnn, where V identifies the field as the version of generation number and nn (in decimal) identifies the version of generation of the file.

Note: BOS and DOS compare the entire field against the file name given in the DLBL card. The generation and version numbers are treated differently by OS.

The remaining fields comprise the DATA portion of the file label:

2.	Format identifier 1 byte, numeric	1 = Format 1

FIG. 11-2. (*continued*)

Field	Name and length	Description
3.	File serial number 6 bytes, alphameric	Uniquely identifies a file/volume relationship. It is identical to the volume serial number of the first or only volume of a multi-volume file.
4.	Volume sequence number 2 bytes, binary	Indicates the order of a volume relative to the first volume on which the data file resides.
5.	Creation date 3 bytes, discontinuous binary	Indicates the year and the day of the year on which the file was created. It is of the form YDD, where Y signifies the year (0-99) and DD the day of the year (1-366).
6.	Expiration date 3 bytes, discontinuous binary	Indicates the year and the day of the year on which the file may be deleted. The form of this field is identical to that of field 5.
7A.	Extent count 1 byte, binary	Contains a count of the number of extents for this file on this volume. If user labels are used, the count includes the user label track as a separate extent.
7B.	Bytes used in last block of directory 1 byte, binary	Used by Operating System/360 only for partioned (library structure) data sets.
7C.	Spare 1 byte	Reserved; at present, show as blanks.
8.	System code 13 bytes	Identifies the operating system or programing language.
9.	Reserved 7 bytes	Reserved; at present, show as blanks.
10.	File type 2 bytes	The contents of this field uniquely identify the type of data file: Hex 4000 = Consecutive organization Hex 2000 = Direct-access organization Hex 8000 = Indexed-sequential organization Hex 0200 = Partitioned library organization Hex 0000 = Organization not defined in the file label.
11.	Record format 1 byte	The contents of this field indicate the type of records contained in the file:

Bit position	Content	Meaning
0 and 1	01	Variable-length records
	10	Fixed-length records
	11	Undefined format
2	0	No track overflow
	1	File is organized by using track overflow (Operating System/360 only)
3	0	Unblocked records
	1	Blocked records
4	0	No truncated records
	1	Truncated records in file

FIG. 11-2. (*continued*)

Field	Name and length	Description
		5 and 6 01 Control character ASA code
		10 Control character machine code
		00 Control character not stated
		7 0 Records have no keys
		1 Records are written with keys.
12.	Option codes 1 byte	Bits within this field are used to indicate various options used in building the file. A 1 bit indicates "on." 0 = No options. 2 = Master index. 3 = Independent overflow area. 4 = Cylinder overflow provided.
13.	Block length 2 bytes, binary	Indicates the block length for fixed-length records or maximum block size for variable-length blocks.
14.	Record length 2 bytes, binary	Indicates the record length for fixed-length records or the maximum record length for variable-length records.
15.	Key length 1 byte, binary	Indicates the length of the key portion of the data records in the file.
16.	Key location 2 bytes, binary	Indicates the high order position of the data record.
17.	Data set indicators 1 byte	Bits within this field are used to indicate the following:

Bit

0   If on, indicates that this is the last volume on which this file normally resides.

1   If on, indicates that the data set described by this file must remain in the same absolute location on the direct-access device.

2   If on, indicates that block length must always be a multiple of 8 bytes.

3   If on, indicates that this data file is security protected; a password must be provided in order to access it.

4-7   Spare. Reserved for future use.

| 18. | Secondary allocation 4 bytes, binary | Indicates the amount of storage to be requested for this data file at end of extent. The first byte of this field is an indication of the type of allocation request. Hex code "C2" (EBCDIC "B") indicates bytes, hex code "E3" (EBCDIC "T") indicates tracks, and hex code "C3" (EBCDIC "C") indicates cylinders. The next three bytes of this field are a binary number indicating how many bytes, tracks, or cylinders are requested. |
| 19. | Last used track and record on that track 5 bytes, discontinuous binary | Indicates the last occupied track in a consecutive file organization data file. This field has the format CCHHR. It is all binary zeros if the last track in a consecutive data file is not on this volume or if it is not consecutive organization. |

FIG. 11-2. (*continued*)

Field	Name and length	Description
20.	Amount of space remaining on last track used 2 bytes, binary	A count of the number of bytes of available space remaining on the last track used by this data file on this volume.
21.	Extent type indicator 1 byte	Indicates the type of extent with which the following fields are associated:

Hex code

	00	Next three fields do not indicate any extent.
	01	Prime area (indexed sequential); or consecutive data area (i.e., the extent containing the user's data records).
	02	Independent overflow area of an indexed sequential file.
	04	Cylinder index or master index area of an indexed sequential file.
	40	User label track area.
	80	Data area with split cylinder.

Field	Name and length	Description
22.	Extent sequence number 1 byte, binary	Indicates the extent sequence in a multi-extent file.
23.	Lower limit 4 bytes, discontinuous binary	The cylinder and the track address specifying the starting point (lower limit) of this extent component. This field has the format CCHH.
24.	Upper limit 4 bytes	The cylinder and the track address specifying the ending point (upper limit) of this extent component. This field has the format CCHH.
25-28.	Additional extent 10 bytes	These fields have the same format as fields 21-24 above.
29-32.	Additional extent 10 bytes	These fields have the same format as fields 21-24 above.
33.	Pointer to next file label within this label set 5 bytes, discontinuous binary	The disk address (format CCHHR) of a continuation label if needed to further describe the file. If field 9 indicates Indexed sequential organization, this field will point to a format 2 file label within this label set. Otherwise, it points to a format 3 file label, and then only if the file contains more than three extent segments. This field contains all binary zeros if no additional file label is pointed to.

Format 2 disk label is for indexed-sequential files. It provides pointers to (disk addresses of) the index, data, and overflow areas used and available.

Format 3 disk label is a continuation of fields 21-24 in the Format 1 label when more than three extents must be specified.

Format 4 disk label is for direct (random) access organized files.

FIG. 11-2. (*continued*)

in accordance with the completion the programer specifies for the ERROPT= in the DTF.

PUT—Put a Record. This macrocommand under OS has one or two operands. The first operand is the name of the DCB. When this is the only operand used, the operating system loads register 1 with the address of the next available place in the buffer. This is known as the "locate" mode. In the "move" mode, the programer specifies as a second operand the address of a work area in storage. The operating system copies the data from the work area into the buffer. Under OS, the programer indicates his intention of using work areas when he writes the MACRF operands for DCB, and having once made a choice, he must adhere to it for that DCB. If the PUT fails, control goes to the address specified as the operand for the SYNAD in the DCB. The programer may assign a name to a PUT.

This macrocommand under DOS may have one or two operands. If the building of the output record is to be done directly in the assigned output area of storage, only one operand, the name of the file, is needed. If the programer wants to have the building done in a work area instead, then the address of the work area is the second operand. If the programer elects to use work areas, he must have specified WORKA= in the DTF, and use them consistently. If the PUT fails for any reason, control goes in accordance with the completion the programer specifies for the ERROPT= in the DTF.

PUTX—Put On an Exchange Basis. This macrocommand under OS has one or two operands. The first operand is the name of the DCB. When this is the only operand used, the operating system returns the record as an output to the same external storage location (usually disk) as it had been found by the previous GET. This permits reading records from a file, modifying them (without changing the length), and then returning them with a PUTX to the original file without rewriting the entire file. The programer can also use PUTX to copy directly from one file to another. This combined GET-PUT operation the programer can have done with a single PUTX by specifying the name of the input DCB as the second operand for the PUTX. In other respects, PUTX operates as a PUT. PUTX is not available under DOS.

Reading and writing data in blocked formats improves the efficiency of magnetic-tape, mass-storage, and magnetic-disk use because the proportion of unused space decreases as blocks grow longer. The IOCS routines for magnetic tape and disk normally assume and make explicit provision for writing data in blocked form. In some cases in a program, however, it will be found that not enough data exist to fill a block completely, yet the block still should be made available as output, since logically no more data should go into it. To handle this function, the TRUNC macro is available. This the programer uses in place of a PUT command when the programer desires to write a variable length or short block—i.e., a block of less than standard length or of variable length as specified by the DTF. The new output block begins with the record for which the TRUNC is given. This macro applies to both tape and disk operations.

The companion on the input side is the RELSE macro. The programer occasionally finds that the records of a block contain data that do not need to be processed. In order to have the computer stop providing logical records from the current input block and to begin providing logical records from the next block of input data, the programer can use the RELSE macro before the next GET macro. This macro interrupts the normal deblocking process, reads in a new physical block of input data, and resumes the logical deblocking with the first record of a new block.

Blocking of input and output is closely tied to buffering. The operating system for the queued-access methods establishes buffers which are queues or waiting lines of logical records. They may be for records waiting to be copied into internal storage by a GET and for those waiting to be written out onto external storage after being copied into the buffer by a PUT. Physically, a buffer is an area of storage large enough to accommodate an input or output block of logical records, together with a set of address pointers to define the start and end of the buffer area and to indicate which is the next portion of the buffer area to be used. Typically, the operating system establishes two buffer areas for each input or output file. This helps isolate the timing of the actual input or output operation from the timing of copying data between the buffer areas and working storage areas in the program. In OS, the programer has available a number of macros (which are beyond the scope of this book) to direct the operating system in its use of buffers.

RELSE—Release. This macrocommand under OS has one operand, the name of the DCB for an input file. Under DOS, it also has one operand, the name of the file.

TRUNC—Truncate. This macrocommand under OS has one operand, the name of the DCB for an output file. Under DOS, it also has one operand, the name of the file. For variable-length blocked records, the programer must use TRUNC for writing each output block after the PUT. This means as a practical matter that the programer must, under DOS, test the VARBLD register before the PUT to determine whether or not the next variable-length records will fit in the block. Under OS, the operating system can take care of this buffering problem automatically for the programer.

One operation that can be performed with magnetic tape and magnetic disks that cannot be performed with punched cards, line printers, or card readers is known as the checkpoint operation. When a long program is being run, the likelihood that the processing may be interrupted by a machine failure increases as the running time increases. If a machine failure should occur, it would be undesirable to have to repeat all the processing from the beginning. To avoid this problem, the programer can design the program so that is can be restarted at certain points.

To provide this restart capability, the programer must build into his program some re-initialization routines to set control fields to their starting values, and must provide information about the amount of processing that has been accomplished. This is provided by what are known as checkpoint dumps or checkpoint records. Checkpoint records are typically written onto tape, disk, or mass storage, when a checkpoint in the program is reached. They typically consist of a partial dump of the contents of storage as it was at that point in time. For the checkpoint records to be useful, the programer must provide at this point in time an indication of what input record has just been processed and what output record had just been produced. The programer also must be careful about the way in which cumulative processing is done. Then, after backing up the input and output to match that at the time of the checkpoint, the computer can use the checkpoint data and the restart routines to resume the processing from the point at which the checkpoint records were taken. Judiciously done, this can save large amounts of computer time in the event of machine failure.

To simplify the writing of checkpoint records, the IOCS routines for tape and disk include the CHKPT macro. This causes the computer to write a set of checkpoint records on the storage device specified. These records are not the same length or in the same format as the physical blocks written as a result of the normal output routines. In the case of magnetic tape, however, they may be interspersed with the normal blocks or be written on a separate tape.

CHKPT—Checkpoint. This macrocommand under OS has one operand, the name of the DCB for a special input-output file. The programer need neither OPEN nor CLOSE that file, but he must provide a DCB macro with at least the following operands: DSORG=PS,MACRF=(W),RECFM=U,BLKSIZE=bytes, DDNAME=somename. The BLKSIZE may not exceed the capacity of one track on a disk file.

This macrocommand under DOS usually has three operands. The first is the SYSnnn identification of the magnetic tape (or less conveniently, disk) unit to receive the checkpoint dump of storage. This can be any output unit, but it is most conveniently handled by assigning a separate unit and giving a separate DTF and OPEN for a logical file to be written on it. The second operand is the address of the restart routine in the program. This the programer must chose carefully to avoid bugs from improper initialization.

The third operand, which is optional, is the address of the high end of the portion of storage to be dumped. Keeping small the amount of storage dumped at a checkpoint reduces the time needed. But it requires that the programer concentrate the working storage parts of his program into one or a few areas and that he place those at low addresses relative to the start of his program. Then by placing the unvarying instructions of his program at the higher addresses, he can avoid dumping them during a checkpoint (by using the third operand) if he can reload them from some other source.

The normal end-of-reel condition for both input and output is handled automatically for magnetic tapes by the IOCS routines. The end-of-job condition for magnetic tape, whether or not end-of-reel is reached, is handled by the CLOSE macro. Occasionally, however, the programer may wish to force an end-of-volume condition at a time when the physical end of a reel of tape or an area on disk has not been reached. For this purpose the FEOV macro is available.

The restrictions on the FEOV macro are that for an input file the IOCS routines do not check the trailer records but terminate the use of the current reel or disk area and go at once to attempt opening the next volume of the same file. For output files the FEOV macro writes the output block (which may be a short block) as needed, produces the standard trailer label, terminates the use of the current reel or disk area, and opens the next volume, if any, of the file.

FEOV—Force End Of Volume. This macrocommand under OS has one operand for magnetic disks and one or two for magnetic tape. The first operand is the name of the DCB, usually for an output file but maybe for an input file. The second operand used with magnetic tape may be REWIND= or LEAVE=. The former rewinds the tape and positions it ready for an OPEN on the file just read or written. The LEAVE= advances the tape to ready for an OPEN on the next file, if any, on the tape. If the programer omits the second operand, the operating system rewinds and unloads the magnetic tape ready for the operator to remove the reel from the tape drive.

This macrocommand under DOS has one operand, the name of the file. The operating system performs a CLOSE on the file without checking any trailer label and then does an OPEN for the next volume of the file, if any.

The CNTRL macrooperation with magnetic tape is very different from its operation with card readers, card punches, or line printers. The reason is that the CNTRL macro operates not upon the data being read or written but with the equipment itself. Since this equipment is different, the codes used are different, and the control operations performed are different.

CNTRL—Control. This macrocommand under OS must be used after each GET or PUT involving a printer, card reader, or card punch. The macro has three operands. The first is the name of the DCB. The second is SK for skip vertically to a printer channel, SP for space vertically, and SS for select a card stacker. The third operand is the identifying number of the stacker, line, or channel desired. Thus, for an immediate space vertically of three lines in order to leave two unprinted (blank) lines between printed lines, with a DCB named TRPT, the macroinstruction would be CNTRL TRPT,SP,3. Under OS, it is not used for magnetic tape and magnetic disks.

This macrocommand under DOS has been described in Chap. 7 for printers, card readers, or card punches. Special operands are available as listed in Fig. 11-3 for magnetic tape. The name of the file is the first operand. The other operands applicable to magnetic tape are described below.

```
CNTRL  TAPEF,REW          REWIND TAPE
CNTRL  TAPEF1,RUN         REWIND AND UNLOAD TAPE
CNTRL  TAPEF2,ERG         ERASE GAP
CNTRL  TAPEF3,WTM         WRITE TAPE MARK
CNTRL  TAPEF4,BSR         BACKSPACE TO INTERRECORD GAP
CNTRL  TAPEF5,BSF         BACKSPACE TO TAPE MARK
CNTRL  TAPEF6,FSR         FORWARD SPACE TO INTERRECORD GAP
CNTRL  TAPEF7,FSF         FORWARD SPACE TO TAPE MARK
```

Fig. 11-3. Control code operands for the CNTRL macro.

The functions performed by the CNTRL macro with magnetic tape enable the programer to specify rewinding of the tape, moving the tape forward or backward, writing tape marks, and erasing gap indicators. These operations can be done if needed before execution of the OPEN macro. The beginning programer should generally avoid the use of the CNTRL macro with magnetic tapes.

The rewind code REW, as shown in Fig. 11-3, rewinds the tape to the first place on the tape where data is recorded—i.e., to the physical beginning of the tape. Rewind and unload (RUN) by contrast goes beyond this, and removes the tape physically from the read mechanism, so that it cannot be further read or written on without first being reloaded by the operator.

The ERG code for an output file causes the computer to write blank tape, in effect erasing the tape without writing any new data (erase the gap marker). The WTM writes a tape mark on the tape. These are normally written at several points on the tape automatically by the IOCS routines, e.g., to separate header and trailer records from the body of the file. If the programer desires to place additional tape marks on the tape, this code gives him the means of doing so.

The two back-space and two forward-space codes apply to input files only. The BSR (Back Space Record) and FSR (Forward Space Record) codes move the tape to the next interblock gap, ready to write or read a physical block on the tape again. The BSF (Back Space File) and FSF (Forward Space File) move the tape until a tape mark is encountered.

TAPE AND DISK DCB DECLARATIVES

The declaratives needed to control input and output operations may take a number of forms. Under DOS and BOS, the DTF declaratives as described in Chap.

7 and in this chapter are the prescribed form. Under OS, the Data Control Block (DCB) declarative is the prescribed form. Under OS, the operating system builds and uses a DCB for each input and each output file. The DCB is like a table summarizing the character of each input and output file.

The programer has three sources for the data needed to complete a DCB. One is the DCB macrodeclarative that the programer must include in his program. The second is the DD job control cards needed, and sometimes changed, for each execution of the program. The third, applying to input data files only, is the file label recorded with the data. For this reason, the programer must often provide a more complete DCB for an output file than for an input file, and for an input file, must avoid unintentional contradictions between the DCB data he provides and what the file label provides.

Under the assumption that the use of buffers is to be left to the operating system, the operands needed to complete a DCB declarative for queued serial data files on magnetic tape or magnetic disk are described below. All of the operands are in keyword format, and the programer may use them in any order or sequence. But the programer must assign a name in the name column to the DCB declarative he includes in his program. And he must not place that declarative within 16 bytes of the start of (lowest address in) a control section. Hence, unlike DTF's, the programer usually puts all DCB's early (toward the left) in his working storage. This has the added convenience of making them easily found in a dump.

In his program, the programer must include for each magnetic tape or disk file a named DCB declarative having at least three operands: DSORG=, MACRF=, and DDNAME=. The programer should also include LRECL=. The DSORG= operand identifies the data organization the programer choses for the file. The usual completion is DSORG=PS for physically serial.

To prepare for the macrocommands the programer wants to use with the file, the programer specifies the MACRF= operand. The usual completions are (GL,PL) for GET and PUT in the "locate" mode using no work areas and (GM,PM) for GET and PUT in the "move" mode for using work areas. Once the programer has made a choice on the use or nonuse of work areas, he must adhere to his decision. If only GET is needed, the ,PL or ,PM portion should be omitted leaving only (GL) or (GM). If only PUT is needed, then the programer should omit GL, or GM, and use only (PL) or (PM).

To crossreference to the portion of the DCB that the programer provides on the DD cards, the programer should include the DDNAME= operand in the DCB in his program. The completion is the name which the programer writes on the DD card starting in column 3. Programers who do not use the file name as the name for the DCB often use it as the name for the DD card, or suffix or prefix one or more D's to it for use on the DD card.

The record length in bytes is the completion for the LRECL= operand. This is the length of the data portion of the logical record and may not exceed the block size.

In his program, the programer may optionally include other operands for the DCB as he feels appropriate. For input files, the programer should specify an end-of-file (EOF) or end-of-data routine as the completion for the EODAD= operand. The significance of the EOF condition was commented upon earlier in this book.

To reduce the chance of input reading failures causing the operating system to abort the execution of the program, the programer can use the EROPT= operand. A completion of ACC accepts the input in spite of the read error. A completion of SKP skips the input having the read error. This means the input data accepted by the program are incomplete. The former alternative may result in accepting erroneous or unprocessable data.

To handle some types of input-output errors, the programer can cite the SYNAD= operand, using as a completion the address of his error analysis routine. When the programer uses both SYNAD= and EROPT=, control goes first to SYNAD= and then to EROPT=. The routine the programer writes must provide its own way of preserving the contents of registers and of restoring them before it returns control to the main program (otherwise, the usual conventions cited in Chap. 13 apply).

To assist the programer, the operating system makes available a 16-byte field of status information and a pointer to the start of the channel program. These are pointed to by register 0. The last three bytes give the address of the status field; the first byte gives the relative address beyond that for the CCW. Register 1 contains the address of the DCB in the low-order three bytes. The high-order byte provides eight status bits. Writing a good SYNAD routine is a difficult task, one rarely assigned to beginning programers.

The programer should specify some of the DCB operands on the DD card that he must provide for the file. These are the operands that reflect the choice of the input-output equipment or that affect the efficiency of that equipment. These operands are BLKSIZE= and RECFM=, all of which are required. These operands, however, may be available in the file labels.

The completion for the BLKSIZE= operand is the length in bytes of the block. This is equal to the number of records the programer wants in a block times the record length. For variable-length records, the programer must add four bytes to the calculated block size.

The completion for RECFM= depends also on the blocking. The usual completions are F for fixed, V for variable-length records, and B for blocked. Thus, RECFM=FB indicates blocked fixed-length records.

When the programer is using magnetic disks, he can have the data written on disk read back for parity checking by specifying the operand OPTCD=W.

```
                 FUNCTION DESIRED         EQUIPMENT USED FOR SEQUENTIAL ACCESS
                                               TAPE                DISK

      REQUIRED OPERANDS

      SPECIFY DATA ORGANIZATION          DSORG=PS            DSORG=PS

      SPECIFY INPUT-OUTPUT MACROS        MACRF=              MACRF=
        GER & PUT IN LOCATE MODE              =(GL,PL)            =(GL,PL)
        GET & PUT IN WORK-AREA MODE           =(GM,PM)            =(GM,PM)

      SPECIFY NAME OF DD CARD             DDNAME=NAME         DDNAME=NAME

      SPECIFY THE RECORD BLOCKING      * RECFM=F           * RECFM=F
        F FIXED                               =FB                 =FB
        V VARIABLE                            =V                  =V
        B BLOCKED                             =VB                 =VB

      SPECIFY LENGTH OF RECORD         * LRECL=BYTES       * LRECL=BYTES

      SPECIFY LENGTH OF BLOCK          * BLKSIZE=BYTES     * BLKSIZE=BYTES

      SPECIFY M. TAPE DENSITY ON         DEN=N               ---
        DD CARD FOR INPUT ONLY

      SPECIFY 7-CHANNEL M. TAPE ON       TRTCH=X             ---
        DD CARD FOR INPUT ONLY; X
        DEPENDS ON CONFIGURATION


      OPTIONAL OPERANDS

      SPECIFY ADDRESS OF INPUT END       EODAD=ADDRESS       EODAD=ADDRESS
        OF FILE ROUTINE

      SPECIFY HANDLING OF ERROR          EROPT=ACC           EROPT=ACC
        CONDITIONS ON INPUT-OUTPUT           =SKP                =SKP

      SPECIFY SPECIAL HANDLING OF        SYNAD=ADDRESS       SYNAD=ADDRESS
        INPUT-OUTPUT ERRORS

      SPECIFY PARITY CHECK FOR           ---               * OPTCD=W
        DATA DATA WRITTEN ON DISK

      NOTE: * INDICATES AN OPERAND NEEDED ONLY FOR OUTPUT IF THE PROGRAMER HAS
            STANDARD LABELS AVAILABLE ON THE INPUT FILES.
```

FIG. 11-4. Summary checklist of DCB operands.

When the programer is using magnetic tape, the usual practice is to specify the density by DEN=. A completion of 2 indicates 800 bits/in., of 3 indicates 1600 bits/in. This operand must reflect actual machine settings on the tape drive. If the tape is 7-channel (a completion of 0 or 1), then an additional operand TRTCH= is needed to specify the conversion and translation, if any, and the parity. Local practice should be observed for this TRTCH= operand, but T is a common completion.

When the programer is using paper tape, he can use the CODE= operand to indicate the code or equipment being used. A completion of A for ASCII code is the most common. The programer usually also must specify when using the ASCII code the operand OPTCD=Q which directs performing a translation between EBCDIC and ASCII on input or output.

When the programer is using punched cards, he can use the MODE= and STACK= operands. The MODE= operand takes a completion of E for EBCDIC punching in the card and C for column binary punching. The STACK= operand takes 1 or 2 as the completion to indicate which stacker the programer wants used. If the programer omits these operands, the default assumption is MODE=E and STACK=1.

When the programer is using a line printer, he can specify the normal printer spacing by the PRTSP= operand. The completion is the number of lines of printing from 0 through 3 to be advanced between each line of printing. The default option is 1, which indicates "single spacing," that is, no space between the lines. Also, if the printer has a "universal character set" feature, the programer can take advantage of it by specifying the operand OPTCD=U but must then also add to the checking done by his SYNAD routine.

TAPE AND DISK DTF DECLARATIVES

Many of the DTFSR operands described in Chap. 7 apply also to magnetic-tape and disk operations, and to mass storage. Some differences appear, however, so a quick review of each of the operands that can be used is appropriate, starting with the required operands (see Fig. 11-6).

For both tape and disk, the TYPEFLE= operand is as described previously, but the DEVADDR= operand is used only for tape, not for disk. For disk files, the needed data are incorporated in the EXTENT control card, which specifies the portion of the disk to be utilized. Only these two operands have no noteworthy changes in their use.

The BLKSIZE= and IOAREA1= operands are used in the same way as noted in Chap. 7, but the programer must take account of the usual data formats used for tape and disk, as diagramed in Fig. 11-5. For disk, the length must be set eight bytes longer for IOAREA1= than the actual byte count to give space for the count field the operating system creates and uses. The fixed-length forms incorporate no length indicators in the record, but the variable-length records provide space for a four-byte binary block-length field at the start (left end) of each block and a four-byte binary record-length field at the start (left end) of each record. For variable-length blocked records, the BLKSIZE= must be long enough to accommodate the longest possible record size.

The completion for the DEVICE= operand is specified as DISK11 for disk and as TAPE for magnetic tape. Otherwise, these two operands are used as described previously, and may be avoided by the use of the varieties of DTFSR—that is, the DTFMT and the DTFSD.

Blocked records are common with tape and disk, and hence FIXBLK is the most commonly used completion for the RECFORM= operand. If variable-length records are being handled, they may be either unblocked or blocked. For unblocked

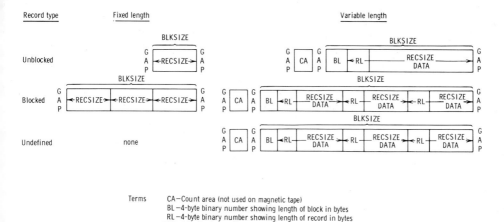

FIG. 11-5. Record and block formats.

records, VARUNB completes the operand, and for blocked records, VARBLK completes it. When either of the variable-length operands is used, a record length is specified in each record and a block length in each block, as noted earlier (see Fig. 11-5). This is to enable the IOCS routines to determine the start and end of each record as it is handled.

The optional operands available with the DTFSR vary considerably from those used with the card readers, card punches, and line printers. To provide two tape units to hold the reels of one input or output file allows the operator to be unloading or loading one tape drive while the other is reading or writing. The operand for this is ALTTAPE=. The completion is the SYS identification for the particular drive to serve as the alternate drive unit. This is needed for BOS, but not DOS, where it is automatic.

When checkpoint records are to be written on magnetic tape, two operands are needed. The CHECKPT= operand indicates that the CHKPT macro is to be used. The completion is the one-digit identification of the DC declarative used in defining the SYSCHKPT are in accordance with local practice at an installation. The CKPTREC= operand is used only for input files, and enables the computer to by-pass the checkpoint records as they are encountered, interspersed among the regular records in the file during a normal GET operation. The CHECKPT= operand is needed for BOS, but not for DOS.

If the CNTRL macro is used with magnetic tape and magnetic disk, the CONTROL operand must be specified in the DTFSR.

For both magnetic-tape and disk operations, the EOFADDR operand can be

| FUNCTION DESIRED | EQUIPMENT USED | |
	TAPE	DISK
REQUIRED OPERANDS		
SPECIFY LENGTH OF BLOCK	BLKSIZE=BYTES	BLKSIZE=BYTES
SPECIFY THE EQUIPMENT BY THE SYS IDENTIFICATION	DEVADDR= SYSXXX	---
SPECIFY THE EQUIPMENT BY MODEL NUMBER CODE	DEVICE= TAPE	DEVICE= DISK11
SPECIFY THE IO AREA RESERVED IN STORAGE	IOAREA1= ADDRESS	IOAREA1= ADDRESS
SPECIFY THE RECORD BLOCKING; FIXUNB IS ASSUMED IF THIS OPERAND BE OMITTED	RECFORM= FIXUNB FIXBLK VARUNB VARBLK UNDEF	RECFORM= FIXUNB FIXBLK VARUNB VARBLK UNDEF
SPECIFY INPUT OR OUTPUT STATUS OF THE FILE	TYPEFLE= INPUT OUTPUT	TYPEFLE= INPUT OUTPUT
OPTIONAL OPERANDS		
SPECIFY SWAP TAPE DRIVE (BOS)	ALTTAPE=SYSXXX	---
SPECIFY USE OF CHKPT MACRO (BOS); INCLUDE FOR EACH FILE; N IS NUMBER OF AREAS UPDATED	CHECKPT= N	---
SPECIFY INTERSPERSED CHECKPOINT ON TAPE INPUT	CKPTREC= YES	---
SPECIFY USE OF CNTRL MACRO	CONTROL=YES	---
SPECIFY ADDRESS OF THE END OF FILE ROUTINE ON INPUT	EOFADDR= ADDRESS	EOFADDR= ADDRESS
SPECIFY HANDLING OF READ ERROR CONDITIONS ON INPUT	ERROPT= IGNORE SKIP ADDRESS	ERROPT= IGNORE SKIP ADDRESS
SPECIFY LABEL CONVENTION	FILABL= STD NO	---
SPECIFY ALTERNATIVE IO AREA AVAILABILITY	IOAREA2= ADDRESS	IOAREA2= ADDRESS
SPECIFY REGISTER NUMBER FOR BLOCKED RECORDS OR ALTERNATE AREAS IN STORAGE	IOREG=(R)	IOREG=(R)
SPECIFY LENGTH OF RECORD WHEN BLOCKED FOR INPUT OR OUTPUT	RECSIZE= N OR (R)	RECSIZE= N OR (R)
SPECIFY TAPE REWIND OPTIONS (PLAIN REWIND IF OMITTED)	REWIND= UNLOAD NORWD	---
SPECIFY SEPARATE COMPILE OF DTF	SEPASMB= YES	SEPASMB= YES
SPECIFY USE OF TRUNC MACRO	---	TRUNCS= YES
SPECIFY WRITE IN READ-FROM AREA ON THE DISK	---	UPDATE= YES
SPECIFY REGISTER FOR CONTROL OF VARIABLE-LENGTH RECORDS OUTPUT	VARBLD=(R)	VARBLD=(R)
SPECIFY PARITY-CHECK READ AFTER WRITE ON DISK	---	VERIFY YES
SPECIFY ROUTINE FOR WRONG-LENGTH RECORDS	WLRERR= ADDRESS	WLRERR= ADDRESS
SPECIFY A WORK AREA FOR USE WITH GET AND PUT MACROS	WORKA=YES	WORKA=YES

FIG. 11-6. Summary checklist of DTF operands for tape and disk operations.

used to specify the programer's end-of-input-file routines. This is used in the manner described in Chap. 7, and the programmer must use it for input files.

In reading magnetic-tape or disk input records, the computer may encounter the case in which it cannot successfully read the records in the file. To handle such cases, the operating system normally provides for terminating the entire job. This is a drastic alternative. To bypass it, the ERROPT= operand is available. If the programer selects the IGNORE completion, then the computer will attempt to process the record in spite of the error. This may give rise to difficulties in the processing itself.

The second alternative completion for ERROPT= is SKIP. If the programer selects this, the IOCS routines do not present that record for processing. This may be permissible in cases in which data may be omitted without seriously violating the integrity of the output. The third completion alternative is to supply a routine name (address), which the programer writes to process erroneous conditions in the record. Intellectually, this is the most satisfying of the alternatives, but it is also the one that places the greatest burden on the programer. All three of these alternatives and the operand itself apply only to input files.

The programer can maintain control over the labeling used in logical IOCS only in the case of magnetic tape. For disks the manufacturer's standard is followed, and only that standard is provided in the logical IOCS routines. For magnetic tape, however, the programer has two main options available for FILABL: standard (STD) and no-label (NO). If the programer elects the standard alternative, the IOCS routines will write and check standard volume, header, and trailer labels in the format shown in Fig. 11-2. If the programer specifies no labels, then no labels are assumed, looked for, or created by the IOCS routines. Thus the programer can, if he likes, specify his own labels and process them in any way he sees fit. The simplest of these alternatives, and the one which gives the greatest uniformity of procedure, is to use the STD completion.

The specification of the input-output areas to be used for magnetic-tape and disk data is done in the same manner as for card readers, card punches, and line printers as described previously. These operands are IOAREA2=, IOREG=, and WORKA=. One difference is that when the programer specifies the WORKA= operand, he must not also specify an IOREG= operand even if it otherwise would be required for IOAREA2= or for blocked records. For fast processing, and maximum input-output speed, the programer should always specify either WORKA= or IOAREA2=. Specifying both usually gives no additional advantage over either alone and uses more storage space. The length set for IOAREA2= must be the same as for IOAREA1=.

For blocked records on both magnetic tape and disk, the programer must specify the RECSIZE= operand. The completion of this operand is the number (count) of characters (bytes) in the record to be written or read (see Fig. 11-5). If undefined records are used, then a register number must be given instead, in the same manner noted in Chap. 7 for card punches and line printers.

The programer has three options available for rewinding (REWIND) magnetic tape. Each time a magnetic tape is read or written to completion, the tape may either be left in its unwound position, rewound, or rewound and unloaded, that is, disengaged from the read mechanism. If the programer desires to rewind at OPEN, CLOSE, and end of volume automatically, he should omit the rewind operand. If he desires the tape to be rewound and unloaded, he should specify the UNLOAD completion. If he desires no rewind of the tape, he should specify NORWD. This alternative is particularly useful when utilizing one magnetic tape for several logical files, since the tape is then automatically positioned for the start of the next file when it completes the reading or writing of the previous file.

The SEPASMB= operand takes the same YES completion described in Chap. 7. This operand permits the programer to compile his IOCS routines separately from his main program and then link-edit together the two resulting object programs. This often saves computer time. For versions of the operating system that do not permit SEPASMB=, the programer can accomplish the same result by using CATALR and ENTRY cards specifying the file name when doing a separate compile of the DTF.

The use of short blocks causes a minor difficulty with magnetic disks. To notify the IOCS routines of the need to handle short blocks on disk, the TRUNCS= operand must be used. If the disk is being written only and the TRUNC macro is to be used, this TRUNCS= operand must be included. If the disk file is used as input, but was created with short blocks included because of the use of the TRUNC macro at the time the file was written, then the TRUNCS= operand must still be included. This operand is not used with magnetic tape.

Because of its precision of operation, the magnetic disk can be used even in the serial data organization for altering a record in storage by writing it at the same place (address) from which it was read. Where this alternative is desired to avoid copying an entire file over, the UPDATE= operand is needed. Then it is possible to write a record, by means of a PUT, exactly in storage where this record was read. When the programer uses UPDATE=, he must specify the TYPEFLE= as INPUT.

Whenever variable-length records are to be used, the programer must provide a register to the IOCS routines to keep track of the length remaining in the output area as records are combined into the output blocks. This operand is required for the variable-length blocked records only. The completion for the operand VARBLD= is a register number from 2 through 11.

One feature available with magnetic disks but not with magnetic tape is the ability to read back the record after writing it. When this alternative is desired, the programer can specify the VERIFY= operand. Its use slows processing time, but does provide an additional check upon the accuracy of writing operations while corrective action is still possible, the data which produced the record still being available in storage. The use of this operand for an output file should be considered in relation to the choice of alternatives available when the same file will be used as input with the ERROPT= operand. If the read-back verify operation is performed, it is less likely that error conditions will arise that will have to be handled by the ERROPT= operand on input.

Occasionally in handling magnetic tape or disk input records an error will be detected in the length of the record being read. If the programer has not provided otherwise, the normal course of events for the supervisor program is to terminate the job. If the programer desires to have the computer attempt correcting the error, he can specify the WLRERR= operand. If the programer has used the ERROPT= operand for an input file, the WLRERR= operand is not required but may still be used to provide a separate routine to handle this specific type of error. If the ERROPT= operand has not been used, then this operand provides the only way of sending control to a programer's routine for handling this type of error.

An example of a tape and a disk DCB and DTFSR and of the use of the macros is given in Fig. 11-7 and in Fig. 11-8. The operation performed is a tape-to-disk copy which used standard labels but does not use any checkpoint.

```
//GO.D70 DD DSNAME=&TTOD,DISP=(NEW,PASS),UNIT=2314,                    X
//            SPACE=(CYL,(9)),DCB=(BLKSIZE=200,RECFM=FB)
//GO.T7Q DD DSNAME=TDFL,DISP=(OLD,PASS),UNIT=2400,                     X
//            DCB=(BLKSIZE=200,RECFM=FB,DEN=3)
```

LOC	OBJECT CODE	ADDR1 ADDR2	ST #	NAME	OP	OPERANDS	COMMENT
			2		PRINT	ON,NOGEN,NODATA	
			3 *				
			4 *	FIGURE 11-7 TAPE TO DISK COPY			
			5 *				
000000			6	FIRST	CSECT		
000000	070007000700		7		CNOP	6,8	
000006	0530		8		BALR	3,0	
000008			9		USING	*,3	
000008	50E0 3044	0004C	10		ST	14,RET	SAVE OS RETURN POINT
			11 *				
			12 *			MAIN ROUTINE	
			13 *				
			14		OPEN	(TAPREC,,DSKREC,(OUTPUT))	
			22	READ	GET	TAPREC,FIELD	
			27		PUT	DSKREC,FIELDA	
000036	47F0 3012	0001A	32		B	READ	
			33	ENDY	CLOSE	TAPREC,DSKREC	
000046	58E0 3044	0004C	39		L	14,RET	PICK UP OS RETURN POINT
00004A	07FE		40		BR	14	EOJ
			41 *				
			42 *			DECLARATIVES	
			43 *				
00004C			44	RET	DS	F	RETURN ADDRESS FOR EOJ
000050			45		DS	0D	FORCE ALIGNMENT
000050			46	FIELDA	DS	0CL50	
000050			47	FIELD	DS	CL50	
			48	TAPREC	DCB	DSORG=PS,MACRF=GM,DDNAME=GO.T7Q,LRECL=50,	X
						EODAD=ENDY,EROPT=ACC	
			104	DSKREC	DCB	DSORG=PS,MACRF=PM,DDNAME=GO.D70,LRECL=50,	X
						EROPT=ACC,OPTCD=W	
00014B			160		LTORG		
000000			161		END	FIRST	

Fig. 11-7. Example of a program using DCB declaratives
for magnetic tape and magnetic disks.

```
LOC   OBJECT CODE    ADDR1 ADDR2  ST #  NAME   OP    OPERANDS              COMMENT
                                            IMPERATIVES
                                   1           PRINT ON,NOGEN,NODATA
                                   2 *
000000                             3           START
                                   4 *
                                   5 *FIGURE11-8          TAPE TO DISK COPY
                                   6 *
                                   7 TAPEREC  DTFMT BLKSIZE=200,                          X
                                                    DEVADDR=SYS181,                       X
                                                    FILABL=STD,                           X
                                                    REWIND=UNLOAD,                        X
                                                    TYPELFE=INPUT,                        X
                                                    EOFADDR=ENDY,                         X
                                                    ERROPT=SKIP,                          X
                                                    IOAREA1=INPUTY,                       X
                                                    RECSIZE=50,                           X
                                                    RECFORM=FIXBLK,                       X
                                                    WORKA=YES
                                  51 *
                                  52 *
                                  53 *
                                  54 DISKREC  DTFSD BLKSIZE=208,                          X
                                                    DEVICE=2311,                          X
                                                    IOAREA1=WRITEY,                       X
                                                    RECSIZE=50,                           X
                                                    RECFORM=FIXBLK,                       X
                                                    TYPEFLE=OUTPUT,                       X
                                                    WORKA=YES,                            X
                                                    VERIFY=YES
                                 103 *
                                 104 *                  MAIN SECTION - COPY THE TAPE RECORDS ONTO THE DISK
000128                           105 FIRST    CSECT
000128 070007000700              106          CNOP  6,8
00012E 0530                      107          BALR  3,0
000130                           108          USING *,3
                                 109          OPEN  TAPEREC,DISKREC
                                 118 READ     GET   TAPEREC,FIELD
                                 124          PUT   DISKREC,FIELDA
000162 47F0 3012           00142 130          B     READ
                                 131 ENDY     CLOSE TAPEREC,DISKREC
                                 140          EOJ
                                 143 *
                                 144 *      DECLARATIVES
                                 145 *
00017C                           146 INPUTY   DS    CL200
000244                           147 WRITEY   DS    CL208
000314                           148 FIELDA   DS    0CL50
000314                           149 FIELD    DS    CL50
                                 150 *
000348                           151          LTORG
000348 5858C2D6D7C5D540          152                =C'$$BOPEN '
000350 5858C2C3D3D6E2C5          153                =C'$$BCLOSE'
000358 00000000                  154                =A(TAPEREC)
00035C 00000314                  155                =A(FIELD)
000360 00000088                  156                =A(DISKREC)
000364 00000314                  157                =A(FIELDA)
000128                           158          END   FIRST
```

Fig. 11-8. Example of a program using DTF declaratives for magnetic tape and magnetic disks.

Do It Now Exercise 11-1. *Prepare a tape-to-printer routine for records 132 characters long blocked ten (records to the block), where print control is to be done by using a printer control character. Be sure to prepare a flow diagram before starting the coding.*

DATA AND INDEX FORMAT FOR INDEXED-SEQUENTIAL FILES

The indexed-sequential file organization makes it possible for the programer to write programs to process data either in a serial or in a random sequence. This capability is obtained by observing some conventions about the way data are recorded and about the use of indexes. The indexed-sequential organization is not available for magnetic tape but is available for magnetic-disk devices. Let us look first at the way in which the programer must structure the data and the indexes in order to use the indexed-sequential IOCS routines.

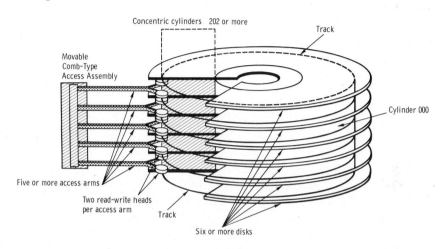

Fig. 11-9. Cylinder and track concepts for disk storage of data.

The data recorded on the magnetic disk can be thought of as being arranged in cylinders and tracks within a particular disk pack. Each disk pack has about 200 or more concentric circular positions over which the set of reading arms can be positioned. All reading heads go at any time to the same concentric circular position on the surfaces of the rotating disks in the disk pack. The area under any one read head on the disk surface is called a track, and the set of tracks that are simultaneously under the set of reading heads at any given time is called a cylinder. A physical analogy gives rise to this use of terms, because the reading heads are arranged vertically one above the other. As the disk surfaces rotate, the arms at any given position in effect act in concert to sweep through a cylinder on the disk surfaces (see Fig. 11-9).

The addresses used for disk and mass-storage devices exist in terms of pack (that is, a physically distinct amount of equipment, usually subject to physical removal by the operator), cell (which is a component only of mass-storage packs), cylinder, head, and record. This address scheme requires a double word, as shown in Fig. 11-10. The head identifies the track, and the record identifies the physically distinct blocks of data recorded on a track.

On any given track, the programer can have the computer record data in any serial format he may choose. In order, however, to use the indexed-sequential IOCS

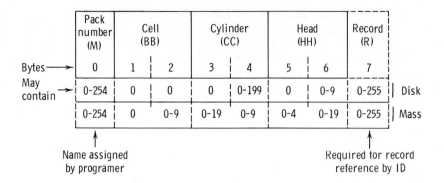

FIG. 11-10. Address format for magnetic disk and mass storage.

routines, the programer must observe some strict conventions on the format of the data. In particular, the programer must give attention to three aspects of the data format: the count, the key, and the record (see Fig. 11-11).

The count field is needed just after the nominal starting position on each track. Since the tracks are essentially concentric circles, this starting point is recorded as a "marker" record. The count field is 11 bytes long, designates the address of the track, and provides the length of the blocks of data recorded on the track. The flag and check bytes are used by the IOCS routines for internal checking operations and can be ignored by the beginning programer.

The key, as in sorting work, is the basis upon which the file is sequenced or ordered. The key may be any length and must occur as a separate record in front (left end) of each block of data recorded. Also, each record in a block must have a key, which is repeated at the start of the record. The key record for the block must be of the same length as the key field in the individual records, and all the key fields must be of the same length. The contents of the key record in front of a block must repeat (be identical to) the key in the final record of the block. For unblocked records this means, therefore, that the key field that precedes the block consisting of one data record must repeat the key within that record.

The data records themselves may be either blocked or unblocked. Variable-length records and variable-length blocking are not permitted. That is, whatever blocking factor the programer selects must be used consistently throughout the entire file. Short blocks are not permitted in the main part of a file, and the programer may have to provide filler records to pad out a block to full length.

Under some conditions, as described later, a field 10 bytes long is added at the start of some records. This 10-byte field, known as the sequence link field, is used to show the address of the next record in sequence when the records are not recorded on the disk track in the correct sort sequence.

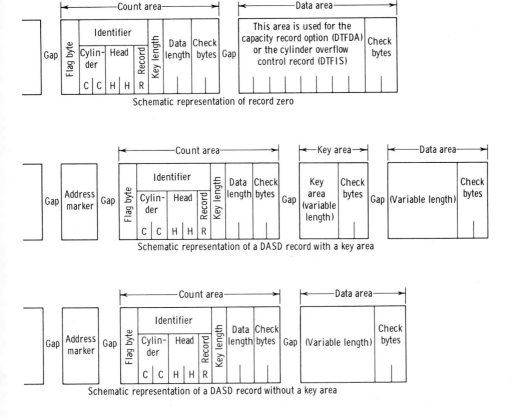

Schematic representation of record zero

Schematic representation of a DASD record with a key area

Schematic representation of a DASD record without a key area

FIG. 11-11. Record layouts for magnetic disk and mass storage.

Records are recorded in two areas on the disk tracks in a cylinder: the prime data area and the overflow data area. The choice between these and the allocation of disk space between them is at the programer's option. In general, the prime area is made larger than the overflow area, and precedes the cylinder overflow area. In addition to the overflow area allotted in each cylinder, the programer usually designates a general overflow area consisting of one or more cylinders set aside for that use only. The distinction between a prime area and an overflow area depends upon the way in which the IOCS routines use them.

In a prime area the IOCS routines write the data records in blocked or un-blocked form in a sequential manner based upon the key, but without a sequence link field. That is, on any given track, the record with the lowest key of those on the track will be found first on the track, and the record with the highest key of those on the track will be found last on the track. The data records are recorded with an interblock gap between the blocks, as in the case of magnetic tape.

By contrast, the IOCS routines write records in the overflow area only in unblocked form. Each data record includes a sequence link field 10 bytes long as the first 10 bytes in the record. Like the leading key field, the sequence link is part of the normal data record. Records in the overflow area are linked together in sequence order by means of the sequence link field, which gives the address of the next higher record in sequence. The order of records in the overflow area, unlike that in the data area, is random.

When an indexed-sequential file of records is initially loaded, the IOCS routines load the records in the prime area only and in a strict sequential order. No records are placed in the overflow area at this time. In each track, the key of the record at the end of the track—that is, the record with the highest key—is used for indexing. Within each block on the track, the last record of each block has its key used as the key for the block. These keys, sequence links, data, and count fields, are diagramed in general terms in Fig. 11-12.

Turning attention now to the matter of indexes, the programer should note that no provision is made in indexed-sequential files for records that have duplicate keys. It is assumed that every record will have a different key and that the records are arranged so that the keys fall in an ascending sequence only. Because of these two facts, provision is made in the index to search for keys on a greater-than-or-equal-to basis.

The reason for this is that the index contains information about only the highest key in each track or cylinder. Thus a comparison of successive entries in the index is needed in order to establish which particular track or cylinder has to be searched to find a record having a particular key. This can be seen more clearly by considering the three different kinds of indexes used with the indexed-sequential files.

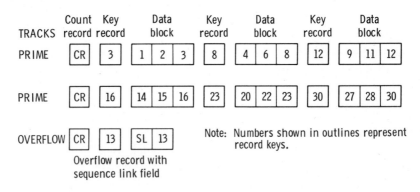

FIG. 11-12. Diagram of indexed-sequential file format.

The track index, which is the lowest level of index, is an index at the start of a cylinder to the records on the individual tracks of the cylinder. The track index has as its first entry a cylinder overflow control record (COCR). This serves as a reference and identifier for use when the data and overflow areas on the cylinder have been fully used. It then directs the IOCS routines to the overflow area (if any).

The entries in the track index change as the track index is used. When a track index is first set up, the same policy noted previously is followed; i.e., the highest key in a track is used as a basis for making an entry in a track index. On this basis, therefore, it would be expected for a disk with 10 tracks to a cylinder as the prime area that a track index would have in it 12 entries: a cylinder overflow control record, ten regular index entries (one for each track), and a dummy entry consisting entirely of 1 bits to signify the end of the track index.

This expectation is not realized in practice because of the need to handle the overflow area. Therefore, when a track index is initially set up, each data entry is made twice in succession in the track index. That is, for the example at hand, the track index initially would contain a total of 22 entries. No entries are made for the overflow areas initially, because no records are placed in the overflow area at the time a track index is initially established (see Fig. 11-13).

The second of the pair of entries for each track is altered as the IOCS routines insert records into the file. The procedure used for this is as follows: The data records on any one track are kept in a strict sequential serial order by key. Therefore, if a new data record is to be inserted into a position that falls between records currently recorded on the track, the last record on the track is moved

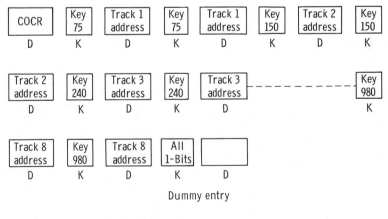

Dummy entry

K = Key area
D = Data area
COCR = Cylinder overflow control record

Fig. 11-13. Diagram of a track index.

("pushed off") to the overflow area, and the remaining records on the track are shifted to permit insertion of the new record. At this time, the first entry in the track index for that track has the key area altered to reflect the new last key now on the data track. This key will always be lower than the original entry at this point in the index, since no duplicate keys are permitted.

The second item of the pair of original entries in the index for that track will not have the key portion altered, since that must remain unchanged to protect the first record on the next data track. Instead the track address in the index for the old highest key will be altered. The reason is that the first record placed in the overflow area, which is always the former last record on the original track, will be marked in the sequence link field with an indication that it is the old end-of-track occupant.

Then, as more new records are inserted into the track and more pushed off the track, it is always the highest remaining record on the track that is pushed off into the overflow area. Each new record pushed off from any given track, however, has a key lower than the key of the first record pushed off the track. Hence each record that is pushed off the track can be linked by the sequence link field to the last record pushed off this data track.

When a record is to be inserted among the records that have been pushed off the end of a track into the overflow area, the new record is added to the overflow area at the next available position and a sequence link field inserted in it to reference the record with the next higher key. The sequence link field of the record with the next lower key is, in turn, altered to link to the record inserted in the overflow area. This is illustrated in Fig. 11-14.

After some additions to the file have been made, the initial overflow area becomes partly filled, and the tracks that previously were filled remain filled, but the records that fill them may now be different. The track index has been adjusted to reflect which record is the last record remaining on each track, and which address in the overflow area has the original final record of each track. The last item in the track index is still a dummy entry containing only 1 bits.

The next higher level of index is the cylinder index. For files which generally do not require more than two disk packs to hold the records, and which require less than two cylinders to hold the cylinder index, the cylinder index is commonly the highest level of index utilized. Not less than one cylinder index is used for each logical file on a disk pack, but multiple pack files are permitted with a single cylinder index. The organization of a cylinder index is simpler than that of a track index. The nature of the entries takes much the same form, but the choice of the information identified in the cylinder index is different (see Fig. 11-15). The cylinder index must occupy a cylinder or cylinders not used for either prime or overflow records of the file.

The cylinder index is an index to individual cylinders on the disk, each of which in turn is a track index, which is the lowest-level index. Thus the address

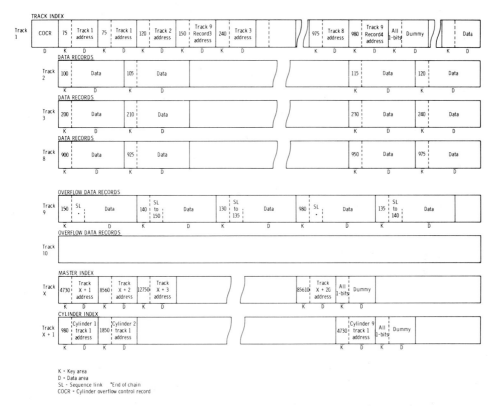

FIG. 11-14. Diagram of an indexed-sequential file.

shown in the cylinder index for a key is the address of the track index that shows that key as the highest key. For instance, if the highest key in the data area and overflow area of a particular cylinder were 986, and the number of the cylinder were 16, then the entry in the cylinder index would be 986, cylinder 16. But the particular address on the cylinder would be the address of the track index covering that cylinder.

The highest level of index is the master index. Its establishment and use is optional. In practice the master index is used only with very large files, such as those which exceed two disk packs. The master index shows a series of entries for the highest entry in each track of each cylinder index. Thus the number of items in the master index is kept small because it has only one key for each track in the cylinder indexes. Each master index entry consists of a key field and a disk address for the track of the cylinder index pertaining to keys up to and including that key. Thus a cylinder index, which itself takes five tracks, would be represented by five entries in

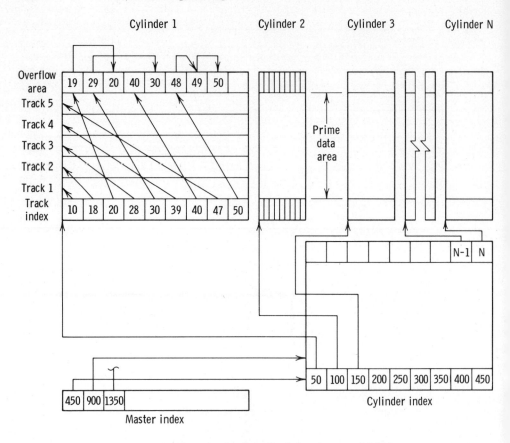

FIG. 11-15. Diagram of indexes for indexed-sequential files.

the master index. The last item in the master index is a dummy entry with a key containing only 1 bits and with no address shown.

By convention, a master index may not be split across two or more disk packs —that is, it must be contained entirely on one disk pack. It must begin with the first track on a cylinder, but may run for as many consecutive cylinders as necessary to accommodate the full index, but it must immediately precede a cylinder index.

OS MACROS FOR INDEXED-SEQUENTIAL FILES

The macros to handle the processing for an indexed-sequential file under OS are, with some exceptions, the OPEN, GET, PUT, PUTX, and CLOSE macros described earlier. These cover the situations of creating an indexed-sequential file, maintaining it sequentially, and using it sequentially. The major exception is using or maintaining it in a random sequence. Each of the situations calls for some differences in what the programer must include in the DCB, and these in turn affect how he uses the macros.

To create an indexed-sequential file, the programer uses the OPEN, PUT, and CLOSE macros. He also uses the following DCB operands besides DSORG and MACRF: BLKSIZE, CYLOFL, KEYLEN, LRECL, NTM, OPTCD, RECFM, RKP, and SYNAD. To delete records from an indexed-sequential file in practice requires copying it, dropping during the copying the unwanted records.

To access (retrieve) records sequentially from an indexed-sequential file, or to update records in sorted sequence, the programer uses the OPEN, SETL, GET, PUTX, ESETL, and CLOSE macros. The DCB operands are usually the same as for the creation of the file originally. The macros SETL and ESETL are described in the subsequent section on DOS macros. The operands for the SETL are the DCB name, followed by ,B. The operand for the ESETL is the DCB name.

To access (retrieve) records in a random sequence from an indexed-sequential file, or to update records in some other sort sequence than the one used in creating the file originally, the programer cannot use the GET and PUT macros because of complications arising from record blocking. GET and PUT work with queues of blocks, but the programer cannot have such queues when he cannot accurately anticipate what the key of the next record will be—as is the case in random operations. Hence, the programer must use the basic, not the queued, IOCS for random operations.

The macros are OPEN, READ, CHECK, WRITE, and CLOSE. The programer must use CHECK after each READ and each WRITE to give time for the reading and writing of data on disk to be completed, one record at a time. If the IOCS routines detect any errors, control goes to the address the programer cites for the SYNAD operand in the DCB. To support these macros, the programer must cite the DCB operands MACRF=(RUSC,WUAC), which permits the use of the macros READ and WRITE in place of GET and PUT, and MSHI=address, which identifies an area of storage to be used for maintaining the index. To select the length for the Define Storage declarative, the programer should seek the recommendations of his lead programer or supervisor.

READ—Read a Record. This macrocommand has two forms. One has seven operands. The first is the name the programer wants assigned to the Data Event Control Block (DECB) created and used by the READ. This requires 26 bytes, and the programer should assign an area in storage at least that size. The second operand is KU to indicate access by key with updating permitted. The third operand is the DCB name. The fourth and fifth operands are 'S' to control the buffering. The sixth operand is the address in storage of the key of the record the programer wants to have read. The seventh operand is MF=L to indicate that this long form of the macro is to establish a DECB for use by the short form. This long macro need be used only once in the program and may be placed in with the DC declaratives.

```
        RELATIVE ADDRESS
            IN DECB
        BYTES     BITS           CONTENTS OF DECB FOR IS READ AND WRITE

          +   0    ALL           EVENT CONTROL BLOCK ADDRESS
          +   4    ALL           TYPE
          +   6    ALL           LENGTH
          +   8    ALL           DCB ADDRESS
          + 12     ALL           ADDRESS OF I-O AREA
          + 16     ALL           ADDRESS OF LOGICAL RECORD
          + 20     ALL           ADDRESS OF KEY
          + 24     ALL           EXCEPTION CODE BITS
                   +  0            RECORD NOT FOUND, READ AND WRITE-K
                   +  1            WRONG LENGTH RECORD, READ AND WRITE
                   +  2            NO SPACE AVAILABLE, WRITE-KN
                   +  3            SYNTAX ERROR IN WRITE-K
                   +  4            UNCORRECTABLE I-O ERROR, READ AND WRITE
                   +  5            BLOCK NOT ACCESSIBLE, READ AND WRITE
                   +  6            OVERFLOW RECORD, READ
                   +  7            DUPLICATE KEY, WRITE-KN
          + 25     ALL           IOCS EXCEPTION CODE BITS
```

Fig. 11-16. Format of the Data Event Control Block (DECB).

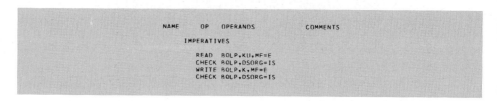

```
        NAME      OP      OPERANDS              COMMENTS

                IMPERATIVES

                  READ    BOLP,KU,MF=E
                  CHECK   BOLP,DSORG=IS
                  WRITE   BOLP,K,MF=E
                  CHECK   BOLP,DSORG=IS
```

Fig. 11-17. Macros for random access to an indexed-sequential file under OS.

The short form of the READ macro is the one used for each READ in the imperative part of the program. This form of the READ macro has three operands. The first is the address of the DECB. The second is KU. The third is MF=E to indicate that this macro is to execute using an existing DECB. Upon execution of the READ, the operating system fills in the fields in the DECB as outlined in Fig. 11-16. The programer's SYNAD routine should test the exception codes. The DECB gives the address of the data in storage. READ makes no provision for the use of work areas. Figure 11-17 gives an example of READ.

WRITE—Write a Record. This macrocommand has three operands. The first is the address of the Data Event Control Block (DECB) used for the READ macro. The second operand is K for the return to the file of an updated record. It is KN for the insertion of a new record, but for that purpose, the programer must first modify the DECB, or create a new different one, to specify the correct address of the record to be written. The third operand is MF=E to indicate that this macro is to execute using an existing DECB. Figure 11-17 gives an example of WRITE.

CHECK—Check for Errors. This macrocommand has two operands. The first is address of the DECB. The second is DSORG=IS. This macro must be used after each READ and WRITE macro. Figure 11-17 gives an example of CHECK. If no errors were detected by the operating system, control goes to the next instruction in sequence. If errors were detected, control goes to the routine named as the completion for the SYNAD operand in the DCB. One infrequent source of error is records stored in the overflow areas in the file. When these are not successfully accessed or read, other errors are flagged. Normally the programmer need not be concerned about whether or not a record is in the overflow area. Overflow records, however, are slower to access, and many of them are an indication that the file should be copied (created again) to pull them up onto the normal position.

DOS MACROS FOR INDEXED-SEQUENTIAL FILES

Situations

The programer must define carefully in advance what functions he wants to have done with indexed-sequential files. This gives a basis for selecting the correct macrocommands to accomplish the work, which in turn determines the character of the DTFIS operands needed. The five major situations are (1) create an indexed-sequential file ("load it onto disk"); (2) insert new records into the file ("add to the file"); (3) delete unwanted records from the file ("purge dead records"); (4) random-access processing of the records in the file ("random update"); and (5) sequential-access processing of the records in the file ("sequential update").

```
               FOR  IOROUT=ADDRTR, ADD, OR RETRVE
BIT POSITION   SIGNIFICANCE OF A 1 BIT
     0         UNCORRECTABLE DISK ERROR OTHER THAN WRONG LENGTH RECORDS.
     1         WRONG LENGTH RECORD DETECTED.
     2         END OF FILE (EOF) ON A SEQUENTIAL RETRIEVE.
     3         RECORD NOT FOUND FOR KEY SPECIFIED IN RANSEQ OR SEQNTL.
     4         ID NOT FOUND WITHIN PRIME DATA FILE LIMITS.
     5         DUPLICATE KEY DETECTED UPON ATTEMPT TO WRITE INTO FILE.
     6         AVAILABLE OVERFLOW AREA IS ALREADY FULL+ CAN NOT PROCESS.
     7         RETRIEVAL WAS FROM OVERFLOW AREA.

               FOR  IOROUT=LOAD
BIT POSITION   SIGNIFICANCE OF A 1 BIT
     0         UNCORRECTABLE DISK ERROR OTHER THAN WRONG LENGTH RECORDS.
     1         WRONG LENGTH RECORD DETECTED.
     2         ONLY ONE MORE TRACK OF PRIME DATA AREA LEFT
     3         CYLINDER INDEX AREA TOO SMALL.
     4         MASTER INDEX AREA TOO SMALL.
     5         DUPLICATE KEYS DETECTED IN RECORDS BEING STORED.
     6         RECORDS NOT IN ASCENDING SORT SEQUENCE.
     7         PRIME DATA AREA EXHAUSTED+ NO ROOM FOR EOF INDICATOR.
```

FIG. 11-18. Index-sequential status bits.

All situations except number 4 require that the programer have records available in sorted order. Situations 1 and 2 permit no records with duplicate or identical keys. Situations 1 and 3 are in practice handled by writing the entire file in sequence, handling once every record in the file. A programer can combine situations 1 and 3, situation 2 with either 4 or 5, and rarely situations 4 and 5. For the convenience of the programer, the presentation that follows groups the macros by situation. These are in addition to the usual OPEN and CLOSE macros.

In using the macros, the programer must take action to detect and dispose of error conditions that may arise. In practice, the programer should check for errors immediately after each macro that directs the movement of data. To make this convenient, the programer can use a Test Under Mask of one byte for any 1 bits. The address of the byte to be tested is the name of the file (the name of the DTF) suffixed with a C. This requires that file names not exceed seven characters in length. The significance of the bits is given in Fig. 11-18. An example of their use is given in Fig. 11-27.

In using DTFIS and the related macros, the programer must be aware that DTFIS is unlike DTFSR and like its subvarieties (such as DTFSD) in one important respect. The DTFIS operands are compiled into a table-like arrangement in storage, much like a DCB under OS. To use this DTFIS data, the operating system uses what is termed a "logic module" to call into play the needed IOCS capabilities. The logic modules are normally maintained by the operating system in a ready-to-use condition and can be incorporated into a program by means of a link-edit operation. This is illustrated in Fig. 11-27, where the routine IJHZLZZZ is the logic module for the indexed-sequential IOCS. At some installations, the available cataloged modules may be unsatisfactory for the options the programer chooses in writing the DTFIS, giving program bugs, usually in execution. The lead programer at an installation can select a new IJH name (thereby resulting in a new logic module) for the programer or use the ISMOD macro to create the new logic module.

Load Macros

Loading an IS file is the process of creating or building an indexed-sequential file, including the indexes, or of adding to the high end of (extending) an existing indexed-sequential file. When new records have keys that all fall beyond the highest key presently in a file, or for the process of creating a file, the programer has three macros available. During this loading process the IOCS routines build the track indexes and the cylinder index. They also build the master index if one has been specified in the DTFIS declarative, as described later. Examples of the macros for loading an indexed-sequential file called DISKF are given in Fig. 11-19.

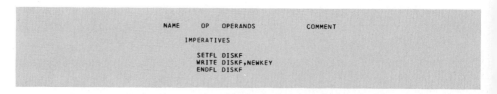

```
NAME     OP   OPERANDS            COMMENT
         IMPERATIVES
         SETFL DISKF
         WRITE DISKF,NEWKEY
         ENDFL DISKF
```

Fig. 11-19. Macros for loading an indexed-sequential file under DOS.

SETFL—Set File Load. This macro has only one operand, which is the name of the file as specified in the DTFIS. If it is for a file which has not yet been loaded, the IOCS routines use the disk area specified as being available by the EXTENT job control card. If the disk area named as being available already contains a file identified with this same name, then the macro prepares the file to have additional records added to the high end of it.

The areas of the disks to be used by this macro are made available by a job control EXTENT card (discussed later in this chapter). One card is required for the area where data records are to be written, one for the cylinder index area, and if desired, one for the master index area.

WRITE—Write. This macro requires two operands. The first operand is the name of the file identified in the DTFIS. The other operand is the word NEWKEY. The two operands are separated by a comma but no space. Sometimes a third operand, IS, is added for "indexed-sequential." In general, the macro WRITE identifies, and is used for, handling records in a random manner as output. The additional operand NEWKEY indicates that entries are to be made into an index, and that the index is to be built, if necessary, by using the keys supplied with the data. So that the right data will be usable for this purpose, the data to be copied onto the disk must be available in a load area of storage as identified in the DTFIS. The records as they are loaded are checked for sequence, and blocked as specified.

By restricting the file name in the DTFIS to a seven-character name, the programer can obtain information, as a result of the WRITE macro, on the position in the track of the record being written. This information is available in an eight-byte field called by the file name suffixed with an H, for example, DISKFH. The final byte in that eight-byte field gives the relative position directly.

ENDFL—End File Load. This macro requires only one operand, the file name as identified in the DTFIS. The operation performed by this macro is to complete the indexes and to finish writing the file of records. In this regard it performs some functions similar to a CLOSE macro. OPEN and CLOSE macros must still be used, however.

Insertion and Deletion of Records

The IOCS routines for the indexed-sequential data organization make no provision for deleting records from the file. To handle deletions, the programer has two main options open to him. One is to copy the file, checking each record as it is read against a delete list in sorted order. If the record is to be deleted, the programer has the computer jump ahead in the program, skipping or bypassing the writing operation. Thus the new copy of the file fails to include the records to be deleted.

The second method of deleting records is to insert a symbol or message in each record to be deleted, marking it as an obsolete record. This second method is the most widely used, since it saves the time that would otherwise be consumed in frequent copying of the file, and automatically provides the deletion list when the file is recopied. The procedure is to insert into the leading byte of the record to be deleted an indicator of FF_x, signifying that it is no longer an active record. This requires that this position in the record be used only as a status indicator or, if it be part of the key, that no keys begin with FF_x. This procedure is also common under OS.

To insert records into an existing file, the programer has two macros available. For the programer to use these, the file must already exist in the indexed-sequential form, e.g., by having been loaded as described previously. If the programer desires to add to the file some additional records which would not all come beyond the high end of the existing file, then he must use macros that make it possible to insert records into the existing file. In practice, this requires that the IOCS routines move some records to the overflow areas as they insert new records into the file and the indexes. Examples of the insertion macros are given in Fig. 11-20 for a file called QFLP.

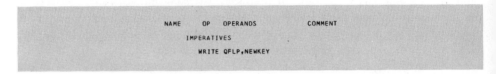

```
          NAME    OP   OPERANDS        COMMENT
               IMPERATIVES
               WRITE QFLP,NEWKEY
```

FIG. 11-20. Macros for inserting records into an indexed-sequential file.

WRITE—Write. This macro has two operands, the file name as specified in the DTFIS and the word NEWKEY. Sometimes a third operand, IS, is added. This macro is the same as the one noted for loading the file, as described previously. It operates in the same basic manner by building the index, but in placing records in the file it moves records to the overflow areas to provide space in the data areas for the records as needed. This difference in the operation of WRITE is triggered by the operands specified by the DTFIS, which call for the insertion of new records into a file.

WAITF—Wait for File. This macro has one operand, the name of the file. It is required after each WRITE macro in order to give the IOCS routines time to perform the building of the index entries and the rearrangement of records on the disk.

Random Processing

One of the major advantages of the indexed-sequential file organization is that records may be processed from the file either in a random sequence or in a strict ascending serial sequence. In the random sequence, the records are not processed from the file in the same order in which they were written into the file originally.

Suppose, for example, that the files were organized and sorted before being loaded on the basis of a stock-number key. If later it were desired to process the transactions for a day, involving additions and withdrawals of stock, the data to be processed could be sorted into the same sequence as the original file. In that case, an ascending sequential processing operation could be done.

However, to save the sorting operation, it would be convenient to be able to process the transactions in whatever order they might occur. This would make it possible to handle the transactions as they occur without waiting to batch them and sort them. To do this, however, requires random access to the file records, because the sequence in which transactions occur during the day will not necessarily follow any stock-number sequencing.

To perform random operations on the indexed-sequential file, the programer has three macros. Since random operations for indexed-sequential files always make reference to the index, and since the index is based upon the key, reference in a random manner to records in an indexed-sequential file can only be made on the basis of the key. Examples of the macros are given in Fig. 11-21 for a file called QFLP.

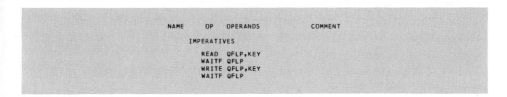

```
        NAME      OP     OPERANDS              COMMENT

              IMPERATIVES
                       READ   QFLP,KEY
                       WAITF  QFLP
                       WRITE  QFLP,KEY
                       WAITF  QFLP
```

FIG. 11-21. Macros for random processing of an indexed-sequential file.

READ—Read. This macro has two operands. The first is the file name as specified in the DTFIS, and the second is the word KEY, separated from the file name by only a comma. Sometimes a third operand, IS, is also used. This macro uses the key specified in the DTFIS entry KEYARG= to search the indexes. It begins with the highest-level index, which is the master index if one exists. It then goes to the cylinder index or, if no master index is present, begins with the cylinder index. After finding the entry or the closest high entry in the cylinder index, it goes to the track index, where it again searches for the equal or closest higher entry. It then goes to the track specified by the track index and searches sequentially through the track until it finds a block with an equal or higher key. It then unblocks (if needed) those records, testing the key of each record to locate the individual record sought. When an equal key is found, the IOCS routines copy the record into the area of storage specified by the DTFIS. If the READ macro cannot find the record sought, control goes to the error routine specified in the DTFIS. If the programer wants to use work areas, he does not specify their address in the READ macro but in the DTF operand WORKR=.

WRITE—Write. This macro has two operands. The first is the file name, as identified in the DTFIS, and the second is the word KEY. Sometimes a third operand, IS, is also used. This macro has the ability to write back into its original position on disk a record which has previously been read from the same position in storage. That is, a record that has been read from disk by the use of the READ macro can be returned (written back) in an updated form to the same position on disk by the use of the WRITE macro with the operand KEY. This macro cannot be used for inserting a new record into a file, since it builds no index entries. It can be used only to return a record to its original position in the file. Since the record, when it is read from the file, includes a key field, the programer must be careful not to permit an alteration in the key field. This helps avoid errors in returning records to the file. If the programer wants to use work areas, he does not specify their address in the WRITE macro but in the DTF operand WORKR=.

WAITF—Wait for File. This macro has one operand, the name of the file as specified in the DTFIS. Its operation is as noted previously. The programer must use it after each READ macro and WRITE macro in order to give the IOCS routines sufficient time to locate and move the records.

If the programer desires, in the course of random processing, to create a new record to be inserted into the file, as occasionally happens, he can use the WRITE macro with the NEWKEY operand noted previously. This requires that the programer move the record to be inserted into an area in storage identified in the DTFIS as being available for loading a new record. The areas in storage used for reading and writing records on a random basis from the file may not also be used for loading or inserting new records into the file.

Sequential Processing

To do an ascending serial (sequential) processing of records from an indexed-sequential file, the programer specifies the key or position of the lowest (earliest) record in the file he wishes to have processed. From that point on, the IOCS routines take the records one after the other in strict key or position sequence until the end of the file is reached. In the case of random processing, no end-of-file indication is appropriate. In the case of sequential processing, however, an end-of-file condition is appropriate and must be provided for. To handle the sequential processing of records from an indexed-sequential file, the programer has four macros available. Examples of the macros are given in Fig. 11-22 for a file called DISKR.

The programer may switch back and forth between random and sequential processing at any time by use of the SETL and ESETL macros. The programer must use one SETL prior to each group of GET and PUT macros and one ESETL at the end of each group. But the programer must be sure that the declaratives he specifies permit both sequential and random processing.

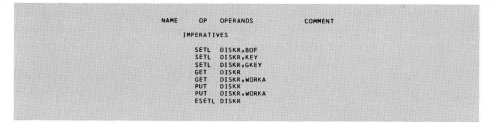

NAME	OP	OPERANDS	COMMENT
	IMPERATIVES		
	SETL	DISKR,BOF	
	SETL	DISKR,KEY	
	SETL	DISKR,GKEY	
	GET	DISKR	
	GET	DISKR,WORKA	
	PUT	DISKR	
	PUT	DISKR,WORKA	
	ESETL	DISKR	

FIG. 11-22. Macros for sequential processing of an indexed-sequential file.

SETL—Set Low. This macro has two operands. The first one of these is the file name as specified in the DTFIS. If the second operand, separated from the first by a comma and no space, is BOF, then the starting point for the sequential operation is the first record in the indexed-sequential file—i.e., the record with the lowest key at the beginning of the file.

Usually the second operand is the word KEY. In this case, the computer uses the address of the field in storage which holds the starting key the programer desires the computer to use, as specified by the KEYARG= operand. If the IOCS routines cannot locate the starting record in the files, control goes to an error routine specified by the DTFIS entry.

GET—Get. This macro has either one or two operands. In either case, the first operand is the name of the file as identified in DTFIS. The second operand, if present, identifies the work area in storage in the same manner noted previously in this chapter and in Chap. 7. Sometimes a third operand, IS, is also used. The operation of this macro is essentially the same as described for magnetic-tape operations, except that the sequence link fields are used automatically when overflow areas are entered. The programer does not use the WAITF macro after the GET macro. If the programer wants to use work areas, he must specify the DTF operand WORKS=YES.

PUT—Put. This macro has either one or two operands, as noted previously. In either case, the first operand is the name of the file as identified in the DTFIS entry. If a second operand is used, it specifies the name of a work area. Sometimes a third operand, IS, is also used. The operation of PUT is essentially the same as noted previously in this chapter and in Chap. 7. The major differences are that the sequence link fields are utilized automatically in the overflow area, and that an interaction (as noted below) exists between GET and PUT. The programer does not use the WAITF macro after the PUT macro. If the programer wants to use work areas, he must specify the DTF operand WORKS=YES.

If the records from a block are handled by a GET operation, and none of the records in that block are subsequently handled by a PUT operation, then the block of records is not returned to disk storage. Since the GET operation is a copying operation, the result is that no change is made in the content of disk storage for that block of records. In other words, if the programer desires to have records on disk storage altered by the processing action, he must issue a PUT macro to have the altered data returned to disk storage. As long as at least one PUT operation has been issued for a record from a block, a GET operation that results in reading a new block will also result in an automatic WRITE operation for the block for which a previous PUT was issued.

This necessitates one precaution for the programer: He must be careful to issue the PUT macro prior to a GET macro for a subsequent record. If he should fail to observe this sequence, the result may be a failure to record in disk storage an altered record content. A GET macro applies to the next higher record in the file than the last prior GET macro. The PUT applies to the same record as the last prior GET. There cannot be a gap of one or more records between the GET and PUT records handled by the IOCS routines in working with indexed-sequential files. The programer can get around this restriction by using the random-processing WRITE for returning records to the file.

ESETL—End Set Low. This macro requires one operand, which is the name of the file as identified in the DTFIS. It finishes writing a block if one is to be written, and performs other CLOSE-like operations. It is not, however, a substitute for CLOSE, which still must be used.

INDEXED-SEQUENTIAL DCB OPERANDS

In his program, the programer must include for each indexed-sequential file a named DCB declarative having at least three operands: DSORG=, MACRF=, and DDNAME=. The operand DSORG=IS specifies an indexed-sequential file. A summary of indexed-sequential DCB operands is shown in Fig. 11-23.

To prepare for the macrocommands the programer wants to use with the file, the programer specifies the MACRF= operand. To select the proper completion, the programer must distinguish between the creation of an indexed-sequential file and its use. To create a file, the usual completion is (PM) or (PL). The choice between them depends upon the use of work areas. If the programer wants to use work areas, the completion is (PM); if not, it is (PL). If the situation is the use of the file, then the programer must decide whether the use is sequential or random. If it is sequential, the completion is (GM,SK), or (GL,SK,PU). The latter permits the use of the PUTX macro but not the use of work areas. The former permits the use of work areas but not the macro PUTX. Both permit the use of search by key. If the use of the file is random, the completion is (RUSC,WUAC). This permits updating records and inserting new records, as well as dynamic buffering. The macros permitted are READ, WRITE, and CHECK.

To cross reference to the portion of the DCB that the programer provides on the DD cards, the programer should include the DDNAME= operand in the DCB in his program. The completion is the name which the programer writes on the DD card starting in column 3. Programers who do not use the file name as the name

```
                FUNCTION DESIRED              INDEXED-SEQUENTIAL OPERANDS

       REQUIRED OPERANDS

       SPECIFY DATA ORGANIZATION                    DSORG=IS

       SPECIFY INPUT-OUTPUT MACROS                  MACRF=
          CREATE FILE AS AN OUTPUT                     =(PM)
          SEQUENTIAL GET, PUTX (LOCATE MODE)           =(FL,SK,PU)
          SEQUENTIAL GET (WORK-A, MOVE MODE)           =(GM,SK)
          RANDOM READ, WRITE                           =(RUSC,WUAC)

       SPECIFY NAME OF DD CARD                      DDNAME=NAME

       SPECIFY THE RECORD BLOCKING                * RECFM=F
          F FIXED                                       =FB
          V VARIABLE                                    =V
          B BLOCKED                                     =VB

       SPECIFY LENGTH OF RECORD                    * LRECL=BYTES

       SPECIFY LENGTH OF BLOCK                     * BLKSIZE=BYTES


       OPTIONAL OPERANDS

       SPECIFY ADDRESS OF SEQUENTIAL INPUT           EODAD=ADDRESS
          END OF FILE ROUTINE

       SPECIFY SPECIAL HANDLING OF                   SYNAD=ADDRESS
          INPUT-OUTPUT ERRORS

       SPECIFY LENGTH OF KEYS                      * KEYLEN=BYTES

       SPECIFY POSITION OF KEY                     * RKP=COUNT

       SPECIFY USUAL OPTIONS                       * OPTCD=RIYULM

       SPECIFY NUMBER OF OVERFLOW TRACKS           * CYLOFL=N

       SPECIFY MASTER INDEX DENSITY                * NTM=N

       NOTE: * INDICATES AN OPERAND NEEDED ONLY FOR OUTPUT IF THE PROGRAMER HAS
             STANDARD LABELS AVAILABLE ON THE INPUT FILES.
```

FIG. 11-23. Indexed-sequential DCB operands.

for the DCB often use it as the name for the DD card, or suffix or prefix one or more D's to it for use on the DD card.

In his program, the programer should include a SYNAD= operand specifying the address of his error-analysis routine. This is important since no EROPT= operand is available for indexed-sequential files. In the routine, the name of which is the completion for SYNAD, the programer can use the considerable amount of status information provided by the operating system. Upon entry to the routine from a GET, PUT, or PUTX, register 0 usually contains the address of a 16-byte status area [the first part of the IOB (Input-Output Block)]. Register 1 usually contains the address in internal storage of the record containing the error. Upon entry from a READ or WRITE, register 0 usually contains the address of the third byte (first "sense byte") of the IOB. Register 1 contains the address of the DECB, the second byte of which contains exception code bits. The other registers are as described previously for magnetic tape and disk operations under OS.

For sequential input of an indexed-sequential file, the programer should include the EODAD= operand, citing as the completion the address of his end-of-data-file routine. The importance of this has been pointed out previously.

For building or creating an indexed-sequential file, the programer should include in his program a number of other operands: CYLOFL=, KEYLEN=, LRECL=, NTM=, OPTCD=, and RKP=. A look at each may clarify the roles they play.

The completion for the CYLOFL= operand is the number of overflow tracks the programer wants in each cylinder. The completion for the NTM= operand is the number of tracks to be represented by each entry in the master index. Local practice and the anticipated size of the file should be followed on this and the operand omitted if no master index is to be built.

The completion for the OPTCD= operand is usually RIYULM. R and Y, respectively, direct the use of independent and cylinder overflow areas. U makes the index building more efficient, and M directs the establishment of a master index. If none is desired, M should be omitted. L indicates that records coded with FF_x in the first byte are not to be placed in the file.

The completion for the KEYLEN= operand is the length in bytes of the key and may not exceed 255 bytes. The completion for the RKP= operand is the relative position of the start of the key field in each record. Note that compound keys are not provided for, and in order to permit the use of the FF_x delete indicator, the key should not start at the first byte (RKP=0) in the record.

The completion for the LRECL= operand is the length in bytes of the record. This must be selected with care, as indicated in Fig. 11-25, and is best if it is some multiple of a double word in length.

For random access to a file with READ or WRITE, the programer can speed the processing by specifying the MSHI= operand. The completion is an address for an area in storage to be used for searches on the index. The size needed depends on the file, and local guidance should be sought.

In the DD job control cards the programer prepares for an indexed-sequential file, the programer should specify the BLKSIZE= and RECFM= operands. These have been described previously. The completion for the BLKSIZE= operand should be chosen with care, taking into account the guidance offered in Fig. 11-25.

DTFIS OPERANDS UNDER DOS

The DTFIS operands for the indexed-sequential file organization consist of two groups: those which are required in all cases, and those which are optional— that is, those whose use depends upon the circumstances. The six required operands are described first in this section; then the remaining, optional operands are de-

REQUIRED OPERANDS FORMAT	DESIRED FUNCTION
DSKXTNT=N	SPECIFY MAXIMUM NUMBER OF EXTENTS FOR THE FILE
IOROUT=LOAD ADD RETRVE ADDRTR	SPECIFY THE FUNCTION TO BE PREFORMED. LOAD, BUILD OR EXTEND A FILE. ADD, ADD NEW RECORDS TO THE DISK. RETRVE RETRIEVE RECORDS FROM THE DISK. ADDRTR, ADD AND RETRIEVE RECORDS.
KEYLEN=N	SPECIFY THE LENGTH OF THE KEY
NRECDS=N	SPECIFY THE NUMBER OF RECORDS PER BLOCK. FOR UNBLOCKED N=1.
RECFORM=FIXUNB FIXBLK	SPECIFY TYPE OF BLOCKING
RECSIZE=N	SPECIFY SIZE OF THE RECORDS

OPTIONAL OPERANDS FORMAT	DESIRED FUNCTION
CYLOFL=N	RESERVE CYLINDER OVERFLOW AREAS
DEVICE=MODELNO	SPECIFY MODEL OF DISK; DEFAULT IS 2311
HINDEX=MODELNO	SPECIFY MODEL OF DISK FOR HIGHEST INDEX
INDAREA=ADDRESS	SPECIFY NAME FOR AREA TO HOLD CYLINDER INDEX IN STORAGE
INDSIZE=BYTES	SPECIFY LENGTH OF INDEX AREA
IOAREAL=ADDRESS	SPECIFY THE I/O AREA. AT LEAST
IOAREAR=ADDRESS	ONE OF THESE MUST BE USED FOR
IOAREAS=ADDRESS	EACH FILE.
IOAREA2=ADDRESS	SPECIFY ALTERNATE I-O AREA
IOREG=(N)	SPECIFY THE REGISTER USED IN CONJUNCTION WITH MORE THAN ONE I/O AREA.
IOSIZE=N	SPECIFY SIZE WHEN USING IOAREAL; N IS AT LEAST 50 MORE THAN SIZE ALLOWED FOR IOAREAL
KEYARG=ADDRESS	SPECIFIES THE ADDRESS OF THE MAIN-STORAGE KEY FIELD.
KEYLOC=N	SPECIFY THE HIGH-ORDER POSITION OF THE KEY FIELD WITHIN THE RECORD.
MSTIND=YES	SPECIFY USE OF A MASTER-INDEX
SEPASMB=YES	SPECIFY SEPARATE ASSEMBLY
TYPEFLE=RANDOM SEQNTL RANSEQ	SPECIFY TYPE OF PROCESSING TO BE PREFORMED. REQUIRED WITH A RETRIEVAL OPERATION
VERIFY=YES	CHECK THE RECORDS AFTER WRITING
WORKL=ADDRESS	SPECIFY THE USE OF A WORK AREA.
WORKR=ADDRESS	MAY NOT BE USED IN CONJUNCTION
WORKS=YES	WITH IOREG.

FIG. 11-24. Summary of DTFIS operands.

scribed. The order within each group is alphabetic. In practice, because of the common situations which arise, many of the optional operands are used routinely by programers. A summary of the DTFIS operands is given in Fig. 11-24.

The completion for the DSKXTNT= operand is the number of disk extents specified by the EXTENT control cards (see later sections). Since an extent is a contiguous area on the cylinder of the disks, the minimum number which may be specified is two, one for the prime data area with its associated overflow and one for a cylinder index. The programer may specify as many more as he may desire or may be required to because of other uses of disk space. The total number of such areas provided by the EXTENT cards is the number to be shown as the completion for DSKXTNT=.

The completion for the IOROUT= operand is one of four words. If the programer desires to build a new file or to lengthen an existing file by adding records with keys greater than the highest key presently in the file, the completion is LOAD. If he desires to insert new records into an existing file where one or more of the records to be inserted has a key less than the highest key presently in the file, the completion is ADD. If he desires to perform either random or sequential processing of data without adding any additional records to the file, the appropriate completion is RETRVE. If he desires to process either randomly or sequentially the records that are in the file, and at the same time occasionally add records to the file, the appropriate completion is ADDRTR.

The completion for the operand KEYLEN= is the number of bytes of the length of the record key. The keys for all records must be of the same length, and each may be anywhere in the record. The key length is also the length of the field that precedes each record to be written on or read back from the disk, plus any check bytes added automatically by the IOCS routines.

The completion for the operand NRECDS= is the number of logical records in a block. This blocking factor must always be included. If records are unblocked, then the appropriate completion is the digit 1, specifying one record per block.

The completion for the operand RECFORM= is one of two choices. It is FIXUNB for fixed-length unblocked records. It is FIXBLK for fixed-length blocked records. Variable-length records are not permitted in an indexed-sequential file. All records in the overflow area on the disk are unblocked, even if the RECFORM= completion specifies blocked.

The completion for the RECSIZE= operand is the number of bytes in the record. Since all records must be fixed in size, only one completion is possible for this operand. Figure 11-25 shows the relationship of RECSIZE= to the KEYLEN=.

The other operands available with the DTFIS for indexed-sequential files are not required, but in practice many are necessary to implement common operations. A brief review of each is incorporated here.

The completion for the CYLOFL= operand is the number of tracks on each cylinder that are to be reserved for use as an overflow area. This operand is required if an overflow area is to be specified for each cylinder, which is the normal case. If an independent overflow area is also specified by an EXTENT control card,

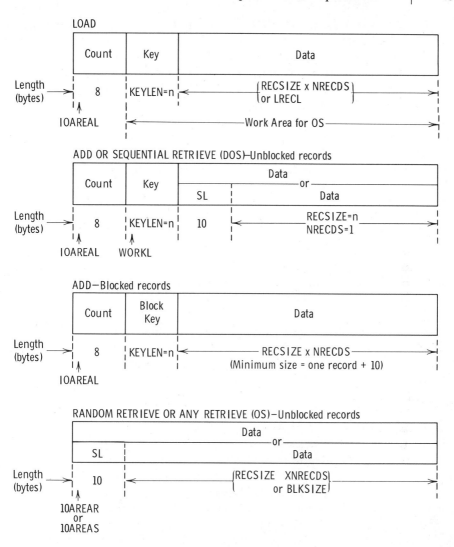

FIG. 11-25. Layout of storage areas for indexed-sequential operations.

then overflows beyond the limits of the overflow tracks reserved by the completion of this operand are automatically placed in the independent overflow area. The appropriate choice of the completion number for this disk operand depends upon the proportion by which the programer expects the file to grow before it is next reloaded (copied). If the programer expects less than 10 percent growth, one track will probably be sufficient. If he expects the files to more than double, he should reserve at least half of each cylinder for overflow.

The completion for the DEVICE= operand is the model number for the type of random-access storage device being used at the installation. Since most installations have only one type of such storage equipment available, the programer can usually omit this operand, and thereby (by default) specify the use of what the installation normally uses. This also applies to HINDEX=, which takes the same type of completion and specifies the storage device used to store the highest-level index for the file.

The programer can usually save computer time by having all of a cylinder index read into internal storage and the index searches performed there. To enable this, the programer can assign with a named DS an area large enough to hold the entire cylinder index. This name then becomes the completion for the INDAREA= operand. The length of the area should be at least equal to the product of three more than the number of cylinders needed for the file times six more than the completion specified for KEYLEN=. This length is then the completion for INDSIZE=.

When he does not specify work areas, the programer can often speed computer operation by specifying IOAREA2= with the address of an area in storage as the completion. Using such an area can sometimes improve the buffering. The length of the area must be the same as that used for IOAREAL= or IOAREAS=.

The completion for the operand IOAREAL= is a symbolic name (address) that the programer has assigned by a DS declarative that defines the area in internal storage from which records are to be copied when they become output into an indexed-sequential file. This operand is required only when the completion for the IOROUT= operand is LOAD, ADD, or ADDRTR. The area in storage must provide eight bytes for the count area or field, the key field bytes, and the length of the block of data record incorporating any imbedded keys. If the IOROUT= operand completion was ADD or ADDRTR, then this DS must also provide 10 bytes for the sequence link field, as shown in Fig. 11-25. Multiple IOAREAL areas are not permitted. If this area in storage is used without also using a work area, then the programer must also use the IOREG= operand.

The completion for the operand IOAREAR= is the name that the programer has assigned by a DS specified area in internal storage, where records are to be read to and written out from, when random processing operations are specified. The space allocated in internal storage must be large enough to accommodate the key field, the sequence link field, and the data area, including any imbedded keys, as shown in Fig. 11-25. If this area in storage is used without also using a work area, then the programer must also use the IOREG= operand.

The completion for the operand IOAREAS= is the name that the programer has assigned by a DS specified area in internal storage for holding records that are to be read or written in a serial (sequential) manner. The area reserved in storage must be large enough to hold the key field, the sequence link field, and the data area, including any imbedded keys. If this area in storage is used without also using a work area, then the programer must also use the IOREG= operand.

The completion for the operand IOREG= is the number in parentheses of the register, from 2 through 12, which the IOCS routine may use for supplying the programer the address of the leftmost byte of the record. The programer must specify IOREG= for blocked records, and must not specify it when he also specifies a WORK= operand.

The completion for the operand KEYARG= is the name of the field which holds the key to be used in a random write and in any read operation. It is the programer's responsibility to copy the key of the record into this area before issuing a GET, READ, or WRITE macro.

The completion for the operand KEYLOC= is the leftmost position of the imbedded key field in blocked data records. This is used only with blocked records, because in that case, the key associated with the block is not the key of the record but the key of the rightmost record in the block. To search for records within a block, therefore, the IOCS routines need the address of the imbedded key. Since only one KEYLOC= operand is specified, it is convenient for the programer to have the key as one field in the record.

The completion for the operand MSTIND= is YES whenever the programer desires a master index to be created or used. The location of the master index is specified by the EXTENT control card and must immediately precede the cylinder index.

The SEPASMB= operand takes the same YES completion described in Chap. 7. This operand permits the programer to compile his IOCS routines separately from his main program and then link-edit together the two resulting object programs. This often saves computer time.

The completion for the operand TYPEFLE= is one of three words. This operand is required whenever a GET or READ operation is to be performed, in order to specify the basis upon which the GET or READ is to be done. The completion is RANDOM if only the READ macro may be used. The completion is SEQNTL if only the GET macro may be used. The completion is RANSEQ if either or both the READ and GET macros may be used.

The completion for the macro VERIFY is YES if the programer desires to have records that are written onto the disk read back again to check parity against the data that were to be written. If the programer omits this operand, no read-and-parity-check operation is performed on the data when they are written on the disk.

The completion for the operand WORKL= is the symbolic name of the DS specified area the programer has assigned in which the individual records to be added to the file are to be built up. This operand is required whenever the programer has used the IOROUT= operand with completions of LOAD, ADD, or ADDRTR. The DS area in storage, so identified, must provide space for the key and data areas, but need not provide space for the sequence link field or the count field. The IOREG= operand may still be used.

The completion for the operand WORKR= is the name of the DS area in storage which the programer has assigned for holding records to be read or written in a random sequence. The space available in this area of storage must provide for one logical record, but need not provide space for a key field or count field. This operand is required only if the programer desires to process data in a work area rather than in an input-output area, and hence the programer may not use IOREG= with this operand.

The completion for the operand WORKS= is YES if the programer desires to have the GET or PUT macros use a work area. Unlike WORKR=, which permits the use of a work area by specifically naming it in the macro, the use of WORKS= provides the programer with the option to specify many work areas, and to name the one he desires to have the GET or PUT use in the GET or PUT macro itself. When the programer uses this operand, he may not also specify IOREG=. Figures 11-26 and 11-27 provide examples of the use of an indexed-sequential file.

Do It Now Exercise 11-2. *Prepare a flow diagram ("post-coding," since the coding exists and is presented in the figure) for the program shown in Figs. 11-26 or 11-27. Explain how each DTFIS or DCB operand contributes.*

TAPE AND DISK LABELS AND JOB CONTROL CARDS

The standard labels utilized for disks and tapes have been described earlier in this chapter. Their use in practice, however, also depends upon the control cards which the programer and the computer operator use in the "job stream." A job stream is a sequence of job control cards directing the operating system programs to have the computer perform the work desired. Control cards, data cards, and program cards may be interspersed. The basic cards in the job stream were described in Chap. 7. Attention is given here to those additional cards which relate specifically to disk and tape operations. The format and function of each of the major job control cards are shown in Fig. 11-28 (see also Fig. 11-26).

```
//FIG#26 JOB (H9-2-867),'MAIL STOP 66',MSGLEVEL=1
//FSTPR EXEC ASMGCLG
//ASM.SYSIN DD *
//GO.DSQ DD DSNAME=TISD(INDEX),DISP=(NEW,PASS),UNIT=2314,          X
//            SPACE=(CYL,(1)),DCB=(DSORG=IS,BLKSIZE=320,RECFM=FB)
//    DD DSNAME=TISD(PRIME),DISP=(NEW,PASS),UNIT=2314,             X
//            SPACE=(CYL,(9)),DCB=*.GO.DSQ
//GO.TSQ DD DSNAME=INREC,DISP=(OLD,PASS),UNIT=2314,DCB=(BLKSIZE=160)
//GO.PSQ DD DSNAME=EROUT,DISP=(,DELETE),UNIT=1403


LEVEL G ASSEMBLER OPTIONS=OS,ESD,ALGN,LIST,LOAD,EXTEN,NORLD,NODECK,NORENT,EXTIME=5,NOBATCH,UTBUFF=3,FULLXREF,
                 INSTSET=67,LINECNT=55,NOEXECUTE,SPACE=MAX-2K,



                              EXTERNAL SYMBOL DICTIONARY

SYMBOL    TYPE ID  ADDR   LENGTH LD ID

FGDCB     SD  01 000000 000490
```

FIG. 11-26. Example of processing an indexed-sequential file under OS.

```
LOC   OBJECT CODE        ADDR1 ADDR2  ST #  NAME    OP     OPERANDS                        COMMENT
                                         2          PRINT  ON,NOGEN,NODATA
000000                                   3  FGDCB   CSECT
000000 070007000700                      4          CNOP   6,8
000006 0530                              5          BALR   3,0
00000A                                   6          USING  *,3
00000A 50E0 322C              00234      7          ST     14,RET                          SAVE OS RETURN POINT
                                         8  *
                                         9  *                MAIN ROUTINE
                                        10  *
                                        11          OPEN   (LODFLE,(OUTPUT),INREC,,PRINTR,(OUTPUT))
                                        21  READ    GET    INREC                           LOCATE INPUT RECORD IN BUFFER
00002A D29F 3240 1000  00248 00000      25          MVC    REC,0(1)                        MOVE TO OUTPUT AREA
00002E D207 323B 32E2  00240 002EA      26          MVC    KEY,ARG                         PULL OFF KEY
                                        27          PUT    LODFLE,REC                      WRITE OUTPUT
000042 47F0 3016              0001E      32          B      READ                            BACK TO READ
                                        33  LAST    CLOSE  LODFLE,INREC,PRINTR             CLOSE FILES
000052 58F0 322C              00234      39          L      14,RET                          PICK UP OS RETURN POINT
000056 07FE                             40          BR     14                              EOJ
000058 D209 3424 32E2  0042C 002EA      41  WRONG1  MVC    KEY2,ARG                        PUT KEY IN MESSAGE
00005F 47F0 3060              00068      42          B      WRONG
000062 D209 3424 1000  0042C 00000      43  WRONG2  MVC    KEY2,0(1)                       PUT KEY IN MESSAGE
                                        44  WRONG   PUT    PRINTR,ERR4                     PRINT ERROR MESSAGE
                                        49          CNTRL  PRINTR,SP,2                     DOUBLE SPACE PAPER
000084 47F0 3016              0001E      54          B      READ                            READ NEXT RECORD
                                        55  *
                                        56  *                DECLARATIVES
                                        57  *
                                        58  LODFLE  DCB    DSORG=IS,MACRF=PM,DDNAME=D50,LRECL=160,KEYLEN=8,      X
                                                           OPTCD=RIYL,RKP=2,CYLOFL=2,SYNAD=WRONG1
                                       126  INREC   DCB    DSORG=PS,MACRF=GL,DDNAME=T50,LRECL=160,RECFM=F,       X
                                                           SYNAD=WRONG2,EODAD=LAST
                                       182  PRINTR  DCB    DSORG=PS,MACRF=PMC,DDNAME=P50,LRECL=132,EROPT=ACC
                                       238  *
000234                                 239  RET     DS     F                               RETURN ADDRESS FOR EOJ
000238                                 240          DS     0D                              FORCE ALIGNMENT
                                       241  *
00023B                                 242  LDREC   DS     0CL176                          IS OUTPUT AREA
00023B                                 243  COUNT   DS     CL8                             COUNT FIELD
000240                                 244  AREA    DS     0CL168
000240                                 245  KEY     DS     CL8                             KEY FIELD
000248                                 246  REC     DS     CL160                           DATA
                                       247  *
0002E8                                 248  WK      DS     0CL160                          INPUT AREA
0002E8                                 249          DS     CL2
0002EA                                 250  ARG     DS     CL8                             EMBEDDED KEY
0002F2                                 251          DS     CL150
                                       252  *
0003B8                                 253  ERR4    DS     CL132                           ERROR MESSAGE
00040C 40E3C8C9C24009C5               254          DC     CL32' THIS RECORD OMITTED FROM FILE: '
00042C                                 255  KEY2    DS     CL10
000436 4040404040404040               256          DC     90C' '                          FILLER OF SPACES
                                       257  *
000490                                 258          LTORG
000000                                 259          END    FGDCB
```

```
                                    CROSS-REFERENCE

SYMBOL    LEN   VALUE    DEFN   REFERENCES

AREA      168   000240   244
ARG         8   0002EA   250      26     41
COUNT       8   00023B   243
ERR4      132   0003B8   253      46
FGDCB       1   000000     3     259
INREC       4   000174   131      17     22
KEY         8   000240   245      26
KEY2       10   00042C   255      41     43
LAST        4   00004B    35     150
LDREC     176   00023B   242
LODFLE      4   000078    63      15     28     37
PRINTR      4   000104   182      19     45     50
READ        4   00001E    22      32     54
REC       160   000248   246      25     29
RET         4   000234   239       7     39
WK        160   0002E8   248
WRONG       4   000068    45      42
WRONG1      6   000058    41      97
WRONG2      6   000062    43     165

NO STATEMENTS FLAGGED IN THIS ASSEMBLY
```

FIG. 11-26. (*continued*)

```
// JOB TEST IS FILE CREATE
// OPTION LINK
// EXEC ASMDVAR


                             EXTERNAL SYMBOL DICTIONARY

SYMBOL    TYPE ID  ADDR  LENGTH LD ID

DKLD       SD  01 000000 0005C8
IJHZLZZZ   ER  02
IJGFIZZZ   ER  03
IJDFCZZZ   ER  04


      DOS LOAD

  LOC  OBJECT CODE    ADDR1 ADDR2  ST #  NAME    OP   OPERANDS                    COMMENT
                                    2            PRINT ON,NOGEN,NODATA
000000                              3  DKLD      CSECT
                                    4  *
                                    5  *         DTF DECLARATIVES FOR FILES
                                    6  *
                                    7  LODFLE    DTFIS DSKXTNT=2,                             X
                                                       IOROUT=LOAD,                           X
                                                       KEYLEN=8,                              X
                                                       NRECDS=1,                              X
                                                       RECFORM=FIXUNB,                        X
                                                       RECSIZE=160,                           X
                                                       CYLOFL=2,                              X
                                                       DEVICE=2314,                           X
                                                       HINDEX=2314,                           X
                                                       IOAREAL=LDREC,                         X
                                                       WORKL=AREA
                                   54  *
                                   55  INREC     DTFSD DEVADDR=SYSO10,                        X
                                                       BLKSIZE=160,                           X
                                                       IOAREA1=GOIN,                          X
                                                       DEVICE=2314,                           X
                                                       EOFADDR=LAST,                          X
                                                       RECFORM=FIXUNB,                        X
                                                       TYPEFLF=INPUT,                         X
                                                       WORKA=YES
                                  100  *
                                  101  PRINTR    DTFPR DEVADDR=SYSO12,                        X
                                                       IOAREA1=OUTPUT,                        X
                                                       BLKSIZE=132,                           X
                                                       CONTROL=YES,                           X
                                                       DEVICE=1403
                                  122  *
                                  123  *         IMPERATIVES
                                  124  *
0001C0 070007000700                125            CNOP  6,8
0001C6 0530                         126  BEGIN     BALR  3,0
0001C8                              127            USING *,3
                                    128            OPEN  LODFLE,INREC,PRINTR     OPEN FILES
                                    138            SETFL LODFLE                  PREPARE TO DO IS LOAD
                                    144  READ      GET   INREC,WK               READ INPUT RECORD
0001FA D29F 3168 3208 00330 003D0   150            MVC   REC,WK                 MOVE TO OUTPUT AREA
000200 D207 3160 320A 00328 003D2   151            MVC   KEY,ARG                PULL OFF KEY
                                    152            WRITE LODFLE,NEWKEY          WRITE OUTPUT
000000                              157            USING LODFLE,1
000212 91FF 101E       0001E        158            TM    LODFLEC,X'FF'          TEST FOR ERRORS
                                    159            DROP  1
000216 4780 3022       001EA        160            BZ    READ                   OK, BACK TO READ
00021A D209 32C8 320A 00490 003D2   161  WRONG     MVC   KEY2,ARG               PUT KEY IN MESSAGE
                                    162            PUT   PRINTR                 PRINT ERROR MESSAGE
                                    167            CNTRL PRINTR,SP,2            DOUBLE SPACE PAPER
00023A 47F0 3022       001EA        173            B     READ                   READ NEXT RECORD
                                    174  LAST      ENDFL LODFLE                 FINISH THE IS FILE
                                    186            CLOSE LODFLE,INREC,PRINTR    CLOSE FILES
                                    196            EOJ
                                    199  *
```

FIG. 11-27. Example of processing an indexed-sequential file under DOS.

LOC	OBJECT CODE	ADDR1 ADDR2	ST #	NAME	OP	OPERANDS	COMMENT
			200	*		DECLARATIVES	
			201	*			
00027R			202		DS	0D	FORCE ALIGNMENT
			203	*			
00027R			204	LDREC	DS	0CL176	IS OUTPUT AREA
00027R			205	COUNTIO	DS	CL8	
00028O			206	KEYIO	DS	CL8	
00028R			207	RECIO	DS	CL160	
			208	*			
00032R			209	AREA	DS	0CL168	
00032R			210	KEY	DS	CL8	KEY FIELD
000330			211	REC	DS	CL160	DATA
			212	*			
0003D0			213	WK	DS	0CL160	WORK AREA FOR INPUT
0003D0			214		DS	CL2	
0003D2			215	ARG	DS	CL8	EMBEDDED KEY
0003DA			216		DS	CL150	
			217	*			
000470			218	OUTPUT	DS	0CL132	PRINTER I/O AREA
000470	40E3C8C9E240D9C5		219	ERR4	DC	CL32' THIS RECORD OMITTED FROM FILE: '	ERROR MESSAGE
000490			220	KEY2	DS	CL10	
00049A	4040404040404040		221		DC	90C' '	FILLER OF SPACES
			222	*			
0004F4			223	GOIN	DS	CL160	DISK INPUT AREA
			224	*			
			225	*			
000598			226		LTORG		
000598	5B5BC2D6D7C5D540		227			=C'$$BOPEN '	
0005A0	5B5BC2E2C5E3C6D3		228			=C'$$BSETFL'	
0005A8	5B5BC2C5D5C4C6D3		229			=C'$$BENDFL'	
0005B0	5B5BC2C3D3D6E2C5		230			=C'$$BCLOSE'	
0005B8	00000000		231			=A(LODFLE)	
0005BC	0000010R		232			=A(INREC)	
0005C0	000003D0		233			=A(WK)	
0005C4	00000190		234			=A(PRINTR)	
0001C6			235		END ,	BEGIN	

RELOCATION DICTIONARY

POS.ID	REL.ID	FLAGS	ADDRESS
01	01	0C	000008
01	02	1C	000010
01	01	0C	0000B8
01	01	0C	0000BC
01	01	0C	0000C0
01	01	0C	000110
01	03	1B	000119
01	01	08	000131
01	01	0C	000134
01	01	08	000149
01	01	0C	000160
01	01	0C	000168
01	01	08	000171
01	01	08	000179
01	01	08	000181
01	01	08	000189
01	01	0C	000198
01	04	1B	0001A1
01	01	0C	0001A8
01	01	08	0001B9
01	01	0C	0001D0
01	01	0C	0001D4
01	01	0C	0001D8
01	01	0C	000268
01	01	0C	00026C
01	01	0C	000270
01	01	0C	0005B8
01	01	0C	0005BC
01	01	0C	0005C0
01	01	0C	0005C4

FIG. 11-27. (*continued*)

```
                                              CROSS-REFERENCE

    SYMBOL    LEN  VALUE  DEFN    REFERENCES

    ARFA      00168 000328 00209   0046  0047
    ARG       00008 000302 00215   0151  0161
    BEGIN     00002 0001C6 00126   0235
    COUNTIO   00008 000278 00205
    DKLD      00001 000000 00003
    ERR4      00032 000470 00219
    GOIN      00160 0004F4 00223   0075  0090  0092  0098
    IJGC0002  00008 000170 00095   0061
    IJJC0011  00004 000264 00191
    IJJ00004  00004 0001CC 00133
    IJJZ0002  00001 000190 00099
    IJJZ0003  00001 0001C0 00121
    INRFC     00006 000108 00058   0135  0146  0193  0232
    INRFCS    00001 000142 00079
    KEY       00008 000328 00210   0151
    KEYIO     00008 000280 00206
    KEY2      00010 000490 00220   0161
    LAST      00004 00023E 00176   0082
    LDRFC     00176 000278 00204   0044
    LODFLE    00002 000000 00011   0023  0134  0140  0154  0157  0176  0192  0231
    LODFLEB   00008 000080 00043   0014
    LODFLEC   00001 00001E 00021   0158
    LODFLEF   00004 0000F8 00052   0023
    LODFLEH   00008 000042 00034
    LODFLEM   00004 000088 00044
    LODFLEP   00024 00006R 00042
    LODFLES   00008 000060 00041
    OUTPUT    00132 000470 00218   0115  0120
    PRINTR    00006 000190 00104   0136  0164  0169  0194  0234
    READ      00004 0001EA 00146   0160  0173
    RFC       00160 000330 00211   0150
    RECIO     00160 000288 00207
    WK        00160 000300 00213   0147  0150  0233
    WRONG     00006 00021A 00161

    NO STATEMENTS FLAGGED IN THIS ASSEMBLY


    /*
    // LBLTYP NSD(2)
    // EXEC LNKEDT
    JOB  TEST      DATE-HERE  DISK LINKAGE EDITOR DIAGNOSTIC OF INPUT

    ACTION TAKEN    MAP
    LIST     AUTOLINK   IJDFCZZZ
    LIST     AUTOLINK   IJGFIZZZ
    LIST     AUTOLINK   IJHZLZZZ
    LIST     ENTRY


    DATE-HERE  PHASE  XFR-AD  LOCORE  HICORE  DSK-AD  FSD TYPE  LABEL     LOADED   REL-FR

               PHASE***  005246  005080  0058A6  92 01 2  CSECT   DKLD      005080   005080
                                                          CSECT   IJHZLZZZ  005870   005870
                                                          CSECT   IJGFIZZZ  005698   005698
                                                          CSECT   IJDFCZZZ  005648   005648
                                                          CSECT             005648   005648

    CONTROL SECTIONS OF ZERO LENGTH IN INPUT


    // DLBL   LODFLE,'TEST DOS IS FILE',72/001,ISC
    // EXTENT SYS001,999999,4,1,39,1
    // EXTENT SYS001,999999,1,2,40,20
    /*
    /&
```

FIG. 11-27. (*continued*)

Under OS, the programer must specify on the DD cards the DCB macro-operands noted earlier in this chapter. To specify the use of magnetic tape and magnetic disk, the programer must complete the UNIT= DD operand with the model number of the equipment used at his installation. For magnetic tape, this is usually UNIT=2400. For magnetic disk it is usually UNIT=2311 or UNIT=2314. By contrast, for a card reader, it is usually UNIT=2540 or UNIT=2520, and for a line printer, it is usually UNIT=1403.

For magnetic disk, the programer must also specify the DD operand SPACE= for an output file. A sample completion is SPACE=(CYL,(10,2,1)). CYL indicates that the allocation of disk space is to be in terms of cylinders, with 10 cylinders allocated for the file, and if more are needed, that 2 more cylinders may be used. One cylinder in addition is to be used for indexes. This and the prior comma are omitted for a serial file. If the programer wants the disk cylinders to be contiguous (a desirable feature to save disk seek time), the sample would be SPACE= (CYL,(10,2,1),,CONTIG).

Under DOS, the format of the ASSGN card depends upon the computer configuration and the level of operating system employed. The ASSGN cards permit the computer operator to specify to the operating system which physical items of peripheral equipment are to be used for which logical files. Under OS, this is accomplished by several parameters on the DD cards.

```
                    IN APPENDIX D, NOTE
                         JOB
                         EXEC
                         ASSGN
                         DLBL
                         EXTENT
                         OPTION
                         PAUSE
                         RSTRT
                         TLBL
```

FIG. 11-28. DOS job control cards used with magnetic tape and disk storage.

Under DOS, two job control cards are needed for each magnetic disk file, and one for each magnetic tape file. The label cards (see Appendix D) differ in format for the tape and disk alternatives, but basically provide the data needed to create or to check the file VOL and HDR labels. For magnetic tape files, these data are more complete on the label card (TLBL) than for magnetic disk (DLBL) for two reasons. First, for magnetic disks, the programer also uses the EXTENT card, and second, disks use a more extensive set of labels, as described earlier. On the label cards, the file name must be enclosed in apostrophies. On the DLBL card, the codes are SD for sequential disk access, DA for random access, ISC for indexed sequential file creation, and ISE for other indexed sequential file access. The use of the data security code depends upon local practice.

For magnetic disk files under DOS, the EXTENT card is very important since it determines how disk space is to be used. The symbolic unit operand is a SYSnnn identification. That and the serial number depend upon local practice, and hence differ from one computer installation to another. The type is 1 for a data area, 2 for an indexed sequential overflow area, and 4 for an index area for an indexed sequential file. The sequence number identifies the logical ordering of the extents for the file, starting with 1. The relative track is the number of the first track in the extent, counting from 0 from the first track of the entire disk pack. Thus, the fifth track

(track number 4) of cylinder 24 on a 20-surface disk pack (on a 2319 or 2314 disk drive) is relative track 484. The number of tracks is a count of the number of contiguous tracks comprising the extent. The remaining two operands are rarely used, and may be omitted.

Do It Now Exercise 11-3. *Prepare the EXTENT cards necessary for an indexed-sequential file to reserve all of cylinders 21 and 22 for a master index; cylinders 23, 24, and 25 for a cylinder index; and cylinders 26, 28, 30 through 42, 51 through 68, and 105 through 186 for the prime data area. For a general overflow area, the following space is available: first three tracks on cylinder 69, last four tracks on cylinder 74, and cylinder 187 through the first five tracks on cylinder 199. What is the correct completion for the DSKXTNT operand for this file?*

EXERCISES

1. Account for the DTF operands that are the same in DTFSR and DTFIS. What generalizations can you draw about the character of input and output on tape and disk from their similarities? What about the DCB operands?

2. Account for the DTF operands that differ in DTFSR and DTFIS. What generalizations can you draw about the character of input and output on tape and disk from these differences? What about the DCB operands?

3. What are the functions of the TLBL, DLBL, and EXTENT cards?

4. Why are the macros used for creating an indexed-sequential file different from those used for making additions to an existing indexed-sequential file?

CHAPTER 12

Floating-point Operations

DECIMAL POINTS AND NUMBER SIZES

In Chap. 5 the programer had the opportunity to gain first-hand experience with the difficulty of determining the correct location of the radix (decimal, binary, or hexadecimal) point, and of scaling numbers to make the radix point come out at the desired position. As the programer undoubtedly noted, preparing a scaling table takes time and thought. To do it, the programer must have some knowledge of the maximum and usually also the minimum size of the numbers, and often even their values, in order to be able to prepare a scaling table correctly.

In some engineering, scientific, and research applications of computers, arithmetic operations tend to dominate the program. In these cases, the labor required in preparing a scaling table for each arithmetic operation in the program becomes unbearably large. The programer typically seeks some way of reducing this burden, while at the same time enabling the computer to perform computations sufficiently accurate to be useful.

Another problem that compounds the difficulty is that the sizes of numbers sometimes become very large and sometimes become very small. Likewise, the number of significant digits is sometimes small, sometimes large. For example, in some work in astronomy, very large numbers are encountered, but the number of filler zero digits in those numbers may be quite large because of the present imprecision of some measurements in that field. Nuclear physics, in contrast, involves some numbers that are extremely small. In organic chemistry some things can be measured with a high degree of precision, thus producing numbers with a large number of significant digits. Handling these diversities in precision and number of significant digits adds to the programer's burden of scaling.

Fortunately, the computer can be equipped with a feature which permits the computer itself to perform automatically many of the operations involved in scaling. This optional feature, known as the "floating-point" or "scientific" command set, makes it possible for the programer to give to the computer much of the labor of keeping track of the proper position of the radix point, while avoiding many of the difficulties involved in adapting to fit different numbers of significant digits and different degrees of precision. This chapter is about the floating-point operations the computer can perform.

In embarking upon this chapter, however, the programer should be wary of one point. There is nothing inherent in floating-point operations that prevents the gradual accumulation of error in computation. Truncation and round-off impair the accuracy of results in extended arithmetic operations. Floating-point operations do little to alleviate the programer's concerns in this area. Selecting algorithms which yield sufficiently accurate results and programing to retain accuracy in computation is still the programer's responsibility.

FLOATING-POINT NOTATION

Numbers of any size can be represented in the decimal system by restating them in terms of an explicit power of ten multiplied by some fraction. This can be illustrated easily, as shown in Fig. 12-1.

Suppose that the fractional number 0.375 be expressed as a fractional number times the power of 10. Since the number is already a fractional number, the question is what is the appropriate power of 10 to multiply it by. Since multiplying a number by 1 leaves the number unchanged, the appropriate power of 10 is the one that

DECIMAL NOTATION	'SCIENTIFIC' NOTATION	'E' NOTATION	EXCESS 64 CHARACTER-ISTIC	FRACTION IN HEXADECIMAL
0.375	$= 0.375 \times 10^{+0}$	$= 0.375E+0 =$	64	600000
3.75	$= 0.375 \times 10^{+1}$	$= 0.375E+1 =$	65	600000
0.0375	$= 0.375 \times 10^{-1}$	$= 0.375E-1 =$	63	600000
3750.0	$= 0.375 \times 10^{+4}$	$= 0.375E+4 =$	68	600000
0.0000375	$= 0.375 \times 10^{-4}$	$= 0.375E-4 =$	60	600000

FIG. 12-1. Floating-point notation for decimal numbers.

equals 1. That, it will be recalled from high-school mathematics, is 10 to the 0th power. Another way of writing this, as shown in Fig. 12-1, is 0.375E+0. The "E" is the general indicator standing for an exponent notation.

Suppose, on the other hand, that the number 3.75 be expressed as a fraction times the power of 10. The fraction is, as before, 0.375, but the power of ten necessary to make that fraction equal the desired number is 10, which is 10 to the 1st power. This also can be written as 0.375E+1.

If the fractional number be 0.0375, this could be represented as 0.375 times 10 to the −1 power. The reason is that multiplying by 10 raised to a minus power is equivalent to dividing rather than multiplying. Hence multiplying 0.375 by 10 to the −1 power, which is 1/10, yields 0.0375, which is the desired number. This can also be rewritten in E notation as 0.375E−1.

If the number be 3,750 the exponent (i.e., the power of 10) becomes larger. The fractional amount is still 0.375, but the power of 10 is now 4. In E notation this is 0.375E+4. The number 0.0000375, on the other hand, would call for an exponent of −4. The fractional part is still 0.375, and the E notation becomes 0.375E−4.

In studying Fig. 12-1, the programer should recall from Chap. 5 that a shift left is equivalent to a multiplication, and a shift right to a division. This equivalence is used to maintain the "normalization" relationship of the exponent and the fraction. The mechanism for this and the methods of notation used require some explanation.

One of the notational schemes used with floating-point operations is known as the "excess notation." This is similar to a modulus notation, as can be seen from Fig. 12-2. The major difference between the two notations is that in an ordinary modulus

Modulus comparison

$\frac{1}{64\overline{)73}}$		$\frac{0}{64\overline{)55}}$	
	+ 73		+ 55
64	− 64		− 64
9	+ 9		− 9

Excess 64 computation

base 64:	64	64	64	64	64
exponent:	+ 0	+ 1	− 1	+ 4	− 4
excess notation:	64	65	63	68	60

Fig. 12-2. Excess 64 notation.

notation the remainder resulting from division is acceptable only if it is a positive number. Hence a modulus notation counts upward from its base until a division with a zero remainder is again possible. In contrast, an excess notation determines the difference in an algrebraic sense, that is, as a plus or minus distance from the starting number.

In Fig. 12-2 an excess 64 notation is illustrated. If the number is 73, it is equivalent to plus 9 in the excess 64 notation. If the number is +55, it is equivalent to minus 9 in the excess 64 notation. An example of the use of excess 64 notation for representing exponents, or powers of a base, is shown in the next to the last column of Fig. 12-1. Thus in the first line the power or exponent is zero. Hence in excess 64 notation this is equivalent to 64 (compare with Fig. 12-2). The next, which is +1, is equivalent to 65, and −1 is equivalent to 63. +4 is equivalent to 68, and −4 is equivalent to 60.

Before leaving Fig. 12-1, one additional definition is worth while. The numbers shown in the second column of Fig. 12-1 are referred to as normalized numbers. Those in the first column of Fig. 12-1 are referred to as unnormalized numbers. By definition, a normalized number is a number placed in a standard fractional format with no leading 0s between the first significant digit and the radix point. That is, the radix point must be immediately adjacent to, and to the left of the first significant digit. Thus the rewriting of the numbers shown in column 1 of Fig. 12-1 into the form shown in column 2 is the process of normalizing. Since this is equivalent to multiplying or dividing the number by doing shifts, this process requires changing the exponent or power to retain the correct value of the number.

FLOATING-POINT REPRESENTATION

The computer uses floating-point numbers in two forms, the short form and the long form. The short form uses six hexadecimal characters for the fractional part of each floating-point number; the long form uses 14 hexadecimal characters for it (see Fig. 12-3). The short form, therefore, can use one aligned full word of storage in the computer, whereas the long form requires an aligned double word. The final column in Fig. 12-1 provides examples of the short-form characteristics in hexadecimal.

The sign occupies the first bit position in either the short or the long form. A 0 bit represents plus; a 1 bit represents minus. This sign applies only to the fractional portion of the floating-point number, and does not apply to the equivalent of the exponent or power of the radix. Negative numbers are represented in true form, not in the two's complement notation. The difference in representation in storage between a negative and a positive floating-point number of the same value except for the sign is only a difference in the sign-bit position. Even though the word "complement" is used with floating-point numbers in the computer, a complement is not actually

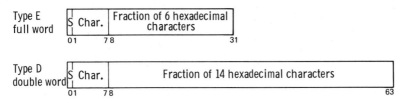

Fig. 12-3. Layout of type E and D floating-point formats.

represented in storage. In storage, floating-point numbers are always represented in absolute form with a sign bit to designate the sign.

The excess 64 code's power of the base is known as the "characteristic" and occupies the next seven bit positions in the first byte in either the long or the short form. The next to the last column in Fig. 12-1 provides examples of characteristics. The base of the characteristic is not 10, as in the decimal system, but is 16, the base of the hexadecimal system. This is consistent with the treatment of the fractional portion of the floating-point number as being composed of hexadecimal characters.

The computer uses an excess 64 notation for the power of the base 16. Since seven bits are used for the "characteristic," the range of numbers that can be represented by the floating-point notation in the computer is about from 0.54×10^{-78} to $0.72 \times 10^{+76}$. Since this range depends primarily upon the size of the characteristic, the length of the fraction, whether long or short, has little effect. In the examples that follow, exponents of various sizes are shown directly. This will give the programer a better feel for the way in which the characteristic is used and expressed in the computer.

For defining constants, the DC declarative is available to the programer in two types: type E for short-form constants, and type D for long-form constants. The type E constants are aligned by the compiler on the full-word boundary and occupy a full word. The compiler aligns the type D constants on the double-word boundary, and they occupy a full double word. Duplication factors are used with both type E and type D in the same manner as for other DC declaratives.

Since the length of the constant is normally specified by its type (E or D), no length operand is normally used with these constants. If the programer does utilize the length operand, the compiler does not align the bytes in storage.

The programer can write the fourth operand of the DC constant in either of two ways. He can write the constant with a decimal point explicitly shown. In such a case, the programer can write the full number in decimal digits that he wishes to have translated into floating-point notation. From this decimal representation the compiler program makes the conversion to binary, builds the characteristic and fraction portions of the constant, and calculates the correct exponent to provide a number normalized in hexadecimal terms. The programer may place a plus or minus sign in front of the number as he chooses. If the programer specifies no sign, the compiler treats it as a plus sign.

The second alternative is to incorporate along with the decimal point the capital letter E followed by a plus sign or a minus sign and one or two digits. This E notation permits the programer to specify the relative location of the decimal point, as was shown in Fig. 12-1. If a plus sign is present, or if no sign is present, the compiler assumes that the exponent indication for the number shown is to be multiplied by 10 to the positive power shown after E. If a negative sign follows the E, the compiler assumes that the number shown is to be divided by 10 to the power indicated. For these operations to be meaningful, the programer must also specify a decimal point in the number to serve as a starting point for the multiplication or division operation. The programer should note that this initial exponent adjustment is made in terms of decimal values, not in terms of hexadecimal values. This is consistent with the practice of writing the floating-point number on the coding sheet in decimal form. The compiler performs the normalization operation automatically later.

The programer should recognize that, as shown in Fig. 12-4, the compiler does a normalization operation so that the first hexadecimal character of the fraction is always nonzero. If this hexadecimal character is a 1, three binary 0s may precede it as part of the first hexadecimal character. If the first hexadecimal character is 2 or 3, two binary 0s may be the lead bits in the hexadecimal character. If the hexadecimal character is 4, 5, 6, or 7, one binary 0 may be the lead bit in the hexadecimal character. Normalization, however, is not in terms of the binary bits but in terms of the hexadecimal character. This is because the characteristic is calculated in terms of powers of the base 16. Thus moving the radix point one hexadecimal position (four binary positions) left or right results in changing the characteristic by one value up or down.

If the programer wishes to have the compiler program establish a type E or type D constant in unnormalized form, he can specify it by the use of an S factor as the third operand of the declarative. For this purpose, the programer writes the

LOC	OBJECT CODE	ADDR1 ADDR2	ST #	NAME	OP	OPERANDS	COMMENT
			669 *				
003200	45165DD0		670	FLOAT1	DC	E'916.13E2'	USE OF A POSITIVE EXPONENT
			671 *				
003204	3E7AE148		672	FLOAT2	DC	E'1.875E-3'	THIS WILL BE NORMALIZED
			673 *				
003208	43349F5C		674	FLOAT3	DC	E'0.84196E+3'	USE OF POSITIVE EXPONENT
			675 *				
00320C	00000000						
003210	44A2E30000000000		676	FLOAT4	DC	D'41699'	NUMBER IS ASSUMED TO BE AN INTEGER
			677 *				
003218	C016CFFA7EB6BF44		678	FLOAT5	DC	D'-.89111E-1'	THIS WILL BE NORMALIZED
			679 *				
003220	3FA3D70A3D70A3D7		680	FLOAT6	DC	DE-2'4,399.11,996,-.0015'	MULTIPLE CONSTANTS
003228	413FDB88AC710CB3						
003230	419F5C28F5C28F5C						
003238	BCFBA8826AA8EB46						
			681 *				
003240	411E0247		682	FLOAT7	DC	E'1.87555555555'	THIS WILL TRUNCATE
			683 *				
003244	44002BF1		684	FLOAT8	DC	ES2'43.943'	PRODUCES AN UNNORMALIZED FORM
			685 *				

FIG. 12-4. Example of DC declaratives for floating-point constants.

capital letter S followed by a one- or two-digit decimal number to indicate the number of hexadecimal 0s that he wishes the compiler program to insert as leading hexadecimal 0s in the fraction. This is also illustrated in 12-4 as FLOAT8.

As can be seen from the examples shown in FLOAT4 and FLOAT7 in Fig. 12-4, the compiler program truncates and pads type D and E constants on the right-hand end. This means that if the constant has fewer significant characters than are needed to fill the number of hexadecimal positions available, the compiler inserts hexadecimal zeros at the right-hand end of the fraction. If it has more significant characters than can be accommodated, the compiler cuts off those on the right to leave only the 6 or 14 most significant hexadecimal characters.

INTERRUPTS AND MASKS

The computer may interrupt floating-point operations for many of the same reasons that it may interrupt other operations. Two examples are improper alignment and use of an address that does not exist in the particular computer configuration. If the programer calls for the use of floating-point operations when no floating-point capability is provided in the particular model and configuration he is using, a specification interrupt occurs.

Floating-point operations are subject to some unique interrupts. Two of the most common involve the size of the exponent. If the exponent becomes too large— i.e., if an attempt is made to increase the characteristic portion of the floating-point number representation beyond seven 1 bits, the situation known as "exponent overflow" arises. The operations that can give rise to exponent overflow are summarized in Fig. 12-5. In all cases, the computer aborts the operation—i.e., it terminates it

CODE	MNEMONIC	COMMAND	FORMAT
2A	ADR	ADD NORMALIZED (LONG)	RR
2B	SDR	SUBTRACT NORMALIZED (LONG)	RR
2C	MDR	MULTIPLY (LONG)	RR
2D	DDR	DIVIDE (LONG)	RR
2E	AWR	ADD UNNORMALIZED (LONG)	RR
2F	SWR	SUBTRACT UNNORMALIZED (LONG)	RR
3A	AER	ADD NORMALIZED (SHORT)	RR
3B	SER	SUBTRACT NORMALIZED (SHORT)	RR
3C	MER	MULTIPLY (SHORT)	RR
3D	DER	DIVIDE (SHORT)	RR
3E	AUR	ADD UNNORMALIZED (SHORT)	RR
3F	SUR	SUBTRACT UNNORMALIZED (SHORT)	RR
6A	AD	ADD NORMALIZED (LONG)	RX
6B	SD	SUBTRACT NORMALIZED (LONG)	RX
6C	MD	MULTIPLY (LONG)	RX
6D	DD	DIVIDE (LONG)	RX
6E	AW	ADD UNNORMALIZED (LONG)	RX
6F	SW	SUBTRACT UNNORMALIZED (LONG)	RX
7A	AE	ADD NORMALIZED (SHORT)	RX
7B	SE	SUBTRACT NORMALIZED (SHORT)	RX
7C	ME	MULTIPLY (SHORT)	RX
7D	DE	DIVIDE (SHORT)	RX
7E	AU	ADD UNNORMALIZED (SHORT)	RX
7F	SU	SUBTRACT UNNORMALIZED (SHORT)	RX

FIG. 12-5. Commands subject to exponent overflow interrupt.

CODE	MNEMONIC	COMMAND	FORMAT
2A	ADR	ADD NORMALIZED (LONG)	RR
2B	SDR	SUBTRACT NORMALIZED (LONG)	RR
2C	MDR	MULTIPLY (LONG)	RR
2D	DDR	DIVIDE (LONG)	RR
3A	AER	ADD NORMALIZED (SHORT)	RR
3B	SER	SUBTRACT NORMALIZED (SHORT)	RR
3C	MER	MULTIPLY (SHORT)	RR
3D	DER	DIVIDE (SHORT)	RR
6A	AD	ADD NORMALIZED (LONG)	RX
6B	SD	SUBTRACT NORMALIZED (LONG)	RX
6C	MD	MULTIPLY (LONG)	RX
6D	DD	DIVIDE (LONG)	RX
7A	AE	ADD NORMALIZED (SHORT)	RX
7B	SE	SUBTRACT NORMALIZED (SHORT)	RX
7C	ME	MULTIPLY (SHORT)	RX
7D	DE	DIVIDE (SHORT)	RX

FIG. 12-6. Commands subject to exponent underflow interrupt.

prematurely, and an interrupt occurs. In the old program PSW the interrupt code is C_x.

A second situation which gives rise to interrupts is "exponent underflow." The smallest characteristic possible in the floating-point representation is a characteristic consisting of seven 0 bits. If an attempt is made to develop or utilize a floating-point number having a still smaller characteristic, exponent underflow occurs. This interrupt, however, is controlled by bit 38 in the PSW. If it is a 1 bit, interrupt is permitted. If it is a 0 bit, the interrupt is suppressed. Whether or not the interrupt occurs, operations subject to exponent underflow are completed with a characteristic of seven 0 bits; the operations are not aborted. The floating-point operations that can give rise to exponent underflow are summarized in Fig. 12-6. When a program interrup occurs, the old program PSW shows a D_x as the interrupt code.

A third interrupt for floating-point operations is the floating-point significance interrupt. This interrupt occurs when the fraction part of the floating-point number becomes all hexadecimal 0s, as from subtracting a floating-point number from itself. What happens to the characteristic part depends upon the setting of the PSW bit 39. If that bit is a 1, the characteristic remains at whatever value it was. If that bit is a

CODE	MNEMONIC	COMMAND	FORMAT
2A	ADR	ADD NORMALIZED (LONG)	RR
2B	SDR	SUBTRACT NORMALIZED (LONG)	RR
2E	AWR	ADD UNNORMALIZED (LONG)	RR
2F	SWR	SUBTRACT UNNORMALIZED (LONG)	RR
3A	AER	ADD NORMALIZED (SHORT)	RR
3B	SER	SUBTRACT NORMALIZED (SHORT)	RR
3E	AUR	ADD UNNORMALIZED (SHORT)	RR
3F	SUR	SUBTRACT UNNORMALIZED (SHORT)	RR
6A	AD	ADD NORMALIZED (LONG)	RX
6B	SD	SUBTRACT NORMALIZED (LONG)	RX
6E	AW	ADD UNNORMALIZED (LONG)	RX
6F	SW	SUBTRACT UNNORMALIZED (LONG)	RX
7A	AE	ADD NORMALIZED (SHORT)	RX
7B	SE	SUBTRACT NORMALIZED (SHORT)	RX
7C	ME	MULTIPLY (SHORT)	RX
7D	DE	DIVIDE (SHORT)	RX
7E	AU	ADD UNNORMALIZED (SHORT)	RX
7F	SU	SUBTRACT UNNORMALIZED (SHORT)	RX

FIG. 12-7. Commands subject to floating-point significance interrupt.

0, then the characteristic is forced to also be the equivalent of 0, which is a 1 bit followed by six 0 bits, and an interrupt also occurs. The old PSW interrupt code shows an E_x. The commands that can give rise to significance interrupts are mostly addition and subtraction as shown in Fig. 12-7.

One additional floating-point interrupt occurs in the case of division. If an attempt be made to divide by 0, the operation is suppressed, and the old program PSW is stored with an interrupt code of F_x. To say that the operation is suppressed means that the division does not occur, and the operands remain in their original condition, unaltered. The floating-point operations that can give rise to the floating-point divide interrupt are summarized in Fig. 12-8.

CODE	MNEMONIC	COMMAND	FORMAT
2D	DDR	DIVIDE (LONG)	RR
3D	DER	DIVIDE (SHORT)	RR
6D	DD	DIVIDE (LONG)	RX
7D	DE	DIVIDE (SHORT)	RX

FIG. 12-8. Commands subject to floating-point divide interrupt.

FLOATING-POINT COMMANDS

All of the floating-point commands available with the computer can be classified into two groups according to the length of the floating-point field they use. If the operation uses an aligned double word with a fraction portion 14 hexadecimal characters long, the mnemonic includes the letter D for double word. If the operation uses an aligned full word containing a six-hexadecimal character fraction portion, the mnemonic includes the letter E. The difference between operations for double-length and single-length operands is usually only in terms of the number of hexadecimal characters being handled. In such cases there is no separate discussion of the differences between the double- and single-length operations. When a difference exists, as in the case of the guard character in addition, subtraction, or division, it is noted.

The floating-point operations use normalization in differing ways. Some operations do not normalize. Others normalize before beginning the arithmetic manipulation and then normalize again afterward. Some only normalize afterward. The normalization done prior to the commencement of the arithmetic operation is referred to as "prenormalization." The normalization done on the result of the arithmetic operation is referred to as "postnormalization."

Some floating-point operations set the condition code. In particular, these are add, subtract, compare, and all of the load register operations except for the simple load register from a register or from storage.

In order to identify the floating-point registers to be used by the commands, the programer usually writes a self-defining decimal value. Only four floating-point registers are provided, numbered 0, 2, 4, and 6. Each is a double word (eight bytes) long. The computer identifies that a floating-point register is to be used by the command specified; hence there is no confusion between these and the general-purpose registers having the same numbers.

Whenever operations are done in floating-point registers, the number of bytes of the register used depends upon the nature of the operation selected. Thus an operation that calls for the use of a double word will use the entire length of the register. An operation that calls only for full-word precision uses only the left half of a register. In these cases, the right-hand half of the register is ignored and remains unchanged.

The sequence of the floating-point commands described in this chapter is as follows: First, ways of loading a floating-point register without setting the condition code are presented. These are followed by ways of storing a floating-point register. These are followed, in turn, by the four normalized arithmetic operations of add, subtract, multiply, and divide. The special divide command known as "Halve" is then presented.

The next group of commands consists of those that set the condition code as they compare or load the contents of a register, e.g., Load and Test, Load Positive, Load Negative, and Load Complement. The last group of commands is the unnormalized add and subtract.

These commands comprise the entire floating-point command repertoire of the computer. For operations not covered by the floating-point command repertoire, the programer can use commands from the regular command repertoire of the computer. For example, to move a floating-point number from one place in storage to another, the programer can use an MVC command.

LDR, LER, LD, LE—Load Register and Load. The LDR and LER are RR commands. The LD and LE are RX commands. These commands copy into the register named by the first-operand address the contents of the field or register named as the second-operand address. The condition code remains unchanged. The commands that make reference to storage are subject to interrupts for improper addressing. Examples of these commands are given in Figs. 12-9, 12-10, 12-11, and 12-12.

STD, STE—Store. These RX commands copy the contents of the register named as the first-operand address into the field in storage named by the second-operand address. The contents of the first-operand address remain unchanged, and the condition code also remains unchanged. This command is subject to interrupts from improper addressing. Examples of these commands are given in Figs. 12-13 and 12-14. The programer should note that to store into a register is the same as to load a register. Hence a "store into register" command is not provided.

ADR, AER, AD, AE—Add Normalized. The ADR and AER are RR commands. The AD and AE are RX commands. In Add Normalized, the computer adds

```
  LOC   OBJECT CODE      ADDR1 ADDR2  ST #  NAME    OP   OPERANDS              COMMENT

                                            IMPERATIVES

000020  6000 2000         00360    17          STD   0,ZKEEP              SAVE REG. CONTENTS
000024  6840 3328         00340    18          LD    4,ZLIXP              LOAD A REGISTER
000028  2804                       19  F12#9   LDR   0,4                  LOAD A REG., LONG FORM -RR
00002A  6000 2010         00370    20          STD   0,ZKEEP+16           SAVE REG. CONTENTS


                                            DECLARATIVES

000340  44262463126E978D           301 ZLIXP  DC    D'9764.387'          F12#9
000348  4040404040404040           302        DC    24C' '               FILLER
000350  4040404040404040
000358  4040404040404040
000360  4040404040404040           303 ZKEEP  DC    32C' '               USED TO DISPLAY STORAGE
000368  4040404040404040
000370  4040404040404040
000378  4040404040404040


                                       DUMP AFTER EXECUTION

001C80  F0404040  40404040  40404040  40404040    40404040  40404040   40404040  40404040
001CA0  44262463  126E978D  40404040  40404040    40404040  40404040   40404040  40404040
001CC0  00000000  00000000  40404040  40404040    44262463  126E978D   40404040  40404040
001CE0  F0404040  40404040  40404040  40404040    40404040  40404040   40404040  40404040


                                       RELOCATION FACTOR   001960
```

FIG. 12-9. Example of Load Register (Long)

```
  LOC   OBJECT CODE      ADDR1 ADDR2  ST #  NAME    OP   OPERANDS              COMMENT

                                            IMPERATIVES

00002E  7020 2080         003E0    22          STE   2,ZHOLD              SAVE REG. CONTENTS
000032  6800 2060         003C0    23          LD    0,ZLIPY              LOAD A REGISTER
000036  3820                       24  F12#10  LER   2,0                  LOAD A REG., SHORT FORM - RR
000038  7020 208C         003EC    25          STE   2,ZHOLD+12           SAVE REG. CONTENTS


                                            DECLARATIVES

0003C0  44262463                   309 ZLIPY  DC    E'9764.387'          F12#10
0003C4  4040404040404040           310        DC    28C' '               FILLER
0003CC  4040404040404040
0003D4  4040404040404040
0003DC  40404040
0003E0  4040404040404040           311 ZHOLD  DC    32C' '               USED TO DISPLAY STORAGE
0003E8  4040404040404040
0003F0  4040404040404040
0003F8  4040404040404040


                                       DUMP AFTER EXECUTION

001D00  F0404040  40404040  40404040  40404040    40404040  40404040   40404040  40404040
001D20  44262463  40404040  40404040  40404040    40404040  40404040   40404040  40404040
001D40  00000000  40404040  40404040  44262463    40404040  40404040   40404040  40404040
001D60  F0404040  40404040  40404040  40404040    40404040  40404040   40404040  40404040


                                       RELOCATION FACTOR   001960
```

FIG. 12-10. Example of Load Register (Short).

```
    LOC   OBJECT CODE    ADDR1 ADDR2  ST #  NAME    OP    OPERANDS          COMMENT
                                            IMPERATIVES

  00003C  6000 2100            00460  27            STD   0,ZSAVE          SAVE REG. CONTENTS
  000040  6800 20E0            00440  28 F12#11     LD    0,ZLOADD         LOAD A REG., LONG FORM - RX
  000044  6000 2110            00470  29            STD   0,ZSAVE+16       SAVE REG. CONTENTS


                                            DECLARATIVES

  000440  41326262CBA732DF            317 ZLOADD    DC    D'3.14902'       F12#11
  000448  4040404040404040            318           DC    24C' '           FILLER
  000450  4040404040404040
  000458  4040404040404040
  000460  4040404040404040            319 ZSAVE     DC    32C' '           USED TO DISPLAY STORAGE
  000468  4040404040404040
  000470  4040404040404040
  000478  4040404040404040


                                       DUMP AFTER EXECUTION

  001080  F0404040   40404040   40404040   40404040   40404040   40404040   40404040   40404040
  001DA0  41326262   CBA732DF   40404040   40404040   40404040   40404040   40404040   40404040
  001DC0  44262463   40404040   40404040   40404040   41326262   CBA732DF   40404040   40404040
  001DE0  F0404040   40404040   40404040   40404040   40404040   40404040   40404040   40404040


                             RELOCATION FACTOR   001960
```

FIG. 12-11. Example of Load (Long).

```
    LOC   OBJECT CODE    ADDR1 ADDR2  ST #  NAME    OP    OPERANDS          COMMENT
                                            IMPERATIVES

  000048  7000 2180            004E0  31            STE   0,ZSTORE         SAVE REG. CONTENTS
  00004C  7800 2160            004C0  32 F12#12     LE    0,ZLOAD          LOAD A REG., SHORT FORM - RX
  000050  7000 218C            004EC  33            STE   0,ZSTORE+12      SAVE REG. CONTENTS


                                            DECLARATIVES

  0004C0  425B10C5                    325 ZLOAD     DC    E'91.0655'       F12#12
  0004C4  4040404040404040            326           DC    28C' '           FILLER
  0004CC  4040404040404040
  0004D4  4040404040404040
  0004DC  40404040
  0004E0  4040404040404040            327 ZSTORE    DC    32C' '           USED TO DISPLAY STORAGE
  0004E8  4040404040404040
  0004F0  4040404040404040
  0004F8  4040404040404040


                                       DUMP AFTER EXECUTION

  001E00  F0404040   40404040   40404040   40404040   40404040   40404040   40404040   40404040
  001E20  425B10C5   40404040   40404040   40404040   40404040   40404040   40404040   40404040
  001E40  41326262   40404040   40404040   425B10C5   40404040   40404040   40404040   40404040
  001E60  F0404040   40404040   40404040   40404040   40404040   40404040   40404040   40404040


                             RELOCATION FACTOR   001960
```

FIG. 12-12. Example of Load (Short).

```
   LOC   OBJECT CODE      ADDR1 ADDR2   ST #   NAME    OP    OPERANDS           COMMENT
                                              IMPERATIVES

000054 D207 2200 21E8 00560 00548      35             MVC   ZHOLD4(8),ZDOUBA   SET UP RECEIVING FIELD
00005A 6840 21E0              00540     36             LD    4,ZSTD             LOAD A REG.
00005E 6040 2200              00560     37  F12#13     STD   4,ZHOLD4           STORE, LONG FORM



                                              DECLARATIVES

000540 43F4768F5C28F5C3                333  ZSTD      DC    D'3911.41'         F12#13
000548 D4D4D4D4D4D4D4D4                334  ZDOUBA    DC    8C'M'
000550 4040404040404040                335            DC    16C' '             FILLER
000558 4040404040404040
000560 4040404040404040                336  ZHOLD4    DC    32C' '             USED TO DISPLAY STORAGE
000568 4040404040404040
000570 4040404040404040
000578 4040404040404040



                                         DUMP AFTER EXECUTION

001E80  F0404040   40404040   40404040   40404040   40404040   40404040   40404040   40404040
001EA0  43F4768F   5C28F5C3   D4D4D4D4   D4D4D4D4   40404040   40404040   40404040   40404040
001EC0  43F4768F   5C28F5C3   40404040   40404040   40404040   40404040   40404040   40404040
001EE0  F0404040   40404040   40404040   40404040   40404040   40404040   40404040   40404040


                              RELOCATION FACTOR    001960
```

FIG. 12-13. Example of Store (Long).

```
   LOC   OBJECT CODE      ADDR1 ADDR2   ST #   NAME    OP    OPERANDS           COMMENT
                                              IMPERATIVES

000062 D207 2280 2260 005E0 005C0      39             MVC   ZSTORE4(8),ZDOUB   SET UP RECEIVING FIELD
000068 7840 2268              005C8     40             LE    4,ZSTE             LOAD A REG.
00006C 7040 2280              005E0     41  F12#14     STE   4,ZSTORE4          STORE, SHORT FORM



                                              DECLARATIVES

0005C0 C6C6C6C6C6C6C6C6                342  ZDOUB     DC    8C'F'              F12#14
0005C8 431410CD                        343  ZSTE      DC    E'321.05'
0005CC 4040404040404040                344            DC    20C' '             FILLER
0005D4 4040404040404040
0005DC 40404040
0005E0 4040404040404040                345  ZSTORE4   DC    32C' '             USED TO DISPLAY STORAGE
0005E8 4040404040404040
0005F0 4040404040404040
0005F8 4040404040404040



                                         DUMP AFTER EXECUTION

001F00  F0404040   40404040   40404040   40404040   40404040   40404040   40404040   40404040
001F20  C6C6C6C6   C6C6C6C6   431410CD   40404040   40404040   40404040   40404040   40404040
001F40  431410CD   C6C6C6C6   40404040   40404040   40404040   40404040   40404040   40404040
001F60  F0404040   40404040   40404040   40404040   40404040   40404040   40404040   40404040


                              RELOCATION FACTOR    001960
```

FIG. 12-14. Example of Store (Short).

the contents of the field or register named by the second-operand address to the contents of the register named by the first-operand address. The sum replaces the contents of the first-operand address, and the contents of the second-operand address remain unchanged. The computer normalizes the numbers before attempting to perform the addition. To do this, it adjusts the number with the smaller characteristic by shifting the fractional portion to the right. This also makes the characteristic larger. When the characteristics of the two fields to be added are identical, addition of the fractional parts then takes place algebraically. If an overflow occurs, the result is again shifted four bits to the right, and the characteristic is increased by 1. After addition is complete, the sum is normalized, if necessary, and the characteristic is appropriately adjusted.

These commands set the condition code in the same manner as for binary addition. That is, if the fractional portion of the floating-point number is 0, the condition code is set to 0. If the sign of the number is negative, the condition code is set to 1. If the sign of the number is positive and the fractional portion is greater than 0, the condition code is set to 2. Condition code 3 is used only for signaling exponent (that is, characteristic) overflow. The reason for this is that the normalization procedure prevents any arithmetic overflow of the fractional portion. Interrupts are possible from a variety of causes, including exponent underflow and overflow, specification, significance, and improper addressing. Examples of Add Normalized are given in Figs. 12-15 to 12-18.

In the case of Add, Subtract, or Divide Normalized, the computer, when the operands are one word long, uses a "guard digit" of one hexadecimal character to improve the precision of the computation. During computation, this guard digit acts in effect as an extension of the fraction portion to seven hexadecimal characters, without altering the contents of the right-hand half of the floating-point registers which are not used for full-word operations. In effect, the guard digit is created during prenormalization and is reabsorbed during postnormalization of the selected full-word (type E) operations. No guard digit is provided for double-word operations.

SDR, SER, SD, SE—Subtract Normalized. The SDR and SER are RR commands. The SD and SE are RX commands. The Subtract Normalized operations follow the same basis as the Add Normalized operations described previously, and are subject to the same conditions and possible interrupts. The only difference is that, before the addition operation is commenced, the sign of the second operand is inverted and the fraction portion is complemented for computation but the second operand remains unchanged in storage or in the registers. A guard digit is used for type E operations. Examples of Subtract Normalized are given in Figs. 12-19 to 12-22.

Do It Now Exercise 12-1. *Prepare a flow diagram for a routine to find the sum of 78 format E numbers, placed consecutively in storage. Store the sum im-*

```
LOC   OBJECT CODE    ADDR1 ADDR2  ST #  NAME    OP    OPERANDS          COMMENT
                                         IMPERATIVES

000070 6800 22E0       00640     43            LD    0,ZADD3           LOAD A REG.
000074 6820 22E8       00648     44            LD    2,ZADD4           LOAD A REG.
000078 05D0                      45            BALR  13,0              SAVE CONDITION CODE
00007A 2A02                      46  F12#15    ADR   0,2               ADD REG., NORMALIZED LONG FORM
00007C 05E0                      47            BALR  14,0              SAVE CONDITION CODE
00007E 6000 2300       00660     48            STD   0,ZKEEP4          SAVE REG. CONTENTS
000082 90DE 230C       0066C     49            STM   13,14,ZKEEP4+12   STORE CONDITION CODES


                                         DECLARATIVES

000640 433AF0353F7CED91          351 ZADD3     DC    D'943.013'        F12#15
000648 4427148000000000          352 ZADD4     DC    D'100045E-1'
000650 4040404040404040          353           DC    16C' '            FILLER
000658 4040404040404040
000660 4040404040404040          354 ZKEEP4    DC    32C' '            USED TO DISPLAY STORAGE
000668 4040404040404040
000670 4040404040404040
000678 4040404040404040


                                         DUMP AFTER EXECUTION

001F80  F0404040   40404040  40404040  40404040   40404040  40404040  40404040  40404040
001FA0  433AF035   3F7CED91  44271480  00000000   40404040  40404040  40404040  40404040
001FC0  442AC383   53F7CED9  40404040  400019DA   600019DE  40404040  40404040  40404040
001FE0  F0404040   40404040  40404040  40404040   40404040  40404040  40404040  40404040


                                RELOCATION FACTOR   001960
```

FIG. 12-15. Example of Add Register Normalized (Long).

```
LOC   OBJECT CODE    ADDR1 ADDR2  ST #  NAME    OP    OPERANDS          COMMENT
                                         IMPERATIVES

000086 7860 2360       006C0     51            LE    6,ZADD            LOAD A REG.
00008A 7840 2364       006C4     52            LE    4,ZADD1           LOAD A REG.
00008E 05E0                      53            BALR  14,0              SAVE CONDITION CODE
000090 3A64                      54  F12#16    AER   6,4               ADD REG., NORMALIZED SHORT FORM
000092 05F0                      55            BALR  15,0              SAVE CONDITION CODE
000094 7060 2380       006E0     56            STE   6,ZSAVE4          SAVE REG. CONTENTS
000098 90EF 238C       006EC     57            STM   14,15,ZSAVE4+12   STORE CONDITION CODES


                                         DECLARATIVES

0006C0 C22E4FAB                  360 ZADD      DC    E'-46.3112'       F12#16
0006C4 41919DB2                  361 ZADD1     DC    E'9.101'
0006C8 4040404040404040          362           DC    24C' '            FILLER
0006D0 4040404040404040
0006D8 4040404040404040
0006E0 4040404040404040          363 ZSAVE4    DC    32C' '            USED TO DISPLAY STORAGE
0006E8 4040404040404040
0006F0 4040404040404040
0006F8 4040404040404040


                                         DUMP AFTER EXECUTION

002000  F0404040   40404040  40404040  40404040   40404040  40404040  40404040  40404040
002020  C22E4FAB   41919DB2  40404040  40404040   40404040  40404040  40404040  40404040
002040  C22535CF   40404040  40404040  600019F0   500019F4  40404040  40404040  40404040
002060  F0404040   40404040  40404040  40404040   40404040  40404040  40404040  40404040


                                RELOCATION FACTOR   001960
```

FIG. 12-16. Example of Add Register Normalized (Short).

```
    LOC   OBJECT CODE      ADDR1 ADDR2   ST #   NAME     OP    OPERANDS              COMMENT

                                              IMPERATIVES

  00009C 6840 23E0            00740      59              LD    4,ZADD6               LOAD A REG.
  0000A0 05E0                            60              BALR  14,0                  SAVE CONDITION CODE
  0000A2 6A40 22E0            00640      61 F12#17       AD    4,ZADD3               ADD NORMALIZED LONG FORM
  0000A6 05F0                            62              BALR  15,0                  SAVE CONDITION CODE
  0000A8 6040 2400            00760      63              STD   4,ZHOLD5              SAVE REG. CONTENTS
  0000AC 90EF 240C            0076C      64              STM   14,15,ZHOLD5+12       STORE CONDITION CODES



                                              DECLARATIVES

  000740 C33AF0353F7CED91                369 ZADD6       DC    D'-943.013'           F12#17
  000748 40404040404040404040            370             DC    24C' '                FILLER
  000750 4040404040404040
  000758 4040404040404040
  000760 4040404040404040                371 ZHOLD5      DC    32C' '
  000768 4040404040404040
  000770 4040404040404040
  000778 4040404040404040



                                           DUMP AFTER EXECUTION

   002080   F0404040   40404040   40404040   40404040       40404040   40404040   40404040   40404040
   0020A0   C33AF035   3F7CED91   40404040   40404040       40404040   40404040   40404040   40404040
   0020C0   00000000   00000000   40404040   50001A02       40001A08   40404040   40404040   40404040
   0020E0   F0404040   40404040   40404040   40404040       40404040   40404040   40404040   40404040



                                  RELOCATION FACTOR    001960
```

FIG. 12-17. Example of Add Normalized (Long).

```
    LOC   OBJECT CODE      ADDR1 ADDR2   ST #   NAME     OP    OPERANDS              COMMENT

                                              IMPERATIVES

  0000B0 7820 2460            007C0      66              LE    2,ZADD5               LOAD A REG.
  0000B4 05B0                            67              BALR  11,0                  SAVE CONDITION CODE
  0000B6 7A20 2360            006C0      68 F12#18       AE    2,ZADD                ADD, NORMALIZED SHORT FORM
  0000BA 05C0                            69              BALR  12,0                  SAVE CONDITION CODE
  0000BC 7020 2480            007E0      70              STE   2,ZSTORE5             SHOW REG. CONTENTS
  0000C0 908C 248C            007EC      71              STM   11,12,ZSTORE5+12      SHOW REG. CONTENTS



                                              DECLARATIVES

  0007C0 409126E9                        377 ZADD5       DC    E'.567'               F12#18
  0007C4 40404040404040404040            378             DC    28C' '                FILLER
  0007CC 4040404040404040
  0007D4 4040404040404040
  0007DC 40404040
  0007E0 40404040404040404040            379 ZSTORE5     DC    32C' '
  0007E8 4040404040404040
  0007F0 4040404040404040
  0007F8 4040404040404040



                                           DUMP AFTER EXECUTION

   002100   F0404040   40404040   40404040   40404040       40404040   40404040   40404040   40404040
   002120   409126E9   40404040   40404040   40404040       40404040   40404040   40404040   40404040
   002140   C220BE84   40404040   40404040   40001A16       50001A1C   40404040   40404040   40404040
   002160   F0404040   40404040   40404040   40404040       40404040   40404040   40404040   40404040



                                  RELOCATION FACTOR    001960
```

FIG. 12-18. Example of Add Normalized (Short).

```
LOC   OBJECT CODE      ADDR1 ADDR2  ST #  NAME    OP   OPERANDS              COMMENT
                                          IMPERATIVES

0000C4 6820 24E0         00840   73          LD   2,ZSUB2               LOAD A REG.
0000C8 6800 24E8         00848   74          LD   0,ZSUB3               LOAD A REG.
0000CC 05D0                      75          BALR 13,0                  SAVE C.C.
0000CE 2820                      76  F12#19  SDR  2,0                   SUBTRACT REG., LONG FORM NORMALIZED
0000D0 05E0                      77          BALR 14,0                  SAVE C.C.
0000D2 6020 2500         00860   78          STD  2,ZKEEP6              SHOW REG. CONTENTS
0000D6 90DE 2510         00870   79          STM  13,14,ZKEEP6+16       SHOW REG. CONTENTS


                                          DECLARATIVES

000840 3E40892DB39771A1          385 ZSUB2  DC   D'.9876E-3'           F12#19
000848 3CB88CA3E7D13511          386 ZSUB3  DC   D'.110E-4'
000850 4040404040404040          387        DC   16C' '                FILLER
000858 4040404040404040
000860 4040404040404040          388 ZKEEP6 DC   32C' '                USED TO DISPLAY STORAGE
000868 4040404040404040
000870 4040404040404040
000878 4040404040404040


                                     DUMP AFTER EXECUTION

002180  F0404040  40404040  40404040  40404040   40404040  40404040  40404040  40404040
0021A0  3E40B92D  B39771A1  3CB88CA3  E7013511   40404040  40404040  40404040  40404040
0021C0  3E4000A1  0FAFA06C  40404040  40404040   50001A2E  60001A32  40404040  40404040
0021E0  F0404040  40404040  40404040  40404040   4040C040  40404040  40404040  40404040


                                RELOCATION FACTOR   001960
```

FIG. 12-19. Example of Subtract Register Normalized (Long).

```
LOC   OBJECT CODE      ADDR1 ADDR2  ST #  NAME    OP   OPERANDS              COMMENT
                                          IMPERATIVES

0000DA 7800 2560         008C0   81          LE   0,ZSUB                LOAD A REG.
0000DE 7860 2564         008C4   82          LE   6,ZSUB1               LOAD A REG.
0000E2 05B0                      83          BALR 11,0                  SAVE C.C.
0000E4 3B60                      84  F12#20  SER  6,0                   SUBTRACT REG., SHORT FORM NORMALIZED
0000E6 05C0                      85          BALR 12,0                  SAVE C.C.
0000E8 7000 2580         008E0   86          STE  0,ZSAVE6             SHOW RESULTS
0000EC 90BC 258C         008EC   87          STM  11,12,ZSAVE6+12      STORE C.C.


                                          DECLARATIVES

0008C0 4414BF03                  394 ZSUB   DC   E'5311.01'            F12#20
0008C4 431D31C3                  395 ZSUB1  DC   E'467.11'
0008C8 4040404040404040          396        DC   24C' '                FILLER
0008D0 4040404040404040
0008D8 4040404040404040
0008E0 4040404040404040          397 ZSAVE6 DC   32C' '                USED TO DISPLAY STORAGE
0008E8 4040404040404040
0008F0 4040404040404040
0008F8 4040404040404040


                                     DUMP AFTER EXECUTION

002200  F0404040  40404040  40404040  40404040   40404040  40404040  40404040  40404040
002220  44148F03  431D31C3  40404040  40404040   40404040  40404040  40404040  40404040
002240  4414BF03  40404040  40404040  60001A44   50001A48  40404040  40404040  40404040
002260  F0404040  40404040  40404040  4040C040   40404040  40404040  40404040  40404040


                                RELOCATION FACTOR   001960
```

FIG. 12-20. Example of Subtract Register Normalized (Short).

```
   LOC  OBJECT CODE    ADDR1 ADDR2  ST #  NAME   OP   OPERANDS             COMMENT
                                          IMPERATIVES

 0000F0 6800 25E0         00940    89          LD    0,ZSUB4           LOAD A REG.
 0000F4 05A0                       90          BALR  10,0              SAVE C.C
 0000F6 6800 24E0         00840    91 F12#21   SD    0,ZSUB2           SUBTRACT, LONG FORM
 0000FA 05B0                       92          BALR  11,0              SAVE C.C.
 0000FC 6000 2600         00960    93          STD   0,ZHOLD7          SHOW REG. CONTENTS
 000100 90AB 2610         00970    94          STM   10,11,ZHOLD7+16   SHOW REG. CONTENTS


                                          DECLARATIVES

 000940 419E04189374BC6A           403 ZSUB4   DC    D'9.876'          F12#21
 000948 4040404040404040           404         DC    24C' '            FILLER
 000950 4040404040404040
 000958 4040404040404040
 000960 4040404040404040           405 ZHOLD7  DC    32C' '
 000968 4040404040404040
 000970 4040404040404040
 000978 4040404040404040


                                          DUMP AFTER EXECUTION

 002280 F0404040  40404040  40404040  40404040  40404040  40404040  40404040  40404040
 0022A0 419E0418  9374BC6A  40404040  40404040  40404040  40404040  40404040  40404040
 0022C0 419E000D  009982F3  40404040  40404040  50001A56  60001A5C  40404040  40404040
 0022E0 F0404040  40404040  40404040  40404040  40404040  40404040  40404040  40404040


                                    RELOCATION FACTOR    001960
```

FIG. 12-21. Example of Subtract Normalized (Long).

```
   LOC  OBJECT CODE    ADDR1 ADDR2  ST #  NAME   OP   OPERANDS             COMMENT
                                          IMPERATIVES

 000104 7860 2660         009C0    96          LE    6,ZSUB5           LOAD A REG.
 000108 05E0                       97          BALR  14,0              SAVE C.C.
 00010A 7860 2560         008C0    98 F12#22   SE    6,ZSUB            SUBTRACT, SHORT FORM
 00010E 05F0                       99          BALR  15,0              SAVE C.C
 000110 7060 2680         009E0   100          STE   6,ZSTORE7         SHOW RESULTS
 000114 90EF 268C         009EC   101          STM   14,15,ZSTORE7+12  SHOW REG. CONTENTS


                                          DECLARATIVES

 0009C0 40FE8A72                  411 ZSUB5   DC    E'.9943'          F12#22
 0009C4 4040404040404040          412         DC    28C' '            FILLER
 0009CC 4040404040404040
 0009D4 4040404040404040
 0009DC 40404040
 0009E0 4040404040404040          413 ZSTORE7 DC    32C' '
 0009E8 4040404040404040
 0009F0 4040404040404040
 0009F8 4040404040404040


                                          DUMP AFTER EXECUTION

 002300 F0404040  40404040  40404040  40404040  40404040  40404040  40404040  40404040
 002320 40FE8A72  40404040  40404040  40404040  40404040  40404040  40404040  40404040
 002340 C414BE04  40404040  40404040  6000A16A  50001A70  40404040  40404040  40404040
 002360 FC404040  40404040  40404040  40404040  40404040  40404040  40404040  40404040


                                    RELOCATION FACTOR    001960
```

FIG. 12-22. Example of Subtract Normalized (Short).

mediately ahead of the list. Code the routine, except for the input-output routines. Use a leading-decisions approach.

Do It Now Exercise 12-2. *Show two alternative ways of clearing to 0 floating-point register number 4. Show the desired contents of the register. Indicate which is the preferred way of accomplishing the clearing, and explain why. Hint: Recall that turning the power off and on in the computer or pressing the reset button can generate non-valid data in a register.*

MDR, MER, MD, ME—Multiply Normalized. The MDR and MER are RR commands. The MD and ME are RX commands. In Multiply Normalized, the computer treats the contents of the second-operand address as the multiplier and the contents of the first-operand address as the multiplicand. The product which the computer generates replaces the multiplicand and becomes the new content of the first-operand address. In multiplication of type D, only the 14 most significant of the resulting hexadecimal characters of the product are retained. The others are lost without round-off. The computer performs normalization before, during, and after the process in order to secure the correct product. The characteristic is calculated by adding algebraically the true values of the excess 64 coded exponents. Exponent underflow is signaled if the characteristic for the product would be less than all 0 bits. No guard digits are provided for either type E or type D. In the case of short precision multiplication (type E), the product is produced in the type D format. The two low-order hexadecimal characters of the product register are always 0, since the two full words participating provide only 6 hexadecimal characters each. The multiplication can yield, therefore, only 12 hexadecimal characters at the most. Since the product register can accommodate 14, the two rightmost characters are always set to 0.

During multiplication the condition code remains unchanged. The sign of the product is determined by the normal rules of algebra. Program interrupts are possible from a variety of sources, including exponent underflow and overflow and, in the case of the RX commands, improper addressing. Multiplication by 0 yields a 0 product without an interrupt. Examples of Multiply Normalized are given in Figs. 12-23 to 12-26.

Do It Now Exercise 12-3. *Prepare a flow diagram for a routine to compute the circumference and area of a circle, where the radius is the only item supplied by input and the radius, the circumference, and area are all desired in the output. Do not code the input-output portions of the program. Code the parts of the program for establishing the constants and work area in storage, and the arithmetic operations to produce the results. Show the contents of storage before and after.*

DDR, DER, DD, and DE—Divide Normalized. The DDR and DER are RR commands. The DD and DE are RX commands. In Divide Normalized, the com-

```
     LOC    OBJECT CODE    ADDR1 ADDR2  ST #  NAME     OP    OPERANDS          COMMENT
                                                 IMPERATIVES

   000118  6820 26E0            00A40  103            LD    2,ZMLT           LOAD A REG.
   00011C  6860 26E8            00A48  104            LD    6,ZMLT1          LOAD A REG.
   000120  2C62                        105  F12#23    MDR   6,2              MULTIPLY REG., LONG FORM
   000122  6060 2700            00A60  106            STD   6,ZKEEP8         SHOW RESULTS




                                                 DECLARATIVES

   000A40  422A30A3D70A3D71            419  ZMLT     DC    D'42.19'         F12#23
   000A48  4080000000000000            420  ZMLT1    DC    D'.5'
   000A50  4040404040404040            421           DC    16C' '           FILLER
   000A58  4040404040404040
   000A60  4040404040404040            422  ZKEEP8   DC    32C' '
   000A68  4040404040404040
   000A70  4040404040404040
   000A78  4040404040404040




                                         DUMP AFTER EXECUTION

   00238C  F0404040  40404040   40404040   40404040    40404040  40404040   40404040  40404040
   0023A0  422A30A3  D70A3D71   40800000   00000000    40404040  40404040   40404040  40404040
   0023C0  42151851  EB851EB8   40404040   40404040    40404040  40404040   40404040  40404040
   0023E0  F0404040  40404040   40404040   40404040    40404040  40404040   40404040  40404040


                                     RELOCATION FACTOR   001960
```

FIG. 12-23. Example of Multiply Register Normalized (Long).

```
     LOC    OBJECT CODE    ADDR1 ADDR2  ST #  NAME     OP    OPERANDS          COMMENT
                                                 IMPERATIVES

   000126  7800 2760            00AC0  109            LE    0,ZMULT          LOAD A REG.
   00012A  7840 2764            00AC4  110            LE    4,ZMULT1         LOAD A REG.
   00012E  3C04                        111  F12#24    MER   0,4              MULTIPLY REG., SHORT FORM
   000130  7000 2780            00AE0  112            STE   0,ZSAVE8         SHOW REG. CONTENTS




                                                 DECLARATIVES

   000AC0  4224028F                    428  ZMULT    DC    E'36.01'         F12#24
   000AC4  41500419                    429  ZMULT1   DC    E'5.001'
   000AC8  4040404040404040            430           DC    24C' '           FILLER
   000AD0  4040404040404040
   000AD8  4040404040404040
   000AE0  4040404040404040            431  ZSAVE8   DC    32C' '           USED TO DISPLAY STORAGE
   000AE8  4040404040404040
   000AF0  4040404040404040
   000AF8  4040404040404040




                                         DUMP AFTER EXECUTION

   002400  F0404040  40404040   40404040   40404040    40404040  40404040   40404040  40404040
   002420  422402BF  41500419   40404040   40404040    40404040  40404040   40404040  40404040
   002440  42B41603  40404040   40404040   40404040    40404040  40404040   40404040  40404040
   002460  F0404040  40404040   40404040   40404040    40404040  40404040   40404040  40404040


                                     RELOCATION FACTOR   001960
```

FIG. 12-24. Example of Multiply Register Normalized (Short).

```
   LOC   OBJECT CODE      ADDR1 ADDR2  ST #   NAME      OP    OPERANDS                COMMENT
                                                 IMPERATIVES

 000134  6820 27E8              00848  114               LD    2,ZMLV2           LOAD MULTIPLICAND
 000138  6C20 27E0              00840  115  F12#25       MD    2,ZMLT2           MULTIPLY, LONG FORM
 00013C  6020 2800              00860  116               STD   2,ZHOLD9          SHOW RESULTS


                                                 DECLARATIVES

 000840  424047AE147AE148              437  ZMLT2        DC    D'64.28'          F12#25
 000848  3F28F5C28F5C28F6              438  ZMLV2        DC    D'.01'
 000850  4040404040404040              439               DC    16C' '           FILLER
 000858  4040404040404040
 000860  4040404040404040              440  ZHOLD9       DC    32C' '           USED TO DISPLAY STORAGE
 000868  4040404040404040
 000870  4040404040404040
 000878  4040404040404040


                                              DUMP AFTER EXECUTION

 002480  F0404040   40404040   40404040   40404040    40404040   40404040   40404040   40404040
 0024A0  424047AE   147AE148   3F28F5C2   8F5C28F6    40404040   40404040   40404040   40404040
 0024C0  40A48E8A   71DE69A0   40404040   40404040    40404040   40404040   40404040   40404040
 0024E0  F0404040   40404040   40404040   40404040    40404040   40404040   40404040   40404040


                                     RELOCATION FACTOR   001960
```

FIG. 12-25. Example of Multiply Normalized (Long).

```
   LOC   OBJECT CODE      ADDR1 ADDR2  ST #   NAME      OP    OPERANDS                COMMENT
                                                 IMPERATIVES

 000140  6840 2868              00BC8  117               LD    4,ZMLV3           LOAD MULTIPLICAND
 000144  7C40 2860              00BC0  119  F12#26       ME    4,ZMLT2           MULTIPLY, SHORT FORM
 000148  7040 2880              008E0  120               STE   4,ZSTORE9         SHOW RESULTS


                                                 DECLARATIVES

 000BC0  4264199A                      446  ZMULT2       DC    E'100.1'          F12#26
 000BC4  40404040                      447               DC    4C' '            FILLER
 000BC8  41500000                      448  ZMLV3        DC    E'5.'
 000BCC  4040404040404040              449               DC    20C' '           FILLER
 000BD4  4040404040404040
 000BDC  40404040
 000BE0  4040404040404040              450  ZSTORE9      DC    32C' '           USED TO DISPLAY STORAGE
 000BE8  4040404040404040
 000BF0  4040404040404040
 000BF8  4040404040404040


                                              DUMP AFTER EXECUTION

 002500  F0404040   40404040   40404040   40404040    40404040   40404040   40404040   40404040
 002520  4264199A   40404040   41500000   40404040    40404040   40404040   40404040   40404040
 002540  431F4800   40404040   40404040   40404040    40404040   40404040   40404040   40404040
 002560  F0404040   40404040   40404040   40404040    40404040   40404040   40404040   40404040


                                     RELOCATION FACTOR   001960
```

FIG. 12-26. Example of Multiply Normalized (Short).

puter treats the contents of the first-operand address as the dividend and the contents of the second-operand address as the divisor. The contents of the first-operand address, the dividend, are destroyed in the division process, and the quotient replaces the dividend. No remainder is developed or available as the result of Divide Normalized. In the D length division, the full 14 hexadecimal characters participate in the dividend and divisor, and are generated for the quotient. In the E length division, the right-hand half of each register is not used and remains unchanged. A guard digit is used for the E length operation.

The computer automatically performs pre- and postnormalization as necessary. The programer, therefore, need give no attention to setting up or calculating a scaling table, as in the case of binary or packed-decimal division. Exponent overflow can arise and is handled as noted earlier. The case of exponent underflow is treated as if it were a program significance interrupt, and the quotient accordingly set to 0 in accordance with the usual procedure for that interrupt. When division by 0 is attempted, an interrupt occurs, and the operation is suppressed, but the program interrupt for significance does not also occur. For Divide Normalized, the condition code remains unaltered. Program interrupts are possible from exponent underflow and overflow, from floating-point divide by zero, and from improper addressing in the case of the RX command. Examples of Divide Normalized are given in Figs. 12-27 to 12-30.

Do It Now Exercise 12-4. *Prepare a flow diagram for a routine to calculate the volume of a cone. The radius and the height are provided as part of the input in floating-point form. The output is to repeat the input and to provide the volume. Include in the flow diagram the input and output operations, but exclude them from the coding.*

HDR, HER—Halve. These RX commands shift the fractional portion of a floating-point number one bit position to the right, truncating off the former rightmost bit. The characteristic and the sign of the number are not changed. No normalization takes place, and no test for 0 value is made. The condition code remains unchanged, and no interrupts occur. Examples of Halve are given in Figs. 12-31 and 12-32.

Do It Now Exercise 12-5. *Prepare the flow diagram for a routine to create a constant equal to one-quarter of pi. Be sure that the resulting constant is correctly normalized. Show the contents of storage after each important step.*

CDR, CER, CD, CE—Compare Normalized. The CDR and CER are RR commands. The CD and CE are RX commands. The Compare Normalized command works in essentially the same manner as the Subtract Normalized. Neither operand, however, is altered as the result of the compare operation. For that reason, exponent underflow, overflow, and significance interrupts cannot occur. The con-

```
LOC   OBJECT CODE    ADDR1 ADDR2  ST #  NAME   OP    OPERANDS           COMMENT
                                        IMPERATIVES

00014C 6840 28E0          00C40   122          LD    4,ZDVS             LOAD A REG.
000150 6860 28E8          00C48   123          LD    6,ZDVD             LOAD A REG.
000154 2D64                       124 F12#27   DDR   6,4                DIVIDE REG, LONG FORM
000156 6060 2900          00C60   125          STD   6,ZHOLD10          SHOW RESULTS



                                        DECLARATIVES

000C40 4264000000000000          456 ZDVS     DC    D'100'             F12#27
000C48 4130000000000000          457 ZDVD     DC    D'3'
000C50 4040404040404040          458          DC    16C' '             FILLER
000C58 4040404040404040
000C60 4040404040404040          459 ZHOLD10  DC    32C' '             USED TO DISPLAY STORAGE
000C68 4040404040404040
000C70 4040404040404040
000C78 4040404040404040



                                   DUMP AFTER EXECUTION

002580  F0404040   40404040   40404040   40404040   40404040   40404040   40404040   40404040
0025A0  42640000   00000000   41300000   00000000   40404040   40404040   40404040   40404040
0025C0  3F7AE147   AF147AE1   40404040   40404040   40404040   40404040   40404040   40404040
0025E0  F0404040   40404040   40404040   40404040   40404040   40404040   40404040   40404040


                        RELOCATION FACTOR   001960
```

FIG. 12-27. Example of Divide Register Normalized (Long).

```
LOC   OBJECT CODE    ADDR1 ADDR2  ST #  NAME   OP    OPERANDS           COMMENT
                                        IMPERATIVES

00015A 7820 2960          00CC0   127          LE    2,ZDIVS            LOAD A REG.
00015E 7840 2964          00CC4   128          LE    4,ZDIVD            LOAD A REG.
000162 3D42                       129 F12#28   DER   4,2                DIVIDE REG., SHORT FORM
000164 7040 2980          00CE0   130          STE   4,ZSTORE10         SHOW RESULTS



                                        DECLARATIVES

000CC0 441A441C                  465 ZDIVS    DC    E'6724.110'        F12#28
000CC4 41200000                  466 ZDIVD    DC    E'2'
000CC8 4040404040404040          467          DC    24C' '             FILLER
000CD0 4040404040404040
000CD8 4040404040404040
000CE0 4040404040404040          468 ZSTORE10 DC    32C' '             USED TO DISPLAY STORAGE
000CE8 4040404040404040
000CF0 4040404040404040
000CF8 4040404040404040



                                   DUMP AFTER EXECUTION

002600  F0404040   40404040   40404040   40404040   40404040   40404040   40404040   40404040
002620  441A441C   41200000   40404040   40404040   40404040   40404040   40404040   40404040
002640  3E137E2A   40404040   40404040   40404040   40404040   40404040   40404040   40404040
002660  F0404040   40404040   40404040   40404040   40404040   40404040   40404040   40404040


                        RELOCATION FACTOR   001960
```

FIG. 12-28. Example of Divide Register Normalized (Short).

```
    LOC   OBJECT CODE    ADDR1 ADDR2  ST #  NAME    OP   OPERANDS              COMMENT
                                                IMPERATIVES

    000168  6860 29E0           00D40  132            LD   6,ZDVS1            LOAD A REG.
    00016C  6D60 29E8           00D48  133 F12#29     DD   6,ZDVD2            DIVIDE, LONG FORM
    000170  6060 2A00           00D60  134            STD  6,ZKEEP10          SHOW RESULTS


                                                DECLARATIVES

    000D40  451719A1C779A6B5           474 ZDVS1      DC   D'94618.1112'      F12#29
    000D48  4120000000000000          475 ZDVD2      DC   D'2'
    000D50  4040404040404040          476            DC   16C' '             FILLER
    000D58  4040404040404040
    000D60  4040404040404040          477 ZKEEP10    DC   32C' '             USED TO DISPLAY STORAGE
    000D68  4040404040404040
    000D70  4040404040404040
    000D78  4040404040404040


                                          DUMP AFTER EXECUTION

    002680  F0404040  40404040  40404040  40404040   40404040  40404040  40404040  40404040
    0026A0  451719A1  C779A6B5  41200000  00000000   40404040  40404040  40404040  40404040
    0026C0  4488CD0E  3BCD35A8  40404040  40404040   40404040  40404040  40404040  40404040
    0026E0  F0404040  40404040  40404040  40404040   40404040  40404040  40404040  40404040


                                    RELOCATION FACTOR   001960
```

FIG. 12-29. Example of Divide Normalized (Long).

```
    LOC   OBJECT CODE    ADDR1 ADDR2  ST #  NAME    OP   OPERANDS              COMMENT
                                                IMPERATIVES

    000174  7800 2A60           00DC0  136            LE   0,ZDIVS1           LOAD A REG.
    000178  7D00 2A64           00DC4  137 F12#30     DE   0,ZDIVD2           DIVIDE, SHORT FORM
    00017C  7000 2A80           00DE0  138            STE  0,ZSAVE10          SHOW RESULTS


                                                DECLARATIVES

    000DC0  42355021                  483 ZDIVS1     DC   E'53.313'          F12#30
    000DC4  41419DB2                  484 ZDIVD2     DC   E'4.101'
    000DC8  4040404040404040          485            DC   24C' '             FILLER
    000DD0  4040404040404040
    000DD8  4040404040404040
    000DE0  4040404040404040          486 ZSAVE10    DC   32C' '             USED TO DISPLAY STORAGE
    000DE8  4040404040404040
    000DF0  4040404040404040
    000DF8  4040404040404040


                                          DUMP AFTER EXECUTION

    002700  F0404040  40404040  40404040  40404040   40404040  40404040  40404040  40404040
    002720  42355021  41419DB2  40404040  40404040   40404040  40404040  40404040  40404040
    002740  41D00001  40404040  40404040  40404040   40404040  40404040  40404040  40404040
    00276C  F0404040  40404040  40404040  40404040   40404040  40404040  40404040  40404040


                                    RELOCATION FACTOR   001960
```

FIG. 12-30. Example of Divide Normalized (Short).

```
   LOC   OBJECT CODE      ADDR1 ADDR2   ST #   NAME     OP    OPERANDS           COMMENT

                                                IMPERATIVES

 000180  6840 2AE0         00E40         140            LD    4,ZHLF             LOAD A REG.
 000184  2404                             141  F12#31   HDR   0,4                HALVE REG. CONTENTS, UNNORMALIZED
 000186  6000 2800         00E60         142            STD   0,ZKEEP9           SHOW RESULTS


                                                DECLARATIVES

 000E40  441A441C28F5C28F                492  ZHLF      DC    D'6724.110'        F12#31
 000E48  404040404040404040              493           DC    24C' '             FILLER
 000E50  404040404040404040
 000E58  404040404040404040
 000E60  404040404040404040              494  ZKEEP9    DC    32C' '             USED TO DISPLAY STORAGE
 000E68  404040404040404040
 000E70  404040404040404040
 000E78  404040404040404040


                                          DUMP AFTER EXECUTION

 002780  F0404040   40404040   40404040   40404040   404C4040   40404040   40404040   40404040
 0027A0  441A441C   28F5C28F   40404040   40404040   40404040   40404040   40404040   40404040
 0027C0  440D220E   147AE147   40404040   40404040   40404040   40404040   40404040   40404040
 0027E0  F0404040   40404040   40404040   40404040   40404040   40404040   40404040   40404040


                             RELOCATION FACTOR   001960
```

FIG. 12-31. Example of Halve Register (Long).

```
   LOC   OBJECT CODE      ADDR1 ADDR2   ST #   NAME     OP    OPERANDS           COMMENT

                                                IMPERATIVES

 0001EA  7860 2E60         011C0         181            LE    6,ZCOM             LOAD A REG.
 0001EE  05D0                             182           BALR  13,0               SAVE CONDITION CODE
 0001F0  3246                             183  F12#38   LTER  4,6                LOAD AND TEST, SHORT FORM
 0001F2  05E0                             184           BALR  14,0               SAVE CONDITION CODE
 0001F4  7040 2E80         011E0         185            STE   4,ZSTORE2          SAVE REG. CONTENTS
 0001F8  90DE 2E8C         021EC         186            STM   13,14,ZSTORE2+12   STORE CONDITION CODES


                                                DECLARATIVES

 0011C0  C422C500                        552  ZCOM      DC    E'-89.01E2'        F12#38
 0011C4  404040404040404040              553           DC    28C' '             FILLER
 0011CC  404040404040404040
 0011D4  404040404040404040
 0011DC  404040404040
 0011E0  404040404040404040              554  ZSTORE2   DC    32C' '             USED TO DISPLAY STORAGE
 0011E8  404040404040404040
 0011F0  404040404040404040
 0011F8  404040404040404040


                                          DUMP AFTER EXECUTION

 002B00  F0404040   40404040   40404040   40404040   40404040   40404040   40404040   40404040
 002B20  C422C500   40404040   40404040   40404040   40404040   40404040   40404040   40404040
 002B40  C422C500   40404040   40404040   60001B50   50001854   40404040   40404040   40404040
 002B60  F0404040   40404040   40404040   40404040   40404040   40404040   40404040   40404040


                             RELOCATION FACTOR   001960
```

FIG. 12-32. Example of Halve Register (Short).

tents of the register named as the first-operand address are compared with the contents of the field or register named as the second-operand address. The comparison is algebraic and takes into account the sign, the fraction portion, and the characteristic of each operand. The CD and CE commands, because they make a reference to storage, may be subject to interrupts for improper addressing. The condition code is set in the following manner: 0 indicates that the operands are equal, 1 that the first operand is smaller or less than the second, and 2 that the first operand is larger or greater than the other. Condition code 3 is not used. In determining the setting of the condition code, the characteristic is considered, as well as the fractional portion of the number and the sign. If the fraction portion, however, is 0, then the characteristic and sign associated with the 0 fraction are ignored. Examples of Compare Normalized are shown in Figs. 12-33 to 12-36.

Do It Now Exercise 12-6. Using the situation and restrictions described for Do It Now Exercise 12-4, incorporate a test to prevent an attempt to divide by 0, and notify the operator by means of an error message. Be sure to prepare a flow diagram.

LTDR, LTER—Load and Test Register. These RR commands replace the contents of the register named as the first-operand address with a copy of the contents of the register named as the second-operand address. They set the condition code as follows: 0 if the fraction portion is equal to 0; 1 if the sign of the fraction portion is negative; 2 if the fraction portion is positive and not zero. When short operands are used (LTER), the right-hand portion of the register is not altered or tested. Interrupt may arise from improper register specification. Examples of LTER and LTDR are given in Figs. 12-37 and 12-38.

Do It Now Exercise 12-7. Prepare a flow diagram for a routine to determine the sign of the double-word-length floating-point number in register 2. Use no other floating-point register. If it is negative, code the routine—without using floating-point operations—that will convert it to positive. For contrast, code the routine again, using the Load and Test Register. Show the contents of storage and the setting of the condition code.

LCDR, LCER—Load Complement Register. These RR commands operate in the same manner as the Load and Test Register commands, but invert the sign of the floating-point number as it is loaded. The condition code is set in the same manner as for Load and Test Register, noted earlier. Improper register specification is the only usual cause of interrupt. Examples of LCDR and LCER are given in Figs. 12-39 and 12-40.

Do It Now Exercise 12-8. Perform the same operations specified in Do It Now Exercise 12-7, but use instead the Load Complement Register commands for altering the sign. Show the contents of storage and the setting of the condition code.

```
   LOC   OBJECT CODE   ADDR1 ADDR2  ST #  NAME    OP   OPERANDS        COMMENT
                                          IMPERATIVES

 000194  6800 2BE0      00F40       148           LD   0,ZCOMD         LOAD A REG.
 000198  6840 2BE8      00F48       149           LD   4,ZCOMD1        LOAD A REG.
 00019C  05D0                       150           BALR 13,0            SAVE C.C.
 00019E  2940                       151 F12#33    CDR  4,0             COMPARE REG., LONG FORM
 0001A0  05E0                       152           BALR 14,0            SAVE C.C.
 0001A2  90DE 2C00      00F60       153           STM  13,14,ZHOLD11   SHOW REG. CONTENTS


                                          DECLARATIVES

 000F40  3F1914D9ABD8607F           508 ZCOMD     DC   D'61.234E-4'    F12#33
 000F48  3E3C40F8EE93C6F2           509 ZCOMD1    DC   D'91.94E-5'
 000F50  4040404040404040           510           DC   16C' '          FILLER
 000F58  4040404040404040
 000F60  4040404040404040           511 ZHOLD11   DC   32C' '          USED TO DISPLAY STORAGE
 000F68  4040404040404040
 000F70  4040404040404040
 000F78  4040404040404040


                                          DUMP AFTER EXECUTION

 002880  F0404040  40404040  40404040  40404040  40404040  40404040  40404040  40404040
 0028A0  3F1914D9  ABD8607F  3E3C40F8  FE93C6F2  40404040  40404040  40404040  40404040
 0028C0  50001AFE  50001802  40404040  40404040  40404040  40404040  40404040  40404040
 0028E0  F0404040  40404040  40404040  40404040  40404040  40404040  40404040  40404040


                                  RELOCATION FACTOR     001960
```

FIG. 12-33. Example of Compare Register Normalized (Long).

```
   LOC   OBJECT CODE   ADDR1 ADDR2  ST #  NAME    OP   OPERANDS        COMMENT
                                          IMPERATIVES

 0001A6  7800 2C60      00FC0       155           LE   0,ZCOME         LOAD A REG.
 0001AA  7820 2C64      00FC4       156           LE   2,ZCOME1        LOAD A REG.
 0001AE  05E0                       157           BALR 14,0            SAVE C.C.
 0001B0  3920                       158 F12#34    CER  2,0             COMPARE REG., SHORT FORM
 0001B2  05F0                       159           BALR 15,0            SAVE C.C.
 0001B4  90EF 2C80      00FE0       160           STM  14,15,ZSTORE11  STORE C.C.


                                          DECLARATIVES

 000FC0  43382029                   517 ZCOME     DC   E'946.01'       F12#34
 000FC4  C33F33AE                   518 ZCOME1    DC   E'-1011.23'
 000FC8  4040404040404040           519           DC   24C' '          FILLER
 000FD0  4040404040404040
 000FD8  4040404040404040
 000FE0  4040404040404040           520 ZSTORE11  DC   32C' '          USED TO DISPLAY STORAGE
 000FE8  4040404040404040
 000FF0  4040404040404040
 000FF8  4040404040404040


                                          DUMP AFTER EXECUTION

 002900  F0404040  40404040  40404040  40404040  40404040  40404040  40404040  40404040
 002920  43382029  C33F33AE  40404040  40404040  40404040  40404040  40404040  40404040
 002940  50001810  50001B14  40404040  40404040  40404040  40404040  40404040  40404040
 002960  F0404040  40404040  40404040  40404040  40404040  40404040  40404040  40404040


                                  RELOCATION FACTOR     001960
```

FIG. 12-34. Example of Compare Register Normalized (Short).

```
   LOC   OBJECT CODE    ADDR1 ADDR2  ST #   NAME    OP   OPERANDS            COMMENT

                                            IMPERATIVES

 0001B8  6820 2CE0            01040   162            LD   2,ZCOMD2           LOAD A REG.
 0001BC  05B0                         163            BALR 11,0               SAVE C.C.
 0001BE  6920 2CE8            01048   164  F12#35    CD   2,ZCOMD3           COMPARE, LONG FORM
 0001C2  05C0                         165            BALR 12,0               SAVE C.C.
 0001C4  908C 2D00            01060   166            STM  11,12,ZKEEP11      STORE C.C.


                                            DECLARATIVES

 001040  481B824068000000             526  ZCOMD2   DC   D'4615.21E5'       F12#35
 001048  4757232100000000             527  ZCOMD3   DC   D'913.7E5'
 001050  4040404040404040             528           DC   16C' '             FILLER
 001058  4040404040404040
 001060  4040404040404040             529  ZKEEP11  DC   32C' '             USED TO DISPLAY STORAGE
 001068  4040404040404040
 001070  4040404040404040
 001078  4040404040404040


                                        DUMP AFTER EXECUTION

 002980  F0404040  40404040   40404040   40404040    40404040   40404040   40404040   40404040
 0029A0  48188240  68000000   47572321   00000000    40404040   40404040   40404040   40404040
 0029C0  5000181E  60001B24   40404040   40404040    40404040   40404040   40404040   40404040
 0029E0  F0404040  40404040   40404040   40404040    40404040   40404040   40404040   40404040


                              RELOCATION FACTOR   001960
```

Fig. 12-35. Example of Compare Normalized (Long).

```
   LOC   OBJECT CODE    ADDR1 ADDR2  ST #   NAME    OP   OPERANDS            COMMENT

                                            IMPERATIVES

 0001C8  7860 2D60            010C0   168            LE   6,ZCOME2           LOAD A REG.
 0001CC  05E0                         169            BALR 14,0               SAVE C.C.
 0001CE  7960 2D64            010C4   170  F12#36    CE   6,ZCOME3           COMPARE, SHORT FORM
 0001D2  05F0                         171            BALR 15,0               SAVE C.C.
 0001D4  90EF 2D80            010E0   172            STM  14,15,ZSAVE11      STORE C.C.


                                            DECLARATIVES

 0010C0  45183800                     535  ZCOME2   DC   E'99.2E3'          F12#36
 0010C4  46975E00                     536  ZCOME3   DC   E'99.2E5'
 0010C8  4040404040404040             537           DC   24C' '             FILLER
 0010D0  4040404040404040
 0010D8  4040404040404040
 0010E0  4040404040404040             538  ZSAVE11  DC   32C' '             USED TO DISPLAY STORAGE
 0010E8  4040404040404040
 0010F0  4040404040404040
 0010F8  4040404040404040


                                        DUMP AFTER EXECUTION

 002A00  F0404040  40404040   40404040   40404040    40404040   40404040   40404040   40404040
 002A20  45183800  46975E00   40404040   40404040    40404040   40404040   40404040   40404040
 002A40  60001B2E  50001B34   40404040   40404040    40404040   40404040   40404040   40404040
 002A60  F0404040  40404040   40404040   40404040    40404040   40404040   40404040   40404040


                              RELOCATION FACTOR   001960
```

Fig. 12-36. Example of Compare Normalized (Short).

```
  LOC   OBJECT CODE    ADDR1 ADDR2  ST #  NAME    OP   OPERANDS              COMMENT
                                            IMPERATIVES

 0001D8 6820 2DE0            01140  174            LD   2,ZTEST              LOAD A REG.
 0001DC 05E0                        175            BALR 14,0                 SAVE CONDITION CODE
 0001DE 2222                        176  F12#37    LTDR 2,2                  LOAD AND TEST, LONG FORM
 0001E0 05F0                        177            BALR 15,0                 SAVE CONDITION CODE
 0001E2 6060 2E00            01160  178            STD  6,ZHOLD2             SAVE REG. CONTENTS
 0001E6 90EF 2E0C            0116C  179            STM  14,15,ZHOLD2+12      STORE CONDITION CODES


                                            DECLARATIVES

 001140 431B41C28F5C28F6           544  ZTEST    DC   D'4361.1E-1'          F12#37
 001148 4040404040404040          545           DC   24C' '               FILLER
 001150 4040404040404040
 001158 4040404040404040
 001160 4040404040404040          546  ZHOLD2   DC   32C' '               USED TO DISPLAY STORAGE
 001168 4040404040404040
 001170 4040404040404040
 001178 4040404040404040


                                         DUMP AFTER EXECUTION

 002A80  F0404040  40404040  40404040  40404040   40404040  40404040  40404040  40404040
 002AA0  431B41C2  8F5C28F6  40404040  40404040   40404040  40404040  40404040  40404040
 002AC0  45183800  3BCD35A8  40404040  5000183E   60001B42  40404040  40404040  40404040
 002AE0  F0404040  40404040  40404040  40404040   40404040  40404040  40404040  40404040


                                 RELOCATION FACTOR    001960
```

Fig. 12-37. Example of Load and Test Register (Long).

```
  LOC   OBJECT CODE    ADDR1 ADDR2  ST #  NAME    OP   OPERANDS              COMMENT
                                            IMPERATIVES

 0001EA 7860 2E60            011C0  181            LE   6,ZCOM               LOAD A REG.
 0001EE 05D0                        182            BALR 13,0                 SAVE CONDITION CODE
 0001F0 3246                        183  F12#38    LTER 4,6                  LOAD AND TEST, SHORT FORM
 0001F2 05E0                        184            BALR 14,0                 SAVE CONDITION CODE
 0001F4 7040 2E80            011E0  185            STE  4,ZSTORE2            SAVE REG. CONTENTS
 0001F8 90DE 2E8C            011EC  186            STM  13,14,ZSTORE2+12     STORE CONDITION CODES


                                            DECLARATIVES

 0011C0 C422C500                   552  ZCOM     DC   E'-89.01E2'          F12#38
 0011C4 4040404040404040          553           DC   28C' '               FILLER
 0011CC 4040404040404040
 0011D4 4040404040404040
 0011DC 40404040
 0011E0 4040404040404040          554  ZSTORE2  DC   32C' '               USED TO DISPLAY STORAGE
 0011E8 4040404040404040
 0011F0 4040404040404040
 0011F8 4040404040404040


                                         DUMP AFTER EXECUTION

 002B00  F0404040  40404040  40404040  40404040   40404040  40404040  40404040  40404040
 002B20  C422C500  40404040  40404040  40404040   40404040  40404040  40404040  40404040
 002B40  C422C500  40404040  40404040  60001B50   50001B54  40404040  40404040  40404040
 002B60  F0404040  40404040  40404040  40404040   40404040  40404040  40404040  40404040


                                 RELOCATION FACTOR    001960
```

Fig. 12-38. Example of Load and Test Register (Short).

```
   LOC   OBJECT CODE      ADDR1 ADDR2  ST #  NAME     OP   OPERANDS           COMMENT
                                             IMPERATIVES

 0001FC 6860 2EE0          01240   188          LD   6,ZCOM2           LOAD A REG.
 000200 05B0                       189          BALR 11,0              SAVE CONDITION CODE
 000202 2346                       190 F12#39   LCDR 4,6              LOAD COMPLEMENT, LONG FORM
 000204 05C0                       191          BALR 12,0              SAVE CONDITION CODE
 000206 6040 2F00          01260   192          STD  4,ZKEEP2          SAVE REG. CONTENTS
 00020A 90BC 2F0C          0126C   193          STM  11,12,ZKEEP2+12   STORE CONDITION CODES


                                             DECLARATIVES

 001240 BE7D2C7B8690D5A5C          560 ZCOM2    DC   D'-1.91E-3'       F12#39
 001248 4040404040404040          561          DC   24C' '            FILLER
 001250 4040404040404040
 001258 4040404040404040
 001260 4040404040404040          562 ZKEEP2   DC   32C' '            USED TO DISPLAY STORAGE
 001268 4040404040404040
 001270 4040404040404040
 001278 4040404040404040


                                      DUMP AFTER EXECUTION

 002B80  F0404040  40404040  40404040  40404040  40404040  40404040  40404040  40404040
 002BA0  BE7D2C7B  8900D5A5C 40404040  40404040  40404040  40404040  40404040  40404040
 002BC0  3E7D2C7B  8900D5A5C 40404040  50001862  60001866  40404040  40404040  40404040
 002BE0  F0404040  40404040  40404040  40404040  40404040  40404040  40404040  40404040


                              RELOCATION FACTOR   001960
```

FIG. 12-39. Example of Load Complement Register (Long).

```
   LOC   OBJECT CODE      ADDR1 ADDR2  ST #  NAME     OP   OPERANDS           COMMENT
                                             IMPERATIVES

 00020E 7800 2F60          012C0   195          LE   0,ZCOM3
 000212 05C0                       196          BALR 12,0              SAVE CONDITION CODE
 000214 3360                       197 F12#40   LCER 6,0              LOAD COMPLEMENT, SHORT FORM
 000216 05D0                       198          BALR 13,0              SAVE CONDITION CODE
 000218 7060 2F80          012E0   199          STE  6,ZSAVE2          SAVE REG. CONTENTS
 00021C 90CD 2F8C          012EC   200          STM  12,13,ZSAVE2+12   STORE CONDITION CODES


                                             DECLARATIVES

 0012C0 444E921A                   568 ZCOM3    DC   E'20114.1'        F12#40
 0012C4 4040404040404040          569          DC   28C' '            FILLER
 0012CC 4040404040404040
 0012D4 4040404040404040
 0012DC 40404040
 0012E0 4040404040404040          570 ZSAVE2   DC   32C' '            USED TO DISPLAY STORAGE
 0012E8 4040404040404040
 0012F0 4040404040404040
 0012F8 4040404040404040


                                      DUMP AFTER EXECUTION

 002C00  F0404040  40404040  40404040  40404040  40404040  40404040  40404040  40404040
 002C20  444E921A  40404040  40404040  40404040  40404040  40404040  40404040  40404040
 002C40  C44E921A  40404040  40404040  60001874  50001878  40404040  40404040  40404040
 002C60  F0404040  40404040  40404040  40404040  40404040  40404040  40404040  40404040


                              RELOCATION FACTOR   001960
```

FIG. 12-40. Example of Load Complement Register (Short).

LPDR, LPER—Load Positive Register. These RR commands operate in the same fashion as the Load and Test Register commands noted earlier, but always set the resulting sign to positive. As a result, only two condition codes are possible: 0 indicates that the fraction portion of the number loaded is 0, and 2 that the fractional portion is positive but greater than 0. Examples of Load Positive Register are shown in Figs. 12-41 and 12-42.

LNDR, LNER—Load Negative Register. These RR commands operate in the same manner as Load Positive Register, but set the sign of the first-operand register to negative. For this reason, only two condition codes are used: 0 if the fraction portion of the floating point number is 0 (note that this is a way of obtaining a negative 0), and 1 when the fractional portion is nonzero. The only interrupt normally possible is from improper register specifications. Examples of LNDR and LNER are given in Figs. 12-43 and 12-44.

Do It Now Exercise 12-9. *Perform the operations specified in Do It Now Exercise 12-7, but use instead the Load Positive Register and Load Negative Register commands to obtain the proper register sign setting. Make sure that the sign is set correctly by performing an explicit operation to set it and to set the condition code to indicate the sign. Show the contents of storage both before and after.*

AWR, AUR, AW, AU—Add Unnormalized. The AWR and AUR are RR commands. The AW and AU are RX commands. The Add Unnormalized operation proceeds as an ordinary floating-point addition operation, the difference being that the sum is not postnormalized to correct for any leading 0s that may be generated. After prenormalization, the computer adds the contents of the register or field named as the second-operand address to the contents of the register named as the first-operand address. Shifting to the right may occur to accommodate carries, and the characteristic adjusted accordingly. For this reason, exponent overflow is possible, but exponent underflow cannot occur. The condition code is set to 0 if the fractional portion of the resulting sum is zero, to 1 if the sum is negative, to 2 if the sum is greater than 0 and positive, and to 3 if an exponent overflow occurs. Interrupt is possible from exponent overflow, from significance, from improper register specification, and in the case of the AU and AW commands, from improper addressing. The W mnemonic indicates a double-word-length operand; the U mnemonic indicates a (short-length) full-word operand. These commands give the programer the option of controlling the normalization himself—a convenience in assessing the buildup of computational error. Examples of Add Unnormalized are given in Figs. 12-45 to 12-48.

SWR, SUR, SW, SU—Subtract Unnormalized. The SWR and SUR commands are RR commands. The SW and SU are RX commands. The Subtract Unnormalized

```
     LOC  OBJECT CODE     ADDR1 ADDR2  ST #  NAME    OP   OPERANDS            COMMENT
                                              IMPERATIVES

  000220 6860 2FE0        01340  202          LD   6,ZPOS2           LOAD A REG.
  000224 05E0                    203          BALR 14,0              SAVE CONDITION CODE
  000226 2026                    204 F12#41   LPDR 2,6               LOAD POSITIVE, LONG FORM
  000228 05F0                    205          BALR 15,0              SAVE CONDITION CODE
  00022A 6020 4000        01360  206          STD  2,ZHOLD3          SAVE REG. CONTENTS
  00022E 90EF 400C        0136C  207          STM  14,15,ZHOLD3+12   STORE CONDITION CODES


                                              DECLARATIVES

  001340 0000000000000000       576 ZPOS2    DC   D'0.0'            F12#41
  001348 404040404040404        577          DC   24C' '            FILLER
  001350 404040404040404
  001358 404040404040404
  001360 404040404040404       578 ZHOLD3    DC   32C' '            USED TO DISPLAY STORAGE
  001368 404040404040404
  001370 404040404040404
  001378 404040404040404


                                          DUMP AFTER EXECUTION

  002C80 F0404040 40404040 40404040 40404040 40404040 40404040 40404040 40404040
  002CA0 00000000 00000000 40404040 40404040 40404040 40404040 40404040 40404040
  002CC0 00000000 00000000 40404040 50001886 4000188A 40404040 40404040 40404040
  002CE0 F0404040 40404040 40404040 40404040 40404040 40404040 40404040 40404040


                                          RELOCATION FACTOR   001960
```

FIG. 12-41. Example of Load Positive Register (Long).

```
     LOC  OBJECT CODE     ADDR1 ADDR2  ST #  NAME    OP   OPERANDS            COMMENT
                                              IMPERATIVES

  000232 7820 4060        013C0  209          LE   2,ZPOS            LOAD A REG.
  000236 05E0                    210          BALR 14,0              SAVE CONDITION CODE
  000238 3002                    211 F12#42   LPER 0,2               LOAD POSITIVE, SHORT FORM
  00023A 05F0                    212          BALR 15,0              SAVE CONDITION CODE
  00023C 7000 4080        013E0  213          STE  0,ZSTORE3         SAVE REG. CONTENTS
  000240 90EF 408C        013EC  214          STM  14,15,ZSTORE3+12  STORE CONDITION CODES


                                              DECLARATIVES

  0013C0 C0F17647               584 ZPOS     DC   E'-.943211'        F12#42
  0013C4 404040404040404        585          DC   28C' '             FILLER
  0013CC 404040404040404
  0013D4 404040404040404
  0013DC 40404040
  0013E0 404040404040404       586 ZSTORE3  DC   32C' '              USED TO DISPLAY STORAGE
  0013E8 404040404040404
  0013F0 404040404040404
  0013F8 404040404040404


                                          DUMP AFTER EXECUTION

  002000 F0404040 40404040 40404040 40404040 40404040 40404040 40404040 40404040
  002020 C0F17647 40404040 40404040 40404040 40404040 40404040 40404040 40404040
  002040 40F17647 40404040 40404040 4000189B 6000189C 40404040 40404040 40404040
  002060 F0404040 40404040 40404040 40404040 40404040 40404040 40404040 40404040


                                          RELOCATION FACTOR   001960
```

FIG. 12-42. Example of Load Positive Register (Short).

```
LOC   OBJECT CODE       ADDR1 ADDR2  ST #  NAME    OP    OPERANDS            COMMENT
                                           IMPERATIVES

000244 6840 40E0        01440         216          LD    4,ZNEG2            LOAD A REG.
000248 05D0                           217          BALR  13,0               SAVE CONDITION CODE
00024A 2164                           218 F12#43   LNDR  6,4                LOAD NEGATIVE, LONG FORM
00024C 05E0                           219          BALR  14,0               SAVE CONDITION CODE
00024E 6060 4100        01460         220          STD   6,ZKEEP3           SAVE REG. CONTENTS
000252 90DE 410C        0146C         221          STM   13,14,ZKEEP3+12    STORE CONDITION CODES

                                           DECLARATIVES

001440 4335D1999999999A               592 ZNEG2    DC    D'861.1'           F12#43
001448 4040404040404040               593          DC    24C' '             FILLER
001450 4040404040404040
001458 4040404040404040
001460 4040404040404040               594 ZKEEP3   DC    32C' '             USED TO DISPLAY STORAGE
001468 4040404040404040
001470 4040404040404040
001478 4040404040404040

                                           DUMP AFTER EXECUTION

002D80  F0404040   40404040   40404040   40404040   40404040   40404040   40404040   40404040
002DA0  43350199   9999999A   40404040   40404040   40404040   40404040   40404040   40404040
002DC0  C335D199   9999999A   40404040   600018AA   500018AE   40404040   40404040   40404040
002DE0  F0404040   40404040   40404040   40404040   40404040   40404040   40404040   40404040

                                     RELOCATION FACTOR   001960
```

Fig. 12-43. Example of Load Negative Register (Long).

```
LOC   OBJECT CODE       ADDR1 ADDR2  ST #  NAME    OP    OPERANDS            COMMENT
                                           IMPERATIVES

000256 7840 4160        014C0         223          LE    4,ZNEG             LOAD A REG.
00025A 05D0                           224          BALR  13,0               SAVE CONDITION CODE
00025C 3104                           225 F12#44   LNER  0,4                LOAD NEGATIVE, SHORT FORM
00025E 05E0                           226          BALR  14,0               SAVE CONDITION CODE
000260 7000 4180        014E0         227          STE   0,ZSAVE3           SAVE REG. CONTENTS
000264 90DE 418C        014EC         228          STM   13,14,ZSAVE3+12    STORE CONDITION CODES

                                           DECLARATIVES

0014C0 00000000                        600 ZNEG     DC    E'0.0'             F12#44
0014C4 4040404040404040                601          DC    28C' '             FILLER
0014CC 4040404040404040
0014D4 4040404040404040
0014DC 40404040
0014E0 4040404040404040                602 ZSAVE3   DC    32C' '             USED TO DISPLAY STORAGE
0014E8 4040404040404040
0014F0 4040404040404040
0014F8 4040404040404040

                                           DUMP AFTER EXECUTION

002E00  F0404040   40404040   40404040   40404040   40404040   40404040   40404040   40404040
002E20  00000000   40404040   40404040   40404040   40404040   40404040   40404040   40404040
002E40  80000000   40404040   40404040   500018BC   400018C0   40404040   40404040   40404040
002E60  F0404040   40404040   40404040   40404040   40404040   40404040   40404040   40404040

                                     RELOCATION FACTOR   001960
```

Fig. 12-44. Example of Load Negative Register (Short).

```
   LOC   OBJECT CODE    ADDR1 ADDR2  ST #  NAME    OP   OPERANDS          COMMMENT

                                           IMPERATIVES

 000268 6820 41E0        01540       230           LD   2,ZWAD            LOAD A REG.
 00026C 6860 41E8        01548       231           LD   6,ZWAD1           LOAD A REG.
 000270 05D0                         232           BALR 13,0              SAVE CONDITION CODE
 000272 2E62                         233  F12#45   AWR  6,2               ADD REG., UNNORMALIZED LONG FORM
 000274 05E0                         234           BALR 14,0              SAVE CONDITION CODE
 000276 6060 4200        01560       235           STD  6,ZKEEP5          SAVE REG. CONTENTS
 00027A 90DE 420C        0156C       236           STM  13,14,ZKEEP5+12   STORE CONDITION CODES


                                           DECLARATIVES

 001540 41922F837B4A233A             608  ZWAD     DC   D'9.1366'         F12#45
 001548 40DD4B599AA60914             609  ZWAD1    DC   D'.864431'        FILLER
 001550 4040404040404040             610           DC   16C' '
 001558 4040404040404040
 001560 4040404040404040             611  ZKEEP5   DC   32C' '           USED TO DISPLAY STORAGE
 001568 4040404040404040
 001570 4040404040404040
 001578 4040404040404040


                                      DUMP AFTER EXECUTION

 002E80  F0404040   40404040   40404040   40404040   40404040  40404040  40404040  40404040
 002EA0  41922F83   7B4A233A   4CDD4B59   9AA60914   4C4C4040  40404040  40404040  40404040
 002EC0  41A00439   14F483C8   40404040   400C1BD2   60CC1B06  40404040  40404040  40404040
 002EE0  F0404040   40404040   40404040   40404040   40404040  4C4C4040  40404040  40404040


                                RELOCATION FACTOR   001960
```

FIG. 12-45. Example of Add Register Unnormalized (Long).

```
   LOC   OBJECT CODE    ADDR1 ADDR2  ST #  NAME    OP   OPERANDS          COMMENT

                                           IMPERATIVES

 00027E 7800 4260        015C0       238           LE   0,ZUAD            LOAD A REG.
 000282 7820 4264        015C4       239           LE   2,ZUAD1           LOAD A REG.
 000286 05E0                         240           BALR 14,0              SAVE CONDITION CODE
 000288 3E20                         241  F12#46   AUR  2,0               ADD REG., UNNORMALIZED SHORT FORM
 00028A 05F0                         242           BALR 15,0              SAVE CONDITION CODE
 00028C 7020 4280        015E0       243           STE  2,ZSAVE5          SAVE REG. CONTENTS
 000290 90EF 428C        015EC       244           STM  14,15,ZSAVE5+12   STORE CONDITION CODES


                                           DECLARATIVES

 0015C0 C2299F83                     617  ZUAD     DC   E'-41.6231'       F12#46
 0015C4 4229628F                     618  ZUAD1    DC   E'41.385'         FILLER
 0015C8 4040404040404040             619           DC   24C' '
 0015D0 4040404040404040
 0015D8 4040404040404040
 0015E0 4040404040404040             620  ZSAVE5   DC   32C' '           USED TO DISPLAY STORAGE
 0015E8 4040404040404040
 0015F0 4040404040404040
 0015F8 4040404040404040


                                      DUMP AFTER EXECUTION

 002F00  F0404040   40404040   40404040   40404040   40404040  40404040  40404040  40404040
 002F20  C2299F83   4229628F   40404040   40404040   40404040  40404040  40404040  40404040
 002F40  C2003CF4   40404040   40404040   60001BE8   500018FC  40404040  40404040  40404040
 002F60  F0404040   40404040   40404040   40404040   4C4C4040  40404040  40404040  40404040


                                RELOCATION FACTOR   001960
```

FIG. 12-46. Example of Add Register Unnormalized (Short).

```
   LOC   OBJECT CODE      ADDR1 ADDR2  ST #  NAME   OP   OPERANDS          COMMENT

                                       IMPERATIVES

 000294  6820 42E0        01640       246          LD   2,ZWAD4           LOAD A REG.
 000298  05D0                         247          BALR 13,0              SAVE CONDITION CODE
 00029A  6E20 41E8        01548       248  F12#47  AW   2,ZWAD1           ADD, UNNORMALIZED LONG FORM
 00029E  05E0                         249          BALR 14,0              SAVE CONDITION CODE
 0002A0  6020 4300        01660       250          STD  2,ZHOLD6          SAVE REG. CONTENTS
 0002A4  90DE 430C        0166C       251          STM  13,14,ZHOLD6+12   STORE CONDITION CODES


                                       DECLARATIVES

 001640  C0DD4B599AA60914              626  ZWAD4   DC   D'-.864431'       F12#47
 001648  4040404040404040              627          DC   24C' '            FILLER
 001650  4040404040404040
 001658  4040404040404040
 001660  4040404040404040              628  ZHOLD6  DC   32C' '
 001668  4040404040404040
 001670  4040404040404040
 001678  4040404040404040


                                       DUMP AFTER EXECUTION

 002F80  F0404040   40404040   40404040   40404040   40404040   40404040   4040C040   40404040
 002FA0  C0DD4B59   9AA60914   40404040   40404040   40404040   40404040   40404040   40404040
 002FC0  00000000   00000000   40404040   50001BFA   40001C00   40404040   40404040   40404040
 002FE0  F0404040   40404040   40404040   40404040   40404040   40404040   40404040   40404040


                                       RELOCATION FACTOR   001960
```

Fɪɢ. 12-47. Example of Add Unnormalized (Long).

```
   LOC   OBJECT CODE      ADDR1 ADDR2  ST #  NAME   OP   OPERANDS          COMMENT

                                       IMPERATIVES

 000008  7800 303C        00044         8          LE   0,ZUAD4           LOAD A REG.
 00000C  05E0                           9          BALR 14,0              SAVE CONDITION CODE
 00000E  7E00 3038        00040        10  F12#48  AU   0,ZUAD1           ADD, UNNORMALIZED SHORT FORM
 000012  05F0                          11          BALR 15,0              SAVE CONDITION CODE
 000014  7000 3058        00060        12          STE  0,ZSTORE6         SAVE REG. CONTENTS
 000018  90EF 3064        0006C        13          STM  14,15,ZSTORE6+12  STORE CONDITION CODES


                                       DECLARATIVES

 000040  4229628F                      26  ZUAD1   DC   E'41.385'
 000044  425B0000                      27  ZUAD4   DC   E'91'             F12#48
 000048  4040404040404040              28          DC   24C' '            FILLER
 000050  4040404040404040
 000058  4040404040404040
 000060  4040404040404040              29  ZSTORE6 DC   32C' '
 000068  4040404040404040
 000070  4040404040404040
 000078  4040404040404040


                                       DUMP AFTER EXECUTION

 001980  F0404040   40404040   40404040   40404040   40404040   40404040   40404040   40404040
 0019A0  4229628F   425B0000   40404040   40404040   40404040   40404040   40404040   40404040
 0019C0  42A4623F   40404040   40404040   4000196E   60001974   40404040   40404040   40404040
 0019E0  F0404040   40404040   40404040   40404040   40404040   40404040   40404040   40404040


                                       RELOCATION FACTOR   001960
```

Fɪɢ. 12-48. Example of Add Unnormalized (Short).

commands operate in the same manner as the Add Unnormalized commands but invert the sign of the second operand before beginning the addition operation. The sign of a difference with a 0 fractional part is always made positive. The setting of the condition code and the interrupts possible follow the same pattern as for Add Unnormalized. Examples of Subtract Unnormalized are given in Figs. 12-49 to 12-52. These commands give the programer the option of controling the normalization himself—a convenience in assessing the buildup of computational error.

A review of the command repertoire of floating-point operations for the computer reveals what at first appears to be one signal omission: some way of converting conveniently from either decimal or binary to floating-point format, and back again. In practice, this is a job for the programer to meet by calling subroutines, or by preparing his own subroutines, using the regular command repertoire of the computer. Numbers received as input normally are in ordinary EBCDIC form, or more rarely in E notation. Most results must be produced in the same form as the input.

Do It Now Exercise 12-10. Prepare the flow diagram for converting an EBCDIC number in E notation into a number in floating-point D format (see, for example, Fig. 12-1). Assume that the fractional portion of the number in the E notation may have from zero through ten digits following the decimal point, and that the integer portion is always an EBCDIC zero. Convert the number to binary as if it were an integer, and then divide by the next larger power of 16 to change it to the fractional form. To avoid problems of converting the number in parts and then combining the parts, consider the use of the Hartmann method of conversion (see Chap. 5). Place the converted number in storage. Code the subroutine and provide an example of calling it. Prepare a storage map.

EXAMPLE OF FLOATING-POINT OPERATIONS

A common mathematical operation frequently encountered in engineering and scientific work is the multiplication of matrices. Consider the simple example shown in Fig. 12-53. The task is to multiply matrices **G** and **H** to obtain as a product matrix **F**. To make the example easy to follow, let us keep the numbers small.

A word about the notation used here is in order. Let us number the rows for the **G** matrix from top to bottom, starting with 1. For convenience, let us identify the rows by the letter i. Thus, the rows start from $i=1$ through $i=m$, where m represents the total number of rows. In the example at hand $m=3$, because there are 3 rows in the matrix. For the same matrix, let us identify the columns by the letter j from left to right in a parallel manner, beginning with $j=1$ and going up to $j=n$, where n represents the total number of columns. In this case, since there are only two columns, $n=2$.

For matrix multiplication of this type to be performed, the number of columns in the first matrix must be equal to the number of rows in the second matrix. For

```
 LOC   OBJECT CODE    ADDR1 ADDR2   ST #  NAME    OP    OPERANDS              COMMENT

                                            IMPERATIVES

0002BC 6840 43E0       01740        260            LD    4,ZWSD               LOAD A REG.
0002C0 6800 43E8       01748        261            LD    0,ZWSD1              LOAD A REG.
0002C4 05B0                         262            BALR  11,0                 SAVE C.C.
0002C6 2F40                         263  F12#49     SWR   4,0                  SUBTRACT REG., UNNORM. LONG FORM
0002C8 05C0                         264            BALR  12,0                 SAVE C.C.
0002CA 6040 4400       01760        265            STD   4,ZKEEP7             SHOW REG. CONTENTS
0002CE 90BC 4410       01770        266            STM   11,12,ZKEEP7+16      SHOW REG. CONTENTS


                                            DECLARATIVES

001740 441B1E1CED916873             642  ZWSD      DC    D'6942.113'          F12#49
001748 4420D61C6A7EF9DB             643  ZWSD1     DC    D'8406.111'
001750 4040404040404040             644            DC    16C' '.              FILLER
001758 4040404040404040
001760 4040404040404040             645  ZKEEP7    DC    32C' '               USED TO DISPLAY STORAGE
001768 4040404040404040
001770 4040404040404040
001778 4040404040404040


                                         DUMP AFTER EXECUTION

003080  F0404040   40404040   40404040   40404040   4C404040   40404040   40404040   40404040
0030A0  441B1E1C   ED916873   4420D61C   6A7EF9DB   40404040   40404040   40404040   40404040
0030C0  C405B7FF   7CED9168   40404040   40404040   60001C26   50001C2A   40404040   40404040
0030E0  F0404040   40404040   40404040   40404040   40404040   40404040   40404040   40404040


                                  RELOCATION FACTOR   001960
```

FIG. 12-49. Example of Subtract Register Unnormalized (Long).

```
 LOC   OBJECT CODE    ADDR1 ADDR2   ST #  NAME    OP    OPERANDS              COMMENT

                                            IMPERATIVES

0002D2 7840 4460       017C0        268            LE    4,ZUSD               LOAD A REG.
0002D6 7860 4464       017C4        269            LE    6,ZUSD1              LOAD A REG.
0002DA 05E0                         270            BALR  14,0                 SAVE C.C.
0002DC 3F46                         271  F12#50     SUR   4,6                  SUBTRACT REG., UNNORM. SHORT FORM
0002DE 05F0                         272            BALR  15,0                 SAVE C.C
0002E0 7040 4480       017E0        273            STE   4,ZSAVE7             SHOW RESULTS
0002E4 90EF 448C       017EC        274            STM   14,15,ZSAVE7+12      STORE C.C


                                            DECLARATIVES

0017C0 4321F4FE                     651  ZUSD      DC    E'543.312'           F12#50
0017C4 428F54FE                     652  ZUSD1     DC    E'143.332'
0017C8 4040404040404040             653            DC    24C' '               FILLER
0017D0 4040404040404040
0017D8 4040404040404040
0017E0 4040404040404040             654  ZSAVE7    DC    32C' '               USED TO DISPLAY STORAGE
0017E8 4040404040404040
0017F0 4040404040404040
0017F8 4040404040404040


                                         DUMP AFTER EXECUTION

003100  F0404040   40404040   40404040   40404040   40404040   40404040   40404040   40404040
003120  4321F4FE   428F54FE   40404040   40404040   40404040   40404040   40404040   40404040
003140  4318FFAE   40404040   40404040   50001C3C   60001C40   40404040   40404040   40404040
003160  F0404040   40404040   40404040   40404040   40404040   40404040   40404040   40404040


                                  RELOCATION FACTOR   001960
```

FIG. 12-50. Example of Subtract Register Unnormalized (Short).

```
  LOC   OBJECT CODE     ADDR1 ADDR2  ST #   NAME     OP    OPERANDS              COMMENT

                                                 IMPERATIVES

0002E8  6800 44E0          01840   276              LD    0,ZWSD4               LOAD A REG.
0002EC  05D0                       277              BALR  13,0                  SAVE C. C.
0002EE  6F00 43E0          01740   278  F12#51      SW    0,ZWSD                SUBTRACT UNNORMALIZED LONG FORM
0002F2  05E0                       279              BALR  14,0                  SAVE C.C.
0002F4  6000 4500          01860   280              STD   0,ZHOLD8              SHOW RESULTS
0002F8  90DE 450C          0186C   281              STM   13,14,ZHOLD8+12


                                                 DECLARATIVES

001840  44181E1CED916873           660  ZWSD4       DC    D'6942113E-3'         F12#51
001848  4040404040404040           661              DC    24C' '                FILLER
001850  4040404040404040
001858  4040404040404040
001860  4040404040404040           662  ZHOLD8      DC    32C' '
001868  4040404040404040
001870  4040404040404040
001878  4040404040404040


                                              DUMP AFTER EXECUTION

003180  F0404040  40404040  40404040  40404040   40404040  40404040  40404040  40404040
0031A0  44181E1C  ED916873  40404040  40404040   40404040  40404040  40404040  40404040
0031C0  00000000  00000000  40404040  60001C4F   40001C54  40404040  40404040  40404040
0031E0  F0404040  40404040  40404040  40404040   40404040  40404040  40404040  40404040


                                       RELOCATION FACTOR   001960
```

FIG. 12-51. Example of Subtract Unnormalized (Long).

```
  LOC   OBJECT CODE     ADDR1 ADDR2  ST #   NAME     OP    OPERANDS              COMMENT

                                                 IMPERATIVES

0002FC  7860 4560          018C0   283              LE    6,ZUSD4               LOAD A REG.
000300  05C0                       284              BALR  12,0                  SAVE C.C.
000302  7F60 4460          017C0   285  F12#52      SU    6,ZUSD                SUBTRACT  UNNORMALIZED SHORT FORM
000306  05D0                       286              BALR  13,0                  SAVE C.C.
000308  7060 4580          018E0   287              STE   6,ZSTORE8             SHOW RESULTS
00030C  90CD 458C          018EC   288              STM   12,13,ZSTORE8+12      STORE C.C.


                                                 DECLARATIVES

0018C0  433DD19A                   668  ZUSD4       DC    E'989.1'              F12#52
0018C4  4040404040404040           669              DC    28C' '                FILLER
0018CC  4040404040404040
0018D4  4040404040404040
0018DC  40404040
0018E0  4040404040404040           670  ZSTORE8     DC    32C' '
0018E8  4040404040404040
0018F0  4040404040404040
0018F8  4040404040404040


                                              DUMP AFTER EXECUTION

003200  F0404040  40404040  40404040  40404040   40404040  40404040  40404040  40404040
003220  433DD19A  40404040  40404040  40404040   40404040  40404040  40404040  40404040
003240  4318DC9C  40404040  40404040  40001C62   60001C68  40404040  40404040  40404040
003260  F0404040  40404040  40404040  40404040   40404040  40404040  40404040  40404040


                                       RELOCATION FACTOR   001960
```

FIG. 12-52. Example of Subtract Unnormalized (Short).

this reason let us, in matrix **H**, again use the subscript j, put here to identify the rows from j=1 through j=n. To identify the columns in matrix **H**, let us use the letter k and identify the columns from k=1 through k=p, where p=2.

$$
\begin{array}{c} \mathbf{F} \\ i \downarrow \begin{pmatrix} 29 & 58 \\ 10 & 20 \\ 8 & 16 \end{pmatrix} \\ m \\ k \longrightarrow p \end{array}
\quad = \quad
\begin{array}{c} \mathbf{G} \\ i \downarrow \begin{pmatrix} 4 & 7 \\ 5 & 0 \\ 1 & 2 \end{pmatrix} \\ m \\ j \longrightarrow n \end{array}
\quad \mathbf{x} \quad
\begin{array}{c} \mathbf{H} \\ j \downarrow \begin{pmatrix} 2 & 4 \\ 3 & 6 \end{pmatrix} \\ n \\ k \longrightarrow p \end{array}
$$

FIG. 12-53. Matrix notation example.

With this notation in hand, it is possible to identify any position in a matrix by the use of subscripts. For example, in matrix **G** the top leftmost element of the matrix, which is a 4, has the location i=1 and j=1. Then if the letter **G** designates the matrix, G_{ij} designates any particular element, and G_{11} designates the top leftmost element. The element at the position i=2, j=2 is the element 0 and is the element G_{22}. The element i=3, j=1 is the element 1 or G_{31}.

In the second matrix **H**, any position can be indicated in the same general way. Thus at position j=2, k=2 is the element 6 or H_{22}.

Identifying things by means of subscripts is convenient for computer use because these subscripts can be incorporated as the effective contents of index registers. Then by changing the contents of the index registers in a systematic manner (e.g., by counting) the programer can have the computer go from one element to another in the matrix in a definite pattern. This suggests, therefore, that the procedure to be followed in handling matrices will probably involve looking at individual elements in each matrix identified by index register contents, and combining these elements in some form to produce a new matrix, matrix **F**, element by element. This will require loading and increasing or decreasing the contents of registers to represent the various subscripts i, j, and k, so that no item in any matrix will be overlooked or omitted.

$$
\begin{aligned}
(4,7) \cdot (2,3) &= 4 \cdot 2 + 7 \cdot 3 = 8 + 21 = 29 \\
(5,0) \cdot (2,3) &= 5 \cdot 2 + 0 \cdot 3 = 10 + 0 = 10 \\
(1,2) \cdot (2,3) &= 1 \cdot 2 + 2 \cdot 3 = 2 + 6 = 8 \\
(4,7) \cdot (4,6) &= 4 \cdot 4 + 7 \cdot 6 = 16 + 42 = 58 \\
(5,0) \cdot (4,6) &= 5 \cdot 4 + 0 \cdot 6 = 20 + 0 = 20 \\
(1,2) \cdot (4,6) &= 1 \cdot 4 + 2 \cdot 6 = 4 + 12 \quad 16
\end{aligned}
$$

FIG. 12-54. Summary of matrix multiplication.

Just for review, Fig. 12-54 summarizes the process of matrix multiplication. In the process of developing the inner products, it does not make any difference whether the rows in one matrix be used first or the columns, as long as the opposite is used in the other matrix. The result matrix, it should be noted, will have m rows and p columns. In studying Fig. 12-54, special attention should be given to distinguishing between decimal points, commas, and multiplication indicators (the dot product).

For a general approach to this example, the programer can begin as indicated in Fig. 12-55 by taking as input the two matrices to be operated upon. He could also use as input explicitly the sizes (dimensions) of the matrices, m, n, and p. These the programer needs later for setting up the exit tests for iterative loops. But the heart of the operation will be the actual matrix multiplication. This will be given particular attention later in this section.

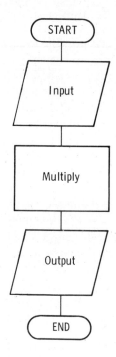

FIG. 12-55. Summary flow diagram for matrix example.

The final part of the program will consist of producing as output the result matrix **F**. In order for the computer to perform this output operation, the program will need some indication of the size of the matrix to be produced. The programer can calculate this from the m, n, and p values of the input matrices, because m and p are the total number of rows and columns in the matrix to be produced.

Before proceeding to a more detailed flow diagram, some attention might well be given to the way in which the matrix data can be arranged in storage. A matrix is normally thought of as being some sort of rectangular array of data. Inside the computer in internal storage, however, a matrix is typically arranged like a long chain or string of beads. As such, the elements in one row or column follow the elements of another row or column of the matrix, as if they ran continuously and consecutively. From the point of view of accomplishing a matrix multiplication, it makes little difference whether the programer used rows or columns first, but the programer must be consistent in whichever he chooses. Arbitrarily and for didactic purposes only here, the programer can assume that the data are to be read into storage with the elements in each row following one after the other in storage in full-length words in floating-point format until the entire row is exhausted for the matrix **G**, and the entire column for the matrix **H**.

A study of Fig. 12-54 can yield some suggestions about an approach a programer might use in developing the algorithm. A review of the data in that figure indicates that the elements have been taken row after row. Each row of the first matrix is first multiplied by *each* column of the second matrix. Thus the first row (4, 7) in matrix **G** is multiplied on an inner product basis by the elements from the first column (2, 3) in matrix **H**. When the entire first column of matrix **H** has been used, Fig. 12-54 indicates that the rows of matrix **G** are then again handled, using this time the second column of matrix **H** (4, 6).

Step or cycle number	Subscript or index values k	i	j
1	1	1	1
2	1	1	2
3	1	2	1
4	1	2	2
5	1	3	1
6	1	3	2
7	2	1	1
8	2	1	2
9	2	2	1
10	2	2	2
11	2	3	1
12	2	3	2

Fig. 12-56. Pattern of subscript (index) change.

In terms of the matrix notation developed earlier, this is equivalent to taking the i rows one at a time until all m rows have been exhausted; then changing to a new k column and repeating the i rows one at a time until they have again been exhausted. The inner product multiplication requires that *within* this row by column operation, the individual elements within the matrices **G** and **H** be taken one at a time. Thus j must be varied on each line in Fig. 12-54 from j=1 through j=n (that is, until j=2) for each pair of values of i and k. After j=n, the programer must re-

k	1						2					
i	1		2		3		1		2		3	
j	1	2	1	2	1	2	1	2	1	2	1	2

FIG. 12-57. Index movement from k (slowest) to j (fastest).

set j back to j=1 and advance i by 1 as shown in Fig. 12-56. After i goes from i=1 to i=2, we see that j goes from j=1 to j=2. When j is reset to j=1, the programer advances i to i=3. Then j again goes from j=1 to j=2. This exhausts not only j but i. At this point, therefore, k is advanced from k=1 to k=2, and the process then repeats, starting again with i=1 and j=1.

On this basis, index j is referred to as the fastest-moving index and index k as the slowest-moving index (see Fig. 12-57). This terminology is only a matter of convention, but it is a convenience to the programer in thinking about the sequence in which he must do indexing in the program.

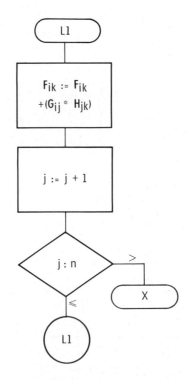

FIG. 12-58. Iterative loop for j index.

The heart of the matrix multiply is the inner product operation. This consists of taking an element from the **G** matrix, identified by the appropriate ij, times the element from the **H** matrix identified by the appropriate jk. This will yield part of an element in the **F** matrix at the position ik. To produce the inner product requires this operation to be done as many times as there are j elements. This requires that this operation be done in a loop or iterative fashion n times. Therefore the programer, as shown in Fig. 12-58, constructs a loop of coding, beginning at L1, down to the comparison of j=n with the exit to L1 for less than or equal to.

Following the analysis made previously, when the computer has executed the loop n times—that is, the comparison of j to n indicates that j is now greater than n—the index i can be advanced and i compared to m (see Fig. 12-59). As long as i is less than or equal to m, control can return to L2, which resets j to its initial value and establishes in matrix **F** the position ik as having a 0 value. Then by entering the loop L1 again, the computer can calculate the new value for this **F** element by the inner loop.

When the value of j again exceeds n, we see that i can again be advanced and again tested against m. When i has been incremented sufficiently (i=m) for the con-

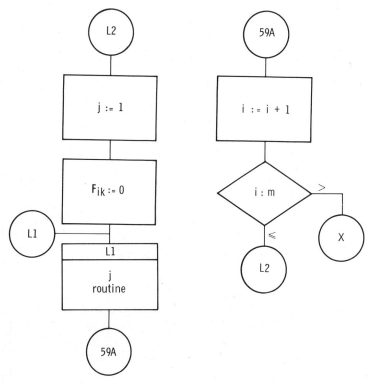

FIG. 12-59. Iterative loop for i index.

trol to drop through the next instruction in sequence, k can be advanced and tested against p. As long as k is less than or equal to p, the computer can execute loop L3 again. This calls for resetting i back to its initial value and then entering loop L2, which resets j back to its initial value and sets to 0 the next element in the **F** matrix, ready to receive its computed value. Thus the whole cycle of operations can then again proceed until such time as k exceeds p. At that time, the matrix multiplication is complete. To initialize this matrix multiplication requires only that k be set to its initial value, as shown in Fig. 12-60.

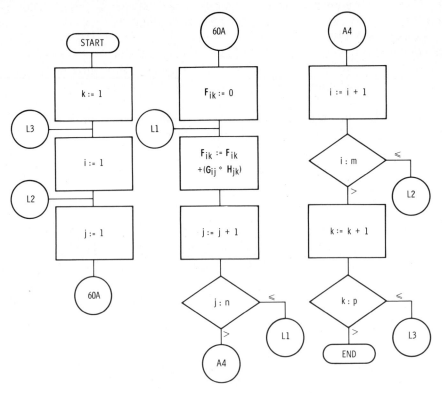

FIG. 12-60. Three indexed loops for matrix example.

The analysis thus far has been in terms of general logic, and has not taken into account the particular features of the computer command repertoire. By taking these into account and using the leading-decision approach, the diagram shown in Fig. 12-61 can be developed. For the three decision outlines, Branch on Index Low or Equal, or Branch on Index High commands can be conveniently used. This permits the programer to set the test amount used in these tests to be equal to the amount by which he must index to have the computer pick up the correct values from or for the **G**, **H**, and **F**, matrices. This is a convenience to the programer.

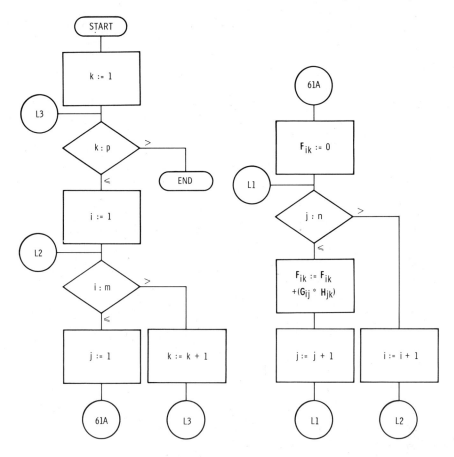

FIG. 12-61. Flow diagram for matrix example.

The coding for the loops L1, L2, and L3, corresponding with Fig. 12-61 is shown in Fig. 12-62. This is the heart of the matrix multiply operation, but excluded from the figure are the input-output operations. The programer should note, however, that the program has been designed because of the DC declaratives to operate with values of m=3, n=2, and p=2 only. This can be generalized by obtaining the values of m, n, and p from the input instead of from DC declaratives. Then the program could be made self-initializing to adapt to a matrix of almost any size within the allowable limits of storage available.

Do It Now Exercise 12-11. *Elaborate the matrix multiply example just shown to accept any values of m, n, and p, as long as the number of input elements is less than 4,096. Complete also the input and output portions of the program, drawing as needed upon the work done in Do It Now Exercise 12-10.*

```
    LOC  OBJECT CODE      ADDR1 ADDR2  ST #  NAME    OP   OPERANDS        COMMENT

                                            IMPERATIVES
                                       1            PRINT ON,NOGEN,NODATA
                                       2 *
                                       3 *          PROCEDURE SECTION
                                       4 *
                                       5 *              FIGURE 12#62  -  MATRIX MULTIPLY
                                       6 *
000000                                 7            START
                                       8            ENTRY BEGIN
000000 070007000700                    9            CNOP  6,8
000008                                10 F12#62     CSECT
000008 05A0                           11 BEGIN      BALR  10,0
00000A                                12            USING *,10
00000A 4120 A092          0009C       13            LA    2,F            ADDR OF OUT. MATRIX *F*  (BY COLS)
00000E 4130 A06A          00074       14            LA    3,G            ADDR OF PRI. MATRIX *G*  (BY ROWS)
000012 4140 A082          0008C       15            LA    4,H            ADDR OF SEC. MATRIX *H*  (BY COLS)
000016 4180 0001          00001       16            LA    8,1            REG  8 = 1   CONSTANT
00001A 41F0 0004          00004       17            LA    15,4           REG 15 = 4   CONSTANT
00001E 1BCC                           18            SR    12,12          REG 12 = 0   INDEX FOR *F*
000020 1BEE                           19            SR    14,14          REG 14 = 0   INDEX FOR *H*
000022 1BCF                           20            SR    12,15          REG 12 =-4
000024 1B55                           21            SR    5,5            K = 0
000026 5890 A05E          00068       22 L3         L     9,P            LOAD K LIMIT
00002A 8658 A05C          00066       23            BXH   5,8,END        ADD ONE TO K AND CHECK LIMIT
00002E 1A4E                           24            AR    4,14           ADVANCE TO NEXT COLUMN OF *H*
000030 1BDD                           25            SR    13,13          REG 13 = 0   INDEX FOR *G*
000032 1866                           26            SR    6,6            I = 0
000034 5890 A062          0006C       27 L2         L     9,M            LOAD I LIMIT
000038 8668 A01C          00026       28            BXH   6,8,L3         ADD ONE TO I AND CHECK LIMIT
00003C 1BEE                           29            SR    14,14          REG 14 = 0   INDEX FOR *H*
00003E 1ACF                           30            AR    12,15          ADVANCE ONE POSITION IN *F* MATRIX
000040 50EC 2000          00000       31            ST    14,0(12,2)     MOVE ZERO TO F(IK)
000044 1B77                           32            SR    7,7            J = 0
000046 5890 A066          00070       33 L1         L     9,N            LOAD J LIMIT
00004A 8678 A02A          00034       34            BXH   7,8,L2         ADD ONE TO J AND CHECK LIMIT
00004E 780D 3000          00000       35            LE    0,0(13,3)      LOAD G(IJ)
000052 7C0E 4000          00000       36            ME    0,0(14,4)      MULTIPLY G(IJ) BY H(JK)
000056 7A0C 2000          00000       37            AE    0,0(12,2)      ADD INTERMEDIATE F(IK) TO PRODUCT
00005A 700C 2000          00000       38            STE   0,0(12,2)      STORE FINAL F(IK) IN OUT. MATRIX *F*
00005E 1ADF                           39            AR    13,15          INCREMENT G(IJ)
000060 1AEF                           40            AR    14,15          INCREMENT H(JK)
000062 47F0 A03C          00046       41            B     L1             RETURN TO PROCESS LOOP
                                      42 END        EOJ
                                      45 *


                                      46 *  DECLARATIVES
                                      47 *
000068 00000002                       48 P          DC    F'2'           LIMIT OF K
00006C 00000003                       49 M          DC    F'3'           LIMIT OF I
000070 00000002                       50 N          DC    F'2'           LIMIT OF J
                                      51 *
000074 41400000                       52 G          DC    E'4.'          *G* MATRIX - PRIMARY
000078 41700000                       53            DC    E'7.'
00007C 41500000                       54            DC    E'5.'
000080 00000000                       55            DC    E'0.'
000084 41100000                       56            DC    E'1.'
000088 41200000                       57            DC    E'2.'
00008C 41200000                       58 H          DC    E'2.'          *H* MATRIX - SECONDARY
000090 41300000                       59            DC    E'3.'
000094 41400000                       60            DC    E'4.'
000098 41600000                       61            DC    E'6.'
00009C                                62 F          DS    6E'0.'         *F* RESULT MATRIX - OUTPUT
000008                                63            END   BEGIN
```

FIG. 12-62. Coding for matrix example.

EXTENDED PRECISION

For some purposes, even the computational precision possible with the long floating-point D format is insufficient. As an optional feature, extended-precision commands are available on some models of the computer.

The extended-precision X format uses the fraction part of two contiguous D format numbers, but ignores the first byte in the righthand double word. Thus, the leftmost double word of an extended-precision number has the usual characteristic and fraction used with the long floating-point format. But the next-higher-addressed double word is treated, except for the first byte, as a continuation of the fraction. When extended-precision numbers are operated on in the floating-point registers, the registers are used in pairs, with numbers 0 and 2 forming one pair to hold one extended-precision operand or result, and registers 4 and 6 forming a second pair to hold one operand or result. Hence, the register operands must be 0 and 4 to avoid specification interrupts.

With one exception, all of the extended-precision commands are of the RR type. Hence they require both operands to be in the floating-point registers. The one exception is an RX multiply. To place operands in the registers requires using two successive load instructions and to copy out results requires two successive store instructions.

The arithmetic commands available are Add Register Normalized Extended (AXR), Subtract Register Normalized Extended (SXR), Multiply Extended Register (MXR), Multiply Long to Extended (MXD), and Multiply Long to Extended Register (MXDR). The first three parallel the corresponding long register commands. The MXD parallels the indexed ME command. The MXDR parallels the MER command.

To round off extended-precision results to the long or short format, two RR commands are available. The Load Register Short Rounded (LRER) rounds the extended fraction down to the E format. The Load Register Long Rounded (LRDR) rounds the extended fraction down to the D format. These register-to-register rounding commands have no parallels for the E or D formats.

EXERCISES

1. What is meant by characteristic, fraction, and exponent?
2. What is E notation? How is it distinguished from type E and type D DC declaratives? How is it distinguished from type E and D imperatives?
3. What is meant by excess 64 notation?
4. Show with an example the changes that take place in a floating-point number under the following circumstances: A change in the value of the number from positive to negative with the absolute value remaining the same; a shift of a number four binary positions to the right; a change of a number from D format to E format.

CHAPTER 13

Subroutines and Macros

SUBROUTINES

Use of Subroutines

Writing subroutines is a common work assignment for programers who use assembly language. The request usually comes from programers in high-level languages, such as COBOL, FORTRAN, or PL/1, who find such languages do not permit or enable them to direct the computer easily for some particular task. The task may be something not provided for at all in the language, such as a floating-point normalization in COBOL, or something done only awkwardly or inefficiently, such as a character-by-character code translation in FORTRAN. The task may involve meeting the requirements of special input or output equipment, as in input validation or output formatting.

The subroutines written in assembly language usually offer a saving in storage space required, and usually take less time to execute, than coding to do the same work in a high-level language. This partly reflects the closer-to-the-computer character of assembly language and partly reflects the "custom tailoring" possible in assembly-language routines.

The subroutines that programers write in assembly language for inclusion in high-level-language written programs generally take a "closed" form. That is, the high-level language will include some coding that "calls" the assembly-language subroutine. It does this basically by a transfer of control to the entry point in the subroutine, with the assumption that after the computer has completed executing the subroutine, control will be transferred back to the main program.

A closed subroutine must therefore be largely complete in and of itself. A closed subroutine does not become an integral part of the program that calls it. Hence, it must include the definition of its own unique work areas and constants. It must provide its own register settings, and it must not disturb register contents and storage areas used by the main program. The exception to this is for the elements of data the subroutine is to produce—its output—that are the evidence of what executing the subroutine accomplished.

Linkage

To minimize the likelihood of bugs from calling a subroutine, each high-level language has a set of conventions the programer can observe about linkage. Linkage is the mechanism by which the call is accomplished. It typically involves conventions on (1) identifying the input to be used by the subroutine; (2) placing this input in the needed form and format at some specific place in storage; (3) saving the contents of all registers, the condition code, and any status indicators (such as the contents of a CSW, for instance) that must be protected from alteration during the execution of the subroutine; (4) transferring control to the subroutine; (5) transferring control back to the main routine upon completion or error; (6) identifying the output or error indication produced by the execution of the subroutine; (7) placing that output at some specific place in storage; and (8) restoring all saved contents and indicators.

Special names are sometimes used for these steps. Thus step 4 is sometimes termed the "entry," and step 5 the "exit." Steps 1 and 2 and 6 and 7 are sometimes termed "the passing of parameters." Steps 3 and 8 are sometimes termed "save" and "restore" or more rarely "preserve" or "push down" and "pop-up."

Unfortunately, the linkage conventions are different for the different high-level languages. Further, they are different for the various operating systems or supervisors that may be used at any given installation. The best practice, therefore, is to ascertain what the local requirements are on each of the eight steps and then program to meet them.

A few general conventions are commonly encountered and merit a brief discussion here. When a calling program transfers control to a subroutine, the entry point for control in the subroutine is normally the contents of register 15. The programer therefore can specify register 15 as his base register in the subroutine by making his first declarative after the CSECT be USING *,15, with no BAL or BALR. However, a better practice is to assign a new register, loading it from register 15 with a BALR and an appropriate USING after saving the register contents.

Because the subroutine must leave the registers as it found them, the first imperative in the subroutine is normally a Store Multiple for the registers, but starting with register 14. Because of the call conventions, register 13 can serve as a base register for that. Therefore, STM 14,12,12(13) does the job in the last part of 18 words of working storage declared in the calling main program. This instruction can well be the first line of the subroutine after the CSECT, saving the register contents so that a BALR and USING can then be done. The programer should then store the contents of register 13 for future use as a safety measure and to free that register for other uses.

Typically register 0 contains a word of data needed as input for the subroutine. Register 1 may contain the address of a string of such input. These two registers are used for the passing of parameters. Determining what their contents may be can only be done by consulting with the programer who writes the calling (main) program—the registers might contain no data of use to the subroutine! The programer writing the subroutine typically uses these same registers to return or identify the output of the subroutine if needed to the calling program.

Upon completion of the work of the subroutine, the programer must restore the contents of registers 2 through 12 and 14. For this, the programer needs to use the original (saved) contents of register 13 with a Load and a Load Multiple instruction. Then he can set register 15 to a zero contents if the subroutine detected no errors in its execution, or can have a nonzero error code loaded into the register as a warning to the calling main program about detected errors. Then he can specify a Branch Register unconditionally using register 14 which should contain the return entry point in the main calling program.

Many complications are possible. One of the most common is that the programer's subroutine uses a system macro or in turn calls another program. For IOCS macros, no special preparation is needed, but some is wise if the original calling main program was not itself written in assembly language. The usual preparations before the subroutine itself issues a call involve typically several steps.

The programer may have to provide a parameter string address in register 1. Such a string often consists of aligned words established by address constants, followed by a marker, such as a word of 80_x, to flag the end of the string. Then the programer must complete the original 18-word-register save area and provide a new one for the use of the routine his subroutine calls. To do this, the programer must have the computer store as the second word in the new register save area the original contents of register 13. Also, the programer must have the computer store the address of the new save area in the third word of the original save area, and as the new contents of register 13. Finally, the programer can have the computer load into register 14 the address in his subroutine to which he wishes control to return, and to load a V-type constant into register 15 for the address of the routine he is calling. Both of these latter operations are usually done automatically for the programer when he is calling system macros.

The usual conventions for closed subroutines do not apply to open subroutines that the programer may be called upon to write. These are always part of another assembly-language program, and the programer usually has full access to all of the declaratives defined in that program. Thus no formal set of linkage conventions are needed, since the context determines what must be done. A special case of open subroutines is macros.

CONVENIENCE OF MACROS

Value of Macros

Some macros instructions have been described in part in earlier chapters. For example, those chapters described the input-output macros available in IOCS, and some system macros, as, for example, those for generating supervisors. But the previous chapters have not described how the programer may write his own macros. Programer-written macros are the subject of the rest of this chapter.

Power, speed, accuracy, specialization, and standardization are the major advantages that programers achieve by writing and using their own macros. The programer adds power to his programing because he needs to write fewer instructions using macros to have the computer accomplish the same work. A single instruction, instead of causing the computer to execute one machine-language operation such as an addition, instead causes the computer to execute from a few to thousands of machine-language instructions in a useful sequence.

The programer gains speed in programing when he uses macros. On the one hand, he can design algorithms in terms of more powerful functions, functions that would need an entire routine to implement. Instead of thinking in terms only of stores, adds, moves, etc., he is able to think in terms of larger building blocks. On the other hand, he needs to write fewer instructions to direct the computer to accomplish the same amount work.

The programer gains accuracy by using macros. Once the programer has written and debugged the macros originally, then every time he uses them, part of the debugging work is already done. Therefore, one source of error vanishes. Appearing to replace it partially is inaccuracy in the use of the macros themselves. Experience has been that this source of inaccuracy is less serious than the inaccuracies commonly encountered in writing equivalent amounts of instructions without macros.

The programer gains specialization. The assembly language is a general-purpose programing language which can be used for any kind of programing work. If there are certain kinds of tasks to which the programer bends his efforts frequently, he can make the assembly language specialized to fit the tasks by designing and using macros. Such extensions of assembly language in no way detract from the general-purpose character of the language but rather add a superstructure enabling a programer to accomplish specialized work efficiently, rapidly, and accurately.

The programer also gains in standardization with the use of macros. The macros can be regarded as building blocks which the programer uses when implementing algorithms. When commonly encountered situations can be handled in a standardized way by using macros, then the amount of diversity different programers may use in approaching the situations is reduced. When this diversity diminishes, the amount of debugging declines, and the work of various programers are more easily made to fit together.

These benefits from the use of macros come at some expense in the initial preparation of macros and in training personnel in their use. Many installations facing relatively routine kinds of work have found these costs to be small in relation to the benefits gained from macros.

Nature of Macros

The term "macro" may designate either a macrocommand or a macroinstruction, depending upon the context. A macroinstruction has a macrocommand as its operation or command part. A macrocommand is a command not found in the normal command repertoire for the language but one which can be implemented or expressed in terms of a sequence of instructions utilizing commands from the regular command repertoire.

The term "macro" suggests a one-to-many relationship. One macroinstruction requires and is translated into many ordinary instructions taken in some explicit sequence. In the case of assembly language, the use of macros provides a way for the programer to get away from machine-language orientation inherent in the command repertoire. It provides a way for the programer to add to the assembly language new commands specifically for his own convenience.

Viewed in another light, using a macro results in producing an open subroutine. A macro is a call which identifies which subroutine is to be executed and how that routine is to direct the computer to perform the work. In the compiling process, the compiler first generates from the single macroinstruction a sequence of ordinary assembly-language instructions. Then it translates those to the object language just like all the other imperatives in the program. The generated instructions physically occupy a place in the program-control sequence where they can be executed without transfers of control to go to the subroutine and to leave the subroutine. No control linkage is needed, no calling sequence appears in the generated instructions, and no passing of data (parameters) occurs.

Underlying this open subroutine form that results from the compiling of the macro call are three significant generalizations. One is a generalization as to operands, the second is as to commands, and the third is as to sequence. First, a macro permits the programer to have the compiler augment and modify some special coding to make the generated coding operationally effective as normal assembly-language coding with an automatic substitution of operands, controlled by the programer. Second, it permits in the same way an alteration in the coding of the commands and operands by automatically adapting the commands and operands generated to fit different data types. An example is a generation of common binary instructions, or alternatively of floating-point instructions from one macro. Third, it permits in the same way alteration and modification of the sequence of instructions generated to fit the computer hardware's requirements for handling different sizes, coding, or addressing of data.

Use of Macros

Programers experienced in working with the assembly language sometimes observe sequences of instructions that recur frequently. They recognize these patterns of instructions in spite of some superficial variation. First, some of this repetition arises from the nature of the computer configuration. This computer hardware must be controlled and its operation monitored. Second, the availability of certain kinds of hardware enables certain kinds of data handling to be done. An off-line data plotter, for example, requires preparing output data in special formats. Third, the kind of applications and kinds of jobs to which the computer is typically applied at any given installation may cause some sequences of operation to be done frequently. For example, if the handling of sorted files of data is common, then sequence checking may be a commonly encountered job.

To write, debug, and maintain macros requires effort on the part of programers. This effort can be regarded as an investment which will yield a benefit if the macros can be used many times. A cost-benefit trade-off therefore must in practice be evaluated in each case. How much investment is justified by how much use of the macro? To answer this question, the programer must consider a number of things. On the benefit side are the five values cited previously. And most of the costs are easily seen.

More difficult to evaluate are the effects of macros on programers' productivity and job satisfaction. How much do more convenient building blocks for algorithms help the programer? How much work is involved in getting a macro to fit? If many situations must be custom tailored, then the implementation gain may be largely offset. Does using macros require doing other work in the program badly or inefficiently? How valuable is the extension of assembly language? Might not COBOL, PL/1, SNOBOL, or some other language be a better choice?

Once the programer has a feel for the cost-benefit balance and has elected to consider seriously the use of macros, the programer must take action on three matters. First, he must decide on and define explicitly the functions the macro is to perform. The programer must unambiguously describe what situations the macro is to cover and what the macro is to do.

Second, the programer must design a macro call format. What will be the command? How are the operands to be specified? This is typically not a difficult matter, but it affects considerably the convenience of macro use since the programer will use it many times.

Third, the programer must provide a macrodefinition. He must do this only once, but it must be in a specific prescribed format in order to direct the compiler how to generate the assembly-language instructions for the macros he writes. The programer may not use a macro unless he has available a supporting macrodefinition. Failure to have available a macrodefinition results in compilation errors.

MACRO CALLS

The programer uses macros by writing macro calls as declarative statements on the coding form. When he does so, the programer must give attention to three things: the name, the macrocommand, and the operands. A look at each is in order.

The programer need not assign a name to the macro at all. The name, if he uses one, will appear in the generated coding in the name column for the first generated instruction. The name must follow the usual rules for symbolic names. A name is needed if the first instruction of the generated coding is also to serve as a control entry point. Otherwise, the common practice is to leave the name blank.

For the macrocommand, the programer must observe more stringent rules. Since the programer writes the macrocommand in the operation (command) column on the coding form, the compiler must be able to distinguish the macrocommand from all the other commands it is likely to encounter. This means that the programer must choose to identify his macrocommand with a combination of letters different from any existing assembly-language command, and different from any system (including input-output) macrocommand available at the installation. Further it should be different from any other programer-written macro utilized at his installation. This is to avoid difficulty if a library of macrocommands is maintained or might in the future be established. The programer is wise to select a combination of letters that have mnemonic value for the function the macro is to cause the computer to execute.

For the operands, the programer needs to consider the role of the macro as a call to generate an open subroutine: What items of data must be identified to the subroutine as variables? Typically, this involves defining the input and the output for the subroutine. In practice, the actual operand names the programer writes are the names of items of data as normally defined in the program by the programer. Or they may be names of items of hardware, such as register numbers, or they may be self-defining operands, such as decimal numbers or literals. The problem the programer faces is how many, and what is the role of each? For the answer, the programer must turn to the macrodefinition described in the next section. Figure 13-1 gives an example of a macro call.

NAME	OP	OPERANDS	COMMENT
	IMPERATIVES		
	KEEP	2	MACRO CALL

FIG. 13-1. Example of a macro call.

For the format of the operands in his macro, the programer has two main options available, keyword and positional. The nature of keyword operands has been described in Chap. 7 on input and output. That chapter also illustrated the positional format for operands, which is the common format used for the operands in assembly language. Most programers in writing macros find it more convenient to use the positional-operand format since it involves less writing on the coding form and serves to remind the programer of the necessity of specifying each of the operands. Any omitted operands in the positional format except for the last operand in a series must have its position marked at least by a comma. Keyword operands may be omitted without commas and be used in any order.

In selecting operands for the macros, the programer needs to consider the effect upon the contents of storage and upon debugging. He can facilitate debugging by choosing operands whose storage values can be easily identified. In this way he can make his interpretation of dumps easier and more rapid. The programer is wise to provide an audit trial in terms of saved intermediate values of variables in storage. To be able to do this, the programer normally must weigh the amount of storage required as well as the placement of that storage.

MACRODEFINITION

Component Parts

Major Parts. The programer needs to provide a macrodefinition only once for each program in which he wishes to use the macro. The programer who wishes to use the macro again in another program may do so simply by copying the macro-definition into the new program. At some installations, he can do this by means of a catalog and copy operation through the assistance of the operating system. At other installations, he may have to incorporate physically the cards for the macrodefinition by copying them himself from another program. To get the most out of using macros, the programer should prepare macrodefinitions with an eye to using them in programs other than the one for which he first writes the definitions.

The programer usually places the macrodefinition in his program just prior to the beginning of the first control section. This is because the compiler does not translate the macrodefinition immediately into imperative object coding, and hence no base-register assignments are needed.

The macrodefinition is a set of declaratives with five major parts: the header, the prototype, the settings, the models, and the trailer. A look at each of these will clarify their roles in the generation process. The macrodefinition is composed of declaratives since it provides directions to the compiler.

A header is required which takes the form of the declarative MACRO written in the operation column of the coding form. It has no name and no operands. It serves to notify the compiler that a macrodefinition is being started (see Fig. 13-2).

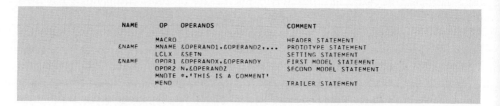

```
        NAME    OP    OPERANDS                    COMMENT

                MACRO                              HEADER STATEMENT
        &NAME   MNAME  &OPERAND1,&OPERAND2,...     PROTOTYPE STATEMENT
                LCLX   &SETN                       SETTING STATEMENT
        &NAME   OPOR1  &OPERANDX,&OPERANDY         FIRST MODEL STATEMENT
                OPOR2  N,&OPERANDZ                 SECOND MODEL STATEMENT
                MNOTE  *,'THIS IS A COMMENT'
                MEND                               TRAILER STATEMENT
```

FIG. 13-2. Example of the general format for a macrodefinition.

The second major part of the macrodefinition is the prototype. The prototype is a statement of the pattern for the macro call that the programer writes, as described previously. As such, it specifies the macrocommand and the number and type of operands. The name may be, and usually is, left blank. If nonblank, it serves only to identify the macrodefinition. Figure 13-2 gives an example.

The operands in the prototype must follow the usual rules for symbolic names but with one exception: The first character of each operand name must be an &. Since the presence of the & makes the name automatically different from the names used elsewhere in the program, the programer can choose the prototype operand names for their mnemonic value with little restriction. The prototype statement must also by example specify the type of operands (keyword or positional) and, if possitional, the sequence of the operands. The number of operands may be from none through as many as 255. Each operand that the programer cites in the prototype must be used in at least one subsequent setting or model statement in the macrodefinition. This is because the compiler uses the prototype statement to identify the operands in the macro call and make the correct substitution in the generated coding.

The third major part of the macrodefinition is the settings. Setting statements, when present, first occur immediately following the prototype statement, but the programer provides them only when he wants to use the conditional-assembly feature. For simple macros, no setting statements are needed. For the more complicated macros, many setting declaratives may be needed. The programer may intermix additional setting statements with model statements as needed. Setting statements and conditional assembly are described in more detail later.

The fourth major part of the macrodefinition is the models. The model statements provide the skeleton basis for the generation process. They serve as the heart of subroutine definitions. As such, the model statement specify the sequence of operations, the particular operations to be performed, and the items of data upon which they are to be performed. They may use any symbolic names used in the program and the & names cited in the prototype operands. To permit easily a wide use of a macro in many programs, the programer should avoid using symbolic names that are unique to any one program. The programer is better off limiting himself to literals and & names. Model statements are described in more detail later.

The fifth and final major part of the macrodefinition is the trailer, which takes the form of a declarative MEND. It has no name and no operands. This serves to notify the compiler that the end of the macrodefinition has been reached. An example is shown in Fig. 13-2.

Other Parts. The other parts, all optional, of the macrodefinition are the MNOTE, the MEXIT, and the sequence symbol. The declarative MNOTE takes no name but takes two operands separated by a comma. The first operand may be an * or an integer number from 0 through 255. The second operand is a comment or message placed within single quote marks or apostrophies. If the first is an *, then the compiler treats the second operand as a comment. If the first operand is a number, then the compiler treats the second operand as a message, printing the number along with the message. Typically such messages serve as diagnostic messages, and the numbers as severity indicators for failures detected by the compiler during macro generation. The convention is to use high numbers for severe (fatal) errors and low numbers for minor difficulties and warnings that merit the programer's attention. An example of an MNOTE is given in Fig. 13-2.

The MEXIT declarative may have a name. If so, the name takes the form of a sequence symbol. No operands are permitted. The MEXIT serves to notify the compiler that macro generation may be terminated. At first this seems a little strange since MEXIT declaratives may appear in a number of places in the macrodefinition. Only one is effective, however, in the process of generating the open subroutine. Which one is effective depends on the conditional-assembly feature described below.

The sequence symbol consists of a period followed immediately by a symbolic name which is not preceded by an &. The sequence symbol may appear as an operand in conditional transfers of control. Each sequence symbol used as an operand must be matched by a sequence symbol used as a name within the macrodefinition. Sequence symbols therefore serve as entry points for transfers of control within the macrodefinition itself. Thus they are used only with the conditional-assembly feature described below.

Model Statements

Simple Macros. The role of model statements and some of the factors affecting the way programers write them can be clarified by considering a few simple examples. Figure 13-3 shows a macrodefinition for a macro called KEEP. The function of this macro is to save in an area called SAVE the contents of the registers beginning with a specified register (called FRSTR) through register 12.

```
   LOC  OBJECT CODE    ADDR1 ADDR2  ST #  NAME     OP    OPERANDS              COMMENT

                                          IMPERATIVES

                                    65             MACRO                       HEADER
                                    66             KEEP   &FRSTR               PROTOTYPE
                                    67             STM    &FRSTR,12,SAVE       MODEL
                                    68             MEND                        TRAILER
                                   111  *
                                   112             KEEP   3                    EXAMPLE OF A MACRO CALL
                                        *
000014 903C 30EC              000F4 113+           STM    3,12,SAVE            GENERATED
                                   114  *
0000F4 0000000000000000             206  SAVE      DC     14F'0'               SAVE AREA IN STORAGE
0000FC 0000000000000000
000104 0000000000000000
00010C 0000000000000000
000114 0000000000000000
00011C 0000000000000000
000124 0000000000000000
```

FIG. 13-3. A simple macrodefinition.

In Fig. 13-3, the header is shown in the first line as MACRO. The prototype, the line with the macrocommand KEEP, shows that one operand is to be written by the programer when he writes a macro call. That one operand is represented symbolically by the name &FRSTR. This macrodefinition has no setting statements. The next statement after the prototype is a model statement.

The first and only model statement in this definition for KEEP has a STM (Store Multiple) command. The three operands are shown as &FRSTR,12,SAVE. As will be recalled from Chap. 4, this serves to place a copy of the contents of the registers starting with the one cited as the first operand through register 12 (the second operand) in an area called SAVE, which must be in an aligned area. The final statement in the macrodefinition is the trailer MEND.

Assume that the programer has just had a sum created in register 3 by an AR instruction. Then, as shown in the middle part of Fig. 13-3, the programer gives a macro call to save registers 3 through 12. Then he loads register 3 with a constant. The compiler for this generates the coding shown in the bottom part of Fig. 13-3.

Several comments about the example are in order.

1. The programer should note that the & operand is never explicitly defined by having its name appear as the name for a Define Symbol (DS) declarative. This is in contrast to the usual requirements for symbolic names outside of macros. This is possible because each & name is really serving as a place holder for the actual operand which the programer uses in the macro call.

2. The symbolic name SAVE is not defined within the macro. This symbolic name therefore must be defined in the usual way elsewhere in the program. The use

of such a name in the macrodefinition limits this macro to programs in which that name is suitably defined and used in a manner consistent with the use in the macro.

3. In examining this simple macro, the programer can note it is unsatisfactory in several ways. Where is the companion macro to reload the saved register contents? If such a macro were to be defined, how could it determine in which register to place the first reloaded material from SAVE? How can the programer determine how large to make SAVE without wasting space? What about successive KEEPs?

Do It Now Exercise 13-1. *Prepare two macrodefinitions: one for KEEP and one for RLOD. Have KEEP save the contents of registers 0 through 12 inclusive in an area called SAVE. Have RLOD enable reloading the same registers with the contents from that same area. Hint: How many operands does the prototype need?*

Do It Now Exercise 13-2. *If your computer installation uses an operating system, does it have SAVE as one of the system macros? If so, obtain a listing of the routine and a description of its purpose, function, and directions for its use. What would you have to change in the KEEP macro of the prior Exercise to enable it to do what the SAVE macro does? Hint: What format does the saved data take in storage? Why?*

4. This macrodefinition used positional operands. Keyword operands could have been specified. This would have had the same effect as far as the compiler is concerned and would not have changed the results of generation. In general, since the use of the keyword format requires additional writing by the programer, the keyword format, for most macros, is less convenient than the positional format for the operands.

5. The number of operands specified could have been less or more than 1. The number depends on what the programer specifies in the prototype. But if the programer required specifying three or more operands, what would be the saving to the programer of using a macro in this case (since STM normally requires three operands anyway)?

Catenation. One of the ways the programer has of adapting macrodefinitions to the situations he encounters is catenating operands to other operands or to commands in the model statements. The way the programer does this depends upon the nature of the operands. Three major cases are symbolic operands, numeric and character literals, and operands involving literal special characters, most commonly parentheses.

Figure 13-4 illustrates catenation with two macros called ARITG and ARITD. Ampersand operands may be catenated by writing them abutted to other symbolic names. Thus the first operand &T is catenated to a letter in the commands for two model statements, as an example. In this case, the programer specifies for the &T operand a letter to designate registers (R) or the type of data: blank for full word,

LOC	OBJECT CODE	ADDR1	ADDR2	ST #	NAME	OP	OPERANDS	COMMENT
						IMPERATIVES		
				71		MACRO		
				72		ARITG	&T,&R,&ONE,&TWO,&THRE	PROTOTYPE FOR NON-PACKED DATA
				73		L&T	&R,&TWO	MODEL
				74		A&T	&R,&ONE	MODEL
				75		S&T	&R,&THRE	MODEL
				76		ST&T	&R,&TWO	MODEL
				77		MEND		
				78 *				
				79		MACRO		
				80		ARITD	&ONE,&TWO,&THRE,&LEN	PROTOTYPE FOR PACKED DATA
				81		AP	&TWO.(&LEN),&ONE.(&LEN)	MODEL
				82		SP	&TWO.(&LEN),&THRE.(&LEN)	MODEL
				83		MEND		
				131 *				
				132		ARITG	H,9,T04,T05,T06	MACRO CALL, HALF-WORD
00002E 4890 3130			00138	133+		LH	9,T05	GENERATED
000032 4A90 312F			00136	134+		AH	9,T04	GENERATED
000036 4B90 3132			0013A	135+		SH	9,T06	GENERATED
00003A 4090 3130			00138	136+		STH	9,T05	GENERATED
				137 *				
				138		ARITD	T01,T02,T03,3	MACRO CALL, PACKED DATA
00003F FA22 3127 3124	0012F	0012C		139+		AP	T02(3),T01(3)	GENERATED
000044 FB22 3127 312A	0012F	00132		140+		SP	T02(3),T03(3)	GENERATED
				141 *				
0012C 00027C				208 T01		DC	PL3'27'	TEST DATA 13-4
0012F 00031C				209 T02		DC	PL3'31'	
00132 00011C				210 T03		DC	PL3'11'	
00135 00								
00136 001B				211 T04		DC	H'27'	
00138 001F				212 T05		DC	H'31'	
0013A 0008				213 T06		DC	H'11'	

Fig. 13-4. Catenation adds adaptability to macros.

H for half word, etc. This takes advantage of a symmetry in the command names used in assembly language, which the observant programer has probably already noticed about the language.

A numeric literal may be catenated, as may equals sign constants, or character literals written with single quote marks or apostrophies in the usual fashion, if the programer precedes the literal with a period and no intervening spaces.

A slight modification of this rule enables special characters to be catenated, most commonly in practice, parentheses. A left parenthesis can be catenated when it is preceded by a period without the intervening space, as noted for literals generally. But a right parenthesis that is preceded by a left parenthesis is catenated without any special notation. It is illustrated in Fig. 13-4 with an operand &LEN for the macro ARITD.

The last prototype operand in the example serves as a length operand when packed-decimal data are to be handled. Such an operand, if present, must be enclosed in parentheses in the generated coding, and if omitted, must be elided entirely including the parentheses. Since the length operand is specified last in the prototype, the programer may omit it entirely when it is not needed (as when the lengths are known to the compiler), without even a comma to indicate the omission. Suppose, for contrast, that the prototype statement was ARTH &T,&LEN,&ONE,&TWO. Then for a register operation with registers 6 and 3, the programer might write the macro called as ARTH R,,6,3. Here the omitted length operand must be indicated by a comma, since it was the last operand.

When the &LEN operand is omitted in the example, then some versions of compiler also automatically delete both the left and the right parentheses. But some versions do not, and for these the programer may have to write separate macros to handle the full range of situations desired.

A review of the example shown in Fig. 13-4 indicates that these macros would be difficult to use as a practical matter. In the first place, they require careful attention to setting up the operands to get them ready. In the second place, they could result in a scaling problem.

Do It Now Exercise 13-3. *Analyze the packed decimal scaling problem indicated in Fig. 13-4 and list some of the actions that would be necessary to handle the problem. Summarize your findings in a table, citing the conditions and the suggested actions.*

Nesting of Macros. The programer may use macros in writing macrodefinitions. He may in this manner nest macros within macros for many levels. An example of a nested macro is shown in Fig. 13-5.

```
  LOC   OBJECT CODE    ADDR1 ADDR2  ST #  NAME    OP    OPERANDS                    COMMENT

                                       IMPERATIVES

                             86            MACRO                     INNER MACRO HEADER
                             87            LABNO  &NUM                PROTOTYPE
                             88            MVC    SAVE(4),&NUM        MODEL
                             89            MEND                       TRAILER
                             90            MACRO                      OUTER MACRO HEADER
                             91            KEER   &CODE               PROTOTYPE
                             92            STM    0,12,SAVE+4         MODEL
                             93            LABNO  &CODE               MODEL
                             94            MEND                       TRAILER
                            123  *
                            124            KEER   =F'256'             MACRO CALL

  000020 900C 30F0              000F8  125+         STM    0,12,SAVE+4         GENERATED
  000024 D203 30FC 31B4 000F4 001BC  126+         MVC    SAVE(4),=F'256'.    GENERATED
                            127  *
                            128 SAVE      DC     2F'0'               HOLD AREA
                            129            LTORG
                            130                   =F'256'
```

FIG. 13-5. Macros may be nested. The macro that incorporates a call to another macro is termed the outer macro.

The two macrodefinitions shown in Fig. 13-5 are for a modified version of the KEEP macro cited previously and a new macro called LABNO to store one word of identifying data represented in the prototype by the operand &NUM. The KEER macro stores all the registers from 0 through 12 into an area called SAVE and reserves the first four bytes of that area for the LABNO macro. A LABNO macro call appears as a model statement within the KEER macrodefinition. LABNO is itself the subject of a separate macrodefinition.

To nest macros, the programer must be able to specify in the macro call he writes on the coding form the operands that may be needed as the nested macros involved. This means in practice that the programer must give his attention to the level of the nesting and to the availability and values of the operands. The macro he calls directly is termed the "outer macro." The other macros invoked by the call are termed "inner macros." The inner macros may be successive—that is, all at the same level—or may be in turn nested or be a combination of both arrangements.

The compiler expands and generates the assembly language to translate the macros in exactly the position that the programer places them by his macro calls. That is, the code is effectively generated "in place"; the compiler does not rearrange code as it generates. The programer therefore may have his macrodefinitions in any sequence, without regard to any nesting. The programer specifies nesting by what he writes within the macrodefinition, not by what he writes in the macro call.

Variations. Programers may use strings of characters, halfwords, words, and doublewords as operands in macros. Strings of fixed-length fields can be used, but not of variable lengths. In the prototype statement, the programer can represent the entire string by a single & name. To designate in a model or setting statement any particular element within the string, he can use a subscript enclosed with parentheses. The count is assumed to start with 1 and must be an integer. The programer uses no period and no space to precede the left parenthesis.

In the macro call, the programer may designate the entire string with a single symbolic name, or he may write the entire string out if he so desires, element by element. In that case, he encloses the entire string in parentheses and uses commas but no spaces to separate the elements. If the programer uses a single symbolic name, then he must have defined in a declarative an appropriate duplication factor and length attribute.

The programer may use keyword operands or positional operands with macros, as he chooses, but given the choice, he must observe some rules for the use of equals signs, single quote marks or apostrophies, parentheses, ampersands, and periods.

Equals signs must be used in the keyword formats with no space on either side of them. If used in the prototype statement, then they must also be used in the model and setting statements in the same way. Equals signs may also be used to define constants in the manner described in Chap. 3. Equals signs may be used too in character literals provided the literal is bounded by the usual single quote marks or apostrophies. And equals signs may be used within enclosing pairs of parentheses, such as (J=K), in setting statements.

Single quote marks or apostrophies may be used in the operands in macrodefinition provided that the usual rules for their use are observed. These have been covered elsewhere in this book but may be briefly summarized as follows. Character strings bounded by defining single quote marks or apostrophies may include single quote marks or apostrophies if they are used in contiguous pairs. Thus a set of two is treated by the compiler as a single literal. A bounding single quote mark or apostrophe may not be a member of such a pair. Thus *""* yields a single *'* as a literal.

Parentheses may indicate a grouping of terms, or may indicate a subscript, or may be required to enclose index or length operands. The rules for the latter two uses have been presented earlier. The groupings may be briefly summarized as follows. Parentheses must appear in left-right pairs with an equal number of each, irrespective of any nesting. Thus $((()())())$ between the left and right parentheses can be thought of as an allowable pattern, but $(( )()())()$ is not. Parentheses can indicate a hierarchy among the names or values cited in them.

Ampersands are used in macrodefinitions to introduce and flag the symbolic operands unique to the macro. Such &'s are the first character of the symbolic name. Programers are advised to limit the use of ampersands to this good practice. Yet, the programer is permitted in assembly language to use an ampersand as an ordinary alphabetic character in framing symbolic names. This he should avoid since the compiler within a macrodefinition takes this as a signal to catenate. The programer who wants to use ampersands must therefore use them in even-number groups. For instance, &EBL&& is acceptable as an ampersand symbolic name.

In macrodefinitions commas play the same role they play in assembly language generally. They are used to separate like elements in a string, such as positional operands. They must never be followed by spaces or blanks except in comments or in literals.

Setting Statements and Conditional Assembly

Global and Local Settings. When the programer is using unnested macros, the symbolic named variables he defines for each macro are normally unique for that macro. When however, he nests macros, and repeats some names, the picture may change. How is the compiler program to evaluate the repeated names?

To resolve this problem, the programer may assign symbolic names for global use for all macrodefinitions in the program, or for local use only within the macro where they are defined. Thus a local variable does not retain its value from one macrodefinition to another. Even though the name may be the same, the compiler treats it as a new and different symbolic name in each different macro if it is a local variable. If it is a global variable, it retains its former value with each different macro, and the compiler treats it as a variable common to all of the macrodefinitions. When macros are nested, the global value applies to all macrodefinitions at the level the variable is first assigned, and at all inner macros to macros at that level, but not to macros more outer in the nesting.

The reason for having both local and global variables is to help the programer control the communication of the values of variables between levels in nested macrodefinitions and from one macrodefinition to another at any given level. To do this, two groups of declaratives are available to the programer. To establish a symbolic name as a local variable, the programer uses declaratives beginning with LCL, with no name assigned in the name column but with the operands assigned in the usual & form.

To establish a symbolic name as a global variable, the programer uses declaratives beginning with GBL, with no name assigned in the name column but with the operands assigned in the usual & form. The operands cited with either LCL or GBL declarative are usually not the same as those in the prototype statement, since, in practice, those are already global.

LCL and GBL declaratives immediately follow the prototype statement and come prior to any model statements in the macrodefinition.

To particularize further the nature of the variables, the programer must affix the letters A, B, or C to the end of the declaratives LCL and GBL to designate the character of the variable. A indicates an arithmetic variable having numeric values; B a binary variable having 0 or 1 values to show logical relationships; and C, character data intended for nonarithmetic operations. These correspond with the setting declaratives SETA, SETB, and SETC, respectively. The choice of SETA, SETB, or SETC must be consistent with the initial declaration of the variables in the LCL or GBL declarative. For example, a value assigned via an LCLB declarative can only be altered with a SETB declarative subsequently.

Operands for Setting Statements.   Operands used with the setting statements take the form of & names, literals, attributes from the symbol table maintained by the compiler, and sequence symbols. Sequence symbols may be used as operands only for the AIF, AGO, and ANOP declaratives described subsequently. The & names and literals used as operands in the statements are the same as those previously described.

The attributes of symbolic names maintained in the compiler's symbol table may be used as operands in setting statements by using an apostrophe or single quote marks to separate an attribute-indicator letter from the symbolic name. The attribute-indicator letters, which are borrowed from the letters used with Define Constant declaratives, are summarized in Fig. 13-6.

T' provides the type designation for the symbolic-named variable. Many of these are the same as the letters normally used in Define Constant declaratives. Thus F represents full word, D represents floating-point long format, and P represents packed-decimal data, etc.

In addition to the letters normally used in the Define Constant declaratives for indicating type, I, J, M, T, W, N, O, U, and $ are also available as the result of the T' qualifier. U, the undefined type, arises primarily as a result of setting statements in macrodefinitions. Programers writing systems software for control of machine functions are mostly concerned with the I, J, and W types.

L' provides the length attribute in bytes. The length attribute is a number usually

```
TYPE ATTRIBUTES FOR DS AND DC NAMES

A    ADDRESS CONSTANT, TYPE A
B    BINARY CONSTANT
C    CHARACTER CONSTANT
D    FLOATING-POINT LONG CONSTANT
E    FLOATING-POINT SHORT CONSTANT
F    FULL WORD CONSTANT
G    FIXED-POINT, SPECIFIED LENGTH
H    HALF-WORD CONSTANT
K    FLOATING-POINT, SPECIFIED LENGTH
L    EXTENDED FLOATING-POINT CONSTANT
P    PACKED DECIMAL CONSTANT
Q    ADDRESS CONSTANT, TYPE Q
R    ADDRESS CONSTANT, SPECIFIED LENGTH
S    ADDRESS CONSTANT, TYPE S
V    ADDRESS CONSTANT, TYPE V
X    HEXADECIMAL CONSTANT
Y    ADDRESS CONSTANT, TYPE Y
Z    ZONED CONSTANT


TYPE ATTRIBUTES FOR NON-DS OR -DC NAMES

I    MACHINE LANGUAGE INSTRUCTION
J    CONTROL SECTION NAME
M    MACRO INSTRUCTION
T    EXTRN SYMBOL (MAY BE DC, DS)
W    CCW INSTRUCTION (CHANNEL PROGRAM)
S    WXTRN SYMBOL (MAY BE DC, DS)


TYPE ATTRIBUTES FOR MACRO OPERANDS ONLY

N    SELF-DEFINING SYMBOL
O    OMITTED OPERAND


TYPE ATTRIBUTES FOR EQU, LTORG, OTHER NAMES

U    UNDEFINED OR MODIFIED SYMBOL
```

Fig. 13-6. Permitted usage of attributes in macros.

in the range from 0 through 255. In practice, the length and the type attributes are the most common attributes used as operands for setting statements.

S' provides a positional-scaling attribute. It applies primarily to fixed-point numbers such as full-word binary data and indicates the number of fractional characters in the number.

L' provides an integer-scaling attribute. It is therefore a companion on the integer side of the S' attribute. For both the S' and I' attributes, the count is provided in terms of the number of characters. Thus, in binary fields, the unit for the count is a bit. For packed decimal, it is the half byte.

N' provides an answer to the question of how many components are there in a macrostring operand. This attribute is available only for variables with & names.

A special case of N' helps the programer in error checking. When the programer specifies N'&SYSLIST as an operand, it provides a count of how many operands are present in the macro call. This the programer can use to check against the number specified in the prototype statement. This special case of N' is not available with some versions of the operating system or supervisor. In general, the programer should avoid asigning operands with names beginning with SYS or &SYS because of the possible confusion with system names assigned through the operating system.

K′ provides a count of the number of characters in the name of the variable that replaces the & name in a macro call. This attribute can be used in analyzing a macro call.

Operations and Relations.   The power and flexibility of the setting statements comes not only from the operands but also from their capability of calling upon the compiler to perform operations and establish relations among the operands. The programer can call upon a substantial range of arithmetic and logic functions.

Arithmetic operations provided are add, subtract, multiply, and divide, represented, respectively, by $+$, $-$, $*$, and $/$. These signs may be used surrounded by spaces. The compiler evaluates the arithmetic statements starting at the left and going forward to the right. The compiler looks ahead enough to give precedence to multiplication and division over addition and subtraction. Thus, for example, &A+&B*&C adds &A's value to the product of &B and &C. If the programer desires by contrast that the sum of &A and &B be multiplied by &C, then he must use parentheses to indicate the desired grouping: (&A+&B)*&C.

Both left and right parentheses are available and must be used in the usual pattern to indicate grouping and levels of operation. In general, operations and relations within parentheses are evaluated by the compiler before those outside the parentheses. If parentheses are used, then the compiler evaluates the innermost relations and operations first.

The comparison relations within parentheses permitted are EQ for equal, NE for not equal, GT for greater than, LT for less than, LE for less than or equal to, and GE greater than or equal to. Each of these must be separated by a space on each side from the surrounding names of variables or constants, with parentheses to indicate levels or groupings.

For logical operations, logical NOT, logical AND, and logical OR are available within parentheses. These are usually separated by a space on each side from the names of variables but may abut parentheses indicating grouping. Logical NOT generally takes precedence over logical AND, and that over logical OR, unless indicated otherwise by the use of parentheses. Definitions for logical AND, logical OR, and logical NOT have been provided in Chap. 10.

Setting Declaratives

LCLA, LCLB, and LCLB.   These three local-variable setting declaratives have been already described. They normally have one operand and no name.

GBLA, GBLB, and GBLC.   These three global-variable setting declaratives have been already described. They normally have one operand and no name.

SETA.   This declarative directs the compiler to do arithmetic operations for variables defined in LCLA or GBLA declaratives. The compiler performs arithmetic operations at compile time, not at the time of execution of the program. The programer usually uses SETA to calculate such factors as the amount of storage space needed, the location of entry points, and addresses of items of data. Operands to enable this typically are length attributes, scaling attributes, addresses, and literals. Parentheses may be used as needed for grouping of the operands. The name shown in the name column must have been an operand of a LCLA or GBLA declarative previously. The name may not be blank. For SETA, the compiler evaluates the arithmetic operations on the operands and assigns the resulting numeric value as the value of the & name in the name column. Figure 13-7 offers several examples of SETA.

NAME	OP	OPERANDS	COMMENT
	LCLA	&VARA	DECLARE LOCAL VARIABLE TYPE A
&VARA	SETA	(R+L'OPND2)*15	SET VALUE OF VARIABLE
&VARA	SETA	&VARA+32	INCREMENT VALUE BY 32
&VARA	SETA	32	SET VALUE TO 32

FIG. 13-7. Examples of SETA and LCLA.

SETB. This declarative directs the compiler to evaluate a logical relationship in binary terms among the variables defined in LCLB or GBLB declaratives. The compiler performs the logical evaluation at compile time, not at the time of execution of the program. The programer usually uses SETB to determine the values of variables used in comparisons leading to conditional transfers of control. The operands may be either numeric or character data and often involve the attributes. The evaluation does not use arithmetic operations but instead uses greater-than, less-than, or equal-to relationships, and logical AND, OR, NOT relationships, with levels of groupings indicated by parentheses as needed. The name shown in the name column must not be blank and must have previously been an operand of a LCLB or GBLB declarative. The result of the evaluation is to assign a numeric value of 0 or 1 as the value of the & name in the name column. Figure 13-8 offers several examples of SETB.

NAME	OP	OPERANDS	COMMENT
	GBLB	&VARB	DECLARE GLOBAL VARIABLE TYPE B
&VARB	SETB	(T'&OPND3 EQ 'P')	SET &VARB TO 1 IF TYPE IS P
&VARB	SETB	(L'&OPND4 LT 5)	SET &VARB TO 0 IF = 5 OR MORE
&VARB	SETB	(T'&OPND3 AND T'&OPND4 EQ NOT 'P')	LOGICAL RELATION

FIG. 13-8. Examples of SETB and GBLB.

SETC. This declarative directs the compiler to assign a character value as the value of the & name specified in the name column. The compiler performs the assignment at compile time, not at the time of execution of the program. The programer usually uses SETC to substitute or modify names for operands and character values of operands. The operands are usually literals enclosed in single quote marks or apostrophies. Under some versions of the operating system, type attributes as well as literals must be enclosed in apostrophies. Arithmetic and logical operations are not permitted. The name shown in the name column must not be blank and must have previously been an operand of a LCLC or GBLC declarative. An example in Fig. 13-9 offers several examples of SETC.

NAME	OP	OPERANDS		COMMENT
	LCLC	&VARC		DECLARE LOCAL VARIABLE TYPE C
&VARC	SETC	'MVC'		SET &VARC TO VALUE OF MVC
&VARC	SETC	'&VARC.L'		CATENATE ON L TO YIELD MVCL

Fig. 13-9. Examples of SETC and LCLC.

AGO. This declarative directs the compiler to make an unconditional transfer of control during compilation. It does not result in any transfers of control during the execution of the program. The name may be present or may be left blank. If it is present, it is normally a sequence symbol. The one operand must be a sequence symbol. The AGO declarative enables the compiler to jump over portions of a macrodefinition in adapting it to particular circumstances indicated in the macro call. An example of the AGO declarative is shown in Fig. 13-10.

NAME	OP	OPERANDS	COMMENT
	AGO	.TWOUP	UNCONDITIONAL TRANSFER

Fig. 13-10. Example of AGO.

AIF. This declarative directs the compiler to make a conditional transfer of control during compilation. It does not result in any transfers of control during the execution of the program. The name may be present or may be left blank, but if present, is usually a sequence symbol. The operand must begin with a left parenthesis which is subsequently paired with a right parenthesis and followed immediately by a sequence symbol. Within the operand parentheses the programer may write relational expressions similar to SETB statements. But he may use operands from SETA, SETB, and SETC declaratives, as well as attributes, & names from the prototype, literals, relations (such as GT), and parentheses if needed. Under some versions of the operating system, operands to be compared to literals must be enclosed in apostrophies, as is also sometimes true in SETB expressions. An example of AIF is shown in Fig. 13-11.

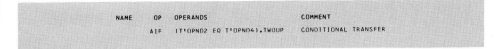

FIG. 13-11. Example of AIF.

ANOP. This declarative provides an entry point for use by the compiler. Some declaratives such as SETA, SETB, and SETC require the name column on the coding form for their own use. Thus the name space may not be available on some lines of coding within the macrodefinition to name an entry point. ANOP provides a means of providing entry points, since it has no operand but must have a name in the name column. The name is normally a sequence symbol. An example of ANOP is shown in Fig. 13-12.

FIG. 13-12. Example of ANOP.

ACTR. This declarative establishes a counter. This counter is used by the compiler and is effective only during the process of compilation. It is not available and not used during the execution of the program. The compiler decrements the value assigned to the counter each time that the compiler handles an AGO or an AIF declarative. Whenever the compiler encounters an AGO or AIF declarative, before handling it, the compiler tests the value of the ACTR counter. If the counter value is zero, the compiler terminates the compilation of the macro call. If it is nonzero, the compiler decrements the value by 1 and continues compilation. For the ACTR declarative, the programer assigns no name. As the operand, he may assign a symbolic name, or a numeric or an arithmetic expression, following the general format for SETA operands. The programer must place the ACTR declaration immediately after the local and global setting statements. The ACTR declarative serves as a bug catcher to protect against endless loops in compiling complex macrodefinitions. An example of ACTR is given in Fig. 13-13.

FIG. 13-13. An example of ACTR.

MACRO EXAMPLE

Adding up a column or row of numbers is a common prelude to further arithmetic operations. For example, assume that nurses have taken readings of a hospitalized patient's body temperature each hour for three days. A first step in analyzing this vector of numeric data is to find the sum; that is, do a sum reduction.

Assuming the data are in a form suitable for computer input, the programer can approach this task in many ways. The usual preferred way is by an iterative

```
LOC  OBJECT CODE   ADDR1 ADDR2  ST #  NAME    OP    OPERANDS                      COMMENT

                                  2  *              PRINT ON,GEN,DATA
                                  3  *
                                  4               MACRO                          HEADER
                                  5               VTSUM  &VEC,&SUM,&VL            PROTOTYPE FOR VECTOR SUM
                                  6  .*  MAKE INITIAL SETTINGS
                                  7               LCLA   &C                      COUNTER
                                  8               LCLA   &L                      LENGTH
                                  9               LCLA   &S                      SCALING
                                 10               LCLA   &SL                     POSITION IN VECTOR
                                 11               LCLC   &RG                     WORK AREA OR REGISTER NAME
                                 12               LCLC   &T                      TYPE
                                 13               ACTR   999                     SET BUG LIMITER
                                 14  &C           SETA   1                       SET COUNT TO 1
                                 15  &L           SETA   L'&VEC                  SET LENGTH
                                 16  &SL          SETA   0                       SET TO FIRST ITEM
                                 17  &T           SETC   T'&SUM                  SET TYPE TO THAT FOR SUM
                                 18  .*  QUALIFY THE CALL
                                 19               AIF    (N'&SYSLIST NE 3).BUG1  NUMBER OF OPERANDS IN CALL
                                 20               AIF    (&VL LT 2).BUG2         CHECK LENGTH OF VECTOR
                                 21               AIF    ('&T' NE T'&VEC).BUG3   TYPES DO NOT MATCH
                                 22               AIF    ('&T' EQ 'F').FULL      DATA ARE TYPE F
                                 23               AIF    ('&T' EQ 'H').REGU      DATA ARE TYPE H
                                 24               AIF    ('&T' EQ 'D' OR '&T' EQ 'E').REGU TYPE D OR E
                                 25               AIF    ('&T' NE 'P').BUG4      REJECT ALL OTHER BUT TYPE P
                                 26  .*  DATA ARE TYPE P
                                 27  &S           SETA   1'&VEC+2-1'&SUM         ESTIMATE SCALING
                                 28               AIF    (&S GT 0).BUG5          SCALING WARNING
                                 29  .PKD         ZAP    &SUM,(&L)'&VEC          CLEAR AND LOAD FIRST ITEM
                                 30  .PK          ANOP                           NEXT NAME SPACE IS OCCUPIED
                                 31  &SL          SETA   &SL+&L                  ADVANCE THE POINTER
                                 32               AP     &SUM,(&L)'&VEC.+&SL     ADD NEXT ITEM
                                 33  &C           SETA   &C+1                    INCREMENT COUNTER
                                 34               AIF    (&C LT &VL).PK          MORE CODE TO GENERATE
                                 35               MEXIT                          NO, FINISHED WITH PACKED
                                 36  .*  DATA ARE TYPE F
                                 37  .FULL        ANOP                           NEXT NAME SPACE IS OCCUPIED
                                 38  &T           SETC   ' '                     BLANK OUT THE TYPE FOR F
                                 39  .*  DATA ARE TYPE F, H, D, OR E
                                 40  .REGU        ANOP                           NEXT NAME SPACE IS OCCUPIED
                                 41  &RG          SETC   '4'                     USE REGISTER 4
                                 42               ST&T   &RG,REGSAVE             SAVE ITS CONTENTS OUT OF MACRO
                                 43               L&T    &RG,&VEC                CLEAR AND LOAD FIRST ITEM
                                 44  .ALL         ANOP                              NEXT NAME SPACE IS OCCUPIED
                                 45  &SL          SETA   &SL+&L                  ADVANCE THE POINTER
                                 46               A&T    &RG,&VEC.+&SL           ADD NEXT ITEM
                                 47  &C           SETA   &C+1                    INCREMENT COUNTER
                                 48               AIF    (&C LT &VL).ALL         MORE CODE TO GENERATE
                                 49               ST&T   &RG,&SUM                STORE THE SUM
                                 50               L&T    &RG,REGSAVE             REPLACE SAVED REGISTER CONTENT
                                 51  .DONE        MEXIT                          CODE GENERATION COMPLETE
                                 52  .*  ERROR MESSAGES
                                 53  .BUG1        MNOTE  3,'IMPROPER OPERANDS IN CALL; NO GENERATION'
                                 54               MEXIT
                                 55  .BUG2        MNOTE  3,'DATA NOT A VECTOR; NO GENERATION'
                                 56               MEXIT
                                 57  .BUG3        MNOTE  3,'SUM AREA TYPE DOES NOT MATCH; NO GENERATION'
                                 58               MEXIT
                                 59  .BUG4        MNOTE  3,'DATA NOT  TYPE P, F, H, D, OR E; NO GENERATION'
                                 60               MEXIT
                                 61  .BUG5        MNOTE  1,'OVERFLOW LIKELY FROM THIS ROUTINE'
                                 62               AGO    .PKD
                                 63               MEND                           TRAILER
                                 95  *
```

Fig. 13-14. Example of a macro to produce straight-line code for addition.

loop, an approach described previously in Chap. 6. Such a code, however, does not execute rapidly because of the substantial overhead necessary to modify and test in the loop. An alternative to gain speed of execution is to write a separate addition instruction for each number to be added. This uses more storage space for instructions and is repetitious and boring for the programer.

A macro, however, can make it a reasonable alternative. This would enable the

```
LOC    OBJECT CODE       ADDR1 ADDR2  ST #  NAME     OP    OPERANDS              COMMENT

000000                                 96 MACFN  CSECT
000000 070007000700                    97        CNOP  6,8
000006 0530                            98        BALR  3,0
000008                                 99        USING *,3
                                      143 *
                                      144        VTSUM PWDS,PSUM,6            MACRO CALL
                                      145
                                            1,OVERFLOW LIKELY FROM THIS ROUTINE
00004E F833 3138 316R 00140 00170     146+      ZAP   PSUM(4),PWDS           CLEAR AND LOAD FIRST ITEM
000054 FA33 3138 316C 00140 00174     147+      AP    PSUM(4),PWDS+4         ADD NEXT ITEM
00005A FA33 3138 3170 00140 00178     148+      AP    PSUM(4),PWDS+8         ADD NEXT ITEM
000060 FA33 3138 3174 00140 0017C     149+      AP    PSUM(4),PWDS+12        ADD NEXT ITEM
000066 FA33 3138 3178 00140 00180     150+      AP    PSUM(4),PWDS+16        ADD NEXT ITEM
00006C FA33 3138 317C 00140 00184     151+      AP    PSUM(4),PWDS+20        ADD NEXT ITEM
                                      152 *
                                      153        VTSUM LWDS,LSUM,4            MACRO CALL
                                      154
                                            3,SUM AREA TYPE DOES NOT MATCH; NO GENERATION
                                      155 *
                                      156        VTSUM DWDS,DSUM,4            MACRO CALL
000072 6040 3148     00150            157+      STD   4,REGSAVE              SAVE ITS CONTENTS OUT OF MACRO
000076 6840 3180     00188            158+      LD    4,DWDS                 CLEAR AND LOAD FIRST ITEM
00007A 6A40 318R     00190            159+      AD    4,DWDS+8               ADD NEXT ITEM
00007F 6A40 3190     00198            160+      AD    4,DWDS+16              ADD NEXT ITEM
000082 6A40 3198     001A0            161+      AD    4,DWDS+24              ADD NEXT ITEM
000086 6040 3140     00148            162+      STD   4,DSUM                 STORE THE SUM
00008A 6840 3148     00150            163+      LD    4,REGSAVE              REPLACE SAVED REGISTER CONTENT
                                      164 *
                                      167        VTSUM FWDS,FSUM,1            TEST OF BUG CATCHER
                                      168
                                            3,DATA NOT A VECTOR; NO GENERATION
                                      184 *
                                      185        VTSUM FWDS,FSUM,6            MACRO CALL
0000BE 5040 3148     00150            186+      ST    4,REGSAVE              SAVE ITS CONTENTS OUT OF MACRO
0000C2 5840 3150     0015R            187+      L     4,FWDS                 CLEAR AND LOAD FIRST ITEM
0000C6 5A40 3154     0015C            188+      A     4,FWDS+4               ADD NEXT ITEM
0000CA 5A40 3158     00160            189+      A     4,FWDS+8               ADD NEXT ITEM
0000CF 5A40 315C     00164            190+      A     4,FWDS+12              ADD NEXT ITEM
0000D2 5A40 3160     00168            191+      A     4,FWDS+16              ADD NEXT ITEM
0000D6 5A40 3164     0016C            192+      A     4,FWDS+20              ADD NEXT ITEM
0000DA 5040 3134     0013C            193+      ST    4,FSUM                 STORE THE SUM
0000DE 5840 3148     00150            194+      L     4,REGSAVE              REPLACE SAVED REGISTER CONTENT
                                      195 *
00013C 00000000                       217 FSUM    DC    F'0'        SUM SHOULD BE X'00FFFFFF'
000140 0000000C                       218 PSUM    DC    PL4'0'      SUM SHOULD BE X'0111111C'
000144 000000                         219 LSUM    DC    RL3'0'      SUM SHOULD BE NONE
000147 00
000148 000000000000000000             220 DSUM    DC    D'0'        SUM SHOULD BE X'40FFFF000000000000
000150 0000000000000000               221 REGSAVE DC    2F'0'
000158 0000000F000000F0               222 FWDS    DC    F'+15,+240,+3840,+61440,+983040,+15728640'   FULL WORDS
000160 00000F000000F000
000168 000F000000F00000
000170 0000001C0000010C               223 PWDS    DC    PL4'+1,+10,+100,+1000,+10000,+100000'   PACKED DECIMAL
000178 0000100C0001000C
0001R0 0010000C0100000C
0001R8 3DF0000R46370059               224 DWDS    DC    D'0.22RR82E-3,0.366211E-2,0.5R5937E-1,0.937500E+0'   LONG
000190 3EF00002AF31DC46
000198 3FEFFFF29406R2A2
0001A0 40F0000000000000
0001A8 00000F                         225 LWDS    DC    XL3'F'      TYPE BINARY VIA HEX
0001AR 0000F0                         226         DC    XL3'F0'     TYPE BINARY VIA HEX
0001AE 000F00                         227         DC    XL3'F00'    TYPE BINARY VIA HEX
0001B1 00F000                         228         DC    XL3'F000'   TYPE BINARY VIA HEX
                                      229 *
                                      230         END   MACFN
```

Fɪɢ. 13-14. (*continued*)

programer to avoid having to write out individually all the repetitive lines of coding. And it would reduce bugs due to clerical errors. A difficulty to be resolved is the need to handle at different times data of different data types. The macro should be self-modifying to handle type F, H, P, D, and E data. And the macro should be easy for the programer to use.

To these ends, a programer must make some decisions about the format and addressing of the data. The compiler must be able to ascertain the attributes of the input and of the desired output from the macro. Defining those inputs and outputs by DS or DC declaratives will generally take care of the problems. Information not available through the compiler-maintained symbol table must be explicitly set forth by the programer in the macrodefinition. Figure 13-14 shows the macro example. A review of it, statement by statement, may clarify the role of each in the macro-definition.

The macrodefinition opens with the header statement which takes the usual form. The prototype statement that follows the header could be assigned a name to identify the macrodefinition in the program listing if the programer wanted to. The mnemonic for the prototype macrocommand, the letters VTSUM, have been chosen arbitrarily. This is what the programer will use in a macro call. The operands speci-fied in the prototype are (1) the address of the vector, &VEC, (2) the address at which the programer desires the sum to be stored, &SUM, and (3) the number of elements in the vector, &VL.

Initial settings are required to enable conditional-assembly operations by the compiler. Since one macrodefinition is being written here and no nesting of macros within this macro is expected, the GBL declaratives should not be used; the LCL declaratives are a more conservative choice. The numeric counter &C requires a LCLA setting since its value will be modified arithmetically. The length, scaling, and position also need a numeric definition. Character values are needed for &T, the type of the operand data. Hence LCLC is used. A literal-register number is needed for &RG, so a LCLC is used since arithmetic operations will not be needed on it. Initially, the counter &C needs a value of $+1$, and &T can be set to show the type attribute of the &SUM area, and &L the length of a vector element.

The cautious programer typically checks for common error conditions before starting the main work of the macrodefinition. These follow the comment line "qualifying the call." First is a test for a match of the number of operands in the prototype with the number of operands in the macro call. If the number differs, the programer directs the compiler to go to BUG1 which prints a message and termi-nates generation. The period in front of the * in the comment line prevents the com-ments from printing in the generated coding when unneeded but permits them to appear in the macrodefinition. Next is a check of the length of the vector. With a length less than 2 there is nothing to add up, so the programer directs the compiler to BUG2 and to terminate generation. The programer then asks the compiler to verify that the type attributes of the &SUM and of the &VEC match. If they do not, the programer directs the compiler to BUG3 to write a message and terminate generation.

Having qualified the call thus far, the programer can turn his attention to identifying the alternative action required. Each data type must be treated differently. Different commands are needed, and packed-decimal data cannot be added in the registers, for example. So the programer directs the compiler to find out the data type and go to a portion of the macrodefinition for the identified type. If the data are not for any of the permitted types, the programer directs the compiler to BUG4 to print a message and terminate generation.

If the data are type P, the programer checks that the &SUM field is at least one byte longer than the individual element fields to be added to estimate the likelihood of overflow. If the &SUM field is small, the programer directs the compiler to print the BUG5 message as a warning, but continue compilation. Control returns to .PKD via an AGO declarative. The next line has the name column occupied with &SL. This requires an ANOP declarative to provide a loop entry point of .PK. The following SETA assigns a pointer, &SL, to the addresses in storage, incrementing it &L at a time. Since packed-decimal operations require lengths, the programer has the compiler obtain and insert the length attribute, &L, in the generated instruction. This operation is not essential, for the programer could have allowed the compiler to use the implied length. To clear and load the first number to be added, the programer writes a ZAP, indexing to the first element in &VEC for the sending operand. Note that the indexing is not in terms of bytes, but in terms of position in the vector.

The main model statement follows. The .(&L) catenates the length in parentheses to the first operand. The .+&SL catenates the relative address factor onto the vector address to serve as a pointer to the next vector element to be added. Then the compiler increments the counter and tests it to determine whether or not to generate more addition instructions.

The commands for handling the type F data do not have the letter F in them as a suffix. Hence, the programer must replace the F value of &T with a blank. For this, he can write a SETC declarative. Then, as is also true for type H, D, and E data, the programer must make a register available by storing off its contents, and then loading the first element from the &VEC. The register number chosen must be an even number from 0 through 6, inclusive, since floating-point commands may be generated. The sequence symbol .REGU requires an ANOP, since the name column for the following statement is occupied by &RG. Then the initial element from &VEC can be loaded into the register &RG with a load operation, where the type of load is indicated by catenating the value of &T onto L in the command column. The generated commands therefore might be L, LH, LD, or LE.

The initialization work is now complete and the main generation sequence can begin. At sequence symbol .ALL, the compiler is directed to generate an add instruction of the correct type by catenating the value of &T onto the A in the command column. The first operand is a register, as designated by &RG. The second operand takes the element from the vector designated by the relative address factor &SL. The remaining loop operations parallel those used for the packed-decimal data alternative.

Then a SETA declarative is needed to advance the value of the counter &C. The new value in &C is set, by an arithmetic operation, to equal one more than the old value of &C. The programer can then ask the compiler to test the number of iterations performed in generation against the length of the vector represented by &VL. Since, at the time of this test, &C has a value one larger than the number of vector elements taken care of by generated coding, the test must be for "less than" to send the compiler back to generate another addition instruction. When the test finally indicates equal or greater (not less than), control falls through to the clean-up operations. The sum in the register must be put into the address named in &SUM in storage, and the register contents must be replaced. Then control exits through the MEXIT declarative.

Do It Now Exercise 13-4.   *The macro just discussed could be improved in a number of ways. Make a list of some improvements that you can think of, starting the list with "eliminate requirement to use register 4." Then select that first item and any other one item from your list and revise the macro to achieve those improvements. What difficulties did you encounter?*

In review, this macro example has illustrated how the macrodefinition directs the compiler in the generation of subroutines adapted to the conditions specified and implied in the macro call. The programer specified the input and the output. The compiler generated an open subroutine. By reference to compiler-maintained tables and to the declaratives in the macrodefinition, the compiler ascertained which commands and operands to generate. The resulting code generation offers the programer considerable savings in programing time, reduced debugging, and increased power in the use of assembly language.

EXERCISES

1.   How does a macrodefinition differ from a macro call?
2.   What are the major parts of a macrodefinition, and what is the role of each?
3.   What is meant by "conditional assembly"? How does it work?
4.   How does the macro AGO differ from the macro B? Hint: Check Fig. 6-22 and the associated text if you need to.
5.   How does catenation make it easier for the programer to write adaptable macrodefinitions?

6.   What are the register conventions usually observed in the linkage for closed subroutines?

7.   What roles do the second and third word play in an 18-word-register save area? Why? Why is register 13 not saved in the numeric sequence of register contents?

Appendix A

HEXADECIMAL AND DECIMAL INTEGER CONVERSION TABLE

HALF WORD (lower order)

BYTE				BYTE			
0123		4567		0123		4567	
Hex	Decimal	Hex	Decimal	Hex	Decimal	Hex	Decimal
0	0	0	0	0	0	0	0
1	4,096	1	256	1	16	1	1
2	8,192	2	512	2	32	2	2
3	12,288	3	768	3	48	3	3
4	16,384	4	1,024	4	64	4	4
5	20,480	5	1,280	5	80	5	5
6	24,576	6	1,536	6	96	6	6
7	28,672	7	1,792	7	112	7	7
8	32,768	8	2,048	8	128	8	8
9	36,864	9	2,304	9	144	9	9
A	40,960	A	2,560	A	160	A	10
B	45,056	B	2,816	B	176	B	11
C	49,152	C	3,072	C	192	C	12
D	53,248	D	3,328	D	208	D	13
E	57,344	E	3,584	E	224	E	14
F	61,440	F	3,840	F	240	F	15
4		3		2		1	

HALF WORD (higher order)

BYTE				BYTE			
BITS: 0123		4567		0123		4567	
Hex	Decimal	Hex	Decimal	Hex	Decimal	Hex	Decimal
0	0	0	0	0	0	0	0
1	268,435,456	1	16,777,216	1	1,048,576	1	65,536
2	536,870,912	2	33,554,432	2	2,097,152	2	131,072
3	805,306,368	3	50,331,648	3	3,145,728	3	196,608
4	1,073,741,824	4	67,108,864	4	4,194,304	4	262,144
5	1,342,177,280	5	83,886,080	5	5,242,880	5	327,680
6	1,610,612,736	6	100,663,296	6	6,291,456	6	393,216
7	1,879,048,192	7	117,440,512	7	7,340,032	7	458,752
8	2,147,483,648	8	134,217,728	8	8,388,608	8	524,288
9	2,415,919,104	9	150,994,944	9	9,437,184	9	589,824
A	2,684,354,560	A	167,772,160	A	10,485,760	A	655,360
B	2,952,790,016	B	184,549,376	B	11,534,336	B	720,896
C	3,221,225,472	C	201,326,592	C	12,582,912	C	786,432
D	3,489,660,928	D	218,103,808	D	13,631,488	D	851,968
E	3,758,096,384	E	234,881,024	E	14,680,064	E	917,504
F	4,026,531,840	F	251,658,240	F	15,728,640	F	983,040
8		7		6		5	

HEXADECIMAL AND DECIMAL FRACTION CONVERSION TABLE

BYTE

1 — BITS: 0123

Hex	Decimal
.0	.0000
.1	.0625
.2	.1250
.3	.1875
.4	.2500
.5	.3125
.6	.3750
.7	.4375
.8	.5000
.9	.5625
.A	.6250
.B	.6875
.C	.7500
.D	.8125
.E	.8750
.F	.9375

2 — BYTE 4567

Hex	Decimal		
.00	.0000	0000	
.01	.0039	0625	
.02	.0078	1250	
.03	.0117	1875	
.04	.0156	2500	
.05	.0195	3125	
.06	.0234	3750	
.07	.0273	4375	
.08	.0312	5000	
.09	.0351	5625	
.0A	.0390	6250	
.0B	.0429	6875	
.0C	.0468	7500	
.0D	.0507	8125	
.0E	.0546	8750	
.0F	.0585	9375	

HALF WORD

BYTE

3 — BYTE 0123

Hex	Decimal		
.000	.0000	0000	0000
.001	.0002	4414	0625
.002	.0004	8828	1250
.003	.0007	3242	1875
.004	.0009	7656	2500
.005	.0012	2070	3125
.006	.0014	6484	3750
.007	.0017	0898	4375
.008	.0019	5312	5000
.009	.0021	9726	5625
.00A	.0024	4140	6250
.00B	.0026	8554	6875
.00C	.0029	2968	7500
.00D	.0031	7382	8125
.00E	.0034	1796	8750
.00F	.0036	6210	9375

4 — BYTE 4567

Hex	Decimal			
.0000	.0000	0000	0000	
.0001	.0000	1525	8789	0625
.0002	.0000	3051	7578	1250
.0003	.0000	4577	6367	1875
.0004	.0000	6103	5156	2500
.0005	.0000	7629	3945	3125
.0006	.0000	9155	2734	3750
.0007	.0001	0681	1523	4375
.0008	.0001	2207	0312	5000
.0009	.0001	3732	9101	5625
.000A	.0001	5258	7890	6250
.000B	.0001	6784	6679	6875
.000C	.0001	8310	5468	7500
.000D	.0001	9836	4257	8125
.000E	.0002	1362	3046	8750
.000F	.0002	2888	1835	9375

POWERS OF 16 TABLE

16^n							n
						1	0
						16	1
						256	2
					4	096	3
					65	536	4
				1	048	576	5
				16	777	216	6
				268	435	456	7
			4	294	967	296	8
			68	719	476	736	9
		1	099	511	627	776	10 = A
		17	592	186	044	416	11 = B
		281	474	976	710	656	12 = C
	4	503	599	627	370	496	13 = D
	72	057	594	037	927	936	14 = E
1	152	921	504	606	846	976	15 = F

Decimal values

Appendix B

ASSEMBLY-LANGUAGE COMPARISON

Feature*	Model 20 Basic Assembler	BPS: Basic Assembler	BPS 8K Tape, BOS 8K Disk Assemblers	BOS 16K Disk/Tape Assembler	TOS, DOS Assembler	OS Assembler
No. of continuation cards/statement (exclusive of macro instructions)	0	0	1	1	1	2
Input character code	EBCDIC	EBCDIC	EBCDIC	EBCDIC	EBCDIC	EBCDIC
Elements:						
Maximum characters per symbol	4	6	8	8	8	8
Character self-defining terms	1 character only	1 character only	X	X	X	X
Binary self-defining terms	NA	NA	X	X	X	X
Length attribute reference	NA	NA	X	X	X	X
Literals	NA	NA	X	X	X	X
Extended mnemonics	NA	NA	X	X	X	X
Maximum location counter value	$2^{14} - 1$	$2^{16} - 1$	$2^{24} - 1$	$2^{24} - 1$	$2^{24} - 1$	$2^{24} - 1$
Multiple control sections per assembly	NA	NA	X	X	X	X
Expressions:						
Operators	$+ -$	$+ - *$	$+ - */$	$+ - */$	$+ - */$	$+ - */$
Number of terms	3	3	3	16	16	16
Levels of parentheses	NA	NA	1	5	5	5
Complex relocatability	NA	NA	X	X	X	X
Assembler instructions, DC and DS:						
Expressions allowed as modifiers	NA	NA	NA	X	X	X
Multiple operands	NA	NA	NA	NA	X	X
Multiple constants in an operand	NA	NA	Except address consts.	X	X	X
Bit-length specifications	NA	NA	NA	NA	X	X
Scale modifier	NA	NA	X	X	X	X
Exponent modifier	NA	NA	X	X	X	X
DC types	Only C, X, H, Y	Except B, P, Z V, Y, S	X	X	X	X
DC duplication factor	Except Y	Except A	Except S	X	X	X
Macros:						
Number of operands	NA	NA	49	100	127	255
Operand sublists	NA	NA	NA	X	X	X
Number of						
SETA, SETC	NA	NA	16	X	X	X
SETB	NA	NA	128	X	X	X

524

Feature*	Model 20 Basic Assembler	BPS: Basic Assembler	BPS 8K Tape, BOS 8K Disk Assemblers	BOS 16K Disk/Tape Assembler	TOS, DOS Assembler	OS Assembler
DC duplication factor of zero	Except Y	NA	Except S	X	X	X
DC length modifier	Except H, Y	Except H, E, D	X	X	X	X
DS types	Only H, C	Only C, H, F, D	X	X	X	X
DS length modifier	Only C	Only C	X	X	X	X
DS maximum length modifier	256	256	256	65,535	65,535	65,535
DS constant subfield permitted	NA	NA	X	X	X	X
COPY	NA	NA	NA	X	X	X
CSECT	NA	NA	X	X	X	X
DSECT	NA	NA	X	X	X	X
ISEQ	NA	NA	X	X	X	X
LTORG	NA	NA	X	X	X	X
PRINT	NA	NA	X	X	X	X
TITLE	NA	NA	X	X	X	X
COM	NA	NA	NA	X	X	X
ICTL	NA	1 operand (1 or 25 only)	X	X	X	X
USING	2 operands (operand 1 relocatable only)	2 operands (operand 1 relocatable only)	6 operands	X	X	X
DROP	1 operand only	1 operand only	5 operands	X	X	X
CCW	NA	operand 2 (relocatable only)	X	X	X	X
ORG	No blank operand	No blank operand	X	X	X	X
ENTRY	1 operand only	1 operand only	1 operand only	X	X	X
EXTRN	1 operand only	1 operand only (max 14)	1 operand only	X	X	X
WXTRN	NA	NA	NA	NA	X	X
CNOP	NA	2 decimal digits	2 decimal digits	X	X	X
PUNCH	NA	NA	X	X	X	X
REPRO	NA	NA	X	X	X	X
Input/output declaratives	NA	DTF	DTF	DTF	DTF	DCB

*Features not shown are common to all assemblers except for macros.

NA = not allowed

X = as defined in Operating System Assembler Language Manual

Type	Implied length (bytes)	Alignment	Length Modifier range	Specified by	Constants per operand	Range for exponents	Range for scale	Truncation/padding side
C	As needed	Byte	1 to 256*	Characters	One			Right
X	As needed	Byte	1 to 256*	Hexadecimal digits	One			Left
B	As needed	Byte	1 to 256	Binary digits	One			Left
F	4	Word	1 to 8	Decimal digits	Multiple	−85 to +75	−187 to +346	Left
H	2	Half word	1 to 8	Decimal digits	Multiple	−85 to +75	−187 to +346	Left
E	4	Word	1 to 8	Decimal digits	Multiple	−85 to +75	0 to 14	Right
D	8	Double word	1 to 8	Decimal digits	Multiple	−85 to +75	0 to 14	Right
P	As needed	Byte	1 to 16	Decimal digits	Multiple			Left
Z	As needed	Byte	1 to 16	Decimal digits	Multiple			Left
A	4	Word	1 to 4	An absolute expression	Multiple			Left
			3 or 4	A relocatable or complex relocatable expression				
V	4	Word	3 or 4	A relocatable symbol	Multiple			Left
S	2	Half word	2 only	One absolute or relocatable expression or two absolute expressions: exp (exp)	Multiple			
Y	2	Half	1 or 2	An absolute expression	Multiple			Left
			2 only	A relocatable or complex relocatable expression				

*In a DS assembler instruction, C and X type constants may have length specification to 65535.

526

Appendix C

This appendix contains a table of the mnemonic operation codes for all commands that can be represented in assembly language, including extended mnemonic operation codes. It is in alphabetic order by the leftmost word of the command name. Indicated for each are both the mnemonic and machine operation codes, explicit and implicit operand formats, program interrupt possible, and condition code set.

The column headings in this appendix and the information each column provides follow.

Command: This column contains the name of the command associated with the mnemonic operation code.

Mnemonic operation code: This column gives the mnemonic operation code for the machine command. .This is written in the operation field when coding the instruction.

Machine operation code: This column contains the hexadecimal equivalent of the actual machine operation code. The operation code will appear in this form in most storage dumps and when displayed on the console control panel. For extended mnemonics, this column also contains the mnemonic code of the command from which the extended mnemonic is derived.

Operand format: This column shows the symbolic format of the operand field in both explicit and implicit form. For both forms, R1, R2, and R3 indicate general registers in operands one, two, and three, respectively. X2 indicates a general register used as an index register in the second operand. Commands which require an index register (X2) but are not to be indexed are shown with a 0 replacing X2. L, L1, and L2 indicate lengths for either operand, operand one, and operand two, respectively.

For the explicit format, D1 and D2 indicate a displacement and B1 and B2 indicate a base register for operands one and two.

For the implicit format, D1, B1 and D2, B2 are replaced by S1 and S2 which indicate a storage address in operands one and two.

Type of command: This column gives the basic machine format of the command (RR, RX, S1, or SS). If a command is included in a special feature or is an extended mnemonic, this is also indicated. The command sets are: the standard set (no designation), packed decimal (designated by Decimal), the floating point (Floating Pt.), the virtual storage address translation (VS), the extended-precision floating point (Ex.F.P.), and the timer and clock-comparator (CK). The commands for the latter three sets are grouped at the end of the listing, since they are much less commonly found than the other commands. The commercial command set consists of the standard and the packed-decimal sets. The scientific command set consists of the standard and the floating-point sets. The universal command set consists of the standard, the packed-decimal, and the floating-point set.

Program interruption possible: This column indicates the possible program interruptions for this instruction. The abbreviations used are: A—Addressing, S—Specification, Ov—Overflow, P—Protection, Op—Operation (if feature is not installed), and Other—other interruptions which are listed. The type of overflow is indicated by: D—Decimal, E—Exponent, or F—Floating Point.

Condition code set: The condition codes set as a result of this command are indicated in this column, as indicated on the next page.

Program interruption possible

Under Ov:	D	Decimal
	E	Exponent
	F	Fixed point
Under Other:	A	Privileged operation
	B	Exponent underflow
	C	Significance
	D	Decimal divide
	E	Floating-point divide
	F	Fixed-point divide
	G	Execute
Condition code set:	H	No carry
	I	Carry
	J	Result $= 0$
	K	Result is not equal to zero
	L	Result is less than zero
	M	Result is greater than zero
	N	Not changed
	O	Overflow
	P	Result exponent underflows
	Q	Result exponent overflows
	R	Result fraction $= 0$
	S	Result field equals zero
	T	Result field is less than zero
	U	Result field is greater than zero
	V	Difference $= 0$
	W	Difference is not equal to zero
	X	Difference is less than zero
	Y	Difference is greater than zero
	Z	First operand equals second operand
	AA	First operand is less than second operand
	BB	First operand is greater than second operand
	CC	CSW stored
	DD	Channel and subchannel not working
	EE	Channel or subchannel busy
	FF	Channel operating in burst mode
	GG	Burst operation terminated
	HH	Channel not operational
	II	Interruption pending in channel
	JJ	Channel available
	KK	Not operational
	LL	Available
	MM	I/O operation initiated and channel proceeding with its execution
	NN	Nonzero function byte found before the first operand field is exhausted
	OO	Last function byte is nonzero
	PP	All function bytes are zero
	QQ	Set according to the new PSW loaded
	RR	Set according to bits 2 and 3 of the register specified by R1
	SS	Leftmost bit of byte specified $= 0$
	TT	Leftmost bit of byte specified $= 1$
	UU	Selected bits are all zeros; mask is all zeros
	VV	Selected bits are mixed (zeros and ones)
	WW	Selected bits are all ones
	XX	Lengths are both zero
	YY	Destructive overlap

Command	Mnemonic operation code	Machine operation code	Operand format Explicit	Operand format Implicit
Add	A	5A	R1,D2(X2,B2) or R1,D2(,B2)	R1,S2(X2) or R1,S2
Add Halfword	AH	4A	R1,D2(X2,B2) or R1,D2(,B2)	R1,S2(X2) or R1,S2
Add Logical	AL	5E	R1,D2(X2,B2) or R1,D2(,B2)	R1,S2(X2) or R1,S2
Add Logical Register	ALR	1E	R1,R2	
Add Normalized, Long	AD	6A	R1,D2(X2,B2) or R1,D2(,B2)	R1,S2(X2) or R1,S2
Add Normalized, Long	ADR	2A	R1,R2	
Add Normalized, Short	AE	7A	R1,D2(X2,B2) or R1,D2(,B2)	R1,S2(X2) or R1,S2
Add Normalized, Short	AER	3A	R1,R2	
Add Packed	AP	FA	D1(L1,B1),D2(L2,B2)	S1(L1),S2(L2) or S1,S2
Add Register	AR	1A	R1,R2	
Add Unnormalized, Long	AW	6E	R1,D2(X2,B2) or R1,D2(,B2)	R1,S2(X2) or R1,S2
Add Unnormalized, Long	AWR	2E	R1,R2	
Add Unnormalized, Short	AU	7E	R1,D2(X2,B2) or R1,D2(,B2)	R1,S2(X2) or R1,S2
Add Unnormalized, Short	AUR	3E	R1,R2	
And Logical	N	54	R1,D2(X2,B2) or R1,D2(,B2)	R1,S2(X2) or R1,S2
And Logical Characters	NC	D4	D1(L,B1),D2(B2)	S1(L),S2 or S1,S2
And Logical Immediate	NI	94	D1(B1),I2	S1,I2
And Logical Register	NR	14	R1,R2	
Branch and Link	BAL	45	R1,D2(X2,B2) or R1,D2(,B2)	R1,S2(X2) or R1,S2
Branch and Link Register	BALR	05	R1,R2	
Branch if Mixed	BM	47 (BC 4)	D2(X2,B2) or D2(,B2)	S2(X2) or S2
Branch if Ones	BO	47 (BC 1)	D2(X2,B2) or D2(,B2)	S2(X2) or S2
Branch if Zeros	BZ	47 (BC 8)	D2(X2,B2) or D2(,B2)	S2(X2) or S2
Branch on Condition	BC	47	R1,D2(X2,B2) or R1,D2(,B2)	R1,S2(X2) or R1,S2
Branch on Condition Register	BCR	07	R1,R2	
Branch on Count	BCT	46	R1,D2(X2,B2) or R1,D2(,B2)	R1,S2(X2) or R1,S2
Branch on Count Register	BCTR	06	R1,R2	
Branch on Equal	BE	47 (BC 8)	D2(X2,B2) or D2(,B2)	S2(X2) or S2
Branch on High	BH	47 (BC 2)	D2(X2,B2) or D2(,B2)	S2(X2) or S2
Branch on Index High	BXH	86	R1,R2,D3(B3)	R1,R2,S3
Branch on Index Low or Equal	BXLE	87	R1,R2,D3(B3)	R1,R2,S3
Branch on Low	BL	47 (BC 4)	D2(X2,B2) or D2(,B2)	S2(X2) or S2
Branch on Minus	BM	47 (BC 4)	D2(X2,B2) or D2(,B2)	S2(X2) or S2
Branch on Not Equal	BNE	47 (BC 7)	D2(X2,B2) or D2(,B2)	S2(X2) or S2
Branch on Not High	BNH	47 (BC 13)	D2(X2,B2) or D2(,B2)	S2(X2) or S2
Branch on Not Low	BNL	47 (BC 11)	D2(X2,B2) or D2(,B2)	S2(X2) or S2
Branch on Not Minus	BNM	47 (BC 11)	D2(X2,B2) or D2(,B2)	S2(X2) or S2
Branch on Not Ones	BNO	47 (BC 14)	D2(X2,B2) or D2(,B2)	S2(X2) or S2
Branch on Not Plus	BNP	47 (BC 13)	D2(X2,B2) or D2(,B2)	S2(X2) or S2
Branch on Not Zeros	BNZ	47 (BC 7)	D2(X2,B2) or D2(,B2)	S2(X2) or S2
Branch on Overflow	BO	47 (BC 1)	D2(X2,B2) or D2(,B2)	S2(X2) or S2
Branch on Plus	BP	47 (BC 2)	D2(X2,B2) or D2(,B2)	S2(X2) or S2
Branch on Zero	BZ	47 (BC 8)	D2(X2,B2) or D2(,B2)	S2(X2) or S2
Branch Register Unconditional	BR	07 (BCR 15)	R2	
Branch Unconditional	B	47 (BC 15)	D2(X2,B2) or D2(,B2)	S2(X2) or S2
Compare Algebraic	C	59	R1,D2(X2,B2) or R1,D2(,B2)	R1,S2(X2) or R1,S2
Compare Algebraic Register	CR	19	R1,R2	
Compare Halfword	CH	49	R1,D2(X2,B2) or R1,D2(,B2)	R1,S2(X2) or R1,S2
Compare Logical	CL	55	R1,D2(X2,B2) or R1,D2(,B2)	R1,S2(X2) or R1,S2
Compare Logical Characters	CLC	D5	D1(L,B1),D2(B2)	S1(L),S2 or S1,S2
Compare Logical Characters Long	CLCL	0F	R1,R2	R1,R2
Compare Logical Immediate	CLI	95	D1(B1),I2	S1,I2
Compare Logical Masked	CLM	BD	R1,I2,D3(B3)	R1,I2,S3
Compare Logical Register	CLR	15	R1,R2	
Compare, Long	CD	69	R1,D2(X2,B2) or R1,D2(,B2)	R1,S2(X2) or R1,S2
Compare, Long Register	CDR	29	R1,R2	

Command	Type of command	A	S	Ov	P	Op	Other	00	01	10	11
								Program Interruption possible / Condition code set			
Add	RX	x	x	F				Sum = 0	Sum < 0	Sum > 0	Overflow
Add Halfword	RX	x	x	F				Sum = 0	Sum < 0	Sum > 0	Overflow
Add Logical	RX	x	x					Sum = 0 (H)	Sum = 0 (H)	Sum = 0 (I)	Sum = 0 (I)
Add Logical Register	RR							Sum = 0 (H)	Sum = 0 (H)	Sum = 0 (I)	Sum = 0 (I)
Add Normalized, Long	RX, Floating Pt.	x	x	E		x	B, C	R	L	M	
Add Normalized, Long	RR, Floating Pt.		x	E		x	B, C	R	L	M	
Add Normalized, Short	RX, Floating Pt.	x	x	E		x	B, C	R	L	M	
Add Normalized, Short	RR, Floating Pt.		x	E		x	B, C	R	L	M	
Add Packed	SS, Decimal	x		D	x	x	Data	Sum = 0	Sum < 0	Sum > 0	Overflow
Add Register	RR			F				Sum = 0	Sum < 0	Sum > 0	Overflow
Add Unnormalized, Long	RX, Floating Pt.	x	x	E		x	C	R	L	M	
Add Unnormalized, Long	RR, Floating Pt.		x	E		x	C	R	L	M	
Add Unnormalized, Short	RX, Floating Pt.	x	x	E		x	C	R	L	M	
Add Unnormalized, Short	RR, Floating Pt.		x	E		x	C	R	L	M	
Add Logical	RX	x	x					J	K		
And Logical Characters	SS	x			x			J	K		
And Logical Immediate	SI	x			x			J	K		
And Logical Register	RR							J	K		
Branch and Link	RX							N	N	N	N
Branch and Link Register	RR							N	N	N	N
Branch if Mixed	RX, Ext. Mnemonic							N	N	N	N
Branch if Ones	RX, Ext. Mnemonic							N	N	N	N
Branch if Zeros	RX, Ext. Mnemonic							N	N	N	N
Branch on Condition	RX							N	N	N	N
Branch on Condition Register	RR							N	N	N	N
Branch on Count	RX							N	N	N	N
Branch on Count Register	RR							N	N	N	N
Branch on Equal	RX, Ext. Mnemonic							N	N	N	N
Branch on High	RX, Ext. Mnemonic							N	N	N	N
Branch on Index High	RX, Ext. Mnemonic							N	N	N	N
Branch on Index Low or Equal	RX, Ext. Mnemonic							N	N	N	N
Branch on Low	RX, Ext. Mnemonic							N	N	N	N
Branch on Minus	RX, Ext. Mnemonic							N	N	N	N
Branch on Not Equal	RX, Ext. Mnemonic							N	N	N	N
Branch on Not High	RX, Ext. Mnemonic							N	N	N	N
Branch on Not Low	RX, Ext. Mnemonic							N	N	N	N
Branch on Not Minus	RX, Ext. Mnemonic							N	N	N	N
Branch on Not Ones	RX, Ext. Mnemonic							N	N	N	N
Branch on Not Plus	RX, Ext. Mnemonic							N	N	N	N
Branch on Not Zeros	RX, Ext. Mnemonic							N	N	N	N
Branch on Overflow	RX, Ext. Mnemonic							N	N	N	N
Branch on Plus	RX, Ext. Mnemonic							N	N	N	N
Branch on Zero	RX, Ext. Mnemonic							N	N	N	N
Branch Register Unconditional	RR, Ext. Mnemonic							N	N	N	N
Branch Unconditional	RX, Ext. Mnemonic							N	N	N	N
Compare Algebraic	RX	x	x					Z	AA	BB	
Compare Algebraic Register	RR							Z	AA	BB	
Compare Halfword	RX	x	x					Z	AA	BB	
Compare Logical	RX	x	x					Z	AA	BB	
Compare Logical Characters	RX	x	x					Z	AA	BB	
Compare Logical Characters Long	RR	x	x		x	x		Z, UU	AA	BB	
Compare Logical Immediate	SI	x						Z	AA	BB	
Compare Logical Masked	RS	S			S	S		Z, XX	AA	BB	
Compare Logical Register	SS							Z	AA	BB	
Compare, Long	RX, Floating Pt.	x	x			x		Z	AA	BB	
Compare, Long Register	RR, Floating Pt.	x	x			x		Z	AA	BB	

Command	Mnemonic operation code	Machine operation code	Operand format	
			Explicit	Implicit
Compare Packed	CP	F9	D1(L1,B1),D2(L2,B2)	S1(L1),S2(L2) or S1,S2
Compare, Short	CE	79	R1,D2(X2,B2) or R1,D2(,B2)	R1,S2(X2) or R1,S2
Compare, Short Register	CER	39	R1,R2	
Convert to Binary	CVB	4F	R1,D2(X2,B2) or R1,D2(,B2)	R1,S2(X2) or R1,S2
Convert to Decimal	CVD	4E	R1,D2(X2,B2) or R1,D2(,B2)	R1,S2(X2) or R1,S2
Divide	D	5D	R1,D2(X2,B2) or R1,D2(,B2)	R1,S2(X2) or R1,S2
Divide, Long	DD	6D	R1,D2(X2,B2) or R1,D2(,B2)	R1,S2(X2) or R1,S2
Divide, Long Register	DDR	2D	R1,R2	
Divide Packed	DP	FD	D1(,L1,B1),D2(L2,B2)	S1(L1),S2(L2) or S1,S2
Divide Register	DR	1D	R1,R2	
Divide, Short	DE	7D	R1,D2(X2,B2) or R1,D2(,B2)	R1,S2(X2) or R1,S2
Divide, Short Register	DER	3D	R1,R2	
Edit	ED	DE	D1(L,B1),D2(B2)	S1(L),S2 or S1,S2
Edit and Mark	EDMK	DF	D1(L,B1),D2(B2)	S1(L),S2 or S1,S2
Exclusive Or	X	57	R1,D2(X2,B2) or R1,D2(,B2)	R1,S2(X2) or R1,S2
Exclusive Or Characters	XC	D7	D1(L,B1),D2(B2)	S1(L),S2 or S1,S2
Exclusive Or Immediate	XI	97	D1(B1),I2	S1,I2
Exclusive Or Register	XR	17	R1,R2	
Execute	EX	44	R1,D2(X2,B2) or R1,D2(,B2)	R1,S2(X2) or R1,S2
Halve, Long	HDR	24	R1,R2	
Halve, Short	HER	34	R1,R2	
Halt Device	HDV	9E01	D1(B1)	S1
Halt I/O	HIO	9E	D1(B1)	
Insert Character	IC	43	R1,D2(X2,B2) or R1,D2(,B2)	R1,S2(X2) or R1,S2
Insert Characters Masked	ICM	BF	R1,I2,D3(B3)	R1,I2,S3
Insert Storage Key	ISK	09	R1,R2	
Load	L	58	R1,D2(X2,B2) or R1,D2(,B2)	R1,S2(X2) or R1,S2
Load Address	LA	41	R1,D2(X2,B2) or R1,D2(,B2)	R1,S2(X2) or R1,S2
Load Control Registers	LCTL	B7	R1,R2,D3(B3)	R1,R2,S3
Load and Test	LTR	12	R1,R2	
Load and Test, Long	LTDR	22	R1,R2	
Load and Test, Short	LTER	32	R1,R2	
Load Complement, Long	LCDR	23	R1,R2	
Load Complement Register	LCR	13	R1,R2	
Load Complement, Short	LCER	33	R1,R2	
Load Halfword	LH	48	R1,D2(X2,B2) or R1,D2(,B2)	R1,S2(X2) or R1,S2
Load, Long	LD	68	R1,D2(X2,B2) or R1,D2(,B2)	R1,S2(X2) or R1,S2
Load, Long Register	LDR	28	R1,R2	
Load Multiple	LM	98	R1,R2,D3(B3)	R1,R2,S3
Load Negative, Long	LNDR	21	R1,R2	
Load Negative Register	LNR	11	R1,R2	
Load Negative, Short	LNER	31	R1,R2	
Load Positive, Long	LPDR	20	R1,R2	
Load Positive Register	LPR	10	R1,R2	
Load Positive, Short	LPER	30	R1,R2	
Load PSW	LPSW	82	D1(B1)	
Load Register	LR	18	R1,R2	
Load, Short	LE	78	R1,D2(X2,B2) or R1,D2(,B2)	R1,S2(X2) or R1,S2
Load, Short Register	LER	38	R1,R2	
Move Characters	MVC	D2	D1(L,B1),D2(B2)	S1(L),S2 or S1,S2
Move Characters Long	MVCL	0E	R1,R2	R1,R2
Move Immediate	MVI	92	D1(B1),I2	S1,I2
Move Numerics	MVN	D1	D1(L,B1),D2(B2)	S1(L),S2 or S1,S2
Move with Offset	MVO	F1	D1(L1,B1),D2(L2,B2)	S1(L1),S2(L2) or S1,S2
Move Zones	MVZ	D3	D1(L,B1),D2(B2)	S1(L),S2 or S1,S2
Multiply	M	5C	R1,D2(X2,B2) or R1,D2(,B2)	R1,S2(X2) or R1,S2

532

Command	Type of command	A	S	Ov	P	Op	Other	00	01	10	11
Compare Packed	SS, Decimal	x				x	Data	Z	AA	BB	
Compare, Short	RX, Floating Pt.	x	x			x		Z	AA	BB	
Compare, Short Register	RR, Floating Pt.		x			x		Z	AA	BB	
Convert to Binary	RX	x	x				Data, F	N	N	N	N
Convert to Decimal	RX	x	x		x			N	N	N	N
Divide	RX	x	x				F	N	N	N	N
Divide, Long	RX, Floating Pt.	x	x	E		x	B, E	N	N	N	N
Divide, Long Register	RR, Floating Pt.		x	E		x	B, E	N	N	N	N
Divide Packed	SS, Decimal	x	x		x	x	D, Data	N	N	N	N
Divide Register	RR		x				F	N	N	N	N
Divide, Short	RX, Floating Pt.	x	x	E		x	B, E	N	N	N	N
Divide, Short Register	RR, Floating Pt.		x	E		x	B, E	N	N	N	N
Edit	SS, Decimal	x			x	x	Data	S	T	U	
Edit and Mark	SS, Decimal	x			x	x	Data	S	T	U	
Exclusive Or	RX	x	x					J	K		
Exclusive Or Characters	SS	x			x			J	K		
Exclusive Or Immediate	SI	x			x			J	K		
Exclusive Or Register	RR							J	K		
Execute	RX	x	x				G	(May be set by this instruction)			
Halve, Long	RR, Floating Pt.		x			x		N	N	N	N
Halve, Short	RR, Floating Pt.		x			x		N	N	N	N
Halt Device	SI						A	DD	CC	GG	KK
Halt I/O	SI						A	DD	CC	GG	KK
Insert Character	RX	x						N	N	N	N
Insert Characters Masked	RS	x			x	x		UU	TT	SS	
Insert Storage Key	RR	x	x			x	A	N	N	N	N
Load	RX	x	x					N	N	N	N
Load Address	RX							N	N	N	N
Load Control Registers	RS	x	x		x	x	A	N	N	N	N
Load and Test	RR							J	L	M	
Load and Test, Long	RR, Floating Pt.		x			x		R	L	M	
Load and Test, Short	RR, Floating Pt.		x			x		R	L	M	
Load Complement, Long	RR, Floating Pt.		x			x		R	L	M	
Load Complement Register	RR			F				P	L	M	O
Load Complement, Short	RR, Floating Pt.		x			x		R	L	M	
Load Halfword	RX	x	x					N	N	N	N
Load, Long	RX, Floating Pt.	x	x			x		N	N	N	N
Load, Long Register	RR, Floating Pt.		x			x		N	N	N	N
Load Multiple	RS	x	x					N	N	N	N
Load Negative, Long	RR, Floating Pt.		x			x		R	L		
Load Negative Register	RR							J	L		
Load Negative, Short	RR, Floating Pt.		x			x		R	L		
Load Positive, Long	RR, Floating Pt.		x			x		R	L	M	
Load Positive Register	RR			F				J		M	O
Load Positive, Short	RR, Floating Pt.		x			x		R	L	M	
Load PSW	SI	x	x				A	QQ	QQ	QQ	QQ
Load Register	RR							N	N	N	N
Load, Short	RX, Floating Pt.	x	x			x		N	N	N	N
Load, Short Register	RR, Floating Pt.		x			x		N	N	N	N
Move Characters	SS	x			x			N	N	N	N
Move Characters Long	RR	x	x		x	x		J	L	M	YY
Move Immediate	SI	x			x			N	N	N	N
Move Numerics	SS	x			x			N	N	N	N
Move with Offset	SS	x			x			N	N	N	N
Move Zones	SS	x			x			N	N	N	N
Multiply	RX	x	x					N	N	N	N

Command	Mnemonic operation code	Machine operation code	Operand format Explicit	Implicit
Multiply Halfword	MH	4C	R1,D2(X2,B2) or R1,D2(,B2)	R1,S2(X2) or R1,S2
Multiply, Long	MD	6C	R1,D2(X2,B2) or R1,D2(,B2)	R1,S2(X2) or R1,S2
Multiply, Long Register	MDR	2C	R1,R2	
Multiply Packed	MP	FC	D1(L1,B1),D2(L2,B2)	S1(L1),S2(L2) or S1,S2
Multiply Register	MR	1C	R1,R2	
Multiply, Short	ME	7C	R1,D2(X2,B2) or R1,D2(,B2)	R1,S2(X2) or R1,S2
Multiply, Short Register	MER	3C	R1,R2	
No Operation	NOP	47 (BC 0)	D2(X2,B2) or D2(,B2)	S2(X2) or S2
No Operation Register	NOPR	07 (BCR 0)	R2	
Or Logical	O	56	R1,D2(X2,B2) or R1,D2(,B2)	R1,S2(X2) or R1,S2
Or Logical Character	OC	D6	D1(L,B1),D2(B2)	S1(L),S2 or S1,S2
Or Logical Immediate	OI	96	D1(B1),I2	S1,I2
Or Logical Register	OR	16	R1,R2	
Pack	PACK	F2	D1(L1,B1),D2(L2,B2)	S1(L1),S2(L2) or S1,S2
Read Direct	RDD	85	D1(B1),I2	S1,I2
Set Clock	SCK	B204	D1(B1)	S1
Set Storage Mask	SPM	04	R1	
Set Storage Key	SSK	08	R1,R2	
Set System Mask	SSM	80	D1(B1)	S1
Shift and Round Packed	SRP	FD	D1(L,B1),D2(B2),I3	S1(L),S2,I3 or S1,S2,I3
Shift Left Double Algebraic	SLDA	8F	R1,D2(B2)	R1,S2
Shift Left Double Logical	SLDL	8D	R1,D2(B2)	R1,S2
Shift Left Single Algebraic	SLA	8B	R1,D2(B2)	R1,S2
Shift Left Single Logical	SLL	89	R1,D2(B2)	R1,S2
Shift Right Double Algebraic	SRDA	8E	R1,D2(B2)	R1,S2
Shift Right Double Logical	SRDL	8C	R1,D2(B2)	R1,S2
Shift Right Single Algebraic	SRA	8A	R1,D2(B2)	R1,S2
Shift Right Single Logical	SRL	88	R1,D2(B2)	R1,S2
Start I/O	SIO	9C	D1(B1)	S1
Start I/O Fast Release	SIOF	9C01	D1(B1)	S1
Store	ST	50	R1,D2(X2,B2) or R1,D2(,B2)	R1,S2(X2) or R1,S2
Store Channel ID	STIDC	B203	D1(B1)	S1
Store Character	STC	42	R1,D2(X2,B2) or R1,D2(,B2)	R1,D2(X2) or R1,S2
Store Characters Masked	STCM	BE	R1,I2,D3(B3)	R1,I2,S3
Store Clock	STCK	B205	D1(B1)	S1
Store Control Registers	STCTL	B6	R1,R2,D3(B3)	R1,R2,S3
Store CPU ID	STIDP	B202	D1(B1)	S1
Store Halfword	STH	40	R1,D2(X2,B2) or R1,D2(,B2)	R1,S2(X2) or R1,S2
Store Long	STD	60	R1,D2(X2,B2)	R1,S2(X2) or R1,S2
Store Multiple	STM	90	R1,R2,D2(B2)	R1,R2,S2
Store Short	STE	70	R1,D2(X2,B2) or R1,D2(,B2)	R1,S2(X2) or R1,S2
Subtract	S	5B	R1,D2(X2)	R1,S2(X2) or R1,S2
Subtract Halfword	SH	4B	R1,D2(X2,B2) or R1,D2(,B2)	R1,S2(X2) or R1,S2
Subtract Logical	SL	5F	R1,D2(X2,B2) or R1,D2(,B2)	R1,S2(X2) or R1,S2
Subtract Logical Register	SLR	1F	R1,R2	
Subtract Normalized, Long	SD	6B	R1,D2(X2,B2) or R1,D2(,B2)	R1,S2(X2) or R1,S2
Subtract Normalized, Long Register	SDR	2B	R1,R2	
Subtract Normalized, Short	SE	7B	R1,D2(X2,B2) or R1,D2(,B2)	R1,S2(X2) or R1,S2
Subtract Normalized, Short Register	SER	3B	R1,R2	
Subtract Packed	SP	FB	D1(L1,B1),D2(L2,B2)	S1(L1),S2(L2) or S1,S2
Subtract Register	SR	1B	R1,R2	
Subtract Unnormalized, Long	SW	6F	R1,D2(X2,B2) or R1,D2(,B2)	R1,S2(X2) or R1,S2
Subtract Unnormalized, Long Register	SWR	2F	R1,R2	

Command	Type of command	A	S	Ov	P	Op	Other	00	01	10	11
		Program Interruption possible						Condition code set			
Multiply Halfword	RX	x	x					N	N	N	N
Multiply, Long	RX, Floating Pt.	x	x	E		x	B	N	N	N	N
Multiply, Long Register	RR, Floating Pt.		x	E		x	B	N	N	N	N
Multiply Packed	SS, Decimal	x	x		x	x	Data	N	N	N	N
Multiply Register	RR		x					N	N	N	N
Multiply, Short	RX, Floating Pt.	x	x	E		x	B	N	N	N	N
Multiply, Short Register	RR, Floating Pt.		x	E		x	B	N	N	N	N
No Operation	RX, Ext. Mnemonic							N	N	N	N
No Operation Register	RR, Ext. Mnemonic							N	N	N	N
Or Logical	RX	x	x					J	K		
Or Logical Character	SS	x			x			J	K		
Or Logical Immediate	SI	x			x			J	K		
Or Logical Register	RR							J	K		
Pack	SS	x			x			N	N	N	N
Read Direct	SI, Direct	x			x	x	A	N	N	N	N
Set Clock	SI	x	x		x	x	A	Set	Secure		KK
Set Program Mask	RR							RR	RR	RR	RR
Set Storage Key	RR	x	x			x	A	N	N	N	N
Set System Mask	SI	x					A	N	N	N	N
Shift and Round Packed	SS, Decimal	x		D	x	x	Data	S	T	U	O
Shift Left Double Algebraic	RS		x	F				J	L	M	O
Shift Left Double Logical	RS		x					N	N	N	N
Shift Left Single Algebraic	RS			F				J	L	M	O
Shift Left Single Logical	RS							N	N	N	N
Shift Right Double Algebraic	RS		x					J	L	M	
Shift Right Double Logical	RS		x					N	N	N	N
Shift Right Single Algebraic	RS							J	L	M	
Shift Right Single Logical	RS							N	N	N	N
Start I/O	SI						A	MM	CC	EE	KK
Start I/O Fast Release	SI						A	MM	CC	EE	KK
Store	RX	x	x		x			N	N	N	N
Store Channel ID	SI					x	A	Stored	CC	EE	HH
Store Character	RX	x			x			N	N	N	N
Store Characters Masked	RS	x			x	x		N	N	N	N
Store Clock	SI	x			x	x		Set	Not set	Error	KK
Store Control Registers	RS	x	x		x	x	A	N	N	N	N
Store CPU ID	SI	x	x		x	x	A	N	N	N	N
Store Halfword	RX	x	x		x			N	N	N	N
Store Long	RX, Floating Pt.	x	x		x	x		N	N	N	N
Store Multiple	RS	x	x		x			N	N	N	N
Store Short	RX, Floating Pt.	x	x		x	x		N	N	N	N
Subtract	RX	x	x	F				V	X	Y	O
Subtract Halfword	RX	x	x	F				V	X	Y	O
Subtract Logical	RX	x	x						W, H	V, I	W, I
Subtract Logical Register	RR								W, H	V, I	W, I
Subtract Normalized, Long	RX, Floating Pt.	x	x	E		x	B, C	R	L	M	
Subtract Normalized, Long Register	RR, Floating Pt.		x	E		x	B, C	R	L	M	
Subtract Normalized, Short	RX, Floating Pt.	x	x	E		x	B, C	R	L	M	
Subtract Normalized, Short Register	RR, Floating Pt.		x	E		x	B, C	R	L	M	
Subtract Packed	SS, Decimal	x		D	x	x	Data	V	X	Y	O
Subtract Register	RR			F				V	X	Y	O
Subtract Unnormalized, Long	RX, Floating Pt.	x	x	E		x	C	R	L	M	
Subtract Unnormalized, Long Register	RR, Floating Pt.		x	E		x	C	R	L	M	

Command	Mnemonic operation code	Machine operation code	Operand format	
			Explicit	Implicit
Subtract Unnormalized, Short	SU	7F	R1,D2(X2,B2) or R1,D2(,B2)	R1,S2(X2) or R1,S2
Subtract Unnormalized, Short Register	SUR	3F	R1,R2	
Supervisor Call	SVC	0A	I	
Test and Set	TS	93	D1(B1)	S1
Test Channel	TCH	9F	D1(B1)	S1
Test I/O	TIO	9D	D1(B1)	S1
Test Under Mask	TM	91	D1(B1),I2	S1,I2
Translate	TR	DC	D1(L,B1),D2(B2)	S1(L),S2 or S1,S2
Translate and Test	TRT	DD	D1(L,B1),D2(B2)	S1(L),S2 or S1,S2
Unpack	UNPK	F3	D1(L1,B1),D2(L2,B2)	S1(L1),S2(L2) or S1,S2
Write Direct	WRD	84	D1(B1),I2	S1,I2
Zero and Add Packed	ZAP	F8	D1(L1,B1),D2(L2,B2)	S1(L1),S2(L2) or S1,S2

Commands for Virtual Storage, Extended Floating Point, Clock and Timer, and Monitor

Command	Mnemonic operation code	Machine operation code	Operand format	
			Explicit	Implicit
Add Register Normalized Extended	AXR	36	R1,R2	
Load Real Address	LRA	B1	R1,D2(X2,B2) or R1,D2(,B2)	R1,S2(X2) or R1,S2
Load Register Long Rounded	LRDR	25	R1,R2	
Load Register Short Rounded	LRER	35	R1,R2	
Monitor Call	MC	AF	D1(B1),I2	S1,I2
Multiply Extended Register	MXR	26	R1,R2	
Multiply Long to Extended	MXD	67	R1,D2(X2,B2) or R1,D2(,B2)	R1,S2(X2) or R1,S2
Multiply Long to Extended Register	MXDR	27	R1,R2	
Purge Translation Lookaside Buffer	PTLB	B20D		
Reset Reference Bit	RRB	B213	D1(B1)	S1
Set Clock Comparator	SCKC	B206	D1(B1)	S1
Set CPU Timer	SPT	B208	D1(B1)	S1
Store Clock Comparator	STCKC	B207	D1(B1)	S1
Store CPU Timer	STPT	B209	D1(B1)	S1
Store Then AND System Mask	STNSM	AC	D1(B1),I2	S1,I2
Store Then OR System Mask	STOSM	AD	D1(B1),I2	S1,I2
Subtract Register Normalized Extended	SXR	37	R1,R2	

536

Command	Type of command	A	S	Ov	P	Op	Other	00	01	10	11
								Program Interruption possible → A S Ov P Op Other; Condition code set → 00 01 10 11			
Subtract Unnormalized, Short	RX, Floating Pt.	x	x	E		x	C	R	L	M	
Subtract Unnormalized, Short Register	RR, Floating Pt.		x	E		x	C	R	L	M	
Supervisor Call	RR							N	N	N	N
Test and Set	SI	x			x			SS	TT		
Test Channel	SI						A	JJ	II	FF	HH
Test I/O	SI						A	LL	CC	EE	KK
Test Under Mask	SI	x						UU	VV		WW
Translate	SS	x			x			N	N	N	N
Translate and Test	SS	x						PP	NN	OO	
Unpack	SS	x			x			N	N	N	N
Write Direct	SI, Direct	x			x	x	A	N	N	N	N
Zero and Add Packed	SS, Decimal	x		D	x	x	Data	J	L	M	O

Commands for Virtual Storage, Extended Floating Point, Clock and Timer, and Monitor

Command	Type of command	A	S	Ov	P	Op	Other	00	01	10	11
Add Register Normalized Extended	RR, Ex.F.P.		x	E		x	B,C	R	L	M	
Load Real Address	RX, VS	x				x	A	LL	Segment	Page	Length
Load Register Long Rounded	RR, Ex.F.P.		x	E		x		N	N	N	N
Load Register Short Rounded	RR, Ex.F.P.		x	E		x		N	N	N	N
Monitor Call	SI				x		Monitor	N	N	N	N
Multiply Extended Register	RR, Ex.F.P.		x	E		x	B	N	N	N	N
Multiply Long to Extended	RX, Ex.F.P.	x	x	E	x	x	B	N	N	N	N
Multiply Long to Extended Register	RR, Ex.F.P.		x	E		x	B	N	N	N	N
Purge Translation Lookaside Buffer	SI, VS					x	A	N	N	N	N
Reset Reference Bit	SI, VS	x				x	A	R=0,C=0	R=0,C=1	R=1,C=0	R=1,C=1
Set Clock Comparator	SI, CK	x	x			x	A	N	N	N	N
Set CPU Timer	SI, CK	x	x			x	A	N	N	N	N
Store Clock Comparator	SI, CK	x	x			x	A	N	N	N	N
Store CPU Timer	SI, CK	x	x			x	A	N	N	N	N
Store Then AND System Mask	SI, VS	x				x	A	N	N	N	N
Store Then OR System Mask	SI, VS	x				x	A	N	N	N	N
Subtract Register Normalized Extended	RR, Ex.F.P.		x	E		x	B,C	R	L	M	

The listings in the Type and Interrupt columns mean:

A	Addressing exception	IK	Fixed-point divide exception
C	Condition code is set	L	New condition code loaded
D	Data exception	LS	Significance exception
DF	Decimal-overflow exception	M	Privileged-operation exception
DK	Decimal-divide exception	P	Protection exception
E	Exponent-overflow exception	S	Specification exception
EX	Execute exception	T	Decimal command feature
F	Floating-point command feature	U	Exponent-underflow exception
FK	Floating-point divide exception	Y	Direct control command feature
IF	Fixed-point overflow exception	Z	Protection feature

Commands for which no feature is shown after the type are part of the standard command set feature.

Name	Mnemonic	Type	Interrupt		Code
Add Register	AR	RR C		IF	1A
Add	A	RX C	P,A,S,	IF	5A
Add Halfword	AH	RX C	P,A,S,	IF	4A
Add Logical Register	ALR	RR C			1E
Add Logical	AL	RX C	P,A,S,		5E
Add Normalized (Long)	ADR	RR F,C	S,U,E,LS		2A
Add Normalized (Long)	AD	RX F,C	P,A,S,U,E,LS		6A
Add Normalized (Short)	AER	RR F,C	S,U,E,LS		3A
Add Normalized (Short)	AE	RX F,C	P,A,S,U,E,LS		7A
Add Packed	AP	SS T,C	P,A, D, DF		FA
Add Unnormalized (Long)	AWR	RR F,C	S, E,LS		2E
Add Unnormalized (Long)	AW	RX F,C	P,A,S, E,LS		6E
Add Unnormalized (Short)	AUR	RR F,C	S, E,LS		3E

Name	Mnemonic	Type	Interrupt	Code
Divide (Long)	DD	RX F	P,A,S,U,E,FK	6D
Divide Packed	DP	SS T	P,A,S,D, DK	FD
Divide (Short)	DER	RR F	S,U,E,FK	3D
Divide (Short)	DE	RX F	P,A,S,U,E,FK	7D
Edit	ED	SS T,C	P,A, D	DE
Edit and Mark	EDMK	SS T,C	P,A, D	DF
Exclusive OR Register	XR	RR C		17
Exclusive OR	X	RX C	P,A,S	57
Exclusive OR Immediate	XI	SI C	P,A	97
Exclusive OR Character	XC	SS C	P,A	D7
Execute	EX	RX C	P,A,S, EX	44
Halt Device	HDV	SI C,M		9E-1
Halt I/O	HIO	SI C,M		9E-0
Halve (Long)	HDR	RR F	S	24
Halve (Short)	HER	RR F	S	34
Insert Character	IC	RX	P,A	43
Insert Characters Masked	ICM	RS C	P,A	BF

Name	Mnemonic	Format				Opcode
Add Unnormalized (Short)	AU	RX	F,C	P,A,S	E,LS	7E
AND Register	NR	RR	C			14
AND	N	RX	C	P,A,S		54
AND Immediate	NI	SI	C	P,A,		94
AND Character	NC	SS	C	P,A		D4
Branch and Link Register	BALR	RR				05
Branch and Link	BAL	RX				45
Branch on Condition Register	BCR	RR				07
Branch on Condition	BC	RX				47
Branch on Count Register	BCTR	RR				06
Branch on Count	BCT	RX				46
Branch on Index High	BXH	RS				86
Branch on Index Low or Equal	BXLE	RS				87
Compare Register	CR	RR	C			19
Compare	C	RX	C	P,A,S		59
Compare Halfword	CH	RX	C	P,A,S		49
Compare Logical Register	CLR	RR	C			15
Compare Logical	CL	RX	C	P,A,S		55
Compare Logical	CLI	SI	C	P,A		95
Compare Logical	CLC	SS	C	P,A		D5
Compare Logical Characters Long	CLCL	RR	C	P,A,S		0F
Compare Logical Masked	CLM	RS	C	P,A		BD
Compare (Long)	CDR	RR	F,C	S		29
Compare (Long)	CD	RX	F,C	P,A,S		69
Compare Packed	CP	SS	T,C	P,A, D		F9
Compare (Short)	CER	RR	F,C	S		39
Compare (Short)	CE	RX	F,C	P,A,S		79
Convert to Binary	CVB	RX		P,A,S,D	IK	4F
Convert to Decimal	CVD	RX		P,A,S	IK	4E
Diagnose		SI		M,P,A,S		83
Divide Register	DR	RR		S,	IK	1D
Divide	D	RX		P,A,S	IK	5D
Divide (Long)	DDR	RR	F		S,U,E,FK	2D

Name	Mnemonic	Format				Opcode
Insert Storage Key	ISK	RR	Z	M, A,S		09
Load Register	LR	RR		P,A,S		18
Load	L	RX				58
Load Address	LA	RX				41
Load and Test	LTR	RR	C			12
Load and Test (Long)	LTDR	RR	F,C	S		22
Load and Test (Short)	LTER	RR	F,C	S		32
Load Complement Register	LCR	RR	C		IF	13
Load Complement (Long)	LCDR	RR	F,C	S		23
Load Complement (Short)	LCER	RR	F,C	S		33
Load Control	LCTL	RS		M,P,A,S		B7
Load Halfword	LH	RX		P,A,S		48
Load (Long)	LDR	RR	F	S		28
Load (Long)	LD	RX	F	P,A,S		68
Load Multiple	LM	RS		P,A,S		98
Load Negative Register	LNR	RR	C			11
Load Negative (Long)	LNDR	RR	F,C	S		21
Load Negative (Short)	LNER	RR	F,C	S		31
Load Positive Register	LPR	RR	C		IF	10
Load Positive (Long)	LPDR	RR	F,C	S		20
Load Positive (Short)	LPER	RR	F,C	S		30
Load PSW	LPSW	SI		L,M,P,A,S		82
Load (Short)	LER	RR	F	S		38
Load (Short)	LE	RX	F	P,A,S		78
Monitor Call	MC	SI		S		AF
Move Immediate	MVI	SI		P,A		92
Move Character	MVC	SS		P,A		D2
Move Characters Long	MVCL	RR	C	P,A,S		0E
Move Numerics	MVN	SS		P,A		D1
Move with Offset	MVO	SS		P,A		F1
Move Zones	MVZ	SS		P,A		D3
Multiply Register	MR	RR		S		1C
Multiply	M	RX		P,A,S		5C

Name	Mnemonic	Type	Interrupt	Code
Store CPU ID	STIDP	SI	M,P,A,S	B202
Store Halfword	STH	RX	P,A,S	40
Store (Long)	STD	RX F	P,A,S	60
Store Multiple	STM	RS	P,A,S	90
Store (Short)	STE	RX F	P,A,S	70
Subtract Register	SR	RR C	IF	1B
Subtract	S	RX C	P,A,S, IF	5B
Subtract Halfword	SH	RX C	P,A,S, IF	4B
Subtract Logical Register	SLR	RR C		1F
Subtract Logical	SL	RX C	P,A,S	5F
Subtract Normalized (Long)	SDR	RR F,C	S,U,E,LS	2B
Subtract Normalized (Long)	SD	RX F,C	P,A,S,U,E,LS	6B
Subtract Normalized (Short)	SER	RR F,C	S,U,E,LS	3B
Subtract Normalized (Short)	SE	RX F,C	P,A,S,U,E,LS	7B
Subtract Packed	SP	SS T,C	P,A, D, DF	FB
Subtract Unnormalized (Long)	SWR	RR F,C	S, E,LS	2F
Subtract Unnormalized (Long)	SW	RX F,C	P,A,S, E,LS	6F
Subtract Unnormalized (Short)	SUR	RR F,C	S, E,LS	3F
Subtract Unnormalized (Short)	SU	RX F,C	P,A,S, E,LS	7F
Supervisor Call	SVC	RR		0A
Test and Set	TS	SI C	P,A	93
Test Channel	TCH	SI CM		9F
Test I/O	TIO	SI CM		9D
Test Under Mask	TM	SI C	P,A	91
Translate	TR	SS	P,A	DC
Translate and Test	TRT	SS C	P,A	DD
Unpack	UNPK	SS	P,A	F3
Write Direct	WRD	SI Y	M,P,A	84
Zero and Add Packed	ZAP	SS T,C	P,A, D, DF	F8

Name	Mnemonic	Type	Interrupt	Code
Multiply Halfword	MH	RX	P,A,S	4C
Multiply (Long)	MDR	RR F	S,U,E	2C
Multiply (Long)	MD	RX F	P,A,S,U,E	6C
Multiply Packed	MP	SS T	P,A,S,D	FC
Multiply (Short)	MER	RR F	S,U,E	3C
Multiply (Short)	ME	RX F	P,A,S,U,E	7C
OR Register	OR	RR C		16
OR	O	RX C	P,A,S	56
OR Immediate	OI	SI C	P,A	96
OR Character	OC	SS C	P,A	D6
Pack	PACK	SS	P,A	F2
Read Direct	RDD	SI Y	M,P,A	85
Set Clock	SCK	SI	C,M,P,A,S	B204
Set Program Mask	SPM	RR L		04
Set Storage Key	SSK	RR Z	M, A,S	08
Set System Mask	SSM	SI	M,P,A	80
Shift and Round Packed	SRP	SS T,C	P,A D,DF	F0
Shift Left Double	SLDA	RS C	S, IF	8F
Shift Left Double Logical	SLDL	RS	S	8D
Shift Left Single	SLA	RS C	IF	8B
Shift Left Single Logical	SLL	RS		89
Shift Right Double	SRDA	RS C	S	8E
Shift Right Double Logical	SRDL	RS		8C
Shift Right Single	SRA	RS C	S	8A
Shift Right Single Logical	SRL	RS		88
Start I/O	SIO	SI CM		9C
Start I/O Fast Release	SIOF	SI C,M		9C-1
Store	ST	RX	P,A,S	50
Store Channel ID	STIDC	SI C,M		B203
Store Character	STC	RX	P,A	42
Store Characters Masked	STCM	RS	P,A	BE
Store Clock	STCK	SI C	P,A	B205
Store Control Registers	STCTL	RS	M,P,A,S	B6

Appendix D

Omitted are statements that are rarely used or that apply to multiprogramed operation, and statements that may only be entered from the control console. Note: Operands separated by commas are written with no intervening spaces. Omitted operands must be signalled by retaining the comma. Brackets indicate optional operands; braces a choice of operands. "JCC" indicates a job control card.

Name	Operation	Operand	Remarks
/*	Ignored	Ignored	Columns 1 and 2 are the only columns checked
/&	Ignored	[Comments]	Columns 1 and 2 are the only columns checked. Comments are printed on SYSLOG and SYSLST at EOJ.
*		Comments	Column 2 must be blank
//	JOB	Job name [accounting information]	Job name: one to eight alphameric characters Accounting information: 1 to 16 characters
[//]	EXEC	[Program name]	Program name: one to eight alphameric characters. Used only if the program is in the core image library.
[//]	ASSGN	SYSxxx, address $\left[\begin{matrix} ,X'ss' \\ ,ALT \end{matrix}\right]$ [,TEMP]	SYSxxx: can be SYSRDR SYSIPT SYSIN—Invalid for SPI SYSPCH SYSLST SYSOUT SYSLOG SYSLNK SYSREC } Invalid for SPI SYSRLB SYSSLB SYSCLB—Only valid for JCC SYS000—SYSmax Address: can be X'cuu', UA, or IGN X'cuu' c = 0–6 uu = 00–FE (0–254) in hex UA: unassign IGN: unassign and ignore (invalid for SYSCLB, SYSRDR, SYSIPT, and SYSIN)

Name	Operation	Operand	Remarks
			X'ss': used for magnetic tape only.

ss	Bytes per in.	Parity	Translate feature	Convert feature
10	200	odd	off	on
20	200	even	off	off
28	200	even	on	off
30	200	odd	off	off
38	200	odd	on	off
50	556	odd	off	on
60	556	even	off	off
68	556	even	on	off
70	556	odd	off	off
78	556	odd	on	off
90	800	odd	off	on
A0	800	even	off	off
A8	800	even	on	off
B0	800	odd	off	off
B8	800	odd	on	off
C0	800	single density 9 track tape		
C0	1600	single density 9 track tape		
C0	1600	dual density 9 track tape		
C8	800	dual density 9 track tape		

ALT: specifies alternate unit (invalid for SYSCLB)
TEMP: only valid for JCC. Assignment for logical unit is destroyed by next JOB statement.

Name	Operation	Operand	Remarks
[//]	CLOSE	SYSxxx $\begin{bmatrix} \begin{Bmatrix} ,X'cuu'\ [,X'ss'] \\ ,UA \\ ,IGN \\ ,ALT \end{Bmatrix} \end{bmatrix}$	SYSxxx: for magnetic tape — for DASD (JCC only)— for magnetic tape: SYSPCH, SYSLST, SYSOUT, SYS000–SYSmax for DASD (JCC only): SYSIN, SYSRDR, SYSIPT, SYSPCH, SYSLST X'cuu', X'ss', UA, IGN, ALT: Values as described in ASSGN command
//	DATE	mm/dd/yy or dd/mm/yy	mm: Month (01–12) dd: day (01–31) yy: year (00–99)
[//]	DLBL	File name, ['file-ID'], [date], [codes], [data security] (See Note below under EXTENT)	File name: one to seven alphameric characters, the first of which must be alphabetic 'File-ID': 1 to 44 alphameric characters Date: one to six characters (yy/ddd) Codes: two or three alphabetic characters Data security: one to three characters
[//]	EXTENT	[symbolic unit], [serial number], [type], [sequence number], [relative track], [number of tracks], [split cylinder track], [B = bins] Note: If the DLBL and EXTENT statements for a private core image library are in the input stream (that is, the information is not contained on the label cylinder), they must precede the ASSGN SYSCLB command.	Symbolic unit: six alphameric characters Serial number: one to six alphameric characters Type: one numeric character Sequence number: one to three numeric characters Relative track: one to five numeric characters Number of tracks: one to five numeric characters Split cylinder track: one or two numeric characters Bins: one or two numeric characters

Name	Operation	Operand	Remarks
[//]	LBLTYP	$\begin{cases} \text{TAPE [(nn)]} \\ \text{NSD (nn)} \end{cases}$	TAPE: used when tape files requiring label information are to be processed and no nonsequential disk files are to be processed. (nn): optional and is present only for future expansion (It is ignored by Job Control) NSD: nonsequential disk files are to be processed (nn): largest number of extents per single file
[//]	LISTIO	$\begin{cases} \text{SYS} \\ \text{PROG} \\ \text{F1} \\ \text{F2} \\ \text{ALL} \\ \text{SYSxxx} \\ \text{UNITS} \\ \text{DOWN} \\ \text{UA} \\ \text{X'cuu'} \end{cases}$	Causes listing of I/O assignments on SYSLST for JCS and SYSLOG for JCC
[//]	MTC	$\text{Opcode,} \begin{cases} \text{SYSxxx} \\ \text{X'cuu'} \end{cases} \text{[,nn]}$	Opcode: BSF, BSR, ERG, FSF, FSR, REW, RUN, or WTM SYSxxx: any logical unit X'cuu': (only valid for JCC) c = 0–6 uu = FE(0–254) in hex nn: decimal number (01–99)
//	OPTION	Option 1 [, option 2, . . .]	Option: can be any of the following:

Option detail for OPTION:

LOG	Log control statements on SYSLST
NOLOG	Suppress LOG option
DUMP	Dump registers and main storage on SYSLST in the case of abnormal program end
NODUMP	Suppress DUMP option
LINK	Write output of language translator on SYSLNK for linkage editing
NOLINK	Suppress LINK option
DECK	Output object module on SYSPCH
NODECK	Suppress DECK option
LIST	Output listing of source module on SYSLST
NOLIST	Suppress LIST option
LISTX	Output listing of object module on SYSLST
NOLISTX	Suppress LISTX option
SYM	Punch symbol deck on SYSPCH
NOSYM	Suppress SYM option
XREF	Output symbolic cross-reference list on SYSLST
NOXREF	Suppress XREF option
ERRS	Output listing of all errors in source program on SYSLST
NOERRS	Suppress ERRS option
CATAL	Catalog program or phase in core image library after completion of Linkage Editor run
STDLABEL	Causes all DASD or tape labels to be written on the standard label track
USRLABEL	Causes all DASD or tape labels to be written on the user label track
PARSTD	Causes all DASD or tape labels to be written on the partition standard label track
48C	48-character set
60C	60-character set
SYSPARM = 'string'	specifies a value for assembler system variable symbol and SYSPARM

544

Name	Operation	Operand	Remarks
[//]	PAUSE	[Comments]	Causes pause immediately after processing this statement. PAUSE statement is always printed on 1052 (SYSLOG). If no 1052 is available, the statement is ignored.
[//]	RESET	$\begin{cases} \text{SYS} \\ \text{PROG} \\ \text{ALL} \\ \text{SYSxxx} \end{cases}$	Resets I/O device assignments
//	RSTRT	SYSxxx, nnnn [, filename]	SYSxxx: symbolic unit name of the device on which the check-point records are stored. Can be SYS000-SYSmax. nnnn: four character identification of the checkpoint record to be used for restarting File name: symbolic name of the DASD file to be used for restarting
[//]	TLBL	File name, ['file-ID'], [date], [file serial number], [volume sequence number], [file sequence number], [generation number], [version number] *Note*: For ASCII file processing the fourth and fifth operands are called set identifier and file section number, respectively.	File name: one to seven alphameric characters, the first of which must be alphabetic 'File-ID': 1 to 17 alphameric characters Date: one to six characters (yy/ddd or d-dddd) $\begin{cases} \text{[file serial number (EBCDIC): one to six alphameric characters]} \\ \text{[set identifier (ASCII): six alphameric characters]} \end{cases}$ $\begin{cases} \text{[volume sequence number (EBCDIC)]} \\ \text{[file section number (ASCII)]} \end{cases}$ one to four numeric characters File sequence number: one to four numeric characters Generation number: one to four numeric characters Version number: one to two numeric characters
//	UPSI	nnnnnnnn	n: 0, 1, or X

545

Appendix E

PROGRAMING WITH VIRTUAL STORAGE
AND OTHER ADVANCED FEATURES

VIRTUAL STORAGE

Some newer models of the computer provide virtual storage for the programer. When present, virtual storage affects programers in two ways. First, it places on the programer more of the burden of assuring that his assembly language program executes efficiently. Second, it adds to the range of jobs that are likely to be assigned to programers. To work with virtual storage, the programer needs to understand not only the hardware and the commands that call it into play, but also the operating system support and data-access methods available.

The computer executes only one instruction at a time in the CPU. Some of the operands may come from or go to the addresses in internal storage. As the programer sees it, such references to internal storage are to: (1) an input data field; (2) an output data field; (3) a working storage or intermediate result field; (4) a constant; or (5) an instruction other than the one currently being executed. Since the computer is a two-address machine (see pages 63 through 70), when it executes an instruction, it uses at most only two of these references. Often it uses none, or only one.

Consequently, most of the time during program execution, most of the contents of internal storage are idle and unused. The average number of bytes of internal storage referenced by an instruction being executed, except for MVC, MVCL, CLC, CLCL, and I-O instructions, is only about two bytes.

The idea behind virtual storage is to make use of this sparse and spotty storage reference: remove from internal storage all of the program and data that are not being actively referenced; leave in internal storage only what is being actively referenced; and provide an orderly way to change what is permitted to occupy space in internal storage, as the pattern of storage references changes during program execution ("paging"). The gain is that internal storage can then be better used, with the active parts of many programs occupying the space.

548

ADDRESS TRANSLATION

To implement virtual storage, the computer must be equipped with magnetic disks (or drums), with Dynamic Address Translation (DAT) hardware in the CPU, and with paging interrupts. Efficiency is enhanced if the CPU also has both a clock and an interval timer. Some models of the computer also have a Translation Look-aside Buffer (TLB) to speed the DAT operation. Briefly, the manner of operation is as shown in Fig. E-1.

External storage carries the entire program in virtual address sequence.

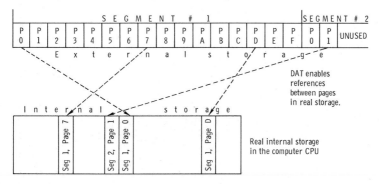

Internal real storage carries only selected active pages.

FIG. E-1. Summary of virtual storage.

The entire program as the programer wrote it, origined at zero and link-edited, is stored in external storage (usually on magnetic disks) in its proper sequence ready for execution. The program may be of any length, and the effective addresses within it, were an attempt made to execute the program as it is stored, may exceed the highest address available in the computer's (real) internal storage.

The entire program is arbitrarily marked off into segments, and each segment into pages. A program stored in external storage always occupies at least one segment. If all the pages possible within a segment are needed by a program, then one or more additional segments may be added for storing the program.

When a program is called for execution, the operating system copies (loads) the control entry-point page of the program from external storage into (real) internal storage and starts executing the program. As the program makes references to effective addresses on other pages, the operating system also loads those into real storage, if space is available for them. If no space is available, the operating system either copies back into external storage a currently inactive page of this or some other program, using the freed space to load the referenced page, or interrupts and holds pending in a queue the further execution of the program until space is available to load in the referenced page.

549

No requirement is made that the available real space in internal storage be contiguous. Rather, pages for a program may be loaded in any sequence at any position (that is itself a multiple of the page size) in real storage. This surpasses the usual relocatable loading requirements commonly used with the computer. Thus, an effective address calling for a storage reference high in storage may be to a page actually placed low in storage. To avoid such problems, the DAT hardware corrects the effective addresses to reflect the absolute (real) addresses of all pages in internal storage, wherever they may be. When DAT is turned off (via bit 5 in the PSW) to be inoperative, the usual effective addresses are not translated, but serve as real absolute addresses as described earlier.

To support virtual storage, DAT, and other functions, the computer has 16 control registers. These are identical in form and identification to the 16 general-purpose registers, but are committed to specific uses. Control register 0 is used for external interruption masks, and for clock and timer masks. Also for DAT, bits 8 and 9 of control register 0 designate the page size (01_b for 2K, and 10_b for 4K). Bits 11 and 12 of control register 0 designate the segment size (00 for 64K, and 10_b for 1M). Control register 1 is used for DAT. Bits 0 through 7 designate for checking purposes the length, in units of 16 entries (64 bytes), of the segment table. Bits 8 through 25 of control register 1 designate the address of the segment table. Control register 2 is used for channel masks. Control register 8 is used for monitor masks. Control registers 9, 10, and 11 are used for program event recording (PER) control. Control registers 14 and 15 are used for machine error functions. Control registers are only addressable through Load Control Registers and Store Control Registers commands.

DAT operates with the control registers and two operating-system-maintained tables, the segment table and the set of page tables. Even though these tables are usually in protected parts of internal storage, DAT references to them are permitted without causing a fetch interrupt. When DAT is turned on, each effective address passes through a translation process as the computer executes each instruction. For this purpose, the effective address is broken into three fields (as shown in Fig. E-2), segment index, page index, and byte index.

24-bit Effective Address in a word

Zeros	Segment Index	Page Index	Byte Index

Table of Field Bit Boundaries

Segment Size	Page Size	Segment Index	Page Index	Byte Index
64 K	2 K	8-15	16-20	21-31
64 K	4 K	8-15	16-19	20-31
1 M	2 K	8-11	12-20	21-31
1 M	4 K	8-11	12-19	20-31

Bit positions 0-7 are not used.

Segment Table Entry

A	B	C	D	E

Bits	Field
0- 3	A—Length
4- 7	B—Zeros
8-28	C—Address of Page Table
29-30	D—Zeros
31	E —Availability Bit for the Segment

Page Table Entry

A	B	C

Bits for Pages of Size

2K	4K	Field
0-12	0-11	A—Page Address
13	12	B—Page Availability bit
14-15	13-15	C—Zeros

FIG. E-2. Fields used by DAT in determining the real address.

550

Translation starts by using the control-register data to mark off the segment index in the effective address. The segment index is added to the address of the segment table to select an entry in the table. That entry gives the address of the page table (see Fig. E-2).

Translation continues by using the control-register data to mark off the page index in the effective address. Three zero bits are appended to the right end of the page-table address found in the prior step, and one zero bit to the right end of the page index from the effective address. The sum of these two numbers is then used as an address to select an entry from the page table. The 12 or 13 leftmost bits of the entry are then catenated on the left with the byte index on the right, to form the 24-bit real address.

That completes the address translation. But the computer also needs to determine whether or not the page sought is in real storage and available for use. For this purpose, the thirteenth or fourteenth bit in the page-table entry indicates whether (0) or not (1) the page is in real storage. And the rightmost bit in the segment-table entry indicates whether (0) or not (1) any pages from the segment are in real storage. If a segment-unavailable bit is encountered, a segment-translation interrupt (code 10_x) occurs that cannot be masked off. If a page-unavailable bit is encountered, a page-translation interrupt (code 11_x) occurs that cannot be masked off. A translation-specification interrupt (code 12_x) may occur if control-register or translation-table formats are not correct. Addressing interrupts (code 5) may occur for absolute addresses that exceed the real storage available.

To support virtual storage and DAT, the format of the PSW is different, as shown in Fig. E-3. The X bit (position 12) is 0 for the "360" or basic control (BC) mode. It is 1 for the extended control (EC) mode, which is required for virtual storage operation. Irrespective of the PSW mode, the commands that affect the program or system masks operate on the correct fields of the PSW.

The major differences between the two PSW formats are in the absence of the interruption code, the channel mask, and the instruction length code. In the EC mode, the control register 2 provides 32 channel mask bits to take over and expand

A	B	C	Z	D	E	Z	Z	F

Bit Positions	Field	Bit Positions	Field
0-7	A—System mask bits	12	EC mode bit if 1
0	Zero bit fill	13	Machine check mask bit
1	PER mask bit	14	Wait state bit
2-4	Zero bit fill	15	Problem state bit
5	DAT switch bit	16-17	Z—Zero bit fill
6	I-O mask bit	18-19	D—Condition Code
7	External mask bit	20-23	E—Program mask bits
8-11	B—Protection key	24-39	Z—Zero bit fill
12-15	C—XMWP control bits	40-63	F—Instruction address

FIG. E-3. Fields in the extended control (EC) mode format of the PSW.

the function of the former channel mask. The interruption and instruction length codes are placed in internal storage at fixed locations, as shown in Fig. E-4. The input-output mask bit applies to all channels in the EC mode. But the external mask bit has the same role in both the BC and EC modes.

Address in Hex	Length in Bytes	Function of the Field	Address in Hex	Length in Bytes	Function of the Field
00	8	IPL or Restart new PSW	86	2	External interrupt code
08	8	IPL first CCW or			in EC mode
		Restart old PSW	88	4	SVC codes in EC mode
10	8	IPL second CCW	8C	4	Program interrupt code
18	8	External old PSW			in EC mode
20	8	Supervisor Call old PSW	90	4	DAT interrupt address
28	8	Program old PSW	94	2	Monitor Call class
30	8	Machine check old PSW	96	2	PER interrupt code
38	8	Input-Output old PSW	98	4	PER address
40	8	CSW (Channel Status Word)	9C	4	Monitor Call code
48	4	CAW (Channel Address Word)	A8	4	Channel identification from
50	4	Interval timer			Store Channel ID command
58	8	External new PSW	AC	4	I-O Extended Logout (IOEL)
60	8	Supervisor Call new PSW			address
68	8	Program new PSW	B0	4	Limited channel logout codes
70	8	Machine check new PSW	BA	2	Input-Output interrupt
78	8	Input-Output new PSW			address in EC mode
			D8	296	Maintenance logout data

Fig. E-4. Fixed addresses used with the EC mode.

The condition code is moved to the left half of the PSW in the EC mode. It is still saved by a BAL or BALR instruction in that mode, because the instruction puts the stored data into the BC-mode format.

The two fields in the EC-mode PSW not found in the BC-mode PSW are the program event recording (PER) mask (bit 1), and the translate control (bit 5) to turn on (1) or off (0) the DAT.

COMMANDS

Nearly all of the commands for controlling virtual storage operations are in the privileged set, and thus usually unavailable to the programer. Hence, only a very brief review of them is given here, with a sumary in Appendix C.

The eight commands most directly involved with virtual storage are Load Control Registers (LCTL), Store Control Registers (STCTL), Load Real Address (LRA), Reset Reference Bit (RRB), Purge TLB (PTLB), Set System Mask (SSM), Store Then AND System Mask (STNSM), and Store Then OR System Mask (STOSM). All are privileged.

The Load Control Registers (LCTL) and Store Control Registers (STCTL) commands work in the same way as the Load Multiple (LM) and Store Multiple (STM) commands work. The main difference is that the control rather than the general-purpose registers are affected. The system mask commands operate with the first byte of the current PSW to record and to change the pattern of interrupts permitted by the PSW.

The Load Real Address (LRA) command operates in the same way as the Load Address command. But instead of loading the effective address into a general-purpose register, it loads the real address if DAT is on and the effective address if DAT is off. Unlike Load Address, however, Load Real Address also sets the condition code. 0 incidates that an address was loaded; 1 that a segment-table error was encountered; 2 that a page-table error was encountered; and 3 that a length error was encountered in the translation tables.

Eight commands less directly involved with virtual storage but useful with it are Set Storage Key (SSK), Insert Storage Key (ISK), Set Clock (SCK), Store Clock (STCK), Set Clock Comparator (SCKC), Store Clock Comparator (STCKC), Set CPU Timer (SPT), and Store CPU Timer (STPT). All but Store Clock are privileged.

The Set Storage Key (SSK) RR command changes the seven-bit storage protection key associated with the specified block of 2K real addresses. The first operand register contains any real address within the block. The second operand register provides, in the seven most significant bits of the rightmost byte, the new storage protection key. The Insert Storage Key (ISK) RR command copies the protection key into the register named as the second operand, in the reverse of the SSK operation.

The seven-bit protection key consists of three parts: four bits of access control code, one fetch protection bit, one reference bit, and one change bit. Bit 5 (the "reference bit") is set to 1 automatically each time any address is referenced in the block. Bit 6 (the "change bit") is set to 1 automatically each time any address in the block has its contents altered. Bit 4, the fetch protection bit, if 0 permits all fetches (accesses to storage that do not alter the existing contents), and if 1 imposes the same access control as for store protection. For store protection access (to alter the contents of storage), the protection key in the current PSW is matched against the access control code applicable to the address desired. If it compares equal, or if the PSW protection key is all zero bits, access is permitted. If not, a protection interrupt occurs.

One other nonprivileged command is available on some models, the Monitor Call. It is an aid to debugging because it permits the programer to generate program interrupts (interrupt code 40_x) for any of 16 classes, and identified with any of as many as 4K codes. The Monitor Call (MC) instruction is most helpful when used with another aid to debugging, the Program Event Recording (PER) interrupt capability. Operating under the masks in control register 9, and addresses in control systems 10 and 11, PER can create a record of all conditional transfers of control executed, selected instruction fetching, selected alterations of storage, and selected alterations of register contents. Unfortunately, to use PER or the MC command requires in practice using either general-purpose utility routines or privileged commands to write specialized routines.

OPERATING SYSTEM SUPPORT

To support the use of virtual storage (VS) and to handle the paging required, varieties of OS and DOS are available. All require the availability of DAT and magnetic disks. All provide for a division of virtual storage into partitions of some size, partly to facilitate multiprogramed operation. All use the input and output operations as described earlier in this book. All offer VSAM as an additional data access method.

DOS/VS is the variety of DOS that supports virtual storage. It divides virtual storage into partitions of fixed size. Only one size of page is permitted, the 2K size. A special partition is provided for VSAM operations.

OS/VS1, also called simply VS1, is an extension of OS/MFT. It divides virtual storage into partitions of fixed length. It maintains job queues and schedules peripheral operations. To assist in this, it uses a job entry subsystem (JES) that may also support the use of remote terminals and job entry equipment through a remote entry system (RES).

OS/VS2, also called simply VS2, is an extension of OS/MVT. It divides virtual storage into partitions of variable length, and permits a more flexible utilization of real storage space. It maintains job queues and schedules a wider range of peripherals with more elaborate priority schemes than does VS1. To assist in this, it uses HASP. For users of time sharing, VS2 offers TSO, the time sharing option.

VM/370 is an operating system that carries the partition idea one step farther. Conceptually, it treats each major storage partition as a separate virtual machine (VM), to make a "computer sharing" operating system. Within each virtual machine, the programer may use VS1, VS2, or DOS/VS, in any combination. In addition, VM/370 offers CMS, a conversational monitor system to provide users through terminals control over the virtual machines.

VSAM

The virtual storage access method (VSAM) is partly similar to the indexed-sequential access method (ISAM) used for indexed-sequential files. But the file organizations supported by VSAM are of two types, not one: key-indexed files, and entry-sequenced files. To take advantage of virtual storage, both types of files are assumed to be composed of 'control areas." These in turn are assumed to be composed of "control intervals," which in turn are composed of records, free space (if any), and control information. A logical record must be entirely contained within a control interval, and may not exceed 64K bytes in length.

An entry-sequenced file has no index provided by the operating system, although the programer may provide his own. Records in an entry-sequenced file are assumed to be in a random order, and are stored as the file is created to fill each control interval as completely as possible before starting to fill the next. No free space is provided deliberately. The assumed addressing is by the relative byte address (RBA), which is the relative address of the leftmost byte of the record counting from the leftmost byte of the first logical record in the file, if the records were placed end-to-end in the order in which they were loaded. This is a virtual address since it is independent of extents, cylinders, and tracks.

All additions to an entry-sequenced file are assumed to be placed at the right-hand end (progressively higher RBA). Updating of existing records can be done in place, if the updated record is no longer than the record as it was originally recorded. Deletions can be made by reloading the entire file. Substitute records can be used to replace records that should be logically deleted, if they are the same length, but this changes the data stored at the given RBA.

A key-indexed file has an index provided by the operating sytem. Each record in the file is assumed to have a key field of uniform length at a uniform relative address within the logical record. Records are stored as the file is created in key sequence, with an average amount of free space in each control interval and control area as specified by the programer. The main index ("index set") is an index to the control areas. Each control area has an index ("sequence set") to its constituent control intervals. Access is normally to the entire control interval. Although each record has an RBA, the RBA is not used for access, since it may change as the file is maintained. Access is by key via the index pointers.

Additions to a key-indexed file are placed as nearly in key sequence order as the available free space permits. If an insert into one control interval would cause a record to overflow, the system uses the free space in unused or adjoining (logically consecutive, not necessariy physically contiguous) control intervals. It attempts to reallocate the records to leave useable amounts of free space in each control interval after making the addition. Corrections are made automatically to the index to reflect the addition.

Updating of records can be done in place. If the record length changes, the amount of free space is adjusted accordingly. Deletions can be made, and the amount of free space in a control interval can be thereby increased. Corrections are made automatically to the index to reflect deletions and length changes.

Imperative macros for the two file organizations are similar to the macros described elsewhere in this book. OPEN prepares the file for use, and CLOSE terminates the use of the file. GET makes the data of a logical record available in real storage. PUT copies the data of a logical record from real storage into a control interval, with the needed changes in the index, if any. But when nonsequential access by the RBA is desired, the POINT macro must precede the GET. To make a deletion from a key-index file, the programer uses GET and then ERASE. For these macros, the programer specifies the operands by referring to a request parameter list, established previously with an RPL declarative.

The declarative macros may be incorporated in the DD card or in the program. A special DD card operand is available, AMP, to override program-specified declaratives. In the program, the programer uses the declaratives ACB, EXLST, and RPL at a minimum. The ACB defines the Access Control Block, somewhat like a DCB. The EXLST specifies the addresses of programer-provided optional routines for the handling of various types of errors and special conditions. A range of other declaratives and imperative macros are available to handle key-indexed and entry-sequenced files.

PROGRAMING CONSIDERATIONS

When writing programs to run on virtual storage models of the computer, the programer can sharply affect the speed of execution of the program by the way he writes it. The effect is small for programs that, in link-edited form and ready for execution, need less than one page. It can be gross for large programs. For the programer to make good use of virtual storage when writing assembly-language programs, he needs to give attention to the following nine considerations.

1. Some addresses are not translated by DAT. Some may be real, some may be virtual (logically), and some may not be addresses at all. It is vital that the programer distinguish correctly among them. The more common fit into three classes.

First are addresses that are always translated if DAT is on. The most common of these are: addresses of operands defined by or calculated from DC or DS declaratives; addresses of instructions; addresses to go into current or new PSW areas, as from a transfer of control; addresses used as operands in Load Real Address instructions; and addresses stored in control registers 10 and 11.

Second are addresses that are always real, not logical (virtual). The most common are: addresses of fixed storage areas within the first 512 bytes of real storage (see Fig. E-4); addresses in old PSW areas and in the current PSW; addresses generated by the computer and provided to the program in the registers (such as from BAL, BALR, EDMK, or TRT instructions); segment-table and page-table addresses; addresses in channel programs (but not the address of a channel program in the main program); and addresses of operands in Set Storage Key, Insert Storage Key, and Reset Reference Bit.

Third, some addresses in instructions do not need to be translated and should not be translated. Among them are shift amounts, peripheral equipment designations, immediate operands (such as in SVC and MC instructions), and the operand in a Load Address instruction. Load Address always gives a virtual address if it is different from the real address.

556

In short, when the programer generates or receives an address in his program, he must know whether it will be treated as real or virtual by the computer at the time of program execution. Which it is will affect how the programer uses it.

2. Control sections should be kept within the page size, but two or more control sections may jointly occupy a page. This encourages the use of EXTRN and ENTRY declaratives for off-page references. This helps debugging by keeping the off-page references visible.

3. By a careful use of BAL, BALR, and USING, the programer can make all on-page virtual addresses be a constant offset from the real addresses. This is just an extension of programing to provide relocatability. This extension does not obviate the need for DAT, or turn it off, but it certainly helps in debugging.

4. Being parsimonious in the use of registers, especially as base registers, makes page-to-page references easier.

5. Using a root page reduces time lost in paging. The control entry point for the program should be here. Frequently executed routines, common closed subroutines, and common work areas used in the program should also be on this page. This page should be origined at zero, and hence be the first page in the first segment.

6. Concentrating the fields that are changed onto as few pages as possible reduces time lost in paging. Switch fields, masks, intermediate data, and input-output areas are examples.

7. Minimizing the number of pages that each page can reference reduces paging. This means minimizing not only the number of different items referenced, but also the number of times such references are likely to be made during program execution. It is more important to minimize references to store than references to access (obtain or fetch). The pages with the most total references between them should be given virtual addresses low enough so that they will be close to the root page.

8. Using MVC and MVCL instructions to copy parts of pages into other pages can reduce the time lost in paging by reducing the number of off-page references. This is feasible if commonly used fields are grouped together, and space is provided in which to move them.

9. Observing the guidelines established at the programer's installation on programing with virtual storage will usually improve the efficiency of the programs the programer writes in assembly language.

557

Index

Entries are alphabetized in ASCII order (see page 44) and hence all-capitalized words are placed at the start of each letter group by their first letter. Major page references are in **boldface** numbers; the names of computer commands are in **boldface** type. Entries are normally under the key noun—thus, for magnetic disk, see Disk, magnetic. But topics which come in varieties are normally listed under the variety—thus, for the binary variety of constant, see under Binary.

560

561

571

574

576